D0782535

The Pharaohs

With the Patronage of the
President of the Italian Republic

The Pharaohs

Edited by
Christiane Ziegler

NEW YORK

© 2002 by Bompiani Arte
Società Editoria Artistica SpA
Gruppo Skira, Milano

First published in the
United States of America in 2002
by Rizzoli International Publications, Inc.
300 Park Aveue South
New York, NY 10010

Printed and bound in Italy

In giving particular prominence to archaeology in its exhibition program, Palazzo Grassi has wished not only to respond to the interests of a growing public, but also to investigate the historical and artistic experiences on which our own civilization is based. In order to reconstruct the most significant moments in the history of mankind, the exhibitions held in recent years have reviewed the major civilizations of the past. It is the world of ancient Egypt that is now being presented, a world full of fascination and beauty, one with a rich history.

In order for the exhibition to measure up to such an important subject, it would not have been sufficient to simply offer a selection of masterpieces, albeit of great prestige; it was necessary to provide an overall view of the entire Egyptian civilization so as to reveal the opulence and complexity of its political, religious and civil life. This has been made possible thanks to the curator of the exhibition, Christiane Ziegler, as she has chosen to focus on the essential and emblematic figure of the pharaoh in order to illustrate Egyptian civilization, making him the key for understanding this important culture.

The opportunity to exhibit this exceptional material from the past has been made possible by the particularly generous cooperation of the major museums of the world, including many from the United States. The Egyptian Museum of Cairo should be singled out for its significant contribution to this effort.

Contributing to the success of the exhibition have been these institutions with their loans, and many individuals—among whom the architect Francesca Fenaroli—with their work. Our gratitude goes to all of them.

Cesare Annibaldi

Baltimore, The Walters Art Museum
Berlin, Staatliche Museen zu Berlin,
 Ägyptisches Museum
 und Papyrussammlung
Bologna, Museo Civico Archeologico
Boston, Museum of Fine Arts
The Brooklyn Museum of Art
Brussels, Bibliothèque Royale de Belgique
Brussels, Musée Royaux d'Art
 et d'Histoire
Cairo, Egyptian Museum
Chicago, The Field Museum of Natural
 History
Cleveland, The Cleveland Museum of Art
Copenhagen, Ny Carlsberg Glyptotek
Darmstadt, Hessisches Landesmuseum
Durham, The Oriental Museum
Edinburgh, The Trustees of the National
 Museum of Scotland
Florence, Museo Egizio
George Ortiz Collection
Hannover, Kestner Museum
Hildesheim, Roemer und Pelizaeus Museum
Leiden, Rijksmuseum van Oudheden
London, The Trustees of the British
 Museum
Lyon, Muséum d'Histoire Naturelle
Munich, Staatliche Sammlung Ägyptischer
 Kunst
New York, The Metropolitan Museum
 of Art
Oxford, The Ashmolean Museum
Padua, Museo Civico Archeologico
Paris, Bibliothèque Nationale de France
Paris, Musée du Louvre, Département
 des Antiquités Égyptiennes
Philadelphia, The University of
Pennsylvania, Museum of Archaeology and
 Anthropology
Pisa, Collezioni egittologiche dell'Università
San Bernardino, Harer Family Trust
 California State University
Turin, Museo Egizio
Toronto, Royal Ontario Museum
Vienna, Kunsthistorisches Museum

3. Saff tombs in western Thebes

its furnishings (no others have reached us), with a radical change of meaning from everyday to everlasting.

It has been suggested that the wider use of metal caused stone vases to go out of fashion, reducing their value and ostentatious function, which may explain their removal to the underground chambers of the pyramid.

One has to wait until the 4th Dynasty to find other royal grave goods, at the great pyramids of Giza. Here, in 1925, George Reisner's American mission found, in an unusual way, the grave goods of queen Hetepheres, the mother of Khufu who built the Great Pyramid. Nothing remains of what was in the latter's tomb, which was raided and sacked already at the end of the Memphite era. What was found in his mother's possession gives us an idea of what was probably in her son's mortuary chamber. The grave contained a rectangular alabaster sarcophagus, without inscriptions, that was empty. This suggested that one was dealing with a reconstruction made after a raiding had taken place elsewhere, which was remedied here by transferring the remaining goods and canopic jars. Recently it has been suggested that this might have been the original grave, from which the body was later removed and buried in a satellite pyramid.

The furnishings are truly regal, consisting mainly of highly refined, rich furniture, including a bed with its canopy (dismounted and placed in a box), two armchairs and a litter that have been reconstructed where the wooden structures—irremediably damaged—were gilded producing the characteristic glowing splendor of the classically simple furniture. Also in gold were the toilet articles, a headrest, and a few vases. A particularly handsome set of silver bracelets, with exquisite butterfly-shaped inlays of cornelians, lapis lazuli and turquoises, was kept in a gilded casket. Then there were stone and earthenware vases and a series of walking sticks. The complex is exemplary for the taste of the "design" of the period, plain in its overall structure, yet without schematic stiffness. Here, for the first time, we touch on what is implicit in Egyptian culture: the everlasting value of gold, the flesh of the gods, that which consigns a series of objects of everyday, earthly meaning to eternity.

4. Gold diadem of Sety II,
New Kingdom, 19th Dynasty.
Cairo, Egyptian Museum
cat. 212

5. Gold and cornelian necklace
with pendants in the shape of flies.
Boston, Museum of Fine Arts
cat. 110

One has to wait until the 12th Dynasty for new documentation of royal grave furnishings; and even in this case they are exclusively the goods of court ladies rather than of the various monarchs.

Splendid ensembles of jewels and personal objects have come down to us from the precincts of the pyramids of Amenemhat II, Senusret III and Amenemhat III at Dahshur, and of Senusret II at el-Lahun, nearly entirely saved from plunderers and carefully excavated by archeologists.

However, in 1895 Jacques de Morgan found an intact sovereign's grave at Dahshur: its occupant a certain King Hor, completely unknown at the time of the discovery, who may have been coregent with Amenemhat III for a short time. The burial chamber contained a sealed shrine with a nude male wooden statue inside it representing the king's *ka*. Inside the coffin was a very damaged mummy with a gilded wooden mask with the *nemes* placed on its face. Next to him were scepters, and on his breast fragments of a flagellum with enamel beads. Necklaces of semi-precious stones, gold finger-guards, and other trinkets, including a dagger of which only the scabbard remains, completed the goods inside the sarcophagus, while beside it was a chest filled with scepters, canes, arrows, and maces. A canopic chest, a round altar, libation cups, and various votive offerings completed the material.

Next to the shaft containing Hor's grave was another one with an identical sarcophagus and canopic chest with identical canopic jars, belonging to a princess Nubhetepthered, perhaps the king's daughter.

The Dahshur and el-Lahun princesses had far more significant offerings. It is worthwhile mentioning that, as far as can be reconstructed from the various materials that were unearthed near the Dahshur pyramids and near el-Lahun, the artifacts comprising them were in the same style and, in some instances, probably made by the same craftsmen. The furnishings include diadems, necklaces, belts, bracelets, ankle bands, enameled brooches, scarabs, pectorals, toilet articles, and a dagger. A large wooden statue of a goose (or a swan) has shown up in one case and a few surviving fragments seem to belong to another. A gilded wooden chest containing a mirror, razors, and obsidian cosmetic jars mounted in gold, found by Petrie in the tomb of Sithathoriunet, can now be seen—reconstructed—in the Metropolitan Museum, New York.

The individual pieces do not always match, and the diadems are of different shapes and makes, but we have here a series of some of the most exquisite jewels, in design, conception and craftsmanship, that have reached us from ancient Egypt and that are evidence of a sophisticated court life. We need only mention the extremely elegant crown made of gold thread joining inlaid rosettes, or the gold band adorned with a *uraeus* and elaborate rosettes. But even if, as someone (Winlock) said, "everything is inspired by a very vital love of beauty and a very vivid vanity," here the presence of ritual offerings recalls the burial function, whereas the daggers and the big statues of geese have a remote meaning that eludes us.

With the end of the 12th Dynasty a darker period loomed, in which the royal function was taken over by Asiatic foreigners (the Hyksos), whose authority remained unchallenged until the 17th Dynasty, when a succession of Theban princes succeeded in reconquering Egypt as far as the Delta, and a new period in Egyptian history began: the New Kingdom (from the sixteenth century BC).

Attributed to that period, still marked by the uncertain political outcome of the "reconquest," were the first royal grave goods found since the ones we heretofore mentioned. Their discovery dates back to the early days of scientific Egyptology, in the mid-XIX century, and a series of circumstances that, even for those times, was unfortunate.

Here again the owner was a princess or a queen: Ahhotep, wife of King Seqenenra who assumed the power of regent at Thebes and whom we know about from other documents. When her grave was discovered, the person in Cairo in charge of the excavations was advised, and he immediately sent someone to preside at the opening. However, the local governor arrived first and, as soon as the sarcophagus was opened and revealed the importance of its contents, he acted on his own sending the treasure to the khedive. The recovery of the goods, during their journey on the Nile, and his subsequent refusal to give some of them to Empress Eugénie, put Mariette's determination to the test, just as he had begun setting up the Egyptian Antiquities Service.

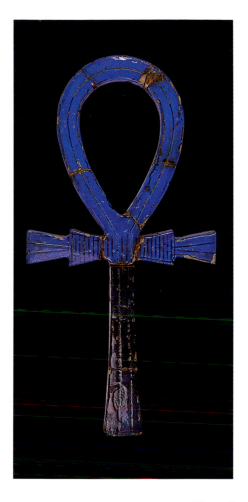

6. Faience *ankh* sign from the tomb of Amenhotep II in the Valley of the Kings, New Kingdom, 18th Dynasty. Cairo, Egyptian Museum
cat. 243

7. Wooden *djed* pillar from the tomb of Amenhotep II in the Valley of the Kings, New Kingdom, 18th Dynasty. Cairo, Egyptian Museum
cat. 242

8. Faience *was* scepter from the tomb of Amenhotep II in the Valley of the Kings, New Kingdom, 18th Dynasty. Cairo, Egyptian Museum
cat. 244

The adventurous circumstances of the discovery prevent us from knowing what really was found aside from the treasure, and how the mortuary complex had been arranged; but at the time the perfection and imagination of Egyptian goldsmiths was a revelation. Besides personal jewelry, the presence of weapons in the queen's grave—although the Dahshur princesses also had them—was unusual: a superb dagger, its blade adorned with inlays of lively animal figures and a ceremonial hatchet with heraldic and warrior figures. These objects all bear the name of King Ahmose, conqueror of the Hyksos, who was the queen's son and had offered them to his mother as a last gift. But even the queen's necklace has a military aspect, being decorated with the golden flies reserved for the heroes of the battlefield. Lastly, among the find are two very unusual boats, a gold one mounted on a stand with wheels (one of the first of its kind found in Egypt) and a silver one, which clearly recalls the aforementioned boats buried in the Protodynastic cemetery of Abydos, that were followed by those buried by the great Giza pyramid and the one by the pyramid of Senusret II at el-Lahun.

The singularity of the goods reflects the singularity of the personality of the dedicatee.

But just as singular is the story of some other contemporary burial goods, from the sarcophagus of Seqenenra's successor, King Kamose, the sovereign who began the victorious campaign against the Hyksos. It is a *rishi* or "feathered" coffin, representing a person entirely wrapped in two wings concealing the body. An obvious parallel with the representation of the winged goddess Isis who protects Osiris, the *rishi* emphasizes the identification of the deceased with the god, lord of the afterlife. We have no idea how and why this coffin ended up, still closed, in an old dump of the Theban necropolis; however, on opening it, Mariette found a decomposed mummy, to whose arm was attached a bronze dagger with a silver handle and a gilded pommel, a bracelet with two figures of lions, and a cartouche with the king's name, quite similar to that of Ahhotep, a mirror, a scarab and a few amulets. These treasures were given to Napoleon III and are now divided between Brussels and the Louvre.

The profound change in the organization of Egyptian society that occurred at the mid-millennium (sixteenth–eleventh centuries BC) of its Imperial period also concerned the arrangement of royal graves, which were no longer marked by pyramids but hidden within bowels of intricate hypogea, and concealed in an inaccessible valley west of Thebes.

Proof that this did not protect them from the avidity of raiders is eloquently demonstrated by the fact that the pharaohs' mummies had to be assembled already at the end of the New Kingdom near Deir el-Bahri, in a nearly inaccessible cache and in a specific tomb, where they were preserved nearly up to our time, for they were discovered not until 1881. Nonetheless, thefts and removals had deprived the sovereigns of their grave goods, and archeological investigations have found only meager, scattered, fragmentary remains, the sparse leftovers of a vanished opulence. In this instance, too, royal graves, even though not of kings, provide some relevant information. Like the tomb of three princesses, the minor wives of Thutmose III, who had a common burial place in a remote canyon southwest of Medinet Habu (the "Valley of the Monkeys"). Like the cache where the royal mummies had been placed, its discovery (and in this case its exploitation as well) is due to the obstinacy and daring of tomb raiders who dropped themselves down the steep mountainside with ropes, and took possession of the grave treasures, selling them piece by piece on the antiquities market. These were methodically redeemed by the Metropolitan Museum, where Winlock, who had already reorganized the el-Lahun treasure, was able to give form and meaning to extremely varied material. We have no idea what was lost due to the carelessness of the clandestine excavation and the successive sales. But what we have been able to put back together is indeed remarkable: the most spectacular of the headdresses is a cascade of gold rosettes, with inlays of cornelians, turquoises and vitreous paste, mounted on a gold plate covering the top of the head and held by tiny gold cylinders. Its original appearance, destroyed at the time of the raiders' hasty recovery of the fragments, has been accurately recomposed, even if there are serious doubts as to the authenticity of several of the rosettes.

There was another crown, simpler but equally elegant: a gold band that circled the head, adorned with rosettes and held by another passing over the head. Where, in royal headdresses, there is the *uraeus* and the vulture, here instead are exquisite gazelle heads: an insignia reserved for high-ranking nobles, and one represented elsewhere. Then there were necklaces, bracelets and ankle bands, belts adorned with gold beads in shell and fish patterns, pectorals, gold sandals, silver vases with lids along with toilet articles and gold, silver, glass and stone ware.

Another grave met with a more felicitous archeological fate. The smallest in the Valley of the Kings, its presence had been concealed ages ago by a deposit of stone chips that came

9. Gold girdle with Nile-fish spacers from Wadi Qubbanet el-Qirud, New Kingdom, 18th Dynasty. New York, The Metropolitan Museum of Art, gift of Edward S. Harkness
cat. 185

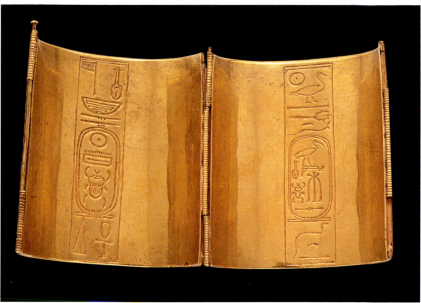

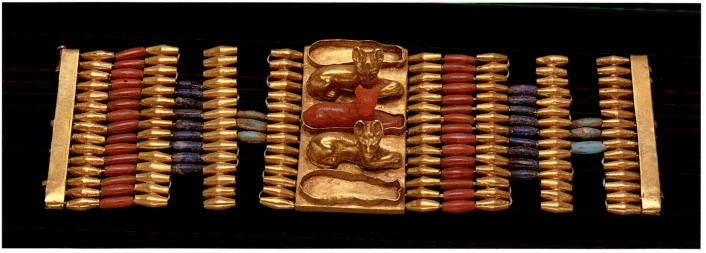

10–11. Inlaid and inscribed bracelet with Thutmose III's cartouche, gold, cornelian, turquoise glass and blue glass, from Wadi Qubbanet el-Qirud, New Kingdom, 18th Dynasty. New York, The Metropolitan Museum of Art, Rogers Fund, 1926
cat. 188

12. Armlet with cats spacer, gold and cornelian, from Wadi Qubbanet el-Qirud, New Kingdom, 18th Dynasty. New York, The Metropolitan Museum of Art, Rogers Fund, 1922
cat. 187

from the excavation of nearby graves. Its entrance had been sealed with the necropolis custodians' seal, but a narrow opening on top showed that someone had nonetheless been inside. The jewelry was missing, but the grave goods themselves were intact. The occupants of the grave, buried in several sarcophagi one inside the other, were the parents of Queen Tiy, in-laws of Amenhotep III. Therefore the tomb held gorgeous regal gifts, decorated furniture (like the famous chair, a gift of the princess Satamon), and other things, but also the grave goods of commoners: food in special boxes, mock vases in painted wood, sandals, a light open basket for a wig, a Book of the Dead (as opposed to the typically royal texts of the Valley tombs). Unusual is the presence of a chariot, in perfect condition, and probably specially made for the tomb (given its size). Yuya, the owner, happened to be a cavalry general.

The religious aspect is represented by two "vegetating Osiris," figures of the god made of earth and filled with seeds that in sprouting augured and bore witness to the hope of renewed life.

The many excavation campaigns in the Valley of the Kings, along with those of the Antiquities Service, which had also attracted sponsors like Theodore Davis and Lord Carnarvon, made it possible to unearth remarkable finds in several royal tombs. Among them, the tomb of Thutmose IV, that Carter explored for the Davis mission. The recovered material was nearly always in wretched condition: big statues of the king, made of wood and blackened with resin as are a group of smaller divine statuettes; the remains of a throne decorated with re-

13. Wooden statue of a panther covered with bitumen from the tomb of Amenhotep II in the Valley of the Kings, New Kingdom, 18th Dynasty. Cairo, Egyptian Museum
cat. 259

liefs commemorating royal exploits; large cow heads; four bricks that were ritually placed at the four cardinal points of the sarcophagus chamber; models in faience and glassware, scepters, elements of apparel; and, most remarkable of all, a gilded chariot, decorated with military scenes, it too broken and incomplete, plus other things. This is all that remains of what was probably a wealth of goods, that was naturally deprived of anything that might have an intrinsic value.

Similar finds—more modest ones—appeared in Davis' excavations in other royal tombs, like that of Hatshepsut, that of a ruler of the Amarna period whose identification is uncertain, and that of Horemheb.

But these dispersed remains, often of questionable interpretation, would be clearly reappraised after the fabulous discovery Howard Carter, commissioned by Lord Carnarvon, made in 1922, of Tutankhamun's intact tomb in the Valley of the Kings.

Actually this tomb had also been visited by thieves, and the seal of the necropolis police stamped on the plaster of the entrance showed that an intervention had interrupted the plundering, so that it was not totally intact. This can be seen from a few absences observed or conjectured, given the indescribable disorder that affected all the goods. The disorder was partly determined by the small size of the tomb which, rather than a royal tomb, seemed to be a private one that had been appropriated due to the sovereign's sudden, premature death. The four rooms contained so many objects that their systematic removal to the Cairo Museum took six years.

The entrance and a small room adjacent to it included furnishings, food supplies in wooden boxes, precious alabaster vases, two chariots, decorated thrones, bows in adorned cases, odd-shaped staffs, and three singular, grandiose ceremonial beds—one shaped like a cow, one like a feline, one with the image of the "Devourer," the fearsome creature who devoured sinners in the afterworld. On the south wall of the first room, on each side of the walled entryway, were two wooden statues of the king, blackened with resin, replicas of the monarch in the other world guarding his own sarcophagus whose entire structure of successive cases took up all the accessible space.

Protected by four successive gold-plated wooden receptacles and by a cloth tester adorned with gilded rosettes, was the quartzite and granite sarcophagus that in turn contained two gilded wooden anthropomorphic cases, inside of which was the true coffin, made of solid

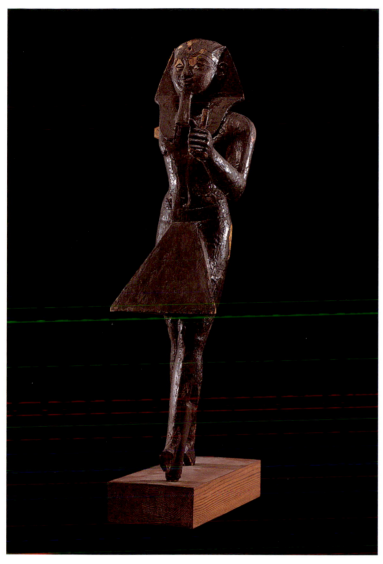

14. Wooden statue of Amenhotep II
covered with bitumen, from the
king's tomb in the Valley of the
Kings, New Kingdom, 18th Dynasty.
Cairo, Egyptian Museum
cat. 258

15. Faience cup from the tomb of
Amenhotep II in the Valley of the
Kings, New Kingdom, 18th Dynasty.
Cairo, Egyptian Museum
cat. 247

16. Faience *hes* vase from the tomb
of Amenhotep II in the Valley of the
Kings, New Kingdom, 18th Dynasty.
Cairo, Egyptian Museum
cat. 245

17. Silver ring inscribed with Thutmose IV's cartouche, New Kingdom, 18th Dynasty. Berlin, Ägyptisches Museum und Papyrussammlung
cat. 138

gold, emulating the ancient model of the *rishi* coffin, with the king's mummy (still conserved in his tomb) enhanced by a gold mask. This complex situation was even further complicated by the fact that in the spaces between the various containers offerings of all kinds were inserted, including the flowers of the funeral day, and insignias of royalty consisting of precious jewels, amulets, and weapons. It was an arduous task to take this complex protective system apart, the recovery of the first receptacle took eighty-four days. But when the chamber was finally emptied, it was possible to enter a fourth room, marked by the presence of canopic jars (the receptacles that contained the viscera removed during mummification) and of ritual boats (the prow significantly facing west as in other instances), which also contained statues, offering objects (from faithful courtiers, too) and jewelry.

It would be impossible to describe this huge quantity of objects. Generally speaking, we know which expressed a religious, symbolic meaning, a specific funerary purport, that was primarily aimed at the monarch's regeneration, and—as far as we can deduce—its arrangement within the modest available space.

The ensemble of different objects reveals the precision, elegance, and perfection of Egyptian craftsmanship, the accuracy of its "design." A comparison of these jewels with those from Dahshur and el-Lisht shows the changed character of the court: the light delicacy of the former contrasting with the emphatic—and opulent—visibility of the latter, as the aristocratic court of the Middle Kingdom contrasts with the "window of appearance" where the king showed himself to his thronged courtiers at the end of the 18th Dynasty. Further comparison with material from other royal graves has given a better understanding of several earlier mentioned finds that had seemed enigmatic. The funerary decoration of other royal graves has also enabled us to understand the meaning of what in this case is not a figurative representation but rather concrete objects.

The discovery of Tutankhamun's tomb soon become legendary, and made one aware of how great the plundering of the Theban royal tombs had been, vividly described in the impressive account of the confessions of thieves during an important trial that exposed the complicity of high-placed Thebans as well toward the end of the Imperial period (eleventh century BC).

After Tutankhamun, the tomb of his successor, Horemheb, gave up scarce remains of goods, some individual articles of which match ones in his predecessor's tomb.

Later, in the Ramesside period, the royal tombs became increasingly remarkable for their size, wealth and variety of the representations (as well as of the grave goods) and inscriptions covering the walls, but very poor in finds for archeologists, except for the splendid

18. Gold and lapis lazuli necklace
with cylinders from the tomb of
Psusennes I at Tanis, Third
Intermediate Period, 21st Dynasty.
Cairo, Egyptian Museum
cat. 264

mummies of some of the most famous sovereigns: Rameses II and Sety I, found in the cache of Deir el-Bahri.

With the last of the Ramessides, Rameses XI, Egypt radically changed its political and social organization, breaking up into more modest state structures, often connected by bonds of kinship, but lacking a central authority. In this situation, the Theban royal necropolis (which kept its ritual and dynastic role even after the court had moved to another capital) was no longer used. That is why the tombs of these local pharaohs are in the individual sites of their authority, especially near the temples of the heavenly gods who were their patrons. Aside from the identification of specific architecture, and the discovery at Leontopolis (Tell el-Muqdam) of the tomb, ruined by water seepage, of a Queen Kama whose sarcophagus contained her lovely jewels, the rich and explicit testimony of these new burial customs is drawn from Montet's excavations in the late 1930s at Tanis, in the eastern Delta.

The breakout of World War II prevented them from receiving due recognition, and it was not until after 1987 that, following an important exhibition held in Paris, these extraordinary finds became widely known to the public.

Concealed under what was left of a Ptolemaic period town district, a group of underground mortuary chambers of kings and princes between the 21st and the 22nd Dynasties (eleventh–eighth centuries BC) came to light, in the southwest corner of the sacred precinct of the temple of Amun, in 1939.

Raiders had entered several of them, which were not of equal importance, and because the environment was less dry and sterile than that of the Theban desert, nearly everything organic deposited there (wood, leather, plant offerings and even the mummies) was destroyed, even the metals were damaged, making the wealth of gold even more impressive. The masks covering the faces of four of the tomb occupants were of gold, and the coffins that contained two of them were of silver; in the place of a human face, one had that of a hawk, probably a particular form of Osiris, or of the god of the dead Sokar with whom the dead king identified. One of the graves, that of Psusennes I, was found intact, and a list of what was found there is instrumental in grasping its coherence, despite the loss of a large part of the goods. The king, a gold mask over his face and his body in a gold wrapping, was in a silver coffin, which in turn was enclosed in an anthropomorphic black granite sarcophagus that was placed inside a larger pink granite one.

The two sarcophagi, on closer examination, turned out to be reused articles: the black one belonging to an unknown personality of the 19th Dynasty, and the pink one to king Merenptah, successor of Rameses II. Tanis is a city where architectural and artistic material was gathered from many ancient capitals. This—like the chest of canopic jars from another royal tomb, that of Osorkon II, which dates back to the Middle Kingdom—might be a specific example of this tendency, contrasting however with the gorgeous opulence of Psusennes I's personal grave goods: two pectorals and four scarabs, eleven lapis lazuli hearts, twenty-six bracelets (one weighing 1,8 kilos of gold), gold finger- and toe-guards for hands and feet, and thirty-six rings slipped on the finger-guards; gold sandals, weapons and scepters were inserted between the two sarcophagi. Particularly impressive are three necklaces made of several rows of gold disks held by a heavy inlaid fastener from which hang chains bearing little bells (one of the necklaces weighs 8,5 kilos). In front, on the ground, were hundreds of *shabti*s, fallen out from the two chests ruined by humidity, a bronze brazier bearing the name of Rameses II upon which was placed a silver altar containing a bowl. The goldware was also fabulously rich.

Given this ostentation of wealth, the thought occurs that the reuse of "antique" material like the sarcophagi and the brazier might not have had to do with a certain collector's taste, which in Psusennes case is represented by a lapis lazuli pendant on one his necklaces bearing a cuneiform inscription, and a Mesopotamian cylinder inserted in a bracelet of Sheshonq II. A comparison of these treasures and Tutankhamun's (the two intact royal tombs) is, like many others, misleading: each has its own cultural and social background, and the artisanal taste of each reflects different artistic intents. In both cases we can observe the soundness on which such a system was based inasmuch as it was a celebration, a role model, an assertion of power and a fulfillment of ritual realities and religious hopes and beliefs.

After the Tanis treasure, the other royal treasures to be mentioned come from the royal

19. Necklace with a sanctuary-
shaped pectoral from Tanis,
22nd Dynasty, reign of Shoshenq II.
Cairo, Egyptian Museum
cat. 266

necropolises of the Ethiopian dynasty and of the Meroitic kings found in Sudanese Nubia. But, while those kings were "Egyptianized" and "Egyptianizing," the overall cultural background of their political and state circumstances differed so much from the classical Pharaonic one that they should not be taken into consideration here.

Nor shall the question of Alexander the Great's tomb be raised or questioned, for it is one of the recurrent problems of Alexandrine archeology. Those were different sovereigns from a very different world, and are entirely unrelated to our survey, which has already dealt with well-known figures.

The Royal Mummies

Francis Janot

The Mummification and Burial of the Pharaohs

For each and every one of us, the contemplation of the mummy of a king who died thousands of years ago is a fascinating experience; it is the tangible proof of the continuing presence of ancient history. Laden with amulets and treasures, this mummified body arouses within us both attraction and repulsion, a mix of emotions that enflames our imagination.

The pharaoh, descendent of Horus of Hierakonpolis, who is the son of Ra, who is the sun of Heliopolis and original Creator of the world, has died. During his life, the pharaoh was the unchallenged master of the Double Land,[1] but now his body—like that of a common mortal—is threatened with corruption; and this decay not only puts the institutions of government at risk but compromises the very order of the world. The ideology of ancient Egypt could not accept this with resignation. Some form of continuity had to be developed, in order to overcome this sense of brusque rupture. The mummification of the body halted the process of corruption, and thus—from that moment on—death might be considered as vanquished. Once it had undergone its physical preparation and magical adornment, the royal mummy became the equivalent of Osiris, the god of the dead. Triumphant, this new Osiris was now ready to live eternally in the afterlife. Hence gold—the incorruptible matter which was "the flesh of the gods"—became the chosen material for the adornment of this deified king.

Making the Royal Body Eternal

Mummification

It was imperative that the physical appearance of the royal body be preserved as completely as possible, thanks to techniques which brought the process of putrefaction to a halt. The magic of the priests was ineffective—that is, incomplete—when not accompanied by appropriate action on the body itself. This preparation of the deceased had a therapeutic aim in its own right; it involved the body as a whole, and was not some accessory stage in the process of burial. Indeed, the "changing" body was in danger, since physical corruption was both rapid and irreversible; in a relatively short space of time, the body might disappear altogether. During this phase, magical formulae and amulets could not yet exert their powers of protection.

The mummification of the king's body could only be carried out by a group of priests from "the great house,"[2] specialists in the preparation of the dead. Possessing the necessary skill and knowledge, only they could make the incision in the royal abdomen. Finally, it was they who recited the all important words when applying the protective amulets to certain parts of the dead king's body.

From the Old Kingdom onward,[3] the sequence of operations in the preparation of an Egyptian mummy were precisely defined, even if their order had yet to be immutably established. The body was washed and shaved; the brain was removed;[4] an incision was made in the abdomen to remove the internal organs; the body was washed a second time; the viscera were treated for preservation; the body was dehydrated using sachets of dried natron, then washed a third time; the skull and the thoracic and abdominal cavities were filled with bitumen; the nails, eyes and external genitals were specially treated; unguents were massaged into the dehydrated body; and finally a covering was placed over the side incision. After this, the viscera were placed in special canopic jars, the bandaging was applied, the nails gilded and, ultimately, the entire body was bound up. These latter stages of the process are described in the two incomplete "Embalming Ritual" papyri which date from the I century AD.[5]

Generally, the entire process lasted some seventy days. The body was dried by filling it with sachets of natron and then covering it with salt, which required something like three weeks to take full effect. It then took a further two weeks to wrap up the limbs and the body as a whole. Certain extant bandages, wadding and winding-sheets bear both individual marks and numbers; prepared in advance, these were then applied in a strictly-established order by the priest officiating at the ceremony.

Herodotus[6] was the first to describe how the Egyptians used different processes of mummification according to the price paid by the relatives of the dead man or woman; and after his account, a number of more or less detailed works on mummification appeared. In the XIX century, the removal of a mummy's bandages became a more scientific procedure; but the archaeologists and doctor who examined the exposed body could only make observations on the basis of what they perceived with the naked eye. Nowadays, museums have in-

1. Lid from the coffin containing the mummy of Rameses II, New Kingdom, 19th Dynasty. Cairo, Egyptian Museum

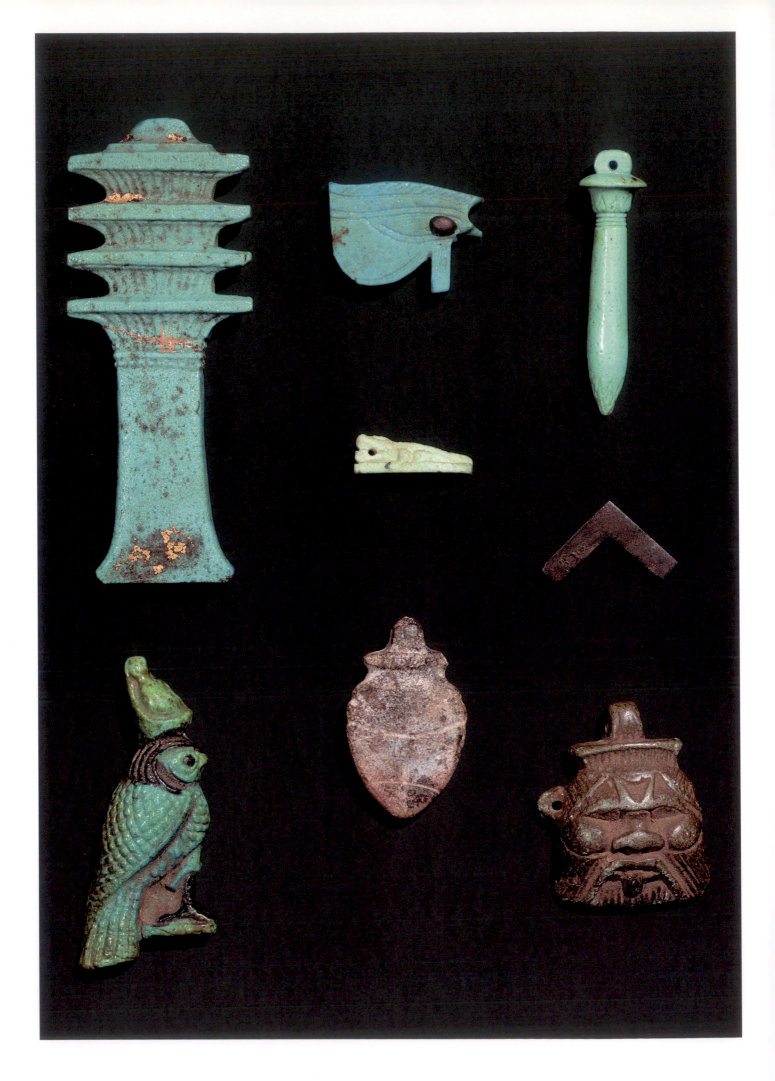

2. Faience funerary amulets, Second Intermediate Period. Berlin, Ägyptisches Museum und Papyrussammlung

terdisciplinary teams that use the most advanced medical techniques—X-rays,[7] tomography, three-dimensional reconstruction and laser-based stereo-photolithography—to examine the material used inside the body, the way the body was remodeled, the techniques used in applying the bandages and the presence of amulets—all without any risk of damaging the mummy itself.[8]

The Work of the Embalmer-priests

The recent reproduction of the instruments that were developed by embalmers to perform their task[9] has given us a clearer idea and closer understanding of how they set about their work.[10] As a matter of fact, two archaeological discoveries have brought to light some of the instruments used by these professionals of death. At Thebes, in the undisturbed tomb of a 30th-Dynasty prophet of Amun named Wahibre, archaeologists found an entire *instrumentarium*, abandoned in circumstances that they could not explain.[11] Furthermore, the waste products of the embalming process found in shaft no. 78 in the Valley of the Queens[12] included a small wooden nostril spoon which was stuck fast in a lump of bitumen that had maintained the form of its original jar container.

The conditions under which such tools were produced is still unclear. Made in wood or metal according to specific models, these instruments had one or more functional features and were obviously developed on the basis of long experience in the practice of embalming.

The best way to understand the function of each object is to actually hold it in one's hand. The position one's fingers take on the handle should be natural, without any constraint or forcing; the hand should have total freedom of action and maneuver when at work. With the tools in one's hand, one feels much closer to the Egyptian embalmer, to the way he worked and thought about his work. Designed specifically for use by the embalmer, the instruments were an extension of his thought processes, responding to well-learned movements.

The instruments that have been duplicated—a cadaver knife, forceps, a hook for excerebration, a nostril spoon and a clyster—have been used by two modern embalmers to remove the organs in the thoracic-abdominal cavities through incision,[13] and then to extract the brain from the brain pan (once the contents were removed, the next step was to fill the skull with resin or hot bitumen poured in through the nostrils). This experiment revealed that at different phases in their work, the embalmers must have shifted their position around the body; and that when the viscera were removed, the officiating clergy must have received them on

3. Bronze embalmer's knife with the god Anubis on the papyrus-shaped handle, New Kingdom, 18th–19th Dynasties.
Paris, Musée du Louvre

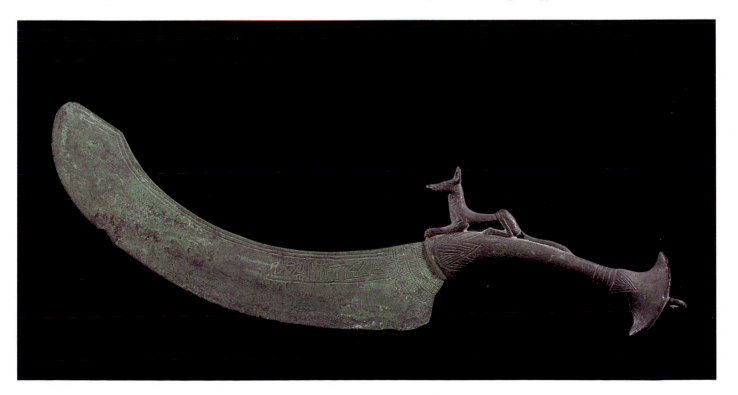

large plates so as to be able to treat them separately. Finally, it emerged that with a little practice and a skillful hand, the embalmer could work without disturbing the position of the heart within the thorax.

The care taken in handling the seven openings in the head—and, in particular, the mouth—was meant to conserve the deceased's mouth and tongue as functional, so that in the afterlife he could take nourishment and express himself before the assembly of the gods. Analysis of textual and archaeological material has thrown light on a whole series of procedures that were previously entirely unknown to us. First of all, the officiating priest had to clean the surface of the mouth, then he pressed on the end of the chin to loosen the teeth. The actual opening of the mouth was achieved by working on the jaw and jaw muscles, requiring the introduction of *medjat* scissors[14] between the teeth (a gold *medjat* was undoubtedly used during the mummification of the Pharaoh Pepy II.[15]) The mouth would then be held wide open using a double instrument such as the *pesesh-kaf*, the " jaw divider"[16] that was part of the *instrumentarium* left in the tomb of Wahibre. Thus, while working, the priest could take the necessary precautions with the organs in the mouth itself.

A Place for Mummification

Where was the body of the king actually mummified? Extant sources provide us with little information on this matter. However, texts do mention the *wabet*, a building where the bodies of humans and sacred animals were prepared. The inscriptions on the statue of Djed-Her the Saviour describe the *wabet* where the falcons sacred to Athribis were embalmed: "68 cubits in height and 64 cubits in length. . . . A large hall was inside it. Six chapels were on the two sides. Their door-frames [carved] in fine white limestone. The doors were in real pinewood. Their hinges and bolts in metal of Asia. A large porch [constructed over] the main door of this *wabet*-sanctuary rested on eight columns. . . . Finally, a large wall was built around the sanctuary."[17]

A second building, known as the *per nefer*, seems to have served the same function as the *wabet*. In effect, texts use the two names interchangeably to indicate the site of embalming, without distinguishing one from the other.

However, there is no certain archaeological trace of such buildings. B. Grdseloff[18] and E. Drioton[19] claim that the ceremony of embalming must have taken place in the valley temple of the funeral complex; the former arguing it was held in the antechamber, the latter on the roof (this embalming facility was only intended for the king, and therefore had to either disappear or be left unused after it had served its royal purpose).[20] The authors claim to have found traces of such a structure—in perishable materials—on the terrace of the building of Khafra. Similarly, in the temple of King Unas "the secondary hall in the main body of the building may have served as the place for the preparation of the mummy."[21]

Nevertheless, archaeological research has yet to discover the precise site destined for the reception of the king's body in the temple. Is this because it was so well-hidden, or because archaeologists simply failed to identify it? Or was it destroyed after it had performed its function? It is difficult to believe that such a prestigious function as the preparation of the king's body was performed in a simple workshop or a tent[22] and not in a solid stone structure that had already been prepared with all the necessary instruments and materials, of which there must have been a detailed inventory, regularly kept up-to-date:[23] One need only think of the preparatory materials and different fabrics, bandages, clothes and adornments that had to be gathered together in one place before starting work on the mummification of King Tutankhamun.

The Remains of Royalty

The Royal Mummies of Saqqara

Archaeological finds dating from the Old Kingdom (*c.* 2700–2200 BC) in the Memphis region—or, more specifically, on the plateau of Saqqara—have brought to light very few undesecrated royal tombs and mummies. The burial chamber of the pyramid of Djoser, founder of the 3rd Dynasty, gradually yielded up "various human bones, including a well-preserved mummified foot";[24] the numerous fragments of the 5th-Dynasty pharaoh Djedkara Isesi seem to have been examined after excavation work on a burial chamber that had unfortunately already been pillaged;[25] the work on the royal chambers of Unas, the last king of the 5th Dynasty, brought to light only "a right arm, a tibia, fragments of a skull and ribs and some linen scattered around the floor";[26] and accounts of the tomb of Teti, founder of the 6th Dynasty, mention a "completely blackened shoulder and arm."[27] Similarly, the sole extant evidence of the royal mummy of Pepy I[28] is to be found in one of four canopic vases, finely bound up in strips of cloth. As for King Merenra, Gaston Maspero[29] mentions that "the mummy, discovered by the *Rais* Mustapha . . . had been stripped by treasure-seekers and was almost completely naked." It would seem that the king's mummy had at least been found intact. But was that the right mummy?[30] The Egyptologist gives the following description of it: "The mummy was found near its sarcophagus. . . . The body was slight, delicate. The head was fine, adorned with the heavy tresses of adolescents, and one could easily make out the features, even though the lower jaw had disappeared and the pressure of the bandages had squashed the nose."[31] However, nothing seems to have been found of the mummy of King Pepy II, since the only thing that was discovered in his burial chamber were "a few scattered rags of linen."[32]

Royal wives also seem to have suffered the outrages inflicted by the tomb-robbers. C.M. Firth and B. Gunn[33] did find the cedarwood coffin of Queen Iput I, wife of King Teti, complete with bone remains and some of her jewelry.[34] Excavations in the burial complexes of queens Nubunet and Inenek/Inti, wives of King Pepy I, have only brought to light some bones. However, the recent work on the burial complex of Queen Ankhesenpepi II, mother of King Pepy II, did discover, scattered around the chamber and within the coffin, various bandages and bone fragments bearing evidence of the processes of embalmment and belonging to the body of a mature female.[35] Once again, however, the grave-robbers had been thorough in their work. One has to move forward to the 11th Dynasty (2064–2013 BC) before finding again royal mummies—those of Queen Ashayt and Henhenet, buried in the temple of Mentuhotep II at Deir el-Bahri.[36]

Royal Mummies in the Theban Mountains

The First Royal Cache at Deir el-Bahri (TT320)

The mummies best known to archaeologists and scientists are those of the kings who ruled over the New Kingdom (*c.* 1550–1075 BC) and were buried in the necropolis of Thebes. Historical events of the day obliged the authorities at the time to actually hide the royal graves from robbers, in order that they be preserved until modern times. The discovery of these tombs in the XIX century provided us with an incomparable source of information.

In order to put an end to the pillage and outrage that was being perpetrated upon royal tombs, the High Priest of Amun Pinudjem II decided during the 21st Dynasty to enlarge his family tomb (TT320)[37] so that it could hold not only the members of his family but also some forty or so coffins complete with burial furnishings; these included the mortal remains of kings Seqenenra Taa II,[38] Ahmose I, Amenhotep I, Thutmose I and II, Rameses I, Sety I, Rameses II, III, and IX. This transfer of royal mummies involved the functionaries who were responsible for gathering together not only the bodies but also the remains of their burial furnishings—no doubt within the enclosure of the temple of Medinet Habu. The pitiful state of these stripped bodies—many of which had been torn open—led the functionaries to decide upon their "reembalming," after which the bodies could be enveloped in new winding-cloths. Finally, royal cartouches were quickly traced on the recycled coffins, whose lids had been scraped and stripped of inscriptions before repainting. Certain of the mummies were accompanied by an account of the different moves and transfers they had been subjected to. For example, the body of Rameses II was buried in a usurped coffin[39] (figs. 1, 4) bearing three inscriptions concerning the changes in location of the mummy; and the lids of the coffins containing kings Rameses I[40] and Sety I[41] also bear identical accounts. The most ancient[42]—and almost illegible—inscription mentions the name of Herihor, high priest of Amun, and a date "year 6 [of the "renaissance era"], the 15th day of the third month of the season of *peret* [winter]"—that is, the twenty-fifth year of the reign of Rameses XI (*c.* 1079 BC). This is partly covered by a second inscription dated "year 10, fourth month of the season of *peret*, day 17." The inscriptions on the coffins of Rameses I and Sety I mention the name of King Siamun of the 21st Dynasty (979–960 BC), during whose reign the mummy "of the great god"

4. Alabaster fragment of a royal sarcophagus showing the Boat of Ra, from the tomb of Rameses II in the Valley of the Kings.
Cliché Y. Rantier, INET-LOUVRE-URA 1064 of the CNRS

(Rameses II) was transferred from the tomb of King Sety I—in which it had been placed before (perhaps during the time of Herihor)—so as to repose in peace in the tomb of Queen Inhapy.[43] The inscription then continues with the names of all the functionaries responsible for the successful completion of the operation. The third inscription, written three days later—that is, "year 10, fourth month of the season of *peret*, day 20"—speaks of the deposition of the coffin in the eternal dwelling-place of Amenhotep I, under the supervision of four other priests of Amun (only the names of the first three have survived).

Thus four whole days were necessary to bring the coffins and the royal contents to the cache of Deir el-Bahri. We do not know exactly what route was taken across the mountains of Thebes[44]—but it must have been safe enough to prevent anyone else taking it before the beginning of the XIX century.

While for archaeologists their most important discoveries are often a matter of chance and good fortune, they can sometimes be aided in their work by external events. In the summer of 1871[45] Mohamed Abd el-Rassul and his two brothers, Ahmed and Soliman—all of whom lived in the village of Qurna, on the west bank of the river Nile in the Theban cliffs—discovered a tomb full of coffins that had been hastily piled up on top of each other. The anthropomorphic coffins were adorned with cartouches and bore the *uraeus* on their foreheads. Their great discovery was to be kept as secret as possible, and thus the brothers decided to unwrap a few bodies to take away amulets, funeral statues, some painted wooden figures of Osiris and some half a dozen papyri. Over the next ten years, they would visit their treasure trove a total of three times.

Sold to rich visitors, the objects arrived in Europe where they aroused the curiosity of Egyptologists; and as early as 1878 Maspero was certain that one or more royal tombs had been discovered. Having arrived in Upper Egypt to investigate, the scholar ordered that the three Abd el-Rassul brothers be arrested and an investigation opened of the chief inhabitants of the village of Qurna. In spite of the pressure applied by the police force—and the two months he spent in prison—Ahmed el-Rassul said nothing; and the entire village testified in support of his family. Then, on June 25, Mohamed Abd el-Rassul went secretly to Qena to ease his conscience and tell the authorities that he knew where the cache was. On July 6, 1881, he led a group of people—including Gaston Maspero, Ahmed Kamal and Emile Brugsch—on a path along the cliffs southeast of Deir el-Bahri.

Maspero gives this account of Emile Brugsch's entry into the tomb (fig. 5): first there was "a descent into a well some 12 meters deep and 2 meters wide. On the west side at the base, an entrance was made into a corridor, which now measures 1.4 meters in width and 0.8 meters in height. The bay in the wall was formed by wooden doors that had since disappeared; after each ceremony they would have been closed with large clay tablets, on which the guardians of the necropolis put the signature of their office. After some 7.5 meters, the corridor turned abruptly north and continued for about 60 meters. Its size varied; sometimes it was about 2 meters wide, sometimes no more than 1.3 meters. Toward the middle, five crudely-cut steps marked a clear change in level; and to the right, a sort of incomplete niche some 3 meters deep revealed that they had once thought of changing the direction of the tunnel yet again. Finally, the tunnel led into a sort of irregular oblong chamber, about 8 meters in length. This was full of wooden sarcophagi, mummies and funeral objects. A white and yellow coffin bearing the name Nibsoni[46] barred the way just 60 centimeters inside the entrance. A little further on there was a solid coffin, that of Seqenenra Taa II, the form of which recalled the style of the 18th Dynasty; then came Queen Henuttawy [wife of Pinudjem I] and Sety I. Alongside, lying on a litter of dried flowers, were boxes of funerary statues, canopic jars and bronze libation vases. Throughout the corridor there was the same clutter, the same disorder; one had to crawl forward without knowing where one was putting one's hands and knees. Glimpsed hastily by the light of a candle, the coffins bore historic names: Amenhotep I and Thutmose II in the niche near the steps, then Ahmose and his son Siamun, Queen Ahhotep II, Ahmose Nefertari, the Pinudjem I that we had searched for so long, and yet others. In the end chamber, the disorder was at its greatest, but at first sight it was clear that the styles of the 20th and 21st Dynasties predominated. The success was beyond what we had hoped for: where I had expected to find two or three obscure kinglets, the Egyptian *fellahs* had unearthed entire families of pharaohs. And what pharaohs! Perhaps the most illustrious of all that had ruled over Egypt. . . ." The inhabitants of Qurna were equally surprised by the importance of the find. People were already letting their imaginations run away with them; there were rumors of "chests filled with gold, of necklaces of diamonds and rubies." This was why two hundred men were employed in two continuous days of work to empty the tomb and thus scotch attempted thefts (in the end, only fifty or so figures in blue enamel disappeared). By the evening of July 11 all the material was in Luxor. Three days later a steamship, the "Menshieh," arrived to take the mummies to Cairo. Having more or less survived their journey to the Bulaq Museum, the mummies were set up in a central hall; and it would take a further four years to draw up a complete inventory of the material discovered. However, in the absence of Maspero, Brugsch set about the unsystematic unwrapping of the bandages enveloping the mummy of Thutmose III and then that of Queen Ahmose Nefertari, which was giving off "a bad smell."[47] This would then oblige Maspero himself to undertake the unwrapping of the mummies "carefully and unhurriedly." The first to be examined, on June 1, 1886, was that of Rameses II. It took the entire month to examine all the bodies (with the exception of that of King Amenhotep I, which was spared because of the quality of its bandaging). Having examined them, Maspero recognized them as being in a poor general state; subsequently the mummies were then rewrapped "so that they could be decently exhibited in the museum." Many are now fittingly exhibited in a special hall of the Cairo Museum.

The Second Royal Cache: the Tomb of Amenhotep II (KV35)

In 1898, Victor Loret,[48] inspector of the Antiquities Service, carried out a series of thorough probes of the rocky terrain in the Valley of the Kings between the anonymous tomb (KV12) and the tomb of Chancellor Bay (KV13), practically opposite the tomb of Rameses III (KV11). On March 8 his hopes of finding a new tomb were fulfilled: an entranceway was discovered at the base of a high sheer wall. It was not until the next day that the opening was made wide enough for a man to pass through "crawling into the unknown." In a feverish atmosphere, the work of excavation continued day and night. Ladders, ropes and candles were necessary; however, progress was hampered by the litter of debris and limestone rubble, and the numerous shattered objects scattered around the floor. Having finally gained access to a large chamber, Loret could—by the light of his candle—make out an open sarcophagus: "Empty? I did not dare to hope the opposite, because no pharaohs had ever been found in the necropolis of Biban el-Moluk. . . . I approached the tomb with difficulty, careful not to crush anything underfoot. All over the outside of the sarcophagus I could read the name and first name of Amenhotep II. I leaned over the edge and raised my candle. Victory! A dark coffin lay at the bottom; near the head a bunch of flowers, near the feet a garland of leaves...." The proprietor of the tomb had just been found! However, the greatest discovery was yet to come; there was one more adjacent chamber left to investigate. Exploration of the western lateral annex revealed the presence of twelve other bodies, including that of a woman

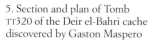

5. Section and plan of Tomb TT320 of the Deir el-Bahri cache discovered by Gaston Maspero

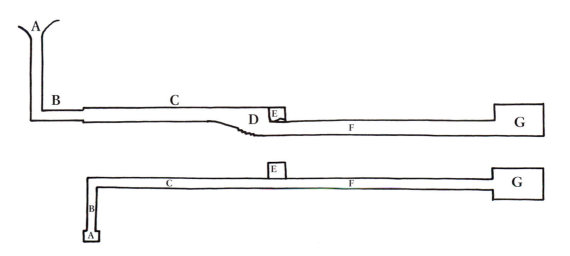

whose "admirably preserved face was of a noble and majestic gravity."[49] The entrance was apparently walled up; except that in the upper corner three stones seemed to have come loose. Pulling himself up to that level, Victor Loret pushed through first his candle, then his head: "The room was large—about three by four meters—and the candle gave scant light. However, I could still make out nine coffins on the floor. Six at the back of the room, three in front." The excavation required that before going any further he complete the inventory and plan of the fragments discovered in the other chambers; but then finally all that was left was this small chamber. Let us leave the archaeologist to describe these moments in his own words: "The coffins and mummies were uniformly gray in color. Bending over the nearest coffin, I blew on it so as to be able to read the name. The gray color was a layer of dust which flew away, enabling me to read the name and first name of Rameses IV. Was I in a cache of royal coffins? I rubbed the dust off the second coffin: a cartouche became visible, which I couldn't read at first; it was painted in matt black against a shiny background. I ran to the other coffins. On all of them, cartouches!"

Most of the mummies were transported in great secrecy to the Cairo Museum; legend has it that these bodies of kings passed through customs as "dried fish." Along with the titular pharaoh of the tomb, there were the bodies of eight other rulers of ancient Egypt: the 18th-Dynasty Thutmose IV and Amenhotep III, the 19th-Dynasty Merenptah, Sety II and Saptah, and the 20th-Dynasty Rameses IV, V and VI.

The discovery of these two caches proved to archaeologists that at some difficult moment in Egyptian history high functionaries had been forced to move the bodies of the dead kings, transferring them to places of burial that were safer than their own tombs. These two particular relocations had turned out to be very fortunate; alongside the coffins of the 21st-Dynasty high priests of Amun (and their families), they had preserved the mummies of most of the kings who had ruled in the period from the 18th to the 20th Dynasty.

The Robbery of Royal Tombs Since Ancient Times

Though highly sacrilegious, tomb-robbery was committed from the very earliest days of Egyptian history; in fact, archaeologists have revealed that tombs were very often robbed soon after being sealed. For the most part, the culprits were those who had built and decorated the tomb itself; and it was always the treasure in the royal burial chambers that these people were after. Obviously, such acts could only be carried out if a number of accomplices were involved—or if various factors worked together to produce a period of social and economic uncertainty, when the state administration and religious authorities could no longer guarantee the security of the tombs.

Various judicial accounts dating from the reign of Rameses IX at the end of the 20th Dynasty (for example, the famous Abbott Papyrus[50]) make mention of tomb-robbery in the Valley of the Kings and Valley of the Queens: among others, a certain Pakhar, "the Syrian," a coppersmith by trade, was accused of looting the tomb of Queen Ese (QV51), the royal wife of Rameses III.[51]

The confession of Imenpanefer reveals the level of corruption behind this practice: "In the year 13 [of Rameses IX], life, health, strength . . . we set out to rob the funeral monuments according to the plan of action that we follow very regularly. . . . Then, some days after, the curators of Thebes learned that we had carried out looting in the west. They seized us and locked me up in the place of the governor of Thebes. I took the twenty gold *deben* that had come to me as my share. I gave them to the scribe of the district of Tameniu Khaemopet; he freed me. I rejoined my accomplices and they gave me back a part. I then again started robbing the tombs of the dignitaries and public figures who were laid to rest to the west of Thebes."[52]

All this tomb-robbery forced the authorities to set up commissions to inspect the state of the tombs in the Valley of the Queens and the royal necropolis of Dra Abu el-Naga. Once these matters became an affair of state, there was veritable rivalry between Paser, the governor of Thebes, and Pauraah, the governor of the west bank; dissension between the two groups resulted in statements and witness reports being altered. Nevertheless, arrests were made. Punishment was severe—most of the culprits were executed—and yet, above all due to the famine of year eighteen, the looting started up again during the reign of Rameses XI. This time it

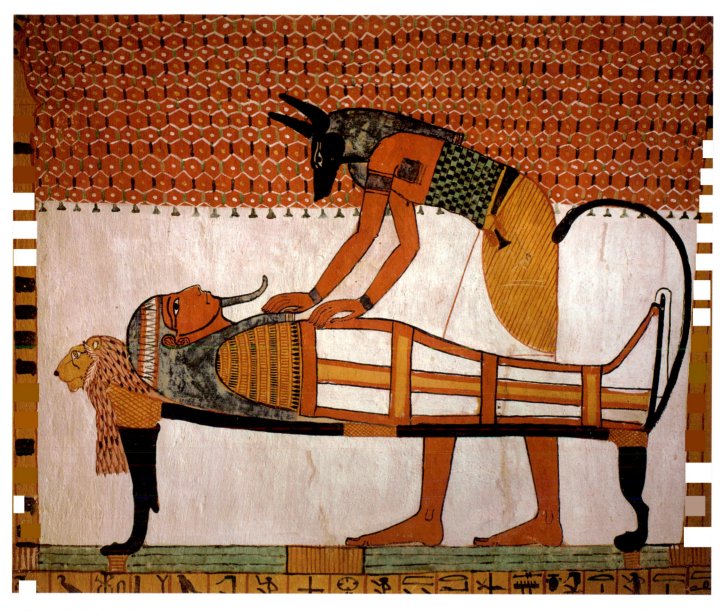

6. Wall-painting depicting Anubis,
god of the dead, leaning over the
mummy of Sennedjem, 18th Dynasty.
Necropolis of Deir el-Medina

7. Wall-painting from the tomb of Sennefer depicting the last journey of the deceased in the netherworld, 18th Dynasty, reign of Amenhotep II. Necropolis of Sheikh Abd el-Qurna

was extended to temples such as the Ramesseum and Medinet Habu. Again new trials were held.

All of this reveals the social instability and uncertainty about the future that prevailed in Upper Egypt at the end of the Ramesside period. It also explains why, after Rameses XI, kings chose not to be buried in the sacred mountain of Thebes. The choice of Tanis as the capital of the 21st and 22nd Dynasties offered only relative security, because only the kings (Psusennes I, Amenemope and Sheshonq II) were safe from looting, while all mummies suffered the irreversible effects of the humidity. But where are the bodies of the last kings who ruled before the arrival of the Greeks? While it seems likely that their burial site in some way coincided with the location of the city chosen as their capital, this supposition has yet to be proved by archaeological evidence.

Throughout classical antiquity, the gold of the pharaohs aroused the avidity of one and all. After all, who hasn't dreamed of discovering an undisturbed tomb, complete with royal mummy and all its rich furnishings? However, archaeologists are generally faced with a much more spartan reality. Still, there can be no doubt that there are fine discoveries yet to be made on the sandy plateau of Saqqara and the mountain slopes of Thebes. And while Saqqara and the necropolis of Memphis still harbor hidden royal tombs, the Valley of the Kings has yet to give up the tomb and mummy of Rameses VIII[53] or that of Nefertiti, the great wife of the heretical pharaoh Akhenaten.[54] Similarly, although we have identified the tomb of Rameses VII (KV1), we have not unearthed his mummy.[55] And again, in the Valley of the Queens, it is certain that during the 20th Dynasty the priests transferred to another cache, "undoubtedly outside the necropolis,"[56] the mummies of various queens (most notably the brides and daughter-brides of Rameses II—Nefertari, Bentanat, Meritamun, Henutmire and Henuttawy, daughter of Nefertari—and Rameses III's wives, Ese and Tyti) together with those of royal children who had been buried during the 19th and 20th Dynasties.

[1] "The reigning sovereign had both a visible, natural and corruptible body and an invisible, political and indestructible body. The two only separated at death: the natural body became a cadaver, the political body—up to then invisible—found concrete manifestation in an effigy." Mathieu 1994.

[2] During the Old Kingdom, a certain Hesy was head of the embalmers of the Great House, PM III.1, p. 122; Junker 1929–1943, p. 167.

[3] The canopic chest in wood containing the remains of Queen Hetepheres, wife of Sneferu, a pharaoh of the 4th Dynasty (c. 2575–2465 BC), reveals that the viscera might be removed through an abdominal incision, Reisner 1955, p. 54.

[4] Leca 1976, p. 54. It was during the 18th Dynasty that the treatment of the brain also became obligatory; from then onward there was a change in embalming procedures as the head became an important anatomical component in its own right. This change brought about technical innovations, and the excerebration hook was developed to serve this specific purpose.

[5] Sauneron 1952; Goyon 1972, pp. 18–182.

[6] Herodotus, *Histories* II, 86, 7–9; Diodorus Siculus would repeat these observations in his *Bibliotheca Historica* V, 91, 4.

[7] Harris, Weeks 1973; Harris, Wente 1980.

[8] Drenkhahn, Germer 1991.

[9] The instruments were reproduced by Alain Neveux, a talented sculptor from Nancy.

[10] Janot 2000.

[11] Nine instruments were discovered, Bietak, Reiser-Haslauer 1982, 191–193.

[12] Franco in Leblanc, de Cenival 1986, p. 30, pl. VI.

[13] Always carried out from the left-hand side. This was due to the religious significance attached to the left side of the individual, Pezin, Janot 1995. The incision was an oblique cut downward, from the outside to the inside, from the far end of the eleventh rib to the upper part of the ilium, Janot 2001.

[14] *Wb* II, p. 188, 5–8; Piccione 1981–1982; Corteggiani 1995.

[15] Discovered in the vestibule of the pyramid, this spatula-shaped instrument has a handle and a flattened end which is wider and softer (so as not to cause rupture), Jéquier 1936, p. 8. fig. 7.

[16] *Wb* I, 555, 2; Janot, Bourrier, Neveux 1999; Janot 2000, pp. 209–217.

[17] Jelínková-Reymond 1956, pp. 97–99.

[18] Grdseloff 1951.

[19] Drioton 1940.

[20] D. Arnold and R. Stadelmann do not agree, Arnold 1977, 12–14; Stadelmann 1985, pp. 213–214.

[21] Labrousse, Moussa 1996, p. 13, no. 1 and p. 58, no. 55.

[22] As soon as the mummification was over, the tent was struck; it was then raised again when needed, Dawson 1927, p. 41.

[23] The only specific list of embalming materials is said to be found on the *Vienna Aeg. 1* ostracon dating from the Ramesside period. The text is said to be the inventory of the contents of an embalmer's workshop at Deir el-Medina, which has never been found, Zonhoven 1979.

[24] Lauer, Derry 1935. Other fragments of the king's mummy—including part of the spine and of the ilium—were thought to have been found by B. Gunn in 1926; however, recent analyses cast some doubt on this attribution, Strouhal *et alii* 1998, pp. 1103–1107.

[25] Batrawi 1947, pp. 98–103.

[26] Maspero 1882, p. 178.

[27] Maspero 1884, p. 3. The complete investigation of the tunnel and chamber of Teti's tomb took two archaeological campaigns, in March 1951 and in 1955–56. The archaeologists found that "the only extant remains of the pillaged mummy were not in the coffin but scattered among the debris of the chamber (some bone fragments and burial bandages)." Lauer, Garnot 1958, p. 260.

[28] This measures 60 centimeters in height and has a diameter of 20 centimeters, Lauer 1970, pp. 582, 583, fig. 2; Lauer 1971, pp. 38 and 40; Leclant 1972, p. 257, figs. 13–14.

[29] Maspero 1887, p. 178. The mummy seems to have been examined by Derry 1947, p. 107.

[30] It seems plausible that the uncompleted tomb was later reused, Grimal 1988, p. 102.

[31] Maspero 1895, p. 43. At the time the mummy was exhibited to the public in a glass case.

[32] Maspero 1892, p. 56.

[33] Firth, Gunn 1935–1936, pp. 11–14.

[34] Dr. D.E. Derry in Firth, Gunn 1935–1936, p. 14.

[35] Fr. Janot in Dobrev, Labrousse, Mathieu 2000, p. 283.

[36] Naville 1907, pp. 50–51, pl. X; Winlock 1942, pp. 41–44.

[37] For a long time this was considered to be the tomb of Queen Inhapy, Winlock 1931. Since then that attribution has been doubted. In fact, the queen's remains would seem to be a "guest" in this 21st-Dynasty tomb created for the high priest of Amun, Pinudjem II, Dewachter 1975.

[38] This is the most ancient body found in this cache, Vandersleyen 1995, p. 189.

[39] CG61020, pls. XX–XXIII. In the form of a statue of Osiris that can be dated to the end of the 18th–beginning of 19th Dynasty, B. Letellier in Desroches Noblecourt 1976, p. 317 (n. LXXII).

[40] The very fragmentary inscription is on a part of the sarcophagus. Fortunately, this account can be pieced together because it is also found on the coffins of Sety I and Rameses II, Maspero 1895, p. 551, no. 17; pl. Xa; CG61018, pp. 26–29, pls. XV–XVII.

[41] Maspero 1895, pp. 553–556, no. 18; pl. Xb and pl. XII; CG61019, pp. 30–31, pls. XVI, XVIII–XIX.

[42] Cerny 1946, pp. 27–30; Thomas 1966, pp. 252–253, 28–29; B. Letellier in Desroches Noblecourt 1976, p. 317 (n. LXXII).

[43] Which thus will also have served as a previous cache, Reeves, Wilkinson 1996, p. 197.

[44] M. Kurz in J. Cerny *et alii* 1969–1970, pp. 46–49.

[45] Maspero 1889; PM I.2, pp. 658–667.

[46] Maspero 1895, p. 575; CG61051–61100, pp. 31–32.

[47] "The mummy was first relegated to the storerooms, and then provisionally buried, since it was on the verge of putrefaction." Maspero 1895, p. 525.

[48] Loret 1899; Reeves, Wilkinson 1996.

[49] The identity of this woman is still a matter of debate. Initially scholars took her to be Queen Tiy, wife of King Amenhotep III; they then identified her as Queen Hatshepsut, el Mahdy 1990, p. 39.

[50] Maspero 1874; Peet 1930; Thomas 1966, pp. 265–273; Reeves, Wilkinson 1966, pp. 192–193.

[51] Vernus 1993, p. 29.

[52] The Léopold II–Amherst Papyrus, II, 2, 1, 12–3, 7; Vernus 1993, p. 19.

[53] Leblanc 2001, pp. 153–172.

[54] A team of archaeologists is currently carrying out surveys in an attempt to locate this tomb and the mummy of its prestigious occupant.

[55] "Nothing is known of the whereabouts of most of his family, with the exception of a son who died before him." Vandersleyen 1995, p. 634.

[56] Leblanc 1999, p. 95.

2. Mummy of Nedjmet.
Cairo, Egyptian Museum

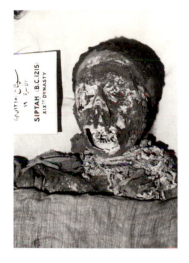

3. Mummy of Saptah.
Cairo, Egyptian Museum

The Display of the Royal Mummies in the Egyptian Museum

In March 1994 the Egyptian Museum in Cairo opened to the public the first phase of the new display of the royal mummies which included those of Seqenenra Taa (late 17th Dynasty), Amenhotep I, Meritamun, Thutmose II, Thutmose IV (18th Dynasty), Sety I, Merenptah, Rameses II (19th Dynasty), Rameses V (20th Dynasty), Nedjmet, and Henuttawy (21st Dynasty). More mummies of the New Kingdom are currently under preparation for display in a second room which is expected to be opened by the end of 2002 (as part of the centennial celebration of the museum). It will include: Ahmose I, Sitkamose, Ahmose Nefertari, Thutmose I, Thutmose III, Amenhotep II (18th Dynasty), Rameses III, Sety II, Saptah XI (19th Dynasty), Rameses IX or XII (20th Dynasty), Maatkara, Istemkheb (21st Dynasty). This display room will have the same conditions as the first one. The vaulted, starry ceiling will be similar to those of 18th-Dynasty royal tombs. The plan and architecture of the first royal mummy room is designed like a tomb with columns to simulate the tomb of Amenhotep II.

The Egyptian Museum possesses twenty-seven royal mummies from two caches.

The Caches

When the Egyptian Antiquities Service was founded in Cairo by Auguste Mariette in 1858, controls were placed on excavations and the export of artifacts for the first time. Anyone planning to dig had first to obtain a signed agreement from the Service, and thereafter inspectors had to be permitted on site at any time. No tomb could be entered without the presence of an inspector, and the contents of any violated tomb had to be presented first to the new Egyptian Museum. After the museum made its selections from the artifacts, the rest would belong to the excavator. Contents of unviolated, or intact, tombs would remain the property of the Egyptian government.

But illicit excavations continued. Amelia Edwards, one of the travelers to Egypt in the late XIX century who recorded her own observations, witnessed such a dig, and saw a coffin brought to light, carved with hieroglyphics and the four Sons of Horus. She further recorded that "Objects of great rarity and antiquity were being brought to Europe every season by travelers who had purchased them from native dealers living on the spot; and many of these objects were historically traceable to certain royal dynasties which made Thebes their royal city."

In 1874, Gaston Maspero, the head of the Egyptian Antiquities Service in Cairo, noticed that on the antiquities market, figures bearing royal names from the 21st Dynasty, a wooden tablet inscribed in ink, a papyrus belonging to Queen Nedjmet, and other artifacts were being sold. Other important objects like papyri, *shabti*-figurines, bronze vessels, inscribed wrappings, and perhaps even at least one mummy (that of the missing Rameses I?), were also leaking out onto the Luxor antiquities market. Maspero knew these came from no licensed excavation, yet, they had to have come from somewhere.

Maspero sent investigators but they learned nothing for years, while antiquities continued to appear. Finally in 1881, Maspero enlisted the aid of Charles Wilbour, a wealthy American collector, who was known to be willing to pay high prices for authentic antiquities. Within a few days after his arrival in Luxor, Wilbour made contact with a local guide who brought him to the village of Qurna and the house of Ahmed Abd el-Rassul. Wilbour was shown a quantity of red leather, looking as fresh as if it had just been opened, and stamped with the titles of a king. Wilbour immediately telegraphed Maspero.

Since the apparent culprits for the illegal sales were three brothers of the family of Abd el-Rassul, Maspero issued warrants for the arrests of Ahmed and Hussein Abd el-Rassul. Mustapha Agha Ayat, the consular agent for Britain, Belgium, and Russia, stationed in Luxor, was also implicated. The governor of Qurna gave Maspero permission to interrogate Ahmed Abd el-Rassul. But Ahmed refused to confess, and the mayor and leading townspeople of Qurna testified to his honesty on his behalf. Hussein was never heard of again however. Shortly thereafter, the authorities heard that quarrels had arisen between the brothers: Ahmed insisted upon taking a half share in profits from the treasure trove, as compensation for his jail time.

Mohamed el-Rassul, the eldest brother, then turned informer, and went to the authorities

4. Mummy of Henuttawy
after restoration.
Cairo, Egyptian Museum

5. Mummy of Henuttawy
before restoration.
Cairo, Egyptian Museum

6. Mummy of Rameses III,
New Kingdom, 20th Dynasty.
Cairo, Egyptian Museum

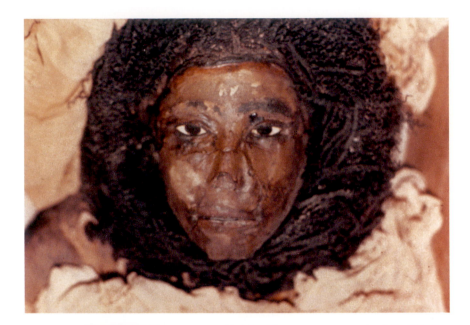

7. Showcase for the display of the royal mummies in the Egyptian Museum, Cairo. From top to bottom: alluminium frame, alluminium base slate, wooden frame under the alluminium base, wood stand frame with bellows

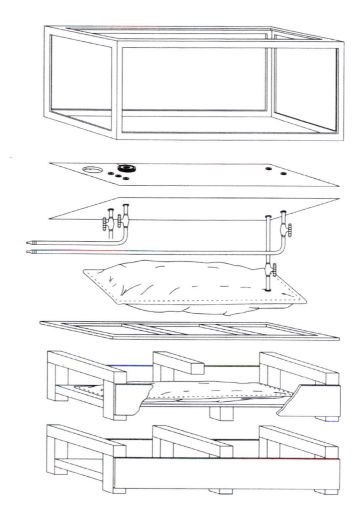

to divulge the location of the hidden tomb. The story Mohamed told of the discovery of the tomb was this: One day, years before, a goat belonging to Ahmed had strayed from its herd on the cliffs in the area of Deir el-Bahri. Ahmed investigated, following the bleating of his animal, and found that it had fallen down one of the vertical tomb-shafts, which honeycombed the cliffs. As he cursed the goat, he descended after it and found himself in a cramped corridor, cluttered with dark shapes. After he lit a candle, he saw that the shapes were a collection of dusty wooden coffins, stretching as far as he could see, heaped one upon another. Ahmed could see the occasional *uraeus*, the royal cobra, and several cartouches inscribed on the coffin lids. He also found *shabti*s, *shabti* boxes, canopic jars, and other funerary paraphernalia. Ahmed's eyes must have widened, as he realized that this was a royal find.

The el-Rassul family lived comfortably off the proceeds of their tomb, until, in the mid-1870s, the growing number of important funerary papyri reaching the West, as well as other objects in circulation on the local antiquities market, gave the game away.

Mohamed then took the officials of the Egyptian Antiquities Service to Deir el-Bahri. He showed them the actual tomb chamber, which contained coffins of some of ancient Egypt's greatest New Kingdom kings. The funerary trappings had disappeared, the gold sarcophagi had been melted down, and the mummies had even been rewrapped. But there they lay, beside the non-royal mummies.

Since Gaston Maspero was in France by this time, Emile Brugsch, an assistant at the Bulaq Museum, was called in to investigate the find. As he lowered himself into the shaft, Brugsch saw a low corridor piled high with "cases of faience funerary offerings, metal and alabaster vessels, draperies, trinkets, and then around a passage, a cluster of mummy cases . . . in such numbers. . . ."

The mummies of kings that were found in this cache were Seqenenra Taa, who had fought the Hyksos and bore a great head wound as apparent evidence, Ahmose I, the founder of the New Kingdom, Amenhotep I, the first three Thutmoside rulers, Siamun,

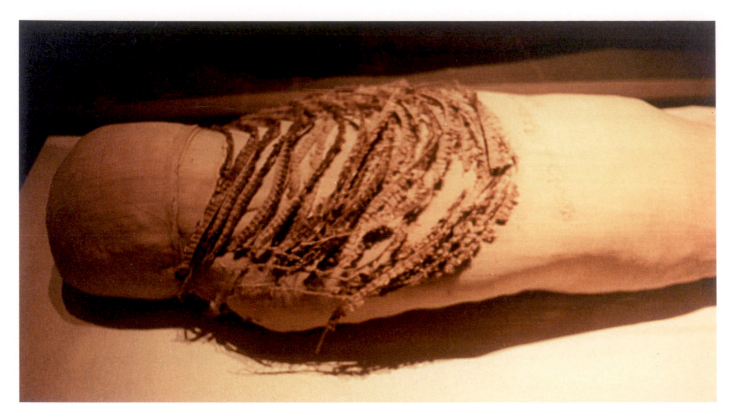

8. Mummy of Ahmose Meritamun, New Kingdom, 18th Dynasty. Cairo, Egyptian Museum

Ahmose Nefertari, Sitkamose, Ahmose Hentempet, Ahmose Henuttimehu, Inhapy, Meritamun, Ahmose Sapair, Sitamun, Baket, Rai, Sety I, Rameses II, III and IX, the coffin of Rameses I, Pinudjem I and II, Henuttawy, Istemkheb, Maatkara, Nedjmet, Neskhons, Masaharta, Tauheret, Nestanebtishru, Djedptahiufankh and eight other anonymous persons.

Within a matter of days, the tomb was emptied, and its occupants, in excess of fifty kings, princes, and courtiers, with almost 6000 accompanying objects, were sent to the Bulaq Museum. Prior to this find, it was already clear that each king was buried separately and independently of his predecessor(s). And each burial certainly had beautiful coffins, and funerary objects laid to rest with them. So why this jumbled collection? And why were some of the coffins in such poor condition, not truly suited to their royal tenants?

One indication was the following text written in ink on the bandages of the mummy of Rameses II: "Year 15, third month of *akhet*, day 6: Day of bringing the Osiris king Usermaatra Setepenra [Rameses II], Life! Prosperity! And Health!, to renew him and to bury him in the tomb of the Osiris King Menmaatra Sety [I] Life! Prosperity! Health! By the High Priest Pinudjem."

So apparently the mummy of Rameses II had been removed from his tomb, and reburied in the tomb of Sety I, and then both those mummies and that of Rameses I, had been removed and reburied within the tomb of Queen Inhapy. With these movements, the kings had lost most of their original burial equipment along the way. Gaston Maspero speculated that these constant moves were prompted by the attentions of tomb-robbers at the end of the New Kingdom. However, experts today believe that the stripping of the dead had not been done by local robbers, but by the state itself, hungry for gold at a time of economic decline. Evidence for this theory comes from the discovery of the funerary equipment and jewels for these earlier kings, reused, in the burials at Tanis of their 21st and 22nd Dynasty successors.

Maspero decided that the mummies fell into two groups, one, dating from the Second Intermediate and New Kingdom periods, poorly coffined, and the second, better equipped and dating from the Third Intermediate Period.

The final royal resting-place at Deir el-Bahri where these fifty and more coffins were found was the family vault of the Theban High Priest Pinudjem II, whose relations had occupied the end chamber of the tomb. Several decades later, after year eleven of Sheshonq I's reign in the 22nd Dynasty, the priestly family was joined by these battered royal mummies.

Mohamed el-Rassul meanwhile took on a job as foreman for the Egyptian Antiquities Service. In 1891 he led an inspector to yet another site in Deir el-Bahri, where the bodies of almost one hundred and sixty priests from Karnak and their relatives, lay at rest. Since it was suspected that Mohamed had known for quite a while about this cache, he was dismissed from the Service.

But the cache of royal mummies found at Deir el-Bahri was not the only one of its kind. In 1898 Victor Loret, excavating in the Valley of the Kings, not only discovered the tomb of Amenhotep II, but another royal cache in the tomb itself. Thirteen mummies, including those of Amenhotep II, Sety II, and Saptah, lay in this second cache.

Moreover, in the same room with the magnificent royal sarcophagus, Loret found other corpses. The first, thought to be King Sethnakhte of the 20th Dynasty, had been laid out on the battered hull of one of Amenhotep II's wooden model boats, left in the antechamber to the tomb. Three further mummies were found, without coffins, and stripped of their bandages. They were neatly placed in a side-room leading off the burial chamber. The first had long flowing hair and a thick veil on her forehead and left eye. This was the mummy later called "The Elder Lady." The second mummy was that of a young boy, his head shaved except on the right temple, where the sidelock of youth flowed. The third mummy was that of a youthful woman, whose face showed evidence of a dislocated jaw. All three corpses had had their skulls pierced with a large hole, and the breast of each was opened. Experts studying the corpses believe this happened when the bodies were robbed, in order to unwrap the bandages faster and take the amulets and jewelry.

The second side chamber contained nine more bodies, with their wrappings intact, but placed in a variety of ramshackle coffins. Loret soon discovered cartouches on the coffins, and realized that he had found yet another royal cache. He determined that the mummies had been reburied in the tomb of Amenhotep II at the end of the second millennium BC. At that time, Amenhotep II himself had also been "restored." However, everything of any value had been stripped from the coffins.

Amenhotep III was there, of course, in his red quartzite sarcophagus but placed in a coffin inscribed for the much later king Rameses III, and covered with a lid inscribed for Sety II; nearby were Thutmose IV, Merenptah (in the lower part of a coffin inscribed for Sethnakhte), Sety II, Saptah, Rameses IV, Rameses V and Rameses VI. The last of these mummies was an anonymous female lying on the upturned lid of a coffin inscribed for Sethnakhte. The heads of Saptah, Sety II, Rameses IV, VI and possibly even V all bore similar cranial holes.

In early 1901, the guards watching over this tomb were overpowered, and the tomb itself rifled once again. The mummy that had been laid in the boat vanished, and the mummy of Amenhotep II itself was unwrapped, the amulets and jewels stolen and one arm even torn off. The inspector who had traced the robberies of Amenhotep II's cache was Howard Carter. He resigned from the Egyptian Antiquities Service but later returned to Luxor. Here he met Lord Carnarvon, and four years later they formed a partnership to begin digging.

The Scientific Basis of Mummification in Ancient Egypt

In all the techniques used, the basic principle of mummification was the dehydration of the body tissues so that the bacteria would not live on its tissues and cause putrefaction and decay. The techniques in mummification first practiced in the Old Kingdom developed steadily in the different periods until it attained its peak. The process of mummification can be summarized in the following steps:

Putting the corpse on the operating table: The body was brought to the house of mummification. It was stripped of all its clothes and put on a wooden board.

Extraction of the brain: This was generally done by passing a chisel through the ethmoid bone into the cranial cavity and then, with a rod hooked at one end, the brain was cut into small pieces and removed with another spoon-shaped instrument. Sometimes other methods were also practiced, including excerebration through the base of the skull or by trepanned orbit. The extracted brain, obviously not preserved since it was reduced to small pieces, was most probably kept with the general remains of mummification.

Extraction of the viscera: The vital organs were extracted through an incision which was usually made on the left side of the abdomen. Diodorus Siculus described the rites which were performed in this process: "First he who is called the scribe, laying the body down, marks the left flank where it is to be cut. Then he who is called the cutter takes an Ethiopian stone and cuts the flesh as the law prescribes, then forthwith escapes, by running away, those who are present pursuing and throwing stones at him and cursing him because of the defilement [of his act]. For whosoever inflicts violence upon, or wounds, or in any way injures a body of his kind, they deem worthy of hatred."

Through this incision, all the contents of the abdominal cavity namely, the stomach, the liver, the spleen, and the intestines, were removed, while the kidneys were sometimes left in their place and sometimes removed. The diaphragm was then cut and the thoracic contents taken out except for the heart and the aorta. The Egyptians attached great importance to the preservation of the heart in the body. To them the heart and not the brain, was the seat of mind and benevolent emotions such as charity and love. It had also a great religious significance, since it was believed to be the organ which recorded all the good and evil deeds of a person during his life, and so was needed for the judgment of the deceased in the afterworld. As illustrated in Spell 125 of the Book of the Dead, the heart is weighed against a figure of Maat, the goddess of truth and justice. If it balanced equally to Maat, the person was considered "true of voice" or innocent, and was introduced to the god Osiris with whom he would live forever in paradise. If the heart proved to be heavier, this meant that his evil outweighed his good deeds and he was therefore thrown to the monster. For this reason they frequently put a heart scarab in the cavity beside the heart, on which Spell 30 was written: "O my heart which I had from my mother; O my heart which I had upon earth, do not rise up against me as a witness in the presence of the lord of things; do not speak against me concerning what I have done . . . . You are my *ka* dwelling in my body and united with it, make strong my members. Come forth to paradise, transport us there too. Do not make my name stink in front of the Divine Lords. Be fair toward us, make fair hearing at the weighing of the words. Speak not lies against me in front of the great God. Surely you will be uplifted living."

Sterilization of the body cavities and viscera: The thoracic and abdominal cavities, as well as the extracted viscera, were then all washed with palm wine and spices. Palm wine, as manufactured in ancient Egypt usually contained about 14 per cent of ethyl alcohol. Ethyl alcohol is known to be one of the most important sterilizing agents for medical purposes.

Embalming the viscera: The viscera were freed of their contents, washed and sterilized as above. They were then dehydrated in solid natron in a small bag for about forty days. After being dried and resterilized, they were anointed with perfumed oil and treated with molten resin. Lastly, they were wrapped separately and, in some cases, put into small gold anthropoid coffins, such as those of Tutankhamun or silver ones such as those of Sheshonq II. These small coffins (or more often the bandaged viscera without coffins) were put into canopic jars, each being identified as one of the four Sons of Horus. The lids of these jars were fashioned in the shape of human heads until the end of the 18th Dynasty. After the 18th Dynasty they were fashioned into the actual shaped of the four Sons of Horus: Imsety (human-headed) cared for the liver; Hapy (baboon-headed) guarded the lungs; Duamutef (jackal-headed) protected the stomach; and Qebehsenuef (hawk-headed) looked after the intestines. These jars were then placed in a canopic chest which was sometimes surmounted by a statue of Anubis, the god of the cemetery and mummification.

Temporary stuffing of the thoracic and abdominal cavities: The thoracic and abdominal cavities were next packed with three kinds of temporary stuffing materials enclosed in linen packets containing dry natron in order to speed the dehydration of the body tissues from inside, other packets of linen to absorb the extracted water that might accumulate in the two cavities, and still other packets of linen impregnated with odoriferous gum-resin that perfumed the body and eliminated the odor of putrefaction during the long period needed for dehydration of the body.

Dehydration of the body: Scientifically, the main operation of mummification depended upon the extraction of the water from the body by osmosis, accomplished by placing the body on a heap of dry natron on a slanting bed, known as the mummification bed; at its end was a small semicircular basin in which the water extracted from the body was collected. This process required forty days, and is supported by Biblical evidence (Genesis 50:3) concerning the mummification of Jacob according to the Egyptian rites. While it is most probable, therefore, that the dehydration process took forty days, the remaining thirty days of the total of seventy days (which were required for the entire mummification process, as is mentioned in many ancient Egyptian texts) were used for carrying out the remaining procedures and ceremonies, as mentioned in the book of the "ritual of embalming."

Removal of the temporary stuffing material: After the dehydration process was completed, the body was taken out of the natron and the temporary stuffing materials removed from the thoracic and abdominal cavities. These had become saturated and would have led to putrefaction if left in the body. They were put in special jars which were buried in sand near the tomb or in a little chamber beside it. Many samples of these refuse embalming materials have been discovered and have provided us with information about the materials used.

Packing the body cavity with permanent stuffing materials: The cranial cavity was then stuffed with resin or with linen soaked in resin. The thoracic and abdominal cavities were most probably washed with palm wine and then stuffed with fresh dry materials, most of which were enclosed in linen bags. These included natron, myrrh, cinnamon, cassia, packets of linen cloth impregnated with resin, sawdust, and occasionally one or two onions. In most cases the two lips of the incision were then drawn together, closed with resinous paste and covered with a small plate of gold or beeswax inscribed with the sacred eye of Horus (the *wedjat*). In a few cases, however, the embalming incision was sewn up with linen string.

Anointing the body: The body was anointed with cedar oil and other precious ointments, and then rubbed with myrrh, cinnamon and other fragrant materials.

Packing the face openings: The mouth, the ears, and the nose were packed with beeswax or linen soaked in molten resin. The eyeballs were pressed slightly down, covered with linen pads dipped in molten resin and the eyelids drawn over them, in order that they appear at their normal level as they had been in life.

Covering the skin with resin: The whole body surface was treated with molten resin that both strengthened the skin and closed its pores to prevent moisture from penetrating.

Adorning and bandaging the mummy: The mummy was adorned with the jewelry that had previously been prepared for it and with amulets. The mummy of Tutankhamun was adorned with 143 fine pieces of jewelry, including rings, earrings, necklaces, collars, pectorals, bracelets, etc. as well as various kinds of amulets. In some cases a girdle of disk beads with a central pendant in the form of a crouching falcon in cornelian was placed around the mummy's abdomen so that the hawk pendent lay over the embalming incision. The falcon of this amulet evidently meant to protect the lower part of the body and magically seal the embalming incision. The body was then wrapped in bandages that stuck to the body by means of molten resin or gum resin.

After these processes and the religious rites in association with them were completed, the priest performed the "opening of the mouth" ceremony. In this ritual, the priest touched the mouth of the mummy so as to restore to the dead person all the faculties of life that, as they believed, would enable him to once more see with his eyes, hear with his ears, open his mouth and speak, eat and move his arms and legs. The last words addressed to him in the embalming rituals were: "You will live again, you will live for ever. Behold, you are young again for ever."

New Kingdom Mummies

The majority of the New Kingdom mummies found date to the 18th and the 19th Dynasties, a time when mummification achieved what can be called its classic phase. This occurred throughout the rest of the New Kingdom, while some splendid innovations subsequent-

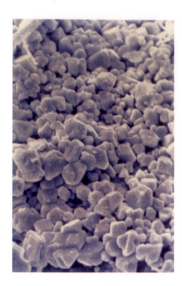

9. Microscopic view of dry natron used for the dehydration of the body

ly occurred in the otherwise rather chaotic Third Intermediate Period. Royal, noble and poor corpses from the New Kingdom indicate that there was simultaneous practice of different types of mummification.

With Ahmose, the first pharaoh of the 18th Dynasty, the brain was removed in an unusual manner. It seems that an incision was made in the left side of the neck, the atlas vertebra removed, the brain extracted through the foramen magnum, and the empty cranium packed with linen. A few isolated examples of this method occurred in the Old and Middle Kingdom, but it never became popular.

The lavish use of resin was common in the New Kingdom. It was carefully applied to the face and body, and poured, via the nose into the emptied cranium, stuffed up nostrils, molded into little balls and used to plug ears and occasionally the anus. Tutankhamun's mummy had so much resin and sacred oils spread over the body that heated knives had to be used to free the body from its coffin in the final unwrapping stage.

Flank incisions were covered by resin smears, and in the case of the wealthy, with a rectangular or oval piece of metal, frequently gold. The location of this incision changed during the New Kingdom. Prior to the mummy of Thutmose III, it was a vertical incision on the left side perpendicular to the rib cage; it then became a diagonal cut from the hipbone to the pubes. Thutmose III's incision is neatly stitched rather than being held together with resin. After his reign, both the stitching and resining of incisions continued; it was not until the 20th Dynasty that stitched incisions became the norm.

Once the embalmers had inserted their hands into the incision and removed the liver, stomach, and intestines, they cut through the diaphragm and pulled out the lungs. During this operation the heart might be inadvertently removed, but it was then replaced, occasionally after having been wrapped separately. In the case of Sety I, it was accidentally loosened and found on the right side of the body. It was imperative to keep the heart in the body because it would be used in the final judgment. The eviscerated organs were treated with natron and spices, wrapped up, and then placed in canopic jars, sometimes shaped like miniature human mummies. It was not until the 20th Dynasty, however, that the practice of returning the internal organs to the body cavity is found. This would subsequently become much more common.

The body cavity would then be washed with water, and then by palm wine, before being packed with natron for desiccation, myrrh for scent, resin for disinfecting and bacterial control, linen for absorbing liquids, and possibly frankincense for perfume. The body would be covered with natron. The natron and incense filler as well as the external natron would no doubt be changed during the drying period. When the final wrapping took place, the body cavities were filled with resin-impregnated linen to maintain the shape and deter insects.

In addition to an elaboration in desiccation methods, many New Kingdom mummies show signs of the cosmetic care lavished on them by embalmers: balding women have false hair woven into their own sparse locks; the nails, especially of the royal mummies, are hennaed; from the 19th Dynasty onward black lines are painted on foreheads to indicate the hair line, while lines are sometimes drawn to emphasize eyebrows. Occasionally the hair has been hennaed, and in the instance of Yuya and Tuyu, the parents of queen Tiy, it is blond, perhaps due to a reaction between the henna and the chemicals used in mummification, or perhaps it is faded henna on white hair.

In the later part of the 18th Dynasty, small pieces of linen with cursorily drawn eyes were placed over the eyes, so as to provide new eyes for the mummies. The 20th-Dynasty ruler Rameses IV had small onions used as eyes as well as onions placed in his ears and nostrils, which had been filled with resin and covered by a piece of onion skin. This may have been because onions are antiseptic agents, or because their strong odor might aid the mummy's nose to function well in the afterlife.

From the 19th Dynasty onward, the body was stuffed very carefully so as to better retain its shape and not be crushed by the bandages.

Rameses II's distinctive nose had been packed with seeds and a small animal bone to make it withstand the pressure of the bandages applied during mummification. The abdomens of Merenptah, Saptah, and Rameses IV, among others, were filled with dried lichen to bet-

10. Gold plaque placed on the abdominal incision of the mummy after the extraction of the viscera

ter preserve the shape of the body. Rameses V was filled with sawdust, an adumbration of a practice that became common in the 21st Dynasty.

A curious feature of New Kingdom embalming is that finger and toenails show evidence of having been tied with string onto the digits for the duration of the natron process. This practice saved the nails from falling off when the surrounding skin shrank because of desiccation. Unusual care was also occasionally taken with male genitalia—the penis of Tutankhamun was mummified fully erected. Strangely, some time after the unwrapping of the king, this member vanished from the mummy, and is yet to be discovered. It is possible that the theft of this part occurred during World War II, when other acts of vandalism took place in the Theban necropolis. The mummy suffered other damage at the same time. On the other hand, the phalluses of Thutmose III and certain other Thutmoside royalty were bound tightly against one thigh, so that they effectively disappeared from view, perhaps to avoid the loss of this important piece of the royal anatomy.

Frequently, when members or extremities of corpses fell off because of desiccation or rapid decomposition, the embalmers tried to provide the dead with reproductions in resin and bandages so that these would not be missing in the afterworld. Embalmers of the 21st Dynasty were particularly gifted in this respect. Certainly, when the New Kingdom mummies from Deir el-Bahri cache were restored, sometimes the embalmers had to provide virtually new bodies since they had been so violently ravaged by robbers. Thutmose II's mummy was so badly damaged that the ancient restorers had to use narrow wooden splints to hold the body together and Rameses VI was so destroyed that the various parts of his body had been tied to a coffin in order to give it some form.

The Position of the Arms

The New Kingdom saw the regularization of the position of the arms. Men's and women's arms lay along their sides with their hands covering their genitalia. An exception to this is the superbly preserved mummy of Yuya, the father of Queen Tiy. His arms were bent at the elbow and crossed under the chin. Perhaps this was due to his semi-royal status as the father of the queen. After Ahmose, whose arms were extended along his body, his hands turned inward along his thighs, and starting with Amenhotep I, the kings had their arms crossed over their breasts with their hands grasping the royal scepters. The mummy of Sety I is the first royal mummy to have the palms flat. This royal arm position is one of the reasons why there is very serious doubt as to the true identity of the mummy frequently attributed to Thutmose I: his arms are stretched down alongside his body, and the hands are broken off.

Few royal women have been found, and thieves have torn off the arms of many of those in search of jewels. For the most part, the arms of royal women, like those of their noble counterparts, are at their sides with the hands covering the pudenda.

Historical Background to the Collection of Royal Mummies
Seqenenra Taa II—17th Dynasty (1558–1553 BC)
The fourteenth king of the Theban dynasty, ruling Egypt contemporaneously with the Hyksos 15th and 16th Dynasties, was the son of Taa I and Queen Tetisheri. When Taa II received word from Apepi, ruler of the Hyksos capital in Avaris, that the hippopotami in the sacred pool at Thebes kept him awake with their snoring, Taa regarded it as an insult. The hippopotami were 650000 kilometers from Apepi's sleeping chambers! Taa declared war but was soon killed. His mummy shows evidence of blows from battle-axes, spears and lances. His ribs, vertebrae and skull were fractured. His heir, Kamose, assumed the throne and the war was victorious.

Ahmose—18th Dynasty (1550–1525 BC)
Egypt's 18th Dynasty that established the New Kingdom is, to most people interested in Egypt, a dynasty of stars. It is the dynasty of Tutankhamun who was a fairly minor king, but perhaps the best known of any of the pharaohs. It was also the dynasty of the well known Akhenaten, and of Queen Hatshepsut.

The founder of this dynasty is less well known to the general public, but unquestionably

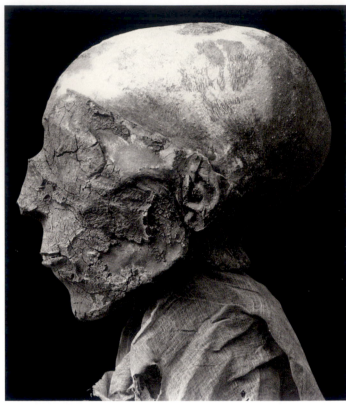

11. Mummy of Rameses IV,
New Kingdom, 20th Dynasty.
Cairo, Egytpian Museum

12. Mummy of Sety II,
New Kingdom, 20th Dynasty.
Cairo, Egytpian Museum

of major importance to Egyptian history. He was Ahmose I, during whose reign Egypt was finally and completely liberated from the Hyksos. Various scholars attribute different dates to his reign, but he probably became ruler of Egypt about 1550 BC, and ruled for a period of around twenty-five years before his death (examination of his well preserved mummy suggest he was about thirty-five when he died).

Ahmose I (Amosis to the Greeks) was given the birth name Ahmose ("The moon is born"). His throne name was Nebpehtyra ("The lord of strength is Ra"). He was probably a boy when he assumed the throne, having lost his father Seqenenra Taa II and his brother Kamose within three years of each other. His mother was Queen Aahotep, a powerful woman who was perhaps his coregent during his early years.

Egyptologists believe that early in his reign, little was accomplished and the Hyksos may have even gained some ground, recapturing Heliopolis. However, by the end of his first decade in power, we know from the autobiography of Ahmose, son of Ibana, a naval officer from Elkab, that he laid siege to Avaris (the tomb of Ahmose Pennekheb, another soldier, also records the campaigns). This long battle was interrupted by the need to put down insurrections in already liberated territories, but was apparently successful sometime between his twelfth and fifteenth regnal year. Afterwards, he attacked the southwest Palestinian fortress of Sharuhen in a six-year siege that finally put an end to the Hyksos control of Egypt.

Next, he turned his attention to Nubia (Kush) and, while Kamose (his predecessor) may have gained some ground prior to his death, Ahmose I pushed the boundaries south to the second cataract. Here, he established a new civil administration at Buhen, probably initially headed by a viceroy named Djehuty.

Apparently, while Ahmose I was in Nubia, former Hyksos allies again attempted a few uprising in the North, led by an archenemy of Kamose named Tetian. In this instance, Ahmose I's mother, Ahhotep, was probably responsible for putting down the rebellion and for this she was awarded the gold flies, an award for valor found on her mummy in her intact tomb at Thebes.

After Ahmose I's campaigns in Nubia, he once again returned to Palestine during his twenty-second year in power and may have fought his way as far as the Euphrates, according to information on a stele of Thutmose I.

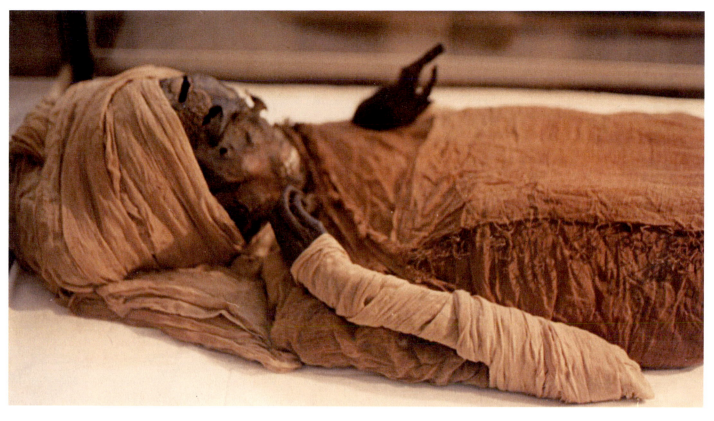

13. Mummy of Seqenenra Taa I,
Second Intermediate Period,
17th Dynasty.
Cairo, Egyptian Museum

Ahmose married his sister, Ahmose Nefertari, and had a number of children including Meritamun, who died young.

He was buried in the Dra Abu el-Naga area, but his tomb has yet to be found. His mummy was found in the Deir el-Bahri cache. He had a cenotaph at south Abydos, consisting of a cliff temple, pyramid and temple on the edge of the Nile valley. The pyramid which measures about 70 meters square is the last known royal example built in Egypt. Some battle scene decorations within the pyramid complex may have depicted his wars with the Hyksos. These scenes contain some of the earliest representations of horses in Egypt.

Amenhotep I—18th Dynasty (1525–1504 BC)
The son of Ahmose and Queen Ahmose Nefertari, Amenhotep I was the second king of the18th Dynasty. He may have ascended to the throne at a relatively early age, for an elder brother had been designated as heir only about five years earlier. He may have even briefly been coregent with his father, however. He evidently continued many of the practices of his father, and his mother certainly played an important part in his reign, acting as "god's wife of Amun." Amenhotep I may have been married to his sister, (Ahmose) Meritamun, though there is apparently little documentation to substantiate this relationship. Better known is this king's daughter, Satamun, who is known both from her coffin, found in one of the royal mummy caches, and from two statues in central and southern Karnak. Because of chronological questions, the dating of the king's rule is uncertain. A heliacal rising of the dog star Sirius is believed to have been seen during his reign, as recorded in the Ebers Papyrus, which states: "Ninth year of the reign of his majesty the king of Upper and Lower Egypt, Djeserkare—may he live forever! Festival of the New Year: third month of summer, ninth day—rising of Sirius."

He was probably the first pharaoh to build his tomb some distance from his mortuary temple, a practice emulated by his successors. While the mortuary temple itself has been located, his tomb remains a mystery. And while some Egyptologists believe it to be an uninscribed tomb at Dra Abu el-Naga, outside of the Valley of the Kings, and others believe it might be KV39 within the valley proper, its location has not yet been established. An inspection of the tomb in year sixteen of Rameses IX's reign reported that the tomb was in-

14. Mummy of Amenhotep I,
New Kingdom, 18th Dynasty.
Cairo, Egytpian Museum

tact at that time. His mummy, along with his father's and a number of others, was found in excellent condition in the royal mummy cache of 1881.

Some information appears to indicate that Amenhotep I's son died in infancy, while other resources tell us he died childless. At any rate, his military commander, Thutmose (I), who was married to the king's sister, princess Ahmose, assumed the throne upon Amenhotep I's death. There is even a possibility that Thutmose I was a grandson of Ahmose, the father of Amenhotep I. He may have even served as coregent prior to Amenhotep I's death.

Thutmose I (Aakheperkara)—18th Dynasty (1493–1481 BC)
The third king of the 18th Dynasty was a commoner by birth. He had married Ahmose, a sister of Amenhotep I, and was named pharaoh when the king died childless. Ahmose bore him two sons who were passed over for Thutmose II, who was born to Mutnofret. Thutmose built an extension to the temple of Amun at Karnak He added pylons, courts and statues. He led a campaign into Nubia where he penetrated beyond the third cataract. He defeated the Nubian chief in a hand-to-hand combat and returned to Thebes with the body of the fallen chief hanging on the prow of his ship. His greatest campaigns were in the Delta. Warring against the Hyksos, he subdued the tribes and finally reached the Euphrates river. To commemorate his victory he built a hypostyle hall at Karnak, made entirely of cedar wood columns. His remains were found in the Deir el-Bahri cache. Thutmose I brought a sense of stability to Egypt and his military campaigns assuaged the wounds of the Thebans.

Thutmose II—18th Dynasty (1492–1479 BC)
Thutmose II might never have ruled Egypt but the early death of Wadjmose and Amenmose, the eldest sons of Thutmose I, left him as the only heir. He became the fourth ruler of Egypt's18th Dynasty. He was apparently the oldest son of Mutnofret, a minor royal queen of Thutmose I, who was herself the sister of Thutmose I's principal queen, Ahmose.

In order to strengthen his position and legitimize his rule, he was married to Hatshepsut, the oldest daughter of Thutmose I and Queen Ahmose Nefertari. She was very possibly older then Thutmose II. During this period, Hatshepsut also carried the title, "god's wife of Amun," a position she may have had even before the death of Thutmose I. Hatshepsut would have been both Thutmose II's half sister and cousin. In the light of history she became a much better known pharaoh than her husband.

We believe that Thutmose II had only one son by a harem girl named Isis (or Iset). However, Thutmose III would have to wait to rule Egypt until after Hatshepsut's death. Thutmose II must have realized the ambitions of his wife, because he attempted to foster the ascent of his son to the throne by naming him his successor before he died. But upon Thutmose II's death, his son was still very young, so Hatshepsut took advantage of the situation by first naming herself as regent, and then taking on the full regalia of the pharaoh. Thutmose may have also had as many as two daughters by Hatshepsut. We are fairly sure one of them was named Neferura while another possible daughter was named Neferubity. We know that Thutmose II was a weak person physically, and many Egyptologists speculate that even during his rule Hatshepsut may have been the real power behind the throne. We believe that Thutmose II ("born of the god Thoth"), ruled for about fourteen years before dying in his early thirties. However, recent scholars wish to shorten his rule to three years. He is also sometimes called Tuthmosis, or Thutmosis (the birth name that the Greeks used), and his throne name was Aakheperenra, which means "great is the form of Ra." *The Oxford History of Egypt* places his reign from 1492–1479, while the *Chronicle of the Pharaohs* provides dates of 1518 to 1504. Aidan Dodson's *Monarchs of the Nile* gives his reign as 1491–1479 BC.

We know that he sent campaigns to Palestine and Nubia, attested to by a short inscription in the temple at Deir el-Bahri and a rock-cut stele at Sehel south of Aswan. We are told that he had to crush a revolt in Nubia in his first year and that this bought about the demise of the kingdom of Kush at Kerma. Apparently, to punish the Kushites for their rebellion, he had everyone put to death with the exception of a royal son, who was brought back to Egypt as a hostage. We are told that the Palestine campaign was against the Shasu bedouin in the region of Nahrin. However, the term Shasu may also refer to Nubians, and some Egyptologists believe that this reference really relates to the campaign in Nubia.

We also have evidence of Thutmose II's building projects. Traces of a temple built by him have been found just north of the temple of Medinet Habu on the west bank at Luxor (ancient Thebes). This small temple, known as *Shespetankh* ("chapel of life"), was finished by his son, Thutmose III. He also had built a pylon-shaped limestone gateway in front of the fourth pylon forecourt at Karnak which also had to be completed by Thutmose III. The material from this gate and another limestone structure were later reused in the building of Karnak's third pylon foundation. However, the gate has since been rebuilt in Karnak's Open Air Museum. Scenes on the gate sometimes depict Thutmose II with Hatshepsut, and sometimes Hatshepsut alone. On one side of the gate, Thutmose II is shown receiving crowns, while other scenes depict his daughter, Neferura, and Hatshepsut receiving life from the gods. We also know of a building project in Nubia at Semna and Kumma, and surviving blocks from his buildings at Elephantine. A statue of Thutmose II, found at Elephantine, was probably commissioned by Hatshepsut.

We have not really identified either a tomb or a completed mortuary complex for Thutmose, though his mummy was found in the royal cache of Deir el-Bahri.

Thutmose III—18th Dynasty (1479–1425 BC)

The son of Thutmose II and a minor royal wife named Aset, Thutmose III Menkheperra, was apparently still a boy when his father died. His "stepmother/aunt" Hatshepsut, the only surviving royal adult (king's daughter, king's sister and king's chief wife), took over the role of regent, but after a few years, assumed the aspect of female pharaoh (some say after two years, others later in his reign). It remains uncertain how this virtual coup was engineered, although the official line was that, as the divine offspring of the god Amun, Hatshepsut had been declared a legitimate successor by her father during his lifetime. Royal propaganda was also later used by Thutmose III himself, claiming that he was singled out as a youth by Amun to be pharaoh. The Hatshepsut "regency" appears not to have been a full usurpation. Various events are dated solely to Thutmose's reign during this period, and the king is shown with Hatshepsut as coruler on some monuments. The subsequent erasure of Hatshepsut's name and figure from monuments, often replaced by those of Thutmose I or Thutmose II, may not have taken place until late in Thutmose III's reign, perhaps to strengthen the legitimacy of his intended successor by removing any reference to an earlier coruler.

Shortly after Hatshepsut's death, in year twenty-two of Thutmose III's reign, the king began a long series of campaigns in Syria–Palestine, "extending the borders" of Egypt and eventually bringing many of the minor principalities of the region under Egyptian control. Initially stimulated by a rebellion by local princes against Egyptian control about the time of Hatshepsut's death, this was also a reaction to the emerging power of the kingdom of Mitanni in northern Syria, to which a coalition of Canaanite rulers, led by the prince of Qadesh, had allied themselves. Egyptian control of the region, established under the pharaohs of the 18th Dynasty following the expulsion of the Hyksos, had been threatened by the decline of military activity in Hatshepsut's reign. Beginning with a stunning victory against the assembled rebel princes at Megiddo, an Egyptian sphere of influence in northern Palestine and southern Syria was solidified, and raids into the lands of the Mitanni across the northern Euphrates checked that kingdom's power. After seventeen campaigns, Egypt's holdings in Canaan and Syria, although still contested by Mitanni, had reached their greatest extent.

Thutmose III also extended Egypt's border to the south, reaching as far as the fourth Nile cataract deep in Nubia, which became the southern frontier of the growing Egyptian empire. The control of the gold mines of the area filled the state and temple treasuries, as did plunder and tribute from the north.

Numerous building activities were carried out during his reign, with substantial additions to temples throughout Egypt and Nubia. In the Theban region, he expanded the Amun temple at Karnak and built his mortuary temple on the west bank, a processional temple at Deir el-Bahri, and additions to the Amun temple at Medinet Habu. In addition to the cutting of his own tomb (KV34) in the Valley of the Kings, he was responsible for a tomb for his chief wife Meritra-Hatshepsut (KV42) and for the reburial of his grandfather Thutmose I in a new sarcophagus in KV38. Outside Thebes, he added to Montu's temples at Medamud, Armant and Tod, and built a shrine for Satet on the island of Elephantine in Aswan. In Nubia, temples and shrines were established or embellished at Amada and Elesiyah, Semna at the second cataract, and at Gebel Barkal near the fourth cataract. In Lower Egypt, he set up two obelisks in the ancient temple of Ra at Heliopolis, northeast of modern Cairo. After being moved to Alexandria by the Romans and subsequently named "Cleopatra's Needles," the obelisks now stand on the Thames Embankment in London and in New York's Central Park.

The reign of Thutmose III is notable for the relatively large amount of "historical" data available. There are several monumental inscriptions detailing events in this king's reign, military and otherwise, such as the *Annals* in the temple of Karnak and stelae erected at Armant and Gebel Barkal. Numerous inscriptions associated with various officials holding office during his reign on stelae, statues and in tomb chapels also add to our knowledge of the period. Later generations looked back to his reign with admiration, and a popular cult developed around him, even to the extent of using his name as an amuletic device on scarabs.

Amenhotep II—18th Dynasty (1428–1397 BC)

As the son and successor of Thutmose III, born of the great royal wife Meritra-Hatshepsut, Amenhotep II continued the military tradition of his father. After his accession at the age of eighteen, and sharing the throne for the last two years of his father's reign, Amenhotep ruled alone for another twenty-three years. His chief wife was Tiaa, the mother of his successor Thutmose IV. Other offspring are known, such as prince Webensenu.

During his time, Egypt's control in the North was consolidated with three campaigns recorded in years three, seven and nine of his reign, and maintained by garrisons outside Egypt and by princely hostages at his court. Two texts record his triumphant return in year three from the Takhsy region of Syria with the bodies of seven rebel chiefs hung from the prow of his boat. Six of the bodies were hung from the walls of Thebes, while the seventh on the wall at Napata in Nubia as a warning.

Amenhotep appeared on many of his monuments as the "heroic king," emphasizing his physical abilities in battle, surpassing other men in his semi-divine prowess as an incarnation of Montu, the warrior-god. A stele erected by the king north of the Giza Sphinx commemorates these so-called "sporting" activities, including running, rowing horsemanship and archery. These citations of athletic prowess continue a motif found earlier in the dynasty. The same concept is carried on into the later 18th and 19th Dynasties, especially with the king depicted as a triumphant chariot warrior.

Some Upper Egyptian sites with evidence of this king's building activities include Dendera, Medamud, Armant, Tod, Elkab, and Elephantine. In Nubia, he added to the construction of the chapel of Senusret III on Uronarti Island and to the decoration of a temple begun by his father at Amada, as well as the northern temple at Buhen and at Kumma. He also built a court in the temple of Luxor that was later decorated by Tutankhamun and Horemheb.

His son, Thutmose IV, assumed the throne when Amenhotep died at the age of forty-five. The mummified remains discovered in his sarcophagus are of a tall, robust male, and show signs of a systemic disease which probably contributed to his death. Some questions have been raised about the correct identification of this mummy, however. His tomb (KV35) is in the Valley of the King in Thebes and was discovered by Victor Loret in 1898.

Thutmose IV—18th Dynasty (1397–1387 BC)

The successor of Amenhotep II, Thutmose IV, was born to the "great royal wife," Tiaa, who was apparently of non-royal origin. There is some suggestion that Thutmose IV was not the first born son of Amenhotep II, and the existence of other brothers, some perhaps older, is known; these include Webensennu, Nedjem and Amenhotep.

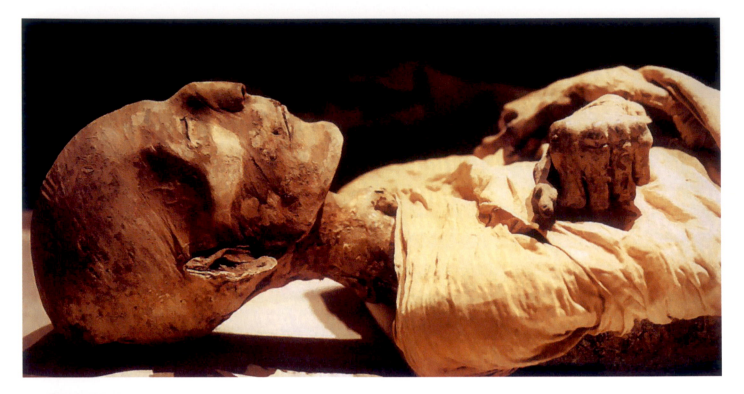

The so-called "Dream Stele," a monumental granite stele erected in front of the Giza Sphinx and perhaps post-dated to Thutmose IV's first regnal year, tells of a vision or a dream the young ruler had while resting in the shadow of the sphinx. The god Horemakhet, identified with the monument, foretold the prince's accession to the throne and asked that he remove the encumbring sands from its body. Egyptologists interpret this as indicating that Thutmose was not the intended heir, but others see it as part of the divine oracle motif prevalent in the royal dogma of the 18th Dynasty.

Three of Thutmose IV's four wives whose names are known to us, Iaret, Nefertiry and Nebetnehet, had royal origins. His fourth wife, Mutemwiya, the mother of his successor Amenhotep III, bore no royal titles of her own. Attempts by some scholars to equate her with a Mitannian princess are not convincing. Two other children are known from burial equipment found in KV43: prince Amenemhat and princess Tenetamen. Possible additional offspring have been suggested but without certainty of parentage.

Unlike his predecessors, Thutmose IV did not engage in many military activities. Some campaigning in southern Syria may have taken place, probably to bring rebellious princes into line and make the Egyptian presence felt. Formal peace with Mitanni may have been sealed by the marriage of a Mitannian princess to Thutmose IV.

There is little evidence of the king's military activity in Nubia. The Konosso Stele, dated to year seven or eight, actually mentions a campaign against southern intrusion into Egypt in the gold mining areas of the Eastern Desert, not a campaign into Nubia as previously interpreted.

Thutmose IV's building activities were mainly concerned with additions to existing structures, rather than to the creation of new monuments. Little remains, other than the foundations and part of the mud-brick first pylon and enclosure wall, of Thutmose IV's mortuary temple, situated south of the Ramesseum on the Theban west bank. The site was excavated by Flinders Petrie and has recently been reexamined by an Italian mission. The decoration of his tomb, KV43, was unfinished at the time of his burial.

He had a peristyle court installed within the existing Festival Hall of Thutmose II, fronting the fourth pylon at Karnak, which was the current entry to the Amun temple complex. The west half of this structure was dismantled and incorporated into the foundations of Amenhotep III's third pylon erected in that area. A monumental entrance porch was also erected in front of the fourth pylon, and a calcite ("Egyptian alabaster") bark shrine

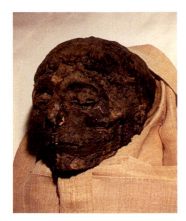

17. Mummy of Ahmose,
New Kingdom, 18th Dynasty.
Cairo, Egytpian Museum

18. Nasry Iskander with the
mummy of King Ahmose

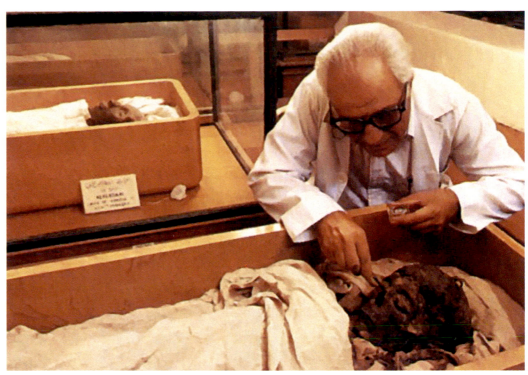

now reconstructed in the Open Air Museum may have been located in the forecourt. A single large obelisk quarried by his grandfather, Thutmose III, was erected in the solar shrine at the east end of temple. It now stands in Piazza San Giovanni in Laterano in Rome. Other monuments, outside of Thebes, include an obelisk and gateways at the solar temple in Heliopolis. At Giza, in addition to the famous Dream Stele, brick retaining walls bearing his name surround the Great Sphinx to hold back the sand. There is evidence of a structure in the Ptah temple at Memphis, and fragmentary stone architectural elements bearing his name have been found at Hermopolis (el-Ashmunein), in Middle Egypt. A small chapel of his was erected at Abydos, a possible building at an earlier Hathor temple at Dendera, and additions to the 18th-Dynasty Montu temple at Medamud are also known. Additions to other Upper Egyptian temples have been noted at Armant, Tod, Edfu and Elephantine. At Amada, in Nubia, he added to the temple constructed by his father and grandfather.

There appears to have been a decrease in the prominence of military officials and an attendant increase of civil and religious bureaucracy during the reign of Thutmose IV. There was an increased emphasis on the solar cult and solar divinity of the king in the official art that became even greater during the reign of his son, Amenhotep III.

Sety I—19th Dynasty (1289–1278 BC)
Sety I was the son of Rameses I by his wife Satra. After a coregency with his father (who reigned less than two years), Sety ruled for fourteen years. At home, Sety devoted substantial energy and wealth to the restoration of temples, erecting hypostyle halls in the temples at Karnak and Gebel Barkal in Nubia and building mortuary temples for himself at Thebes and at Abydos. This last is perhaps his most famous temple, and it is here that the famous king list can be found giving the names of Sety's predecessors (with some notable exceptions) on the throne. Behind the temple at Abydos, Sety I built the Osireion, a temple to Osiris which came to be thought of as the god's tomb. Sety also pursued an active foreign policy, campaigning in Asia in his first and second years on the throne. These military exploits were depicted in reliefs carved on the north wall of the hypostyle hall at Karnak. They show in great detail such events as the battles with the Shasu bedouin, the capture of Raphia and Gaza and the Battle of Qadesh. Sety I continued to exploit the turquoise mines in the Sinai and sent gold-mining expeditions to the desert east of Edfu

15. Mummy of Merenptah,
New Kingdom, 19th Dynasty.
Cairo, Egytpian Museum

16. Mummy of Rameses II,
New Kingdom, 19th Dynasty.
Cairo, Egytpian Museum

19. Black soapstone dyad of
Amenhotep I and Ahmose Nefertari
from west Thebes (?), New
Kingdom, late 18th–early 19th
Dynasties
Durham, The Oriental Museum
cat. 175

and Nubia. Sety's tomb in the Valley of the Kings (KV17) is one of the largest ever dug and the most extensively decorated. The king's alabaster sarcophagus is now in London's Soane Museum. His mummy, found in 1881 in the Deir el-Bahri cache, is in the Egyptian Museum. Sety and his principal wife, Tuya, lost their firstborn son; their second, Rameses, succeeded his father as pharaoh.

Rameses II—19th Dynasty (1279–1212 BC)
Rameses II ascended the throne at the age of twenty and ruled Egypt for sixty-seven years. He is popularly called "Rameses the Great," a title justified by the many achievements of his long reign.

The most celebrated military event of his reign was the Battle of Qadesh. There, on the Syrian frontier, in the fifth year of his reign (1275 BC) Rameses II led an Egyptian army of 20,000 men against the 37,000 troops of the Hittite king, Muwatallis. Though in the end a stalemate, the battle was depicted as a great victory on many of his temple walls. Rameses II was the most prolific builder of all the pharaohs. He added to the temples of Luxor and Karnak; completed the temple of his father, Sety I, at Abydos; and built his own mortuary temples at Abydos, Thebes (the Ramesseum), and in Nubia, the greatest being the two rock-cut temples at Abu Simbel. He also founded a new city in the Nile delta, Pi-ramesse ("The domain of Rameses").

His principal wives were Nefertari (whose tomb is in the Valley of the Queens) and Iset-nofret. By these two queens and a host of lesser wives, Rameses II fathered over one hundred children, many of whose names are not even recorded. His thirteenth son, Merenptah, eventually succeeded him as pharaoh and was buried in KV8 in the Valley of the Kings. Other sons are now believed to have been buried in KV5, where the Theban Mapping Project is currently excavating. Rameses II's own tomb, KV7, is one of the largest in the valley. Like KV5, however, it was robbed and repeatedly flooded in antiquity, suffering great damage.

The body of Rameses II was found in 1881 at Deir el-Bahri, part of a hidden cache of royal mummies.

Merenptah—19th Dynasty (1212–1202 BC)
Merenptah was the thirteenth son of Rameses II and his wife Isetnofret. Rameses II ruled for sixty-seven years and by the time Merenptah succeeded to the throne he was nearly sixty years old. During his ten-year reign he tried to maintain the peaceful foreign relations that his father had established. When the Hittite king in Syria faced a possible invasion from the north and widespread famine, Merenptah answered his call for help by sending much-needed grain. On Egypt's western borders there was a conflict with the Libyans, who had been filtering into the Delta, and in the fifth year of his reign the Libyans attempted to invade Egypt and incite a revolt against the pharaoh in Nubia. Merenptah was successful in crushing the Nubian revolt and the Libyan invasion.

The military victories of Merenptah are recorded in three major inscriptions: eighty lines on the sixth pylon in the temple of Amun at Karnak; a stele from Athribis in the Delta; and a victory stele found by Flinders Petrie in 1896 in the ruins of Merenptah's mortuary temple at Thebes, the oldest surviving Egyptian text to mention the people of Israel. Because Merenptah was already nearly sixty when he became king, he began early in his reign to build his tomb, KV8, and his mortuary temple in Thebes, for which he used the mortuary temple of Amenhotep III as a quarry. He also added to the Osireion at Abydos and built at Dendera. In addition, he moved the administrative center of Egypt from Piramesse to Memphis and constructed a royal residence there, next to the temple of Ptah. Some believe that Merenptah was the pharaoh of the biblical Exodus, mainly because Israel is mentioned in his inscription at Thebes, but there is no evidence to support this claim. Merenptah was buried in KV8 in the Valley of the Kings, close to KV7, the tomb of his father. The mummy of Merenptah was found in 1898 in the royal cache of Amenhotep II's tomb (KV35).

Sety II—19th Dynasty (1199–1193 BC)
Sety II was the eldest son of Merenptah and as crown prince bore the name of Sety-

the designated successor, his reign was either challenged or usurped by Amenmessu, whose three to four year reign either preceded or coincided with that of Sety II. Sety II is known to have reigned for six years, the surviving texts record both the date of his accession and of his death. At least two women are thought to have been his queens, one named Tauseret is thought to have borne his designated successor also named Sety Merenptah, who predeceased him. The other, Takhat, appears on the sides of some of his statues, although these seem to have been taken over from Amenmessu whom some have claimed to be her son.

Thebes is the location for several of his monuments, which include, in addition to his tomb in the Valley of the Kings, a bark shrine at Karnak and several statues at that temple site. No mortuary temple for this king has been found. His reign is commemorated elsewhere by inscriptions, monuments and artifacts ranging from Serabit el-Khadim in the Sinai to the temples of Abu Simbel and Buhen in Nubia. He erased the name of Amenmessu, previously inscribed on many Upper Egyptian and Nubian monuments, and added his own in its place.

Rameses III—20th Dynasty (1184–1153 BC)

Rameses III became the second ruler of the 20th Dynasty immediately following the death of his father Sethnakhte. Though not related, he sought to mirror the actions of Rameses II, even choosing a similar titulary. He modeled his own mortuary temple on the Ramesseum and in like manner glorified himself by depicting great war victories on his monuments. In addition to his mortuary temple at Medinet Habu he was responsible for building projects in the Karnak and Luxor temples, and added to sites all over Egypt, Nubia, and Syria. He also ran trade expeditions to Punt. An important historical document of his reign is the famous Great Harris Papyrus. This not only lists his benefits to the temples of Egypt's major gods, but gives a summary of the events leading up to his reign as well as his own acts in war and peace.

The first few years of his reign were relatively peaceful but year five marked the beginning of a series of invasions by Libyans with their allied troops, the Sea Peoples, from the Eastern Mediterranean. The Egyptian army crushed the enemies and enslaved the survivors. These battles are documented on the walls of Rameses III's mortuary temple in Medinet Habu in western Thebes.

Despite the strength of the army, Egypt's power had begun to wane and the economy had weakened toward the end of his reign; the papyrus documents from the workmen's village at Deir el-Medina speak of delays in the payment of grain to the workers due to lack of resources. Strikes occurred and even though the workmen were eventually paid, these incidents show the weakness of the government.

The economy was not the only problem Rameses III had to deal with at the end of his reign as pharaoh. A secondary wife, Tiy, along with members of her harem and court officials, planned to assassinate the pharaoh, so that Tiy's son Pentaur could become heir to the throne instead of prince Rameses (later Rameses IV). The plot was discovered, all suspects were tried and most were condemned to death or suicide. But the pharaoh died before the outcome.

Rameses III outlived several of his offspring, and buried a number of them in the Valley of the Queens along with his queens. Rameses III himself was buried in KV11 a tomb that his father Sethnakhte began before abandoning it for KV14. His mummy was rewrapped by the 21st-Dynasty priests of Amun, moved to the Deir el-Bahri cache, and discovered in 1881. The mummy is remarkably well-preserved and was not at all damaged by tomb robbers.

Rameses VI—20th Dynasty (1143–1135 BC)

When Rameses V died, Rameses VI became pharaoh. By the time of his reign, Egypt was a weakened state. The turquoise mines in Sinai were abandoned and the eastern borders drawn back. Rameses VI tried to improve his reign by adding his name to the list of the sons of Rameses III at Medinet Habu. This act linked him to the admired leaders of the past. But nothing could help restore royal power. Egypt was heading for a downfall and his son, Rameses VII, also had difficulty keeping the central government together. Rameses VI was buried in KV9, which he usurped from his predecessor, Rameses V, and then enlarged. His mummy was destroyed by tomb robbers. In an attempt to restore the mummy's shape, priests placed body parts from other people in the wrappings, some of Rameses VI's body parts were even put back incorrectly.

Rameses IX—20th Dynasty (1126–1108 BC)
Evidence of the events at the end of the New Kingdom is sparse. Rameses IX, ruled for eighteen years, longer than his dynastic predecessors, and seems to have accomplished more than the previous 20th-Dynasty rulers in terms of foreign relations: inscriptions mention his travels to Palestine and Nubia. His major architectural work was built at Heliopolis, but he also added to the seventh pylon at Karnak.

The most important event during Rameses IX's reign was the pillaging of the royal necropolises at Thebes, in the Valley of the Kings and the Valley of the Queens, and some 17th-Dynasty royal tombs. The investigations and trials of thieves, which took place in years nine and sixteen, resulted in the sealing of tombs and the transfer of the royal mummies to tomb DB320 at Deir el-Bahri.

Rameses IX was buried in KV6 opposite the tomb of Rameses II. His mummy was rewrapped at Medinet Habu and moved to the Deir el-Bahri cache during the 21st Dynasty reign of Pinudjem II. In the cache, the mummy was laid to rest in the coffin of Neskhons, the wife of Pinudjem II.

Catalog of the Works

Texts by:

A.G.	Alfred Grimm
A.H.	Alice Haynes
A.Hel.	Abeer Helmi
A.M.	Adel Mahmoud
B.S.	Bettina Schmitz
C.B.	Christophe Barbotin
C.Br.	Catherine Bridonneau
C.H.	Christianne Henry
C.L.	Christine Lilyquist
C.Z.	Christiane Ziegler
D.L.	Domenico Lavarone
D.M.D.	Denise M. Doxey
D.P.	Daniela Picchi
D.P.S.	David P. Silverman
D.R.-M.	Dorren Martin-Ross
D.W.	Dietrich Wildung
E.D.	Elisabeth Delange
E.E.F.	Rita E. Freed
E.F.M.	Elisa Fiore Marocchetti
E.G, B.M.	Elizabeth Goring, Bill Manley
F.S.	Flora Silvano
FT	Francesco Tiradritti
G.O.	George Ortiz
G.P.	Geneviève Pierrat
H.H.	Halla Hassan
H.S.	Helmut Satzinger
I.F.	Isabelle Franco
J.H.	Joyce Haynes
J.H.W.	Jennifer Houser Wegner
J.T.	John Taylor
J.W.W.	Josef W. Wegner
K.G.	Krzysztof Grzymski
K.J.B.	Kenneth J. Bohac
L.M.B.	Lawrence M. Berman
M.B.	Matilde Borla
M.C.G.	Maria Cristina Guidotti
M.E.	Marc Étienne
M.E.C.	Madeleine E. Cody
M.J.R.	Maarten J. Raven
M.M.	Marcel Maree
M.S.	Mohammed Saleh
M.T.	Marcella Trapani
N.S.	Neal Spencer
O.P.	Olivier Perdu
P.R.	Patricia Rigault
S.D.	Sara Demichelis
S.E.	Silvia Einaudi
Y.J..M.	Yvonne J. Markowitz
Z.T.	Zainab Tawfik

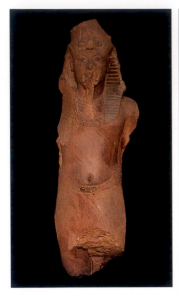

1
Colossal statue of Tutankhamun
New Kingdom, 18th Dynasty,
reign of Tutankhamun
Quartzite, painted
H. 285; W. 73; D. 87 cm
Thebes, funerary temple of Ay
and Horemheb
Cairo, Egyptian Museum, JE 59869

This statue most likely represents Tutankhamun, as can be seen from the
youthful face and serene expression,
the eyes, eyebrows and lips are outlined, and distinctive post-Amarna
artistic features: narrow eyes and
bulging belly.
The king is depicted in the classical
striding pose, wearing the double
crown (partially preserved), the striped
nemes headdress (painted yellow and
blue and adorned with the *uraeus*),
the ceremonial beard, a broad collar
and the traditional pleated *shendjyt*
kilt. A dagger with a falcon-headed
handle is slipped under his belt. On
the belt buckle, the name of Horemheb has been inscribed over the
name of a former king which, for the
above-mentioned reasons, belongs to
Tutankhamun.
A.M.

2
Statue of Sekhmet
New Kingdom, 18th Dynasty,
reign of Amenhotep III
Diorite
H. 2.05 (2.55 with base); W. 0.53;
D. 0.99 m
Provenance unknown (probably
from the temple of Mut at Karnak)
Padua, Museo Civico Archeologico

Visitors to the main collections of
Egyptian art will be familiar with this
lion-headed goddess, innumerable effigies of whom can be found in museums throughout the world.
In ancient Egypt the rays of the sun
could be personified as a goddess.
Like the energy she represented, she
was an emanation of Ra and considered to be his daughter. A beneficial
force on the banks of the Nile, the
rays of the sun could also become a
devastating weapon used to destroy
those who had rebelled against the divine order. This especially dangerous
aspect of the sun is represented by the
goddess Sekhmet. She was particularly terrible on the eve of the Day of the
Year—that is, that fearful period when
Egypt awaited the return of the Nile
flood waters under an implacable sun.
At this time of the year, Sekhmet not
only poured forth her ferocious heat,
but also spread all sorts of pestilence
among men. She was, therefore, a goddess who had by any means to be ap-
peased.
However, Sekhmet was only one aspect of the irascible daughter of the
Sun. Within her slumbered also that
female goodwill which was the other
aspect of her nature. Men, therefore,
would use specific rituals to avert her
terrible rage; and if one is to believe
the *Book of the Heavenly Cow*, then
some of these ceremonies were actually
instituted by Ra himself.
To guarantee the goodwill of Sekhmet
throughout the year, King Amenhotep
III had two series of 360 effigies of
the lioness-goddess made. Originally,
most of these were placed in the temple of Mut at Karnak—the Theban
goddess sometimes taking over the
functions of Sekhmet. Some of the figures, however, were set up on the other side of the Nile, near the jubilee
temple of the king. Since then they

have traveled widely, and those which
have not been taken abroad can now
be found in collections all over Egypt.

Bibliography
Siliotti 1987, p. 31; Zampieri 1994,
pp. 172–174.
I.F., D.L.

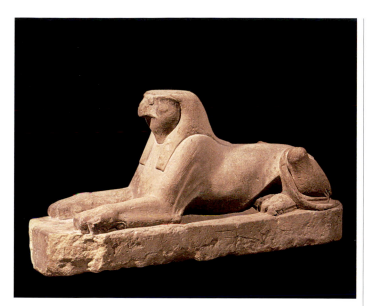

3

Falcon-headed sphinx
New Kingdom, 19th Dynasty,
reign of Rameses II
Sandstone
106.5 × 33 cm
Abu Simbel, great temple
London, The Trustees of the British
Museum, EA 13

Courtyards, processional avenues and
doorways of pharaonic temples were
frequently embellished with a variety
of sphinx statues; this example was
one of a pair flanking the entrance to
the second hypostyle hall in the rock-
cut temple of Abu Simbel. Such statues commonly portray a human head
upon a lion's body, but the features of
other animals could be used. In the
reign of Rameses II, ram- and jackal-
headed sphinxes are also known. The
falcon head on this example indicates
that the statue represented the god
Ra-Horakhty. A tripartite wig creates
a transition between the falcon head
and the leonine body; the latter form
intimated the might of the pharaoh.
Alongside Amun-Ra and Ptah, Ra-Horakhty was one of the three principal
gods to whom the temple of Abu Simbel was dedicated. Statues of these
three deities and Rameses II were
carved into the rock at the back of the
temple's sanctuary.
N.S.

4

Decorated gateway
New Kingdom, 19th Dynasty
Limestone
Memphis, palace of Merenptah,
south portal
Philadelphia, The University
of Pennsylvania, Museum of
Archeology and Anthropology,
E13575

Standing limestone gate jambs were
excavated in a number of locations by
Clarence Fisher during his work for
the Coxe Expedition. The most important were the main gate to the
palace of Merenptah (located at its
north end) and a gateway termed the
"south portal." The south portal connected the palace precinct with poorly preserved areas to the south. The
decoration of both sets of gates were
similar and depict divine aspects of
Merenptah's kingship. The gateway of
the south portal reached a height of
approximately 8 meters. The jambs of
the gateway are decorated with a set of
scenes showing Merenptah in the company of gods and his role as pharaoh
on earth. This fragment is the uppermost of a set of 5 scenes arranged vertically on the jamb. It depicts Merenptah standing before the creator god
Atum. The king is receiving the emblems of rulership, the crook and the
flail from the god. Scenes below this
on the gateway represent Merenptah's
interaction with Ptah, the main god
of Memphis, and his role as the defeater of foreign enemies (as seen on
cat. no. 91).

Bibliography
Horne 1985; Sourouzian 1989;
O'Connor 1991; Murnane 1995b; Sil-
verman 1997, pp. 155–176.
J.W.W.

The Pharaohs and History.
The Change in Permanence

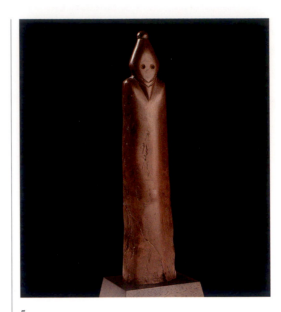

At first glance all the pharaohs are very much alike, adorned with the same attributes, and fixed in identical attitudes. Their faces affect an ideal youthfulness while their bodies reveal the physique of an athlete. Ancient Egypt refuses, notwithstanding some exceptions, the idea of realizing the "portrait" of a being, a fortiori when it has to do with a king. As in all figurative representations, it is necessary to transcend imperfection and the precariousness of a terrestrial existence in order to leave an effigy to eternity that is the sum and symbol of each individual.

In the case of a monarch, it is the function first of all of which he is the titular that is emphasized. The image of a sovereign corresponds to a concept: that of a man in his prime, qualified to succeed to the gods, be he seven or seventy-seven years old! And even when it is a woman who ascends to the throne of Horus, she must appear like the male pharaoh.

Nonetheless, when we contemplate the faces of those who, one after the other or simultaneously, wear the double crown, we see that beyond the constraints and rules of representation, the man is present behind the king. Certainly, his features are idealized but the artist never forgets that the sovereign is the living image of the divine function that he assumes. Moreover, an attentive observation makes it possible to recognize the human being in the wrappings of the Son of the Sun.

Thus it is impossible to confuse the son and heir of Khufu, Djedefra, with his half-brother, Khafra. The features of Menkaura with his round face are recognizable among certain of his successors. Family resemblance or an academic artifice in a period in which the legitimacy of the sovereigns may have been questioned?

After the solar triumphalism of the pyramid builders, the monarchs of the Middle Empire radically changed their image. The change is subtle, but revealed on careful observation. Here, the humanity of the king seems to have taken precedence over his divine essence and the sovereign's features are marked by the weight of his heavy burden. The effigies of the New Kingdom sovereigns reveal, in the same way as the splendors of Egypt of that period, the zenith of a civilization. The turmoil that haunted their immediate predecessors seems to have disappeared; the confident look and at times even the smile that characterize the majority of the pharaohs' "portraits" of this auspicious period reveal the total confidence that the Nile dwellers then had in their country and its system of values; the "Akhenaten case" represents an entirely special excursus in the history of royal Egyptian art.

Thus, on perusing this gallery of sovereigns, we actually meet only one king with the features of a simple mortal who succeeds to the throne of the gods.

I.F.

5

Statuette of a bearded man
Predynastic period, Naqada I,
Amratian period
Schist
H. 31.5; W. 7; D. 5 cm
Gebelein
Lyon, Muséum d'Histoire Naturelle,
90000172

About 4000 BC the banks of the Nile were gradually emerging from prehistory, and the very first evidence of a dawning civilization begins to appear. The objects of the so-called "Naqada period"—named after a site in Upper Egypt—are of great quality. Certain techniques—for example, the cutting of hard stone—had already achieved a high degree of perfection and thereafter would never be abandoned.

The artistic works of this era include two main types of statuettes. Alongside the female figurines—often in fireclay—there are also carved stone statues of male figures, revealing a simplicity of line. The "bearded man" of Lyon, found at Gebelein to the south of Luxor, is remarkable. The face is made up of a lozenge in which only the eyes are inscribed; two chevron-type incisions indicate either his beard or, perhaps, his chin and mouth. The figure appears to be wearing a cap surmounted by some sort of bobble. Certain Egyptologists justifiably see this headgear as the precursor of the white crown that would become the emblem of the sovereign of Upper Egypt (cat. no. 44).

The body of the bearded man is rendered rather summarily; however, the treatment of the shoulders suggests that he wore some sort of cape draped around him. This could have already been the famous mantle the kings of the historic era wore for the feast of *sed*, their jubilee celebration. We know, in fact, that the origins of that ceremony go back to the very earliest days of pharaonic power.

Bibliography
Ziegler, Bovot 2001, p. 87.
I.F.

6

Pottery shard with red crown
Predynastic period, Naqada I,
Amratian period
Glazed fireclay
H. 8. 9 cm
Naqada
Oxford, The Ashmolean Museum,
1895.795

The Naqada I period (cat. no. 5) was
marked by the production of fireclay
ceramics with a red glaze. As a result
of the firing technique, the neck and
inside of this type of vases is shiny
dark black. There are a number of unbroken vases extant, whose shoulder
or belly are decorated with various figures (generally animals) or geometric
motifs. This decoration is either incised or painted on in white.
The fragment from the Ashmolean
Museum is of great interest: it bears
the image of a crown modeled in light
relief—rather like a stamp. In spite of
its schematic nature, one can easily
recognize this as the red crown, the
distinct headdress of the kings of Lower Egypt. Found in a tomb at Naqada,
to the north of Luxor, this shard is a
rich source of information. It is highly probable that the royal emblem was
used to indicate the provenance of the
product contained in the vase it
adorned. Thus we know that even at
this very early period contacts between
the two halves of Egypt did exist. We
also learn that the red crown, which
subsequently would be traditionally
associated with the North, was—some
thousand years before the foundation
of the Double Kingdom—already being used to identify the sovereigns of
the Delta.

Bibliography
Moorey 1988, p. 12.
I.F.

7

Label with the name of King Den
Thinite period, 1st Dynasty
Wood
H. 6.35; L. 7.6; D. 0.65 cm
Abydos, Umm el-Qa'ab,
tomb of Den
Paris, Musée du Louvre, E 25268

The royal tombs discovered at the
Umm el-Qa'ab site of Abydos by Emile
Amélineau have yielded up a large
quantity of furnishings and materials,
from the deposits both within and
alongside the tombs.
These objects included wood or ivory
labels that were either incised or inscribed in ink. These all had one hole
drilled in the upper right corner; but
only one—"recycled"—tag was actually found in context, next to a leather
bag in the tomb of Chancellor Hemaka. The present piece was found along
the approach to the tomb of King Den,
the fourth king of the 1st Dynasty.
These labels were probably attached to
receptacles to identify what they contained. Those dating from the very beginning of the 1st Dynasty were laid
out in horizontal bands one above the
other; that format was then replaced
by what we can see here, with the
space on the tag divided into two areas. That on the left contains information of an economic-financial nature: the name of the recipient (here
King Den, whose name appears in a
rectangle surmounted by a falcon); the
name of the sender, of the person responsible for the transaction (the
Chancellor Hemaka), of the product
(here, oil) and of the number of vases
delivered (indicated using hieroglyphs
that are larger than those which appear
elsewhere on the label).
The right-hand side is edged with an
indication of the year. This serves to
date the arrival of the product. The
date is not given in figures but by
means of small graphic renderings of
the key events of the year concerned.
On this label, one recognizable event
(in the section nearest the corner hole)
is the passage of the king between two
half-moon-shaped boundary mark-
ers—one of the rituals that were part
of the celebration of the *sed*, the feast

of the king's jubilee. Other recognizable events are the manufacture of
statues, the king's visits to sanctuaries
and a hippopotamus hunt. This event
is associated with the name of the king
of Upper and Lower Egypt, Khasety of
Horus Den. The information contained here enables us to reconstruct
the history of the monarch, and can be
checked against the royal annals contained in the Palermo Stone, which
was compiled during the Old Kingdom. Hence, these labels are a find of
prime historic importance.

Bibliography
Paris 1982, (cat. 20); de Cenival 1992,
p. 37 fig. 4; Amélineau 1905, pp.
425–431, pl. 37 (cat. 8).
M.E.

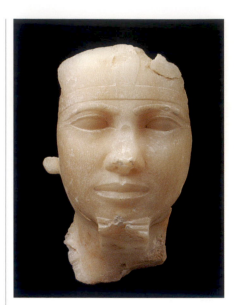

8

Stele of King Qahedjet
Old Kingdom, 3rd Dynasty
Lithographic limestone
H. 50.5; W. 31; max. D. 2.8 cm
Provenance unknown
Paris, Musée du Louvre, E 25982

The sole decoration of this delicate bas-relief stele is the figure of a sovereign embraced by a falcon-headed god. This scene occupies a slightly overhanging rectangular frame that is off-center.

The pharaoh is shown standing; he is wearing the white crown, has a "false" beard, a girdle and a pagne decorated with the tail of an animal. His belt holds a dagger, while in his right hand there is a mace with a pear-shaped head, and his left hand holds a long pointed cane that bulges out toward the middle (such canes occur frequently in Old Kingdom material). The falcon-headed god Horus faces him, griping his forearm with his left hand while his (unseen) right hand passes round the pharaoh's shoulders in sign of protection. This seems to be one of the earliest known representations of Horus as a falcon-headed human figure. Above the figures are two facing inscriptions which identify them: "Horus Qahedjet" and "Horus in the Great Dwelling." Of all his multiple names, the pharaoh is here identified using that which places him under the protection of Horus, the tutelary deity of royalty; while the god himself is referred to using the title that occurs at Heliopolis near Cairo. We know nothing more of this "Qahedjet," who has sometimes been identified with Huni, the last king of the 3rd Dynasty.

This delicate low relief, which seems sunk into the stone, is comparable to those found on the six stelae decorating the cavities of the burial complex of Djoser in Saqqara. There is the same subtlety in the handling of the human body, rendered through slight gradations of surface. These shifting planes highlight the structure of the pharaoh's face, the more accentuated face of Horus, the musculature of the legs and the knee joints. The same simple and perfectly ordered composition can be found in the hieroglyphics above the scene. Though smaller than the Djoser stelae, it is legitimate to suppose that, like those, this was meant to be set in a niche, where it would stand out against a background of blue-green ceramic.

Bibliography
Ziegler 1990, pp. 54–57, (cat. 4) with extensive bibliography; Valbelle 1998, p. 38; Paris 1999, p. 155 (cat. 9) with extensive bibliography.
C.Z.

9

Face of Khafra
Old Kingdom, 4th Dynasty
Egyptian alabaster
H. 20.5 cm
Giza, West Cemetery, northeast corner of mastaba G 5330
(Harvard University–Museum of Fine Arts Expedition)
Boston, Museum of Fine Arts, 21.351

For the absolute power of the monarchy and its expression in sculpture, the Old Kingdom served as the model which later ages attempted to emulate. The divinity of kingship is nowhere better expressed than in the faces of King Khafra, builder of the second pyramid at Giza who is generally credited with the sculpting of the sphinx. Remains of the *nemes* headscarf, *uraeus* (divine snake), and beard identify this striking face as a king, and his identity is confirmed by the cartouche of Khafra found beside it.

Its abstract forms and minimal modeling contribute to the aloof and imperial impression the face projects. Arched brows in raised relief add emphasis to the large eyes, whose inner corners are marked by deeply cut canthi. The upper eyelid rim extends out to the temples in a cosmetic line. Faint folds of flesh continue diagonally from the nostrils to the corners of the mouth and set off the cheeks. The straight lips are outlined by a slight ridge. Most likely, it is not a true portrait of the king, but rather an idealized image and the way he wished to be remembered for eternity.

Once as many as 200 statues of Khafra stood in his funerary complex at Giza, but today the vast majority have been reduced to indistinguishable fragments in order to reuse the stone. The rest of this once life-size statue undoubtedly suffered the same fate.

In addition to the cartouche mentioned above, it was found with debris associated with a stonecutter's workshop.

Bibliography
Chr. Ziegler in: New York 1999, p. 255.
R.E.F.

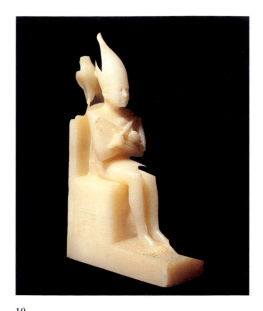

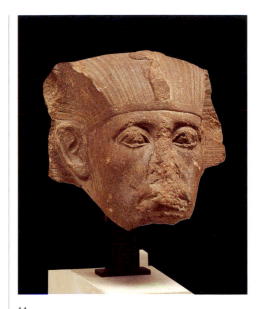

10

Sed-festival statuette of Pepy I
Old Kingdom, 6th Dynasty,
reign of Pepy I
Egyptian alabaster
26.5 × 6.6 × 15.7 cm
Provenance unknown
New York, The Brooklyn Museum
of Art, Charles Edwin Wilbour
Fund, 39.120

Statues depicting kings and queens of ancient Egypt served religious functions, reinforcing belief in divine kingship: the ruler might be mortal but his office was divine. Pepy I, third king of the 6th Dynasty, is shown here with regalia and symbols that proclaim his status as divine ruler: he wears the white crown of Upper Egypt and holds the crook and flail, his ceremonial beard is broken away, only the rectangular support on his chest remains. His throne is decorated on its sides with the *sm3-t3wy* motif, representing the joining of the Two Lands; the *serekh*, or palace façade, is carved on its back below his Horus name, *Mry-t3wy*. Pepy is robed in the *sed*-festival garment, worn for the ceremony of rejuvenation and renewal of powers celebrated by reigning kings. An inscription on the base commemorates this occasion as the "first time of *sed* festival." It is likely that this refers to an actual event, not an expressed wish. The concept of the king as the earthly embodiment of the god Horus is expressed here in the round by the falcon behind Pepy's head. The placement of the falcon parallel to the back of the king's head instead of enfolding it within his wings is unusual; a fragmentary example is known from the earlier reign of Khafra. This statuette was probably originally placed in a temple; repaired at least twice in antiquity, it may have been a cult image in later reigns.

Bibliography
Romano 1998.
M.E.C.

11

Portrait of Senusret III
Middle Kingdom, 12th Dynasty,
reign of Senusret III
Sandstone
H. 20.6; W. 20.8 cm
From Ehnasya, according
to the donor
Paris, Musée du Louvre, E 25370

The features of this fragmentary head enable us to identify it as a portrait of Senusret III wearing a pleated *nemes* above which stretches the *uraeus* (cat. no. 28). The face reveals both the monarch's determined temperament and, in an unusual fashion, his advanced age. The rather prominent eyes are half-shaded by large eyelids, which are the same from one corner of the eye to the other; the upper eyelid is shown overlapping the lower. Gentle creases run from the folds of flesh at the corners of the mouth, giving the pharaoh sunken cheeks; and the jawbones mold the face to a very square shape. After his harsh campaigns of repression in Nubia, the undiminished energy of the pharaoh led him to set up a string of eight defensive fortresses, running right up to the second cataract, in order to impose order on the rebellious Nubians. There, he proclaimed himself "the Shepherd of his people," adding with great firmness that "to keep silent is to embolden the heart of the enemy, [while] it is an act of courage to be aggressive, an act of cowardice to retreat. . . ."
His actions in those campaigns led to him being recognized as a god, and the warrior king *par excellence*. More than three hundred years later, Thutmose III would make reference to this deified ancestor, symbolically recognizing himself as his successor in the field.
Senusret's political energy also found expression in the reorganization of the Egyptian administration. Local potentates having become independent, he abrogated their authority to set up a more centralized power—and stimulate the growth of families lower down the social scale.
The breaks in the statue indicate that it was probably part of a sphinx, because the *nemes* (cat. no. 29) reaches very far back and spreads out, as if the bow that held the folds of the headdress were placed horizontally on the back of a feline.

Bibliography
Delange 1987, pp. 44–45.
E.D.

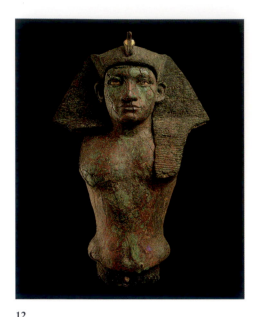

12

Bust of Amenemhat III
Middle Kingdom, 12th Dynasty,
reign of Amenemhat III
Copper alloy
H. 46.5 cm
Allegedly from Hawara (Fayum)
George Ortiz Collection (formerly
Maurice Tempelsman Collection,
1971–1986)

Introduction

The Old Kingdom centered in Lower
Egypt started dissolving at the end of
the 6th Dynasty as local governors became too powerful. Toward the end of
the 11th Dynasty Mentuhotep II reunited Upper and Lower Egypt, laying
the groundwork for the 12th Dynasty
when the administrative center moved
from Thebes to Memphis, close to the
Old Kingdom pyramids.

The Middle Kingdom (2050–1750 BC)
was considered by the Egyptians to
be the classical period of their civilization, its apex. Writing in the form
of hieroglyphic script, begun around
3000 BC and achieved formal perfection around 2000 BC.

Art influenced by the Nile valley with
its ever renewing life cycle reflected
time and space. Its artistic standards,
with their thematic formality and rigid-
ity of pose, were perfected in centralized royal workshops retaining the
same monolithic aesthetic for three
millennia. It served to express religious and political truths that represented the immutability of the natural order and embodied universally accepted ideals. There was always an intimate correlation between art and religion. Its supreme virtues were mod-
eration and constancy; its achievement
perfect balance and harmony.

Being a representational art, whose
function was to illustrate the purpose
of present life and after life, its statues
were considered as animate beings

perpetuating and inseparable from the
person represented. Statuary fulfilled
a crucial religious and mortuary role
for both king and commoner.

Even before the creation of an organized state, which took place during
the Dynastic period (*c.* 3100 BC),
sculpture was a means of manifesting
royal power. Flourishing and sometimes realistic during the Old Kingdom, the arts add a new dimension to
classical perfection during the extra-
ordinarily creative reign of Senusret
III.[1] Bodies remain totally idealized
conforming to type, whereas the faces
are realistic and reveal in conjunction
with an awareness of self [2] the wear
and tear of absolute power. Individual
portraiture revealing human character
and royal icon are combined in abstract formalism to convey the official mood. In his statues a subtle modeling gives life to his features which
express a new realism revealing his
energy, his autocratic power undiminished, ". . . a new way of expressing an unchanging view of divine kingship."[3] The kings of the Middle Kingdom used art as an effective means of
representing sovereignty.

Sculpture of the Middle Kingdom thus
achieved its apex under Senusret III
and his son Amenemhat III in a culmination of classical measure, a happy
mean between the severe realism of
the Old Kingdom and the almost man-
neristic humanism of the New Kingdom. Senusret III became the archetype of the pharaoh (Herodotus, Diodorus). This period so impressed later dynasties that its sculpture, both
royal and civilian, was to be reused
and imitated—in the measure that it
was possible and appropriate—by future pharaohs, officials and priests.
During the early Middle Kingdom a
major evolution in ideas leads to a secularized and absolute conception of

sovereignty embodying considerable
realism and individualism in art.[4]

Technical data[5]
Lost wax casting was practiced from
the Middle Kingdom onward. The
bust of Amenemhat III, as other statues of the group,[6] was executed in this
technique. He was solid-cast of copper
alloy[7] by the lost wax method, with
parts hollow-cast, carefully chased in
the cold, incised and polished.

Condition
Once heavily incrusted with cuprite
and copper carbonate (malachite)[8] as
usually produced by sandy desert contexts. The bust was first subjected to
rapid manual stripping[9] and in a subsequent[10] operation was most carefully and ably cleaned and restored.
The surface of contrasting patches of
red cuprite, malachite green and varying shades of dark green, brownish
red.
G.O.

*The author is indebted to Dietrich
Wildung's excellent study of the Middle
Kingdom (1984), from which he has
gleaned much information for the present entry. Naturally, he bears full responsibility for all and any mistakes.*

[1] Senusret III (1862–1844) who recreates
one kingdom centralizing the power that
had been enjoyed by provincial governors
and is the father of Amenemhat III.
[2] Wildung 1984, p. 203.
[3] Bourriau 1988, p. 42.
[4] Wildung 1984, p. 17.
[5] Resulting from visual observation only;
scientific analysis to be conducted in the
future will confirm or invalidate and supply
the answer to certain questions.
[6] Another figure of the king, standing and
solid-cast (Munich, Staatliche Sammlung
Ägyptischer Kunst ÄS 6982), a kneeling figure of him (*The George Ortiz Collection,*
cat. no. 37), two more high officials (Paris,
Louvre E 27153 and Munich, Staatliche
Sammlung Ägyptischer Kunst ÄS 7105),
two viziers (*The George Ortiz Collection,*
cat. nos. 33, 34), a statue of a Queen (*The
George Ortiz Collection,* cat. no. 35), a large
wig of a queen (Geneva, private collection),
and the figure of a crocodile (Munich, Staatliche Sammlung Ägyptischer Kunst ÄS
6080), though the appurtenance of this last
to the group has been questioned by H.-W.
Müller (1989), and this author had his
doubts. D. Wildung states that it unquestionably belongs.
[7] Technical analysis will reveal whether the
alloy is natural or induced by human action. This should be by AAS = Atomic Ab-
sorption Spectral Analysis. (Unfortunately
several drill holes 1 mm in diameter are necessary for samples.)
[8] Possibly copper chloride (atacamite),
analysis will determine.
[9] Carried out in Switzerland.
[10] Work carried out by Anna Plowden before it entered the Tempelsman collection.

The statue of Amenemhat III

Bust and head hollow-cast together, thick-walled bronze upward of 1 cm. A recessed thick ring section extending 3.5–4.5 cm below enabled insetting into lower body. The arms, now missing, were cast separately and fixed by means of tangs slotted into longitudinal grooves inset from the shoulders down. The right one broken off, remains still in place.

A recessed rim around the head holds in place the royal headcloth, cast separately by the lost wax process and worked in the cold.

Eyes inlaid of polished crystalline limestone (calcite, Egyptian alabaster), the cornea inset of rock crystal. For the left eye the rock crystal cornea and the pupil underneath missing; for the right eye the pupil would appear to be indicated here by a painted black dot.[1] The outline of the eyes formed by silver or electrum inlay.[2] The temples inlaid with silver or electrum strips. Right nipple still extant, left missing. At lower right of navel a silver rivet-like protuberance and straight above it under the breast a round hole for another rivet, a large protruding silver rivet on the left side of the back halfway between shoulder-blade and waist and on the right remains of a cavity for receiving an identical nail; these surely served to fix a sheet of silver[3] over the bust.

Condition: the head and neck and the upper bust with large fissures, three below the left breast attest the difficulty of casting such a mass of metal at such an early stage of a new technological development.

The circlet is missing that would have hidden the join between the head and the royal headcloth, deeply fissured in places, the lower right lappet broken off and reattached, the lower left one missing. The *uraeus* cast separately and inlaid with gold; its right cheek with a gold rectangle, the right eye of an indeterminate substance (garnet?) inset in gold; the left eye and cheek inlay missing; the dilated hood below the head once with seven gold inlays, two of quarter moon shape, serrated on the curving edge, still in place.

Great king of the 12th Dynasty, Amenemhat III was responsible for transforming the swamps of the Fayum into rich cultures. He built a first pyramid at Dahshur, and then a pyramid at Hawara accompanied by a vast funerary temple. The present group and all the other pieces belonging to it possibly come from this funerary ensemble, maybe buried in antiquity during the Hyksos period.[4]

We are told[5] that from early times royal statues were placed in the temples of the gods. In certain texts the king appears as the central figure and the population's well-being depends on its loyal attitude toward him. Venerating Amenemhat III included a spiritual side as he was the high priest, the only human in contact with the gods.[6]

The alleged find-spot would be in keeping since, during the Middle Kingdom, the pharaoh's protection and patronage was sought for the afterlife as much as for actual life. Thus the setting for sculptures could be a temple or mortuary temple celebrating the king's cult, but palace or tomb were also possible. It was necessary to be buried close to the royal tomb, which explains the enormous cemetery complexes.[7]

This bust is what remains of what was surely the central figure of the whole group, his consort on his left. The author is unsure as to whether he would have been seated or standing and what the rest of his body would have been made of. If wood, probably acacia since it would have been covered with a sheet of precious metal—gold, silver or electrum. The standing figure of the King[8] from the same group may have been added to it toward the end of his life or slightly thereafter, since "his sunken cheeks and other characteristics represent the traits of an aging personality." The universal image of an absolute monarch, in appearance untouchable, with his distant dignity, "rarely in Egyptian art has a king been represented so directly and frankly, so revealing in his deep psychology, his personality so little disguised."[9] He epitomizes the new style of the end of his dynasty with his contained expression of interior life. To look at him is to admire him, he is the greatest of monarchs for though he will suffer no contradiction his presence is promise of protection and well-being in this world and the next.

Bibliography

Wildung 1984, pp. 208 (fig. 184), 210–211; Schoske 1988, 212, (n. 20); Müller 1989, p. 27; Schoske 1992, pp. 177–181; Michalowski 1994, p. 137 (pl. 91), pl. 91; Phillips 1994, pp. 60–61 (n. 8), ill. p. 63; Ortiz 1996, cat. 36; Smith 1998, p. 183.

G.O.

[1] Possibly made from charcoal or ground antimony.
[2] This is also how the outline of the eyes of the Louvre high official is described (E 27153 : Delange, 1987, p. 211ff.). However, for the standing king in Munich (Staatliche Sammlung Ägyptischer Kunst ÄS 6982: Schoske 1988, pp. 207–210) the outline of the eyes is stated as being inlaid with electrum, but for the statue of a high official in the same museum (Schoske 1992, pp. 177–181 figs. 3-5), the eye inlays are said to be of silver. It is to be noted that silver on Egyptian objects is seldom pure since it was used as an alloy with gold and copper; thus without analysis it is difficult to differentiate between silver and electrum (verbal communication A. Giumlia-Mair, 26–27 November 1994).
[3] Possibly electrum.
[4] Schoske 1988, p. 210.
[5] Russmann 1981, p. 153 n. 17.
[6] Wildung 1984, p. 211.
[7] Of which the most popular site was the "terrace of the great god" at Abydos, the great god is Osiris, primeval king of Egypt and ruler of the dead.
[8] Munich, Staatliche Sammlung Ägyptischer Kunst ÄS 6982: Schoske 1988
[9] Wildung 1984, p. 210.

13

Head of a colossal statue of
Hatshepsut as Osiris
New Kingdom, 18th Dynasty,
reign of Hatshepsut
Painted limestone
H. 106.8; L. 34.9; D. 58.4 cm
Western Thebes, Deir el-Bahri
New York, The Metropolitan
Museum of Art, Rogers Fund,
31.3.164

Hatshepsut is undoubtedly one of the most famous of Egyptian sovereigns, because her destiny was so remarkable. The daughter of Thutmose I, she married her half-brother, Thutmose II. He would reign for only three years, leaving a very young son as heir to the throne. As "great royal wife," Hatshepsut became regent, then arrogated to herself the full powers of a monarch. However, she did not supplant the heir to the throne, Thutmose III, who was her nephew, her stepson and soon her son-in-law. Hatshepsut had, in fact, had a daughter by the dead king, princess Neferura, who would marry the heir; the daughter's tutor was the famous Senenmut (cat. no. 171) who was the queen's factotum, accumulating the most prestigious offices and honors.

Hatshepsut's reign (*c.* 1479–1458) would see a most remarkable form of power-sharing. Thutmose III and his "regent" often appeared side by side, sharing the titles of royal protocols as if their two persons formed one single monarch. The queen-pharaoh and her coruler enjoyed years of relative calm—but not as peaceful as it is sometimes claimed. The most celebrated expeditions under Hatshepsut were those she sent into the land of Punt, in search of the trees which would provide the precious incense she needed for her temples.
She had numerous monuments built

throughout the country. In Thebes, this work involved alterations to the temple of Amun; but, most importantly, she had her own jubilee temple built at Deir el-Bahri on the west bank of the Nile, just opposite Karnak. She was the first sovereign to be buried in the Valley of the Kings, choosing for her tomb a site that was behind the rocky cirque where she had had her Temple of Millions of Years built. This latter was subsequently the object of important restoration work, but many of its statues have not survived the passage of time. The site has yielded up various heads of the sovereign, now in the Metropolitan Museum. Like many other pharaohs, Hatshepsut here appears in the form of a colossus representing Osiris. She is wearing the double crown—the *pshent*—and has the curved beard that denotes divinity, an indication of the future deified status of the queen.
Simply because she was a woman, Hatshepsut was judged rather unfairly by early Egyptologists, while in fact a number of the anomalies they noted in her reign can be easily explained. Represented with a masculine body, she was not trying to pass herself off as a man but simple remain faithful to traditional royal iconography, appearing both as pharaoh and as the heir of the gods. Her disappearance from the Egyptian king lists is due to the fact that her period on the throne was considered to be an extension of her period of regency and not a reign in itself. Finally, the damage done to certain of her monuments during ancient times was due not to her so-called usurpation of the throne but to her audacity in religious matters.

Bibliography
Tefnin 1979, p. 41.
I.F.

14

Bas-relief of Thutmose III
18th Dynasty, reigns of Hatshepsut
and Thutmose III
Polychrome sandstone
L. 1.08 m; H. 67.5 cm
Elephantine, temple of Satet
Paris, Musée du Louvre, B 72,
E 12921 bis

Famed for his triumphant imperialism, King Thutmose III was victor in seventeen campaigns in Asia and is here shown wearing the *atef* crown (cat. no. 30). This composite crown of majestic size and twisted horns identifies the king with the god Khnum, worshipped on the island of Elephantine, along with the local goddesses. The king is also wearing all the insignia of his office: the *uraeus* (cat. no. 26), the royal beard and the wide necklace. The differences in level in the bas-relief show that the work was altered—particularly in the two cartouches, where yellow ochre covers the alterations around the names of the king "Menkheper[ra]" and "Thutmose" (the second cartouche was subsequently completed with rather coarse hieroglyphics for "*heka* Maat" and "Lord of Maat").
The temple of Satet was begun by Hatshepsut and completed by Thutmose III, and the walls are decorated with clearly-differentiated faces revealing the individual characters of each of the sovereigns—though sometimes the names have been changed. For a long time this was thought to be the young king's revenge against his aunt Hatshepsut, who had arrogated his royal power to herself when he was young. However, the continuation of the queen's architectural work on this Elephantine temple—and the fact that her face appears therein more or less intact, together with her name—suggests perhaps that this idea of a conflict

between the two corulers is, in fact, ill-founded (see Ch. Desroches-Noblecourt 2002).
The bas-relief in the Louvre shows that prominent nose typical of the Thutmoside family; there is also the typically beady eye, with its long line of eye makeup reaching round to the temple, and the chin receding into the beard (a specific feature of this king). Larger than life-size, this portrait of Thutmose was meant to be a statement of the sovereign's dignity.

Bibliography
Berman, Letellier 1996, pp. 50, 51, 95;
Desroches-Noblecourt 2002.
E.D.

15
Block with relief of Amenhotep III
New Kingdom, 18th Dynasty
Pinkish sandstone, traces of red
paint
102 × 38 × 20 cm
Soleb, area of the temple of
Amenhotep III
Pisa, Collezioni Egittologiche
dell'Università, 29

The block bears, carved in low relief, a figure of Amenhotep III, wearing the blue crown with the *uraeus* adorning the brow and two ribbons hanging behind. The king is facing left and extending his right arm perhaps to offer an incense-burner or else in the consecration gesture of offerings; his left arm, that appeared on a different block which completed the scene (presently in Sudan), was lowered and partly bent. Facing the king, level with the crown, is the lower part of a sign *nb* ("every") (to be completed: "every feast-day" of the jubilee) and the lower tip of two cartouches, that conserve the last signs of the king's names: [*Imn-Htp*] *HkA Wast* for the first, and [*Nb-Maat-Ra*] for the second. Carved behind the king's head one can make out a sacred cane or religious insignia decorated with a small head that recalls the sovereign's profile; the staff of the insignia was probably held by a figure of the royal *ka*.

Bibliography
Schiff Giorgini 1961; Schiff Giorgini 1962, pl. XLII; Bresciani, Silvano 1992, p. 24 (cat. 1).
F.S.

16
Portrait of Akhenaten
New Kingdom, 18th Dynasty
Plaster
H. 26 cm
Tell el-Amarna, house P 47,2
(excavations of the Deutsche
Orientgesellschaft, 1912)
Berlin, Ägyptisches Museum und
Papyrussammlung, 21351

During the reign of Amenhotep IV/Akhenaten, the image of the pharaoh became an individual portrait of the sovereign rather than a symbolic representation of royalty. Neither before nor after this period were the features of the monarch ever rendered with such realism. This stylistic change was the direct result of a radical change in official religious beliefs. Amenhotep IV shifted the focus of belief away from the afterlife and a world of gods of multiple forms and names to a monotheistic veneration of the sun-god Aten. Human life now occupied the span between birth and death; and this new importance of mankind's terrestrial existence became a leitmotif of artistic expression. A royal portrait that actually resembled the king became the new ideal for images of mankind.

Bibliography
Grimm, Schokse 2001, p. 140, (cat. 11), frontispiece.
D.W.

17
Kneeling figure of a ruler
New Kingdom, 18th Dynasty
Bronze, with traces of gold
H. 20.5 cm
Provenance unknown
Philadelphia, The University
of Pennsylvania, Museum of
Archeology and Anthropology,
E 14295

This figure has been cast in a material referred to as black bronze, and traces of gold still survive on the *nemes* headdress, the nipples and the kilt. Perhaps these areas had originally been entirely gilded. Inlays of stone were used in the eyes and eyebrows, and these parts may have been outlined in metal as well. While the arms are missing, the pose suggests that when the statue was complete, they extended forward, offering *nw* jars, probably to a deity. Artifacts of this type occur among the implements and utensils stored in the temple that the priests used during rituals and ceremonies. No inscriptions appear on the statuette to identify it, but the style of the costume, the shape of the body, and the physiognomy indicate the individual to be a ruler of the Amarna period. Often referred to in the past as either Akhenaten or Tutankhamun, it has most recently been attributed with some certainty to the latter. Tutankhamun is the young ruler who came to the throne shortly after the death of Akhenaten, who had instituted a new belief system that focused on a single god, the Aten. During the reign of Tutankhamun the restoration of the orthodox religion took place, and it is precisely this kind of ritual object that would have been prominent in the services that were again taking place in the temples. He is also the pharaoh whose modern fame rests predominantly on the discovery of his tomb in the Valley of the Kings in 1922.
D.P.S.

18

Portrait of Sety I (ostracon)
New Kingdom, 19th Dynasty
Limestone, red paint and black
charcoal
H. 51; W. 38 cm
Qurna
Florence, Museo Egizio, 7618

This big slab of limestone is a drawing exercise, probably executed by one of the decorators of the tombs in the Valley of the Kings. Draftsmen had reached a very high level of expertise as can be seen from the hundreds of decorated stone or terra-cotta ostraca that have been found in the western area of Thebes. On one side, the Florentine slab presents the picture of a pharaoh's head, identifiable by the trace of the *uraeus* on the brow, a striped wig and the face that conserves traces of red paint; above, the bust of a sovereign wearing a red crown is sketched in red paint: we can recognize the ribbons that hang from the crown, the wide *wesekh* necklace on the breast and bracelets. On the back of the slab a prince's profile is outlined, with wig, sidelocks of hair, and ribbons, that typify his being a king's son. On stylistic grounds, the front figure has been identified as the portrait of the Pharaoh Sety I: thus, the ostracon might be a drawing sketch done by the decorator of his tomb.
M.C.G.

19

Relief of Rameses II
New Kingdom, 19th Dynasty,
reign of Rameses II
Polychrome limestone
L. 93.5; H. 40 cm
Abydos, temple of Rameses II
Paris, Musée du Louvre, B 13,
N 128

The *hauteur* of this king in his *khepresh* crown (cat. no. 29) befits the hero who crushed the Hittite alliance at the famous Battle of Qadesh. Everything about this king was larger-than-life, even his reign: sixty-six years, the longest in Egyptian history. His family, for example, comprised a total of at least four wives, as well as the daughters who were promoted to the rank of "great royal wives," and around a hundred children, whom his listed with arrogance. His colossal statues covered Egypt, as he "recycled" those of his predecessors; there is no temple on the banks of the Nile that does not have some trace of his royal cartouches. And his taste for the grandiose is confirmed by the rock-cut temple of Abu Simbel, saved during the creation of Lake Nasser. Omnipresent in both North and South Egypt, Rameses II was the very stuff of legend, and he remains the pharaoh best known to the wider public.

The relief from the Louvre is mostly concerned on illustrating the harmony resulting from his reign. Hollow-carved with a firm chisel, the work has sharply-defined surfaces and still maintains some of the original colors used to enliven the figure. The adornments of the king contrast with the red ochre of his face, just as the "Egyptian blue" of the crown and *wesekh* necklace contrast with the gold of the borders and the *uraeus*.

Characteristically, the line of the blue crown continues that of the profile of the nose; the long neck incised with two creases seems to be reaching forward; the finely-carved pierced ear is placed obliquely, parallel to the cheek; and the ribbons of the crown float behind the pharaoh. All of these details reveal the continuation of the earlier style favored by the artists at Abydos. The block of the upper section—also in the Louvre—shows a tutelary vulture. Moving in the opposite direction to the king, the inscription breaks the wall scene into two pictures; it actually accompanies the ritual gesture of the goddess, part of whose shoulder can be seen to the right and of whom it is said "[her] two arms bear the *menat*, the headdress of the Lady of heaven, which reward for. . . ." The king is moving to the back of the chapel toward other deities.

The walls of Egyptian temples reproduced the permanent dialogue that existed between the king and the gods; on this uninterrupted exchange depended the maintenance of order within the country.

Bibliography
E. Delange in: Corzo 1994, pp. 135–137.
E.D.

20

Statuette of King Rudamon
Third Intermediate Period,
reign of Rudamon
Blue glassy faience
H. 19 cm
Hermopolis Magna, the temple
of Thoth (according to inscriptions)
Private collection

The bust and part of the front of a pedestal supporting the base of a vase is all that is left of this statue of a kneeling king. Adorned with the attributes that indicate his rank—frontal *uraeus*, *nemes* and "false" beard—the monarch is holding up a jar of unguents in front of himself; thus the sculpture immortalizes those divine ablutions that the pharaoh was supposed to perform daily for the statue of the deity in his temple. The face here is rather resolute—if not severe—and is clearly too expressive to be just an idealized portrait. In effect, it commemorates King Rudamon, the last of a rather short-lived line which spread from Thebes to impose its power in the South of the country, undermining the influence of the Libyans of the 22nd Dynasty, the first members of which had—with a certain success—tried to restore the grandeur of the Ramesside period just some hundred years or so after the collapse of the New Kingdom. If the throne name of this king is easily legible on various parts of this statuette, his actual birth name—the only one which makes for certain identification—can be seen solely in a fragmented form on from the front of the vase: just beneath the break there are enough significant traces for one to read in the last part of the cartouche the "rud" of Rudamon.

It is this king's predecessors- his father Osorkon III and brother Takelot III—who are best known to us; of Rudamon we have relatively little trace. Among the three most significant extant products of his reign, are two small alabasters in limestone in the Louvre, and a fragment of a votive *sistrum* in faience recently identified in the British Museum. So, this statue is the only known representation of the monarch, which naturally adds to its interest. If its modest size reflects the

modest reign of the pharaoh himself—one of a number of rulers who, together with various princelings and local chieftains, divided up the territory before the Ethiopian conquest—it is also true that the craftsmanship here reveals that technical mastery one often finds in the work of the Third Intermediate Period. In certain ways this statue can be compared to such admirable sculptures as the statuette of Pimay in London or what may be a torso of Osorkon II in Paris; in all three there is the same quality in the treatments of facial features and the details of the headdress. The very choice of materials reveals the innovation of which the craftsmen of the time were capable, perhaps to meet the restrictions imposed by the political situation of the time. In effect, this use of "glassy faience"—often to be found in the Libyan period—was one way of making do without such expensive materials as feldspar, lapis lazuli and turquoise, and yet at the same time produce a monument that was solid and durable—essential qualities when, as here, the object was destined for a temple.
O.P.

21

Head of Ahmose (?)
Late Period, 31st Dynasty
Graywacke
H. 24 cm
Sais
Berlin, Ägyptisches Museum
und Papyrussammlung, 11864

The personality of the Late Period pharaohs emerges primarily from Greek textual evidence—rather than Egyptian. However, the individuality of the sovereigns takes second place to an idealized image of kingship in the visual art of this period. Inspiration was drawn from the great eras of the past—above all the Middle and New Kingdoms—since that "classical" art seemed to express the legitimacy of the sovereign. The facial features of this head are so impersonal, and the fact that there is no inscription make it almost impossible to identify the actual pharaoh concerned. A stylistic comparison with inscribed works of the same period has led us to identify this bust from Berlin with King Ahmose.

Bibliography
Priese 1991, pp. 172–173 (cat. 103).
D.W.

22

Nectanebo II adoring the Apis bull
Late Period, 30th Dynasty
Limestone
H. 40; L. 63.5; W. 9.5 cm
Saqqara, approach to the Serapeum
Paris, Musée du Louvre, N 423

Egypt took advantage of the dynastic disputes among the Achaemenids—and of its own position on the periphery of their empire—to regain a certain autonomy, which for a short while withstood Persian reconquest. From the beginning of the reign of Nectanebo I (Nakhtnebef), first king of the 30th—and last Egyptian—Dynasty, the country recovered a certain vitality and prestige, as one can see from the works carried out in all the temples. The tendency would continue and grow during the reign of Nectanebo II (Nakhthorheb).

This bas-relief is part of the restructuring and decoration of the approaches to the Serapeum in Saqqara, the Memphite necropolis, which took place during that latter king's reign. It comes from a building dedicated to the Apis bull which stood at the end of the paved road leading to the burial place of these sacred animals.

The bull "the living Apis, the replica of the (god) [Ptah]," a local deity, is shown here in a hybrid form, with the body of a man and the head of a bull. To the left, King Nectanebo II is shown "adoring the god [four times]." The pharaoh is identified by his birth name and his throne name, both included within a cartouche. In the former, the mention of Onuris, tutelary deity of Sebennytos, recalls that this city in the Delta was the place of origin of the 30th Dynasty.

In 343 BC Nectanebo II fled into Upper Egypt before the advancing armies of Artaxerxes III—a flight which marked the end of Egyptian independence. After ten years of a new Persian occupation, the kingdom of the pharaohs would pass into the hands of another power, that of Alexander the Great.

Bibliography
B. Letellier in: Berman, Letellier 1996, pp. 86, 87, 98.
M.E.

23

*Bas-relief from a temple
of Ptolemy VIII*
Ptolemaic period
Sandstone
H. 84; W. 77 cm
Karnak, East Temple
Berlin, Ägyptisches Museum
und Papyrussammlung, 2116

Nothing in this bas-relief betrays the fact that the pharaonic couple concerned were of European origin. Formal structure and iconography are entirely traditional, and the stylistic idealization avoids any touch of the personal. The king, wearing the crown of Lower Egypt, is shown making an offering to a (no longer extant) figure of a deity to the left. The queen follows him, presenting flowers. It is the hieroglyphics alone which enable us to identify the two as Ptolemy VIII and Cleopatra II (or III). In spite of their Macedonian origin, the sovereigns of the Ptolemaic dynasty (340–30 BC) ruled the country in total respect of the pharaonic traditions of ancient Egypt. The religious dogma of royal power remained unchanged, and—as one can see here—the pharaoh was still seen as the guarantor of the continued existence of the world.

Bibliography
Prese 1991, pp. 188–189, (cat. 112).
D.W.

The Images of Royalty.
The Pharaoh as Man or God

Catalog of the Works

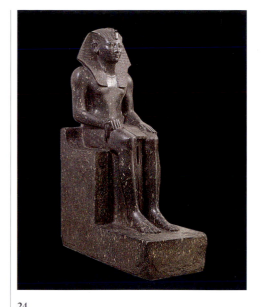

Among the clichés often encountered in literature, that of the divinity of the pharaoh has been the hardest to die. It is true that the inscriptions qualify the sovereign as the "perfect god," but he was really only a man and far from being perfect. There also exist multiple representations in which the king seems to be the equal of the gods. Let us take, for example, the famous temple of Abu Simbel. Rameses II is seated on the sanctuary walls between two divinities, who appear to pay homage to him in the cult scenes. In the central part of the holy of holies, the figure himself is seated among divine entities. One can note there a form of despotic megalomania, but it is merely Rameses II who inscribed his image among those of the gods. The cult consecrated to a king could also be expressed by the veneration of his colossal effigies or more simply by his name. In reality, the "divinity" of the pharaoh had to be varied. It was not meant to be a total assimilation with one god, as in the case of the Roman emperors. The personality of an Egyptian sovereign totally reflected the conception of the world of a civilization. The god creator had set up the established order at the beginning of the world. He then delegated men with the task of administering Egypt through the intermediary of one single person, the king. The latter was therefore first and foremost a human being, but the divine heritage conferred on him a supernatural aura; at the moment of his coronation, he was invested with a part of divinity. Thus the divinity of the royal function received a cult and not its momentary titular, a simple mortal elected by the gods.

Since it was necessary that this special divine form, the solar essence of the monarchy, receive material support, the latter was chosen from the real world. No one better than the king in person could serve as a living receptacle for the divine sovereignty that was therefore represented with the features of the reigning pharaoh. The utilization of his images fully entered the traditional iconographic vocabulary, and the least of his attributes was invested with a meaning.
I.F.

24

Statue of Thutmose I
New Kingdom, 18th Dynasty,
reign of Thutmose II
Diorite
H. 168; W. 53; D. 108 cm
Thebes (Karnak?)
Turin, Museo Egizio, Drovetti
Collection, 1374

The statue was discovered by J.J. Rifaud, Drovettis' agent, in 1818 at Thebes, probably in the temple of Karnak. The king is seated on a backless throne. He is wearing the striped cloth headdress (*nemes*) with the *uraeus* on his brow and the short pleated linen kilt (*shendjyt*) attached to the hips by a belt with a fastener on which is written: "The perfect god, lord of the execution of the rites, Aakheperkara [Thutmose I], to whom life is given forever." From it hangs the feral tail that can be seen between his legs. The right hand is closed in a fist, the left lying on his thigh. Under his bare feet nine arches have been carved, symbolizing the subjected foreign peoples. On the sides of the throne the union of the Two Lands is represented by the sign *sema*, "union," combined with lotus flowers and papyri. On the surface of the seat a vertical column of hieroglyphs reads on the right side: "the son of the sun Djeutymes kha-[mira] [Thutmose I], the beloved of Amon-Ra, king of the gods, to whom is given life"; on the left: "the perfect god Aakheperkara [Thutmose I], the beloved of Amun, giver of life"; on the right side of the legs: "the perfect god, the lord [of the Two Lands] Aakheper[en?]ra [Thutmose II], the beloved of Amun, to whom is given life"; on the left: "he made as a monument for his father Djeutymes khami-ra, justified." In all likelihood the name of the dedicator Thutmose II, whose descent from Thutmose I is uncertain, was erased by hammering, perhaps by Hatshepsut, as in the case of the obelisk raised by the queen west of the fourth pylon in the temple of Karnak, which was dedicated by Thutmose II to Thutmose I. They both seem to want to legitimatize their own descent with monuments dedicated to their father.

Bibliography
Tefnin 1979, pp. 62–64, pl. XV [b];
PM VIII, pp. 609, 700, 800 (with earlier bibliography).
E.F.M.

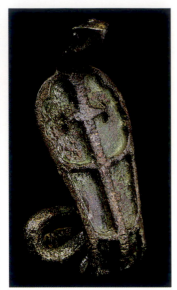

25

Stele of Nakhtsu
New Kingdom, 19th–20th Dynasties
Limestone
H. 46; L. 28 cm
Deir el-Medina
Turin, Museo Egizio, Drovetti
Collection, 1454 (CGT 50041)

Ribbed stele dedicated by the "Servant of the Lord of the Two Lands in the Seat of the Truth, Nakhtsu." Together with his son Panakht, Nakhtsu is holding an incense burner and kneeling in adoration of Ahmose Nefertari and Djeserkara (Amenhotep I), to whom a sanctuary at Deir el-Medina was dedicated. Below them are the kneeling figures of his wife, son and daughters, wearing long, wide-sleeved robes, and carrying a vase in their left hand. The queen is wearing a long robe and the crown with the *modius* and the vulture cast. The king is wearing a skullcap wig with the *uraeus* held by a ribbon and the *khemkhem* headdress. On the front of the long skirt, hanging from the belt there is the *djebau-biti*, "the adornment of the king of Lower Egypt," and he is holding the *ankh* scepter in his left hand and the staff and the flail in the right.

Bibliography
Tosi, Roccati 1972, pp. 75–76.
E.F.M.

26

Bronze uraeus
Late Period
Coppered metal
H. 8.7; W. 5.1; D. with tenon 7 cm
Paris, Musée du Louvre, E 19930

This is the typical form of the *uraeus*, with a rearing serpent. The current name is the latinized form of the Greek *ouraios*, which came from the Egyptian *iaret*, the name for a female cobra. When it feels threatened, this serpent puffs out its neck into an extended "racket" shape, to better spit its poison in the face of its enemies. According to Egyptian myth, the cobra was the daughter of the sun-god, the eye of Ra, who broke away from her father then returned, and has since been placed on his forehead in the form of a serpent. Hence it was only natural that the divine *uraeus* appeared on the forehead of the king, the sole legitimate heir of the sun-god on earth. A symbol of destructive power, this was a weapon at the service of the king, ready to destroy his enemies and those who were enemies of Egypt. However, also associated with the goddess Wadjyt of Lower Egypt, it protected the king and symbolized the river floodwaters that were essential to the life of Egypt. Thus, the *uraeus* symbolized both destructive energy and protective power. In an ivory tablet in the British Museum, King Den (1st Dynasty) is shown wearing the *uraeus* as he brandishes a *hedj* and grips an enemy by the hair. From Sneferu's reign onward (4th Dynasty), one finds the *uraeus* on the *seshed* headband, while in the reign of Djedefra it appears adorning the *nemes* (cat. no. 27), and in the Middle Kingdom would also appear on other royal crowns. The *uraeus* here has a horizontal tenon which must have served to fix it to a crown or other royal ornament.

Bibliography
Mysliwiec 1976.
C.Br.

27

Bronze nemes
Coppered metal
H. 8.3; W. 7.2; D. 6.7 cm
Provenance: unknown
Paris, Musée du Louvre, N 783

This small bronze model of a headdress represents a *nemes*, the most simple of the royal headdresses but the one that occurs most often in depictions. From the vertical position of the large bow holding the hair at the back of the neck, it must have been placed on the head of a statue of a standing, sitting or kneeling king. A small hole in the front served to fix the—unfortunately lost—*uraeus* in place (this would have been made separately). The *nemes* was a wig-covering made of a heavily-starched rectangle of striped material. Bound closely against the forehead, it passed behind the ears forming a pouch; two round-ended side sections hung down either side of the neck onto the chest, with a third section—in the form of a large bow—serving to hold the headdress in place at the back. The *nemes* first appears in statuary of the 3rd Dynasty—on the statue of King Djoser (Cairo Museum)—but not yet entirely covering the wig. During the reign of Djedefra (4th Dynasty) the front *uraeus* makes its appearance. In the New Kingdom, the stripes of the *nemes* were lapis lazuli blue and gold, as in the funeral mask of Tutankhamun; these were the colors of the rising sun. It would remain in use right up to the time of the Romans. Extant statues and bas-reliefs show us kings—either in human or sphinx form—wearing the *nemes* in tomb portraits or in scenes of religious worship.
C.Br.

28

King wearing the ibes *wig (sculptor's model)*
Late or Ptolemaic period
Limestone
L. 11.5; H. 8.7; D. 2 cm
Provenance unknown
Paris, Musée du Louvre, E 9289

This small limestone block fragment is a sculptor's model, with the lightly-carved right profile of a royal figure in bas-relief. The king is wearing the short, curled *ibes* wig that covers his ears and is bound by the *seshed* headband, the front of which is adorned with a rearing serpent.
The *ibes* wig was part of ceremonial royal costume and was shown in those scenes where the king is in contact with the gods, or else shown deified after his own death. The wig appeared during the Old Kingdom, would enjoy great popularity during the New Kingdom and remain in use right up to the period of the Ptolemies. From the reign of Sneferu onward, it was often decorated—as here—with the *seshed* headband, whose royal character is underlined by the presence of the *uraeus* (cat. no. 26). On the basis of representations and extant examples from royal tombs, we know this band was in gold (though those of Intef V, in the Leiden Museum, and of Tutankhamun, in the Cairo Museum, were in silver); around it was wrapped a cobra, whose head and upper body reared up at the front. The back closed with a decorative motif of two papyrus reed umbels, back to back, and two long ribbons which reached down between the shoulders. Sometimes there might also be two short side ribbons. From the 11th Dynasty onward, these latter might end in a *uraeus*, adorned with perhaps a crown, a solar disk or—as here—the Hathoric headdress. When he wore his *ibes* wig, the king also wore the straight royal beard; unfortunately, this cannot be seen here because of the break in the fragment.
C.Br.

29

Head of Amenhotep III
New Kingdom, 18th Dynasty,
reign of Amenhotep III
Quartzite
22.5 × 16 × 16.5 cm
Provenance unknown
London, The Trustees of the British Museum, EA 30448

Apart from suppressing a rebellion in Nubia, Amenhotep III undertook little military activity and was content with consolidating the empire that he inherited. Peaceful foreign relations with other powerful nations found a climax in his marriage to two princesses from Mitanni, Egypt's one-time arch-enemy across the Euphrates. Within Egypt, his was a time of unprecedented prosperity and highly refined artistic achievements, and Amenhotep's monuments superseded by far those of his predecessors in grandeur and delicacy. His best known monuments are the Luxor temple and his destroyed mortuary temple in western Thebes, marked by the so-called "Colossi of Memnon." This head from one of the king's numerous statues shows Amenhotep wearing the helmet-like blue crown (*khepresh*). It iconographically marked the king as a man of deeds—both in military and ritual contexts. The highly stylized, youthful features with almond-shaped eyes are a hallmark of the art from his reign.
M.M.

30

Head of a king wearing the atef *crown (ostracon)*
New Kingdom, 20th Dynasty (?),
reign of Rameses VI (?)
Limestone
H. 39; W. 42 cm
West Thebes (?)
Vienna, Kunsthistorisches Museum, ÄS 5979

The high quality of the king's head sketch on this Vienna ostracon—together with the unusual size of the piece—suggests that it was used for one of the tombs in the Valley of the Kings. In fact, outlines, plans and sketches for bas-reliefs were often produced on such limestone shards (ostraca).
The figure depicted is wearing the *nemes* (cat. no. 27) with the *uraeus* at the front (cat. no. 26), surmounted by the *atef* crown. This latter comprised a conical mitre made out of cane fixed to a base and adorned at the front with the solar disk. It is surmounted by the head of a ram bearing the solar disk (one of the ways Amun was depicted) and flanked by two ostrich feathers. Lower down to the sides one can see two ram's horns with two *uraei* with cow's horns and a solar disk (probably representations of the goddesses of Upper and Lower Egypt).
The king is holding the symbols of his office: the *heka* scepter (in the form of a cross, cat. no. 32) and the flyswatter (flabellum, cat. no. 31). Originally the drawing was done in light red; one can still make out the corrections in darker red.

Bibliography
Seipel 1992, pp. 55, 455 (cat. 186); Satzinger 1994, p. 89, fig. 61.
H.S.

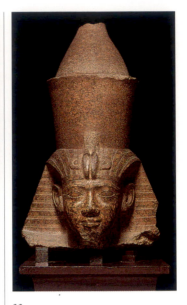

31

Parts of a flabellum
New Kingdom, 18th Dynasty,
reign of Tutankhamun
Egyptian faience
L. 10.5–10.4–9.5 cm; max. diam.
2.2–2.5–2.2 cm
Saqqara, Serapeum, tomb of the
bull-god Apis which died during
the reign of Tutankhamun
(A. Mariette excavations)
Paris, Musée du Louvre, N 2271 A,
B and C

These three long drop-shaped pendants in Egyptian faience are inscribed with the name of king Tutankhamun, "the good god, Nebkheperura, beloved of Apis" and must have been part of a flabellum (the Egyptian name for which was *nekhakha*). This object consisted of a handle from which hung three series of threaded beads (either round or cylindershaped) that ended in pendants similar to the ones here.
Like the *heka*, with which it is often associated, the flabellum was one of the royal scepters, an instrument of royal authority bestowed upon the king at his coronation so that he might successfully carry out his mission. The two examples found in the tomb of Tutankhamun, together with two *heka* scepters (cat. no. 32), are the only flabella belonging to a pharaoh that have come down to us. The king also appeared in public with the flabellum during the feast of *sed*, when he was seated under a canopy (as depicted in the Narmer macehead in the Ashmolean Museum, Oxford), or during the ritual race depicted on the stelae in the tomb chambers of King Djoser at Saqqara (one of the most ancient extant depictions of this event).
The flabellum has been interpreted as a flyswatter, as an implement for collecting and sprinkling *ladanum* (an odoriferous resin collected from the leaves and buds of the rockrose) or else as a symbol of rebirth.

Bibliography
PM III.1, p. 205; Mariette 1857, pp. 125–126, pl. II.
C.Br.

32

Heka scepter
Wood
L. 46.5; W. base 2.3; H. crook 10.5 cm
Paris, Musée du Louvre, N 1519

This wood baton ending in a sharplydefined crook which rises slightly at the end is a model of a *heka* scepter. Round in cross-section, the handle gets much thicker toward the end, terminating in an oval. Perhaps the form of this scepter was originally inspired by the crooks shepherds used to defend and guide their flocks, or catch hold of wandering animals. It very soon became one of the royal scepters of the Old Kingdom, and might appear, along with other royal insignia, painted on the friezes decorating sarcophagi, or else be placed in the tomb itself. The funeral furnishings in the tomb of Tutankhamun include not only two flabella (cat. no. 31) and two *hedj* war clubs (cat. no. 102) but also two *heka*. These latter are made up of a series of cylinders in lapis blue glasspaste and gold leaf covered metal which are threaded on a core of wood. The *heka* was in some way the Egyptian baton of command, the very symbol of sovereignty that the king received on the day of his coronation and which he would again appear holding during the *sed* festival, when the divine nature of his governance was reiterated and renewed; the object is a fundamental part of the hieroglyphs for "chief," "to command" and "to direct." The *heka* scepter is almost always associated with the flabellum. Both appear together in the hands of the king, just as they appear together in the hands of Osiris when represented as the very first king of Egypt, to whose throne each pharaoh was the legitimate successor.
C.Br.

33

Colossal head of Shabaqo
Late Period, 25th Dynasty,
reign of Shabaqo
Pink granite
H. 97 cm
Karnak, temple of Amun,
cachette court
Cairo Egyptian Museum, JE 36677=
CG 42010

King Shabaqo, the first ruler of the 25th Dynasty, strengthened the Kushite control over Egypt, which was started by his father Kashta, and followed by Shabaqo's own brother Piy. Their empire extended from Napata to the Mediterranean Sea. During their dynasty, the title of "god's wife of Amun," which had belonged to the Egyptian queens since the reign of Amenhotep III, was transferred to the daughters of the Kushite kings who were allowed to choose their successor during their lifetime. This is how Shepenwepet I adopted Amenirdis, Shabaqo's sister, and this line of succession followed the same rule also during the 26th Dynasty. The title gave its bearer religious power on the Theban west bank, which was equal in importance to that of the high priests of Amun on the east bank.
The head, part of a colossal statue of Shabaqo, bears the specific features of the royal statuary of the 25th Dynasty: projecting eyebrows, mouth with folds at the corners, and double *uraeus*. On his head, the king wears a combination of the double crown and the *nemes*. From this period onward, the pillar at the back of the statue surmounted by a *pyramidion*, occasionally became a form of support. Shabaqo built his tomb in el-Kurru, and left many monuments in Egypt and Nubia.

Bibliography
Kaiser 1967, p. 81 (cat. 816).
Z.T.

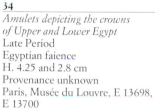

34

*Amulets depicting the crowns
of Upper and Lower Egypt*
Late Period
Egyptian faience
H. 4.25 and 2.8 cm
Provenance unknown
Paris, Musée du Louvre, E 13698,
E 13700

These amulets of rather late date reproduce the most significant symbols in pharaonic civilization. In fact, the crowns of North and South Egypt, each known as "Great," were veritable objects of veneration, and considered to have fearsome power.
The crown of Upper Egypt was a tall smooth mitre that was rounded at the top; the first traces of its ultimate form can be seen in such prehistoric statues as the "Bearded Man" of Gebelein on show here (cat. no. 5). It was called the "white crown" (*hedjet*) and was often of the color of the purest white linen; the faience here, however, has a greenish hue—as if there were a pale reflection of moonlight upon it (the white crown was compared to the moon in the Book of the Dead, Spell 80).
The crown of Lower Egypt was surmounted by a stalk and decorated with a volute in the front; it would seem to reproduce a bundle of fibres. Called the "red crown" (*deshret*), after the blazing color of the sun, it here appears to be azure blue—but amulets often used imaginary colors, creating these paradoxical images. In fact, the Egyptians held more firmly to what they knew to be the case that what they saw to be the case: naming the crowns by their real names created them as they really were, quite apart from their present appearance.
The dual crowns were complementary and inseparable. They indicated the plenitude of royal power; were an in-

tegral part of the very personality of the king, communicating their might to him. This is why the king often performed rituals or made offerings "symmetrically"—wearing first one crown, then the other. He truly was "the king of Upper and Lower Egypt".

Bibliography
Delange 2001, pp. 184–185 (cat. 67).
E.D.

35

Model of a sculpture
Ptolemaic period
Limestone
H. 16,5; W. 20 cm
Heliopolis (Schiaparelli excavations, 1903–04)
Turin, Egyptian Museum, inv. Suppl. 2898

Model of a sculpture consisting of a rectangular panel on which are reproduced, in relief, the "Two Ladies" Wadjyt and Nekhbet, tutelary deities of Lower and Upper Egypt. The goddesses are respectively represented as a cobra and a vulture above the hieroglyph for basket: *nb*. The ensemble, to be read *nebty* ("two ladies"), introduced the second of the five names forming the royal titulary. This name referred to the duality and at the same time the union of Egypt of which the king was warrant.

Bibliography
Donadoni Roveri 1989, p. 245, fig. 373.
S.D.

36

*Bas-relief depicting the veneration
of the royal name*
New Kingdom, 19th Dynasty
Sandstone
H. 48; L. 123 cm
Provenance unknown
Copenhagen, Ny Carlsberg
Glyptotek, ÆIN 1724

This bas-relief probably formed the
lintel of a tomb; but the name of the
deceased is unknown because parts of
the inscriptions are no longer extant.
The man himself is shown twice, on either side of a central motif comprising
the cartouches of Amenhotep I. Contrary to the use of a similar theme that
occurs on Pairy's lintel (cat. no. 57),
here the titles are not those of the
reigning king but of a pharaoh who
had been dead for two centuries (cat.
nos. 59, 60, 174, 175).
The double name of the king is placed
over an image that itself summarizes
the dual nature of Egypt. The *sema-
tawy*, in fact, was the symbol of the
union of the Two Lands, and comprised the heraldic plants of the South
(yet to be clearly identified, but traditionally referred to as a "lily") and the
North (the papyrus reed), both enveloping the hieroglyph for the concept of "unity". Placed directly under
the name of the king, this symbolizes
the very basis of pharaonic government.
Surmounting the cartouches are two
ostrich feathers flanking a solar disk;
these form a very ancient symbol that
sometimes appears as the headdress
for falcon images of the god Horus. In
this way, the king is directly identified
with the deity who was the patron of
the institution of monarchy. The predecessor of all pharaohs, the falcon-
god appears on either side of the cartouches above the Horus name of
Amenhotep I, who was the "bull who

brought the Two Lands into submission," probably an allusion to the political equilibrium the land recovered
after the military victories of his father, Ahmose.
Quite apart from the homage rendered
to the deified sovereign, it is the very
function of kingship that the praying
figure on this relief is venerating. This
is a good example of how ordinary
mortals perceived the institution of
the monarchy. The current earthly
monarch, whose existence was finite,
was only the "living image" in which
an office inherited from the gods was
embodied. It was not so much the
names and statues of the reigning
monarch that were venerated as the
symbols of royalty itself. Here, that
veneration concerns the divine cartouches and insignia (incorporated
within figurative representations); it
is the solar attributes of the pharaoh
which are being worshipped.

Bibliography
Jørgensen 1998, cat. 100.
I.F.

37

Plaque with figures of gods
Third Intermediate Period
Blue-glazed faience
5.5 × 4.0 cm
Provenance unknown
London, The Trustees
of the British Museum, EA 14556

This plaque served as a spacer-bar for
inclusion in an item of jewelry. It is
decorated in openwork with figures
of deities. In the center stands the falcon-headed sun-god, with the solar
disk on his head. In his right hand he
holds the *ankh* (sign of life), while
grasping a bound prisoner with his
left hand. To the right stands Montu,
wearing double plumes, and behind
him the goddess Mut. This pair is balanced by figures of Horus, wearing
the double crown, and a lion-headed
goddess, perhaps Sekhmet. The scene
emphasizes the kingly aspect of the
sun-god, and the motif of the ruler's
triumph over enemies serves to reaf-
firm the principle of *maat*.
On the other side the central figure is
the sovereign, thus placed in exact
parallel to the sun-god. The pharaoh is
flanked by two male deities holding
hes libation vases (cat. no. 246). To
the right is Thoth, recognizable by his
ibis head surmounted by the symbol of
the moon (combined disk and crescent). Behind him is a reared cobra
surmounted by a solar disk, whose
body is wrapped around the stalk of a
plant. On the opposite side of the king
is a falcon-headed deity—undoubtedly Horus, even if the headdress (similar to that of Thoth) suggests he could
be a lunar deity such as Khons. Behind
this god is a divinity with the head of
a lioness (one of the dangerous goddesses, such as Sekhmet or Mut).
Thoth and Horus are two deities who
are very often to be found together
like this in a ritual that was part of an

ensemble of ceremonies forming the
"Royal Ascension." As depicted on
the walls of temples, this involved the
new king being presented to the main
deities of a sanctuary and, once accepted, recognized as the legitimate
heir and the religious officiant *par excellence*. The "Royal Ascension" was
essentially predicated on the notion
of coronation and of the dual government of Egypt united in the figure of
a single sovereign. Here, one sees a
depiction of what is often described as
a "baptism." The liquid flowing from
the two *hes* vases is symbolized by the
two hieroglyphs *ankh* and *was*, which
embody life and the power to protect
it. These qualities originated with the
sun-creator but were then bestowed
on all the gods, who are often depicted holding these two symbols. This
purification of the king was also linked
with the Two Lands of Egypt that were
materially bound together by the Nile.
The liquid that the gods Thoth and
Horus are pouring on the sovereign
might thus be identified with the flood
waters of the river. This recalls the
necessary unity embodied in royal
power, and also indicates that the
anointed king in his turn will be able
to pour forth for others the life forces
which issue from the gods.
J.H.T., I.F.

38

Faience plaque with the royal name of nesw-bit
New Kingdom, 19th Dynasty,
reign of Sety I
Egyptian faience
H. 26; W. 12.3; D. 2.1 cm
Qantir
Paris, Musée du Louvre, E 11518

Excavations at Qantir in the Delta have unearthed a number of bricks in Egyptian faience that must originally have decorated the gateway to a royal palace. With subtle nuances of color, varying from turquoise blue to green, the monumental hieroglyphs stand out against a sky-blue background of dazzling beauty. Set in vertical and horizontal bands, these faience tiles followed the outline of the architectural structure, which was thus encased within the complete "roll-call" of the king's royal titles.

This single brick contains signs and symbols characteristic of royal honors which dated back to the very earliest days of Egyptian history. The "sedge and the bee" used to indicate one of the "five great names" of the king are two symbols referring to the North and the South of the Nile valley before they were united as a single kingdom. Curiously, it is the more commonplace "sedge" that is chosen to indicate the South, rather than the "lily" which appears elsewhere—for example, in the pictogram of the "Reunion of the Two Lands." And the bee, forever fixed as the symbol of the king of the North, would never find any other use in the Egyptian bestiary. It would seem that these two signs of the reed and the bee bear witness to an ancient name of the king which is now unknown to us. "The king of Upper and Lower Egypt, lord of the Two Lands," proclaims the tile with the usual rhetorical redundancy, underlining the permanent du-alism that was the basis of this monarchy and which was reflected in the way plants and tutelary deities associated with the North and South could play a role in the iconography of monarchy. The "double land" was reflected by a dual organization within the kingdom, and by the dual performance of pharaonic ritual.

Bibliography
Delange 2001, pp. 44–45.
E.D.

39

Rameses II's foundation brick bearing the royal titulary
New Kingdom, 19th Dynasty,
reign of Rameses II
Faience, vitrified
L. 35.9; W. 18; H. 6.7 cm
Hildesheim, Roemer- and Pelizaeus Museum, 6339

This type of brick, one of the foundation elements in a royal edifice, is inscribed with the names and titles of the sovereign whose edifice it was. Since the Middle Kingdom, the full form of address consisted of five epithets, comprising fixed titles and individual names. Three parts of the "royal protocol" are shown on this brick.

The upper and lower sides bear the birth name ("Rameses-loved-by-Amun") and throne name, both encircled by a royal cartouche. The throne name was bestowed on accession to the throne and contained a programmatic declaration, which placed the ruler in relation to the sun and creator-god Ra. Rameses II called himself "Mighty-in-relation-to-the-world-system-of-Ra, chosen-by-Ra," thereby stressing the divine authority of every pharaoh: namely, as guarantor on earth of the world order (*maat*).

On the narrow side is an extended form of address. Already in existence since the Early Period, the "Horus name" announces the king as a manifestation of the celestial falcon Horus. During the New Kingdom, the appellation "mighty bull" was added: "Long live Horus, mighty bull, who-loves-Maat." The birth and throne names then followed, combined with various titles like "King of Upper and Lower Egypt," "Lord of the Double Land [Egypt], "Lord of the ritual" (before the throne name), "son of Ra" and "Lord of the Crowns" (before the birth name). The royal titulary, there-fore, comprised declarations of the ruler's authority, divinity and divine empowerment.

Bibliography
Kozloff, Bryan, Berman, Delange 1993, pp. 184–185.
B.S.

40

*Plaquette with the names
of Horemheb*
New Kingdom, 19th Dynasty,
reign of Horemheb
Faience
H. 5.4 cm
Provenance unknown
Copenhagen, Ny Carlsberg
Glyptotek, ÆIN 41

The two sides of this faience plaquette are simply decorated with the two cartouches of King Horemheb. The royal names, preceded by their epithets, are to be read vertically. The line above which they are placed contains the traditional wishes for long life, and is to be read horizontally. The whole thing is contained within a rectangular frame with rounded corners, with the edge being echoed by a line that completes the composition.

On one side is the name the sovereign received at the moment of his coronation, and which he always bore from that moment on: "The king of Upper and Lower Egypt, Lord of the Two Lands, Djeserkheperura, Setepenra, the son of Ra, Lord of Crowns, Horemheb, Beloved of Amun, who has given life as Ra for the whole of created time." This very common title at the end is often translated as "gifted with life," but it really conveys the idea of the ability that the gods have granted the king to bestow upon his subjects the vital force that they themselves have bestowed upon him.

On the other side is a similar text in which the only royal epithets are "perfect god" and "Lord of the Two Lands." The scene is dominated by a winged disk that symbolizes the great heavenly god, Horus. Opposite the first cartouche of the king is a vulture wearing the white crown flanked by two ostrich feathers; it is perched on the hieroglyph for a basket (*neb*),

which rests on a tuft of papyrus reeds. The bird is holding out the sign of royal power (*was*) toward the royal name. This is an interesting combination of symbols. The vulture is the animal symbol of the goddess of the South, Nekhbet. However, if one "reads" the hieroglyphs it comes above, one learns that she is "Lady of the Delta," which is the role of her counterpart, Wadjyt, usually depicted as a cobra. This is not a mistake by some careless engraver, but rather a combination of icons—a practice that was highly developed among the Egyptians. The resulting ensemble thus evokes both of the tutelary deities of the pharaonic monarchy.

Bibliography
Jørgensen 1998, cat. 140.
I.F.

41

"Golden Horus"
Ptolemaic period
Polychrome ceramic
H. 15.5; L. 12.7; D. 1.2 cm
el-Ashmunein
New York, The Metropolitan
Museum of Art, gift of Edward
S. Harkness, 26.7.996

The five names of the royal titulary (see cat. no. 39) underline the subtle links between the pharaoh and the gods. The guarantor of the unity of the two regions of the country (King of Upper and Lower Egypt, *nesw-bit*), he placed himself under the aegis of the tutelary goddesses of the Valley and the Delta (named the "Two Ladies," *nebty*). From the 4th Dynasty onward, the king would proclaim himself "son of Ra" (*sa Ra*). And finally the last two parts of his titulary linked him directly with the god who was the clearest patron of the pharaonic monarchy: Horus. This was the name used in referring to the most ancient of the Egyptian sovereigns. The identification with the falcon-god is taken up with insistence in the name of "Golden Horus" which was also borne by kings. In effect, the precious metal mentioned was the very flesh of the gods—and of the sun-god in particular. Thus the king is identified with the solar falcon, lord of the heavens and of the whole of the created universe.

As well as monuments and texts, there are a number of objects that bear inscriptions of the royal titulary in more or less complete form. This ceramic plaque comes from one of these formulations, which originally comprised more than one of the royal titles. The quality of finish here proves the exceptional technical mastery of the craftsman, while the very fragility of such ceramic pieces of this size means

that very few have come down to us intact. The falcon dominating the hieroglyph signifies "gold," while the combination forms the transcription of the name "Golden Horus."

This image must have been an inlay for a wood panel bearing the entirety of the royal titulary of a king from the Ptolemaic era.

Bibliography
Friedman 1998, p. 200.
I.F.

42

Statue of a falcon
New Kingdom, 19th Dynasty,
reign of Rameses II
Black granite
86.5 × 35.5 cm
Tell el-Maskhuta
London, The Trustees of the British
Museum, EA 1006

This statue of a falcon represents the sun-god Ra-Horakhty, described in the inscription upon the base as "great god, lord of heaven." The falcon stands above the cartouche of Rameses II, which is topped with two feathers. Originally, the falcon was embellished with a crown, perhaps of gilded wood, attached through the hole carved into the upper surface of the head. The statue proclaimed the strong link between king and this creator god, and intimated the notion that the pharaoh was under the protection of the divine world. This example contrasts with earlier works, in which a diminutive figure of a falcon spread its wings behind the king's head, as on the famous diorite statue of Khafra in the Cairo Museum. Edouard Naville excavated the statue within the temple enclosure of Tell el-Maskhuta in the Wadi Tumilat. However, ceramic evidence indicates that the earliest permanent occupation of the site occurred in the Saite period, five centuries after this statue was carved. Thus the statue must have been brought from another site and reused in the temple of Atum, a Heliopolitan god often identified with Ra-Horakhty.
N.S.

43

*Statuette of the goddess Isis
suckling the king*
Late Period
Bronze
H. 16 cm
Provenance unknown
Berlin, Ägyptisches Museum
und Papyrussammlung, 8288

The pharaoh was already being depicted as a child suckled by his divine mother in the bas-reliefs of the pyramids of ancient Egypt. Although intimate in aspect, these depictions were a powerful expression of dogma for they stressed the divine descent of the sovereign. Through his Horus name, the king was linked to the son of the goddess Isis. This bronze statuette shows the naked child wearing the royal headdress complete with *uraeus*, thus underlining the royal status of the pharaoh protectively embraced by the goddess Isis.

Bibliography
Cat. Berlin 1967, p. 81, (cat. 816).
D.W.

44

*Rameses II suckled by a goddess
(ostracon)*
New Kingdom, 19th Dynasty,
reign of Rameses II or later
Painted limestone
H. 31.2; W. 18.2; D. 3.3 cm
Cleveland, The Cleveland Museum
of Art, gift in honor of James
N. Sherwin, 1987.156

Among Egypt's most celebrated kings, Rameses II (or Rameses "The Great") was also its greatest builder. The king's colossal statues and sprawling temples are among the largest and most numerous monuments of any ruler in Egypt. The scene on this limestone flake or ostracon was probably a preliminary sketch or study for a larger composition. The king (identified by the cartouche behind him) stands beside a goddess. The artist has combined meticulous detail with a vibrantly colored palette to masterful effect. The tall, slender goddess wears an elaborate vulture-feather garment. Though she is unnamed, her costume links her with a number of motherly sky goddesses such as Isis, Mut or Nekhbet. She cups her breast in her right hand, signaling the king to suckle. Although he is surely an adult, the great ruler has shrunk to a child's size under the divinity's protective embrace. Dressed in fine linens, he holds the shepherd's crook and flail, the dual emblems of Egyptian kingship. His crown is the blue crown or *khepresh*, a type reserved for royal ritual or cult activity.

The motif of a king suckled by a goddess has a long history in Egyptian art, beginning at least as early as the Old Kingdom. Various matronly goddesses can appear. Similar scenes include the feline Sekhmet and Bastet, the bovine Hathor, the monstrous hippo-crocodile figure Taweret, and Isis, cast in the guise of a tree. Depending on the context, the scene can refer to the king's birth, his entry into the world of the gods after death, or to the ritual rebirth of his kingship celebrated in the *sed*-festival jubilee. In all cases, the meaning is clear. The goddess' nourishment reaffirms the Egyptian king's divine nature as well as rejuvenating him in his role the earthly embodiment of the sun-god and cosmic creator, Amun-Ra.

Bibliography
A.K. Capel in: Capel, Markoe 1996, pp. 117–118, (cat. 51); L.M. Berman in: Berman, Bohac 1999, pp. 248–249, (cat. 179).
K.J.B.

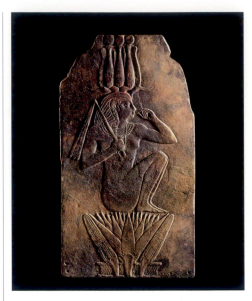

45

Stele of Rameses II as a child
New Kingdom, 19th Dynasty,
reign of Rameses II
Limestone
H. 18; W. 13 cm
Provenance unknown
Paris, Musée du Louvre, N 522

This stele was raised by the vizier who is shown to one side of the monument adoring the god Ptah. However, there is more to this object than a high functionary's dedication of perpetual prayer to the deities; on the other side, there is a very interesting image, with a figure recognizable as a pharaoh from his *uraeus* (here worn wrapped around the *seshed* headband, see cat. no. 28) and identified by the cartouche as Rameses II. Quite exceptionally, this king is here shown as a young boy. This emphasis on boyhood clearly contradicts what one would expect from a royal portrait, which should show the sovereign as an adult at the height of his powers, capable of both governing and leading an army. The image used here to depict the king is thus drawn from another area of iconography.
Rameses is shown with a finger to his lips and with the typical sidelock of hair—two features that indicate youth. However, the elegantly-pleated pagne, a very fashionable item during his reign, is not part of the iconography of children. He is seated on a cushion, the center of which gives under his weight. Indeed, the key to reading this image is to be found in the iconography used in depictions of the deities. The childhood of Horus was an essential component in Egyptian foundation myths. The youth of the god symbolized immaturity and inability to act. Nevertheless, the youthful and inexperienced god embodied a key phase in creation—that of perpetual

renewal and rejuvenation. From the Third Intermediate Period onward, the reigning monarch was continually being associated with images of Horus the Child, thus underlining the permanent renewal of the strength within the monarchy. This representation of Rameses is simply the prototype of what would become a commonplace of royal iconography. However, in the Ramesside period there was a god who was depicted in an almost identical way: Herymaat, who first appears at the beginning of the 19th Dynasty (in the Valley of the Queens) and was an embodiment of the deceased on the point of being reborn, just like the rising sun on the horizon.

Bibliography
Andreu, Rutschowskaya, Ziegler 1997, p. 144.
I.F.

46

Plaque of Iuput II
Third Intermediate Period,
23rd Dynasty
Faience (discolored)
H. 29.5 × W. 16.0 cm
Edinburgh, The Trustees of the
National Museums of Scotland,
A.1956.1485

The plaque probably represents Iuput II, a little-known king of the Third Intermediate Period (731–720 BC), in the form of the infant Horus. He wears a composite crown, *nemes* headdress with lappets and *uraeus*, a sidelock, broad collar and necklace. The king seems to have Kushite facial features, which was the fashion in art of that period. The plaque may have originally decorated a shrine that was damaged by fire.

Bibliography
Friedman 1998, p. 199 (cat. 59).
E.G., B.M.

47

*Statue of the cow Hathor suckling
the Pharaoh Horemheb*
New Kingdom, 18th Dynasty,
reign of Horemheb
Pink granite
H. 103; base 74.5 × 70.5 cm
Rome, Iseo Campense
Florence, Museo Egizio, 5419

This statue represents the cow goddess Hathor suckling the Pharaoh Horemheb. All that remains of the animal is the rear part, resting on a parallelepiped-shaped base; the pharaoh is shown in profile on the right side of the cow, kneeling on his left leg. With his right hand he draws to his mouth the goddess' udder; he is wearing on his head the *nemes* headdress. Around the base is carved a fragmentary hieroglyphic inscription, with the remains of a cartouche bearing the name of the Pharaoh Horemheb. The pose in which the pharaoh is represented is extremely rare in Egyptian statuary, whereas it is more common in the reliefs in the temples adorning the chapels consecrated to the cult of the goddess Hathor, featuring images of the goddess nursing the pharaoh: actually the Egyptians attached important purification and resurrection meanings to milk.
This statue was discovered, along with other important finds, during the excavations carried out in 1881 in Rome in the place where rose the ancient Iseo, known as Iseo Campense, by the church of Santa Maria sopra Minerva, and was purchased by the Ministry of Public Education for the Egyptian Museum of Florence.

Bibliography
Schiaparelli 1887, pp.152–154 (cat. 1225); M.C. Guidotti, in: Walker, Higgs 2000, p. 261 (cat. IV.43).
M.C.G.

48

Sphinx attributed to Akhenaten
New Kingdom, 18th Dynasty,
reign of Amenhotep IV
Quartz or gneiss (?)
H. 33; L. 53 cm
Karnak, temple of Amun,
cachette court
Cairo, Egyptian Museum,
CG 42090, JE 37485

Found in the "cachette court" at Karnak, this sphinx has been attributed to Akhenaten and dated at this period, because found among other objects of the same era. If it did belong to the heretic pharaoh, then it is very interesting because we have very few three-dimensional statues of Amenhotep IV as a sphinx. However, the motif does figure in Amarna iconography, because the sovereign appears in this form in various bas-reliefs. The sphinx was one of the most powerful evocations of the solar origin of kingship, and it is well known that Akhenaten was someone who took this identification of the pharaoh with the divine son of the sun to most daring extremes.
However, the stylistic clumsiness of the work has puzzled archaeologists. Voicing all the doubts an Egyptologist would have about this piece, if he simply came across it in some antique dealer's, Legrain remarks that "the whole thing reveals a complete ignorance of the traditions of the Theban school of the 18th Dynasty and of Khuiatonu [Akhenaten]." In fact, the basis for the dating is essentially the objects found along with the sphinx, even if the "cachette" contained statues from various eras—from the 12th to the 30th Dynasties.
It is true that the piece is rather unskillful, undoubtedly because the stone is hard and difficult to work. Contrary to tradition, the figure is not shown full-on, but with its head slightly to the right. The lion's body is out of proportion, and the head and the face seem to have been recut (a suggestion I owe to Elisabeth Delange, whom I thank for her considered opinions). If this work does not exercise great aesthetic appeal, it is indicative of certain royal statues that are not very well known to the public at large. It might also perhaps attract further attention from researchers: the study of its numerous unusual details and stylistic incoherence might well lead to some interesting conclusions.

Bibliography
CG 42001–42250, pp. 52–53 (pl. LV)
I.F.

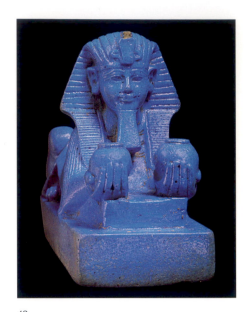

49

*Small sphinx representing
Amenhotep III*
New Kingdom, 18th Dynasty,
Amenhotep III
Ceramic
H. 13.7; L. 25; W. 7 cm
Provenance unknown
New York, The Metropolitan
Museum of Art, gift of Lila Acheson
Wallace, 1972.125

The sphinx is one of the most famous symbols of pharaonic Egypt—the most obvious example being the colossal figure that has been a haunting presence on the Giza plateau for thousands of years and which the ancient Egyptians ultimately venerated as an incarnation of the god Horemakhet ("Horus in the Horizon"). The deification of the Great Sphinx should not, however, obscure the original significance of the composition—a significance which it had throughout the Pharaonic period.
Having always used images to describe the forces of the gods, the Egyptians chose the lion as one of the icons to represent the energy of the sun (see cat. no. 53). Associated with sovereignty, it meant that the king was seen as enjoying the supernatural qualities attributed to the god Ra. The sphinx was, in fact, the very symbol of the function performed by the monarch. The reigning sovereign only held his title temporarily, with the timeless governance of Egypt being in the hands of the gods, and passed down from one reign to the next. Simple mortals with a transcendent divine heritage, those who ascended to the throne may have lent their faces to royal effigies, but what was being honored was not the individual but the wearer of the double crown. The sphinx echoes this very special duality of pharaonic theocracy, which brought together the supernat-

ural essence of the gods and the human nature of a king who was responsible for seeing to it that the world functioned fairly and justly.
Like so many other symbols of royal power linked with the sun, the sphinxes stood guard over the processional ways leading to the temples. The forms of the animals could vary according to which deity the temple was dedicated to, just as there could be variation in the composite image of king and god. For example, at Karnak, the ram of Amun is used, sometimes together with features from the body of a lion. At Gebel Barkal, the great Theban god is shown protecting Amenhotep III between his paws; but this is not the traditional image of the sphinx. The Metropolitan Museum piece, therefore, is one of the multiple expressions of this genre, and is remarkable both for its size and its state of preservation: extant ceramic objects generally being rather small and often in poor condition. Like most sphinxes, this too wears the *nemes*, the solar headdress (cat. no. 257) which was inspired by the first rays of the rising sun. This wig-covering thus underlined the king's identification with the sun, but it also enabled artists to achieve a smooth transition between the body of the lion and the face of a man.
The tense feline body representing the sun is surmounted here by the rather impassive face of Amenhotep III, holding two small globular pots in his hands. These are the *nw* jars (cat. no. 258) which were originally used in presenting the wine to the gods during ceremonies. One of those plays on object-for-word which were so popular with the Egyptians occurs here, with the arm holding the spherical receptacle serving to write the term for an offering in general (*henek*). Thus, the

arm holding out the *nw* refers to any ritual offering, not just the presentation of wine. The inscription between the outstretched arms here is rather laconic, simply naming the king "The perfect god, Nebmaatra, who has given life." Fixed for eternity in this pose as a sovereign officiating at religious worship, the sphinx of Amenhotep thus shows the pharaoh maintaining the mysterious dialogue that links men and the gods. Shown as his people's intermediary with the sun—the very source of all life—the monarch thus deserves the epithet given.

Bibliography
Paris 1993, pp. 184–185.
I.F.

50

Plaque with cartouches of Sety I
New Kingdom, 19th Dynasty,
reign of Sety I
Blue faience
H. 1.3; L. 1.9 cm
Florence, Museo Egizio, 10367

The longitudinal hole in this parallelepiped plaque would indicate that it was meant to be hung. It is a seal, showing on both sides the cartouches with the name and first name of Sety I. On the front surface the pharaoh's first name is accompanied by the image of a sphinx shown in profile, with a lion's body and human head, wearing a wig bound by a ribbon and the ceremonial beard. On the back side the name of Sety I appears, flanked by two winged *uraei*, with a solar disk above the head.
The plaque belongs to a series of articles that the pharaoh used as means of "propaganda" in the territory of the country: like for instance the famous celebrative scarabs of Amenhotep III, they were vehicles of information throughout Egypt, and even beyond, about the important events of the pharaoh's reign, as well as the sovereign's authority and power.
M.C.G.

51

Finger-ring
18th Dynasty, reign of Thutmose IV
or Amenhotep III
Gold and glazed composition
W. 1.7 cm (bezel)
Provenance unknown
London, The Trustees of the British
Museum, EA 4159

The gold stirrup-shaped hoop, albeit modern, copies authentic examples supporting the longitudinally pierced bezel by means of a gold pin and twisted wire. The swiveling bezel bears an incised representation of a king as a couchant sphinx with the blue crown (*khepresh*). Pharaoh's divine protection is signified by the cobra, representative of the sun-god, spreading its wings behind his head, and by the cross-shaped amuletic hieroglyph for "life" (*ankh*). The reverse of the bezel bears the figure of a goose adjoined by the name of Amun, and with the amuletic hieroglyph for "perfection" (*nefer*) in front. This configuration appears to be deliberately ambiguous. The goose is a depiction of one of the sacred animals through which Amun revealed himself, but is also the hieroglyph for "son," whereby the full inscription reads "The son of Amun [viz. the king] is perfect."
M.M.

52

Finger-ring
New Kingdom, 18th Dynasty,
reign of Thutmose III
Gold and blue glass
W. 1.5 cm (bezel)
Provenance unknown
London, The Trustees of the British
Museum, EA 14349

The swiveling bezel of this ring holds a plaque with delicate decoration incised on both sides. The obverse shows king Thutmose III as a striding sphinx with a prostrate enemy under his feet. The caption to this well-attested icon asserts he is "trampling all foreign lands." The king is given the traditional epithet of Perfect God, and the cartouche contains his throne name. The hieroglyphs on the reverse present Thutmose's Golden Horus name, one of the five traditional elements of an Egyptian ruler's full titulary, and linking him to the principal god of kingship in his role of glorious victor.
Thutmose III ranks among the greatest rulers of ancient Egypt. Through a long series of military campaigns he restored Egyptian supremacy in Syria–Palestine after the warless interlude of Queen Hatshepsut's reign. He was posthumously deified and frequently figures on amulets down to the Late Period. The present ring must have belonged to a high-ranking contemporary, but must partly have served as just such a protective amulet.
M.M.

53

Scarab with lion and crocodile
Second Intermediate Period
Green-enameled soapstone
L. 3.2; W. 2.3; D. 0.6 cm
Provenance unknown
New York, The Metropolitan
Museum of Art, T.M. Davis
Collection, bequest of T.M. Davis,
30.8.767

Inspired by natural models, motifs taken from the animal kingdom could have different meanings according to the context in which they appeared. A dangerous wild animal symbolized aggression. When the creature appeared in a scene evoking the fearsome forces against which the Egyptians had to fight, it was considered as an emblem of chaos. However, given that such animals were also endowed with remarkable strength, they might well feature as a beneficent image: the belligerent power symbolized by the animal being thus turned back upon the milieu inhabited by that animal itself. The lion is a perfect example of this ambivalence in the Egyptian use of animal images. It might be hunted without pity (see cat. no. 95), or else taken as am emblem of the power ruling over the desert. In the latter case, its valor was compared to the implacable rays of the sovereign sun. Thus the lion might become part of the vocabulary used to describe deities; it appears in this way, for example, in the image of the sphinx (see cat. no. 49).
Here, the lion probably represents the king, and is shown passing over the body of a crocodile. The interpretation of this latter animal is much more delicate. As ambiguous as the lion in significance, it could be associated with the god Sobek, in which case it was an allegory for the combination of the forces of water and light, mutually as-sisting each other. However, the position of the lion here naturally suggests that of the conqueror, treading his enemy into the dust. Crocodile-hunting, in fact, focused on the negative associations of this animal, and although it was not very common in objects dating from before the Ptolemaic period, it does sometimes occur in Predynastic works. It also forms the subject matter of Spell 32 of the Book of the Dead.

Bibliography
Hayes 1959, p. 36, fig. 17.
I.F.

54

Lion devouring an enemy (ostracon)
New Kingdom, Ramesside period
Limestone, painted
H. 5; W. 11 cm
Deir el-Medina
Cairo, Egyptian Museum, JE 63802

Shards of limestone or fragments of pottery, ostraca have been unearthed in large quantities in Egypt, particularly near the village of Deir el-Medina. Among other things, they were used for rough drafts of the decorative schemes to be carried out in the tombs of the Valley of the Kings or in temples. Sometimes, the artists took advantage of these "sketchbooks" to give free reign to their imagination or else offer a very personal treatment of a conventional theme.

This is the case here, with this ostracon from the Cairo Museum. The lion motif was a frequent one in Egyptian art, often linked with royal iconography; the most striking instance of this is the use of the lion's body as part of the sphinx. Here, the artists shows that he is familiar with the habits of his subject: the fearsome predator seems to be dragging off its prey to devour it undisturbed in its lair. The inspiration also comes from another motif: that of statues showing a lion holding an enemy's head in its mouth. Lions like this have been found in audience palaces, decorating the string wall of the staircase leading up to the royal podium. In that case, the animal is shown rearing up, resting its forepaws on a victim reduced to helplessness. Depictions of the feline also appear in other contexts. For example, on the walls of temples celebrating a pharaoh's victories the predator can be seen fighting in the thick of the enemy alongside the king. However, this does not mean that this animal accompanied the pharaoh into battle (as has

sometimes been claimed); if that were the case, the feline would have had to be remarkably discerning in choosing to savage only the pharaoh's enemies and not his own troops! Once again, what we have here is simply a visual allegory of the strength and vigor of the king as he leads his army to victory. Like the destructive rays of the sun, the arrows of the son of Ra pierce the enemies of Egypt. The lion is only present (in the image) as an emblem of the solar origin and power of royal might.

Bibliography
Peck 1980, no. 94.
I.F.

55

Relief with the names of Rameses II
New Kingdom, 19th Dynasty,
reign of Rameses II
Polychrome limestone
H. 57; W. 57 cm
Abydos, temple of Rameses II
Paris, Musée du Louvre, B 21,
N 133

The inscriptions in the two hollow-engraved vertical bands mention Rameses II's first and third royal names. Above these names and enclosed within the plan of the royal palace are two large falcons of Horus wearing the *pschent*, the double crown of Upper and Lower Egypt (cat. no. 34). The missing fourth side of the rectangle would have shown the wall of the salient and projections typical of early fortifications. At first glance, the two "Great Names of Horus"—"Powerful Bull, beloved of Maat" and "Powerful Bull, rich in years"—reveal that the king is the equal of the god Horus, that he is his incarnation. The names use various symbols. In effect, the bull, always associated with the sign for "power" or "victory" (comprising an arm and weapon), was the incarnation of the pharaoh. A picture-narrative palette from Predynastic times reveals that even then the thick-set bull with aggressive horns and solid, threatening hooves represented victorious Strength trampling its enemies underfoot and guaranteeing continuing order through its triumph. The royal title, therefore, takes up the meaning of a primitive iconography that preceded writing. A further confirmation of this comes from one of the ceremonial attributes of the pharaoh, the bull's tail he often wore hanging from his belt.

The sequence of Rameses II's names in this relief is confirmed by the ones on the doorjambs of the king's temple at

Abydos. The reliefs that were left in place at Abydos are today severely deteriorated, but one can still see that they have the same stylistic characteristics and the bright colors.
E.D.

56

Statuette of a king in falcon garb
Ptolemaic period
Faience
H. 18 cm
Provenance unknown
Leiden, Rijksmuseum van
Oudheden, F 1937/6.9

The reigning pharaoh was regarded as the earthly incarnation of the god Horus. Usually this divinity manifested himself as a falcon. Therefore he was associated with the sky, the celestial bodies (sun and moon were regarded as his eyes), and also with kingship. The close association between the king and the falcon is a theme first conceived by the earliest pharaohs. The royal name was written inside a rectangular frame surmounted by the falcon of Horus. In monumental form, the theme was first expressed by King Khafra, the builder of the second pyramid at Giza. A majestic seated statue (now in the Cairo Museum) depicts the king seated, with the falcon standing on the high back of the throne and enveloping the king's head with its wings. In succeeding periods, this theme developed into an ever closer association of the man and the animal, as is illustrated by this seated statuette of the Ptolemaic period. In frontal view, it merely shows a king enthroned on a low chair, wearing the royal headcloth (*nemes*) and a short kilt. The rear aspect, however, shows how the human body has been transformed into the back, wings, and tail of a falcon. Two kneeling prisoners are depicted under the throne.
M.J.R.

57

Lintel of Pairy
New Kingdom, 18th Dynasty,
reign of Amenhotep III
Sandstone
74 × 163 × 20 cm
Qurna
London, The Trustees of the British
Museum, EA 1182

This lintel adorned the entrance to the offering chapel of Pairy's tomb in western Thebes. At left Pairy appears with his title of "overseer of fields of Amun," and in keeping with this worldly office wears contemporary fashion and a wig. But being also high priest of Ptah, he is shown at right clad in a leopard-skin and bald.
Pairy raises his hands in worship of king Amenhotep III, who is addressed with lofty epithets. The king is symbolically represented by the centrally-placed cartouches and Horus names, whose hieroglyphs "look" at Pairy. The cartouches contain Amenhotep's throne and birth names, while the Horus names identify him as manifestations of the falcon-god Horus. The cartouches are placed over a sign with entwined papyrus and lily stalks symbolizing the king's rule over the united lands of Upper and Lower Egypt. Amenhotep aspired to self-glorification in ever closer assimilation to the sun-god, whom he particularly revered. An allusion to this union between divine father and son are the sun-disks atop his cartouches.
M.M.

58

*Stele dedicated to Rameses II
by Rahotep*
New Kingdom, 19th Dynasty,
reign of Rameses II
Limestone
H. 95; W. 62 cm
Probably from Qantir (on the
evidence of the scene depicted)
Munich, Staatliche Sammlung
Ägyptischer Kunst, Gl 287

There are works intended to express
the divinity of the pharaoh that date
from the reign of Amenhotep III, but
it was only under Rameses II that such
representations became the dominant
mode of depicting the king. Rameses
encouraged the cult of himself as a deity—particularly in Piramesse, his residence in the eastern Delta, near the
modern city of Qantir. To this end, he
had colossal statues of himself erected
with such names as "Rameses, Sun of
Sovereigns," "Rameses, Montu in the
Double Land" or "Rameses Loved as
Atum." He also had colossi bearing
identical or similar names raised in
Memphis, Luxor, the Ramesseum (his
temple on the west bank at Thebes)
and Abu Simbel.
But there are also numerous small-size
stelae from the era of Rameses II
which bear statues of the sovereign
whose name is being adored by the
donor of the stele itself. In other
words, the colossi of Rameses II obviously met a felt need for an object of
religious veneration that was entirely
concrete, a divinity embodied in the
reigning monarch.
Many of these votive stelae come from
Qantir—that is, Piramesse. This Rahotep stele from Munich occupies a
special place among them. With a
slight curve, it has two sections. In the
lower, there is the donor on the right,
the vizier, city mayor and royal fanbearer, Rahotep, shown bald and

kneeling. He is wearing the typical
garments of a vizier and in his left
hand has a flabellum of ostrich feathers. His right is raised in the gesture indicative of prayer, and the hymn he is
reciting is incised in front of him: "To
Rameses, the great god, who hears the
prayers of men." The Rameses invoked
here is the reigning monarch, Rameses
II, who appears in the upper part, to
the right. As a terrestrial monarch, he
is wearing the long pagne typical of
the Ramesside period and the blue
crown. Standing beside a table of offerings, he stretches out his hands,
holding a thurible and a libation vase
to present incense and water to the
deity before him on the left.
As one can see from its specific characteristics, this deity is a statue. It
stands on a thick base, with a slim
back pillar; the arms hanging lifeless-
ly at the side of the body. Given the
iconography—with *nemes* (cat. no. 27)
and double crown—this must be a
statue of a royal figure; but the costume deliberately contrasts with the
clothing and headdress of the Ramesside monarch. In front of this divine
manifestation of the king as a colossal
statue is the following inscription:
"Rameses, King of Kings, the Great
God, Lord of Heaven, for Eternity."
The four large ears at the edge of the
stele, behind the depiction of the statue, are the iconographical transcription of the epithet for king Rameses II
mentioned in the hymn: "he who hears
prayers." In other words, this stele uses both words and images to express
the fact that the deified sovereign was
ready to hear the requests of his subjects and to listen to their prayers.

Bibliography
Roeder 1926, p. 63 no. 2; Scharff 1934;
Habachi 1966; de Meulenaere 1966,
p. 231 (e); Habachi 1969, pp. 33–34

with fig. 21 p. 34, and pl. XIIIb;
Müller, Wildung, 1976, p. 146 (no. 88)
with fig. p. 147; Sadek 1988, p. 15 no.
5 and pl. XXV, 1; D. Wildung in:
Grimm, Schoske, Wildung 1997, pp.
164–66 (cat. no. 123) with fig. p. 165;
Blumenthal 2001, pp. 54–55 with fig.
42 p. 55.
A.G.

59

Stele of regal cult
New Kingdom, 19th Dynasty
Limestone
H. 29; L. 18 cm
Deir el-Medina
Turin, Museo Egizio, Drovetti
Collection, CGT 50049 (Cat 1454bis)

Ribbed stele on which is represented a
statue of Amenhotep I, carried on a litter with a frieze of serpents and *uraei*,
seated on a stool. The king, protected
by a winged divinity and by a fan, is an
object of worship on behalf of the *wab*
priest, Atumnakht, who is holding an
incense-burner in front of a table of offerings. Behind the portable chapel
there is the *was* scepter supporting the
flay. Next to one of the litter rods a lion is carrying on his back a human-
headed sphinx, representing the king.
The inscription underneath, arranged
in ten columns, is a praise to Amenhotep I and Thutmose IV, who had votive chapels at Deir el-Medina, and
Amenhotep is invoked as protector
against calamities: "Give praise to the
Lord of the Two Lands Amenhotep
who is life; to Menkheperura, great living god, who loves the truth. He saves
whoever prays to you [=him], gives the
breath of life to whom he loves. Whoever enters your home with an afflicted
heart goes out joyful and jubilating. He
comes to you greatly because your
name sounds out loud. He who puts his
trust in you is joyful, trouble for whoever assails you; to put a crocodile in
front of a . . . [resist to?] a ferocious lion, you will extend your hand against
the den in which lies a great serpent and
will see the glory of Amenhotep, who is
life, while he accomplishes a prodigy for
your city."

Bibliography
Tosi, Roccati 1972, p. 83.
E.F.M.

60

Votive stele
New Kingdom, late 18th–early
19th Dynasties
Limestone, hollow relief
H. 26; W. 17 cm
Deir el-Medina
Turin, Museo Egizio, Drovetti
Collection, CGT 50029

The dedicator is this votive stele is a certain Huy, whom we cannot identify since the name is very common in Deir el-Medina. The ribbed stele represents him upright, his forearms bent in prayer addressed to Amenhotep I followed by the god Ptah. The pharaoh, shown with the *khepresh* crown, is wearing a long draped skirt, enhanced by a *djebau-biti* ("adornment of the king of Lower Egypt"). This regal accessory was usually made of gold and decorated with beads of semi-precious stones and/or faience. Ptah is represented according to the traditional iconography, his body wrapped in the *sudarium* and wearing a skullcap. The incised inscription says: "Offering every good and pure thing! Offering every pure and good thing! To your *ka*, Imenhotep [Amenhotep I], endowed with life, on behalf of Huy, justified. The perfect god, lord of the Two Lands, Djeserkara, endowed with life, like Ra forever, eternally Ptah, lord of Maat, Sovereign of the Two Lands." The worship of Amenhotep I, often associated with his mother Ahmose Nefertari, is attested at Deir el-Medina since the time the village was founded. Countless rock chapels built by the workmen along the path leading to the Valley of the Queens were dedicated to Ptah, and he was also celebrated with votive chapels even inside the houses.

Bibliography
Tosi, Roccati 1972, pp. 61–62.
M.B.

61

Fragment of furnishing with Ahmose Nefertari and Amenhotep I
New Kingdom
Fretworked and painted wood
H. 18; L. 40 cm
Deir el-Medina (?)
Turin, Museo Egizio, Drovetti collection, 2457

In all likelihood the item on exhibit was (along with two other examples conserved in the Museo Egizio of Turin) a piece of furnishing such as a chair, a litter for the cult statue of the divinity, or part of a *naos*. Queen Ahmose Nefertari and her son, King Amenhotep I—certainly the object of worship ever since the 19th Dynasty—are shown seated in front of a table laden with offerings, including flowers and plants in baskets, and are protected by the winged goddess Mut, kneeling on the sign that signifies gold and holding in both hands the *ankh* sign. The king is wearing a short skullcap wig with a band topped by the *uraeus*, the two extremities of the ribbon ending with a cobra head. He is wearing a linen robe and holding a flabellum and the staff in one hand and the *ankh* sign in the other. A wide necklace and bracelets adorn the figure. Above, over the offerings we can read the first name of Amenhotep I, Djeserkara. The queen is represented with black skin. She wears the tripartite wig covered by a vulture cast upon which rests a *modius*. Her pose is conventional: she is holding the flyswatter in her right hand bent toward her breast and the *ankh* sign in the other hand. The flowing robe, down to her ankles and flared at the bottom, leaves her breasts bare.

Bibliography
Fabretti, Rossi, Lanzone 1882, p. 349.
E.F.M.

62

Statue of a pharaoh between Osiris and Horus
New Kingdom, 19th Dynasty
Granite
H. 1.34 m; L. 78 cm
Probably Karnak
Paris, Musée du Louvre, A 12, N 12

Set against a monolithic stele, the three statues are organized in a hieratic arrangement. In the center, Osiris—in a winding-cloth and wearing the *atef* crown (cat. no. 30)—is shown holding the sceptres. He is embraced by Horus—recognizable by his falcon's head—and by a king whose symmetrical position in the group indicates his divine status.

In spite of the absence of inscriptions—normally present on the pedestal or the back plaque—one can identify this king as Rameses II, thanks to a parallel group in the Turin Museum, in which the king is shown in the same fashion with the gods Amun and Mut. It might, however, also be that king's son, Merenptah, who had himself depicted in a very similar group at Abydos. The style of the slender figures does not enable us to date this Louvre group with any precision.

The king is wearing a heavy *nemes* headdress (cat. no. 27) and the crowns of Upper and Lower Egypt (cat. no. 34), and thus—in accordance with a specific iconographical tradition—the work presents him as "the divine king" identified with Amun-Ra. In the group itself, the king is linked with Osiris by facial resemblance, and with Horus by similarities of crown and gesture; hence the triad offers the three aspects of the sun-god Ra. According to myth, this god appeared in the morning as Horus, in the zenith as Amun-Ra, and declined to the horizon as Osiris. This interpretation of the monument reveals that each statue was part of the iconographical program of a temple, designed to give a contemporary reading of the old religious myths.

Bibliography
Zayed 1964, pp. 204–206; Sourouzian 1989, pp. 132, 223, pl. 23c,d; Delange 2001, pp. 36–37 (cat. 2); see Museo Egizio di Torino cat. 747 in: Donadoni Roveri 1989, p. 155, fig. 240.
E.D.

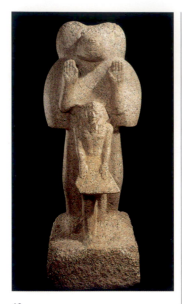

63

*Statue of a praying baboon,
with a royal figure*
New Kingdom, probably
18th Dynasty
Red granite
H. 130; L. 61.5; D. 42 cm
Memphis (?)
Vienna, Kunsthistorisches Museum,
ÄS 5782

In religious iconography, the dog-headed baboon was not only seen as connected with the god Thoth. The monkey with raised hands was also an evocation of the adoration of the sun at dawn. This is explained by reference to a phenomenon that could be seen in the natural world: when baboons leave the place where they have slept during the night, the whole group is very animated and noisy. In the iconography of ancient Egypt this image became the symbol of worship of the rising sun.
The rising and setting of the sun were key events, as the star passed from one world to another. The pharaoh himself played a role here, assisting the god at each of these essential moments, just like the "solar monkeys." One should also recognize that this statue uses another key iconographical theme—that of the god who protects the sovereign. This idea is conveyed by the enormous difference in scale between the colossal baboon and the small royal figure in front of him. The same motif can be found in the ram-headed sphinxes who protect the royal figure standing between their outstretched forepaws (cat. no. 64).
H.S.

64

*Amun depicted as a ram protecting
the king*
New Kingdom, 18th Dynasty
Granite
H. 130; L. 207; W. 87 cm
Soleb (found in 1844 by the Prussian archaeological expedition to Gebel Barkal)
Berlin, Ägyptisches Museum
und Papyrussammlung, 7262

The small statue of a praying king stands under the powerful animal image of the god Amun. The depiction of the "god of gods" as a ram originated in Nubia. This is one of the first examples of those statues which show the pharaoh under the protection of the deity in his animal form. For the jubilee marking the thirtieth anniversary of his coronation, Amenhotep III had a temple built at Soleb (near the third cataract) which was approached along an avenue lined with ram statues. The model of Soleb would soon be taken up at the Temple of the Kingdom in Karnak.

Bibliography
Priese 1991, pp. 93–94 (cat. 58); Paris 1997, pp. 138–139 (cat. 141).
D.W.

The Pharaoh, Intercessor between Men and the Gods. The Temples

*The temple walls invariably present us with the pharaoh in the act of performing different rituals before the gods. Thus when he officiates, the king is first of all a human being; he is also in certain respects, the man, he who in the holy of holies represents all the Egyptian people and also all of mankind. This mission was more ponderous than it seemed because a face-to-face with the gods was not granted to everyone. In theory, no simple mortal could stand up to a confrontation with the divine entities whose images, in the central part of their sanctuaries, were charged with a particle of supernatural energy.
As in many other cases, it was the divine essence of the Pharaonic monarchy that conferred the king with the possibility therefore of dialoguing with the gods almost as an equal. A great number of rituals existed in Egypt and they all had a precise function. The divinities were the object of a daily cult added to which were countless ceremonies, like those proper to one god or more specifically destined to maintaining the cosmic equilibrium. In all these cases, through the intermediary of their sovereign, men offered to the invisible powers on which their existence depended the fruit of their own contribution to the common good. This gift, for the most part in the symbolic form of food gifts, had to attract the goodwill of the gods and provoke their beneficial action in the cosmos.
In practice, it was obviously quite impossible for one individual, the Son of the Sun, to officiate at the same time in all the temples of Egypt. Just as the functionaries were the sovereign's delegates, the priests seconded the king and performed different rituals in his place.
They were refined scholars and possessed the required knowledge, according to their place in the clerical hierarchy, for warding off the danger to their person represented by the formidable divine presence. The sovereign generally participated, however, in the great ceremonies that were essential for the proper functioning of the kingdom, such as the Opet Festival at Karnak. Nor can it be excluded that at times he carried out daily rites, through personal piety, in a particular sanctuary. However, it is more than likely that only Akhenaten officiated in this way regularly, although he did have priests who could substitute for him.
I.F.*

66

Foundation brick
New Kingdom, 19th Dynasty,
reign of Rameses II
Faience
H. 11.7 cm
Provenance unknown
Cairo, Egyptian Museum, JE 84388

Copies of such bricks—along with
other objects—were at the time of construction placed in "foundation deposits," cavities dug near the weak
parts of a structure which were considered to require extra "magical" support if they were to resist over time.
Reproduced in miniature, the bricks
were in such valued materials as
faience or vitrified limestone (those
used in the construction proper were
normally made of sun-dried clay). In
the case of a royal building (for example, a palace or a temple), the building bricks were stamped with the name
of the reigning sovereign, the
power of whose name thus served an
apotropaic purpose and guaranteed
greater solidity and resistance over
time. Here, that practice has been imitated, and the name of the sovereign
is painted in black on the vitrified surface. The two cartouches, surmounted by a double feather enclosing a solar disk, are placed over the hieroglyphic sign for "gold"; they bear the
birth name (Ramessu Meramon) and
coronation name (Usermaatra) of
Rameses II.
F.T.

67

"Foundation deposit" at Matmar
New Kingdom, 19th Dynasty,
reign of Rameses II
Faience
Cartouche H. 1.9; L. 1.1 cm
Models H. 1.7–3.9 cm
Matmar
Cairo, Egyptian Museum, JE 54354,
54357, 54358, JE 54365

From the Early Dynastic to the Late
Period in Egyptian history, evidence
reveals the presence of "foundation
deposits," groups of objects buried in
a cavity or well near the crucial points
(i.e. corners, entrances) of religious or
mortuary buildings. Intended to protect the structure and guarantee its
survival through time, these objects
were mainly models of building tools
and utensils, food offerings (either real or miniature) and amulets with mag-
ic-apotropaic powers.

Near a no longer extant temple of
Rameses II at Matmar, three such deposits were found, containing dozens
of small faience objects depicting:
bound calves, the heads or hooves of
cattle (JE 54354), ducks, birds (JE
54337), fruit (JE 54365), fish and cartouches with the name of Rameses II
(JE 54358). The name of the pharaoh
also appears on two faience blocks
from the same deposits—one rectangular, the other semi-circular—which
reproduce the bricks or stone blocks
used in the actual construction work.

Bibliography
B. Letellier in: Desroches-Noblecourt
1976, pp. 47–48.
S.E.

68

Tablet with cartouches of Rameses IX
New Kingdom, 20th Dynasty,
reign of Rameses IX
Wood with blue paint
H. 103; W. 7 cm
Thebes, Valley of the Kings
Florence, Museo Egizio, 6197

This rectangular tablet presents on the
front surface delicately carved cartouches bearing the name and first
name of Rameses IX; the two cartouches are topped with the sun-disk
and double feather, while below them
we find the sign *nwh*. The incision is
filled with blue color. The tablet belongs to a group of small items, consisting mainly of faience plaques figuring parts of oxen as burial offerings,
forming the foundation deposit of a
prince's tomb. Ernesto Schiaparelli,
who found the deposit in the Valley of
the Kings, left a brief annotation, unfortunately practically illegible, in
which he indicated that the series of
objects came from the "tomb of prince
Mentuxopries," that is, Rameses Mon-
tuherkhopshef, Rameses II's son.

Bibliography
Rome 1992, p. 24.
M.C.G.

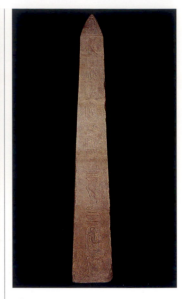

69

Dovetail joint
New Kingdom, 19th Dynasty
Granite
L. 39; W. 20 cm
Provenance unknown
Berlin, Ägyptisches Museum
und Papyrussammlung, 14199

In the construction of their temples, the Egyptians fixed together large blocks of stone using dovetail joints in wood, stone or metal within the space corresponding to the mortises of two neighboring blocks. Guaranteeing the stability of the building, these joints became a symbol of the role of the king as the builder of the structure; and his name might be incised upon them. Here we see the name of Sety I inscribed in the granite. The pharaoh held together the world—a world of which the temple was a metaphor in stone.

Bibliography
Grimm, Schoske, Wildung 1997, p. 140 (cat. 104).
D.W.

70

Obelisk of Hatshepsut
New Kingdom, 18th Dynasty,
reign of Hatshepsut
Red granite
H. 165 cm
Qasr Ibrim
London, The Trustees of the British Museum, EA 1834

This small obelisk was inscribed on one side with the Horus name and prenomen of Queen Hatshepsut. The ruler was described as "beloved of Horus, lord of Miam [Aniba], living forever like Ra." The queen's names were later intentionally erased, as were the words "beloved" and "living," while the names of the gods were left intact. This selective defacement was probably carried out on the orders of Thutmose III, in whose reign the memory of Hatshepsut was persecuted, perhaps because in ideological terms the rule of a woman was regarded as an offence against *maat*, the principle of cosmic order.
The obelisk was discovered reused as a step in a stairway east of the Podium at Qasr Ibrim, a strategically important spot on the east bank of the Nile in Lower Nubia. Its original location is unknown, but it may have been transported as building material from the temple of Horus at Aniba, mentioned in the inscription.
J.H.T.

71

Cast of the obelisk of Rameses II, known as the Dogali Obelisk
Modern reproduction
Plaster and iron reinforcing
H. 630; base 60 × 80 cm
Turin, Museo Egizio, 7084

This is a cast of an obelisk raised at Heliopolis by the Pharaoh Rameses II, whose royal titles are cut into the four sides of the monument. Probably moved to Rome during the period of the Roman empire, it was—together with other works of Egyptian sculpture—rediscovered in 1883 by the archaeologist Rodolfo Lanciani during excavations at a site in Via Sant'Ignazio near Santa Maria sopra Minerva. In Roman times, this area had been occupied by a sanctuary to the goddess Isis—the Iseo Campense—and the obelisk (and other material) will have been brought here to decorate the *peribolos*. In 1887 the obelisk was used as part of the monument to the memory of the Italian soldiers who had died at the Battle of Dogali in Africa—a monument which at the time was variously described as a "piece of artistic knavery" and "like the neck of some table ornament" (*Osservatore Romano*). Initially placed outside the Central Station, in 1924 it was moved to the gardens of the Terme Diocleziane, where it still stands. After the fascist conquest of Abyssinia, to the base of the monument was added a bronze statue of the Lion of Judah which had originally been a gift from the French Railways to the Negus of the conquered country. The lion disappeared after the Allied troops entered Rome at the end of the World War II. Together with copies of other Egyptian monuments—including that of the "hidden column"—this cast was presented to the Museo Egizio in Turin by Baron Barracco.

Bibliography
Marucchi 1898, pp. 96–100; D'Onofrio 1965, pp. 303–308; Iversen 1968, pp. 174–177.
M.B.

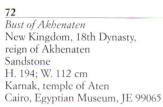

72

Bust of Akhenaten
New Kingdom, 18th Dynasty,
reign of Akhenaten
Sandstone
H. 194; W. 112 cm
Karnak, temple of Aten
Cairo, Egyptian Museum, JE 99065

Akhenaten erected his principal temple of Aten on the east side of the temple of Amun-Ra, called *Gempaaten*. This temple was demolished by the rulers of the late 18th and early 19th Dynasties following the condemnation of the "heretic" king.
The temple contained a peristyle court whose twenty-eight pillars supported colossal statues of the king. Six of these statues are to be found in the Egyptian Museum, Cairo, two others in the Luxor Museum, one in the Louvre, one in Munich, others in the museum depots at Karnak. Other fragments are stored in the basement of the Cairo Museum from which this recently restored bust comes.
The upper part of the statue shows the king wearing the *nemes* headdress and the tall plumes of the god Shu, god of the air and son of the creator-god Atum. Akhenaten would have appeared in the typical Osirian pose, arms crossed and carrying the crook and flail. Only two cartouches of the royal names have survived, stamped on his arms.
The king's characteristic features that include the long, tapering half-closed eyes with heavy eyelids, long delicate nose, large protruding mouth, exaggerated chin, and long ears with pierced lobes are present in the bust.
A.M.

73

Statue of Rameses III
New Kingdom, 20th Dynasty
Limestone
H. 1.25 m
Provenance unknown
Philadelphia, The University
of Pennsylvania, Museum of
Archeology and Anthropology,
E 15727

The youthful king depicted in this statue is identified as Rameses III in several of the inscriptions that are carved on its surface. The figure has a "false" beard and wears a short, curled, wig that ends at the broad collar that the pharaoh has around his neck. Below, mid-chest, is his name, Usermaatra Meryamun, Rameses, HekaIoun, in hieroglyphs; the two protective deities, Wadjyt and Nekhbet flank the left and the right sides. His diadem consists of a simple band with a cobra at the front, projecting forward. A belt with a cartouche encircling his name, Usermaatra Meryamun, is atop his short pleated kilt, and a dagger with a double-headed falcon with solar disk is tucked under it. A bracelet is on his right wrist and a cloth is in that hand. His left hand and arm support a lioness-headed staff that he holds in place next to him. Preserved on the king's left side, and sculpted in low relief, is the upper part of a female figure wearing a long garment, a tall crown, and she extends her arm, Both the crown she wears and the titulary inscribed before her indicate that she was a queen.
The full titulary of Rameses III is carved on the staff, oriented from left to right: "Horus, Strong Bull, Great of Kingship; the Two Ladies, Great of *heb-sed*s [jubilees] like Amun; Horus of Gold, Strong of Years like Atum; The King of Upper and Lower Egypt; The Lord of the Two Lands, User-

maatra Meryamun [Son] of Ra. . . ." A back pillar originally had a similar inscription: "[. . . Great] of *heb-sed*s like Amun; Horus of Gold, Strong of Years like Atum; The King of Upper and Lower Egypt; The Lord of the Two Lands, Usermaatra Mery-[Amun . . .]."
Rameses III was the last of a long line of powerful military pharaohs of the empire that Thutmose III established earlier in the 18th Dynasty. Faced with formidable adversaries threatening the borders of Egypt, Rameses successfully held back both the Sea Peoples and the Libyans. Issues within the palace also created problems for him, but he contended successfully with a plot against him, called in modern times "the *harim* conspiracy."

Bibliography
Monnet 1965; Ranke 1950, p. 54; Chadefaud 1982, pp. 67–8; PM VIII, p. 71; Mojsov 1992, pp. 160–163.
D.P.S.

74

Akhenaten raising the cartouches of Aten
New Kingdom, 18th Dynasty
Alabaster (calcite)
H. 8.9; W. 4.2; D. 1.3 cm
Provenance unknown
Berlin, Ägyptisches Museum
und Papyrussammlung, 2045

The king and god were mutually interdependent: The pharaoh received his office from the gods, but the gods needed him for the preservation of the cosmic order. The pharaoh's role is clearly illustrated by this votive plaque. The royal figure is shown with raised arms, and the names of the sun-god are inscribed in cartouches: "He lives, Ra-Horakhty, who rejoices on the Horizon, in his name of Light, who is in the disk of the sun." This is the name of Aten, the single god with which Amenhotep IV/Akhenaten replaced the traditional pantheon. On either side of the figure of the kneeling king are inscribed the names of Akhenaten and Nefertiti.

Bibliography
Grimm, Schoske, Wildung 1997, pp. 112–113 (cat. 86).
D.W.

75

Procession of the boat of Amun (ostracon)
New Kingdom, 19th–20th Dynasties
Limestone
H. 11.2; W. 17.5 cm
Deir el-Medina
Berlin, Ägyptisches Museum
und Papyrussammlung, 21446

The king was the only person authorized to come into direct contact with the gods. The bas-reliefs in the temples respect this fundamental principle when, in their innumerable scenes of worship, the one figure they show before the gods is the pharaoh himself. The temple decorations that depict the occasions when the deity left his sanctuary in solemn procession also show the pharaoh accompanying the boat that contained the veiled image borne by priests. This ostracon shows a sketch of the procession of the divine boat of Amun, decorated with the ram's head of the god both fore and aft. In the middle of the scene, the priest is taking the place of the king. This realistic depiction of an officiant standing in for the pharaoh somewhat qualifies the official dogma that the king was omnipresent in all the temples of the country.

Bibliography
Kaiser 1967, p. 64 (cat. 725).
D.W.

76

Kneeling statue of Hatshepsut
New Kingdom, 18th Dynasty,
reign of Hatshepsut
Red granite
H. 77 cm
Deir el-Bahri
Cairo, Egyptian Museum, JE 47702

At the death of King Thutmose I, Hatshepsut married her half-brother, Thutmose II. The latter died early, leaving the throne to Thutmose III, son of a secondary wife. Hatshepsut was appointed regent and taking advantage of the young age of Thutmose III, she assumed power as sole pharaoh. She was not the first female to rule Egypt, but she is the only one who chose to be portrayed as a man. Her reign was peaceful, and full of architectural achievements. She built a three-terraced funerary temple at Deir el-Bahri. The decoration of the second terrace on the southern portico has as its main subject the expedition sent by Hatshepsut to the land of Punt to collect the incense trees for the god Amun-Ra.
The statue represents Hatshepsut kneeling. She is portrayed as a king, wearing the *khat* headdress (similar to the *nemes* but fuller in the lower back part) surmounted by the *uraeus* and a ceremonial beard attached to her chin. She holds a ritual vase, decorated with a *djed* pillar.
Despite the masculine character of the figure, this idealized portrait nevertheless bears distinctive feminine features, such as the gently curving eyebrows, large almond-shaped eyes outlined with kohl, delicate aquiline nose, full cheeks and gracefully outlined mouth. The queen wears the traditional pleated skirt.
A.M.

77

Statue of Rameses IV
New Kingdom, 20th Dynasty,
reign of Rameses IV
Mudstone
68.3 × 25.5 cm
Provenance unknown
London, The Trustees of the British
Museum, EA 1816

This is one of very few surviving three-dimensional sculptures of Rameses IV, who reigned for seven years, during which several temples were left unfinished and inscriptions were added to buildings erected by his more illustrious predecessors. The king is depicted with the banded *nemes* headdress, fronted by a uraeus, and wears the *shendjyt* kilt. He adopts a kneeling pose, offering two *nw* pots in his upturned hands. Such a stance is one of the classic types of royal statuary, and reveals the pharaoh's piety and humility toward the god. His names are carved in four places: cartouches on his shoulders, the remains of his titulary around the base and again on the back-pillar, and another cartouche on his belt. The form of his first name, Hekamaatra, suggests the statue was carved in the latter part of his reign, as his early monuments bore another name, Usermaatra Setepenamun. The knees, *nw* pots and most of the base are modern.
N.S.

78

Statuette of Akhenaten
New Kingdom, 18th Dynasty
Alabaster (calcite)
H. 12.2; W. 2.4; D. 5.8 cm
Tell el-Amarna, house N 48,15
(excavations by the Deutsche
Orientgesellschaft, 1912)
Berlin, Ägyptisches Museum
und Papyrussammlung, 21835

In spite of the absence of an inscription, it is not difficult to identify the subject of this small royal statue. The thin legs, full thighs, almost feminine bust and the face with its pronounced chin, fleshy lips, long nose and half-closed eyes are all stylistic characteristics of depictions of King Akhenaten. He is holding in front of him a rectangular stele whose height exceeds its width. This was a space on which a text would have been incised—undoubtedly one of the hymns that the king addressed to the sun-god Aten when he was praying.

Bibliography
Kaiser 1967, p. 67 (cat. 744); Grimm, Schoske, Wildung 1997, pp. 132–133, (cat. 98).
D.W.

79

*Ramesside pharaoh making
an offering of Maat*
New Kingdom, 19th Dynasty,
reign of Sety I (?)
Gold-plated silver
H. 19.5 cm
Provenance unknown
Paris, Musée du Louvre, E 27431

The pose of this sovereign—undoubtedly Sety I—is very familiar from the corpus of representations of the king officiating at religious worship. What distinguishes the statuette is the material used and the quality of craftsmanship. Silver, in fact, was rare in Egypt, and relatively few objects in precious metals have come down to us. This is even more interesting because the tenons under the feet of the small effigy indicate that it must have been attached to a base, doubtless a model of a processional boat.

Bare-footed, the pharaoh is wearing the royal pagne and the *uraeus* headdress much prized by the Ramessides; it was a variant of the *khepresh*. He is shown holding an image of the goddess Maat. This latter personified all aspects of divine order—cosmic harmony, social equilibrium, justice and truth. Maat, born of the demiurge, came into existence at the same time as the created world. The incarnation of all that which must come about if creation is to take place and the universe continue, she symbolized the ideal toward which the actions of gods and men must strive in order to renew the great work of the Sun after that "First Time," the beginning of time. Thus when a sovereign presented an image of Maat to a deity it symbolized an offering of the joint efforts of mankind. Maat, in fact, embraced all the gifts that the gods received in their temples. This offering by the king, therefore, brought about a favorable re-

sponse from the supernatural powers on whom he depended; it served to guarantee the continuance of creation.

Bibliography
Andreu, Rutschowskaya, Ziegler 1997,
pp. 110–112.
I.F.

80

Prostrate statue of Rameses II
New Kingdom, 19th Dynasty,
reign of Rameses II
Gray schist
H. 27.5; L. 38; W. 12.5 cm
Karnak, temple of Amun,
cachette court
Cairo, Egyptian Museum, JE 37423
= CG 42144

The statue represents Rameses II, prostrate and holding a shrine in front of him. Above the shrine are three squatting figures, the first (on the viewer's left) represents the god Ra, the second probably the god Amun, the third probably that of a child (corresponding to the hieroglyph *mes*). In front of the three figures is a singe-*mer*. This last element indicates that the statue may represent a veritable graphic puzzle giving a rebus for the reading of Rameses II's birth name: *Ra* (the god Ra)–*messu* (the child)–*mry* (the singe-*mer*)–*Imen* (the god Amun). The shrine is inscribed with four columns of hieroglyphs. The dedicatory inscription states that Rameses II is beloved by Amun-Ra, lord of the thrones and of the heaven, and by Ra-Horakhty, the great god lord of the heaven.

Rameses II is portrayed as a young man wearing a striped *nemes* headdress, surmounted by the *uraeus*. He wears only a pleated skirt.

The prostrate attitude is well attested since the New Kingdom, the oldest example being in the tomb of Rekhmira at Thebes, where a scene depicting a sculptor's studio shows the representation of a statue of Thutmose III in the same attitude. A similar statue of Amenhotep III, prostrate and pushing an altar, is in the Metropolitan Museum of Art, New York. Later on, in the 19th Dynasty, Sety I was represented prostrate in the reliefs decorating the

base of the model for a temple gateway from Tell el-Yahudiya, now in the Brooklyn Museum.

The Egyptian Museum in Cairo has three prostrate statues of Rameses II, and one of Osorkon III.
A.M.

81

*Decorative element in the name
of Sehibra*
Third Intermediate Period,
23rd Dynasty
Wood
25.5 × 15 × 1 cm
Provenance unknown
Bologna, Museo Civico
Archeologico, Palagi (Nizzoli)
Collection, KS 289

The panel, fretworked and once enhanced with inlays of vitreous paste
and/or other precious material, belonged to a small *naos*, of which the
Louvre possesses a second decorative
element, specular to this one. Together they form the accurate graphic
transposition of a religious ceremony:
its only officiant is the pharaoh Sehibra, identified by the cartouche bearing his name inscribed in hieroglyphs.
The king, kneeling between the large
wings of the goddess Isis, holds in his
outstretched, upturned hands a basket
topped by the *wedjat* eye and the *nefer* sign to be offered to the divinity.
This kind of ritual was repeated every
day inside a great number of Egyptian
temples, and it was the king, as supreme warrant of *maat* (truth, justice
and cosmic order) on earth, and as
privileged intermediary between the
human and divine worlds, who had to
celebrate it, even if, in order to perform the rite at the same time all over
the land, he had priests replace him.
The wall reliefs, sculptures, and decorative elements found inside the sacred precinct and representing the
king, reiterated his indispensable role
in the presence of the divinity for the
purpose of the rite.
D.P.

82

*Standard-bearer statue usurped
by prince Sheshonq*
New Kingdom, late 18th Dynasty
and 22nd Dynasty, reign of Osorkon I
Green breccia
H. 48 cm
Karnak, temple of Amun,
cachette court
Cairo, Egyptian Museum, JE 36988
= CG 42194

The statue represents a striding man
wearing a double wig. The well preserved face is a skilful example of late
18th-Dynasty sculpture. The facial features (elongated eyes enclosed by
heavy eyelids, small straight nose,
fleshy unsmiling mouth, and side dimples) recall those of Tutankhamun.
The neck is adorned with a double-
ring necklace, the so-called "gold of
valor" given to functionaries and soldiers who achieved remarkable deeds.
The dress is made of a tunic with wide
pleated sleeves and a loose pleated
skirt knotted at the waist and decorated on the front with a triangular element. The upper arms have armlets,
the wrists are decorated with bracelets;
the right hand holds a piece of cloth,
the left a standard topped with the
head of a goddess wearing a wig and
uraeus. The latter is surmounted by a
sun-disk enclosed in a pair of cow
horns, elements that identify the goddess as Hathor or Isis.
Stylistically, the sculpture can be dated to the late 18th Dynasty. However,
the inscription on the back pillar "The
first prophet of Amun-Ra, the king of
the kings, the supreme commander of
the army, the prince Sheshonq, justified, son of the lord of the Two Lands,
Osorkon Meramon," proves that the
statue was reused at a later date by
Sheshonq, and consequently modified
to suit the new ruler. In addition to the
inscription, the figures of Amun-Ra
and Osiris were also carved on the
chest and skirt. The restoration of part
of the right sleeve (in the same stone as
the statue, fixed by a dovetail joint)
can be dated when the statue was
reused.
A.M.

83

Fragment of a stele of Horemheb
New Kingdom, 18th Dynasty,
reign of Horemheb
Quartzite
H. 187; W. 57 cm
Heliopolis (?)
Cairo, Egyptian Museum, JE 34189

This large block of stone is all that is left of a stele of Horemheb; probably it was cut down to this size so that it could be reused as building material. What survives is the right side of the original monument. The scene depicted shows the god Horus, in the form of a falcon with spreading wings, over Horemheb, who is wearing the blue crown and a short robe. The bas-relief reveals the fluidity of form that was typical of post-Amarna art, and heralds the measured luminosity of style achieved in the bas-reliefs produced shortly after the period of Sety I. In his left hand, Horemheb is holding an incensor; in his right, a vase from which flows a trickle of water onto the altar in front of him, which is loaded with foodstuffs. The inscription to the scene tells us that the king is in fact purifying offerings with incense and water. Unfortunately, the image of the god to whom these offering are being made is no longer extant; however, the surviving inscription informs us that it was the god Khepri, who in exchange for these gifts gave Horemheb "the period of life of Ra and the regality of Horus in joy."
The hieroglyphic text beneath comprises sixteen lines, of which only one half is extant. The other inscriptions suggest that the main subject matter of this text was a series of offerings that the king had decided to make to the sanctuary of the god (Khepri). In exchange, he would receive long life and a long, prosperous and peaceful reign.

Though the stele is generically referred to as coming from Cairo (where it was probably reused as building material after the advent of the Muslims), the mention of Khepri - the god of the morning sun - suggests a provenance from Heliopolis, where there was an important sanctuary to this deity, or in Giza, whose famous Sphinx was (from the New Kingdom onward) gradually taken as a manifestation of the god Khepri.

Bibliography
Urk IV, 2129–2131.
F.T.

84

Censer
Late Period
Bronze
L. 48 cm
Provenance unknown
Paris, Musée du Louvre, E 13531

Very well-preserved, this censer is made up of three parts cast using the lost-wax technique and then fitted together. All the components are still in place. From the umbel of a flowering papyrus reed emerges an extended hand on the palm of which was fixed the cup in which the perfumed incense would burn. In the center is a small royal figure respectfully presenting the balls of resin which must have been kept in the cartouche-shaped receptacle. The handle ends in an elegantly curved falcon's head, the symbol of Horus.
The officiating priest or king held the handle horizontally, thus the open hand was the substitute of his own, and he himself was offering the incense. The pharaoh was the only high priest, the sole intermediary between the gods and mankind, and this is why in the bas-relief wall decorations from temples he is always the figure shown officiating at religious ceremonies (as, for example, the relief of Horemheb, cat. no. 83). It was the pharaoh who carried the offerings, who presented the perfumed resin to the nostrils of the gods, who poured the water of libations, offered the vases of wine, and proffered the effigies of the goddess Maat or the *wedjat* eye. However, not being omnipresent, the pharaoh could delegate to priests who thus represented him. "The servant of god," literal translation of the word "priest," was in fact then only a substitute who guaranteed the continuance of worship "in the name of the king." This is what is recalled by the symbols used in this censer

Bibliography
Beinlich 1978, pp. 19, 20.
E.D.

85

*Statue of Queen Nefertari
as a standard-bearer*
New Kingdom, 19th Dynasty,
reign of Rameses II
Black granite
H. 94; W. 28; D. 28.4 cm
Provenance unknown
San Bernardino, Harer Family Trust,
California State University

Well-known to the wider public because of the romantic passion she is said to have inspired in her husband Rameses II, Nefertari seems to be omnipresent in the main monuments raised by the great pharaoh in the first decades of his reign (For a biography of the queen, see Leblanc 1999). Rameses, in fact, always had at his side two "great royal wives," but the second—Isetnofret—appears very little during this period. After the death of the two queens, the sovereign would marry his own daughters by each, in order to maintain that shared role that had been played by the two "first ladies" of the kingdom.

While one cannot simply rule out that there was true affection between Rameses and Nefertari, there are also at least two other very good reasons for the pre-eminence of this "beloved." One should also bear in mind that this preference shown to her was relatively short-lived: during the course of the pharaoh's long reign, Nefertari would be gradually eclipsed by other women—a disappearance that cannot simply be explained by her early death. Already during the 18th Dynasty one can see that the "great royal wife" was playing an ever more important role alongside the pharaoh. This underlining of the position of the reigning female presence would culminate during the reign of Akhenaten, and then receive a new breath of life during the Ramesside period. Rameses II placed greater emphasis than his predecessors on the divine nature of royal power, increasing the number of images of the pharaoh, the living incarnation of that originally supernatural function; and, naturally, these statues and bas-reliefs were in the image of the present sovereign himself. It was undoubtedly this identification with the Sun-Horus which led Rameses to have

at his side his two "great royal wives," just as the solar deity was accompanied by two goddesses. Perhaps this is also the reason why he married his daughters, just as Ra took Hathor to wife in order to give rebirth to his own works. Thus the queen who appears next to Rameses is present above all as the mother of the heir to the throne. After the death of her elder sons, Nefertari would cede pre-eminence to her "rival." Unfortunately for this latter, Rameses had already raised the main monuments of his reign, and that is why there are few depictions of Isetnofret, the mother of Merenptah, who would eventually succeed his father. While her eldest son was alive, Nefertari benefited from her rank as mother of the future pharaoh, and thus appeared in pride of place in all the monuments raised by her husband. This is why at Abu Simbel, in a sanctuary essentially reserved for him, she appears in the role of the goddess Sopdet; in the nearby *speos*, Rameses figures among the gods as Horus. The queen is also buried in a splendid tomb in the Valley of the Queens, which was dug and decorated during the first years of the reign; one cannot list here all the temples in which Nefertari accompanies her husband in the celebration of ritual. What is more, she also figures in those colossal effigies of the sovereign, in a smaller-sized statue standing at his feet.

The statue from the Harer Collection is unique of its kind. In fact, it shows Nefertari holding one of the standards of the gods in her left hand. These wooden stakes surmounted by an image of the deity were borne in procession by officiants as they accompanied the god from one temple to another. The depictions of the king as such a standard-bearer are relatively common; there are also some such statues

of private individuals who were honored with the right to take part in the feasts of deities to whom they had a particular devotion. However, this statue of Nefertari seems to be the only three-dimensional work showing a queen in such a role. The divine standard she is bearing is that of the goddess Mut, a secondary divinity to the god Amun of Karnak. This image shows the liturgical role that must have been played by the "great royal wives" when, alongside the sovereign, they took part in religious ceremonies at the great temples.

Bibliography
Scott III 1992, no. 82; Capel, Markoe 1996, (cat. 47).
I.F.

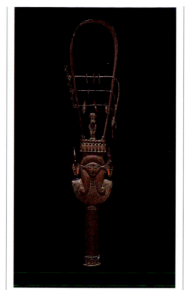

86

Menat *counterpoise*
New Kingdom, 18th Dynasty,
reign of Amenhotep III
Bronze
H. 13.8; max. W. 4.5; D. 0.2 cm
Semna, Sudan
(Harvard University-Museum
of Fine Arts Expedition)
Boston, Museum of Fine Arts,
29.1199

*Menat*s, necklaces made of multiple strings of beads with decorative counterpoises, were used as musical instruments by queens and elite women serving in divine cults, especially that of Hathor. The *menat*s were shaken to produce soft music believed to appease the deity.

Three images of Hathor adorn this openwork counterpoise from the Egyptian fort at Semna in Nubia. The upper part takes the form of Hathor's head. While the cow's horns and sun disk indicate that she is a goddess, the style of the wig and vulture headdress identify her as Queen Tiy, who was worshipped with Hathor throughout Nubia, especially at the temple of Sedeinga. The facial features, including the almond-shaped eyes, soft cheeks and pursed, slightly smiling lips, are characteristic of the reign of Amenhotep III.

In the central portion, she stands under a canopy and holds a *was* scepter, the symbol for dominion, while below she appears as a cow standing in a papyrus bark. The sun disk between her horns emphasizes her role as a sky goddess, and a lotus blossom arching over her back alludes to her role as mistress of the marshes, a goddess of fertility and sexuality. An identical counterpoise discovered at el-Amarna probably traveled to the site along with the royal family after Amenhotep's death.

Bibliography
Capel, Markoe 1996, p. 101, (cat. 35d); D'Auria, Lacovara, Roehrig 1988, pp. 135–136, (cat. 72); Dunham, Janssen 1960, p. 48, pl. 128a; Freed 1982, p. 306, (cat. 418); Kozloff, Bryan 1992.
D.M.D.

87

Sistrum
Greco-Roman period
Bronze, gilded and inlaid
H. 21 cm
Provenance unknown
Cairo, Egyptian Museum,
TR 14/5/75/1

The *sistrum* was a musical instrument sacred to Hathor, the goddess of joy, love and music, which dates back to the Old Kingdom. In the Greco-Roman period it became a cult object of the goddess Isis. It is believed that the rattle still used in Coptic rituals and other similar Ethiopian instruments are derived from this ancient Egyptian prototype. Priestesses, musicians and singers were often represented shaking the *sistrum* during temple ceremonies to produce a rattling sound that warded off evil and harmful spirits. This type of *sistrum*, called *sesheshat*, consists of a handle in the form of a simple column surmounted by the double human-head of Hathor wearing her typical wig with two *uraei*, one bearing the red crown of Lower Egypt and the other the white crown of Upper Egypt. On her head a diadem of *uraei* is surmounted by a large *uraeus*. Hathor's head supports a frame with three horizontal crossbars and rings shaped like snakes that, when shaken make the typical rattling sound. Some *sistra* discovered in Dendera were a manifestation of the goddess Hathor. The "god's wives of Amun" were often shown holding the *sistrum*. The strange sound produced when it is shaken was intended to introduce an altered state of consciousness in ritual participants, as much as the bull-roarer does in African and other traditional societies.

Bibliography
CG 69201–69852, pp. 80–81; Saleh, Sourouzian 1987 (cat. 264).
Z.T.

88

Sistrum
Third Intermediate or Late Period,
21st–26th Dynasties
Bronze
H. 43.7; W. 14.5; D. 10 cm
Thebes
Boston, Museum of Fine Arts, Edward J. and Mary S. Holmes Fund, 1970.572

The *sistrum*, a ceremonial rattle shaken by priestesses and temple singers, is most closely associated with the worship of Hathor, whose image appears on both sides of the handle of this superb example. The goddess is shown as a woman with the ears of a cow. She wears her characteristic heavy wig with lappets ending in tightly wound curls, and a band of rearing cobras with sun disks encircles her crown.

This *sistrum*, however, was intended for the worship of Amun-Ra, whose temple dominated Theban religious and political life by the end of the New Kingdom. Amun's consort, the goddess Mut, Mistress of Isheru, is the subject of much of the decoration. On each side of the loop, she appears in the role of a temple singer, shaking a pair of *sistra* with Hathor-headed handles. The object of her worship is her husband, Amun-Ra, who takes the form of a recumbent ram. At the top of the loop is the solar bark, occupied by the three deities of the Theban triad, Amun-Ra, Mut and the lunar deity Khons.

Bibliography
Ziegler 1977; Simpson 1987, pp. 52–53.
D.M.D.

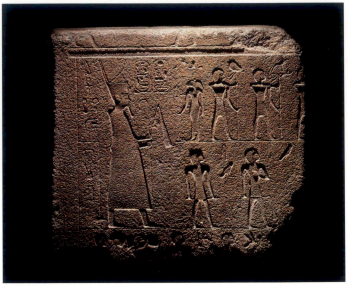

89

Bas-relief showing Rameses II with his mother, Tuya, playing a sistrum
New Kingdom, 19th Dynasty,
after year 40 of Rameses II's reign
Limestone
H. 53.5; W. 46.5; D. 6 cm
Memphis (?)
Vienna, Kunsthistorisches Museum,
ÄS 5091

This bas-relief was perhaps part of a door lintel. The king is shown standing before an enthroned deity, presenting offerings; his mother is behind him. One cannot make out much of the deity, but the inscription informs us that it is "Osiris, Lord of Rosetau, the Great God, Master of Heaven." The sovereign, who is wearing the blue crown (cat. no. 29), offers the god a small cup of incense from his left hand, while in his right he holds a libation vase. On top of her wig, the queen-mother is probably wearing vulture plumage, surmounted by a cap.
The text alongside the king gives the two names of Rameses II in cartouches: "The Lord of Two Lands, Usermaatra Setepenra, the Lord of Crowns, Rameses, Beloved of Amun, the Lord and Sovereign of Heliopolis." The name of the queen also appears in a cartouche: "The mistress [?] of the Two Lands, Tuya." In line with the traditional female role in worship, she is shown holding a *sistrum*; but she is also pouring out a libation from a vase.

Bibliography
Radwan 1978.
H.S.

90

Relief of Osorkon II
Third Intermediate Period,
22nd Dynasty
Red granite
Tell Basta (Bubastis)
Philadelphia, The University of Pennsylvania, Museum of Archeology and Anthropology, E225

Originally part of the temple of Bastet at Tell Basta, this impressive relief fragment depicts King Osorkon II taking part in a ceremony known as "Coming Forth around the wall"—one of the rituals associated with the celebration of the *sed* festival. Located in the north, Bubastis was the capital city of this dynasty of Libyan origin. Osorkon II and his grandfather, Osorkon I, were responsible for the rebuilding of the temple of Bastet at this site. Osorkon II added a pylon gateway to the temple with scenes of his *heb-sed* celebration (from which this fragment comes).
The *heb-sed* undoubtedly has its origins in the Predynastic period, and is perhaps best known from the reliefs and associated structures that comprise the Step Pyramid complex of King Djoser of the 3rd Dynasty (2675–2625 BC). This celebration traditionally took part after 30 years of reign and its goal was the rejuvenation of an aging monarch. In the case of Osorkon II, this celebration took place a few years early, in year twenty-two. While there were many parts of the *heb-sed*, this scene seems to correspond with the recording of the king's veneration of gods from Lower Egypt, who have gathered to bless the king's continued reign.
In this scene, the king is shown standing before the resident goddess of the temple, the feline-headed Bastet. The king wears a long cloak peculiar to the *sed* festival. He carries the crook and the flail as traditional symbols of his kingship. He also wears the red crown of Northern/Lower Egypt. The procession is led by a series of priests who are shown in two registers. In the top register, the figures carry standards depicting divine images associated with the opening of the way.

Bibliography
Altenmüller 1975; Mysliwiec 1988; Naville 1892; R.K. Ritner in: Silverman 1997, p. 168 (cat. 51); Spalinger 2001, pp. 521–525; Van Siclen 1999, pp. 776–778.
J.H.W.

The Pharaoh, Guarantor of World Equilibrium. The Victories over the Enemies

91

Decorated doorjamb
New Kingdom, 19th Dynasty
Limestone
Memphis, palace of Merenptah
Philadelphia, The University of
Pennsylvania, Museum of
Archeology and Anthropology,
E17527

Each visitor to an Egyptian temple finds himself at first facing the image of a king in the act of slaughtering his enemies. Wandering through the rooms of a museum of Egyptology, one again encounters the sovereign in the same attitude on monuments from all periods. And yet, the history of the Pharaonic civilization spanned more than thirty centuries! There seems to be no change between Narmer striking a prostrate enemy with his club about 3200 years before our era and a Roman emperor eliminating Egypt's traditional adversaries with the same ritual gesture on the walls of a sanctuary built in a country where he most certainly never set foot. When one looks more closely, one quickly notes that the pharaoh's exploits seem exaggerated. The young Tutankhamun, for example, uses a similar gesture to run through his enemies and the lions in the scenes decorating a processional coffer discovered in his tomb. It is highly improbable that the king ever participated in person in these warlike exploits. Before the image of the pharaoh conqueror, as before all Egyptian representations, one need bear in mind that these scenes express conceptions of "art" that are totally extraneous to our own. The victory of the sovereign is not the expression of an avenging animosity over adversaries reduced to impotence, but it has a twofold value. It is above all an effigy of the guarantor of order, established by the gods, who is represented in the act of protecting the country from the dangers threatening it; the latter are able to assume the many forms of the natural world that exist as actual dangers along the banks of the Nile. Fixed in stone, the triumph of the pharaoh has a conspiratorial role: existing eternally on the walls is a perfection that could hardly be acquired in the terrestrial world.

The majority of the New Kingdom sovereigns, who were in fact victors on the battlefields, used their own military successes to illustrate the victory of the divine order. At times, their expectations did not measure up to the results achieved on the ground. The image then compensated for human failings. One need only consider the way in which Rameses II multiplied the evocations of the famous Battle of Qadesh so as to convince one and all. The combat ended at best in a "drawn match." Still, the "defeat" of the Hittites was represented in the main sanctuaries built by the great pharaoh. They vie in celebrating the unequalled courage of the king; in this case, as in others certainly, the personal exploit of the sovereign cannot be excluded, but catastrophe really was brewing in Egypt. One has the impression that the proclamations of victory were as many as the conspiracies of a disaster avoided by a hairbreadth. Nor must one forget that the representation of the victorious sovereign at the portals of the temple had a prophylactic meaning: at the entrance of a sanctuary, it magically prevented troublemakers from penetrating into the sacred precinct.
I.F.

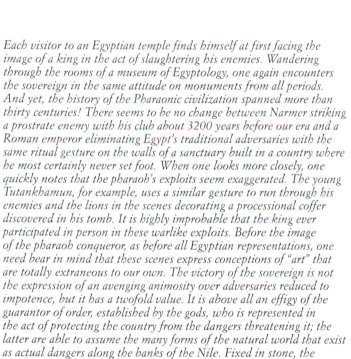

The well-preserved remains of the palace of Pharaoh Merenptah at Memphis were excavated by the Coxe Expedition of the University of Pennsylvania Museum between 1914 and 1918. The palace ranks as the best preserved of all ancient Egyptian palaces, due largely to the fact that the wooden roof of the building burned in antiquity and collapsed into the interior. The main palace building was a massive rectangular structure measuring 110 by 30 meters. The building was constructed of mud-brick, plastered and painted. Limestone, carved and inlaid with faience, was used extensively for architectural elements such as doorjambs, columns, thresholds and windows. This fragment is the lower part of a decorated doorjamb that marked the entrance from the outside of the palace into one of the rooms (room 14) adjacent to the throne room of the palace. The throne room itself occupied roughly one third of the innermost part of the building. The palace of Merenptah was not a standard residential palace but rather a ceremonial one built adjacent to the main temple precinct of Ptah at Memphis. The king would have used the palace during important royal visits and rituals at Memphis.

Decorated with a scene of the king smiting Asiatic enemies, the upper parts of the doorjamb have two columns of vertical inscriptions in hieroglyphs with the titulary and epithets of the pharaoh. The smiting scene is a very standard representation on Egyptian temples and royal buildings and often is found protecting the entrances into the building interior. In this case the king's role as defeater of foreign enemies is emblematic but also real through virtue of the fact that Merenptah was a king actively involved in military campaigning particularly in Syria–Palestine and on Egypt's Libyan frontier.
J.W.W.

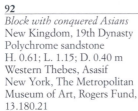

92

Block with conquered Asians
New Kingdom, 19th Dynasty
Polychrome sandstone
H. 0.61; L. 1.15; D. 0.40 m
Western Thebes, Asasif
New York, The Metropolitan
Museum of Art, Rogers Fund,
13.180.21

This block was discovered by Metropolitan Museum archaeologists in the jubilee temple of Rameses IV at Asasif, the northern area of the Thebes necropolis. Probably it originally came from a temple built by Rameses II, and was then recycled in building the foundations of his distant successor's Temple of Millions of Years. This bas-relief fragment comes from a wall decoration representing one of the triumphs of the great Rameses. The battle scenes not only refer to the real wars that the Egyptians had to fight to conquer—then maintain—their empire, but also to the eternal combat between the positive forces of the universe and those which aimed to disturb the balance of the world established by the gods.

The pharaoh's artists were always careful in these works to mark a clear distinction between those who guaranteed universal harmony (in this battle scene, the armies of the pharaoh) and the enemies they were fighting against. In the combat, therefore, the Egyptian forces are always shown in regular disciplined ranks—as befits soldiers who are the representatives of divine order; on the other hand, the enemies of the country—and thus, the emissaries of chaos—are always shown in the most totally disarray. This confusion is also due to the fact that the enemies of Egypt are always the losers and thus shown in complete rout.

Bibliography
Dorman 1987, pp. 70–71.
I.F.

93

Fragment of bas-relief
New Kingdom, 19th Dynasty
Sandstone
H. 70; W. 75 cm
Provenance unknown
Cairo, Egyptian Museum, JE 69306

The original location of this bas-relief is not known; but it was probably part of the external decoration of a temple pillar. It shows a group of prisoners being pulled by the hair; among these, the figures on the right can be identified as inhabitants of southern Egypt by their characteristic facial features and snub noses. Originally produced in painted versions, these scenes became part of Egyptian iconography during the period of the New Kingdom, when it was common to celebrate the strength of the pharaoh by showing him triumphing over his enemies. However, in its rigorous symmetry this bas-relief shows the central enemies face-on, and thus breaks with the profile rendition that was the norm in Egyptian bas-reliefs. The prisoner in the foreground wears a necklace with a fly pendant; like his companions, he raises his hands in surrender and as a plea for mercy.

Bibliography
M. Trapani in: Bongioanni, Croce 2001, p. 208.
S.E.

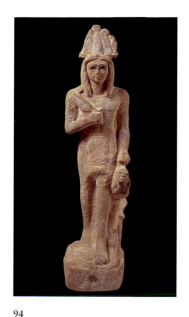

94

Statue of pharaoh with captive
New Kingdom, 20th Dynasty
Sandstone
H 58.5 cm
Provenance unknown
Turin, Museo Egizio, Drovetti
Collection, 1392

The statue, without an epigraph, represents a king striding forward wearing the *shendjyt* skirt and on his head a wig topped by the composite crown. He holds a hatchet in his right hand, while with the left he grasps the hair of a Libyan captive whose hands are bound behind his back. Between the captive's legs is a lion biting him. The lion's tail runs along the front side of the base of the statue, parallel to the king's advancing leg.

The striding king holding a captive by his hair becomes a widespread subject matter toward the middle of the 20th Dynasty, beginning with the reign of Rameses VI. It borrows the traditional theme of the ruler massacring the enemies, who embody chaos and evil, from the regal statuary of the Ramesside period, but known since Protodynastic representations. It was echoed throughout all of Egyptian history, in particular on the external walls of the New Kingdom temples, especially on those of Amun at Karnak and those of Rameses III's temple at Medinet Habu. These figures, aside from glorifying the sovereign's past heroic feats, also had an apotropaic role as the representation of the defeat of Egypt's enemies meant to be everlastingly repeated. Probably this statue too has that aim, not as the representation of a precise event but as the timeless image of the king vanquishing Egypt's enemies.

The king was supreme chief of the army and thus assumed the role of custodian of law and order that subjected the enemies and insured the security of the country, in keeping with the dispositions of *maat*.

Bibliography
Curto 1984, pp. 160, 164; Donadoni 1989, pp. 166 (fig. 256), 170; E. Leospo in: Donadoni Roveri, Tiradritti 1998, p. 316, fig. 319; Seipel 1992, pp. 302–03.
M.T.

95

Sketched scene of a lion hunt (ostracon)
New Kingdom, Ramesside period
Limestone, pigments
H. 12.1; L. 19; D. 2.8 cm
West Thebes, Valley of the Kings
New York, The Metropolitan
Museum of Art, gift of Edward
S. Harkness, 26.7.1453

Lion-hunting was the royal sport *par excellence*, and the fearsome wild cat was a frequent subject matter in Egyptian religious iconography. Here we do not have an image of the power of the sun (see cat. no. 49), nor an invocation of a tutelary divinity (cat. no. 2), but rather a rendition of the wild beast itself. Given it lived on the very margins of the arid lands, the lion symbolized those negative forces couched within the sands of the desert. In effect, for the Egyptians the fertile banks of the Nile were constantly under threat from all that lay beyond the country's borders; quite soon in its history, the Valley would be the object of raids by marauding Bedouins. What is more, the enemies of the country very often had to make their way across desert spaces if they were to invade the country; and the wild beasts of the desert were a constant danger to those who ventured to travel along the caravan routes. In the symbolic language of the Egyptians everything that came from the desert was synonymous with disorder and chaos. Thus lion-hunting was more than a simple expression of a sovereign's pleasure in the joys of the chase. Here, the pharaoh is the very guardian of Egypt as he transfixes those powers that are a danger to universal order. The very way he is dressed shows just how far Egyptian images can stray from a strict depiction of reality. Wearing the red crown, with a ceremonial pagne and girdle, the king is here in traditional court garb rather than the outfit of a hunter. The dog accompanying him is not only the faithful companion of man but also an ally in this battle against chaos. One finds an echo of that constant Egyptian preoccupation with the need to stand against the forces of the desert even in the tombs of high functionaries—who, for their part, are shown more modestly hunting smaller mammals.

Bibliography
Arnold 1995, pp. 16–17.
I.F.

96

Signet ring with smiting scene
New Kingdom, 18th Dynasty,
reign of Amenhotep II
Silver
Diam. 2.2 cm; 1.4 × 1.35 cm (bezel)
Saqqara
New York, The Brooklyn Museum
of Art, Charles Edwin Wilbour
Fund, 37.726E

The motif of the pharaoh smiting an
enemy illustrates the concept of the
divine king defending universal order
(*maat*) against chaos (*isfet*). Here the
king, Aakheperura (Amenhotep II),
wears the *khepresh* or blue crown,
symbolizing victory in this context.
His label of "good" or "perfect" god
and the hieroglyph for life behind him
accord with his role as defender of
maat. The foreigner he smites may be
a Syrian; Egypt's enemies and certain
wild animals were identified with the
forces of *isfet*.
Developed before the 1st Dynasty,
this motif and its variants occur in a
variety of media. It appears on small
objects in the later New Kingdom but
it is always unusual on rings. The
provenance of Saqqara claimed for
this ring by the XIX-century collector
Henry Abbott suggests that it came
from an official's tomb. If so, the ring
may have been a royal gift. Certainly,
its decoration, conveying the wish for
triumph over evil, could have served
an amuletic purpose for the wearer.

Bibliography
R.A. Fazzini in: Fazzini, Bianchi, Ro-
mano, Spaniel 1989 (cat. 38).
M.E.C.

97

Forepart of a sphinx holding
a captive
Middle Kingdom, early 12th Dynasty
Ivory
6.1 × 2.9 cm
North Abydos, Tomb 477
London, The Trustees of the British
Museum, EA 54678

The sphinx, an image of the pharaoh
with the body of a lion, was introduced as early as the 4th Dynasty to
symbolize his half human, half divine
nature. It became a popular form of
representing the king's invincible power as protector of the ordered world
that was Egypt. The present figure is
the only known three-dimensional representation of a sphinx holding a subdued enemy between its paws. From
the victim's hairstyle, we are probably
dealing with a Nubian, Egypt's traditional enemy in the south. The flat underside and two peg-holes suggest that
the figure once adorned a chest or
some piece of furniture. Once thought
to date to the Second Intermediate
Period, stylistic features seem to point
to the early 12th Dynasty.
M.M.

98

King crushing an enemy (ostracon)
New Kingdom, 20th Dynasty
Limestone with black ink drawing
H. 31; W. 33 cm
Deir el-Medina (Schiaparelli
excavations, 1905)
Turin, Museo Egizio, Suppl. 6279

On this limestone slab one of the most
typical scenes of the royal repertory is
reproduced, widely used on pylons
and external walls of temples: the king
in the act of crushing the defeated enemy. The sovereign is shown upright,
in battle dress, his head adorned with
the red crown topped by the two
feathers and the ram's horn; leaning
forward, with both hands he grasps
the tightly bound arms of a kneeling
Nubian captive. The prisoner's ethnic
group is identified by the typical garb
with large festooned neckpiece and by
the short curly hair. In front of the
king are the cartouches containing the
sovereign's name over a short line of
text: "The Lord of the Two Lands,
Usermaatra Meryamun, the Lord of
the Two Lands, Rameses, is the one
who crushes the foreign countries."

Bibliography
Curto 1984, p. 162.
S.D.

99

Stone relief
New Kingdom, late 18th–early
19th Dynasties
Limestone
H. 22.3 × W. 19.0 cm
Probably from Saqqara
Edinburgh, The Trustees of the
National Museums of Scotland,
A.1961.438

This relief fragment shows two har-
nessed horses with elaborate trappings
being calmed by a Nubian groom.
This is an unusually naturalistic rendering of horses, which were high-sta-
tus animals. The relief probably came
from the tomb chapel of a high official.

Bibliography
Houlihan 1996, p. 34, fig. 27.
E.G., B.M.

100

Military camp (fragment of bas-relief)
New Kingdom, 18th Dynasty
Limestone
H. 51; W. 41 cm
Saqqara, tomb of Horemheb
Berlin, Ägyptisches Museum
und Papyrussammlung, 20363

Archaeological discoveries often bear
out what we see in depictions of ancient Egypt, enabling us to put together a fair picture of what life was
like. This fragment of a bas-relief from
the tomb of General Horemheb depicts, in the context of a military camp,
the utensils and furnishings that were
actually present in the tomb: two-
wheeled war chariots, jars and stands,
water basins and jugs, folding seat,
stools and headrests.

Bibliography
Priese 1991, pp. 130–131 (cat. 81).
D.W.

101

Khepesh with the name of Rameses II
New Kingdom, 19th Dynasty,
reign of Rameses II
Bronze
L. 57.5; W. 4.8 cm
Paris, Musée du Louvre, E 25689

By the end of the Middle Kingdom, the Egyptians could no longer contain the threat posed by the Hyksos, who thus founded their own kingdom in the Delta. Their success was undoubtedly due, in part, to internal divisions within Egypt; however, it is also true that their weapons were of better quality. This period saw the introduction of horses, chariots and the use of bronze—creating armaments for the Egyptian army that were ultimately used to drive out the intruder. In fact, these borrowings from the Hyksos would lead to the pharaohs of the New Kingdom having an army that for several centuries was the most powerful in the Mediterranean basin. As if flaunting their new superiority, the pharaohs of the New Kingdom often had themselves depicted on the walls of their temples holding a large curved bronze blade. Borrowed from the invaders, this sword would replace the traditional war club in numerous ritual scenes. The weapon was a cross between an axe and a scimitar; its ancient Egyptian name, *khepesh*, is written in the same way as the term used for the vital energy of the animals offered up in sacrifice. In fact, the shape of the front right hoof of sacrificed cattle—the select morsel offered up to the gods or placed on the altars of the dead—recalls that of this weapon. The coincidence was obviously used in images and pictures to bring together the pharaoh's animal power and his invincibility. The *khepesh* from the Louvre is inscribed with the name of Rameses II. This does not necessarily mean that the illustrious sovereign himself will have used it in combat; perhaps this weapon—from the workshops of royal craftsmen—was presented by the pharaoh to one of his valiant officers.
I.F.

102

Wooden war club
Stuccoed and painted wood
L. 55.7; diam. 2.5; H. head 8 cm
Paris, Musée du Louvre, E 5983

This model of a war club with a pear-shaped head (the Egyptian name was *hedj*) is carved out of a single piece of wood. There are still traces of yellow-painted stucco on the handle, and white on the head. The head is wider at the base and has a small bulge at the top, showing that the handles of real war clubs extended through the head and were fixed at the other end. The round-section handle gets wider toward the base, ending in a tenon of smaller diameter (which suggests the club was to be fixed in the hand of a statue).

This weapon first appeared in Neolithic Egypt, and the pear-shaped war club would replace all others from the period of Naqada II onward. Thereafter, it became a symbol of power, remaining so in Pharaonic period. The king was a war chief who had to maintain order within the country, protect its borders and—why not?—extend its power abroad. In the scenes depicting the massacre of the nation's enemies, the pharaoh is most frequently shown wielding a *hedj* over the minute figures of his adversaries, whom he grips by the hair. This scene is first known to us from the Narmer Palette (Cairo Museum), and would be repeated frequently right up to the Roman period—above all, on the outer faces of the monumental columns of temples, where it also had an apotropaic significance.
C.Br.

103

The dagger of Kamose
Second Intermediate Period,
17th Dynasty, reign of Kamose (?)
Bronze, silver and gold
L. 31.8 (blade: L. 23; W. 3.1 cm)
West Thebes, Dra Abu el-Naga
(Mariette excavations, 1857)
Brussels, Bibliothèque Royale
de Belgique

The 17th Dynasty ruled in Thebes while the Delta area was under the control of the Hyksos. It comprised various valiant sovereigns who lost their life in fighting to drive the intruders out of Egypt. The mummy of Seqenenra (Taa II) still bears traces of the wounds that led to his death. His son, Kamose, would carry on the fight, but would die less than three years after ascending to the throne. His half-brother, Ahmose, would eventually win the conclusive victory—around 1550 BC—which marked the beginning of the New Kingdom and 18th Dynasty.

Kamose's tomb was discovered to the north of the Theban necropolis of Qurna, at Dra Abu el-Naga. This dagger from the Brussels Cabinet des Médailles undoubtedly belonged to the king. Given the shape of its handle and the delicacy of the goldsmith work involved, it was certainly not designed for use in combat. It will have been a ceremonial weapon, placed alongside Kamose's body by his successor in recognition of his valor. The necropolis of Dra Abu el-Naga also contained the tomb of Queen Ahhotep, Seqenenra's wife. This queen, who played a vital role in these troubled times, received similar funeral gifts, now in the Cairo Museum.
I.F.

104

Dagger of General Djehuty
New Kingdom, 18th Dynasty,
reign of Thutmose III
Bronze and wood
L. 35.5; W. 4.3 cm
Provenance unknown
Darmstadt, Hessisches
Landesmuseum, Ae: I, 6

General Djehuty is well known to us because of the number of objects bearing his name that can now be found in museums throughout Europe. He was certainly a man of courage and valor, given that his sovereign, Thutmose III, bestowed gifts of exceptional quality upon him.

Is this general to be identified with the hero of the same name who appears in a famous story recounting the capture of Joppe by Egyptian troops? It is tempting to believe so. In this case, Djehuty was the architect of the fall of a city which seemed capable of resisting siege forever. The cunning officer hid his men in baskets, and thus was able to smuggle them into the city. It is striking to note that this incident is not only conserved in Egyptian chronicles but also seems to have inspired the Arabian tales of Ali Baba.

Even if he is not the daring solider mentioned in that story, our Djehuty was clearly an effective general, given the rewards heaped upon him by his sovereign. Among other valuable prizes was this magnificent dagger, the quality of whose workmanship reveals that it must have come from royal craftsmen. This is a ceremonial weapon, the handle of which is decorated with hieroglyphs. The pommel is dedicated to Onuris, a god of war originating in the city of Thinis. This evocation of the warrior god was clearly intended to recall the bravery of Djehuty himself. The inscription mentions the joys of eternal life that will be granted to a man who has proved himself a faithful servant of his sovereign.

Bibliography
Eggebrecht 1987, pp. 120–121.
I.F.

105

Cup of General Djehuty
New Kingdom, 18th Dynasty,
reign of Thutmose III
Gold
H. 2.2; diam. 17.9 cm;
weight 371.5 gr.
Provenance unknown
Paris, Musée du Louvre, N 713

It was customary for the sovereign to honor his most zealous servants with gifts; and one of the most highly prized of these rewards was the "gold of valor." However, royal largesse was not always limited to somber necklaces; the bestowal of a tomb and part of the funeral furnishings might well be one of the ways the monarch showed his favor. Along with these gifts went various luxury objects, of which this is an example. The presentation of the royal gift is recorded here in a short inscription that says that this cup was given to General Djehuty by Thutmose III in recognition of his devotion in campaigns in foreign lands.

This is more than a valuable object in gold; its prestige is heightened by the quality of the workmanship, which reveals it must have been produced by royal craftsmen. The decor at the base of the cup is far from ordinary. It opens out from a central core into a floral pattern around which six fish form a circle enclosed by papyrus umbels—a charming scene which recalls the Egyptians' delight in fountains and gardens. However, this goes beyond a simple evocation of the delights of an aristocratic lifestyle.

In ancient Egypt water was the realm par excellence of regeneration—and particularly of the regeneration of the sun. This latter might well be depicted on the point of sinking beneath the sea in the form of a Nile perch (*tilapia nilotica*)—a depiction of which can be seen here (cat. no. 145). What is more, papyrus reed thickets were the haunt of the goddess Hathor, the great universal mother, often shown as a cow whose head rises above the tops of the reeds. It seems, therefore, that Thutmose was not content with simply rewarding his general with a magnificently-produced object; he wanted to present him with a symbolic evocation of the milieu within which the processes of eternal rebirth take place.

Bibliography
Andreu, Rutschowskaya, Ziegler 1997, pp. 110–112.
I.F.

106

Relief fragment with dignitaries
New Kingdom, 19th Dynasty,
reign Rameses II
Sandstone, painted
H. 102; W. 117 cm
Thebes, Asasif
Cairo, Egyptian Museum,
TR 14/6/24/20

This fragmentary relief scene with a procession of dignitaries was preserved between two blocks of sandstone in a noble's tomb on the Theban west bank. The processional scene is divided in two registers—the upper one is only partly preserved—showing two lines of officials who bow in respect and proceed to the right, most likely toward the king. The men are barefoot with shaved heads and wear long linen gowns held by two straps tied at the back of the neck. This is the traditional dress of the vizier, the man second in command under the king (during the New Kingdom, there were two viziers, one for the northern region or Lower Egypt, and one for the South, or Upper Egypt). One of the figures carries the flabellum which places him "to the right of the king," and on his arm a great ceremonial scarf is also tied; the other dignitaries carry other insignia of their rank: scepter, baton, palette, or papyrus roll. At the extreme left a man carries a stand with vessels and gold collars. These dignitaries are most likely going to a ceremony to receive awards and make various donations. In the fragmentary band below the scene, the word *djadjat* "masteries" appears, referring to the men in the procession.

Bibliography
PM I.2, p. 627.
A.M.

107

Tomb relief of Ay receiving a reward
New Kingdom, 18th Dynasty,
reign of Akhenaten
Limestone
H. 27.5; W. 54 cm
Tell el-Amarna, tomb of Ay
Cairo, Egyptian Museum,
TR 10/11/26/1

Ay was an important official during the reign of Akhenaten and increased his power and privileges throughout his lifetime. He ruled Egypt for four years after the death of King Tutankhamun and erected small buildings in Karnak and temples in Luxor, as well as dedicating a stone to the god Min at Akhmim.
On the northern wall of Tutankhamun's burial chamber, Ay is depicted as a priest administering the final rituals (the "opening of the mouth") to the deceased king. This scene is proof that Ay became Tutankhamun's heir. Ay constructed two tombs, one in el-Amarna and a later one in the Valley of the Kings. His unfinished Amarna tomb, in the northern group, is one of the largest private tombs. A relief portrays Ay with his wife Tey receiving gold necklaces and other valuable gifts from the king. The couple wears wigs fastened by a band and surmounted by ointment cones, around their necks are gold collars. In his tomb inscription, Ay proudly records that the king "doubled rewards for me like the number of sands while I was first of the officials in the front of the subjects."

Bibliography
Freed, Markowitz, D'Auria 1999, p. 270; Aldred 1973, pp. 19–20, fig. 5.
A.M.

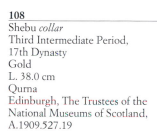

108

Shebu *collar*
Third Intermediate Period,
17th Dynasty
Gold
L. 38.0 cm
Qurna
Edinburgh, The Trustees of the
National Museums of Scotland,
A.1909.527.19

This collar (like the earrings, cat. no. 232) comes from an intact and exceptionally wealthy burial within the 17th-Dynasty royal cemetery at Qurna, Thebes. Excavated by Petrie in 1908, this burial of a woman and child is remarkable for the quality and quantity of its grave offerings. The woman, almost certainly a member of the royal house, was buried in a spectacular tall *rishi* coffin decorated in blue and gold. She was fully equipped with food, jewelry, ceramics, furniture and other offerings, much of it with foreign connections. At her feet lay the simple coffin of a three-year old child, who was also richly furnished with jewelry. The *shebu* collar, which was found around the woman's neck, is the earliest known example of a type that became popular in the 18th Dynasty. It consists of four rows of tightly strung gold beads, fastened with a pin inserted into loops in interlocking rings. The gold is purer than most known examples from the Middle Kingdom.

Bibliography
Eremin, Goring, Manley, Cartwright 2000; Andrews 1990, pp. 23 (fig. 14b), 181–182.
E.G., B.M.

109

Stele of Ay
New Kingdom, 18th Dynasty,
reign of Akhenaten
Limestone, painted
H. 72 cm
Tell el-Amarna
Cairo, Egyptian Museum,
JE 29748 = CG 34177

Ay was overseer, royal scribe of the Two Lands and scribe of the offering table. In his tomb at el-Amarna were six votive stelae placed in three niches beneath the entrance portico. These were dedicated to Ay by his brother and other members of his household, including his charioteer.
This round-top stele represents Ay standing in his chariot; on the left side is his charioteer, Thay, holding the reins in his hands; the chariot is equipped with a quiver of arrows. Ay wears a heavy wig and around his neck hangs an unguent vase with the so-called "gold of valor" necklace. He wears a tunic with short, wide pleated sleeves and a loose skirt. The Amarna style is obvious in the bulging belly and high buttocks, as well as in the facial features and head of the charioteer, all of which recall Akhenaten's daughter's head with its elongated skull and tapering half-closed eyes. The stele includes six columns with hieroglyphic inscriptions which mention Ay's name and titulary, and three short lines for the charioteer Thay.
A.M.

110

Fly necklace
New Kingdom
Gold and cornelian
L. 26.7; H. of flies 1.1–1.7 cm
Boston, Museum of Fine Arts,
William Stevenson Smith Fund,
1980.167

Small, stylized flies of stone, precious metal, and faience were part of the amuletic repertoire of ancient Egypt. Early examples, carved from hard stone, were recovered from Naqada II burials while examples from the first millennium BC include complex hybrid forms.
Fly ornaments were also worn in Nubia, Egypt's neighbor to the south. Their presence is documented in several classic Kerma (1700–1550 BC) burials identified as belonging to male warriors. Unlike Egyptian flies, these adornments were typically large (c. 6 cm high), made of ivory, silver, or gilded bronze, and worn in pairs around the neck. George A. Reisner, who excavated the site early in the XX century, classified them as military decorations awarded for heroism in battle. Two exceptional sets of large fly pendants from Egypt were found in the early 18th Dynasty burial of Queen Ahhotep. The more elaborate grouping consists of three flies fabricated from thick gold sheet and suspended from a loop-in-loop chain. The second set is a matched pair of flies with electrum wings and gold heads. This pair closely resembles Nubian military flies and may, in fact, derive from Kerma models. Other examples of foreign influence, both Aegean and West Asian, are also evident in the jeweled metalwork from the queen's burial so that the treasure is best described as an amalgam of traditional and new motifs. That Queen Ahhotep was interred with flies symbolic of strength, valor, and endurance is best interpreted in the context of her family's role in expelling foreign rulers and reestablishing Egypt's northern and southern borders.
During the New Kingdom, Egypt became a military power and worthy officers were routinely honored by the king. The "Order of the Golden Fly" was one of several awards given for bravery and meritorious action. Worn around the neck, it consisted of a series of small, gold flies. Although the individual elements in this necklace are authentic, the composition is modern.

Bibliography
Reisner 1923; Dunham 1963; Wilkinson 1971; P. Lacovara in: Eggebrecht 1987, p. 231 (cat. 161); Andrews 1994; Müller, Thiem 1999; A.M. Roth in: Hornung, Bryan, 2002, pp. 106–107 (cat. 22).
Y.J.M.

The Pharaoh, Guarantor of the Country's Prosperity. The Art of Good Government

111

Fabric with cartouches of Rameses II
New Kingdom, 19th Dynasty,
reign of Rameses II
Linen
L. 153; W. 74 cm
Qurna
Florence, Museo Egizio, 7951

This rectangular-shaped linen fabric appears in good condition, with just a few vertical tears. The cartouches with Rameses II's name and first name are painted in red, in the center area, slightly to the right. The fabric comes from an unidentified tomb of the Theban necropolis of Qurna, and must have belonged to the burial goods of a noble dignitary. This official had probably distinguished himself for his pharaoh, who in return for his services, offered him a delicate textile produced by the royal laboratories, as the Rameses II cartouches indicate. The item ended up by becoming a part of his grave goods.
M.C.G.

The decoration of the palace in which a sovereign held his audiences had to reflect the prestige of the Pharaonic monarchy. Apart from the collaborators of the sovereign, emissaries of foreign states, ambassadors and representatives of vassals could enter the official rooms of the residence. Whoever approached the pharaoh had to be fully cognizant that the person he was about to meet was much more than a simple human being. Therefore everything was carried out in order to give the royal audiences a setting worthy of the host of the premises. Like every Egyptian image, the smallest detail of the decoration in the official part of the palace had a meaning and was meant to give the visitor the impression that he was nothing but a tiny element in the gigantic mechanism destined to make the world function, and ruled over by the pharaoh.

The sovereign was at the center of the universe like the sun creator. Immediately around him reigned order as it had been established at the beginning of time. This ideal equilibrium was supported by two basic elements. On the one hand, those depending directly on the Egyptian government and benefiting from the good offices of a just rule. On the other hand, the foreigners to that universe who constituted a threat and therefore had to be integrated in one way or the other into the Egyptian world.

Like the priests in the temples, all the functionaries were emanations of the king, his delegates throughout the country who were to insure the equilibrium he was responsible for. Though only the highest state officials could approach the sovereign, even the lowest-ranking scribe working for the government felt that he had also been invested with a part of royal power. The administration was organized according to a strict hierarchy and the hereditary transmission of responsibilities was a current practice, at any rate, in certain periods.

On the borders of Egypt, the foreigners adopted an attitude that varied according to the times, and often according to the power of the pharaoh's armies. As long as the country only had to drive back Bedouins incursions, the local police sufficed for establishing order, while the king commanded commercial expeditions protected by his troops. It was not until after Egypt had been subject to foreign invasions that it created a professional army. In the New Kingdom, the army with its assault chariotry was reputed to be the most powerful force in the Near East. When faced with it, principalities, cities and foreign kingdoms very often became the vassals of the Two Lands; some moreover had always been its trading partners, like Byblos. Egypt's influence was threatened when new states came into being and contested its control of the Fertile Crescent. The decline of the land of the pharaohs began when its armies could no longer keep in check its adversaries' fleets.
I.F.

112

*Model of the throne room
in the palace of Merenptah*
Modern reproduction
Painted wood
H. 119; L. 246; W. 190 cm
Philadelphia, The University
of Pennsylvania, Museum of
Archeology and Anthropology

The Egyptians only used stone for monuments destined to last for eternity; for other structures—including most parts of royal palaces—they used perishable materials. The extant remains of the palace of Merenptah discovered at Memphis, however, are sufficient to give us a fairly exact idea of the structure of a royal residence. Though the buildings themselves have disappeared, one can reconstruct them with a certain precision through comparison with temples (the architecture of which was, after all, inspired by that of buildings in unfired brick). The batter of the walls, for example, is typical of that of structures in clay, with the base of the wall thicker than the top in order to guarantee stability. This aspect is particularly noticeable in the monumental pillars of temples. Thus we know that the façade of a palace must have resembled that of a temple (this hypothesis has been amply borne out by archaeological evidence). Merenptah's residence at Memphis was largely an official building, intended for royal audiences and the reception of petitioners and ambassadors. Extant evidence reveals the layout of the halls (which can also be reconstructed from the mural paintings in tombs). The ruins of the unfired-brick sections used as the private apartments and communal spaces of the palace are more difficult to interpret; but the official areas of the royal palace contained numerous elements in stone, which means these

spaces can be reconstructed with some precision. The throne room was designed to make an impression upon visitors—be they the king's ministers, court personages or representatives of foreign countries. These mere mortals were being brought before the living incarnation of royalty, and thus entered an almost sacred space, conceived of as a sort of temple. An imposing colonnade led up to the podium and raised throne, from which the pharaoh dominated those before him. The entire decor was intended to recall the role of the sovereign as the guarantor of cosmic order and the representative of the gods on earth.
I.F.

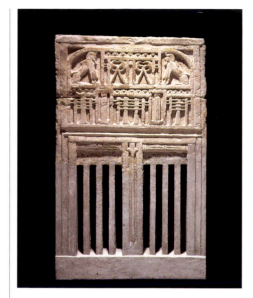

113

*Window from the palace of
Merenptah*
New Kingdom, 19th Dynasty
Limestone, with traces of coloring
H. 128; L. 79 cm
Memphis, palace of Merenptah
Philadelphia, The University
of Pennsylvania, Museum of
Archeology and Anthropology,
E. 13564

Few traces remain of the residences of the pharaohs; not only were they, like more humble homes, largely built in perishable materials, they also stood in urban areas which are often still occupied (and thus unavailable for archaeological research).

The palace of Merenptah is exceptional because it is relatively well preserved and could be studied through painstaking archaeological excavation. Various prestigious features give us an insight into the layout of the halls which were the setting for royal audiences.

Alongside these spectacular rooms, there is more modest evidence which gives us a glimpse of how the Egyptians actually lived. This is the case with this open-work window. Part of a royal residence, it is decorated in a way that reflects the role of the monarch. The arch shows two figures of the king as seated sphinx opposite a double motif of papyrus stalks tied in pairs under the umbel. This ensemble surmounts a frieze of *djed* pillars; the small animal heads here could be an allusion to the rising sun.

The window proper starts under this lintel. The plant motifs in the decoration recall that the more common parts of this house were in unfired brick and other perishable materials. For example, one can clearly make out a representation of the rolled-up rush mats that were used to close openings.

Normally in wood, the open-work here is in limestone.

Windows were placed high up in houses, leaving the rooms in a penumbra that protected them from direct sunlight. This layout was also intended to guarantee a slight breeze; and in palace or the homes of the wealthy the system was made even more efficient. Along with the openings in the walls, there might be a central colonnade raising part of the ceiling. It was at this difference in ceiling level that such open-work windows were installed, to allow light into the middle of the room. This architectural feature can also be seen in the large hypostyle halls of temples, of which the most famous is that in the sanctuary of Amun at Karnak.

Bibliography
Horne 1985.
I.F.

114

Frieze with lotus flowers
New Kingdom, 20th Dynasty
Faience inlaid with colored paste
L. 59; H. 8 cm
Tell el-Yahudiya
Cairo Egyptian Museum, JE 21842

This fragment of a glazed faience frieze
was once part of the wall decoration of
a Ramesside palace in Tell el-Yahudiya,
in the Delta. The frieze is composed of
separate elements representing blue
lotus flowers alternating with blue
grapes and a sort of red fan-shaped
flowers. At the bottom of the frieze, all
these motifs are punctuated by small
white rosettes. In ancient Egypt, the
blue lotus was used in the preparation
of perfumes. It was considered the
symbol of resurrection and rebirth and
one of the sacred flowers, because it
was believed that Nefertem (god of
the primeval lotus blossom, who completed the Memphite triad with Ptah
and Sekhmet) arose every morning
from a lotus flower, which opens at
sunrise. It was also considered an eternal source of life and was represented
everywhere in temples. In tomb furnishings, the blue lotus is placed on the
offering tables with a pile of vegetables
and trussed birds, so that the deceased
could enjoy them eternally in the afterlife.

Bibliography
Griggs 1985, p. 31; Montréal 1986,
(cat. 18); H. Khatab, in: Le Caire 2002,
p. 65.
Z.T.

115

Floor-tiles with images of foreigners
New Kingdom, 20th Dynasty,
reign of Rameses III
Faience
35.1.12 (H. 31.2; W. 20.7;
D. 4.8 cm); 35.1.19 (H. 22.3; W. 22;
D. 4 cm); 35.1.16 (H. 33; W. 34.3;
D. 6.1 cm); 35.1. 21 (H. 12.1;
W. 18.9; D. 6.1 cm); 35.1.18
(H. 33.3; W. 33.6; D. 6.7 cm);
35.1. 20 (H. 21.9; W. 33.6;
D. 10.2 cm)
Qantir
New York, The Metropolitan
Museum of Art, Rogers Fund, gift
of Edward S. Harkness, 35.1.12–19,
35.1.16–21, 35.1.18–20

Depictions of the overpowered enemies of Egypt bound hand and foot
(cat. nos. 116, 117) were not the only
way of including images of "foreigners" within the decoration of the royal palace. Recent archaeological research has enabled us to reconstruct
certain features of the decor of the
hall in which royal audiences were
held. It has thus been possible to piece
together the appearance of the podium on which the pharaoh's throne
rested.

These Metropolitan Museum floor-
tiles, which decorated the base of the
royal podium in the palace of Qantir,
are made up in two parts. The lower
has a frieze in which the images of the
salient of a palace enclosure alternate
with motifs of the heraldic plants of
Upper and Lower Egypt. Above, are
representatives of the various peoples
subject to Egyptian rule; these are
shown kneeling in homage to the
pharaoh.

Egypt's dominion over its enemies reflected the gods' continual struggle
against the forces of disorder and
chaos. In the physical world of the
Egyptians themselves, these latter
forces were either annihilated
or—willy-nilly—included within the
organized universe. The use of images
of this type—and particularly the way
they are distributed within the architectural space—had a double purpose;
their position was never casual. Placed
as they were, these floor-tiles with their
figures of foreigners served to decorate
the base of the royal podium, just as
the submission of vassal states was the
effective base of the Egyptian empire.
Hence, the position of the image reflected the situation in the real world.
But there was also another idea at
work here: rebellions were frequent,
and the magic of this image served to
guarantee the continuance of a politi-

cal equilibrium that was repeatedly challenged. So, the foreigners are shown not only fixed in an attitude of subjection, but also symbolically immobilized on the royal podium—that is, right "under the feet" of the pharaoh and his authority.
I.F.

116

Tile with an Asiatic chief
New Kingdom, 20th Dynasty, reign of Rameses III
Polychrome faience
H. 25; W. 6 cm
Medinet Habu
Boston, Museum of Fine Arts, Emily Esther Sears Fund, 03.1573

Egypt's New Kingdom rulers decorated their royal palaces and mortuary temples with a variety of images portraying vanquished foreigners intended to emphasize and perpetuate symbolically the domination of foreign lands, potential enemies and other hostile forces by Egypt and its king. This inlay tile in brilliant polychrome faience originally derives from the palace adjacent to Rameses III's mortuary temple at Medinet Habu. One of a group of tiles portraying chiefs from a range of foreign lands, it probably adorned the lower jamb of a doorway near the "window of appearance," where the king appeared before his subjects surrounded by imagery intended both to impress and to intimidate.
The chief represented is from the Syro-Palestinian region, and exemplifies Egypt's stereotype of its northern neighbors. His short pointed beard, large nose, sidelock, and yellow flesh identify him as a Northerner. Wrapped around his body over a pale blue undergarment is a gray woolen cloak decorated with floral motifs and secured by a characteristically Asiatic wide sash. He stands on his toes with his arms tightly tethered in front of him and a rope around his neck. His face, contorted with pain, effectively conveys his discomfort and submission.

Bibliography
Rowe 1908, p. 48; Smith 1960, p. 147.
D.M.D.

117

Fragments of inlay with images of prisoners
New Kingdom, Ramesside period
Faience
E 7691 A (H. 8.7; W. 9.5; D. 2.4 cm); E 7691 B (H. 14.2; W. 9.7; D. 2.7 cm); E 7691 C (H. 11.2; W. 8.3; D. 2.8 cm); E 7691 D (H. 9.5; W. 7.1; D. 1.9 cm)
Medinet Habu (?), E 7691 D
Tell el-Yahudiya, E 7691
Paris, Musée du Louvre, E 7691 A–D (AF 2890, AF 2888, AF 2889, AF 2887)

The decor in the audience chambers of a royal palace reflected Egyptian notions of world order.
Innumerable tiles in polychrome faience were used to decorate door and window frames. Certain were adorned with hieroglyphs that were an endless repetition of the royal titles of the pharaoh. Others, as is the case here, were decorated with low reliefs showing foreigners, always depicted in the position of prisoners. This was not an expression of xenophobia but a magical use of the plastic arts: in a real and symbolic sense, the images vanquished Egypt's enemies and made them subject to its power. However, it is also probable that such decoration also had a propaganda purpose and was intended to make an impression on the foreigners being received by the king. Note that the ethnic diversity of the enemies is rendered with great attention to detail in facial features, types of headdress and, above all, costume.
These precise details made it possible for the eye to immediately pick out the various enemies of the nation. However, the refinement shown in these depictions reveals that concern for elegance which was typical of the Ramesside period—even finding ex-

pression in the portrayal of those who threatened that universal order embodied by pharaoh.

Bibliography
Wien 1994, pp. 277–278 (E 7691 A and D); Etienne 2000, p. 105.
I.F.

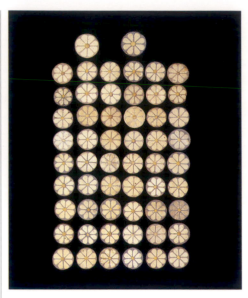

118

Two fragments of paneling
from Qantir
New Kingdom, 19th Dynasty,
reign of Rameses II
Siliceous faience
H. 19.2; W. 19.6; D. *c.* 3.5 cm
(E 14360)
H. 18.8; W. 12.5; D. 3 cm (E 11098)
Qantir, palace of Rameses II
Paris, Musée du Louvre, E 14360,
E 11098

The use of siliceous faience for wall
decoration began in the early Old
Kingdom, and the most complete extant example from that period is to be
found in the blue tiles adorning the
underground chambers of Djoser at
Saqqara. The tradition most probably
carried on uninterrupted; but the most
copious examples of this decorative
art date from the period of the New
Kingdom. As a matter of fact, the
range of metal oxides used increased
from the 18th Dynasty onward, and
more and more colors became available.
The palette and quality of these two
pieces make it possible for us to date
them to Rameses II's Qantir palace—a
building which, on the basis of extant
evidence, would seem to have marked
a high point in the decorative use of
faience. But while public apartments
will have been decorated with official
art depicting the king's dominion over
the universe, these are more relaxed
scenes of Nile life, and therefore were
more appropriate for the palace's private apartments. The zigzags representing water run horizontal to the lotus flowers (the opposite is the case in
the fragment from the same palace
now in New York).
The panels are covered with 1 mm of
blue-gray glaze as the basis for the water motif. The lotus flowers are painted in more or less pastel turquoise

enamel; the stalks were in attached
red faience. Black lines pass through
the different areas to outline the motifs. The pieces are too incomplete for
us to be able to reconstruct the wall
decoration as a whole.
G.P.

119

56 decorative rosettes
New Kingdom, 19th Dynasty,
reign of Rameses III
Siliceous faience
N 8142 and N 8147: diam. 4.3;
D. of roundel 0.7–0.9; D. of yellow
stud 1.2 cm
All the others: diam. 0.35–0.39;
D. of roundel 0.4–0.6 cm
Tell el-Yahudiya, palace of
Rameses III
Paris, Musée du Louvre, dépôt
du département des Antiquités
orientales, N 8142, N 8147,
N 8151–N 8169, N 8173, N 8177,
N 8178, N 8180–N 8182,
N 8186–N 8192, N 8194, N 8195,
N 8197–N 8207; dépôt
du département des Antiquités
égyptiennes, E 10840, A, B, C, D, E;
E 5118 A, B, C, D

Perhaps we should let Gaston
Maspero describe the now-lost building of Tell el-Yahudiya—a site some
twenty kilometers to the northeast of
Heliopolis—in his own words: "The
core of the building is in limestone
and alabaster; but instead of the usual sculpted panels, there is a sort of
mosaic, made up in almost equal parts
of cut stone and painted clay. The most
commonly used feature is a roundel in
friable fireclay coated with blue or
gray glaze, against which simple rose
forms, geometric frameworks, spider's
webs or open flowers are picked out in
shades of cream. The central core is in
relief, with leaves and designs pressed
into the mass of the clay. These
roundels vary in diameter from one to
ten centimeters, and were attached to
the walls using a very fine cement."
(*L'Archéologie égyptienne*, Paris, 1887,
pp. 257–258).
This is the only written record of a
now totally destroyed building and its
decor, of which the Cairo Museum

contains a valuable old reconstruction.
Probable method of production: a
roundel of pure sand quartz siliceous
paste without color was molded on
two sides, so that the upper side was in
the form of hollowed out petals. Blue-
gray paste was then added to these
hollows; a stud of yellow faience was
fixed in the center hole.
G.P.

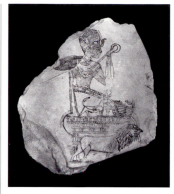

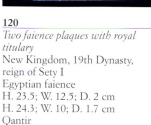

120

Two faience plaques with royal titulary
New Kingdom, 19th Dynasty, reign of Sety I
Egyptian faience
H. 23.5; W. 12.5; D. 2 cm
H. 24.3; W. 10; D. 1.7 cm
Qantir
Paris, Musée du Louvre, E 11518

Excavations at the palace of King Sety I unearthed decorative bricks that bear witness to its "dazzling halls of lapis lazuli and turquoise." Faience reproduced the gleam of these semi-precious stones on plaques that were used to adorn the high doorjambs and gateways of the palace; following the outline of the architectural form, these tiles will have been fixed in place using wooden pins.

In Egypt the whole architectural decor served as a basis for writing. So great was the power of royal "names," that each monument became a page on which to write out the honors and titles of the king. Pronouncing a name or fixing its image in hieroglyphic script made that name come back to life—hence the endless repetition in a sort of litany. The 160 panels from the Louvre form a puzzle of multiple fragments that comprise the full royal titulary, the "Five Great Names," chosen by Sety I when he came to the throne. The throne name given here is Menmaatra and appears within a cartouche—that is, an enclosure of rope that recalls the closed cycle of the sun around the earth; the combination serves to indicate the privileged relationship between the pharaoh and the essential deities Maat and Ra.

The second piece of faience must have preceded the birth name of "Sety," qualifying him as "son of Ra, of the womb that he loves." This formula indicated that the king was the actual carnal son of the sun-god, conceived in the divine womb and loved just like a son. Hence, the divinity of "Menmaatra Sety" was proclaimed throughout his royal palace.

Bibliography
Delange 2001, pp. 44–45.
E.D.

121

King carried in a chair by porters (ostracon)
New Kingdom, 19th–20th Dynasties
Limestone
H. 18; W. 20 cm
Deir el-Medina (excavation by de G. Möller)
Berlin, Ägyptisches Museum und Papyrussammlung, 21434

In Egypt, the pharaoh never appeared on horseback on official occasions; in public processions, he was either in his war chariot or in a chair borne by porters. The sketch on this ostracon is either a design for—or copy of—a depiction of such a scene. The chair is flanked by a representation of a lion, and next to the armrest one cán see a statue of a standing sphinx. The reclining position of the king, whose right arm rests on the back of his throne, contrasts with his official garb of long pleated robe, blue crown (cat. no. 29), *heka* scepter in the form of a cross (cat. no. 32) and flabellum (cat. no. 31).

Bibliography
Kaiser 1967, p. 64 (cat. 720).
D.W.

122

Window of appearance (ostracon)
New Kingdom, 19th–20th Dynasties
Limestone
H. 13.5; W. 16 cm
Thebes
Berlin, Ägyptisches Museum und Papyrussammlung, 3316

The palace was the locus of sovereignty; its layout was an expression of the pharaoh's dominion both at home and abroad. The sketch on this ostracon (perhaps a project for a bas-relief in a temple or tomb) shows the central part of a palace façade, the "window of appearance" at which the king would appear to a selected public on official occasions. Beneath the window we can see bound foreign captives, who are easily recognizable as Asians and Nubians. They are linked with a hieroglyph for "Reunion" in the center of the image. On both sides of the pharaoh are *rekhyt* birds, which symbolize the king's subject peoples.

Bibliography
Kaiser 1967, p. 64 (cat. 723).
D.W.

123

Representation of foreign lands paying homage to the king
New Kingdom, 18th Dynasty, reign of Akhenaten
Sandstone
H. 22; W. 54 cm
Karnak, temple of Aten
Cairo, Egyptian Museum, TR 10/11/26/1

Amenhotep IV, who later changed his name to Akhenaten, turned away from Amun and the gods associated with him soon after his accession to the throne.

He began the construction of several shrines to the god Aten east of the temple of Amun at Karnak. The principle temple of Aten at Karnak was called *Gempaaten*, which can be translated literally as "finding of the Aten," a name that refers to the king's active role with the sun-god. Recent excavations have cast light on the processional avenue, depicted in reliefs, that leads from the palace to the temple of Aten: in the colonnade corridor of the temple, a number of foreign delegates throw themselves at the feet of the god-king; their hairstyle, shape of face, and skin color indicate their ethnic origin. From right to left: a Nubian with characteristically treated eyes, curly hair, and one earring; a northern Syrian with shaven head and sideburns; a Palestinian with shoulder-length hair, a headband, and full beard; and a Libyan with curls at his temples and a pointed beard.

Bibliography
Freed, Markowitz, D'Auria 1999, pp. 57–58, fig. 39; Schulz, Seidel 1998.
A.M.

124

Base with two prostrate figures
Middle Kingdom, 12th–13th Dynasties
Red quartzite
H. 11.5; L. 26.5; W. 25.7 cm
Baltimore, Walters Art Museum, 22.373

This enigmatic sculpture depicts two provincial governors lying prostrate in a position known as "kissing the earth," a ceremonial posture assumed in the presence of a deity or pharaoh. A third official between the two has been removed and his name erased. Does this indicate the Egyptian custom of obliterating the memory of an individual in disgrace? This remarkable work poses a number of such challenging questions.

Its context is unclear. Perhaps it may have been placed near a statue of a king in a temple setting, reflecting the respectful intent of the donors to appear humble and obedient before a ruler. During the 12th Dynasty, administrative reforms in Egypt removed power from provincial governors. The donors may have hoped to obtain favor from the king with their gift. By the late 12th and 13th Dynasties, a network of bureaucratic organization effectively ran the country.

The inscriptions below the faces indicate their status as *haty-a*, the administrative title of a local prince or mayor. The names of the officials and their mothers are inscribed on the left, Hatankh, born of Satwosret, and on the right, Nakht the Elder, born of Maket.

The sculpture is unique in Egyptian art, as there are no known examples depicting multiple prostrate figures in three-dimensional form. Also noteworthy is the unusual stylistic contrivance of the figure's elongated hairstyle. Perhaps the figures represent "Egyptianized" foreigners or vassal rulers of Asiatic origin. The work is without doubt an extraordinary artistic creation, yet many questions remain unanswered.
C.H.

125

Bust of a Ramesside king, probably Merenptah
New Kingdom, 19th Dynasty, reign of Merenptah
Gray granite
H. 52 cm
Medinet Habu
Cairo, Egyptian Museum, JE 601

Merenptah was the thirteenth son and successor of Rameses II. The eldest son alive at the end of that long-lived sovereign's sixty-seven-year reign, Merenptah must have been about fifty years old when he came to the throne, as his mummy indicates, and he ruled for ten years.

This bust is probably of King Merenptah and comes from a colossal statue. The king wears a striped *nemes* headcloth, whose two lappets fall behind his ears over his shoulders; it is surmounted by the *uraeus*, which represents the divine protection of the king and is the symbol of royalty, as was the "false" beard, which is held in place by straps over the large ears. He wears a wide collar of several strands. He has wide-open staring eyes framed by heavy lids, a broad, straight nose, a fleshy mouth with down-turned corners, and dimples.

This idealized portrait shows the sovereign at a much younger age, and emphasizes his personality and power rather than his features for he was probably over fifty years old. Unfortunately the back pillar shows only the beginning of his royal titulary: "King of Upper and Lower . . . ."

Bibliography
PM, I.2, p. 776.
A.M.

126

Statue of Paser
New Kingdom, 19th Dynasty,
reign of Rameses II
Gray granite
H. 110 cm
Karnak, temple of Amun,
cachette court
Cairo, Egyptian Museum, CG 42164 =
JE 36935

The so-called "cachette court" at Karnak is located in front of the seventh
pylon. The excavation of its floor between 1901–05 unearthed more than
two thousands statues of kings, deities
and private individuals, dating from
the 11th Dynasty to the Ptolemaic period. Deposited for generations in the
temple, these statues eventually filled
the passages and the courts. Hence
they were buried and hidden under
the temple floor for they were not to
be destroyed.
The statue of Paser is one of these.
He was city mayor and vizier during
the reigns of Sety I and Rameses II,
and was buried in Tomb no. 106, located in the west bank of Luxor.
Paser kneels and holds an altar. He
wears a double wig, which recalls the
models in vogue during the New Kingdom. His neck is adorned with a chain
with a Hathoric and Tyet ("knot of
Isis") amulet. Paser's remarkable features have been preserved for us in
this 19th-Dynasty portrait: feline eyes,
full cheeks, and delicate mouth with a
slightly curved lower lip. His long skirt
covers his body up to his chest with
flaps crossing at the front, where they
are supported by a strap around the
neck. This type of costume was generally worn by viziers.
The altar is hollow for an offering; depicted on the front are scenes of the
goddess Mut, Mistress of Isheru
(precinct of Mut at Karnak), and the
god Khons. On the back pillar, three

columns of hieroglyphic inscriptions
mention Paser's name and titulary
". . . of the lord of Two Lands, dignitary, mayor and vizier." On the shoulders of the statue are his titles: "Priest
of the . . . judge," and "priest of all the
henmemet."

Bibliography
CG 42001–42250, pp. 31–32, pl.
XXVIII; Hornemann 1957, pl. 587.
A.M.

127

Statue of Ramessnakht as a scribe
New Kingdom, second half of the
20th Dynasty, reigns of Rameses
IV, V, VI
Gray granite
H. 75; W. 43 cm
Karnak, temple of Amun,
cachette court (1904)
Cairo, Egyptian Museum, JE 36582
= CG 42162

Ramessnakht held many positions in
his life, the most important being that
of first prophet of Amun. He is known
to have led an expedition to the Wadi
Hammamat quarry in the Eastern
Desert, reputed for the quality of the
stone from the beginning of Egyptian
history. Ramessnakht built a recently
discovered mortuary temple on the
top of the cliff in Dra Abu el-Naga
(western Thebes).
The statue represents Ramessnakht in
the traditional posture of the scribe:
He is sitting on the ground, legs
crossed, a partly unrolled papyrus on
his lap. His right hand is closed so as
to hold a brush, while the left one
grasps a papyrus roll. Ramessnakht
gazes at the unrolled papyrus on his
lap as if he were reading the text inscribed on it. The scribe is a typical figure of Egyptian art, but the baboon
perched on the head and shoulders is
not attested elsewhere. The baboon
was the sacred animal of Thoth, the
god of the scribe, the inventor of writing, so the portrait symbolically places
Ramessnakht under the protection of
Thoth. Ramessnakht is represented as
a youth with narrow elongated eyes; he
wears a typically Ramesside garment:
a transparent tunic with pleated
sleeves covers his chest. The hieroglyphic inscriptions mention his name
and titles.
A.M.

128

Statue of the architect May
New Kingdom, 19th Dynasty,
reigns of Rameses II and Merenptah
Gray granite
H. 74 cm
Memphis
Cairo, Egyptian Museum, JE 67878

The statue of May was found by
chance near the temple of Merenptah
in the ruins of ancient Memphis.
May was an architect under Rameses
II, who continued in the reign of his
son and successor, Merenptah. May is
seated on a base that is rounded in
the back, his palms are turned up,
waiting to receive offerings. His wig
falls in a triangular shape onto each
shoulder, pushing his ears out on both
sides; this old style wig was common to
Middle Kingdom statues. He has
slightly closed, almond-shaped eyes,
a rounded nose and a small, tight-
lipped mouth; his short chin is covered
by a small beard. He wears a kilt, that
is tied at the waist and completely covers his legs, its rippling edge running
diagonally across his lap.
A cartouche of King Merenptah is
carved on each shoulder.
The inscription incised between his
hands is a prayer to the god of Memphis, Ptah, the lord of Justice, asking
him, to give life, health and prosperity to May, identified as the chief of
works in the temples of Ra and Ptah
and chief of the craftsmen in the Great
Palace of the prince at Heliopolis, and
the son of the chief of works Bakena-
mun, his grandparents being the chief
Chancellor Nebiot and lady Takartia.
A.M.

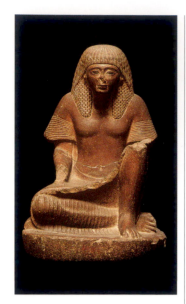

129

Statue of Hapy
New Kingdom, 19th Dynasty,
reigns of Sety I and Rameses II
Quartzite
H. 69 cm
Karnak, temple of Amun
Cairo, Egyptian Museum, CG 42184
= 36914

Hapy, the steward of Amun, is portrayed as a scribe seated on a cushion;
his left leg is raised and he holds a papyrus roll in his left hand, which is
stretched across is lap; in his right
hand he holds a quill pen. The god is
wearing a tripartite wig, and a typical
Ramesside transparent tunic with
pleated short sleeves.
Two columns with hieroglyphic inscriptions stand at his back. The first
one reads: "The offering which the
king gives Amun-Ra, the great one . . .
divine wife Ahmose Nefertari may she
give them . . . beautiful purification, for
the *ka* [soul] of the steward of . . .
Hapy." The second pillar reads: "The
offering which the king gives Amun-
Ra, the lord of the throne of the Two
Lands, the foremost of Ipet-isut [Kar-
nak] Mut the eye of Ra may [she] give
. . . invocation offering in Thebes for
the steward Hapy."
The inscription mentions the name of
Ahmose Nefertari, wife of King Ahmose, founder of the 18th Dynasty,
and mother of King Amenhotep I.

Bibliography
PM II, p. 147.
A.M.

130

*Stele of an anonymous vizier
of Sety I*
New Kingdom, 19th Dynasty,
reign of Sety I
Limestone
H. 56; W. 65; D. 11 cm
Deir el-Medina
Turin, Museo Egizio, CGT 50090
(= C. 1466)

This incised stele, that has kept some
traces of polychromy, features a scene
representing King Sety I in the act of
offering a brazier to two divinities,
identified by the hieroglyphic inscription as Amenhotep I and his mother
Ahmose Nefertari. The text reads:
"The perfect god Djeserkara [Amen-
hotep], Ahmose Nefertari."
On the right of the scene, behind Sety I, we have the figure of a vizier of
which all that remains is his titles, but
not his name. The text pronounces:
"Burn incense, make offerings. The
Lord of the Two Lands, Menmaatra,
the lord of apparitions, Sety Merenptah. The superintendent of Thebes
and vizier. . . ."
Under Sety I's reign there two attested viziers, both of Upper Egypt:
Paser and Nebamon. Our stele seems
to indicate the titular was also a vizier
of the South, but it is not clear
whether he is one of the viziers mentioned or else a third, undocument-
ed one.
The vizier played an essential role in
the administration of justice on the
central level, based on the principle of
maat, as equilibrium and recomposi-
tion of order troubled by an offense.
In fact he also had the title of "priest
of Maat." The duties of the vizier are
minutely described in a text, *Instructions for the Vizier*, inscribed in several
18th-Dynasty tombs, but formulated
in the administrative terminology of
the late Middle Kingdom.
Bibliography
Tosi, Roccati 1972, pp. 126, 301.
M.T.

131

Stele of Parahotep
New Kingdom, 19th Dynasty,
reign of Rameses II
Basalt
H. 63; W. 41 cm
Sedment el-Gebel
Cairo, Egyptian Museum, JE 47001

Parahotep was vizier during the reign
of Rameses II. His large tomb in Sedment el-Gebel overlooked both the
Nile and the Fayum, and consisted of
eight chambers branching in different
directions, with two shafts. The tomb
contained two red granite sarcophagi
in low relief, a granite altar for offerings, a pair of indurated limestone figures, two wooden pectorals and two
fragmented stelae.
This stele was unfortunately broken
on one side, and split into two symmetrical scenes. It now comprises
three registers: In the first one Parahotep is represented wearing his vizier
costume and raising his hands in adoration of the god Nefertem, the lion-
headed goddess Sekhmet, and an
unidentified god; the vizier is followed
by the royal messenger Hatiaay.
In the second register, Parahotep is
shown adoring two sets of gods: the
falcon-headed god Ra-Horakhty, Maat
and Hathor, and in the back Horus
with his son Isis; here Parahotep is
followed by his priest Thay; Rameses'
name appears in front of the vizier.
In the third register, Parahotep adores
Heryshef, Hathor, and in the back the
goddess Mehit; Parahotep is followed
by the chief of the archers Ipwia.
All the gods holds a staff in one hand
and the *ankh* sign of life.

Bibliography
PM IV, p. 117; Petrie, Brunton 1924,
pp. 29 (52), 30 (55), pls. XXI (4),
LXXIII.
A.M.

132

Libation basin of Neferrenpet
New Kingdom, 19th Dynasty,
reign of Rameses II
Black granite
78 × 64 × 39 cm
Provenance unknown
London, The Trustees of the British
Museum, EA 108

This monument stood outside a temple or in one of its outer courtyards, allowing Neferrenpet to share in offering rituals performed for the gods. It was a receptacle for water that escaped from the spout of an adjoining offering table as libations were administered. Neferrenpet is shown kneeling to drink from the life-giving water that poured in straight opposite him, where the cross-shaped hieroglyph for "life" is carved on the rim. Offering prayers on the edges and sides address the gods Ptah, Amun-Ra, Maat and Hathor, and confirm that Neferrenpet be granted a long life in perfect health. Neferrenpet held office as vizier during the later years of Rameses II. The highest official of state, he was only subservient to the great king himself, on whose behalf he performed a wide range of governmental duties. The end of the basin that was nearest the offering table shows Neferrenpet adoring cartouches with the principal names of his king, already worshipped as a god during his life. Rameses is thus invoked as a benevolent mediator between Neferrenpet outside and the gods within the temple. The cartouches are framed by symbols of the king's all-embracing power. Over his names is the heavenly vault, while the floral motif below, a more stylized variant to that on Pairy's lintel, symbolizes a unified Egypt. The hieroglyphic configurations that flank the king's names invoke for him millions of regnal years.
M.M.

133

Relief with scribes
New Kingdom, 18th Dynasty,
reigns of Tutankhamun and Ay
Limestone
H. 24; W. 31.5 cm
Saqqara
Florence, Museo Egizio, 2566

This fragment of wall relief represents four scribes intent on their task. The figures, standing but slightly bent forward, repeat with small variants the same gesture: with their left hand they grasp the scribe's tablet, showing the hollows containing the inks, and with the right hand they hold the calamus with which they are writing, probably on a papyrus placed on the tablet. They all feature a short wig and are wearing a pleated tunic with wide sleeves and puffed up aprons in front; notice the attempt to render the figures in perspective, even causing the last scribe's body to disappear.
The fragment comes from a wall of General Horemheb's tomb at Saqqara, decorated with a scene representing the pharaoh consigning the gold necklaces to Horemheb: thus, the scribes are writing the chronicle of the event, one of the many tasks of their profession. The style of the relief reflects the influence of the Amarna manner, which was felt in Tutankhamun's reign; later, Horemheb, raised to pharaoh, had his royal tomb excavated in the Valley of the Kings.

Bibliography
Guidotti 2000, p.100 no. 24 (with previous bibliography).
M.C.G.

134

*Scribe palette bearing the name
of Tutankhamun*
New Kingdom, 18th Dynasty,
reign of Tutankhamun
Wood
L. 37; W. 5.5; D. 1.3 cm
From the region of Thebes (?)
Paris, Musée du Louvre, N 2241

A long rectangular tablet of wood, with the center hollowed out to hold reed brushes, this object conforms perfectly to the usual models of palette. A sliding cover made it easier to arrange the brushes. Two small cups contained the cakes of red and black paint that were indispensable to the work of the scribe; the thick traces of color around them reveals that this object must actually have been used. Within the incised cartouche at the top there is the coronation name of Tutankhamun "the perfect god, master of the Two Lands, Nebkheperura, beloved of Thot."
In all likelihood not from the tomb of Tutankhamun—though that was amply furnished with scribe materials—this palette probably belonged to a, now anonymous, scribe who exercised his craft during the reign of the young king. (A plate in the *Monuments of Egypt and Nubia*, pl. 191 bis, claims that this piece comes from the "tombs of Kurna," but gives no further details.) Simple functionaries or high-court dignitaries with important functions, scribes—educated and sometimes cultured people—played an important role in the administrative machinery of pharaonic Egypt. This role was, in fact, the first step in the career of any good functionary. Indeed, whatever the field in which the high functionaries of the state operated, they necessarily included the title of "scribe" among their sometimes abundant official titles.

Bibliography
Paris 1982, p. 345 (cat. 292); Chr. Ziegler in: Paris 1990, p. 29 (cat. E9).
P.R.

135

Model of a scribe's palette
New Kingdom, 19th Dynasty,
reign of Sety II
Blue faience
H. 4.1; W. 8.2; L. 22.5 cm
Luxor
Chicago, The Field Museum
of National History, gift of Mrs.
Edward Ayer, 31551

There is no need to argue the importance of writing in ancient Egypt.
Words could bring into existence the
state of affairs they described, and—a
fortiori—that power was enhanced
when they were written. Scribes'
palettes (cat. no. 134)—or models
thereof—have been found in various
tombs. This one from the Field Museum is a model in faience, inscribed
with the name of King Sety II. This is
not an object that was actually used
but a copy, which was perhaps part of
the precious furnishings placed in the
tomb chamber.
Accompanying the deceased into the
afterlife, this object did much more
than simply satisfy an eternal craving
to write. To understand this one only
has to look at the scenes decorating
one of the annex chambers in the
tomb of queen Nefertari. There one
can see the deceased receiving a
scribe's palette from the hands of
Thoth himself, the very god who had
invented hieroglyphs and the calen-
dar. It was a gift that conferred on the
dead queen powers similar to those of
the gods, because writing gave her the
unfailing ability to master time.
I.F.

136

Papyrus knife
Third Intermediate Period (?)
Bronze and gold
L. 15.5 cm
Deir el-Bahri
Cairo, Egyptian Museum, JE 65359,
SR 9390

Like most of the extant examples of
such objects, this elegant papyrus knife
is in bronze. The quality of workmanship reveals it was owned by a person
of rank. The knife consists of a blade
and a handle ending with the head of
a duck turning back on itself, a common decorative motif in objects of
everyday use (cat. no. 200). There is also an inscription in damascened gold
mentioning the scribe Neferhor who
owned it. This figure was part of the
immediate entourage of the priestess
performing the role of the "god's
wife."
Contrary to what one might think, papyrus was used relatively little in ancient Egypt, because it was costly. Production was a royal monopoly, and the
finished papyrus was used sparingly,
generally for important official or ritual documents.
To make a sheet of papyrus, two fine
perpendicular layers were cut from
the stem of the reed and then placed
one on top of the other. These were
then put in a press, and the natural
substances of the plant bound them together. Several such sheets might then
be glued together at their edges, so
that the scribe could write out a long
document. However, a parsimonious
functionary might cut down a sheet
to the size he required for a short message or report. To do so, he will have
used a knife similar to this one.
I.F.

137

Seal ring with the name of Horemheb
New Kingdom, late 18th Dynasty,
reign of Horemheb
Gold
Diam. 3.85 cm
Paris, Musée du Louvre, N 747

This impressively-sized seal ring comprises a thick band and a pivoting rectangular bevel in solid gold. The incised mold decoration covers four
sides and was clearly carried out with
great care. One of the longer sides
bears a cartouche containing the
throne name of the Pharaoh Horemheb (Djoserkheperura Setepenra),
while on the other is a majestic lion,
the symbol of royal power, surmounted by the hieroglyphs *neb khepesh* (*nb
xpS*, "lord of valor"), an epithet of the
king's which appears on other monuments. The short sides have images of
a crocodile and scorpion—the latter
being very frequent on this type of
royal object.
Its form and size rule out that this ring
was ever worn; it probably served to
seal official documents. Seal rings first
made their appearance during the
Middle Kingdom and were widely
used during the New Kingdom. The
iconography that one finds on rings
of this type associates various figures,
such as lions, crocodiles and scorpions,
with the royal name—as is the case
here. These animals might be seen as
symbolizing forces that the pharaoh,
the guardian of order, has mastered
and brought to heel. However, there
are also other interpretations: images
of lions and crocodiles could be seen
as having apotropaic powers. And the
same could be said of the scorpion,
which was also associated with the notion of regeneration.

Bibliography
Boreux 1932, p. 349; Hari 1965,
p. 398.
P.R.

138

Ring of Thutmose IV
New Kingdom, 18th Dynasty,
reign of Thutmose IV
Silver
H. 2.4; W. 2.4; W. of bezel 1.7 cm
Provenance unknown
Berlin, Ägyptisches Museum
und Papyrussammlung, 8943

The pharaoh was appointed by the
gods to establish order in the world, a
task which also involved him in being
a leader of warriors. This motif is very
common in temples from the third
millennium onward, but it became a
political reality when, around the time
of the New Kingdom, Egypt came up
against the states of the Near East. Images and texts referring to war thence-
forward become realistic accounts of
actual fighting. The inscription on this
solid silver ring should thus be read in
a literal sense: "Menkheperura [Thut-
mose IV], beloved of Amun, supreme
general." In fact, during this king's
reign various campaigns were fought
in Nubia and the Near East.

Bibliography
Schäfer 1910, p. 52 (cat. 80), pl. 13;
Grimm, Schoske, Wildung 1997,
p. 114 (cat. 87).
D.W.

139

Gold finger-ring of General Djehuty
18th Dynasty, reign of Thutmose III
Gold
L. of bezel 1.85; W. of bezel 1.6;
diam. 2.95 cm
Saqqara
London, The Trustees of the British
Museum, EA 71492

This large and substantial gold ring,
weighing 35.8 grams, has a rotating
rectangular bezel bearing an incised
inscription on both faces. One side
carries the prenomen of King Thutmose III, who is described as "beloved
of Ptah, radiant of face." On the other is the pharaoh's "Two Ladies"
name, "Great of terror in all lands."
This ring formed part of the rich burial assemblage of General Djehuty, an
army commander who played an important part in Thutmose III's con-
quests in the Levant. Djehuty became
a popular hero and was immortalized
in a folk-tale, preserved on papyrus
British Museum EA 10060. In this story, he captures the port of Joppa by
smuggling soldiers into the city in baskets. His tomb at Saqqara, discovered
in the 1820s, contained many items of
jewelry, besides gold and silver vessels
inscribed with a dedication from the
king. This ring was perhaps also a gift
by Thutmose III to the general, in
recognition of his good service.
J.H.T.

140

Seal ring of Rameses II
New Kingdom, 19th Dynasty,
reign of Rameses II
Electrum (64% gold, about 30%
silver and 5% copper)
L. of bezel 2.95; W. of bezel 1,90;
diam. of ring 2.15–2.20 cm;
weight 52 gr.
Provenance unknown
Munich, Staatliches Museum
Ägyptischer Kunst, ÄS 5851

The oval seal bezel of this single-cast
ring—probably produced using the
lost-wax technique—bears an indent-
ed inscription of the name of King
Rameses II. The oval bezel has the
form of a royal cartouche within which
the name of the king was always written: "It is Ra who put him in the
world, the Beloved of Amun" reads
the translation of the birth name of
Rameses II (*c.* 1279–1213 BC), the third
sovereign of the 19th Dynasty and one
of the most important of all pharaohs
(cat. no. 19).
The hieroglyphs were cast with the ring,
and then finely tooled and polished,
which explains the extraordinary refinement of the characters. One can
see small imperfections in the casting
process and fissures in the metal, above
all in the solar disk on the upper edge
of the seal. The ring is made of an alloy
of precious metals containing primarily gold, silver and copper—an alloy
that was called "electrum" in the days
of classical antiquity. Modern analyses
reveal that Egyptian jewelry in electrum dating from the 18th and 19th
Dynasties contained between 67 to
80% gold, 15 to 19% silver and 3 to
8% copper. The composition of the alloy in this ring, therefore, conforms to
the known proportions for "electrum."
Apart from a slight scratch in the upper border of the seal bezel, this ring
is perfectly intact, and there is no sign

that it was ever worn or used. Thus it
was probably part of the funeral furnishings for the king's tomb. The inside diameter is unusually large (2.2
cm at most), which suggests it may
have been worn over a glove. We know
that linen gloves were found in the
tomb of Tutankhamun, and the king
also wore gloves when holding the
reins of his war chariot and firing his
bow. The middle and ring finger of
the left hand of Tutankhamun's mummy bore two seal rings of the same
form, though much lighter in weight.
With its precious funeral furnishings,
the tomb of Rameses II in the Valley of
the Kings had already been pillaged in
the 20th Dynasty—that is, very shortly after the pharaoh's burial. The papyri that contain accounts of the trials
of tomb robbers (the Abbott and the
Leopold II-Amherst Papyri) describe
these thefts in detail. Around the year
1000 BC, the High Priest Pinudjem ordered that the mummy of Rameses II
be rebound in new bandages and
transferred to the Deir el-Bahri cache,
where other royal mummies were kept
safe from further pillage. When the
bandages were removed in modern
times (1886), no jewels were found,
which proves they had been removed—and perhaps hidden—in ancient times. This Munich ring of
Rameses II is undoubtedly one of the
finest known examples of this type of
seal ring dating from the days of the
pharaohs. Going by the inscription on
the flat bezel, it may very well come
from the tomb of Rameses II in the
Valley of the Kings (KV7).
A.G.

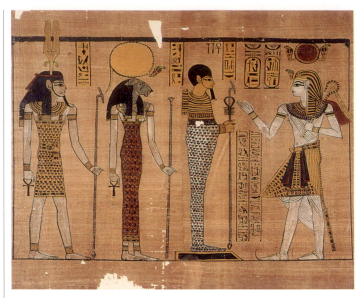

141

*Papyrus ledger; accounts of deliveries
of corn and dates*
New Kingdom, 18th Dynasty
Papyrus, red and black ink
H. 17; L. 445 cm
Provenance unknown
Paris, Musée du Louvre, E3226

This papyrus ledger is the longest administrative document of the 18th Dynasty that has come down to us. Made up of two parts of the same papyrus scroll, it bears two distinct texts written, front and back, in hieratic cursive. One is concerned with deliveries of grain, the other with deliveries of dates made in exchange for that grain. The layout of the document respects a ledger's rigid classifications, producing a practical document which can be easily compiled and consulted. The back bears the accounts of the teams of the scribe Hapu, while on the front are those of the team of the scribe My. The accounts are laid out in horizontal lines, with figures and quantities given in the left-hand margin. Though independent of each other, the two texts are the product of the same administrative service, and deal with the same agents, the same transactions and the same places.
The record covers seven years of activity by the two teams at the Central Granary (from year 28 to year 35 of the reign of Thutmose III). These men traveled to different cities to collect corn from state institutions and from the estates of temples and private individuals, sometimes redistributing it on site. This corn also served as exchange merchandise for the acquisition of dates, the other foodstuff component in the salaries of granary employees.
In theory, the king was the sole owner of all land, which he then granted to individuals, landed estates or temples.

From these he received income in the form of taxes "in kind," which could then be distributed to various institutions. The collection of these dues was the responsibility of those under the authority of the vizier. This document reveals that internal trade seems to have been a state monopoly which—in the absence of money—was one vast system of barter.

Bibliography
Megally 1971; Megally 1977.
M.E.

142

The Great Harris Papyrus
New Kingdom, 20th Dynasty,
reign of Rameses IV
Papyrus, paint
H. 46; W. 58.7 cm
Thebes
London, The Trustees of the British
Museum, EA 9999/43

The Great Harris Papyrus, 42 m long, contains an exhaustive account of the reign of Rameses III. The first section records his actions in favor of the gods, in the form of temple building and endowments throughout Egypt. Lists provide details of the scale of offerings at major temples, with emphasis on Thebes, Heliopolis and Memphis. In total, 2954 km of land and 107,615 men were provided for temples, alongside livestock, agricultural produce, precious metals and stones, imported goods and cult equipment. The second part of the papyrus is formulated as an address to mankind, and includes an account of Rameses III's military campaigns, mining expeditions and the prosperity enjoyed by Egypt during his rule. The final section of the text relates his death and the accession of Rameses IV, followed by a short *Instruction* text advising the new pharaoh about his conduct while ruling. It has been suggested that the work was produced in order to legitimize the accession of Rameses IV, particularly in light of the turbulent end to his predecessor's, who was the victim of an assassination attempt.
This vignette, one of only three, preceded the section on actions in favor of the Memphite gods. Rameses III is shown offering to Ptah, Sekhmet and Nefertem, the principal deities of the temple at Memphis. The king wears the banded *nemes* headdress with *uraeus*, a complex collar and a triangular kilt, with the lion's tail trailing be-

hind him. The three gods face the king, holding divine scepters. Ptah, the Memphite creator-god, is shown in his typical mummiform guise, while Sekhmet is depicted with the head of a lioness and the body of a woman. The figures are all identified in the hieroglyphic labels; the two lines of text between the figures states that the king "says before you the humble praise, glorifications, hymns, prayers, the great actions and deeds which I accomplished in your favor, him-who-is-south-of-his-wall [an epithet of Ptah]."
N.S.

143

Donation stele
New Kingdom, 18th Dynasty, year
45 or 47 of the reign of Thutmose III
Limestone
H. 42; W. 29.5 cm
Heliopolis (?)
Cairo, Egyptian Museum, JE 65830

This small stele is a stone record of an
act of donation made by Thutmose
III to the Mnevis bull in the year 45 or
47 of his reign (the inscription is incomplete at this point). To meet the
needs of the animal, whose worship
was closely linked with that of the sun-
god at Heliopolis, the pharaoh ceded
sixty *arure* of land, which were entrusted to the management of the Superintendent of the treasury and the
Superintendent of the Benermerut
works (perhaps the very man portrayed in cat. no. 172, even if this work
has always been dated to the 19th Dynasty due to the presence of a princess
whose name—Meritamun—is the
same as that of Rameses II's famous
daughter). The land donated was to
serve as pasture for the herds of
Mnevis.
This is a particularly important piece
because the hieroglyphic inscription
defines the Mnevis bull as "the messenger of Ra and true traveling companion of Aten." There is claimed to
be a link between this sacred animal
and the setting sun (Aten), and Mnevis
thus becomes an embodiment of dusk;
this would explain why the bull chosen
as the embodiment of the deity (to be
venerated as a hypostasis of his divine
nature) had to be completely black.

Bibliography
URK IV, 1372–1373; Kakosi 1982,
c. 165.
F.T.

*It is well known that Egyptian archeology has essentially bequeathed
to us its stone constructions, temples and tombs, dedicated to eternity.
Daily life unfolded in houses of mud-brick that were more suitable
for the climate and perishable, just like human lives. Destined to be
rapidly rebuilt, the dwellings of the ancient Egyptians still today lay
for the most part under modern cities, making them inaccessible for
excavations.
Like those of his subjects, the house of the king was built in perishable
materials. It extended over a large area, since dwelling there were
not only the sovereign and his numerous family, but also the palace
officials, innumerable servants and other personnel responsible for
the upkeep of that institution. The "Residence" moved at the same
time as the pharaoh and his court. Each monarch possessed several
palaces throughout Egypt, traveling there with his court according
to the needs of the moment.
Because of their importance, the royal palaces often extended beyond
a strictly urban area, and this has preserved them. Recent excavations
have made it possible to understand them better. Far from the official
rooms, they often included elements built in stone, and the living
quarters were spread out in the middle of sumptuous gardens.
The royal residences of Malkata on the west bank of Thebes or of Tell
el-Amarna are particularly well-preserved, so much so that one can still
today admire a part of their decoration, wherein the paintings on
the floors and walls reproduce the fresh landscape of the Nile banks.
Outside of the official residence where the "great royal wife" regularly
resided, the sovereigns had sumptuous dwellings built for their
secondary wives and numerous concubines, "tokens" of the good
relations Egypt entertained with its foreign neighbors. At Gurob,
the vestiges of important constructions were discovered that were
destined for the wives of the Crown and their young offspring. Far
from languishing in the harim of the pharaohs, the wives of the
sovereign managed their own properties and carried out economic
activities, of which weaving was the most renowned.
I.F.*

144

Westcar Papyrus
Second Intermediate Period
Papyrus
L. 33.5 cm
Provenance unknown
Berlin, Ägyptisches Museum
und Papyrussammlung, p3033

Written down on papyrus around
1600 BC, this text itself probably dates
from the era of the pyramids (middle
of the third millennium BC) and gives
a lively description of an eastern court.
Khufu, the builder of the Great Pyramid of Giza, has his sons tell him stories of marvels, and then has magicians perform their tricks before him.
The first of the five stories dates back
to the period of King Djoser; in the
last, the future is foretold and the beginning of a new dynasty is prophe-
sied. The atmosphere at King Khufu's
court as revealed in these stories is the
only direct (though fictional) insight
we have into the personal existence of
an Egyptian pharaoh of the Old Kingdom.

Bibliography
Simpson 1982, cc. 744–746; Parkinson
1997, pp. 102–127.
D.W.

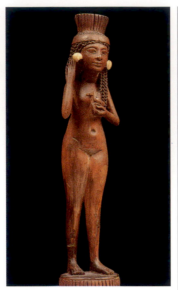

145

Makeup spoon in the form of a fish
New Kingdom, 18th Dynasty,
reign of Thutmose III
H. 9.5; L. 18.1; D. 1.9 cm
Green-enameled soapstone
Provenance unknown
New York, The Metropolitan
Museum of Art, gift of James
Douglas, 90.6.24

Cosmetics containers could take many
forms, with animal shapes being some
of the most favored. Nevertheless, it
was not very common for such makeup
spoons to come in the shape of fish
(such inhabitants of the river did, however, figure on the votive plaques from
the Predynastic period). The fish whose
hollow body serves here as the container for precious unguents is the bulti or chromis fish of the Nile (*tilapia
nilotica*), which was associated with the
powers of regeneration proper to water.
It represents the rising sun. After having been laid and fertilized, the eggs of
this fish are actually kept within a cavity in the female's mouth until they
hatch; and at the least sign of danger,
the alevins can thereafter flee back into this maternal refuge. Keen-eyed ob-
servers of the natural world, the Egyptians took the bulti fish as one of the numerous natural emblems for the different phases of rebirth. The spoon we
have here is an object of very high quality. The cartouche of Thutmose III inscribed on the fin indicates that this
must have been a royal gift. Perhaps a
zealous high functionary was accompanied to his tomb by this precious
fish, which not only contained the
unguents indispensable for the preservation of the body but was also a symbol of the promise of eternal rebirth.

Bibliography
Arnold 1995, p. 37; Lilyquist 1995, p. 50.
I.F.

146

Mirror handle
New Kingdom, late 18th–early
19th Dynasty
Wood and ivory
14.5 × 3.4 × 3 cm
Provenance unknown
Bologna, Museo Civico
Archeologico, Palagi Collection,
KS 1859

The graceful, sensuous body of this
young girl formed the handle of a met-
al-plate mirror, a favorite toilette article among rich Egyptian ladies. A
bronze or silver disk, now lost, was
joined to the head of the statuette by
a tenon whose hole is visible at the
center of the feathered *modius* crown-
ing the wig. Although the viewer's attention is at first drawn to the long
curls held by a ribbon behind the head
and the large ivory earrings, the careless gesture with which the girl casts a
lock of hair over her right shoulder,
pressing to her bosom a tiny open-
winged bird, while she barely moves
her left leg, incites to discover the entire nudity of her body, modeled with
balanced harmony, delicate fullness
and vital tension. Perhaps it was like
this—forever youthful—that the owner of the mirror wished to see herself,
while using it every morning.
D.P.

147

Stool
New Kingdom
Wood (restored), ivory inlay
H. 36.3; L. 38; W. 46.1 cm
West Thebes (?)
Brussels, Musées Royaux d'Art
et d'Histoire, E 2409

The decoration of the tombs of high
functionaries gives us some idea of the
environment in which they lived.
There are very few extant urban sites,
and those traces there are have yielded up very slight information on the
daily life of a high-ranking Egyptian.
The wall decorations in tomb chapels
show us that the members of the upper levels of society ate their meals
seated on low chairs or stools, with
the food placed in front of them on little occasional tables.
This Brussels stool is a very fine example of quality furniture. As was often the case, the feet are sculpted in the
form of lion paws; and a luxury detail
here is the use of ivory inlay to depict
the claws. On either side of the seat,
the furniture-maker has created the
figure of an animal, whose body is
stretched out between the two feet of
the stool. This motif recalls some features of royal furnishings known to us
through the tomb of Tutankhamun,
which contained beds modeled in the
shape of a cow, a hippopotamus and a
large feline.

Bibliography
Seipel 1989.
I.F.

148

Stool
New Kingdom, mid-18th Dynasty
Wood, stuccoed and painted linen
seat
40 × 40 × 24.5 cm
Thebes
Turin, Museo Egizio, Drovetti
Collection, 6404

Square stool with wooden frame and seat made of stuccoed and painted linen. The frame consists of four cylindrical legs that are slightly tapered in the lower part, joined at mid-height by horizontal, cylindrical crossbars. The legs, painted black to simulate precious ebony wood, are adorned at the upper tips with a geometric motif emulating ivory inlays. In the point where they connect with the crossbars, the legs are enhanced on the outer side with painted red and white concentric squares that simulate polychrome inlays, and on the inner side with a yellow papyrus plant corolla, it also ivory. The concave seat is formed by overlaid pieces of linen fabric, stuccoed and decorated in red, the color recalling leather seats of precious chairs. The center is enhanced with a pictorial decoration of concentric squares with floral and geometric motifs, blue and red on a white background, probably reproducing a cushion. The slight structure of the stool and the material with which it is made suggest that this furnishing was not an article of everyday use but had been made exclusively for the grave goods. This typology is attested in the first half of the 18th Dynasty and is comparable to the stool from the grave of Kha (Suppl. 8507) or to the wooden stool of the British Museum (2472), with ivory inlays and leather seat.

Bibliography
Donadoni Roveri 1987, fig. 211 p. 157.
M.B.

149

Folding stool
New Kingdom, 18th Dynasty
Ebony, ivory inlays, bronze pivot
pins
L. of base 54; L. of top 43; H. 37 cm
Toronto, Royal Ontario Museum,
914.2.1

The elegant wooden folding stool was made of two round base bars with bent duck's head finials, two crossbars also terminating with duck's heads and two thin, flat rails to support the seat. Most stools have leather sets, but the small holes in the top indicate that the Toronto piece, like the one in New York was designed to hold a woven seat.

Although the folding stools, called by the Egyptians *isbwt*, first appeared during the Middle Kingdom, they become most popular during the New Kingdom, especially the 18th Dynasty. Several folding stools were found in the tomb of Tutankhamun. In the tomb paintings, such as in the Theban tomb of Nebamen and Ipuki, it is the officials who sit on such stools suggesting their role as a status symbol.

Bibliography
P. Der Manuelian in: Freed 1982, pp. 63–76; Desroches-Noblecourt 1963; Hayes 1959; Zonhoven 1979.
K.J.

150

Casket of Rameses IX
New Kingdom, 20th Dynasty,
reign of Rameses IX
Wood, ivory and colored inlays
H. 22; L. 24; W. 22.5 cm
Thebes, Deir el-Bahri cache
Cairo, Egyptian Museum, JE 26271

The sides and top of this small, short-legged casket have inset panels coated with black resin, in imitation of ebony, now badly cracked. The sides and panels are joined by tenon and mortise with adhesive glue to the four legs. The panels have borders of colored inlay and lines of hieroglyphic inscriptions, written on an ivory facing, with the titulary of the king. The front panel has a small knob.

This splendid casket was found in the tomb of Queen Inhapy at Deir el-Bahri, which was used by the Theban high priests of Amun of the 21st Dynasty for their burials and those of their families. At the end of the dynasty, when they were no longer able to protect the royal burials in the Valley of the Kings from pillage, the priests transferred some of the royal dead and what remained of their burial equipment to this tomb as well. There they remained undisturbed there their modern discovery at the end of the XIX century.

It was during Rameses IX's reign that the scandal of the tomb robberies broke out and royal commissions were formed to carry out investigations. While meeting with temporary success, they did not abate the looting and Rameses IX's own burial suffered the same fate.
A.M.

151

Tamit's chest
New Kingdom, second half
of the 18th Dynasty
Painted wood
36 × 36 × 30 cm
Thebes
Turin, Museo Egizio, Drovetti
Collection, 2448

Wooden chest with square base and rectangular sides, fitted with a square lid. The sides of the chest are decorated at the center with an "imitation wood" panel emulating a coniferous wood, and are trimmed with a cornice featuring polychrome geometric patterns. The decorative motif of the central panel that we might describe in modern terms as *trompe l'œil*, is rather widespread in Egypt, where precious wood is quite rare. Instead the cornice emulates inlays in precious materials such as ivory, ebony, turquoise, lapis lazuli and cornelian. The feet of the chest as well are decorated with polychrome geometric motifs, green, red and blue, reproducing precious stone inlays. The flat lid is enhanced with two rectangular "imitation wood" panels, also framed by a cornice with polychrome geometric designs. It was attached to the chest by hinges made of wooden bars, of which all that remains is a trace of their housing. The fastening consists of two button knobs, held by a rope tie with buttonhole tips, in part still conserved. On one of the knobs we can read the name of the owner of the chest, Tamit. The simple assembling technique it suggests it was meant only for the burial goods and not for everyday use.

Bibliography
Donadoni Roveri 1987, fig. 212 p. 157.
M.B.

152

Game of senet *belonging to Imenmes*
New Kingdom, 18th Dynasty
Wood
L. 36; W. 12; H .17 cm
Provenance unknown
Paris, Musée du Louvre, E 2710

The game of *senet* was played on a board of thirty squares, on which the pieces moved in the order of boustrophedon script—from left to right, then right to left. If the rules of this ancient ancestor of the game of "Snakes and Ladders" are still not totally clear, we do know that the players had to avoid certain squares that a hieroglyph identified as unlucky, and try to land on others with hieroglyphs indicating perfection. (On the various Egyptian table games, see the exh. cat. *Jouer dans l'Antiquité*, RMN, 1992.) The very name of the game means "to pass," thus referring to the movement of the pieces.

The introductory paragraph to Spell 17 of the Book of the Dead announces the various transformations that the deceased may go through before achieving his eternal destiny. This process is like a game of *senet*, and the vignette of the deceased—in papyri or on the walls of tombs (for example, that of Queen Nefertari)—often shows him playing this game (sometimes accompanied by his wife, who is seated alongside him). Obviously, here *senet* is not an agreeable pastime for whiling away the afterlife; it probably serves as an image of the deceased's passage through the various difficulties present in the netherworld.

Boxes with the game were a fixed part of funeral furnishings, as one can see from the numerous examples that have come to light in necropolises. This one for Imenmes is very finely made. The inscription along the two long sides of the box mention the traditional of-ferings of the king, who in gratifying a god with a surfeit of food and drink attracted the beneficence of the deity upon the deceased.

On one of the short sides one sees Imenmes playing against an invisible opponent, while a cupbearer holds out a goblet of wine. As in most of the depictions of games of *senet*, the pieces are cylindrical or bobbin-shaped.

Bibliography
Decker, Herb 1994.
I.F.

153

*Game pieces modeled in the form
of prisoners*
New Kingdom (?)
Blue, green and black glazed faience
E 1660 (H. 2.9; diam. 2.5 cm);
E 1661 (H. 2.8; diam. 2.7 cm);
E 1662 (H. 2.5; diam. 2.1 cm);
E 3624 (H. 2.7; diam. 2.5 cm);
E 8396 (H. 2.2; diam. 1.9 cm);
E 22704 (H. 3.6 cm)
Provenance unknown
Paris, Musée du Louvre, E 1660,
E 1661, E 1662, E 3624, E 8396,
E 22704

Indispensable for the players of board
games, the pieces could come in various forms—depending on the type of
game involved. Certain were modeled
in the form of animals or of deities
such as Bes. Probably these were not
used for *senet* (see cat. no. 152) but for
other types of board games. (On the
various Egyptian table games, see the
exh. cat. *Jouer dans l'Antiquité*, RMN,
1992.) Undoubtedly, their significance
was positive, because during the
course of the game the player would
be handling images of the protectors of
divine order.
These game pieces from the Louvre
are not the only examples of those
which are modeled as bound prisoners. We do not know exactly in what
game they figured. However, they take
up a theme that was constant in Egyptian iconography, symbolizing the enemies of Egypt and—by extension—of
the equilibrium established by the
gods. Neutralized by the magic of the
image, they are now rendered forever
harmless. If they were used in a board
game, they were the opposite to pieces
modeled as the forces of good—rather
like the black and white pieces in modern games. Thus the two players will
have been doing more than simply engaging in a pastime; they will have
been acting out the eternal combat between good and evil. Defeat of the enemies of the order incarnated in Egypt
and its pharaoh might thus become a
motif taken up by the most modest
accessories of everyday life.

Bibliography
Etienne 2000, p. 101 (E 1660).
I.F.

154

Cylindrical box
New Kingdom, 18th Dynasty
Cedarwood, linen, gesso, ebony, ivory,
gold
H. 21.6 × D. 12.1 cm
Thebes
Edinburgh, The Trustees of the
National Museums of Scotland,
A. 1956.113

This box was found by the Scottish
excavator Alexander Henry Rhind at
Thebes in 1857. It is probably from the
Rhind Tomb. Two of the ivory inlay
plaques bear cartouches of Amenhotep II. The most striking feature of
this unique box is the high-relief figure
of Bes.

Bibliography
Petrie 1895–1896; Aldred 1961, pp.
58–59, no. 56.
E.G., B.M.

155

Fan head (flabellum)
New Kingdom, 18th Dynasty,
reign of Amenhotep III
Wood
H. 20.3; W. 5.1;
diam. of head 1.2 cm
Provenance unknown
Paris, Musée du Louvre, E 17112

This part must have been fixed at the
end of a long handle. Sculpted from a
single piece of wood, it has an entirely hollowed summit in which the clip
held the ostrich feathers that have now
disappeared. The fixture is in the form
of a papyrus reed with an opened umbel, while the clip is in the form of a
palmetto, one side of which is decorated with the double cartouche of
King Amenhotep III enclosed within
an Egyptian frieze. The engraving was
encrusted with blue paste—undoubtedly that pigment known as "Egyptian
Blue"—obtained from the baking of a
mixture of finely-ground quartz, limestone, copper oxide and a few alkalis
(natron or vegetable cinders). In a
country with such a hot climate, a fan
waved by a servant was clearly a sign
of great social status; and inevitably it
became an accessory of the parades
in which the pharaoh and the statues
of the gods appeared in public. It was
a great honor to be appointed as fanbearer for such occasions; from the
18th Dynasty onward, the title "fanbearer on the king's right hand" was
one reserved to the highest dignitaries.
There are various types of extant fans;
in the tomb of Tutankhamun, three
fans in the form of elongated buds
were found, one still complete with
its plumes.
G.P.

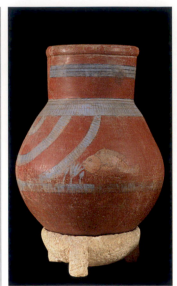

156
Painted vase
New Kingdom, 18th Dynasty
Painted ceramic
H. 43 cm
Provenance unknown
Berlin, Ägyptisches Museum
und Papyrussammlung, 14412

We do not know if the owner of this painted vase drove a war chariot or worked in the royal stables. The artist who decorated this food jar with two galloping stallions was clearly fascinated by a subject matter that was still unusual. In effect, it was only from around 1600 BC that the Egyptians began to raise horses. When this vase was painted, Egyptian art had yet to establish fixed rules for this new iconographical motif. The use of such a motif by itself—as on this jar—is most unusual.

Bibliography
Settgast 1989, pp. 64–65 (cat. 33).
D.W.

157
Painted vase
New Kingdom, 18th Dynasty
Painted ceramic
H. 62 cm
Tell el-Amarna, house O 50,2
(excavations of the Deutsche
Orientgesellschaft, 1912)
Berlin, Ägyptisches Museum
und Papyrussammlung, Inv. 22355

We have scant knowledge of the layout and furnishings of an ancient Egyptian palace. For a long time archaeology neglected domestic architecture, which appeared less spectacular than that of tombs or temples. The excavations carried out at el-Amarna, the capital of Akhenaten, are an exception. In the well-preserved ruins of palaces and private homes, archaeologists have found numerous utensils and pieces of furniture. This large ceramic vase found in a house at Amarna offered refreshment not only through its contents of cold water but also through its cooling decoration of fish and lotus flowers.

Bibliography
Priese 1991, pp. 123–124 (cat. 75).
D.W.

158
Goblet
New Kingdom, 19th–20th Dynasties
Glazed blue faience
H. 14; L. sides of the mouth
8 and 7 cm
Florence, Museo Egizio, Nizzoli
Collection, N. 3254

This elegant goblet, with a truncated cone-shaped foot, represents a partly closed lotus flower whose petals are outlined in light relief on the body. The goblet's square mouth is a rare feature in Egyptian vessel production: the angles of the mouth probably indicate the tips of the lotus petals that are about to blossom. Lotiform faience goblets made their appearance during the 18th Dynasty and are attested until the 22nd. This kind of container, destined for high-ranking personalities, must have been used for religious rituals, especially funerary ones, here underlined by the lotus which symbolizes resurrection: at least that is what the representations on tomb walls and the funerary stelae lead us to suppose.

Bibliography
Guidotti 1991, p. 262 (cat. 432) with previous bibliography; Saleh 1999, p. 230 (cat. 65).
M.C.G.

159
Bowl of Maiherpri
New Kingdom, 18th Dynasty
Blue faience
Diam. 14 cm
Thebes, Valley of the Kings,
tomb of Maiherpri (KV36)
Cairo, Egyptian Museum, CG 24058
= JE 33825

Maiherpri, "fanbearer on the king's right hand" and "child of the nursery," was probably of Nubian descent. His tomb was discovered intact by Loret in 1899 in an uninscribed tomb in the Valley of the Kings at Thebes. This small bowl, part of his funerary goods, is made of faience, fritted ground quartz. It was probably modeled over a core, then decorated with black ink on the inside and outside, and fired to give the vessel its lustrous finish. The outside is painted with an open lotus flower, depicted from the top. Inside the bowl are aquatic scenes, two bulti fish are about to hatch their eggs, while a third fish holds a papyrus blossom in its mouth. Both the bulti fish and the papyrus are symbols of rebirth and resurrection. An oryx with two horns and one ear eats a plant while her baby suckles. The upper edge of the bowl is decorated with triangles. This bowl probably served as a drinking vessel for the afterlife.
A.M.

160

Amphora
New Kingdom
Light-red fireclay. Inscription almost totally erased
H. 65; max. diam. 22;
diam. of opening 9.5 cm
Probably Abydos (Amélineau excavations)
Paris, Musée du Louvre, E 30547

Innumerable scenes reflecting the production of wine show two-handled amphorae like this one. If one is to believe the—undoubtedly cryptic—depictions, the crushed grape was poured directly into the amphorae from the wine press. The opening was then closed with a bundle of vegetable fibers covered with a large "capsule" of dried mud. Most amphorae show no trace of any resinous coating on the inside (to prevent evaporation); hence it would seem that the wine was drunk quite quickly after being "bottled."
G.P.

161

Fragment of an amphora bearing a "wine jar label" inscription
New Kingdom, 19th Dynasty, reign of Rameses III
Red-brown fireclay
H. 10.8; W. 17.6; D. *c.* 0.5 cm
Abydos (Amélineau excavations)
Paris, Musée du Louvre, E 22395

Wine played an important part in the palace economy. Produced in state vineyards—the most famous of which were in the Delta and the Fayum area—it was one of the rations distributed by the palace administration. These two fragments come from the shoulder of a wine amphora similar to cat. no. 160. The inscription—in very casual hieratic cursive—indicates that the contents were produced in the vineyards of Rameses III, probably in the Delta region. The name of the vintner appears on the last line, and is almost totally destroyed. Documents of this type are of great help in dating when areas were occupied by the pharaoh's functionaries. Such jar labels are among the oldest extant examples of hieroglyphic inscriptions.
G.P.

162

Small bottle
New Kingdom
Brown fireclay
H. 21; max. diam. 9 cm
Deir el-Medina (B. Bruyère excavations. Share of the finds, 1935)
Paris, Musée du Louvre, E 14619

In the paintings of banquets decorating the Theban tomb-chapels of the New Kingdom, small elongated vases like this one—with a round base and a slightly narrowed opening—are shown in the hands of servants as they pour drinks for the guests. Indeed, it would not have been very practical to try and serve wine straight from the large amphorae. One did not drink directly from this vase, put poured the wine or beer from it into the cup held by the guests.
G.P.

163

Grooved free-standing cup
New Kingdom
Red wood
H. 3.5; diam. 9 cm
Provenance unknown
Paris, Musée du Louvre, E 198

For generations, Egyptians had been using round-based cups as drinking vessels when—during the New Kingdom—new, more elaborate, forms of tableware began to appear. One such is this cup with its elegantly modeled base. In the tomb of the sculptor Nebamun, his wife is shown holding out a similarly-shaped vessel, encouraging her husband to drink and enjoy the present. The cup on exhibition here is turned in a core of very fine red-colored hardwood. Other receptacles of similar form but made in alabaster were undoubtedly used to contain the perfumed pomades that were passed around during banquets.
G.P.

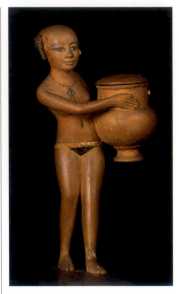

164

Large cup
New Kingdom, first half
of the 18th Dynasty
Brown fireclay, with vegetable
and mineral additions
H. 6.3; diam. 20 cm
Deir el-Medina, eastern cemetery
(B. Bruyère excavations)
Paris, Musée du Louvre, E 14638 a

This very flared open cup was the most
common type of tableware. The only
intact examples come from tombs.
Such cups were used to contain the
food that was placed in the burial
chambers of the 18th Dynasty. The
polishing of the slip on the inside was
designed to make the vessel less
porous and protect the contents from
contact with the dusty ground.
G.P.

165

Unguent vessel of Siamun
New Kingdom, 18th Dynasty,
reign of Amenhotep IV-Akhenaten
Painted wood inlaid with ivory
H. 14 cm
West Thebes, Sheikh Abd el-Qurna,
tomb of Hatiay (G. Daressy
excavations, 1896)
Cairo, Egyptian Museum, JE 31382

This cosmetic vessel together with other toiletry articles was discovered in lady Siamun's coffin in the tomb of the
head of the family, Hatiay, a scribe and
granary official of the temple of Aten.
The statuette represents a servant in
the process of rising from a kneeling
position with a heavy vessel on his
shoulders. His head is shaven and he
wears a short pleated kilt. The load
he carries is a miniature version of a
Syrian amphora inlaid with ivory. The
tall, wide neck is decorated with geometric and stylized flower patterns and
the belly with a scene in which three
calves frolic under the trees. The lid,
inlaid with a figure of a calf, is attached
to the handle by a string sealed with
clay. It was intended to contain cosmetic unguents imported from Crete.

Bibliography
Daressy 1901, p. 9, fig. 9; Le Caire
2002, p. 39.
Z.T.

166

*Statuette of a young girl holding
a vase*
New Kingdom, 18th Dynasty,
reign of Amenhotep III
Wood, traces of paint, dyed ivory,
gold and pigments
H. 13.3; W. 7.1; perim. 4 cm
West Thebes, Sheik Abd el-Qurna
Durham, The Oriental Museum,
N 752

Unguents, perfumes and makeup were
part of the refinements of life for those
who belonged to the upper classes in
Egypt. Such products might be contained in small bowls or, as here, in
small vases held by servants (cat. nos.
165, 167). Cosmetics were considered
of such importance that they were included with the tomb furnishings that
might be useful to the deceased in the
afterlife. A—now lost—tomb was the
site where this small statuette of a nude
servant girl bearing a receptacle was
found.
In Egyptian statuary the figures were
depicted face-on, a hieratic pose that
reflected concern with rendering sovereigns and high functionaries eternal. The same criteria were followed in
the paintings and bas-reliefs adorning
tombs, which show the figures frozen
in conventional poses. However, if one
looks at the scenes of so-called everyday life, one sees that many of the rules
have disappeared. Given that they are
not present as themselves but only as
figures performing specific actions,
the different characters acquire a certain freedom of movement, which enables Egyptian painters to give free
rein to their imagination. This same
breaking-away from traditional canons
can be seen in the Durham statuette of
a young girl. Though small in size, this
young servant has remarkable presence and seems to be on the point of
moving. Seen from the front, the

unguent jar she carries on her hip
seems heavy, and the balance of the
composition is maintained by her shifting her weight onto one leg. The tor-
sion in the body and the bending of
the right knee are better seen from the
side, where one can also see the twist-
ing of the shoulders; and from the
back, the impression of movement is
even stronger. A pure rendition of
physical grace, this small figure of a
young girl has a dynamism that is astonishing in Egyptian sculpture.

Bibliography
Kozloff, Bryan, Berman, Delange
1993, pp. 319–320.
I.F.

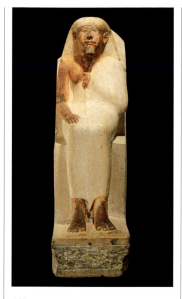

167

Dwarf carrying a jar
New Kingdom, 18th Dynasty,
reign of Akhenaten
Wood
5.9 × 1.8 × 2.6 cm
Said to be from Tell el-Amarna
Boston, Museum of Fine Arts, Helen
and Alice Colburn Fund, 48.296

Although at first glance this tiny statuette of a dwarf appears to be uninscribed, closer examination reveals cartouches of Akhenaten and Nefertiti barely half a centimeter high incised on the jar he carries. Dwarves had afforded great fascination to kings at least since the Old Kingdom when a young King Pepy II expressed his excitement at the pair the nomarch Harkhuf had captured for him on an excursion to Nubia. In Akhenaten's household, they seem to have been especially favored, based on the evidence provided by relief representations in Amarna's rock-cut tombs, where groups of dwarves dance with abandon at the arrival of the royal family. Based on these frequent representations, it seems likely that dwarves like the one pictured here were present in Akhenaten's court.
Although Akhenaten's artists are best known for the stylizations with which they portrayed human figures, they also realistically captured unusual character types and extremes of youth and age. Accordingly, it is not surprising to find this dwarf so accurately portrayed, both in terms of his figural proportions and his movement. In order to accommodate the weight of the jar he carries, a vessel nearly half his size, his left hip is raised, his upper torso bends to the right and his head thrusts forward. In this way, the artist has successfully captured a single moment in time. The container has been hollowed out, and probably once held a cosmetic unguent. Such naturalistically rendered figures of both men and women bearing vessels were in vogue from the middle to the end of the 18th Dynasty. Unusually, here the figure and its base were carved from a single piece of wood.

Bibliography
S. D'Auria in: Freed, Markowitz, D'Auria 1999, pp. 123, 264.
R.E.F.

168

Statue of the fanbearer Thenuna
New Kingdom, 18th Dynasty,
reign of Thutmose IV
Painted limestone
H. 56; W. 15.8; D. 35.7 cm
West Thebes (?)
Vienna, Kunsthistorisches Museum,
ÄS 63

Down to the slightest details, this statue of "Director of the [Tribunal] Hall, Director of the Works of Construction . . . Thenuna," who was also honored with the office of "fanbearer to the king's right hand," reveals him to have been a great dignitary. He is sitting on a high-backed chair wearing a long wig of parallel plaits, as well as a fashionable goatee. With his left hand, he holds across his chest his long white cloak with a decorated border.
The inscriptions appear on the base of statue and its back (which takes the form of a stele). They were very carefully produced, but some time later a hammer was deliberately taken to them. The texts on the base have entirely disappeared. However, on the back, one can still read the name and some of the titles of the figure, which are included in the traditional offering formula. The tomb which can most probably be identified as created for Thenuna (TT76) also bears marks of the same hammering. This *damnatio memoriae* was carried out officially: for some reason unknown to us, Thenuna had fallen into disgrace.
H.S.

169

Lintel of Nebmose
New Kingdom, 19th–20th Dynasties
Limestone
215 × 75 cm
Provenance unknown
London, The Trustees of the British
Museum, EA 1465

This lintel, from above a doorway in a tomb-chapel, depicts two near-identical scenes of the deceased, Nebmose, seated before a table of offerings. He receives offerings from a chantress of Isis, Baketankhet. Small details differ between the scenes, such as the style of chair in which the deceased is seated and the nature of the offering. Nebmose's titles reveal an association with royalty, as he is a "fanbearer on the king's right" and royal scribe, but also more specific roles such as overseer of the treasury and high priest of Isis lord of Hebyt. The latter is the ancient Egyptian term for Behbeit el-Hagar, where a massive granite temple to Isis was erected in the 30th Dynasty. This lintel provides evidence for a precursor in Ramesside times, but as no cemetery has been identified in the area, it is impossible to ascertain whether the relief comes from a nearby tomb. Alternatively, Nebmose may have been buried at Saqqara, as with so many elite officials of the period.
N.S.

170

*Statue of Manakhtef, cupbearer
to the king*
New Kingdom, 18th Dynasty, reign
of Amenhotep II (on the evidence of
the cartouche engraved on the right
shoulder)
Diorite
H. 50; W. 23; perim. 29.5 cm
Medamud (north of Thebes), temple
of Montu
Paris, Musée du Louvre, E 12926

This work of sculpture is a veritable archetype of temple statuary, not only because of its cubic form but also because the scribe has, very obligingly, given us "Instructions for use" in the inscription on the right side of the figure. These take the form of an invocation to the temple of Montu: ". . . May you grant that this statue of the cupbearer to the king, Manakhtef, may remain within the great hall of feasts, may breathe the myrrh and the incense in the flame . . . . May eat of what is offered by the hands of the pure priests at the moment of divine offering . . . . May accompany his god when he moves around his temple during his feast . . . just like I did when I was on earth." Thus the statue was an exact substitute for Manakhtef, replacing him in all the actions he might have performed in the temple.
This cupbearer clearly was a considerable figure. Nine columns of hieroglyphs are engraved in front of his legs (in a format characteristic of the 18th Dynasty) to list his prerogatives in administering temple and royal estates. At the end of the list, the title "cupbearer to the king" appears almost as a sign of apotheosis. This clearly indicates that the real influence of the king's "cellarman" went well beyond the management of royal libations. The power of these "cupbearers to the king" is well documented within the pharaonic administration of the second half of the 18th Dynasty. However, both power and life pass. A shrewd man, Manakhtef has completed his monument with an inscription (on the left side) taken from Spell 106 of the Book of the Dead, which makes his demand for food and drink ever present, now and for evermore.

Bibliography
Drioton 1927, no. 354, pp. 49–51 and fig. 23 (*editio princeps*); Schulz 1992.I, pp. 456–457, no. 272 (with previous bibliography) and 1992.II, pl. 120 (b/w reproduction).
C.B.

171

Statue of Senenmut
New Kingdom
Black granite
Luxor
Chicago, The Field Museum of
Natural History, gift of Stanley Field
and Ernest Graham, 173800

Senenmut was a chief official for Queen Hatshepsut, functioning as a statesman, architect, administrator, and favored supporter. He raised the queen's daughter, Princess Neferura, who is depicted here in his arms. Senenmut wears an elaborate shoulder length wig. Neferura has the royal insignia or *uraeus* on her brow, wears her hair in the heavy sidelock distinctive of royal youth, and holds a scepter. Senenmut fell into disfavor with subsequent rulers, and the hieroglyph of his name has been effaced (the first character to the left in the first and third rows of hieroglyphs). The inscription on the statue may be translated: "Given as a favor from the king [to] the hereditary noble, count and steward of Amun, Senenmut. A boon which the king gives to Amun, Lord of the Thrones of the Two Lands, that he may give all that is issued from his offering table in the course of every day to the ka of the Good God, overseer of the double granaries of Amun, Senenmut.
He says, 'I was a dignitary, beloved of his lord, who was familiar with the behavior of the Lady of the Two Lands [Hatshepsut], for he had aggrandized me before Two Lands and appointed me to be master of his house, one who rendered judgment in the entire land inasmuch as I was efficient in his opinion. I reared the eldest princess, the god's wife [Neferura], may she live. It was as Father of the Goddess that I was appointed for her inasmuch as I was serviceable to the king.'
Chancellor of the Lower Egyptian King, Senenmut; hereditary noble, guardian of the Shrine of Geb, master of the servants of Amun, Senenmut, justified. It is the steward, Senenmut, who has come from the flood, to whom inundation has been given, so that he has power over it as the Nile-flood."
D.R.-M.

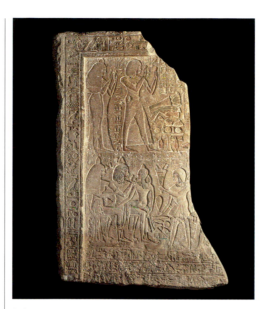

172

*Statue of Benermerut with
the princess Meritamun*
New Kingdom, 19th Dynasty,
reign of Rameses II
Gray granite
H. 70 cm
Karnak, temple of Amun,
cachette court
Cairo, Egyptian Museum,
CG 42171 = JE 36922

The block statue, one of ancient
Egypt`s most original sculptural types,
was found in extremely diversified
forms during the course of Egyptian
history. In this case, the child`s head
emerging from its tutor's mantle represents an 18th-Dynasty innovation,
as does the statue of Senenmut with
Hatshepsut`s daughter. This combi-
nation touchingly displays the exclu-
sivity of the tutor`s charge.
Benermerut, sits on a high rounded
base, and wears a round, tight mush-
room-like wig that hides his ears; his
facial features represent the style of
the 19th Dynasty. The chubby child's
hair is plaited, her finger is at her
mouth, and her name inscribed
around her head.
Benermerut was superintendent of the
treasury of Upper and Lower Egypt
and the chief of all the royal works.
Nine lines of hieroglyphic inscriptions
are on his mantle; the inscription is a
traditional offering formula which invokes the god to give provision to the
statue's owner.
A.M.

173

Bas-relief of Merira
New Kingdom, 18th Dynasty,
reign of Amenhotep III
Limestone
H. 97; L. 130; D. 15 cm
Saqqara, bas-relief from a tomb
Vienna, Kunsthistorisches Museum,
ÄS 5814

The Saqqara tomb of Merira, director
of the Treasury and tutor to the prince,
was discovered in the XIX century,
but then all trace of it was lost. It is only in the last few years that it has been
rediscovered.
This, originally polychrome, bas-relief
mural presents the iconographic program of a tomb stele in two sections.
The upper shows the deceased, with
his wife, adoring the sun-god under
the name of Ra-Horakhty-Atum. In
the lower section, he is shown receiving funeral offerings. There is an insistence here on his role as tutor to
the prince: the deceased is depicted
offering some fruit to a son of the royal family who is sitting on his knee.
Child and tutor both wear a pleated
robe with a perfumed ointment cone
on their heads. The child has the "sidelock of youth" which consists of a
strand or lock of head falling down to
one side of an otherwise shaven head.
The inscription gives the name of the
prince: Satum. There is only one other piece of evidence which bears out
the existence of a royal son of that
name in this period.
H.S.

174

*Stele of Amenhotep I and Ahmose
Nefertari*
New Kingdom, late 18th Dynasty
Limestone
H. 52; W. 41 cm
West Thebes, Sheikh Abd el-Qurna
Cairo, Egyptian Museum, JE 27573
= CG 34337

This stele is one of numerous objects
found scattered along the west bank of
the river at Luxor which can be interpreted as *ex-voto* to a deified dead sovereign whose apotheosis had made
him into one of the tutelary deities of
the Theban necropolis.
The upper part is entirely occupied
by a scene in which two royal couples
sit either side of a table loaded with offerings. To the left is Ahmose and Ahmose Nefertari; to the right, Amenhotep I and, again, Ahmose Nefertari.
The double presence of the queen is
explained by the fact that she was wife
of Ahmose and mother of Amenhotep.
Ahmose is wearing the blue crown, a
sort of war helmet (perhaps to record
his military exploits, which finally
drove the Hyksos from Egypt). In the
lower part of the monument are two
figures identified by inscriptions as
priests: on the left is the *wab* Se-
mentawy; to the right, the *sedjem-ash*
Huy. Both are kneeling and looking
toward the center, with their hands
raised in front of the faces in the typical gesture of prayer. The object of
their veneration is a double expression of adoration for Amenhotep I (on
the left) and Ahmose (on the right).
Though rather stylized, the rendering
of the scene reveals that fluidity of
form which enables us to date this
stele the post-Amarna period.
F.T.

175

*Statuette of Amenhotep I
and Ahmose Nefertari*
New Kingdom, late 18th–early
19th Dynasties
Black soapstone
H. 20.3 cm (with the head of the
king)
Probably from western Thebes
Durham, The Oriental Museum,
N 495

This statuette depicting Amenhotep I and his mother Ahmose Nefertari is interesting for more than one reason. The queen and her son were worshipped as deities, and there are numerous stelae which bear witness to the popular devotion of which they were the object (cat. nos. 60, 61, 174). However, this is the only extant three-dimensional depiction of the famous couple known to us. The date put forward by Cl. Vandersleyen is based on convincing stylistic considerations, which would make this one of the earliest posthumous depictions of Amenhotep I and Ahmose Nefertari we have—indicating that the veneration of the couple was very ancient, going back to the beginning of the Ramesside period, or even a little earlier.
The history of this object itself as related by Cl. Vandersleyen is a perfect example of the good luck that is sometimes the basis of archaeological work. When found, at the beginning of the XIX century, the statue was damaged: a corner of the base was broken, and the king was missing his head and his right elbow. It was in this state that the piece became part of the collection at the Durham Oriental Museum. However, Amenhotep was not destined to remain headless forever, because Cl. Vandersleyen identified his head among the pieces of a private collection. That fragment came from the left bank at Thebes, which sug-

gests that was also the origin of the statue. This "matching" of scattered fragments is becoming more and more frequent: the Durham Museum, for example, has a small figure of Amenhotep III in glazed soapstone (N. 496), the head of which is in the Egyptian Museum in Cairo.
In accordance with the conventions of Egyptian sculpture, the statute of Amenhotep I and his mother depicts the two characters as if they were husband and wife. The symmetrical composition shows Ahmose Nefertari holding the floral scepter of queens in her left hand, and Amenhotep holding the *heka* scepter, one of the very insignia of royalty (cat. no. 32), in his right. A cast of the head of Amenhotep I now completes the statue. The king is wearing the blue crown (or *khepresh*, cat. no. 29), the wide necklace and a royal pagne with an elaborately worked front section. The queen's headdress comprises the symbols of royal and divine maternity: a vulture, with the wings falling down to frame a wig of fine plaits. The cap that surmounts the headdress is also a typical feature of the iconography of goddesses and "great royal wives."
The two figures are wearing sandals, which means they are not shown as if officiating at a temple, the sacred ground of which was only to be trodden by bare feet.
The back prop to this double statue is incised with the names and titles of mother and son. The queen is referred to using the epithets that regard her role when alive. As sovereign, she was the woman whose words enabled each person to rejoice. She was also the "god's wife"—that is, priestess of Amun at Thebes—and in that role her hands were pure while she held the *sistrum* (cat. nos. 87, 88). As for the son, he is identified with the usual ti-

tles of a pharaoh, but he is also described as Son of Amun and of divine seed—underlining the close bonds between the great god of Karnak and the monarchs of the 18th Dynasty.

Bibliography
Birch 1880; Vandersleyen 1983.
I.F.

176

Wesekh necklace of Ahhotep
New Kingdom, 18th Dynasty,
reign of Ahmose I
Gold and semi-precious stones
W. 37.5 cm
Thebes, Dra Abu el-Naga, tomb
of Queen Ahhotep
Cairo, Egyptian Museum, JE 4725 =
CG 52672

As attested from the wall decorations in temples, Egyptian kings used to wear *wesekh* necklaces with falcon heads on both sides for many reasons. First, because the falcon head refers to the sun-god Horus, the patron deity of royalty and state; secondly, it put the wearer king under the protection of that god, thus providing him with a magical protection; thirdly, because of its majestic design and form; and lastly because of the materials used in the collar and their symbolic meanings. In addition to all the above-mentioned reasons and the beautifully encrusted falcon heads, the beads are in wonderful tiny designs of hieroglyphic signs of animals, stars, drops and spirals.
This royal collar of intricate workmanship was found among the jewelry of Queen Ahhotep's tomb at Dra Abu el-Naga, Thebes. It is a testimony that this queen was a true hero and deserved such items of warfare, as the daggers, axes and the order of valor that were also found in her tomb.
M.S.

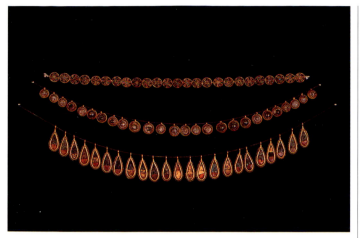

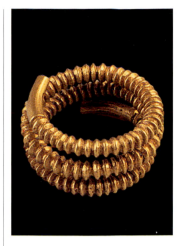

177

Necklace pendants of Ahhotep
New Kingdom, 18th Dynasty,
reign of Ahmose
Gold and semi-precious stones
W. 25.5 cm
Thebes, Dra Abu el Naga, tomb
of Queen Ahhotep
Cairo, Egyptian Museum, JE 4725 =
CG 52673

The jewelry remains found among the funerary equipment of Queen Ahhotep indicate that the queen's treasure must have included many more items than the ones that became part of the Cairo Museum collections. These pendants come from two different necklaces and another unknown ornament. The drop and round-shaped pendants (with an amethyst in the center) most certainly belonged to a necklace, as indicated by the ringlets on each of them; while the small rosettes—with turquoise, cornelian and lapis lazuli petals— may have been applied to a fabric by the hole on their back. These were probably not the only jewelry pieces that were lost in the course of the troubled events leading to the acquisition of Ahhotep's treasure on the part of the Cairo Museum.
F.T.

178

Bead bracelet of Ahhotep
New Kingdom, 18th Dynasty,
reign of Ahmose
Gold, feldspar, cornelian and lapis
lazuli
H. 4.35; diam. 4.8 cm;
weight 61.5 gr.
Thebes, Dra Abu el-Naga, tomb
of Queen Ahhotep
Cairo, Egyptian Museum, JE 4685 =
CG 52070

The tomb of queen Ahhotep, wife of Seqenenra Taa and mother of Ahmose was discovered by Mariette in Dra Abu el-Naga, Thebes, in 1959. A collection of very interesting artifacts was found inside the tomb, such as daggers and axes inscribed with the name of Ahmose, a golden necklace with three flies, which was an order of valor, models of silver and gold canoes, bracelets and collars.
This bracelet, one of a pair, was found with other jewelry inside the sarcophagus of the queen and was a present from her son Ahmose. The birth name of the king is on the golden clasp: "The son of Ra, Ahmose, beloved of Ra." The throne name is in gold on a blue background: "The good god, Nebpehtetra ("Lord of power is Ra"), may he be given life forever."
The bracelet has thirty rows of beads of gold and semi-precious stones alternating to form a design of triangles and squares. The clasp is made of two gold sheets that slide into each other so as to close the bracelet.

Bibliography
Saleh, Sourouzian 1987, cat. 125.
M.S.

179

Fastener for hair of Princess Ahmose
New Kingdom, 18th Dynasty
Gold
Diam. 2 cm
Valley of the Queens (Schiaparelli
excavations, 1903–1905)
Turin, Museo Egizio, S. 5053

The clasp comes from the grave of princess Ahmose. The processing of the fastener and the spiralform typology recall Near Eastern style jewelry. On one of the fragments of the princess' shroud the following text is written, containing the princess' titles and family origins: "Daughter of the king, Sister of the King Ahmose, created by the perfect god Seqenenra, son of King, Taa and generated by the royal wife Sathot, twice justified by voice." The princess is also known by a statue conserved in the Louvre Museum (E. 15.692), dedicated to prince Ahmose by his relatives: his father, King Seqenenra, his mother Ahhotep and his two sisters, one being our Ahmose. Both sisters are named Ahmose, but one is defined "older royal daughter" and she is perhaps the future queen Ahmose Nefertari, wife first of Kamose and then, at his death, of Ahmose. The princess to whom the fastener belongs must instead have been the king's younger daughter and was never a "great royal wife." This royal family, arisen in Thebes, strongly marked the transition from the 17th to the 18th Dynasty; in all likelihood it sought an alliance with the city of Hermopolis, center of the cult of the moon and of the god Thoth, as might be proved by the family anthroponymy composed of the terms *iaH* (moon) and *Hwty* (Thoth).

Bibliography
Ronsecco 1996, pp. XXV–XXIX;
Schiaparelli 1923, pp. 13–21.
M.T.

180

Braids of Princess Ahmose's wig
17th Dynasty (C. Vanderslayen:
18th Dynasty, between the reign of
Ahmose and that of Thutmose III)
Hair
L. *c.* 36; D. *c.* 1 cm
Valley of the Queens (Schiaparelli
excavations, 1903–1905)
Turin, Museo Egizio, C. 6506

The braids of princess Ahmose's wig
come from her grave in the eastern
sector of the Valley of the Queens.
Schiaparelli found the tomb (QV47)
already opened and ransacked; he discovered there, along with the braids,
the mummy of the princess (C. 5050),
her shroud inscribed with the Book
of the Dead, decorative fragments in
leather, pieces of a wooden sarcophagus and of a chest for canopic jars, a
pair of leather sandals, two wooden
*shabti*s and a hair clasp.
Princess Ahmose was the daughter of
the king of the 17th Theban Dynasty,
Seqenenra Taa II, as indicated by one
of the written fragments of fabric that
bears the princess' cartouche, her titles
and the name of her mother, queen
Sathot. This king fought against the
Hyksos rulers and died a violent death,
probably struck by a cudgel of a common type found in the eastern Delta
during the Second Intermediate Period; this is proved by the traces found
on his mummy conserved at the Cairo
Museum (CG 61051). The first
episode of the battles is related in the
Papyrus Sallier I that dates back to
the New Kingdom and is known as
the *Quarrel of Apophis and Seqenenra*.
The campaign against the Hyksos was
continued by his successor, Kamose,
who pursued them all the way back to
Avaris, their capital in the Delta, and
then was concluded by King Ahmose
who chased them out of the country.
Kamose left us the memory of his battles against the Hyksos in two stelae
raised in the temple of Karnak and
dated to the third year of his rule.

Bibliography
Ronsecco 1996, pp. XXV–XXIX;
Schiaparelli 1923, pp. 13–21; Vander-
sleyen 1971, pp. 214–215.
M.T.

181

*Small percussion rod of Princess
Ahmose*
New Kingdom, early 18th Dynasty
Ivory
L. 20 cm
Turin, Museo Egizio, Drovetti
Collection, Cat. 6921

The small rod is shaped like a right
hand with a curved forearm. The fingers are long and tapering; level with
the wrist is carved a bracelet with concentric rings, under which the name
and the title of the "Royal Wife Ahmose" is inscribed. She was a princess
of the early 18th Dynasty, known only by this document. According to
some authors, the name might be an
abbreviation of that of the queen Ahmose Nefertari, daughter of the
Pharaoh Seqenenra and sister of the
princess Ahmose, and therefore the
owner of the staff might be identified
with the latter.
During the New Kingdom, the members of the royal dynasty, especially
the women, generally remained on the
sidelines with respect to the actual
conduct of affairs, unless they belonged to a segment of the direct line.
Important political positions were held
only by the crown prince, heir to the
throne, who was often "great general
of the army," and by the king's main
wife, the "great royal wife" who, by the
beginning of the 18th Dynasty, also
assumed the title of "god's wife of
Amun." This title was justified by the
fact that the kings of the Theban dynasty mythologically attributed their
origin to the god Amun, who had
miraculously fecundated their mothers. From a political point of view, the
creation of this role, whose first holder was precisely the queen Ahmose
Nefertari, put a substantial part of
Amun's possessions under the direct
control of the king.

Bibliography
Donadoni Roveri 1987, fig. 334 p. 237;
M. Gitton, *S.v. "Ahmose Nofretere"*,
in: LÄI, Wiesbaden 1977, cc. 102–109.
M.T.

182

Cup with the name of Ahmose Nefertari
New Kingdom, 18th or 19th Dynasty
Egyptian faience
H. 6; diam. 23 cm
Abydos (Pétrie excavations, 1921–22)
Copenhagen, Ny Carlsberg Glyptotck, ÆIN 1600

This type of cup in shiny blue-green faience was relatively widespread. Its color evokes the watery medium in which the sun is reborn, and in which all life comes into being. It has bccn argued that these vases are somehow related to Nun, the primordial liquid chaos from which all life emerged; the depths of this primitive ocean were generally symbolized by the dark blue of lapis lazuli. The light color of this faience work recalls the water of canals and basins, enlivened by light. In imitating the shades of turquoise, the cup is placed under the aegis of Hathor, a goddess closely associated with this semi-precious stone.
The presence of the benevolent deity of maternity and rebirth is also clear in the decoration on the inside of the vessel. The opulent wig of the female head depicted reveals the ears of a cow, the animal that was the symbol of this goddess and was often used in the decoration of *sistra* (cat. nos. 87, 88). As if to suggest the frame of a water-basin, the lotuses flower in a sort of round. The plant, which each day emerged from the water in which it grew, was considered a symbol of the womb that give birth to a new sun every morning. The overall composition, predicated on the notion of perpetual renewal, is dedicated to Ahmose Nefertari, the "great royal wife" of Ahmose and mother of Amenhotep I. Even though the epithet "living" appears in her cartouche, this object was probably a posthumous act of homage to the famous queen (cat. nos. 174, 175, 184).
While it gives us a fair idea of the luxury quality of the ceramics used by the upper echelons of society during the New Kingdom, this piece itself was probably purely votive, as it is in tombs and in sanctuaries dedicated to the goddess Hathor that these "cups of Nun" have been found.

Bibliography
Jørgensen 1998, cat. 137.
I.F.

183

Hes vase of Ahmose I
New Kingdom, 18th Dynasty, reign of Ahmose
Gold
H. 14.6; diam. 5; base diam. 4 cm
Tanis, Tomb no. 3, burial of Psusennes I
Cairo, Egyptian Museum, JE 85895

This kind of vessel was used for the libation of sacred water during the funerary or religious ceremonies in temples, especially by royal personalities or high priests.
They were manufactured mostly of faience, like those found in the tomb of Tutankhamun, or of gold.
This *hes* vase is formed of five individual pieces that have been delicately soldered together: the rim, neck, spout, body, and base.
Although the vase bears the name of King Ahmose, first ruler of the 18th Dynasty, and may have been among his funerary equipment or that of his mother's, Queen Ahhotep, at Thebes, it was discovered in the Delta residence of the 21st–22nd Dynasties at Tanis with other artifacts in the tomb of King Psusennes I.
The dedication text incised on the vase refers to the cult of Osiris at Abydos and reads as follows: "The good lord, Nebpehtyra [Ahmose], true of voice [or justified], beloved of Osiris, lord of Abydos."
M.S.

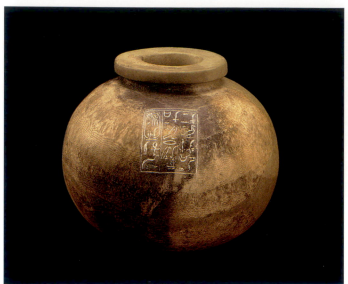

184

*Vase with the name of Ahmose
Nefertari*
New Kingdom, 18th Dynasty,
reign of Ahmose
Travertine ("Egyptian alabaster")
H. 16.5; diam. 20.5 cm
West Thebes
Hannover, Kestner Museum, 1979.2

The queens of the early New Kingdom period played a full role in the efforts of the Theban sovereigns, who
were engaged first in driving out the
Hyksos and then reestablishing order
in a country that had been torn by almost a century and a half of division
and civil war.
Ahmose Nefertari was the "great royal wife" of Ahmose. She ably supported his victorious efforts against
the invader and then later served as regent for their son, Amenhotep I, who
ascended to the throne when still a
boy. After years of strife, the government of the young king and his mother were able to reorganize the kingdom
in relative peace. Temples in particular benefited from royal largesse in
this period; and the efficacious rule of
Ahmose and Amenhotep led to them
achieving divine status and being worshipped as gods—particularly at Deir
el-Medina.
Most of the numerous monuments celebrating the queen date from the
Ramesside period (cat. nos. 60, 61,
174, 175). It is therefore particularly
moving when one finds an object that
dates from the lifetime of the queen
herself. This is the case with this small
finely-made vase, the shoulder of
which is inscribed with Ahmose's full
royal title. Her blood links with the
most important monarchs of this key
period of change are amply underlined: we are told she is the daughter
of a king, sister of a king, "god's wife,"
"great royal wife" and mother of a

king. While they may appear redun-
dantly rhetorical to us, these titles express the key status and role of the
queens of the early New Kingdom.

Bibliography
Eggebrecht 1987, p. 108.
I.F.

185

Girdle with Nile-fish spacers
New Kingdom, reign of Thutmose III
Gold
L. as strung 83.8; L. of fish 2.4 cm
Wadi Qubbanet el-Qirud
New York, The Metropolitan
Museum of Art, Fletcher Fund,
26.8.61a

Twenty-two spacers of golden Nile
perch (*tilapia nilotica*) have three holes
through the body; they were among
the art market items thought to be
from the Wadi Qirud tomb. Only one
other such spacer is known, also of
gold but with holes for only two
strings. The spacers here have been
strung with gold ring beads, but colored beads may have been used instead. Also, the number of fish is
greater than that expected for a single
girdle, so there may have been two.
The material and workmanship of the
spacers and ring beads show them to
be of royal workmanship.

Bibliography
Winlock 1948, p. 38, pl. 21.
C.L.

186

Gazelle diadem
New Kingdom, reign of Thutmose III
Gold, cornelian, turquoise glass,
blue glass
L. of forehead band 48 cm;
W. of proper right gazelle head
at ear tips 2.3 cm
Wadi Qubbanet el-Qirud
New York, The Metropolitan
Museum of Art, gift of Mr. G.F.
Baker and Mr. and Mrs. Everit Macy,
26.8.99

This diadem is composed of a t-shaped
band terminated by feline heads, probably leopards. A ring at the tip of each
nose would have allowed the fillet ends
to be tied together by string at the
back of the head. Six cloisonné rosettes attached to the band are inlaid
with cornelian and glass. But the two
animal protomes are the finest part of
the diadem, representation's of the
dorcas gazelle. They appear here in
what seems to have been a new fashion reflecting an association with
Hathor.

Bibliography
Winlock 1948, 16f, pls. 6–7; pl. 41b.
C.L.

187

Armlet with cats spacer
New Kingdom,
reign of Thutmose III
Gold, cornelian, turquoise glass,
lapis lazuli
L. 16.8; W. of spacer 2.9 cm
Wadi Qubbanet el-Qirud
New York, The Metropolitan Museum
of Art, Rogers Fund, 26.8.121A

This armlet is one of four reconstructed from purchased elements.
The beads repeat the scheme found on
jewels certainly from the tomb, and
the feline spacers find parallels in spacers inscribed for King Nubkheperra
Intef and his Queen Sobkemsaf of the
17th Dynasty. One of the sets form
the Wadi Qirud has lion cub spacers
and the other cats; both probably refer to Hathor.

Bibliography
Winlock 1948, pp. 29–31, pl. 16b.
C.L.

188

Inlaid and inscribed ornament
New Kingdom, reign of Thutmose III
Gold, cornelian, turquoise glass,
blue glass
H. 7.2 cm
Wadi Qubbanet el-Qirud
New York, The Metropolitan
Museum of Art, Rogers Fund,
26.8.130

This massive gold ornament is of the
highest Egyptian workmanship, and
is both inlaid with cornelian and glass
and superlatively traced with royal inscriptions giving the nomen and
prenomen of Thutmose III. It is common to find the name of a ruler on a
jewel (rather than the female owner's)
although no name at all could have
been seen on these ornaments when
worn. This one of six ornaments re-
trieved has a wider diameter at the
bottom than the top.

Bibliography
Winlock 1948, 31f, pl. 17 bottom.
C.L.

189

Mirror
New Kingdom, reign of Thutmose III
Silver with gold foil
H. 30 cm
Wadi Qubbanet el-Qirud
New York, The Metropolitan
Museum of Art, Fletcher Fund,
26.8.97

Royal burials in the Middle Kingdom
and Late Period yielded silver disks,
undoubtedly preferable to the standard copper or bronze examples that
gave reflection more commonly in ancient Egyptians. The gold foil handle
here, once covering wood, is in the
shape of a papyrus column to which
two cow faces representing the goddess Hathor have been applied. On
the front is the cartouche Menkheperra, for Thutmose III. The goddess
Hathor was especially associated with
attractiveness and vitality.

Bibliography
Winlock 1948, 49f, pl. 29 left.
C.L.

190

Libation vessel of Menwi
New Kingdom, reign of Thutmose III
Silver
H. 19.5 cm
Wadi Qubbanet el-Qirud
New York, The Metropolitan
Museum of Art, Rogers Fund,
18.8.21a-b

This is one of three such ritual vessels
found in the tomb, one for each of the
foreign wives. The inscription on each
vessel states that it was the gift of the
king, and the material and craftsmanship indicate the regard that the king
had for these women.

Bibliography
Winlock 1948, 60f, pl. 36 lower left.
C.L.

191

Cosmetic jar
New Kingdom, reign of Thutmose III
Travertine ("Egyptian alabaster")
and gold
H. with lid 9.8 cm
Wadi Qubbanet el-Qirud
New York, The Metropolitan
Museum of Art, Fletcher Fund,
26.8.31a-b

This inscribed jar has characteristics
similar to cat. no. 191bis, but has re-
tained its lid, inscribed with the name
Menkheperra in a cartouche. The jar
has an unusual shape; its long slender
neck indicates that its contents would
have been more liquid or prone to
evaporation than those of cat. no.
191bis.

Bibliography
Winlock 1948, 52g, pl. 30.7.
C.L.

191bis

Cosmetic jar
New Kingdom, reign of Thutmose III
Travertine ("Egyptian alabaster")
and gold
H. 10.5 cm
Wadi Qubbanet el-Qirud
New York, The Metropolitan
Museum of Art, gift of Edward
S. Harkness, 26.7.1434

This stone lotiform vessel with gold
trim no doubt once held a precious
substance, probably a thick viscous
unguent. A flat lid, also trimmed in
gold, would have fit the recessed rim,
and been held in place by a cloth
bound around the outside with linen
string. The inscription on the vessel is
similar to that on other precious vessels from the tomb, and names Thutmose III. The missing lid probably
had his prenomen in a cartouche,
Menkheperra.

Bibliography
Winlock 1948, 61f, pl. 35b right.
C.L.

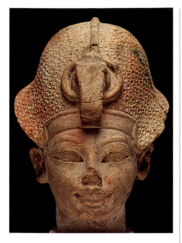

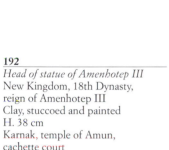

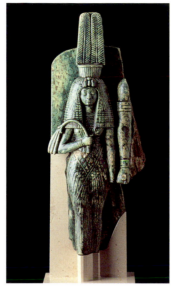

192

Head of statue of Amenhotep III
New Kingdom, 18th Dynasty,
reign of Amenhotep III
Clay, stuccoed and painted
H. 38 cm
Karnak, temple of Amun,
cachette court
Cairo, Egyptian Museum, JE 38597

Amenhotep III, the son of Thutmose
IV and Mutemwiya, was no more than
ten or twelve years old when his father
died. His first recorded acts as king are
dated to his first and second years in a
quarry chamber at Tura. Already by
his second regnal year, Amenhotep III
was married to his great royal wife,
Queen Tiy.
Of all the ancient Egyptian sovereigns,
the greatest number of known statues
are of him (more than 250).
This statue represents him with the
khepresh headdress, or blue crown,
which was normally used in military
representations of the sovereign. It has
sharp edges and is decorated with circle motifs; the front is adorned with
the cobra, the symbol of royalty, the
coil of which after having encircled
the forehead, extended over the top of
head. The king has a fleshy face, with
long, slanting almond-shaped eyes,
arched eyebrows, a small flattened
nose, distinctive mouth—outlined by
an incised lipline, ending with two lateral dimples—and full lips, the upper
one with a deep "V" in the center and
a slight bulge where it meets the lower one.

Bibliography
Bryan 1992; Hornung, Bryan 2002,
pp. 63, 165.
A.M.

193

Statuette of Tiy
New Kingdom, 18th Dynasty,
reign of Amenhotep III
Soapstone, glazed
H. 30; W. 12; D. 6 cm
Provenance unknown
Paris, Musée du Louvre, N 2312 =
E 25493

Numerous representations of queen
Tiy have come down to us. The luck
involved in all archaeological finds is
clearly not enough to explain this, and
the quality of the objects reveals profound religious, ritual—and perhaps
political—changes which, at the end of
the 18th Dynasty, led to a rethinking of
the role of the "great royal wives."
Wearing a cap surmounted by two tall
straight feathers that have solar con-
notations, the queen has a full wig that
falls down to her shoulders. The vulture plumage adorning the headdress
symbolizes divine maternity and indicates that Tiy was the mother of the
heir to the throne when this image was
produced. The head of the bird is
framed by the two cobras, another
symbol of the goddesses of generation
(this type of *uraeus* sometimes also
bore the crowns of Upper and Lower
Egypt). The body of the queen is enveloped in a braced tunic, which emphasizes the Egyptian ideal of femininity: high, small breasts, narrow
waist, wide hips and curving buttocks.
The clothing is again adorned with
vulture plumage, with the wings enfolding the body of the queen—stressing her identification with the great
mother goddess (an identification further underlined by the floral scepter
the queen holds in her left hand). The
"great royal wife" here must have been
portrayed standing next to her husband, Amenhotep III, but his figure
has unfortunately disappeared. Accompanying her sovereign, who was

the Son of the Sun, Tiy played the role
of those goddesses who accompanied
the solar god, of whom they were
daughter, spouse and mother, thus embodying all aspects of vigorous wom-
anhood.

Bibliography
Kozloff, Bryan, Berman, Delange
1993, p. 164.
I.F.

194

Queen Tiy (fragment of a stele)
New Kingdom, 18th Dynasty
Quartzite
H. 36.5 cm
Thebes, mortuary temple
of Amenhotep III
Berlin, Ägyptisches Museum
und Papyrussammlung, 23270

Royalty's key role in the maintenance
of the order of the world was borne by
the queen as much as by the pharaoh.
The complementary role of male and
female was one of the bases essential to
the good working of the cosmos. Always important, the role of the queen
was underlined particularly during the
reign of Amenhotep III, whose wife,
Tiy, is shown alongside him in numerous official scenes. This fragment of a
bas-relief is part of a large-format representation of the royal couple on a
five-meter-high stele found in the innermost part of Amenhotep III's mortuary temple.

Bibliography
Priese 1991, pp. 92–93 (cat. 57); PM
II, p. 451.
D.W.

195

Scarab of the reign
New Kingdom, 18th Dynasty
Green-enameled steatite
L. 9.15; W. 6.3; H. 4 cm
Provenance unknown
Paris, Musée du Louvre, N 787 a

During his reign, Amenhotep III had various series of scarabs with commemorative inscriptions produced. The divine coleopteran beetle symbolizes both the rising sun and the sun in its perpetual mutations. The text is inscribed within an oval that recalls the shape of royal cartouches; the fine cord around it represents the course of the sun encircling the whole of a created world which was under the joint protection of the creating god and his emissary on earth, the pharaoh.

Certain of these scarabs celebrate the valor of the king in hunting the wild bull—a variation on the theme of the monarch combating all the forms of chaos that pushed at the borders of Egypt. An artifact of this type, in soapstone, also announces the arrival of a new bride for Amenhotep, the Mitanni princess Kilughepa.

Given their similarity to this record of what was substantially a diplomatic event, the sixty-odd objects of comparable content bearing the name of queen Tiy are referred to as "marriage scarabs." However, the text mentions only the name and title of the queen, after those of her husband. Then comes the concise formula: "This is the wife of the victorious king, whose southern frontier is Karopy and whose northern frontier is Naharina." This, far from ritual, mention of the extent of the pharaoh's dominions does not correspond to the area of his effective political control but rather to a traditional sphere of influence.

These scarabs are not the only evidence of the importance of the "great royal wives" during the reign of Amenhotep III. In the tomb of Kheruef, for example, Tiy is portrayed in the form of a sphinx showing as much confidence and determination as her husband while she crushes the enemies of Egypt underfoot. In another scene she is directly associated with Maat, the goddess who guaranteed cosmic order.

All the depictions and texts which bring together king and queen on the same monument serve to celebrate the union of the couple and their joint action at the head of the state. Hence, these scarabs were more than simple wedding announcements; they were a statement of the royal couple's effective performance of their duties, guaranteeing Egypt fair government in the eyes of the gods.

Bibliography
Kozloff, Bryan, Berman, Delange 1993, p. 58.
I.F.

196

The daughters of Amenhotep III
(bas-relief from a tomb)
New Kingdom, 18th Dynasty
Limestone
H. 40; W. 42; D. 5.5 cm
Thebes, tomb of Kheruef (no. 192)
Berlin, Ägyptisches Museum
und Papyrussammlung, 18526

The royal couple—Amenhotep III and Tiy—are depicted various times in the tomb of Kheruef, "director of the sovereign's palace." At the ceremony for the raising of the *djed* pillar—part of the celebrations for the pharaoh's jubilee—the king and queen are shown followed by sixteen princesses. It is striking that here as elsewhere the royal princes are not depicted. Even the heir to the throne Thutmose, who would die prematurely, and his younger brother, who would become Amenhotep IV/Akhenaten, are absent from bas-reliefs in tombs and temples.

Bibliography
PM I.1, p. 299 (7); Epigraphic Survey 1980, pl. 57.
D.W.

197

Kohl tube
New Kingdom, 18th Dynasty,
reign of Amenhotep III
Faience and glass
H. 12.5; diam. 2 cm
Provenance unknown
Turin, Museo Egizio, Drovetti Collection, 6236

Cylindrical tube, in yellow faience with blue vitreous paste inlays. The inside of the container, hollow to mid-height, contains a tapered wooden stick, pointed at the tip, that was used like a stylus for makeup. Nothing remains of the contents. The lower part of the tube bears a horizontal groove and on the back a decoration of concentric triangles. These motifs can be found on other kohl tubes of the same period and are a naturalistic refinement: they emulate the ring and growth knots seen on bamboo canes, a rather widely used material for this kind of container. The inscription, arranged in a column, bears the cartouches of King Amenhotep III and his wife: "The perfect god, lord of the Two Lands, Nebmaatra, the royal wife, Tiy, long life!" The provenance of this kohl tube is unknown but it is likely this elegant and refined toilette article belonged to royal grave goods.

Bibliography
Kozloff, Bryan, Berman, Delange 1993, pp. 345–346.
M.B.

198

Kohl tube with the name of Satamon
New Kingdom, 18th Dynasty,
reign of Amenhotep III
Ceramic
H. 14.5; diam. 2 cm
Provenance unknown
New York, The Metropolitan
Museum of Art, gift of Edward
S. Harkness, 26.7.910

From quite early times the Egyptians used galena powder kohl as part of their cosmetics; it soon replaced the malachite that had been used at the very beginning of the Old Kingdom. Men and women applied the kohl to the edge of the eyelids and along the corner of the eye. There was naturally a practical purpose here, as the kohl kept off insects and reduced the dazzle of sunlight; however, given that it also made the eyes more striking, the aesthetic results of this treatment were certainly not overlooked. What is more, the made-up eye recalled that of Horus, the *wedjat* that was a symbol of physical wholeness and well-being.
The kohl was kept in small tubes, great numbers of which—of varying quality—have come down to us. Members of the royal family and high-ranking court functionaries had containers that naturally reflected their status. Several of the extant makeup tubes belonged to those close to Amenhotep III (cat. no. 197). The king is in fact mentioned on this object from the Metropolitan Museum as "The perfect god Nebmaatra." His name is immediately followed by that of his daughter, whose titles reveal that she sat as queen alongside her father: "the daughter of the king, Great Royal Wife, Satamon, who is alive."

Bibliography
Kozloff, Bryan, Berman, Delange 1993, p. 347.
I.F.

199

Unguent jar
New Kingdom, 18th Dynasty,
reign of Amenhotep III
Polychrome faience
H. 8.4; diam. 6.6 cm
Provenance unknown
Paris, Musée du Louvre, E 4877

This small jar is noteworthy for its bright yellow faience and the use of three different colors, which reveals a great mastery of technique on the part of the person who made it. Slightly pear-shaped, the jar vaguely resembles a bundle of clothes. Its wide-lipped neck is decorated with a floral motif alternating four lotus flowers and petals. The delicate stopper in the form of a daisy completes the bouquet.
The inscription on the side links the jar with a famous royal couple. The two columns on the left contain the two cartouches of Amenhotep III in the short formula: "The perfect god Nebmaatra, the son of Ra, Imenhotep, sovereign of Thebes, who has given life eternally." The signs under the double royal name are to be read side to side and not as a continuation of the columns.
Opposite, as if his alter ego, there is "the king's wife, Tiy, who is living." The names of the husband and wife are inscribed within a rectangle, as if to emphasize their union. It is therefore legitimate to suppose that the significance of this magnificent object goes beyond its aesthetic excellence; just like the commemorative scarabs (cat. no. 195), it celebrates the royal couple as a single entity.

Bibliography
Kozloff, Bryan, Berman, Delange 1993, p. 344.
I.F.

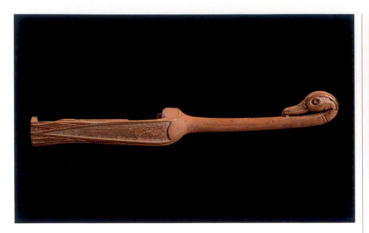

200

Spoon of Mutemwiya
New Kingdom, 18th Dynasty,
reign of Amenhotep III
Wood (acacia?) with traces
of pigments
L. 20; W. 3.5 cm
Provenance unknown
Paris, Musée du Louvre, E 3671

Among the luxury objects most prized by the upper echelons of Egyptian society, the various containers for unguents held a special place. These could come in a wide variety of forms. Odoriferous balms might be kept in a spoon-shaped vessel—most often in wood—the handle of which could be worked in various ways. Here, the receptacle opens out into a lotus bud, and must have been closed with a lid that has now disappeared. The handle is in the form of the stretched neck of a duck (or goose), whose head is turned back. The neck is inscribed with the name of the illustrious owner of the object: "The great royal wife, mother of God, Mutemwiya," mother of King Amenhotep III. In Egyptian myths, the lotus is associated with the rebirth of the sun, for which it served as a sort of symbolic womb. In the Book of the Dead, the deceased becomes a rising sun emerging from a fully-flowered nenuphar; and this perfumed flower was also linked with femininity and a woman's sexual appetites.

The motif of the duck with the twisted neck appears in various objects. For a long time it was thought that the bird was associated with chaos. In the tombs of private individuals, it is shown in marshland hunting-scenes, where it suggests the agents of unrest and perturbation that must be overcome by all those striving for eternity. A new hypothesis is that the duck is not an animal of devastation but a symbol of the god Geb. Its association with the lotus of femininity is thus said to refer to the daily birth of the sun from the womb of the goddess Nut.

This makeup spoon is very precious because it is inscribed with the name of the mother of Amenhotep III, a figure who is not often mentioned in texts. However, she does occupy center-stage in the famous so-called "theogamy" scenes in the temple of Luxor, which describe the divine descent of the sovereign. There is no mention of Mutemwiya as the "great royal wife" of Thutmose IV, and it is probable she had no official title before the ascent of her son to the throne. The spoon, therefore, was made after the pharaoh raised his mother to the rank befitting her.

Bibliography
Kozloff, Bryan, Berman, Delange 1993, p. 302.
I.F.

201

Akhenaten and Nefertiti
(fragment of a stele)
New Kingdom, 18th Dynasty
Limestone
H. 12 cm
Provenance unknown
Berlin, Ägyptisches Museum
und Papyrussammlung, 14511

The frieze of *uraei* and the cornice indicate that this fragment of bas-relief must have come from a small domestic altar in the form of a chapel. Such depictions of the royal couple were venerated in the homes of el-Amarna. Nefertiti is shown very close to her husband, Akhenaten, and is passing a necklace around his neck. The sun-god Aten emerges from the hieroglyph for the sky and surrounds the royal couple with his rays, which end in hands. This is an image of the harmony between heaven and earth, in a setting of natural munificence (indicated by the thicket of papyrus on the left side).

Bibliography
Priese 1991, pp. 105–106 (cat. 64).
D.W.

202

The royal family (household altar)
New Kingdom, 18th Dynasty
Limestone
H. 32.5; W. 39; D. 3.8 cm
Provenance unknown
Berlin, Ägyptisches Museum
und Papyrussammlung, 14145

The scene depicted in the bas-relief on this stele has a familiar, almost intimate, air. It comes from an altar in a private house. The sovereign couple—Akhenaten and Nefertiti—are accompanied by three of their six daughters. Their gestures are natural and animated. The sun of Aten hangs over the royal family in the sky; its rays end in hands that hold out the sign of life (*ankh*) to the king and queen. The deity offers light and life, and the royal family responds with gestures of love. During the monotheistic period of Akhenaten, the strictly ritualized relationship between mankind and the gods was replaced by one focused on the plenitude of life, an expression of the harmony between heaven and earth.

Bibliography
Settgast 1989, pp. 90–91 (cat. 46).
D.W.

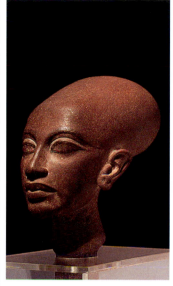

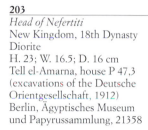

203

Head of Nefertiti
New Kingdom, 18th Dynasty
Diorite
H. 23; W. 16.5; D. 16 cm
Tell el-Amarna, house P 47,3
(excavations of the Deutsche
Orientgesellschaft, 1912)
Berlin, Ägyptisches Museum
und Papyrussammlung, 21358

No Egyptian queen was depicted as often as Nefertiti, wife of Akhenaten. She is present in nearly all the bas-reliefs from temples and tombs that depict her husband. There are also numerous extant statues in various sizes and materials. This life-size head in dark stone is fascinating because of the slight asymmetry in the depiction of the face, and because the unfinished quality of the surface gives the impression that the eyes are covered with a veil.

Bibliography
Priese 1991, pp. 112–113 (cat. 68):
Grimm, Schoske, Wildung 1997, pp.
90–91 (cat. 66).
D.W.

204

Head of princess
New Kingdom, 18th Dynasty,
reign of Akhenaten
Brown quartzite
H. 21 cm
Tell el-Amarna, workshop of the
sculptor Thutmose
Cairo, Egyptian Museum, JE 44869

The workshop of the sculptor Thutmose contained, in addition to many plaster heads, a number of heads in quartzite, now in the Cairo Museum and in the Ägyptisches Museum, Berlin. This egg-shaped head has a broad, elongated cranium, slim neck and severe features. The head is rendered in the Amarna style which, influenced by religious concepts, emphasized hereditary traits and natural representations. On this beautifully modeled head, the sculptor outlined the eyes and eyebrows in black, perhaps intending to carve them out for inlay; additional black lines on the neck designated areas for further work. When such a piece was completely finished, the superb high polish of the face would extend to the neck as well. The tenon at the base of the neck indicates that this head was attached to a separately sculptured torso and was part of a composite statue that was assembled after both parts were finished.
A.M.

205

*Bead showing Akhenaten
and Nefertiti*
New Kingdom, 18th Dynasty,
reign of Akhenaten
Egyptian faience
H. 3.5; diam. 4.2 cm
Provenance unknown
Copenhagen, Ny Carlsberg
Glyptotek, ÆIN 1791

This object is unusual for various reasons. First of all, it may be in the form of a bead but it is much too big to have been used in a necklace. It has been suggested that it was to be threaded onto a sleeve or that it was part of some composite object that served a ceremonial purpose. The chasing of the background which suggests the rippling surface of water reveals exceptional craftsmanship.
The surround of the "bead" shows two boats bearing a solar disk behind which sits a figure raising its arms in adoration. On one side, the white crown makes it easy to identify the figure as a king of Upper Egypt; on the other, the headdress is equally revealing, because it is that favored by the queen Nefertiti. All doubt about the identity of the couple is removed by the cartouches which appear on the upper surface of the object. Shaped rather similarly to the red crown, Nefertiti's headdress here seems to be chosen as an echo of that of her husband.
During the Amarna period, the royal couple were considered as a single entity, just like the children of the sun-creator, Shu and Tefnut. Various signs were used to express this intimate union between husband and wife, which was necessary to the correct working of the world. Taking his identity with "the son of Ra" to its limit, Akhenaten played the role of Shu on earth. The function of the god—who

personified the light and breath of life that issued from the sun-creator—was entirely taken over by the king, who thus became responsible for bestowing this light and breath of life on mankind. At his side, Nefertiti played a complementary role, and sometimes appeared as his wife and spouse, Tefnut. Like the divine twins, the king and queen had to restore to their solar parent the energy which he lavished upon them.
The lotus flowers separating the two barks are themselves solar symbols, while the turquoise of the water recalls the liquid medium from which the sun was reborn each day. Akhenaten and Nefertiti here take the place of the deities who were normally depicted on the divine bark. They are not only furthering the progress of the sun, but they are also benefiting from the course it follows, caught up in the daily cycle on which the permanent renewal of the cosmos depends.

Bibliography
Jørgensen 1998, cat. 138; Freed,
Markowitz, D'Auria 1999, cat. 97.
I.F.

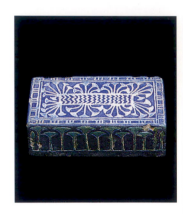

206

*Block of vitrified limestone
with papyri*
New Kingdom, 18th Dynasty,
reign of Akhenaten
Vitrified limestone
H. 3.2; L. 11; W. 6.5 cm
Tell el-Amarna
Cairo, Egyptian Museum, JE 55524

The surfaces of this rectangular block of limestone are vitrified and decorated with a refined plant motif in blue and green. The center of the upper side contains a stylized depiction of a rectangular lake (rendered using zigzags to indicate water), on whose banks are fan-shaped thickets of green papyrus reeds seen against a blue background. The entire decoration is framed by a geometrical motif in two colors. The side faces all bear the same schema of decoration: alternate tall and short stems of flowering papyri, delimited at either end by papyrus reeds with unopened umbels. It has been assumed that this block served scribes to hold a papyrus unfurled—a hypothesis supported by the fact that all the decoration centers on the very plant that supplied the Egyptians' most prized writing material.

Bibliography
Hildesheim 1976, no. 42.
S.E.

207

Fragment of a painted floor
New Kingdom, 18th Dynasty,
reign of Akhenaten
Painted plaster
H. 101; W. 160 cm
Tell el-Amarna, Maru-Aten
Cairo, Egyptian Museum,
JE 33030/1

While most ancient Egyptian buildings were built mainly of brick and wood and thus disappeared very quickly, some rare remains have come down to us to bear witness to the grandeur and refined construction and painting techniques.

Among the features of the royal palaces at el-Amarna were gorgeously painted pavements, walls and pillars. In the *harim*, columned courts were painted with cooling false ponds containing fish, ducks, and lotuses amid rippling water.

Several fragments of a painted floor from the southern palace at el-Amarna, the Maru-Aten (which was built for Meritaten, Akhenaten's eldest daughter) depict one of those marsh scenes with wild ducks flying over tufts of reeds and papyrus which intermingle with the floating leaves of a flowering plant. These scenes were a favorite subject for palace decoration.

Bibliography
PM IV, p. 208; Peet, Wolley 1923, pp. 118–189; Pendlebury 1951, pp. 40–41; Badawy 1968, pp. 82–84, 209–14, pl. 5; Kemp 1995B, pp. 411–62; Freed, Markowitz, D'Auria 1999, p. 229, cat. 82, 83.
A.M.

208

Palace interior
New Kingdom, 18th Dynasty,
reign of Akhenaten
Limestone
23 × 43 × 3.5 cm
Tell el-Amarna, found at Hermopolis
Boston, Museum of Fine Arts,
Marilyn M. Simpson Fund, 1997.98

At el-Amarna, capital city of Akhenaten and Nefertiti, what we know about palaces comes from both the archaeological record and relief representations such as the present example. To date, three palaces have been identified at Amarna, one in the "central city" probably used for ceremonial purposes based on its enormous size (15,000 m2), and two smaller residential palaces in the "north city." It has been suggested that the king and queen lived in the northernmost, beautifully situated near the riverbank and cooled by breezes from the north, while the second palace in that area was used by Akhenaten's lesser wife, Kiya.

Palaces shared large, open courts, altars, columned hallways, windows of appearance, throne rooms and other reception areas, kitchens, storerooms, servants' quarters, pools, gardens, and, in an area toward the back and separated from the rest by a transverse hall, the private apartments of the royal family. Several of those elements are featured in this relief.

In the upper right is a bedroom, furnished with low tables and a bed made comfortable by a thick bolster and headrest. Below may be a bathroom with curtain suspended for privacy. A more public area of the palace may be seen on the left side, where an attendant burns incense on an altar in a columned court. Small doorways connect the different areas of the palace. Palaces were depicted not only on the buildings of the city itself, the likely provenance of the present example, but also on the walls of about a third of the private tombs at el-Amarna.

Bibliography
P. Lacovara in: Freed, Markowitz, D'Auria 1999, p. 224.
R.E.F.

209

Window of appearances
New Kingdom, 18th Dynasty,
reign of Akhenaten
Limestone
23.8 × 43 × 3.5 cm
Tell el-Amarna, found at Hermopolis
Boston, Museum of Fine Arts, Helen
and Alice Colburn Fund, 63.427

The daily journey by chariot of the king and his family from their palaces in the north of el-Amarna to the Aten temples in the "central city" and back offered one opportunity for the populace to view their monarch. The "window of appearance," a raised and partly screened dais overlooking a courtyard in the palace, provided another. Based on its representation in reliefs such as the present example and on the walls of nearly every private tomb at Amarna, this window formed an important component of the palaces there. From the window of appearance, the king, accompanied by Nefertiti and often their children as well, bestowed the gold of honor on deserving courtiers as their households celebrated with great abandon. Although to date no actual examples have been identified at Amarna, windows of appearance may be found in the ceremonial palaces of the funerary temples of Rameses II and Rameses III in western Thebes.
This relief provides a detailed view of the structure of the window of appearance and its context within the palace. For the window itself, two small doorways lead up to a balcony-like structure. The central area is framed by an interrupted lintel topped by a frieze of cobras, both elements characteristic of Amarna architecture. The bottom half is masked by a low screen wall topped by a thick bolster that offered a soft surface for the royal family to lean upon. The double-

leaf doorway above it is now shut. The four columns with palm capitals supported a roof that provided shade. Outside, the tall columns with papyrus capitals marked the courtyard in which a servant and guard engage in conversation. Meanwhile another attendant is about to pour water to settle the dust as another takes a brief break from sweeping.

Bibliography
P. Lacovara in: Freed, Markowitz, D'Auria 1999, p. 224.
R.E.F.

210

Statue of a queen
New Kingdom, 19th Dynasty
Black granite
27 × 19 cm
Provenance unknown
London, The Trustees of the British Museum, EA 1133

This small statuette bears the remains of an inscription: "great royal wife, lady of the Two Lands, Nefertari [beloved of] Mut." The person depicted may be Rameses II's principal queen, Nefertari. Indeed, the style of the sculpting places this statuette in the early 19th Dynasty, when the effects of Amarna art are still clearly visible. Here, this is most notable in the elongated almond-shaped eyes. The queen is shown wearing a heavy tripartite wig, originally topped with a crown, and fronted by the double *uraeus*. A floral collar is carved between the front lappets of her wig. Below her right shoulder, a hand rests on her back. With the angle of her left arm, this indicates that the figure of the queen was part of a pair statue, depicting the queen seated next to a deity.
N.S.

211

Lid of chest
New Kingdom, 19th Dynasty,
reign of Rameses II
Painted wood
13 × 9 cm
Valley of the Queens,
tomb of Nefertari (Schiaparelli excavations, 1904)
Turin, Museo Egizio, Suppl. 5199

Arched lid belonging to a chest from the burial goods of Nefertari, royal wife of the sovereign Rameses II. It is decorated with polychrome blue, green and red stripes. The yellow central panel bears a partly erased dedicatory inscription: ". . . everywhere, Nefertari, beloved by Mut, lady of the Two Lands." There are traces of the housing of the knob, probably button-shaped. Chests with arched lids are attested in New Kingdom burial goods. The dimensions of the lid and comparison with coeval exemplars suggest an oblong rectangular-shaped container like the ones destined to contain one or two *shabti*s.

Bibliography
Donadoni Roveri 1988, p. 150, fig. 201; Corzo 1994, p. 196 (cat. 54).
M.B.

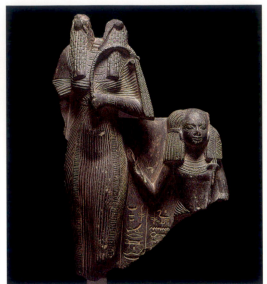

212

Sandals
New Kingdom, 19th Dynasty,
reign of Rameses II
Plant fibre
29 × 10 cm
Valley of the Queens, tomb of
Nefertari (Schiaparelli excavations,
1904)
Turin, Museo Egizio, Suppl. 5160

Thong sandals with flat pointed sole
and palm-leaf straps. The technique
used for making the sole comes from
the processing for baskets called "spi-
ralled," formed by a nucleus that coils
around itself in spirals (see drawing).
In the crafting of sandals the weft of
the sole is formed by horizontal strips
of palm leaves, overcast with a strip of
the same material. The sole itself is
trimmed all along the edge with dou-
ble-triple overlying stitches, using the
same technique. These sandals were
found by Schiaparelli in the tomb of
Nefertari and testify to the furnishings of the queen's burial goods, unfortunately for the most part lost because the tomb was looted.

Bibliography
Schiaparelli 1923, p. 55, fig. 51; Cor-
zo 1994, p. 197 (cat. 57); Nicholson,
Shaw 2000, p. 256.
M.B.

213

Double statue of a queen and prince
New Kingdom, 19th Dynasty,
reign of Rameses II
Schist
H. 27 cm
Karnak, temple of Amun,
cachette court
Cairo, Egyptian Museum, CG 42154
= JE 37337

This exquisite sculpture carved in
schist, one of the hardest of all stones,
depicts an unknown queen and prince.
It is the work of an artist of exceptionally fine taste, one capable of
sculpting a masterpiece of beauty and
elegance. The queen wears an elaborate tripartite wig of braided hair and
a broad necklace composed of many
strands of beads. Her head is missing
but it is clear that it was originally
carved from a separate piece of stone
that was attached to the neck with a
tenon. Earrings were, on the contrary,
sculpted on the main piece of stone
and are still visible. Her robe is composed of an inner and outer garment
of fine, pleated linen that is tied in the
front and seductively reveals the form
of her body. She holds a floral scepter
that covers the wig and one arm and a
bracelet adorns her wrist.
The prince, a child, on the left side of
the queen, touches her with his right
hand. He has the sidelocks of braided
hair gathered with bands traditionally
worn by children. The prince wears a
necklace of several strands, but only
part of his pleated skirt remains. On
the left-hand side of the prince's head
a small portion of a fan can be seen,
which is composed of an ostrich plume
set in a handle terminating in a papyrus flower.
There are two incomplete columns of
hieroglyphic inscriptions between the
prince and the queen that read: "his
beloved great royal wife, lady of. . . ."
and "the prince from his body. . . ." On
the back, there are five columns of inscriptions. The sculpture, dating from
the 19th Dynasty, is possibly from the
reign of Rameses II, while the style of
the dress is similar to that of the mother of Rameses II (cat no. 224).
A.M.

214

Stele of Mai
New Kingdom, 19th Dynasty,
reign of Sety I
Limestone
H. 94.5 cm
Abydos
Brussels, Musées Royaux d'Art
et d'Histoire, E 5300

Mai, the scribe-recorder of offerings,
worked in the jubilee temple of King
Sety I at Abydos. He is depicted praying at the bottom of this stele that he
dedicated to the family of Osiris; the
long hymn to Osiris himself that he is
reciting is inscribed in front of him.
Mai has, however, left the place of hon-
or to his sovereign, who is shown in the
arch of the stele opposite the holy trinity of Abydos: Osiris, Isis and Horus.
Sety is wearing the blue crown and a
fine cloak that is light enough to reveal
the ceremonial pagne underneath. In
his outstretched hand he receives the
hieroglyphics for the divine gifts which
enable all kings to rule effectively over
Egypt: life, stability and power. The
king is followed by a prince whose
youth is indicated by the lock of hair he
wears to the side of his head. A short
inscription reveals his identity: the future Rameses II, eldest son of Sety and
here fan-bearer to his father. The titles of Mai himself show that the Abydos temple of the king, his Temple of
Millions of Years, was already in operation when he dedicated this stele. The
fact that Sety is shown as the reigning
and officiating sovereign reveals that
such sanctuaries were already used
during the lifetime of the kings in those
annual ceremonies which associated
royal power with the might of Amun,
and celebrated the renewal of both.

Bibliography
Limme 1979, p. 31.
I.F.

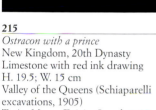

215

Ostracon with a prince
New Kingdom, 20th Dynasty
Limestone with red ink drawing
H. 19.5; W. 15 cm
Valley of the Queens (Schiaparelli
excavations, 1905)
Turin, Museo Egizio, Suppl. 5637

On this ostracon we have prince Sethherkhepeshef, Rameses III's son, accurately drawn in red ink. It is probably a sketch the artists used later to
decorate the walls of the prince's tomb
(QV43).
The prince's hair is gathered in a side
braid held by metal barrettes, a hairstyle typical of youth; he is wearing a
long skirt in light fabric, that shows his
legs and is held at the waist by a belt,
the ends of which hang down in front.
His feet are shod in sandals with upturned points. His right hand is raised
in an act of adoration while the left
holds a fan, whose feather has been
lost. The inscription behind him in hieroglyphic writing says: "The son of
the king, of his bowels, his beloved,
Sethherkhepeshef."
The back bears five lines in hieratic
writing, in black ink, very dim, and
containing administrative annotations
dated to the year 30 of Rameses III.

Bibliography
Donadoni Roveri 1988, p. 161.
S.D.

216

Glazed tile with a fish
New Kingdom, 19th Dynasty
Faience
31.5 × 16 cm
Qantir
Cairo Egyptian Museum, JE 89479

Together with many others, this glazed
tile decorated either the floor or the
lower section of the wall of the magnificent Ramesside palace at Qantir. It
shows a fish, the *tilapia nilotica* (of
the Cichlidae family), still common in
the Nile River, which was depicted
on tomb walls since the Prehistoric
Period. The ancient Egyptians called
it *inet* and later also referred to it as
wajd (the green or fresh). It was considered a symbol of rebirth and resurrection. Here the fish is heading toward a lotus flower, the vertical zigzag
lines in the background represents the
flow of water. Representations of natural scenes used for floor decorations
in royal palaces, indicate the influence of the Amarna style on the artist.

Bibliography
Griggs 1985, p. 31; Montréal 1986,
cat. 18.
Z.T.

217

Tile with rekhyt *bird*
New Kingdom, 20th Dynasty
Faience inlaid with glass paste
12 × 8 cm
Medinet Habu
Cairo Egyptian Museum, JE 33968

This tile shows the so-called *rekhyt*
("people") bird, a species of plover
bird crowned with a distinctive crest,
whose representation dates as far back
as the Early Dynastic period.
Together with many other tiles, it decorated the mortuary temple of Rameses III at Medinet Habu on the Theban west bank. The horizontal tail and
long legs are shown resting on a basket, which reads *neb*, meaning "all."
Similar tiles with a more complete decoration represent the *rekhyt* bird raising its arm in adoration; this interpretation is confirmed by the star which
reads *dua* and means "worship." Thus,
the symbolic idea behind the tile can
be translated as: "All the people are
worshipping [you]."

Bibliography
Griggs 1985, p. 38; Montréal 1986,
cat. 21.
Z.T.

218

Collar
New Kingdom, 19th Dynasty (?)
Gold and cornelian
W. 36 cm
Tell Basta (Bubastis)
Cairo, Egyptian Museum, JE 39875
= CG 53184

The Egyptians mastered the cutting,
forming, polishing and piercing of
hard gems and inlay stones as well as
the manufacture of colored glass and
faience in imitation of natural stones.
Here is an example of the production
of tiny beads of cornelian and gold
that suit the taste of both artisan and
owner. This collection of beads was
found loose in one of the two treasures at Bubastis (eastern Delta). The
arrangement and mounting of the gold
and cornelian drop beads on the collar, which resemble hanging cornflowers, is not the original one.

Bibliography
CG 52001–53855, p. 388, pl. LXXXIII;
Wilkinson 1971, p. 152, pl. LVIII B.
M.S.

219

Necklace
New Kingdom, 19th Dynasty,
reign of Sety I
Gold
L. 61 cm
Valley of the Kings, cache of the
jewels of Sety II and Tausret (KV56)
Cairo, Egyptian Museum, JE 39679
= CG 52679

This necklace comes from a burial
chamber which yielded up vases in
terra-cotta and alabaster, together with
various pieces of jewelry; some of the
latter bears the names of Sety II and
Tausret, but the chamber was undoubtedly dug during the period of
the 18th Dynasty (the presence of material from the 19th Dynasty reveals
that it was reused at a later date). The
discoverer of the chamber, E.R. Ayr-
ton, took it to be the cache for the
jewelry of Sety II and Tausret; C. Aldred gave another interpretation, arguing that what we see here are the remains of the furnishings from the
tomb of a son of Sety II and Tausret.
The filigree parts of this necklace were
found scattered among other pieces
of jewelry, and were later divided between the Egyptian Museum in Cairo
and the Metropolitan Museum of New
York (30.8.66; 26.7.1346, 1348). The
two necklaces now on display in those
museums, therefore, should be considered as forming a single piece. The
links are in the form of cornflowers
and small spheres, which in the reconstruction were placed alternately.
Each is an *à jour* mounting with different gold-wire rings of varying diameter welded together.

Bibliography
CG 52001–53855; Andrews 1990, pp.
126–127; Reeves, Wilkinson 1996, p.
153.
F.T.

220

Earrings of Sety II
New Kingdom, 19th Dynasty
Gold
H. 13 cm
Valley of the Kings,
cache of Tomb 53
Cairo, Egyptian Museum, JE 39657
= CG 52397

Earrings and ear ornaments as beauty
accessories for both sexes were known
since the New Kingdom, either
clasped on the ear lobes or hanging
from the sides of the wig, near the
ears. Pierced ears were first attested in
the mummy of Thutmose IV and statues from the time of Akhenaten. Different forms and shapes of ear ornaments are known from the tomb of
Tutankhamun, and are also depicted
on the wall decorations of temples and
royal or private tombs.
The owner of this piece of jewelry was
Sety II who ruled Egypt at the end of
the 19th Dynasty for about six years.
He built the triple shrine of Amun-
Ra, Mut and Khons at Karnak and his
tomb in the Valley of the Kings (KV15).
Sety II had two wives, Takhat and
Tausret.
This ear ornament was found together with other artifacts belonging to the
king and Tausret in a cache in the Valley of the Kings in 1908. It is composed of a flat trapezoidal centerpiece
from which hang seven pendants in
the form of cornflowers. At the ends of
the upper hollow tube of the earring
which keep the wig in place is a concave corolla of eight petals on one side
and a stud on the other. The birth and
throne names are incised on the flat
piece.

Bibliography
Vernier, Bijoux and Orfevreries (CG),
pp.137–38.
M.S.

221

Diadem of Sety II
New Kingdom, 19th Dynasty
Gold
Diam. 17.5 cm; weight 104 gr.
Valley of the Kings, cache of Tomb
53
Cairo, Egyptian Museum, JE 39674
= CG 52644

This golden diadem consists of 16 concave corolla of ten petals each fixed to
a narrow band. Some of the petals are
incised with the names of Sety and his
royal wife Tausret, before she assumed
the full royal titulary as the female
ruler after the king's death.
Diadems were worn during the lifetime and after death by royal and
wealthy personalities. They can be
seen on the statue of Nofret, wife of
Rahotep (Egyptian Museum of Cairo
CG.4) from the 4th Dynasty, in the
relief showing the daughters of Dje-
hutyhotep (Egyptian Museum of Cairo
JE 30199), and on the statue of Queen
Meritamun (Egyptian Museum of
Cairo JE 31413). They are made either of gold or silver and inlaid with semi-precious stones and glass paste or
frit, or are simply of pure gold. Of the
Middle Kingdom jewelry found in the
12th-Dynasty burials of the princesses in Dahshur, Hawara, the diadem of
Sat-Hathor-Yunet (Egyptian Museum
of Cairo JE 44919) is the most exquisite. It was used as an ornament
and also to keep the wig in place.

Bibliography
CG 52001–53855, p. 204, pl. XLI.
M.S.

222

Cup of Tausret
New Kingdom, 19th Dynasty
Gold
H. 9.5; diam. 8; base diam. 4.3 cm
Tell Basta (Bubastis)
Cairo, Egyptian Museum, JE 39872
= CG 53260

This delicate gold chalice, a royal
drinking vessel in the shape of a lotus
flower, belonged to Queen Tausret
when she became the ruler of Egypt after the death of her husband Sety II. It
consists of two pieces soldered together: the open blossom of the lotus
and the stem in the shape of an upside
down papyrus stalk.
The royal cartouche contains the name
of Queen Tausret surmounted by
feathers and a disk.

Bibliography
Griggs 1985, (cat. 25).
M.S.

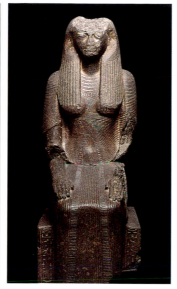

223
Sieve
New Kingdom, 19th Dynasty
Gold
H. 3.5; diam. 12 cm
Bubastis
New York, The Metropolitan
Museum of Art, T.M. Davis
Collection, bequest of T.M. Davis,
30.8.369

This prized object is a reproduction in precious metal of what is still an implement of everyday life. Even if its precise use cannot be determined, it seems probable that it was used to strain drinks. For example, beer was made by breaking up loaves of barley into vats of water and leaving the whole thing to ferment, which obviously meant there was quite a lot of residue floating in the finished drink. Having been poured into a drinking vessel (cat. no. 164), the liquid would then be drunk through a straw, complete with a small filter in the form of a cube. Wines, too, contained impurities.

The Metropolitan Museum sieve will have been used when the drinks were already presented to the guests in goblets (cat. no. 162). Its center consists of a number of concentric circles of small holes, and the handle is in the form of a flowering lotus, which extends into the inside of the receptacle in a semicircle frieze in which there are geometrical motifs and a floral corona. As was often the case, in producing objects for everyday use Egyptian craftsmen used decorative motifs that were both highly elegant and symbolically significant.

Bibliography
Seipel 2001, pp. 97, 100 (cat. 110).
I.F.

224
The queen mother of Rameses II
Middle Kingdom 12th Dynasty (?)
and New Kingdom, 19th Dynasty,
reign of Rameses II
Gray granite
H. 150 cm
Tanis
Cairo, Egyptian Museum, JE 37484

The queen sits on a small cushion on a cubical seat with a low back. She wears an elaborate tripartite wig of braided hair and a headpiece with a winged vulture. Her chest is adorned with a necklace made of several strands. Her dress, an inner and outer garment of fine pleated linen, is tied under her right breast. This pleated dress style was common during the 19th Dynasty. The queen has a round face, elongated eyes, a rather wide nose and a full mouth. Originally, her ears were visible, but they have been cut away. Her features are characteristic of the late Middle Kingdom.
Examination of the sculpture reveals that other changes have been made to the statue. There are remnants of stone around the waist, beside the hands, wrists, arms, and on the breasts that indicate that the queen's figure was recarved to create a more slender form. The hieroglyphic inscriptions on the front seem to be original, while those on the back and two sides are more deeply carved, suggesting recarving by another sculptor. These later inscriptions refer to the great royal mother of King Rameses II. One can only surmise that a sculpture of a Middle Kingdom queen was recarved as the queen mother of Rameses II.
A.M.

225
Rollin Papyrus
New Kingdom, 20th Dynasty
Papyrus, ink
H. 27.6; W. 50 cm
Thebes
Paris, Bibliothèque Nationale, 195
(*papyrus Rollin* 1888)

At the end of the reign of Rameses III a dark plot was hatched among the king's entourage. A secondary wife, the queen Tiy, had organized everything so that power would pass to her son, Pentaur. However, his access to the throne was barred by the legitimate heir, prince Rameses, and by the reigning sovereign himself. The conspiring queen used all the means at her disposal, intending to eliminate her husband and get rid of her son's rival. The number—and rank—of the people involved in the so-called "*harim* conspiracy" gives us some idea of the prevailing climate in the court of the day. Before it could be put into effect, however, the plot was discovered and the conspirators executed. The records of the various trials have come down to us, providing us with a range of information concerning the main figures involved (even if their real names are generally replaced with derogatory nicknames).
The Rollin Papyrus is one of the numerous documents that deal with this conspiracy, the main figure in which seems undoubtedly to have been queen Tiy, who in order to achieve her ends suborned various functionaries in the king's *harim*. This latter—modern—term is, in fact, a misnomer, because the so-called *harim* was a royal institution that was the home not only of the pharaoh's wives and concubines but also of his daughters. The text here is particularly interesting because it reveals that the accused, contemptuously referred to as Pabakka-

men—"The Blind Servant"—was responsible for getting the other conspirators into queen Tiy's apartments without anyone noticing. The traitor performed this task by using his knowledge of magic to cast a spell on the guards and making them fall into a deep sleep. Even if it is very likely that he also used powerful narcotics, Pabakkamen's misdeeds nevertheless reveal that sorcery might well be used by those close to the crown.

Bibliography
Goedicke 1963; Vernus 1993, p. 151;
Grandet 1993, p. 334; Grandet 1994.ll,
p. 113, no. 116.
I.F.

226
Plaque
New Kingdom, 18th Dynasty
Terra-cotta
H. 9.5 × W.11.8 × D. 2.0 cm
Gurob (Fayum), Tomb 474
Edinburgh, The Trustees of the
National Museums of Scotland,
A.1921.1482

The plaque represents two female fan-bearers wearing Nubian-type wigs, ointment cones and fillets.

Bibliography
Brunton, Engelbach 1927, pl. 28.9.
E.G., B.M.

227
Spoon in the form of an ibex
New Kingdom, 18th Dynasty, reigns
of Amenhotep III and IV
Tamarisk wood
L. 18.5; W. 8 cm
Gurob (Fayum), cemetery of the
palace
Paris, Musée du Louvre, E 11124

At the beginning of the XX century, near the present-day village of Medinet el-Gurob tombs of court ladies were found who—along with their personal effects—had been buried close to the palace in which they had lived. Unfortunately, this was a chance discovery, and the articles were soon snapped up by various Cairo antique dealers. The quantity of toilette implements in carved wood found in Gurob would suggest that the palace actually contained a workshop that produced such goods.
Wild game with bound feet, shown turning to lick its back, was a classic theme in the adornment of spoons, whose decoration was very varied: from young girls at the water's edge to servants carrying jars of water, from swimming girls to ducks, dogs and shells, etc. As usual, no trace of greasy unguent was found inside: hence the use of these spoons remains as uncertain as the significance of their decoration.

Bibliography
Vandier d'Abbadie 1972, p. 29, fig. 65 (cat. 65); Freed 1982, pp. 213, 214 (cat. 257); Delange 1993, p. 30.
G.P.

228
*Mirror for a court lady from
the Gurob palace*
New Kingdom, 18th Dynasty, reigns
of Amenhotep III and IV
Wood and bronze
L. 26; W. 5.1; diam. 12.7 cm
Gurob (Fayum), cemetery of the
palace (purchased in 1904)
Paris, Musée du Louvre, E 11042

The application of makeup required the use of mirrors, whose highly polished metal surfaces reflected the face more or less accurately. The handle of this mirror uses the curved form that was very common among accessories of the period, while the mirror itself is not a perfect circle but a more "organic" shape, fanning out at the bottom and rather flattened at the top. This work of adorned craftsmanship, therefore, is an example of the elegant style of the day. Like all objects from these tombs, this mirror reveals signs of wear and tear, which shows that it must have actually belonged to the deceased and followed her into the grave, for use in the afterlife.

Bibliography
Vandier d'Abbadie 1972, p. 169, fig. 756 (cat. 756); Kozloff, Bryan, Berman, Delange 1993, p. 360 (cat. 113bis).
G.P.

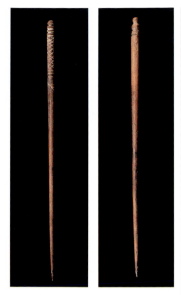

229

Two hairpins from Gurob
New Kingdom, 18th Dynasty,
reigns of Amenhotep III and IV
Wood
L. 17.5 cm (E 11049 1); L. 17 cm
(E 11049 2)
Gurob (Fayum), cemetery of the
palace (purchased in 1904)
Paris, Musée du Louvre, E 11049
1 and 2

These large wooden pins do not appear in depictions of Egyptian women but only in the scenes of hairdressing that took place in their private apartments. They were indispensable here for the dressing of either real hair or wigs. As a matter of fact, Egyptian hairstyles were made up of small plaits; so in dressing hair it was necessary to separate the strands for plaiting and hold the mass of the remaining hair in place at the same time. Whether made of wood, bone or ivory, these pins were only decorated at the head. Here, the decoration is a simple geometrical pattern; perhaps the end of one might be interpreted as a pomegranate.
G.P.

230

*Cosmetic Spoon in the shape
of a swimmer holding a goose*
New Kingdom, 18th Dynasty
Painted wood
L. 30. 5, H. 6.2 cm
Gurob (Fayum)
Cairo, Egyptian Museum, JE 28737,
CG 45117

This period abounded in cosmetic toilet articles in all manner of forms; private and royal tombs were equipped with unguent vessels, caskets, kohl containers, combs, mirrors, and variety of cosmetic spoons. The most popular was of a girl swimming, holding in her outstretched hands a container in the shape of a gazelle, fish or duck. The object illustrated here is often called a "swimming-girl spoon." The container is in the form of a duck, its body hollowed out to hold some precious ointment. Its head, with open beak and protruding tongue, was made separately and joined. Sliding wings, now missing, would have acted as a lid that fit into the hole at the base of the neck.
The incised linear decorations around the body and base of the neck are filled with blue paste. The handle consists of a slender nude girl in a swimming pose, her face is enhanced with color, her fringed wig is painted black, and her collar is inlaid with blue paste. The girl probably represents a servant or concubine supplying her master or mistress with a cosmetic unguent.
A.M.

231

Statuette of young girl with a cat
New Kingdom, 18th Dynasty
Wood
H. 17.3 cm
Abuzir el-Melek (excavations of
1903)
Berlin, Ägyptisches Museum
und Papyrussammlung, 16400

This delicate statue of a young girl served as the handle for a bronze mirror, which slotted into the fissure in the ointment cone on the young girl's head. In her left hand she holds a cat, while with her right she throws her wig back over her shoulder—an erotic gesture one finds in representations of couples. This mirror handle was found in a woman's tomb; however, the clear signs of wear on the figure's face and forehead reveal that the object must have been used in everyday life.

Bibliography
Priese 1991, p. 239 (cat. 145).
D.W.

The Eternity of a Pharaoh

232

Earrings
Second Intermediate Period,
17th Dynasty
Gold
Diam. 3 cm
Qurna
Edinburgh, The Trustees of the
National Museums of Scotland,
A.1909.527.18

These earrings came from the same
intact burial as the *shebu* collar (cat.
no. 108). They were found in place by
the woman's head. They are the earliest known examples of an open-end-
ed type that became popular in a modified form in the 18th Dynasty. Simple
in appearance, they are unusually elaborate in construction and are made of
exceptionally pure gold.

Bibliography
Andrews 1990, pp. 23 (fig. 14b), 111;
Eremin, Goring, Manley, Cartwright
2000.
E.G., B.M.

233

Toiletry implement
New Kingdom, 18th Dynasty
Gold
L. 8.6 cm
Provenance unknown
New York, The Metropoli-
tan Museum of Art, gift of Lila Acheson
Wallace, 1977.169

Such implements of toiletry can be
found in various museums, though
their exact use has never been established with certainty. It has been said
that they were scissors or pincers for
depilation; however, the arrangement
of the arms would not seem to lend itself to this use. Others have said that
they could have been used as hair-curl-
ing tongs. Part of the two copies of
such objects in the Hildesheim collection could well have been used as a
razor.
Usually these small instruments were
in bronze. The one in the Metropolitan Museum is in gold, and was clearly more of a luxury object. A further
peculiarity is that the upper arm is
shaped in the form of a dog, but the
proportions and outline do not correspond to the usual canons.

Bibliography
E. Haslauer in: Seipel 2001, p. 104
(cat. 118).
I.F.

*When one evokes ancient Egypt, images of pyramids and the Valley
of the Kings often come to mind and one may have the impression that
only the pharaoh had access to eternity. This was not, however, the
case, even though the intellectual conceptions of the other world are
more developed in the royal sepulchers.*
*The most ancient testimonies of a belief in a post mortem
transformation are constituted by the burials themselves and the
material that accompanied the deceased. In the Predynastic period, the
tombs were not only reserved to the local chiefs. In the historic period,
there was a sharp distinction between the funerary monuments of a
sovereign and those of his subjects. Naturally, this had to do with the
more privileged among the latter, those holding the highest state
offices. Nevertheless, cemeteries did exist for the common people, but
these were ignored by archaeology for a long time and contemporary
excavations have only begun to bring them to light.*
*Two main elements denote the basic difference existing between a
royal tomb and a private one. On the one hand, the cut and shape of
the sepulcher; on the other, the contents of its decoration. In the Old
Kingdom, for example, the pyramid and its complex of two temples
connected by an ascending causeway can be distinguished from the
mastabas of the high officials. Further, while the decoration of the
royal and private cult places seems quite close, at the end of the 5th
Dynasty the chambers in the pyramids began to be decorated with
extremely important texts that enable us to understand what happened
to the king after his death. One discovers this same distinction in the
New Kingdom; the hypogea in the Valley of the Kings developed
complex descriptions of the cosmos and the nocturnal course of the sun
with which the deceased sovereign was associated. The latter merged
into the divine world and was identified primarily with the sun-god.
The different transformations that enabled him to be eternally reborn
in the image of the sun constituted several stages in which one of the
most important was his identification with Osiris, the divinity who
presided over the renewal of life. These preoccupations are quite
similar to those that appear in private chapels. Nonetheless, their form
of expression is completely different. This is due to the very nature of
the Egyptian monarchy that required that the sovereign, originally a
simple mortal, be transcended by the divine function with which he
was entrusted. This special essence enabled him to mingle with the
gods after his death, while his subjects, who aspired to the same
destiny, had to employ images that were closer to the real world.
Another notable characteristic: each period of decline in royal power
seems to have given the officials access to the corpus of texts that until
then were reserved to the king, a sign that the transformation of the
pharaoh was the model par excellence of the entire destiny of eternity.*
I.F.

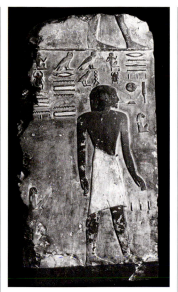

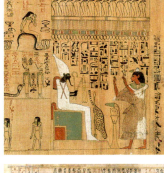

234

The work organization in the tomb of Rameses IV
New Kingdom, 20th Dynasty
Cyperus papyrus
H. 23; W. 24 cm
Deir el-Medina
Turin, Museo Egizio, Drovetti Collection, 1891

This papyrus, dating to Rameses IV's second year, was found in the archives of the village of Deir el-Medina. The hieratic text on the front of the papyrus regards the work organization in the king's tomb (KV2) in the Valley of the Kings, of which Cat. 1885 reproduces the plan. According to other sources, work on the tomb did not begin until the second year of Rameses' rule, the delay being due to the political and economic unrest that marked the end of Rameses III's reign and the beginning of his successor's. To hasten the work, the vizier Neferrenepet went to Thebes, with the treasury superintendent Montuematawy and other officials, where, on behalf of the king, he ordered that the number of craftsmen be increased in order to complete the royal burial. Their number was doubled from 60 to 120, an increase that had never before been registered and one that would never again occur in the history of the Valley of the Kings. In spite of the organizational effort and the human resources, the tomb was left unfinished: at the king's death, the corridor and the annexes behind the burial chamber were hastily completed.

Bibliography
Pleyte, Rossi, pls. 49–50; Valbelle 1985.
S.D.

235

Fragment of the Book of Gates
New Kingdom, 19th Dynasty
Painted limestone
H. 100; W. 53 cm
Thebes, Valley of the Kings, tomb of Sety I
Berlin, Ägyptisches Museum und Papyrussammlung, 2079

In the New Kingdom pharaohs' tombs in the Valley of the Kings at Thebes, the dead sovereign is surrounded by several descriptions—of the afterlife both in words and images—wherein the deceased accompanies the sun during the night until it rises again in the morning. In Sety I's hypogeum, one of the largest royal tombs, the illustrations and texts from the book of *Amduat* are accompanied by others from the *Book of Gates*. These include a depiction of the kingdom of the sun-god, whose rays also fall onto foreign countries, where alongside the Egyptians, Asians and Libyans can also be seen.

Bibliography
PM I.2, p. 541 (33)–(34).
D.W.

236

Book of the Afterlife *of the priest Amenhotep*
New Kingdom, 20th Dynasty
Papyrus
L. 30 cm
Provenance unknown
Berlin, Ägyptisches Museum und Papyrussammlung, 3005

In twelve successive scenes involving various figures, the *Book of the Emergence of the Day* describes the journey of the sun from when it sets in the evening to when it rises in the morning. Initially limited to the royal tombs in the Valley of the Kings, toward the end of the New Kingdom it would begin to appear in the tombs of private individuals, as well as on coffins and—above all—religious papyri that were available to everyone.

Bibliography
Luft, Poetke 1977, pp. 35–36, pl. III.
D.W.

237

Coffin of Ahmose
18th Dynasty, reign of Ahmose
Painted wood
L. cm 178
Thebes, Deir el-Bahri cache (TT320)
Cairo, Egyptian Museum, CG 60001

This coffin is one out of many discovered in 1881 by Maspero in the Deir el-Bahri cachette, where the high priests of Amun reburied the mummies of the most famous pharaohs of the New Kingdom to preserve them from robberies.
King Ahmose was the first ruler of the 18th Dynasty, son of the Theban 17th-Dynasty ruler Seqenenra Taa II. He came to the throne of a reunited Egypt after having definitively repulsed the Hyksos rulers from the Delta region. Little has survived of his architectural achievements: a few additions to the temples of Amun and Montu at Karnak and a mud-brick cenotaph for himself and his grandmother Tetisheri in Abydos.
The coffin of King Ahmose is of the *rishi* type. The Arabic word means "feathers" and refers to the wing motif decorating the coffin. These are interpreted as the wings of the goddess Isis who protectively embraces the deceased. The coffin also shows the introduction of a new technique. Rather than simply scoring the feathered patterning and other elements into the plaster that overlays the relatively poor local wood, cedar was used. The royal craftsmen made use of this finer medium to carve the strips of the headdress and collar into the wood itself. The whole surface was then gilded over a fine layer of whiting so that the gold leaf could adhere. The strips were then probably inlaid with colored glass paste or semi-precious stones.
An examination of the mummy of Ahmose, which was still in the coffin when it was found, suggests that the king was about 35 years old when he died. The location of his tomb is not yet known, but it is thought to be somewhere on the cliff of Dra Abu el-Naga, in the west bank of Thebes.

Bibliography
CG 61001–61044; CG 61051–61100.
A. Hel.

238

The linen shroud of Thutmose III
New Kingdom, 18th Dynasty,
reign of Thutmose III
Linen and black ink
L. 111; H. 63.5 cm
Thebes, Deir el-Bahri cache (TT320)
Boston, Museum of Fine Arts,
gift of Horace L. Mayer, 60.1472

This inscribed fragment of fine linen is a portion of a shroud that once enveloped the mummy of Thutmose III. Protective spells and prayers are artistically rendered in cursive hieroglyphs in black ink in one horizontal band at the top and 50 vertical columns. (According to Dunham 1972, pp. 15–16, shortly before 1885 this fragment was part of the Luigi Vassali collection, it then passed into the collection of Clement Maraini from whose heirs it was acquired by Mr. Horace Mayer about 1928.)
Tomb robbers during the New Kingdom had ripped the mummy of Thutmose III into pieces, subsequently priests in the 21st Dynasty rewrapped and reburied the mummy in a royal cache in Deir el-Bahri. (Smith 1912, p. 33; Reeves 1990, p. 245 suggests a time "after year 11 of Shoshenq I.") When discovered in 1881, the shroud was found in fragments in the burial. (Maspero 1889, p. 548, states that it was in three fragments. The Museum of Fine Arts, Boston, possesses two additional very small fragments, 60.1473 and 60.1474; Note also that Porter and Moss 1964, p. 660 mention two additional fragments: Cairo Museum Ent. 26203 and another fragment formerly in Amherst Collection, in Sothebys' Sale Catalog June 13–17, 1921, no. 353.) While the mummy was unwrapped and then rebandaged at that time by Emil Brugsch, it is not stated whether the shroud was on the rewrapped remains or even lying on or inside the coffin. (Nagel 1949, pp. 317–318; Smith 1912, p. 32; Maspero 1883, p. 317.)
The Boston fragment of the shroud is torn along the top, bottom and left sides. A selvedge edge on the right indicates the right end of the shroud. The left side of the Boston piece joins directly to a larger one in the Cairo Museum (40001) which forms the left end of the shroud. The entire shroud is greater than 5 m in length (Nagel 1949, p. 320). The entire lower half of the shroud is missing. A decorative border of blue sky with yellow stars tops the Cairo length and originally the Boston piece as well (Nagel 1949, p. 32).
The Book of the Dead Spells 1, 21–24, 90, 125, 154 and Pyramid Texts Spells 52 and 53 are inscribed on the Boston linen (Nagel 1949, pp. 322–325). The Cairo portion contains additional Book of the Dead spells (17, 18, 68, 69, 70, 75, 83–86, 88, 105) as well as the Litany of Ra. One fascinating passage in the Cairo portion reveals that the shroud was made for Thutmose III by his son, and successor Amenhotep II ("made as a monument for his father").

Bibliography
PM I.2; CG 61051–61100; Maspero 1883, pp. 315–317; Maspero 1889; Dunham 1931; Nagel 1949, pp. 317–329; Smith 1962; Dunham 1972, pp.15–16; Reeves 1990.
J.H.

239

Shroud of princess Ahmose
New Kingdom, late 17th Dynasty
Linen
H. 110; W. 45 cm
Valley of the Queens (Schiaparelli
excavations, 1903–1906)
Turin, Museo Egizio, CGT 63001

Fragment of the shroud of princess Ahmose, daughter of the King Seqenenra I and coming from her burial place in the Valley of the Queens (QV47). The grave, at the time of the discovery, had already been ransacked of its treasures and the shroud was found in fragments, along with a few items of the burial goods. Originally 1 m high and 4 m wide, it must have entirely enveloped the mummified princess' body. On the shroud are written several chapters of the collection of magic-religious texts known as the Book of the Dead, and of which it is one of the oldest exemplars conserved on fabric. The following Spells in particular were preserved: 124, 83, 84, 85, 82, 77, 99, 172, 7, 102, 38a, 27, 14, 39, 65, 116, 91, 64. This sequence matches that of other shrouds in the Cairo Museum, all datable to the beginning of the 17th Dynasty. The texts, in hieroglyphic writing, are arranged in vertical columns, with spaces left for the titles of the formulas. The fragment on exhibit features Spell 64, that presents a synthesis of the entire Book of the Dead, as specified by the title—known by other versions, but not conserved here: "formula to know the formulas to come to light in a single formula."

Bibliography
Ronsecco 1996.
S.D.

240

Heart scarab of King Sobkemsaf
Second Intermediate Period,
17th Dynasty
Gold and green jasper
3.6 × 2.4 × 1.8 cm
Thebes
London, The Trustees of the British
Museum, EA 7876

The heart scarab was an important funerary amulet, and was usually inscribed with Spell 30B from the Book of the Dead. This text was intended to prevent the heart of the deceased from revealing to the gods of the judgment hall any potentially incriminating information about its owner's conduct during life.

This example is the earliest known heart scarab made for a king, one of two rulers of the Second Intermediate Period named Sobkemsaf. The body of the scarab is carved from green jasper and has a rudimentary human face. The gold setting reproduces the beetle's legs, and is inscribed around the edge and on the base with the appropriate spell. In the inscription, the legs of the bird-hieroglyphs have been deliberately omitted in order to render them harmless should they (by some mischance) become animated and cause harm to the deceased. This reflects the belief that an image, even when acting as a phonetic sign, was capable of becoming reality and possessed a latent power.

The Leopold II-Amherst Papyrus records the confession of robbers who plundered the pyramid tomb of Sobkemsaf II on the Theban west bank about 1110 BC, and includes a description of the valuable objects stolen from the royal mummy: "A large number of amulets and jewels of gold were upon his neck, and his headpiece of gold was upon him." This heart scarab, which may well have been among the loot, was perhaps hidden by the robbers before their capture or subsequently recovered by the authorities of the necropolis.
J.H.T.

241

Canopic jar
New Kingdom, 18th Dynasty,
reign of Akhenaten
Alabaster
H. 38.5 cm
Thebes, Valley of the Kings (KV55)
Cairo, Egyptian Museum, JE 39637

Canopic jars were used to preserve the viscera (liver, lungs, stomach and intestines) removed during mummification. This jar was one of four found inside a niche in tomb KV55. One was taken to the Metropolitan Museum of Art, New York, the other three remained in Cairo. Although the inscriptions on the bodies have been carefully chiseled away so that the neither the name of the deceased nor the title are legible, the jars have been attributed over the years to several members of Akhenaten's family, from Queen Tiy to the pharaoh himself. Recently, however, scholars have attributed the vessels to Akhenaten's secondary wife Kiya, though it has been suggested that they originally did not match the lids. At present, most scholars favor one of Akhenaten's daughters as the original owner.
The female royal head which forms the stopper of each jar is a masterpiece of Amarna art. It is an elegant portrait, its face framed by a short wig ending with two side braids cut diagonally in front. On the forehead was once the *uraeus* whose body is carved on top of the wig. The eyes are narrow with heavy lids; the eyebrows and eyes are outlined in blue paste, while the whites and the pupils are in quartz and obsidian. Traces of red color are still visible at the corners. The nose is small and narrow, the mouth fleshy and slightly downturned.

Bibliography
Arnold 1996, pp. 116–17, fig. 116;
Tiradritti 1998, p. 293.
A.M.

242

Djed pillar
New Kingdom, 18th Dynasty,
reign of Amenhotep II
Painted wood
H. 51 cm
Thebes, tomb of Amenhotep II
Cairo, Egyptian Museum,
CG 24436, JE 32548

Like the blue faience *ankh* (cat. no. 243), the *djed* pillar was among the objects excavated by Victor Loret in 1898–99 in the tomb of King Amenhotep II in the Valley of the Kings. Many similar objects were excavated there.
The *djed* pillar probably represents a pole to which sheaves of grain were attached, or it may be a schematic representation of a sacred tree. Whatever it may have been, it was a very ancient sacred object. The *djed* pillar was carried by the pharaoh himself, no doubt to ensure the continuing fertility of the fields and to guarantee that the god himself as corn king was periodically revived.
The *djed* pillar is one of the most important symbols of Osiris, the lord of the netherworld, protector of justified souls, and judge of the dead. Osiris is also the symbol of resurrection and a plant fertility deity.
The *djed* pillar emblem was associated not only with Osiris but also with the Memphite god Ptah, and probably also with Sokar. These connections suggest its origin in Memphis, capital of Egypt during the Old Kingdom. Ptah, Sokar, and Osiris were merged into a single composite deity in the course of the New Kingdom.
It was represented on the bottom of the New Kingdom coffin in line with the backbone, so the hieroglyphic word must mean stability, capacity to endure.
A.M.

243

Ankh sign
New Kingdom, 18th Dynasty,
reign of Amenhotep II
Faience
H. 42; W. 21 cm
Thebes, tomb of Amenhotep II
Cairo, Egyptian Museum,
CG 24348, JE 32491

Amenhotep II's tomb was excavated by Victor Loret in 1898–99 in the Valley of the Kings. This faience sign of the *ankh*, the Egyptian symbol of life, was found in the king's tomb together with about forty similar objects.
Ankh signs made of faience or other materials were among the most popular Egyptian amulets. Their precise function is not certain although they most probably were used as a magical protection, and as guarantee of the pharaoh's renewed life in the tombs.
The *ankh* is one of the most effective symbols in Egyptian art, and it was frequently depicted in scenes which show the gods placing it near the king's face or nose to symbolize the conferral of eternal life. In the Amarna period, when the sun-disk is represented with rays that end with an arm or a hand, the *ankh* is shown being offered to Akhenaten by the sun. *Ankh* signs were also commonly carried by deities in human or partly human form. The sign survived into the Christian era and was used by the Copts on their funerary stelae.
A.M.

244

Was *scepter*
New Kingdom, 18th Dynasty,
reign of Amenhotep II
Faience
H. 60 cm
Thebes, Valley of the Kings,
tomb of Amenhotep II (KV35)
Cairo, Egyptian Museum, CG 24396
= JE 96898

The *was* sign is a scepter whose handle is in the form of a canine head and whose base ends in two prongs. A symbol of power, it is usually carried by gods. The sky is also supported by *was* scepters. Innumerable depictions show the gods passing it on to the king along with the *ankh* and *djed* signs which are traditionally translated as dominion, life and stability.
This scepter, which was broken into five pieces, bears Amenhotep II's cartouche. The head of the animal is barely marked with black ink.

Bibliography
CG 24001–24990, p. 126, pl. XXIX.
A.H.

245

Hes *vase*
New Kingdom, 18th Dynasty,
reign of Amenhotep II
Faience
H. 21.5; Diam. max. 7.6 cm
Thebes, Valley of the Kings,
tomb of Amenhotep II (KV35)
Cairo, Egyptian Museum, CG 3870
= JE 32543

The tombs of the pharaohs in the New Kingdom were filled with vessels of all shapes and materials that were filled with oil, wine, cereals, unguents, cosmetics etc. to provide the dead with everything needed for the afterlife. Other vessels were primarily used for cultic rites. The *hes* vase was usually used for water, i.e. libation for the gods or for purifying rituals. The inscription reads: "Beautiful god, lord of the Two Lands, Aakheperura [prenomen of Amenhotep II], beloved of Osiris, justified."

Bibliography
CG 3618–4000, 18001–18037, 18600, 18603; CG 24001–24990, p. 220, pl. XLVI.
A.H.

246

Faience hes *vase of Amenhotep II*
New Kingdom, 18th Dynasty,
reign of Amenhotep II
Blue-glazed faience, painted
H. 21 cm; diam. at shoulder 8.0 cm
Thebes, Valley of the Kings,
tomb of Amenhotep
London, The Trustees of the British Museum, EA 43042

Faience hes *vase of Amenhotep II*
New Kingdom, 18th Dynasty,
reign of Amenhotep II
Blue-glazed faience, painted
H. 21.5 cm
Thebes, Valley of the Kings,
tomb of Amenhotep
London, The Trustees of the British Museum, EA 48656

The tombs of the pharaohs of the New Kingdom contained numerous ritual vessels in a variety of materials. Many of them were manufactured in faience, and were models of functional jars, which would have been made of metal or pottery. The tomb of Amenhotep II, discovered by Victor Loret in 1898, yielded several of these dummy-vessels. The first example bears a single column of inscription in black paint, reading "The good god, lord of the Two Lands, Aakheperura [prenomen of Amenhotep II], beloved of Osiris." The second vase also carries the king's name and epithets, here arranged in two columns.
J.H.T.

247

Cup
New Kingdom, 18th Dynasty,
reign of Amenhotep II
Faience
H. 6; upper diam. 8.8;
lower diam. 6 cm
Thebes, Valley of the Kings,
tomb of Amenhotep II (KV35)
Cairo, Egyptian Museum, CG 3926

The cup has the form of a truncated
cone and is decorated with black lines.
The two columns of inscription read:
"Beloved of Osiris, justified, the beautiful god, lord of the Two Lands,
Aakheperura [prenomen of Amenhotep II]." Cups like this could be
used as drinking-vessels or for libation before the gods.

Bibliography
CG 3618–4000, 18001–18037, 18600,
18603; CG 24001–24990, p. 230, pl.
XLVI.
A.H.

248

Model throw-stick
New Kingdom, 18th Dynasty,
reign of Amenhotep II
Blue faience
L. 21.5 cm
Thebes, Valley of the Kings,
tomb of Amenhotep II (KV35)
Cairo, Egyptian Museum, CG 24346
= JE 32648g

Throw-sticks were used to hunt birds,
a sport often depicted in private
tombs. As part of the funerary equipment, the model of the throw-stick
not only symbolized the joy of hunting,
but also the destruction of evil and regeneration. This example is decorated
with two eyes on the curved part and
with a lotus flower at the end of the
handle. The inscription reads: "The
perfect god, Aakheperura [prenomen
of Amenhotep II], [lord of] the Two
Lands, justified b[y] Osiris."

Bibliography
CG 24001–24990, p. 118.
A.H.

249

Model of a scroll
New Kingdom, 18th Dynasty,
reign of Amenhotep II
W. 10 cm
White faience
Valley of the Kings,
tomb of Amenhotep II (KV35)
Cairo, Egyptian Museum, JE 39645

This cylindrical object is generally tak-
en to be a model of a papyrus scroll.
However, its width does not really correspond with that of the scrolls actually in use in this period (the standard
during the reign of Thutmose III was
36 cm per scroll, and 16–17 cm for a
half scroll). Similarly, the slightly diagonal incision across the cylinder
does not exactly reflect how the final
part of a papyrus was cut. It is thus
possible that this cylinder, like others
found in the tomb of Amenhotep II,
was a model not of a papyrus scroll but
of a roll of bandages. This interpretation is perhaps supported by the total
absence of any inscription. The placing of this model of mummification
bandages in the tomb would have
been intended to offer further protection of the body of the pharaoh—giv-
en that the model was more long-lasting than the perishable fabric actually
used. If the cylinder is seen as a papyrus scroll, then its contents would
have been rather particular: scrolls of
ten-fifteen centimeters in width were
used above all for literary text, which
means that these ceramic models were
intended to form a veritable library of
reading matter.
F.T.

250
Model of unrolled papyrus
New Kingdom, 18th Dynasty,
reign of Amenhotep II
Blue faience
L. 12.4; W. 9.2 cm
Thebes, Valley of the Kings,
tomb of Amenhotep II (KV35)
Cairo, Egyptian Museum, CG 24473
= JE 32646

The object imitates a partially opened papyrus that is still rolled at both ends. The inscription reads: "The perfect god, Aakheperura [prenomen of Amenhotep II], justified by Osiris, the great god." Models of rolled and unrolled papyri as well as usable writing palettes were given as funerary equipment so that the dead would be able to write in the netherworld.
A.H.

251
Ankh *sign*
New Kingdom, 18th Dynasty,
reign of Thutmose IV
Bichrome faience
H. 23.5; W. 12.8 cm
Thebes, Valley of the Kings,
tomb of Thutmose IV (KV43)
Boston, Museum of Fine Arts,
gift of Theodore M. Davis, 03.1089

"You have not gone away dead, you have gone away alive." So begins the Resurrection Ritual from the ancient Egyptian Pyramid Texts, inscribed in the burial chambers of the Old Kingdom pyramids. A lifetime like Ra, the sun-god, was the ultimate gift from the gods to the king. Innumerable scenes on temple walls show the gods presenting the sign of life to the king's nostrils.

This object takes the form of the hieroglyph for *ankh,* the Egyptian word for "life." On the shaft a papyrus plant supports the cartouche of the king. Similar large faience *ankh*s were found in the tomb of Amenhotep II, Thutmose IV's father. One gathers they were standard items of royal funerary equipment. Blue faience as a material was believed to have regenerative properties and would thus have been appropriate for a funerary amulet connoting new life in the hereafter.

Bibliography
Carter, Newberry 1904, p. 102; A.M. Roth in: Eggebrecht 1987, pp. 359–230 (cat. 310); P. Lacovara in: Thomas 1995, p. 182, (cat. 83B); Y.J. Markowitz in: Nagoya/Boston 1999, pp. 79, 184 (cat. 77).
L.M.B.

252
Model papyrus roll
New Kingdom, 18th Dynasty,
reign of Thutmose IV
Bichrome faience
L. 14; diam. 2.8 cm
Thebes, Valley of the Kings,
tomb of Thutmose IV (KV43)
Boston, Museum of Fine Arts,
gift of Theodore M. Davis, 03.1095

Among the objects Carter found in the tomb of Thutmose were twenty-six model papyrus rolls. Each is a simple cylinder of faience. Spirals painted on the ends give the effect of the rolled up papyrus while a single line painted lengthwise simulates the outer edge of the roll. These are clearly magical objects for obviously the "roll" cannot be unrolled and there is a not a word to be read or recited. But just as in Egyptian art a container may also stand for its contents so might the outward form of a papyrus roll call up the magical spells inscribed thereon. Not a shred of papyrus was found in the tomb.

Sixteen model papyrus rolls were found in the Tomb 55 in the Valley of the Kings. These were evidently made in pairs, there being eight pair.

Bibliography
Carter, Newberry 1904, p. 115; P. Lacovara in: Thomas 1995, p. 182 (cat. 83C); Yvonne J. Markowitz in: Nagoya/Boston 1999, pp. 79, 184 (cat. 78).
L.M.B.

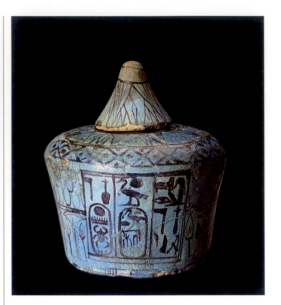

253

Model throw-stick
New Kingdom, 18th Dynasty,
reign of Thutmose IV
Bichrome faience
L. 26; W. 4.1 cm
Thebes, Valley of the Kings,
tomb of Thutmose IV (KV43)
Boston, Museum of Fine Arts,
gift of Theodore M. Davis, 03.1086

This model throw-stick inscribed with
the name of Thutmose IV is one of
nineteen found in the tomb. Real
throw-sticks for fowling were made of
wood. Faience throw-sticks, impracti-
cal for use in daily life, were made for
the afterlife. Fowling in the marshes is
mentioned in funerary spells as one of
the activities of Osiris: "There shall
come to you waterfowl in thousands,
lying on your path; you cast your
throw-stick at them, and it means a
thousand are fallen at the sound of its
wind." Implicit in every hunt is the
victory of order over chaos, embodied
in the sun-god's triumph over his enemies, and made manifest by the dawn
of each new day, which is a renewal of
creation. The throw-stick is itself a visual pun, for the same Egyptian root,
qema, is used both for the actions of
throwing a throw-stick and for the
verb "to create."
A standard item of royal tomb equipment in the New Kingdom, the model throw-stick is both the symbol and
guarantor of the king's successful rebirth in the afterlife.

Bibliography
Carter, Newberry 1904, p. 112 [10]; P.
Lacovara in: Thomas 1995, p. 182 (cat.
83A); Yvonne J. Markowitz in: Nago-
ya/Boston 1999, pp. 79, 184 (cat. 76).
L.M.B.

254

Shabti *of Thutmose IV*
New Kingdom, 18th Dynasty,
reign of Thutmose IV
Faience
H. 18.5 cm
Thebes, Valley of the Kings,
tomb of Thutmose IV (KV43)
Boston, Museum of Fine Arts,
gift of Theodore M. Davis, 03.1098

Just as agriculture and division of agricultural labor served as the basis for
organizing the Egyptians' daily life,
these ideas also served as the basis for
the next life. The Egyptian vision of
the afterlife was one spent performing
agricultural tasks in service to the gods.
To avoid having to serve personally, the
deceased could hire a substitute work-
er to act on his or her behalf. Made in
the image of their owner, these funerary
figurines, called *shabti*s, magically fulfilled the owner's obligations, and in
the process, allowed him or her to enjoy an afterlife of peace and relaxation.
Strangely enough, not only high officials
and their ladies but also kings and
queens, who never did menial work in
their lives, still felt it was necessary to
take this precaution against the chance
they might be called upon to work in
the fields. To enable them to perform
their tasks *shabti*s were often equipped
with small hoes and baskets. The
*shabti*s of Thutmose IV found in his
tomb were the first funerary figurines to
be shown holding these implements.
A column of inscription proclaims his
royal status as "The son of Ra, of his
body, Thutmose, beloved of Osiris, the
great god."
L.M.B.

255

Libation vessel (nemset jar)
New Kingdom, 18th Dynasty,
reign of Thutmose IV
Bichrome faience
H. 19; diam. 16 cm
Thebes, Valley of the Kings,
tomb of Thutmose IV (KV43)
Boston, Museum of Fine Arts,
gift of Theodore M. Davis, 03.1103

The tomb of Thutmose IV was discovered in 1903 by Howard Carter, at
that time chief inspector for Upper
Egypt, on behalf of Theodore M.
Davis, a wealthy American business-
man, who from 1902 to 1914 held the
concession to excavate in the Valley of
the Kings.
The tomb had of course been ransacked in antiquity, though it still contained the king's magnificent quartzite
sarcophagus and his wooden chariot
decorated with scenes of the king triumphing over his enemies. As was the
arrangement, these objects were re-
tained for the Cairo Museum while
the duplicates among the small finds
were given to Davis who generously
divided them between the Metropolitan Museum, New York, and the Museum of Fine Arts, Boston.
The tomb was particularly rich in
faience. Among these were twenty-
three *nemset* jars (a type of libation
vessel) with lids in the form of invert-
ed lotus blossoms glazed a brilliant
blue with details in purple-black paint.
These vessels were used in the funerary cult to purify the deceased with
water in the "opening of the mouth"
ceremony, performed over the mummy. The inscription linking the king
with the god of the dead reads, "the
good god Menkheperra, the son of Ra
Thutmose, beloved of Osiris, the great
god."

Bibliography
Carter, Newberry 1904, p. 58 [1], pl.
XVIA–B; Smith 1960, pp. 120, 124,
fig. 70 center; P. Lacovara in: Thomas
1995, p. 182 (cat. 83D); Y.J. Markowitz in: Nagoya/Boston 1999, pp. 79,
184 (cat. 79).
L.M.B.

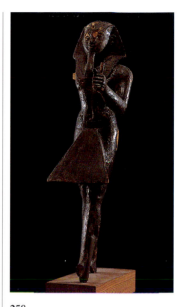

256

Model throw-stick
New Kingdom, 18th Dynasty,
end of reign of Akhenaten
Glazed composition
38.5 × 4.4 × 1.7 cm
Tell el-Amarna
London, The Trustees of the British
Museum, EA 34213

King Akhenaten, successor of Amen-hotep III, was determined to impose on Egypt his personal belief in only one god, the sun-disk Aten. Rapidly abolishing worship of the traditional deities, his doctrine failed to appeal to the masses and he made many ene-mies. On his death the old gods were quickly restored, and Akhenaten's newly-created residential city at el-Amarna, along with its temples, was abandoned and demolished. Stigma-tized as "the heretic king," Akhenaten was soon wiped out of history. But al-though his tomb in the Eastern Desert was thoroughly pillaged, part of the burial equipment did survive into modern times. This throw-stick—un-fit for actual use and of mere ritual significance—was probably taken from the tomb before archaeologists discovered it. Similar examples were found in tombs of two earlier 18th-Dynasty kings, and parallels are known for many other New Kingdom rulers, the most striking being from the fol-lowing reign of Tutankhamun. The decoration consists of lotus flowers, amuletic *wedjat* eyes and the king's cartouches.
M.M.

257

*Dummy bag with the name
of Rameses II*
New Kingdom, 19th Dynasty,
reign of Rameses II
Wood, plastered and gilded
H. 11.5 cm
Provenance unknown
London, The Trustees of the British
Museum, EA 35274

*Dummy vessel with the name
of Rameses II*
New Kingdom, 19th Dynasty,
reign of Rameses II
Wood, plastered and gilded
H. 7.2 cm
Provenance unknown
London, The Trustees of the British
Museum, EA 35275

Models of implements and containers used in important rituals were some-times included among the equipment placed in tombs. It was believed that such replicas could function by mag-ic as effectively as the real objects. These models represent a globular jar and a bag, tied at the neck and in-scribed with the name of the supposed contents: *mesdemet*, or black eye paint. One context in which this substance was used was the "opening of the mouth," a crucial ritual which reani-mated the mummified body so that it could function as a base for the *ka*, or spirit, in the afterlife.
The models undoubtedly formed part of a more extensive set of items, which would have enabled the deceased to perform the ritual him/herself, there-by ensuring an eternal existence in the hereafter. Both pieces (together with a third in the British Museum, EA 35273) are inscribed with the names of Rameses II, which suggests that they may have come from the burial of a royal personage—possibly even that of the king himself.
J.H.T.

258

Statue of Amenhotep II
New Kingdom, 18th Dynasty,
reign of Amenhotep II
Wood (cedar), covered with bitumen
H. 80; W. 22 cm
Thebes, Valley of the Kings,
tomb of Amenhotep II (KV35)
Cairo, Egyptian Museum, CG 24598
= JE 32305

King Amenhotep II is represented walking in the traditional regal cos-tume with the *nemes* headdress, straight beard, and short apron with a triangular front. The whole statue was covered with bitumen and painted, but only traces are left. An *uraeus*, probably made of metal must have been in the hole on the forehead. The inlaid eyes are missing. The arms and feet were worked separately and at-tached with wooden dowels. The plugs under the feet indicate that the statue was mounted on a base. The king holds a stick in his left hand which runs through a ring in the form of a pa-pyrus, the heraldic plant of Lower Egypt and the symbol of youth and regeneration.

Bibliography
CG 24001–24990, p. 155, pl. XXXI.
A.H.

259

Statue of a panther
New Kingdom, 18th Dynasty,
reign of Amenhotep II
Wood covered with bitumen
H. *c.* 28; W. *c.* 70 cm
Thebes, Valley of the Kings,
tomb of Amenhotep II (KV35)
Cairo, Egyptian Museum, CG 24621
= JE 32632 and 32531

The panther represented a protective
force for the life of the king, but was
also venerated inasmuch as it was related to the sun-god and the goddess
of the sky, being described as "mother and sky" for the dead. Its skin was
worn by priests as a symbol of regeneration.
This statue of a panther is covered
with bitumen, and its eyes are painted
yellow. On the back are two plugs,
others are under the paws; therefore it
is possible that this object carried a
statue of the king, like the ones on a
leopard found in the tomb of Tutankhamun.

Bibliography
CG 24001–24990, p. 160f.,
pl. XXXIV.
A.H.

260

Statue of a deity
New Kingdom, 18th Dynasty,
reign of Amenhotep II
Wood (cedar)
H. 61 cm
Thebes, Valley of the Kings,
tomb of Amenhotep II (KV35)
Cairo, Egyptian Museum, CG 24620
= JE 32327

Among the many different lion-deities
in ancient Egypt, the most popular
was the wild goddess Sekhmet,
who—once tamed—turned into the
gentler shape of a cat. Sekhmet was also the divine mother of the king and
protectress against illnesses. The body
of this seated statue is mummified.
The statue was composed of several
pieces and painted black. The four
plugs at the bottom indicate that it
was probably mounted on a base.

Bibliography
CG 24001–24990, p. 160, pl. XXXIII.
A.H.

261

Model boat
New Kingdom, 18th Dynasty, reign
of Amenhotep II
Wood, painted (sycamore and cedar)
L. 213; W. 36; H. 22 cm
Thebes, Valley of the Kings,
tomb of Amenhotep II (KV35)
Cairo, Egyptian Museum, CG 4945
= JE 32217

The ship was the most common means
of transport in ancient Egypt. Therefore it is not surprising that the sun-
god on his journey is also depicted in
a boat. Real shipping was largely restricted to the Nile, for the sea was
rather sinister to the Egyptians. Model boats (then still mostly of clay) were
placed into the tombs of the deceased
from prehistoric times onward, a usage
that became fashionable in the Middle
Kingdom. The boats were thought to
symbolize the ritual journey to Abydos, during which the mummy or the
statue of the deceased was brought to
that Upper Egyptian cult center. The
boat of King Amenhotep II lacks the
central cabin, as well as the bow and
stern shields. The hull is decorated
with sphinxes—symbolic representations of the king—smiting enemies,
and several images of the falcon-headed god of war Montu, who also spears
enemies.

Bibliography
CG 4798–4976, 5034–5200, p. 98; CG
24001–24990, p. 241ff., pl. XLVIII;
Landström 1970, p. 107ff.
A.H.

The treasures buried in the tombs of the pharaohs belong to a collective imaginary. Since antiquity they have whetted the appetite of thieves so that only a few royal sepulchers have remained intact in Egypt. That of Tutankhamun, which is known to everyone, was discovered in 1922 by Howard Carter in the fascinating site of the Valley of the Kings. The only ensemble that can be compared to it is that of Tanis where, between 1939 and 1946, the Egyptologist Pierre Montet brought to light six royal tombs, some of which had remained inviolate for millennia. They belonged to lesser-known sovereigns from the 21st and 22nd dynasties (about 1069–730 BC) who had chosen that northern city called Tanis as their capital.
Buried under the constructions of a more recent period, these tombs had escaped being plundered thanks to their original architecture. Indeed, at Tanis one finds neither pyramids nor hypogea comparable to those in the Valley of the Kings: inside the sacred precinct of the temple of Amun, the pharaohs had had simple stone vaults built that were buried at a shallow depth. It seems that these were surmounted by chapels that have disappeared today in which the funerary cult was celebrated.
Because of the humidity of the region, the mummies and organic materials decomposed. The funerary furniture that has survived is sumptuous. Unlike Tutankhamun, the deceased had brought objects that were essentially ritual and very few elements of daily life to the beyond. Among the thousands of objects found in the necropolis that has come down to us from ancient Egypt is a dazzling collection of golden masks. There is also gold jewelry, often adorned with brightly colored stones: dark blue lapis lazuli, green feldspar, red cornelian. The series of vases worked in gold, silver, and electrum is unequalled. And lastly, there are two unique sarcophagi in silver that belonged to the pharaohs Psusennes I and Sheshonq II.
All these objects are conserved in the Egyptian Museum of Cairo where a whole room has been devoted to them.
I.F.

262

Necklace with a snake's head pendant
Third Intermediate Period,
21st Dynasty, reign of Psusennes I
Gold, cornelian and obsidian
L. of necklace 75; L. of amulet 6 cm
Tanis, tomb of Psusennes I
Cairo, Egyptian Museum, JE 85800

At the end of a thin gold circle hangs a snake's head amulet, known by various names in Egyptian: *menkebyt*, *menkeryt* or *mekeryt*. Generally made of red material (apart from cornelian—diaspore, glass paste and faience were also commonly use) these amulets very often contained eyes made of a different substance (in this specific case they are set in obsidian). The snake's head was considered to have prophylactic powers; and here it is interpreted as a protection for the throat. A spell in the Book of the Dead in the Busca Papyrus (19th Dynasty) identifies the *menqeryt* amulet with the eye of Horus, crediting it with generic apotropaic powers.
On the back of the serpent are two columns of engraved hieroglyphics, with the name of Psusennes I and phrases of good wishes.
F.T.

263

Pendant in the form of a heart
Third Intermediate Period,
21st Dynasty, reign of Psusennes I
Lapis lazuli and god
H. 4.6 cm
Tanis, tomb of Psusennes I
Egyptian Museum of Cairo,
JE 85804

The heart controlled the body and was the symbol of consciousness and knowledge. A heart amulet or a scarab was worn as talisman during life or put on the body or within its bandages in place of the real one after death. According to ancient Egyptian funerary beliefs, the heart was one of the seven elements that constituted the human personality. The other six were the *ka* (guardian spirit), the *ba* (immortal spirit), the *khet* (body), the *shwt* (shadow), the *akh* (the benevolent spirit) and the *ren* (name). Spell 30 of the Book of the Dead explains how the heart was not to stand or speak against its owner during the judgment in the court of Osiris. Other spells describe how to prevent the heart from being stolen, how to give a heart to the dead in the underworld, let the heart go through its transformations according to the deceased's deeds, and give him the power to have control over his members, or provide him with a heart of cornelian.
Engraved upon this scarab is the cartouche of Psusennes with the figures of the sun in its different human forms: The rising sun Khepri, with the scarab on his head, the midday sun Ra, falcon headed, and the evening sun Atum wearing the double crown. These deities assure the protection of the king in the afterlife.

Bibliography
Paris 1987, p. 250, pl. 86.
M.S.

264

Necklace with cylinders and the cartouche of Psusennes I
Third Intermediate Period,
21st Dynasty, reign of Psusennes I
Gold and lapis lazuli
L. 95.5 cm
Tanis, tomb of Psusennes I
Cairo, Egyptian Museum, JE 85757

When compared to other pieces of jewelry from the rich tomb furnishings of Psusennes I, this necklace is striking in its sobriety. Its decorative effect relies solely on the richness of its materials and the powerful, yet measured, contrast between their colors. This same contrast between the yellow of the gold and the blue of the lapis lazuli occurs frequently in Egyptian jewelry—from those of the Middle Kingdom princesses to the tomb furnishings of Tutankhamun. The clasp is modeled on a cartouche and bears the name and title of the sovereign: "the High Priest of Amun, Psusennes."

Bibliography
Stierlin, Ziegler 1988, p. 35, figs. 12, 15.
F.T.

265

Pendant of Psusennes I with winged scarab
Third Intermediate Period,
21st Dynasty, reign of Psusennes I
Gold, black stone, jasper and feldspar
H. of pendant 10.5, of scarab 6.5, of counterpoise 4 cm; L. of chain 42 cm
Tanis, Tomb no. 3, burial of Psusennes I
Cairo, Egyptian Museum, JE 85788, JE 85799

The Khepri scarab, the self-creator, was the symbol of the morning sun. The ancient Egyptians observed that this beetle emerged from the earth in the early morning with the rising sun and rolled a ball of mist containing its eggs all day long. When the sun set, the beetle disappeared again in the earth. A relationship was made between the beetle rolling the ball and the rolling of the sun disk in the sky. It was thought that the scarab incarnated the morning sun-god, so that it became a symbol of good omen, fertility and resurrection, and was manufactured primarily in blue stone or faience. Spell 30 in the Book of the Dead engraved on the base of the scarab wished that the heart of the deceased not be taken from its owner nor oppose him in the judgment of the afterlife.
Four of such pendants were found on the mummy of Psusennes I. The main element of the composition is a big scarab of black stone in a golden frame with two large wings encrusted with multicolored glass. The scarab lies on the *shen* sign of universal power inlaid with brown jasper. The name of Psusennes (Pasebakhaenniut) meaning "the shining star in the city, beloved of Amun" is written in the cartouche. The necklace chain and counterpoise are composed of beads of gold, green and brown jasper, and feldspar.
F.T.

266

Necklace with a pectoral in the form of a sanctuary
Third Intermediate Period, 22nd Dynasty, reign of Shoshenq II
Gold, glass paste and semi-precious stones
L. of chain 75; H. of sanctuary 15.6 cm
Tanis, tomb of Psusennes I, burial chamber of Sheshonq II
Cairo, Egyptian Museum, JE 72170

From a thin band of gold hangs an elaborate pectoral in the form of a sanctuary, the center of which is occupied by a scarab with a winged heart; the inscription on the base is taken from Spell 30 of the Book of the Dead and was intended to prevent the heart—for the Egyptians, the seat of human intellect—from testifying against the deceased in the tribunal of the afterlife. Alongside the heart, almost as if they were holding up the wings, are the goddesses Isis and Nephthys—Osiris's wife/sister and sister, respectively—who had the ungrateful task of collecting his limbs after they had been scattered all over Egypt by Seth. In this particular context, they simply stand in protection of the heart. Over the figures, the solar disk spreads its wings, thus adding another symbol of apotropaic power. The counterpoise to the pectoral—in gold lamina—hungs at the opposite side of the necklace.
This precious piece of jewelry was found around the neck of Sheshonq II, a short-lived pharaoh of the 22nd Dynasty—he reigned for one year only—whose mummy was buried in a secondary chamber of the tomb of Psusennes I (along with a man and a woman whose identity it has not been possible to establish).

Bibliography
S. Einaudi in Tiradritti 1998, p. 328.
F.T.

267

Two Amulets of Psusennes I
Third Intermediate Period,
21st Dynasty
Gold
H. 3.5; L. 3.5 cm (JE 85820)
H. 3.6; L. 4 cm (JE 85814)
Tanis, Tomb no. 3, burial of
Psusennes I
Cairo, Egyptian Museum,
JE 85814, JE 85820

These elegant amulets belonged to the same king, Psusennes I. One is in the shape of a human-headed bird, the *ba*, which symbolized the immortal spirit that came back after death "to attach itself to its corpse in the god's domain" (Book of the Dead, Spell 89), or to "assume the form of a [living] soul who did not enter the place of execution" (Book of the Dead, Spell 85) or to "open the tomb for the soul and for the shadow, going forth by day, and controlling one's feet" (Book of the Dead, Spell 92). Through these acts, the ancient Egyptians believed that the deceased would resurrect in the afterlife and live forever.

The human head of the bird resembles the king himself, wearing the royal *nemes* headdress, the protective cobra (*uraeus*) on his forehead, and the "false" beard of dignity. The claws of the bird hold the *shen* sign, symbol of the universal power bestowed upon the wearer.

The other piece, the so-called amulet of the "Two Ladies" is in the form of a miniature *wesekh* ("broad") collar, with a pendant. It hung from a wire or string that passed through a loop on the back of the amulet. The vulture-goddess *Nekhbet* and the cobra-goddess *Wadjyt*, who represented dominion over Upper and Lower Egypt respectively, share the wings of one bird. Both deities in this tiny amulet extend their divine protection to the king and kingship. The details of the bird's feathers, the wings and claws with the *shen* circles of universal power, and the cobra's body and tail, are all elaborately incised.

Bibliography
Montet 1951, p. 148, pl. CXIX; Paris 1987, p. 250, pl. 88.
M.S.

268

Bracelet of plain and striped rings
Third Intermediate Period,
21st Dynasty, reign of Psusennes I
Gold
Diam. 7; H. 4.8 cm
Tanis, Tomb no. 3,
burial of Psusennes I
Cairo, Egyptian Museum, JE 85760

The jewelry found in Tanis displays a variety of designs, mostly with stone scarabs and/or inlays of semi-precious stones and glass. This bracelet, however is of an unusually delicate and simple design. It was found on the mummy of King Psusennes I. It consists of two parts of seven tubes connected by a kind of hinge and a clasp using a nail (not found) that passes through the tubes. The tubes are soldered together, three of them are of alternating stripes, the other four are plain.

The bracelet is incised from with a two-lined hieroglyphic text. The upper one bears the name of the owner: "The king, lord of the Two Lands, the first prophet of Amun-Ra, king of the gods, son of Ra, Psusennes, beloved of Amun." The lower line specifies the queen's dedication of the bracelet to her husband: "The first great royal wife of his Majesty, lady of the Two Lands, Mutnedjemet.

Bibliography
Paris 1987, p. 250, pl. 86.
M.S.

269

Bracelet
Third Intermediate Period,
21st Dynasty, reign of Psusennes I
Gold, agate
Diam. 5.8 cm
Tanis, tomb of Psusennes I
Cairo, Egyptian Museum, JE 85764

The many pieces of jewelry found with the mummy of Psusennes I included this bracelet, one of the most sober works of Tanite goldsmiths. It consists of a twisted wire of gold passing through two hemispheres between which is set an almost cylindrical bead of agate. Large quantities of this stone were available in Egypt, and yet it appears to have been only periodically used in Egyptian jewelry, from the Predynastic period onward. In tomb murals dating from the 18th Dynasty, the stone is shown in association with diaspore; in fact, in the Eastern Desert, a deposit has been identified where both of these stones occur together.
F.T.

270

Ring with a scarab inset
Third Intermediate Period,
22nd Dynasty, reign of Shoshenq II
Gold and lapis lazuli
Diam. 2.5 cm
Tanis, tomb of Psusennes I,
burial chamber of Shoshenq II
Cairo, Egyptian Museum, JE 72190

This lapis lazuli scarab inset is hinged
to the two short gold bars of the ring;
hence it could be rotated and used as
a seal. In fact, on the base is a hieroglyphic inscription which, though difficult to read, seems to bear the name
and title of a functionary: "The con-
troller of the Great Palace who has
access to the holy things, Hore-
makhbyt." Thus the ring belonged to
a court figure close to the sovereign;
the fact that it was found on the finger
of Shoshenq II himself might be explained by a final act of devotion to the
dead pharaoh by the functionary who
had served under him.
The figure of the scarab was widely
used on seals from the Old Kingdom
onward, when such rings tended to
replaced the old cylindrical seals. They
soon became very widespread, largely
because the beetle—associated with
the solar cycle of eternal return—was
a symbol of rebirth and regeneration.

Bibliography
J. Yoyotte in Paris 1987, pp. 268–269
(no. 103).
F.T.

271

*Ring with an inset engraved
with the* wedjat *eye*
Third Intermediate Period,
21st Dynasty, reign of Psusennes I
Gold, lapis lazuli
H. 1.1; W. 1.5 cm
Tanis, tomb of Psusennes I
Cairo, Egyptian Museum,
JE 85824 B

The many rings found in the tomb of
Psusennes I included some with an inset engraved with the *wedjat* eye in
deep relief. This symbol was a representation of the eyes of Horus,
which—according to myth—had been
torn from their sockets by Seth (the
curl across the pupil is, in fact, a tear)
and then put back in place by the god
Thoth. This story is the basis of the
powers of regeneration that amulets
with this type of decoration were supposed to possess.
The ring from the Psusennes I tomb
consists of a short rod of gold, the
ends of which have been wound in
gold wire. The inset in lapis lazuli is
framed by a thin strip of gold, welded
to two rings around the hole that runs
through the stone. In fact, the inset is
reversible. The other side is engraved
with the name of the pharaoh, and it
is possible that Psusennes I used it as
a seal ring.
F.T.

272

Finger ring with lozenges
Third Intermediate Period,
21st Dynasty, reign of Psusennes I
Gold, lapis lazuli, cornelian and
glass paste
Diam. 2.2; H. 1.6 cm
Tanis, Tomb no 3,
burial of Psusennes I
Cairo, Egyptian Museum,
JE 85222 A

Finger rings were of many forms and
designs and were made of gold,
faience, or stones. The bezels of the
rings were sometimes used as seals for
kings and high officials, bearing their
names, epithets or titles. Sometimes
they were decorated with the figures,
names and symbols of deities. This is
especially true for the quantity and
quality of the finger rings found in the
tomb of Tutankhamun.
This ring with lozenges has a unique
form which imitates a bracelet. It is
made of gold sheet and encrusted with
semi-precious stones and glass paste in
the manner of cloisonné, a technique
mastered in Egypt since the Middle
Kingdom (*c.* 1950 BC).
M.S.

273

Toe-stalls for mummy
Third Intermediate Period,
21st Dynasty
Gold
H. 5.5–8 cm
Tanis, Tomb no. 3,
burial of Psusennes
Cairo, Egyptian Museum,
JE 85822–85826

The mummification process, in which
natron salt was used for the dehydration of the corpse, needed to find a
way to protect the softer tissues of the
body, especially the fingers and toes
since the nails could fall off. Thus it
was necessary to cover the royal fingers
and toes, protecting them with golden
stalls on the bandages. This would also enable the deceased king to use his
fingers and toes perfectly. Each mummy was then furnished with ten long
finger stalls and ten shorter toe ones.
There are five gold toe stalls belonging
to Psusennes I, each with a golden
ring or amulet, a magical circle for
protection.

Bibliography
Montet 1951, pp. 155–157, pl.
CXXIV; Paris 1987, pp. 220–221, pls.
69.
M.S.

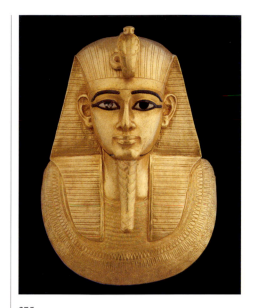

274

Two shabtis *from the reign of Psusennes I: foreman and workman*
Third Intermediate Period,
21st Dynasty, reign of Psusennes I
Painted faience
H. 14.3 and 13.5 cm
Tanis, tomb of Psusennes I
Cairo, Egyptian Museum,
JE 85920N, JE 85920

Bibliography
L. Aubert in: Paris 1987, pp. 128–129
(no. 12).
H.H.

The etymology of the word *ushabti* is uncertain in some respects. Some scholars claim the word comes from *shub* ("avocado"), because the first were produced using the wood of this plant; others argue for a derivation from the verb *ushab* (" to respond"), because the figures were placed alongside the deceased to respond to any demands for labor that might be made on him in the afterlife. Equipped with shovels and baskets for carrying earth (agricultural work in Egypt was primarily concerned with keeping irrigation canals in working order), these figures were organized in teams of ten with a foreman, depicted wearing a skirt and holding a whip. The standard number of *shabti*s in any tomb was 365 (one for each day of the year), with 36 foremen.

The tomb of Psusennes I also contained a large number of such figures (some in bronze). Even if here the foremen do not wear the typical robe, their authority is clear not only from their whips but also from their "false" beards. The workmen are shown with a shovel in each hand. The lower part of their bodies bears a painted text taken from Spell 6 of the Book of the Dead—the phrase with which the *shabti*s respond to the call to work. Thanks to these substitutes, the deceased could repose in peace, unburdened by the earthly duties that he would otherwise have to meet in the afterlife.

275

Mask of Psusennes I
Third Intermediate Period,
21st Dynasty
Gold and semi-precious stones
Max. H. 48 cm
Tanis, Tomb no. 3,
burial of Psusennes I
Cairo, Egyptian Museum, JE 85913

According to the ancient Egyptian funerary beliefs, the body and the soul were resurrected in the afterlife. The soul was kept alive by providing it with a magical formula from the Book of the Dead. The corpse on the other hand was preserved by embalming it and then wrapping it with linen bandages for protection. Since the soul had to find its corpse in the necropolis, the tomb was provided with an image of the deceased's actual features. Instead of placing stone heads in the burial chambers of 4th-Dynasty tombs, or preparing plaster death masks in the 6th Dynasty, Egyptians began to make cartonnage masks in the Middle and New Kingdoms for this purpose. Only kings had gold masks of exquisite craftsmanship.

This mask of Psusennes I is made of two pieces of beaten gold, soldered and joined together by five nails visible from the back. The king wears the *nemes* headdress, usually made of linen, surmounted by the sacred *uraeus*, which protected the king against opponents and enemies in life and after death. The king wears a "false" beard, the symbol of dignity, and a broad *wesekh* collar incised with floral decorations. The eyelids, eyebrows, and straps fixing the beard are inlaid with lapis lazuli, the eyes with black and white stones.
M.S.

Appendix

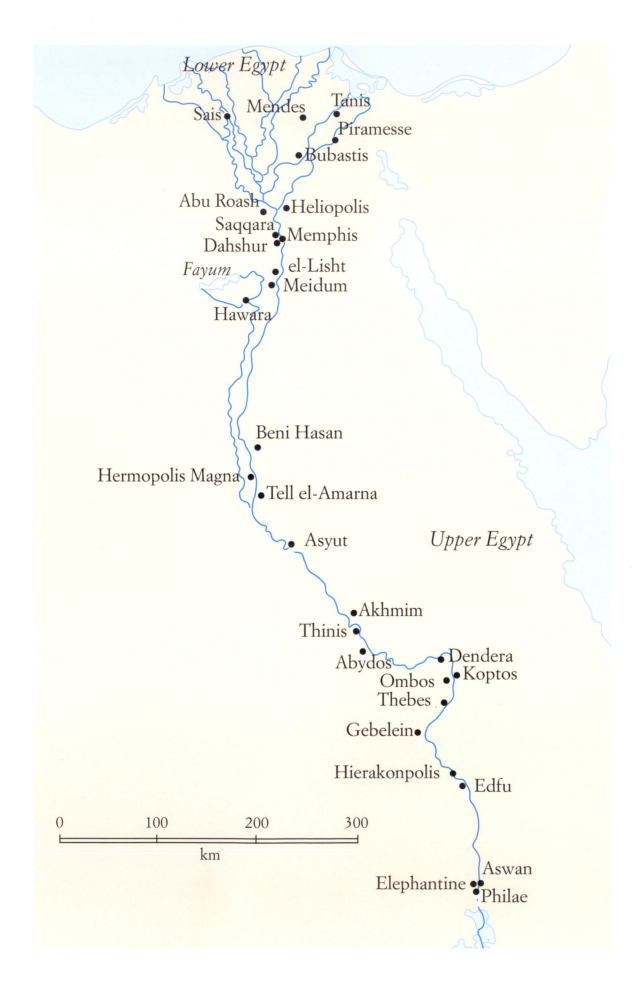

Lower Egypt

Sais
Mendes
Tanis
Piramesse
Bubastis

Abu Roash
Heliopolis
Saqqara
Memphis
Dahshur
el-Lisht
Fayum
Meidum
Hawara

Beni Hasan

Hermopolis Magna
Tell el-Amarna

Asyut

Upper Egypt

Akhmim
Thinis
Dendera
Abydos
Koptos
Ombos
Thebes
Gebelein

Hierakonpolis
Edfu

Aswan
Elephantine
Philae

0   100   200   300
km

Thebes

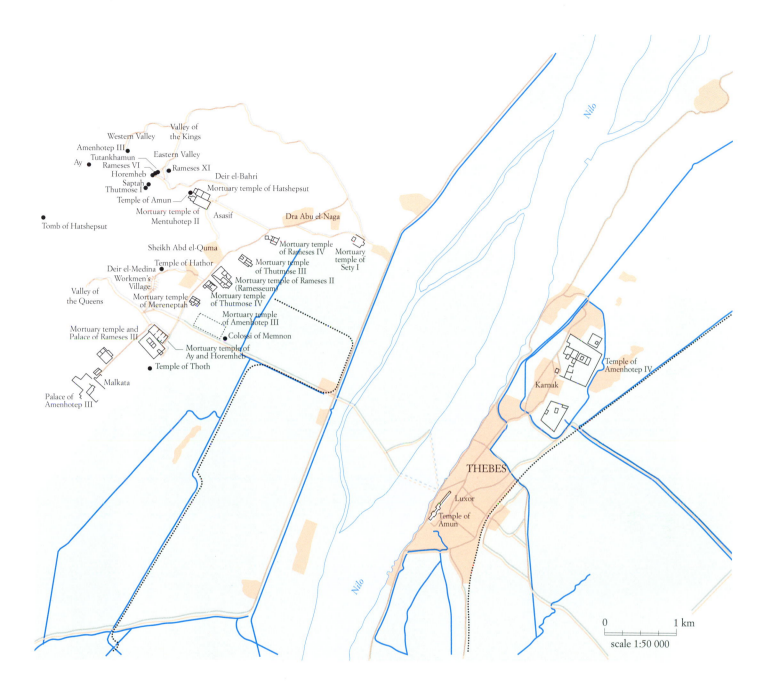

Valley of
the Kings

Western Valley

Amenhotep III

Eastern Valley

Ay

Tutankhamun

Rameses VI

Rameses XI

Horemheb

Deir el-Bahri

Saptah

Thutmose I

Mortuary temple of Hatshepsut

Temple of Amun

Mortuary temple of
Mentuhotep II

Asasif

Dra Abu el-Naga

Tomb of Hatshepsut

Sheikh Abd el-Quma

Mortuary temple
of Rameses IV

Mortuary
temple
of Sety I

Temple of Hathor

Mortuary temple
of Thutmose III

Deir el-Medina

Mortuary temple of Rameses II
(Ramesseum)

Workmen's
Village

Mortuary temple
of Thutmose IV

Valley of
the Queens

Mortuary temple
of Mereneptah

Mortuary temple
of Amenhotep III

Mortuary temple and
Palace of Rameses III

Colossi of Memnon

Mortuary temple of
Ay and Horemheb

Malkata

Temple of Thoth

Palace of
Amenhotep III

Nilo

THEBES

Temple of
Amenhotep IV

Karnak

Luxor

Temple of
Amun

Nilo

0   1 km

scale 1:50 000

Neolithic period
Badarian period (c. 4400–3800 BC)

PREDYNASTYC PERIOD (4000–3000)

Naqada I or **Amratian period** (3900–3650 BC)
Naqada II or **Gerzean period** (3650–330 BC)
Naqada III or **Semainan period** (3300–3050 BC)
Dynasty 0 (3000 ca.)
King Scorpion
Narmer

EARLY DYNASTIC PERIOD (2920–2575)

1st Dynasty (2920–2770)
Aha (Menes ?)
Djer
Djet
Den
Anedjib
Semerkhet
Qa'a

2nd Dynasty (2770–2650)
Hetepsekhemwy
Raneb
Nynetjer
Peribsen
Khasekhemwy

3rd Dynasty (2650–2575)

Sanakht	2650–2630
Djoser (Netjerikhet)	2630–2611
Sekhemkhet	2611–2603
Khaba	2603–2600
Huni (?)	2600–2575

OLD KINGDOM (2575–2135)

4th Dynasty (2575–2465)

Sneferu	2575–2551
Khufu (Cheops)	2551–2528
Djedefra	2528–2520
Khafra (Chefren)	2520–2494
Menkaura (Mycerinus)	2490–2472
Shepseskaf	2472–2467

5th Dynasty (2465–2323)

Userkaf	2465–2458
Sahura	2458–2446
Neferirkara Kakai	2446–2426
Shepseskara	2426–2419
Raneferef	2419–2416
Nyuserra	2416–2392
Menkauhor	2396–2388
Djedkara Isesi	2388–2356
Unas	2356–2323

6th Dynasty (2323–2150)

Teti	2323–2291
Userkara	2291–2289
Pepy I	2289–2255
Merenra	2255–2246
Pepy II	2246–2152

FIRST INTERMEDIATE PERIOD (2150–1994)

7th Dynasty
Inexistent dynasty. Manetho mentions "Seventy kings of Memphis who ruled for seventy days" to indicate the period of instability at that time in Egypt.

8th Dynasty (2150–2135)
Numerous ephemeral kings are known to have belonged to this dynasty.

9th and 10th Dynasties (2135–2040)
Dynasties in which the rule of most of Egypt passed to the kings of Herakleopolis.

11th Dynasty (2135–1994)

Mentuhotep I	
Intef I	
Intef I	2123–2073
Intef III	2073–2065
Mentuhotep II Nebhepetra	2065–2014
Mentuhotep III	2014–2001
Mentuhotep IV	2001–1994

MIDDLE KINGDOM (1994–1650)

12th Dynasty (1994–1781)

Amenemhat I	1994–1964
Senusret I	1974–1929
Amenemhat II	1932–1898
Senusret II	1900–1881
Senusret III	1881–1842
Amenemhat III	1842–1794
Amenemhat IV	1798–1785
Queen Sobekneferu	1785–1781

13th Dynasty (1781–1650)
Some seventy ephemeral rulers from Memphis.

14th Dynasty (1710–1650)
Indefinite number of ephemeral kings.

SECOND INTERMEDIATE PERIOD (1650–1550)

15th Dynasty (1650–1550)
Salitis
Sheshi
Jaqobher
Khayan
Apepi
Khamudi

16th Dynasty (1650–1550)
Minor Hyksos rulers contemporary with the 15th Dynasty.

17th Dynasty (1650–1550)
Fifteen kings based in Thebes, of which the most prominent ones are:
Intef V
Sobkemsaf I
Sobkemsaf II
Intef VI
Intef VII
Senakhtenra Taa I
Seqenenra Taa II
Kamose

NEW KINGDOM (1550–1075)

18th Dynasty (1550–1291)

Ahmose	1550–1525
Amenhotep I	1525–1504
Thutmose I	1504–1492
Thutmose II	1492–1479
Hatshepsut	1479–1458
Thutmose III	1479–1425
Amenhotep II	1428–1397
Thutmose IV	1397–1387
Amenhotep III	1387–1350
Amenhotep IV/Akhenaten	1350–1333
Smenkhkara	1335–1333
Tutankhamun	1333–1323
Ay	1323–1319
Horemheb	1319–1291

19th Dynasty (1291–1185)

Rameses I	1291–1289
Sety I	1289–1278
Rameses II	1279–1212
Merenptah	1212–1202
Amenmessu	1202–1199
Sety II	1199–1193
Saptah	1193–1187
Tausret	1193–1185

20th Dynasty (1187–1075)

Sethnakhte	1187–1184
Rameses III	1184–1153
Rameses IV	1153–1147
Rameses V	1147–1143
Rameses VI	1143–1135
Rameses VII	1135–1127
Rameses VIII	1127–1126
Rameses IX	1126–1108
Rameses X	1108–1104
Rameses XI	1104–1075

THIRD INTERMEDIATE PERIOD (1075–664)

21st Dynasty (1075–945)

Smendes I	1075–1049
Neferkara	1049–1043
Psusennes I	1045–994
Amenemope	997–985
Osorkon the elder	985–979
Siamun	979–960
Psunennes II	960–945

22nd Dynasty (945–718)

Sheshonq I	945–924
Osorkon I	924–899
Sheshonq II	ca. 890
Takelot I	889–883
Osorkon II	883–850
Takelot II	853–853
Sheshonq III	827–775
Pimay	775–767
Sheshonq V	767–729
Osorkon IV	729–718

23rd Dynasty (820–718)

Pedubastis	820–795
Sheshonq IV	795–788
Osorkon III	788–760
Takelot III	765–756
Rudamon	752–718

24th Dynasty (730–712)

Tefnakht	730–718
Bakenrenef (Bocchoris)	718–712

25th Dynasty (775–653)

Alara	775–765
Kashta	765–745
Piye (Piankhy)	745–713
Shabaqo	713–698
Shabitqo	698–690

Taharqo   690–664
Tanutamani   664–653

LATE PERIOD (664–332)

26th Dynasty (664–525)
Psamtek I   664–610
Nekau   610–595
Psamtek II   595–589
Apries   589–570
Ahmose   570–526
Psamtek III   526–525

27th Dynasty (525–404)
Cambyses   525–522
Darius I   521–486
Xerxes I   486–465
Artaxerxes I   465–424
Xerxes II   424
Darius II   423–405
Artaxerxes II   405–404

28th Dynasty (404–399)
Amyrtaios   404–399

29th Dynasty (399–380)
Nepherites I   399–393
Hakor   393–380

30th Dynasty (380–342)
Nectanebo I   380–362
Teos   362–360
Nectanebo II   360–342

31st Dynasty (342–332)
Artaxerxes III   342–338
Arses   338–336
Darius III   336–332

GRECO-ROMAN PERIOD (332 BC–313 AD)

Macedonian dynasty (332–305)
Alexander the Great   332–323
Philip Arrhidaeus   323–317
Alexander IV   317–305

Ptolemaic dynasty (305–30)
Ptolemy I Soter   305–282
Ptolemy II Philadelphus 285–246
Ptolemy III Euergetes   246–222
Ptolemy IV Philopator   222–205
Ptolemy V Epiphanes   205–180
Ptolemy VI Philometor   180–164,
163–145
Ptolemy VII Neos Philopator   145
Ptolemy VIII Euergetes   170–163,
145–116
Ptolemy IX Soter   116–110,
109–107, 88–80
Ptolemy X Alexander   110–109, 107–88
Ptolemy XI Alexander   80
Ptolemy XII Neos Dyonysos 80–58, 55–51
Berenice IV   58–55
Cleopatra VII Philopator 51–30
Ptolemy XV Caesarion   36–30

Roman empire (30 BC–313 AD)

Notice
This chronology is based on J. Baines's and J. Malek's Cultural Atlas of Ancient Egypt (Oxford 2000, pp. 36–37) up to the First Intermediate Period (c. 2135 BC), and on J. von Beckerath's Handbuch der ägyptischen Königsnamen (Müncher/Berlin 1984, pp. 158–166), from the 11th Dynasty to the end of Pharaonic history.

Bibliography

Abbreviations

AAWL = Abhandlungen der Sächsischen Akademie der Wissenschaften zu Leipzig, phil. hist. Kl. (Berlin).

AAWMun = Abhandlungen der bayerischen Akademie der Wissenschaften, phil. hist. Kl. (München)

AAWWien = Anzeiger der österreichischen Akademie der Wissenschaften in Wien, phil. hist. Kl. (Wien).

ADAIK = Abhandlungen des Deutschen Archäologischen Instituts Kairo, Ägyptologische Reihe.

ÄF = Ägyptologische Forschungen (Glückstadt / Hamburg / New York).

Ägypten und Levante = Ägypten und Levante. Internationale Zeitschrift für ägyptische Archäologie und deren Nachbargebiete (Wien).

ASAE = Annales du Service des Antiquités de l'Égypte (Le Caire).

AV = Archäologische Veröffentlichung des Deutsche Archäologische Institut von Kairo (Mainz am Rhein).

BdE = Bibliothèque d'Études de l'Institut Français d'Archéologie Orientale (Le Caire).

BIE = Bulletin de l'Institut égyptien, *puis* Bulletin de l'Institut d'Égypte (Le Caire).

BMFA = Bulletin of the Museum of Fine Arts (Boston).

BMMA = Bulletin of the Metropolitan Museum of Arts (New York).

BSAE = British School of Archaeology in Egypt (London).

BSFE = Bulletin de la Société Française d'Égyptologie (Paris).

CAA = Corpus Antiquitatum Aegypticarum (Mainz am Rhein).

CRAIBL = Comptes Rendus de l'Académie des Inscriptions et Belles-Lettres (Paris).

CSA = Cahiers de la Société Asiatique (Paris).

DFIFAO = Documents des Fouilles de l'Institut d'Archéologie Orientale (Le Caire).

EA = Egyptian Archaeology. The Bulletin of the Egypt Exploration Society (London).

EAAE = K.A. Bard, *Encyclopaedia of the Archaeology of Ancient Egypt*, London/New York 1999.

EEF = Egypt Exploration Fund (London).

EES = Egypt Exploration Society (London) (fino al 1918 = EEF).

EPRO = Études Préliminaires aux Religions Orientales dans l'Empire Romain (Leiden).

ERA =Egyptian Research Account (London).

ET = Études et Travaux. Travaux du Centre d'archéologie méditerranéenne de l'Académie de sciences polonnaise (Warsaw).

FIFAO = Fouilles de l'Institut Français d'Archéologie Orientale (Le Caire).

HdO = Handbuch der Orientalistik (Leiden).

JARCE = Journal of the American Research Center in Egypt (Boston).

LÄ = W. Helck und W. Westendorf (a cura di), *Lexikon der Ägyptologie, begründet von W. Helck und E. Otto*, Band I-VII, Wiesbaden 1972-1992.

LAPO = Littératures anciennes du Proche Orient (Paris).

MÄS = Münchner Ägyptologische Studien (München/Berlin).

MAIBL = Mémoires présentés par divers savants à l'Académie des Inscriptions et Belles - Lettres de l'Institut de France *puis* Mémoires de l'Académie des Inscriptions et Belles - Lettres (Paris).

MDAIK = Mitteilungen des Deutschen Archäologischen Institut, Abt. Kairo (Mainz am Rhein).

MIFAO = Mémoires publiés par les membres de l'Institut Français d'Archéologie Orientale (Le Caire).

MMMAF = Monuments des Membres de la Mission Archéologique Française (Le Caire).

OBO = Orbis Biblicus et Orientalis (Freiburg/Göttingen).

OEAE = D.B. Redford (Edited by), *The Oxford Encyclopaedia of Ancient Egypt*, Vols. 1-3, Oxford 2001.

OIP = Oriental Institute Publications (Chicago).

PMMAEE = Publications of the Metropolitan Museum of Arts Egyptian Expedition (New York).

PSAS = Proceedings of the Society of Antiquaries of Scotland (Edinburgh).

RdE = Revue d'Égyptologie (Le Caire/Paris).

SAOC = Studies in Ancient Oriental Civilizations (Chicago).

SDAIK = Sonderreihe des Deutsche Archäologische Institut von Kairo (Mainz am Rhein).

Sinuhe = A.M. Blackman, *Middle Egyptian Stories*, Monumenta Aegyptiaca II, Bruxelles 1972.

UPMB = University of Pennsylvania Museum Bulletin (Philadelphia).

UZKÖAI = Untersuchungen der Zweigstelle Kairo des Österreichischen Archäologischen Institut (Wien).

VDI = Vestnik Drevnej Istorii (Moskva/Leningrad).

VO = Vicino Oriente (Roma).

Wb = A. Erman und H. Grapow (Hrsg.), *Wörterbuch der ägyptischen Sprachen*, 13 Bande, Berlin 1982 (unveränderter 4. Nachdruck der Auflage von 1926-1953).

WVDOG = Wissenschaftliche Veröffentlichung der Deutschen Orient-Gesellschaft.

ZÄS = Zeitschrift für ägyptische Sprache und Altertumskunde (Berlin).

BIBLIOGRAPHY

Abd El-Maqsoud 1983
M. Abd El-Maqsoud, *Un monument du roi 'Aa-sh-R' Nhsy à Tell el-Haboua (Sinaï Nord)*, ASAE 69, 1983, pp. 3-5.

Abitz 1995
F. Abitz, *Pharao und Gott in den Unterweltbüchern des Neues Reich*, Göttingen/Fribourg (Schweitz) 1995.

Abu Bakr 1937
Abd el-Moneim Y. Abu Bakr, *Untersuchungen über die ägyptischen Kronen*, Glückstadt 1937.

Aldred 1961
C. Aldred, *New Kingdom Art in Ancient Egypt During the Eighteenth Dynasty 1570 to 1320 B.C.*, (Second Edition Revised & Enlarged), London 1961.

Aldred 1973
C. Aldred, *Akhenaten and Nefertiti*, New York [1973].

Altenmüller
H. Altenmüller, *S.v. "Feste"*, in: LÄ I, Wiesbaden 1975, cc. 172-191.

Altenmüller 1981
H. Altenmüller, *Amenophis I. als Mittler*, MDAIK 37, 1981, pp. 1-7.

Amélineau 1905
É. Amélineau, *Les nouvelles fouilles d'Abydos : compte rendu in extenso des fouilles, description des monuments et objets découverts. Part 3: 1897-1898*, Paris 1905

Andreu, Rutschowskaya, Ziegler 1997
G. Andreu, M.-H. Rutschowskaya, Ch. Ziegler, *L'Égypte ancienne au Louvre*, Paris1997.

Andrews 1990
C. Andrews, *Ancient Egyptian Jewellery*, London 1990.

Andrews 1994
C. Andrews, *Amulets of Ancient Egypt*, Austin 1994.

Arnold 1977
D. Arnold, *Rituale und Pyramidentempel*, MDAIK 33, 1977, pp. 1-14.

Arnold 1982
D. Arnold, *S.v. "Palast"*, in: LÄ IV, Wiesbaden 1982, cc. 644-646.

Arnold 1992
D. Arnold, *Die Tempel Ägyptens. Götterwohnungen, Kultstätten, Baudenkmäler*, Zürich 1992.

Arnold 1994
D. Arnold, *Lexikon der ägyptischen Baukunst*, Zürich 1994.

Arnold 1995
D. Arnold, *An Egyptian Bestiary*, BMMA 52.4, Spring 1995.

Arnold 1996
D. Arnold, *The Royal Women of Amarna. Images of Beauty from Ancient Egypt*, New York 1996.

Arnold, Ziegler 1999
D. Arnold, Ch. Ziegler (Edited by), *Catalogue of the Exhibition "Egyptian Art in the Age of the Pyramids"*, New York 1999.

Assmann 1970
J. Assmann, *Der König als Sonnenpriester*, ADAIK 7, Glückstadt 1970.

Assmann 1989
J. Assmann, *Maât, l'Egypte pharaonique et l'idée de justice sociale*, Paris 1989.

Assmann, Blumethal 1999
J. Assmann, E. Blumenthal (Hrsg.), *Literatur und Politik im Pharaonischen und ptolemäischen Ägypten*, BdE 127, Le Caire 1999.

Aufrère 1980
S.H. Aufrère, *Le Livre des Rois de la XIIᵉ dynastie*, Thèse de l'Université Paris IV-Sorbonne 1980.

Aufrère 2000
S.H. Aufrère, *Les vétérans de Montouhotep Nebhepetrê. Une garnison funéraire à Deir el-Bahari?*, Égypte, Afrique & Orient 19, 2000, pp. 9-16.

Aufrère 2001
S.H. Aufrère, *Le roi Aouibrê Hor. Essai d'interprétation du matériel découvert par Jacques de Morgan à Dahchour (1894)*, BIFAO 101, 2001, pp. 1-41.

Aufrére, Golvin, Goyon 1991
S.H. Aufrére, J-Cl. Golvin, J-Cl. Goyon, *L'Égypte Restituée*, Paris 1991.

Badawy 1956
A. Badawy, *Maru-Aten: Pleasure Resort or Temple?*, JEA 42, 1956, pp. 58-64.

Badawy 1968
A. Badawy, *A History of Egyptian Architecture: The Empire (the New Kingdom)*, Berkeley/Los Angeles, 1968.

Baines 1995A
J. Baines, *Kingship, Definition of Culture, and Legitimation*, in: O'Connor, Silverman 1995, pp. 3-47.

Baines 1995B
J. Baines, *Origins of Egyptian Kingship*, in: O'Connor, Silverman 1995, pp. 95-156.

Baines, Málek 1993
J. Baines, J. Málek, *Atlas of Ancient Egypt*, New York 1993.

Barbotin 1999
Chr. Barbotin, *Le Papyrus Chassinat III*, RdE 50, 1999, pp. 5-49.

Barta 1968
W. Barta, *Aufbau und Bedeutung der altägyptische Opferformel*, ÄF 24, Glückstadt/Hamburg/New York 1968.

Barta 1970
W. Barta, *Das Selbstzeugnis eines altägyptischen Künstler (Stele Louvre C 14)*, MÄS 22, München/Berlin 1970.

Batrawi 1947
A. Batrawi, *The Pyramids Studies. Anatomical Reports*, ASAE 47, 1947, pp. 97-111.

Baud 1999
M. Baud, *Famille royale et pouvoir sous l'Ancien Empire Egyptien*, BdE 126, Le Caire 1999.

von Beckerath 1984
J. von Beckerath, *Hanbuch der ägyptischen Königsnamen*, MÄS 20, München/Berlin 1984.

Beinlich 1978
H. Beinlich, *Ein ägyptischer Räucherarm in Heidelberg. Mit einem Exkurs von W. Brunsch*, MDAIK 34, 1978, pp. 15-31.

Bell 1985
L. Bell, *Luxor Temple and the Cult of the Royal Ka*, JNES 44, 1985, pp. 251-294.

Berman, Letellier 1996
L.M. Berman, B. Letellier, *Catalogue of the Exhibition "Pharaohs. Treasures of Egyptian Art from the Louvre"*, Cleveland 1996.

Berger, Clerc, Grimal 1994
C. Berger, G. Clerc, N. Grimal (Édité par), *Hommages à Jean Leclant. Vols. 1 - 4*, BdE 106/1-4, Le Caire 1994.

Berger, Mathieu 1997
C. Berger et B. Mathieu, *Études sur l'Ancien Empire et la nécropole de Saqqâra dédiées à Jean-Philippe Lauer*, Orientalia Monspeliensia, 9/1-2, Montpellier 1997.

Berlandini 1997
J. Berlandini, *Contribution aux "Princes du Nouvel Empire à Memphis". Le prince Thoutmès, fils d'A-menhotep III. Le prince Senakhtenamon, fils de Ramsès II*, in: Berger, Mathieu 1997, pp. 99-112.

Berman, Bohac 1999
L.M. Berman, K.J. Bohac, *The Cleveland Museum of Art. Catalogue of Egyptian Art*, Cleveland 1999.

Bertrac, Vernière 1993
P. Bertrac, Y. Vernière, *Diodore de Sicile, Bibliothèque historique, Livre I*, Paris 1993.

Bierbrier 1991
M. Bierbrier, *Elements of Stability and Instability in Ramesside Egypt: the Succession to the Throne*, in: Bleiberg, Freed 1991, pp. 9-14.

Bietak 1996a
M. Bietak, *Avaris. The Capital of the Hykos. Recent Excavations at Tell el-Dab'a*, London 1996.

Bietak 1996b
M. Bietak (Hrsg./Edited by), *Haus und Palast im Alten Ägypten / House and Palace in Ancient Egypt. Internationales Symposium 8. bis 11. April 1992 in Kairo / International Symposium in Cairo, April 8 to 11, 1992*, UZKÖAI 14, Wien 1996.

Bietak, Reiser-Haslauer 1982
M. Bietak, E. Reiser-Haslauer, *Das Grab des 'Anch-Hor, Obersthofmeister der Gottesgemahlin Nitokris. II*, UZKÖAI 5, Wien 1982.

Bickel, Mathieu 1993
S. Bickel, B. Mathieu, *L'écrivain Amennakht et son Enseignement*, BIFAO 93, 1993, pp. 31-51.

Birch 1880
S. Birch, *Catalogue of the Collection of Antiquities at Alnwick Castle*, Londra 1880.

Blankenberg-van Delden 1969
C. Blankenberg-van Delden, *The Large Commemorative Scarabs of Amenhotep III*, Documenta et Monumenta Orientis Antiqui 15, Leiden 1969.

Bleiberg, Freed 1991
E. Bleiberg, R. Freed (Edited by), *Fragments of a Shattered Visage. The Proceedings of the International Symposium on Ramesses the Great*, Monographs of the Institute of Egyptian Art and Archaeology 1, Memphis (Tennessee) 1991.

Blumenthal 1970
E. Blumenthal, *Untersuchungen zum ägyptischen Königtum des Mittleren Reiches I: die Phraseologie*, AAWL 61.1, Berlin 1970.

Blumenthal 2001
E. Blumenthal, *Kuhgöttin und Gottköng. Frömmigkeit und Staatsreue auf der Stele Leipzig Ägyptisches Museum 5141.11*, Siegfried-Morentz-Gadächtnis-Vorlesung (Leipzig 2000), Leipzig 2001.

Boardman 1980
J. Boardman, *I greci sui mari*, (traduzione italiana di: *The Greeks Overseas. Their Early Colonies and Trade* 1980) Firenze 1980.

Boas 1950
G. Boas, *The Hieroglyphics of Horapollo*, Bollingen Series 23, New York 1950.

Bogoslovsky 1973
E.S. Bogoslovsky, *Pamjatniki i dokumenty iz Dèr-èl'-Mèdina, xranja_ciesja v muzejax SSSR. Vypusk V* ("Monuments and Documents from Deir el-Medîna in Museums of the USSR. Part V"), VDI 1 (123), 1973, pp. 78-104 (English summary).

Bongioanni, Croce 2001
A. Bongioanni, M.S. Croce (a cura di), *I tesori dell'antico Egitto nella collezione del Museo Egizio del Cairo*, Vercelli 2001.

Bonhême, Forgeau 1988
M.-A. Bonhême, A. Forgeau, *Pharaon. Les secrets du pouvoir*, Paris 1988.

Bonnet, Valbelle 1976
Ch. Bonnet, D. Valbelle, *Le village de Deir el-Médineh. Étude archéologique (suite)*, BIFAO 76, 1976, pp. 317-342.

van den Boorn 1988
G.P.F. van den Boorn, *The Duties of the Vizier. Civil Administration in the Early New Kingdom*, London/New York 1988.

Boreux 1932
Ch. Boreux, *Musée National du Louvre, Département des Antiquités Égyptiennes : guide-catalogue sommaire*, Paris 1932.

Boston 2002
Catalogue of the Exhibition"Egypt in the Age of the Pyramids", Boston 2002.

Bourriau 1988
J. Bourriau, *Catalogue of the Exhibition "Pharaohs and Mortals. Egyptian art in the Middle Kingdom"*, Cambridge 1988.

Bowman 1997
A. Bowman, *L'Egitto dopo i faraoni*, (traduzione italiana di: *Egypt after the Pharaohs. 332 BC - AD 642 from Alexander to the Arab Conquest*, 1996), Firenze1997.

Breasted 1906
J.H. Breasted, *Ancient Records of Egypt, Historical Documents from the Earliest Times to the Persian Conquest. Vol. 1*, Chicago 1906.

Bresciani 1985
E. Bresciani, *The Persian Occupation of Egypt*, in: Gershevitch 1985, pp. 502-528.

Bresciani 2000
E. Bresciani, *Sulle rive del Nilo. L'Egitto al tempo dei faraoni*, Roma/Bari 2000.

Bresciani 2001
E. Bresciani, *Nove faraoni*, Pisa 2001.

Bresciani, Silvano 1992
E. Bresciani, F. Silvano, *La Collezione Schiff Giorgini*, Catalogo delle Collezioni Egittologiche I, Pisa 1992.

Brissaud, Zivie-Coche 1998
Ph. Brissaud, Chr. Zivie-Coche, *Tanis. Mission Française des Fouilles de Tanis*, Paris 1998.

Brunner 1979
H. Brunner, *Die südlichen Räume des Tempels von Luxor*, AV 18, Mainz am Rhein 1979.

Brunton, Engelbach 1927
G. Brunton, R. Engelbach, *Gurob*, BSAE/ERA 41, London 1927.

Bruyère 1929
B. Bruyère, *Rapport sur les fouilles de Deir el Médineh (1928)*, FIFAO 6.2, Le Caire 1929.

Bryan 1992
B.M. Bryan, *Royal and Divine Statuary*, in: Kozloff, Bryan 1992, pp. 125-192.

Cabrol 2000
A. Cabrol, *Amenhotep III le Magnifique*, Monaco 2000.

Cannuyer 1993
Chr. Cannuyer, *Encore la date de l'accession au trône de Ramsès XI*, GM 132, 1993, pp. 19-20.

Capel, Markoe 1996
A.K. Capel, G.E. Markoe (Edited by), *Ctalogue of

the Exhibition "Mistress of the House, Mistress of Heaven. Women in Ancient Egypt", New York 1996.

Carter, Newberry 1904
H. Carter, P.E. Newberry, *The tomb of Thoutmôsis IV with an essay on the king's life and monuments by Gaston Maspero, and a paper on the physical characters of the mummy of Thoutmôsis IV. by G. Elliot Smith*, Westminster 1904.

de Cenival 1992
J.L. de Cenival, *Les tablettes à écrire dans l'Egypte pharaonique*, Bibliologia 12, 1992

Cerny 1927
J. Cerny, *Le culte d'Aménophis Ier chez les ouvriers de la nécropole thébaine*, BIFAO 27, 1927, pp. 159-203.

Cerny 1946
J. Cerny, *Studies in the Chronology of the Twenty-first Dynasty*, JEA 32, 1946, pp. 24-30.

J. Cerny et alii 1969 – 1970
J. Cerny et alii, *Graffiti de la montagne thébaine. Vol. I: cartographie et étude topographique illustré*, Le Caire 1969-1970.

CG 3618-4000, 18001-18037, 18600, 18603
F.W. von Bissing, *Catalogue Général des Antiquités Égyptiennes du Musée du Caire. Nos. 3618-4000, 18001-18037, 18600, 18603: Fayencegefäße*, Wien 1902.

CG 4798-4976, 5034-5200
G.A. Reisner, *Catalogue Général des Antiquités Égyptiennes du Musée du Caire. Nos. 4798-4976, 5034-5200: Models of Ships and Boats*, Cairo 1913.

CG 24001-24990
G. Daressy, *Catalogue Général des Antiquités Égyptiennes du Musée du Caire. Nos. 24001-24990: Fouilles de la Vallée des Rois 1898-1899*, Le Caire 1902.

CG 25001 – 25385
G. Daressy, *Catalogue Général des Antiquités Égyptiennes du Musée du Caire. Nos. 25001-25385: Ostraca*, Le Caire 1901.

CG 34001 – 34189
P. Lacau, *Catalogue Général des Antiquités Égyptiennes du Musée du Caire. Nos. 34001-34189: Stèles du Nouvel Empire. I-III*, Le Caire 1909-1957.

CG 42001 – 42250
G. Legrain, *Catalogue Général des Antiquités Égyptiennes du Musée du Caire. Nos. 42001-42250: Statues et statuettes des rois et des particuliers. Tomes I-IV*, Le Caire 1906-1925.

CG 44001-44102
G. Bénédite, *Catalogue Général des Antiquités Égyptiennes du Musée du Caire. Nos. 44001-44102: Miroirs*, Le Caire 1907.

CG 52001 – 53855
E. Vernier, *Catalogue Général des Antiquités Égyptiennes du Musée du Caire. Nos. 52001-53855: Bijoux et orfèvreries, Tomes I-II*, Le Caire 1927.

CG 61001 – 61044
G. Daressy, *Catalogue Général des Antiquités Égyptiennes du Musée du Caire. Nos. 61001-61044: Cercueils des cachettes royales*, Le Caire 1909.

CG 61051 – 61100
G. Elliot Smith, *Catalogue Général des Antiquités Égyptiennes du Musée du Caire. Nos. 61051-61100: The Royal Mummies*, Cairo 1912.

CG 69201 – 69852
H. Hickmann, *Catalogue Général des Antiquités Égyptiennes du Musée du Caire. Nos. 69201-69852:*

Instruments de musique, Le Caire 1949.

Chadefaud 1982
C. Chadefaud, *Les statues porte-enseignes de l'Égypte ancienne (1580 - 1085 av. J.C.). Signification et insertion dans le culte du Ka royal*, Paris 1982.

Chappaz 1987
J.-L. Chappaz, *Un nouvel assemblage de talâtât: une paroi du Rwḏ-mnw d'Aton*, Karnak 8, 1987, pp. 81-119.

Cherpion 1999
N. Cherpion, *La statue du sanctuaire de Medou-nefer*, BIFAO 99, 1999, pp. 85-101.

Clayton 1994
P.A. Clayton, *Chronicle of the Pharaohs. The Reign-by-Reign Record of the Rulers and Dynasties of Ancient Egypt*, London 1994.

Clère 1961
P. Clère, *La porte d'Evergète à Karnak*, Le Caire 1961.

Comitato Organizzativo 1993
Comitato Organizzativo, *Atti del VI Congresso Internazionale di Egittologia. Volume I-II*, Torino 1993.

Condon 1978
V. Condon, *Seven Royal Hymns*, MÄS 37, München/Berlin 1978.

Corteggiani 1995
J.-P. Corteggiani, *La " butte de la Décollation " à Héliopolis*, BIFAO 95, 1995, pp. 149-151.

Corzo 1994
M.A. Corzo (a cura di), *Catalogo della mostra "Nefertari. Luce d'Egitto"*, Roma 1994.

Curto 1965
S. Curto, *La satira nell'antico Egitto*, Torino 1965.

Curto 1981
S. Curto, *L'antico Egitto*, Torino 1981.

Curto 1984
S. Curto, *L'antico Egitto nel Museo Egizio di Torino*, Torino 1984.

Daressy 1901
G. Daressy, *Rapport sur la trouvaille de Hatiay*, ASAE 2, 1901, pp. 1-13.

D'Auria, Lacovara, Roehrig 1988
S. D'Auria, P. Lacovara, C.H. Roehrig, *Catalogue of the Exhibition "Mummies and Magic: The Funerary Arts of Ancient Egypt"*, Boston 1988.

Davies 1903
N. de Garis Davies, *The Rock Tombs of El Amarna. Part I: The Tomb of Meryra*, London 1903.

Davies 1906
N. de Garis Davies, *The Rock Tombs of El Amarna. Part IV: Tombs of Penthu, Mahu, and Others*, London 1906.

Davies 1908
N. de Garis Davies, *The Rock Tombs of El Amarna. Part VI: Tombs of Parennefer, Tutu, and Ay*, London 1908.

Davies 1930
N. de Garis Davies, *The Tomb of Ken-Amun*, London 1930.

Dawson 1927
W.R. Dawson, *Making a mummy*, JEA 13, 1927, pp. 40-49.

Decker, Herb 1994
W. Decker, M. Herb, *Bildatlas zum Sport im Alten*

Ägypten. Corpus der bildlichen Quellen zu Leibesübungen, Spiel, Jagd, Tanz und verwandten Themen, HdO Erste Abteilung: Der Nahe und Mittlere Osten 14.1-2, Leiden 1994.

Delange 1993
E. Delange, *Rites et beauté, objets de toilette égyptiens*, Paris 1993.

Delange 1987
E. Delange, *Musée du Louvre. Catalogue des statues égyptiennes du Moyen Empire (2060 – 1560 avant J.-C.)*, Paris 1987.

Delange 2001
E. Delange, *Catálogo da Exposiçao"Egito faraônico Terra dos deuses"*, Casa França – Brasil 2001.

Delia 1980
R.D. Delia, *A Study of the Reign of Senwosret III*, Ann Arbor 1980.

Derchain 1965
Ph. Derchain, *Le Papyrus Salt 825 (B.M. 10051), rituel pour la conservation de la vie en Égypte*, Académie royale de Belgique. Classe des Lettres et des Sciences Morales et Politiques. Mémoires, Tome 58.1a-b / Koninklijke Academie van België. Klasse der Letteren en der Morele en Staatkundige Wetenschappen. Verhandelingen, Boek 58.1a-b, Bruxelles 1965.

Derry 1947
D.E. Derry, *The Pyramid Studies, Anatomical Reports*, ASAE 47, 1947, pp. 97-111.

Desroches-Noblecourt 1947
Chr. Desroches-Noblecourt, *Une coutume égyptienne méconnue*, BIFAO 45, 1947, pp. 185-232.

Desroches-Noblecourt 1963
Chr. Desroches-Noblecourt, *Tutankhamen. Life and death of a pharaoh*, New York 1963.

Desroches-Noblecourt 1976
Chr. Desroches-Noblecourt, *Catalogue de l'exposition " Ramsès Le Grand "*, Paris 1976.

Desroches-Noblecourt 1991
C. Desroches-Noblecourt, *Abou Simbel, Ramsès, et les dames de la couronne*, in: Bleiberg, Freed 1991, pp.127-166.

Desroches-Noblecourt 2002
Ch. Desroches-Noblecourt, *La reine mystérieuse Hatchepsout*, Parigi, 2002.

Dewachter 1975
M. Dewachter, *Contribution à l'histoire de la cachette royale de Deir el-Bahari*, BSFE 74, 1975, pp. 19-30.

Dobrev, Labrousse, Mathieu 2000
V. Dobrev, A. Labrousse, B. Mathieu, *La dixième pyramide à textes de Saqqâra : Ânkhesenpépy II. Rapport Préliminaire de la campagne de fouilles 2000*, BIFAO 100, 2000, pp. 275-296.

Dodson 1990
A. Dodson, *Crown Prince Djhutmose and the Royal Sons of the Eighteenth Dynasty*, JEA 76, 1990, pp. 87-96.

Donadoni 1989
S. Donadoni, *L'immagine e la forma: l'esperienza della scultura*, in: Donadoni Roveri 1989, pp. 98-185.

Donadoni 1990
S. Donadoni (a cura di), *L'uomo egiziano*, Roma/Bari 1990.

Donadoni 1993
S. Donadoni, *Encyclopédies d'aujourd'hui : l'art*

égyptien, (Traduction française de *L'Egitto*, [Torino 1981]), Paris 1993.

Donadoni 1999
S. Donadoni, *Tebe*, Milano 1999.

Donadoni Roveri 1987
A. M. Donadoni Roveri (a cura di), *Museo Egizio di Torino. Civiltà degli Egizi. La vita quotidiana*, Milano 1987.

Donadoni Roveri 1988
A.M. Donadoni Roveri (a cura di), *Museo Egizio di Torino. Civiltà degli Egizi. Le credenze Religiose*, Milano 1988.

Donadoni Roveri 1989
A.M. Donadoni Roveri (a cura di) *Museo Egizio di Torino. Civiltà degli Egizi. Le arti della celebrazione*, Milano 1989.

Donadoni Roveri, Tiradritti 1998
A.M. Donadoni, F. Tiradritti (a cura di), *Catalogo della mostra "Kemet. Alle sorgenti del tempo"*, Milano 1998.

D'Onofrio 1965
C. D'Onofrio, *Gli Obelischi di Roma*, Roma 1965.

Dorman 1987
P.F. Dorman (Introduction by), *The Metropolitan Museum of Art. Egypt and the Ancient Near East*, New York 1987.

Dorner 1999
J. Dorner, *Die Topographie von Piramese - Ein Vorbericht*, Ägypten und Levante IX, 1999, pp. 77-83.

Dothan, Dothan 1992
T. Dothan, M. Dothan, *People of the Sea: The Search for the Philistines*, New York 1992.

Drenkhahn, Germer 1991
R. Drenkhahn, R. Germer, *Mumie und Computer, ein multidisziplinäres Forschungsprojekt in Hannover*, Hannover 1991.

Drioton 1927
E. Drioton, *Rapport sur les fouilles de Médamoud (1926). Tome 2: les inscriptions*, FIFAO 4.2, Le Caire 1927.

Drioton 1940
É. Drioton, *Compte rendu de: B. Grdseloff, das Ägyptische Reinigungszelt*, ASAE 40, 1940, p. 1014.

Drioton, Vandier 1984
E. Drioton, J. Vandier, *L'Égypte : Des origines à la conquête d'Alexandre,* (6e édition), Paris 1984.

Dunham 1963
D. Dunham, *The Royal Cemeteries of Kush. Vol. 5: The West and South Cemeteries at Meroë*, Boston 1963.

Dunham, Janssen 1960
D. Dunham, J.M.A. Janssen, *Semna Kumma Excavated by George Andrew Reisner Published by Dows Dunham and Jozef M. A. Janssen*, Second Cataract Forts, Volume I, Boston 1960.

Dunham 1931
D. Dunham, *A fragment from the mummy wrappings of Tuthmosis III*, JEA 17, 1931, pp. 209-210.

Dunham 1972
D. Dunham, *Ancient Egyptian and Near Eastern Acquisitions and Loans from the Horace L. Mayer Collection*, BMFA 70, 1972, pp. 14-21.

Eggebrecht 1987
A. Eggebrecht, *Katalog zur Ausstulleng „Ägyptens Aufstieg zur Weltmacht"*, Mainz am Rhein, Verlag Philipp von Zabern, 1987

Eigner 1996
D. Eigner, *A Palace of the Early 13th Dynasty at Tell el-Dab'a*, in: Bietak 1996b, pp. 73-80.

Elgood 1951
P.G. Elgood, *Later Dynasties of Egypt*, Oxford 1951.

Engelbach 1929
R. Engelbach, *A head of king Shabaka*, ASAE 29, 1929, pp.15-18.

Epigraphic Survey 1970
Epigraphic Survey, *Medinet Habu. Volume VIII: Plates 591-660. The Eastern High Gate*, OIP 94, Chicago1970.

Epigraphic Survey 1980
Epigraphic Survey, *The Tomb of Kheruef. Theban Tomb 192*, OIP 102, Chicago [1980].

Eremin, Goring, Manley, Cartwright 2000
K. Eremin, E. Goring, B. Manley, C. Cartwright, *A 17th Dynasty Egyptian Queen in Edinburgh?*, KMT 11.3, Fall 2000, pp. 32-40.

Ertman 1980
E.L. Ertman, *The Search for the Significance and Origin of Nefertiti's Tall Blue Crown*, in: Comitato Organizzativo 1993.I, pp. 189-193.

Étienne 2000
M. Étienne (Édité par), *Catalogue de l'exposition " Heka. Magie et envoûtement dans l'Égypte ancienne "*, Paris 2000.

Eyre 1998
C.J. Eyre (Edited by), *Proceedings of the 7th Congress of Egyptologist*, OLA 82, Leuven 1998.

Fabretti, Rossi, Lanzone 1882
A. Fabretti, F. Rossi, R.V. Lanzone, *Regio Museo di Torino: antichità egizie. Vol. I*, Catalogo generale dei musei di antichità e degli oggetti d'arte raccolti nelle gallerie e biblioteche del Regno, Serie 1.1, Torino 1882.

Fay 1999
B. Fay , *Royal Women as Represented in Sculpture during the Old Kingdom*, in: Ziegler 1999, pp. 99-148.

Fazzini, Bianchi, Romano, Spaniel 1989
R.A. Fazzini, R.S. Bianchi, J.F. Romano, D.B. Spanel, *Ancient Egyptian Art in the Brooklyn Museum*, New York/London 1989

Feucht 1995
E. Feucht, *Das Kind im Alten Ägypten. Die Stellung des Kindes in Familie und Gesellschaft nach altägyptischen Texten und Darstellungen*, Frankfurt/New York 1995.

Firth, Gunn 1935 – 1936
C.M. Firth, B. Gunn, *The Teti Pyramid Cemeteries. Vol. I*, Cairo 1935-1936.

Fox 1985
M.V. Fox, *The Song of Songs and Ancient Egyptian Love Songs*, Madison 1985.

Franco 1993
I. Franco, *Rites et Croyances d'éternité*, Paris 1993.

Freed 1982
Rita E. Freed (Edited by), *Catalogue of the Exhibition "Egypt's Golden Age: The Art of Living in the New Kingdom"*. Boston 1982.

Freed, Markowitz, D'Auria 1999
R. Freed, Y. Markowitz, S. D'Auria (Edited by), *Catalogue of the Exhibition "Pharaohs of the Sun: Akhenaten, Nefertiti, Tutankhamen"*, Boston 1999.

Friedman 1998
F.D. Friedman (Edited by), *Gifts of the Nile, Ancient Egyptian Faience*, Rhode Island 1998.

Gaballa 1972
G.A.Gaballa, Some Nineteenth Dynasty Monuments in the Cairo Museum: A new Monument of May, Chief of Works, BIFAO 71, 1972, pp.129-133.

Gabolde 1988
L. Gabolde, *Le " grand château d'Amon " de Sésostris Ier à Karnak*, Mémoire de l'Académie des Inscriptions et Belles-Lettres, Nouvelle série, tome 17, Paris 1998.

Gardiner 1947
A.H. Gardiner, *Ancient Egyptian Onomastica*, Oxford 1947.

Gardiner 1953
A.H. Gardiner, *The Coronation of King Haremhab*, JEA 39, 1953, pp. 13-31.

Gardiner 1958
A.H. Gardiner (Edited by), *The Temple of King Sethos I at Abydos. Volume IV: the Second Hypostyle Hall*, London/Chicago 1958.

Gardiner 1959
A.H. Gardiner, *The Royal Canon, of Turin*, Oxford 1959.

Gardiner 1997
A.H. Gardiner, *La civiltà egizia*, (traduzione italiana di *Egypt of the Pharaohs. An Introduction*, 1961), Torino 1997.

Gardiner, Carter 1917
A.H. Gardiner, H. Carter, *The Tomb of Ramesses IV and the Turin Plan of a Royal Tomb*, JEA 4, 1917, pp. 130-158.

Gauthier 1907
H. Gauthier, *Le Livre des rois d'Égypte. Tome I*, MIFAO XVII, Le Caire1907.

Gauthier 1912
H. Gauthier, *Le Livre des rois d'Égypte. Tome II*, MIFAO XVIII, Le Caire 1912.

Gauthier, Sottas 1925
H. Gauthier, H. Sottas, *Un décret trilingue en l'honneur de Ptolémée IV*, Le Caire 1925.

Gershevitch 1985
I. Gershevitch (Edited by), *The Cambridge History of Iran. Volume 2: The Median and Achaemenian Periods*, Cambridge 1985.

Gitton 1977
M. Gitton, *S.v. "Ahmose Nofretere"*, in: LÄ I, Wiesbaden 1977, cc. 102-109.

Gitton 1981
M. Gitton, *L'épouse du dieu Ahmès-Néfertary. Documents sur sa vie et son culte posthume*, Paris 1981.

Gitton 1984
M. Gitton, *Les divines épouses de la 18e dynastie*, Annales Littéraires de l'Université de Besançon, 306, Paris 1984.

Goedicke 1963
H. Goedicke, *Was Magic used in the Harem Conspiracy against Ramses III?*, JEA 49, 1963, p. 71-92.

Golvin, Goyon 1989
J-Cl..Golvin, J-Cl. Goyon, *Karnak Le temple d'Amon restitué*, Paris 1989.

Gomaa Farouk, Hebenu (pp. 1075-76) in Wolfgang Helck and Wolfhart Westendorf, eds, Lexikon der Ägyptologie, vol. 2 (Wiesbaden, 1977).

Goyon 1972
J.-Cl. Goyon, *Rituels funéraires de l'ancienne Égyp-*

te. Introduction, traduction et commentaire, LAPO 4, Paris 1972.

Grandet 1993
P. Grandet, Ramsès III : histoire d'un règne, Paris 1993.

Grandet 1994
P. Grandet, Le Papyrus Harris I (BM 9999). Volume I-II, BdE 109.1-2, Le Caire 1994.

Grandet, Mathieu 1990
P. Grandet, B. Mathieu, Cours d'Égyptien hiéroglyphique. Volume I, Paris 1990.

Gratias 1999
R. Gratias, Der "Turiner Ramses", Kemet 8.1, 1999, pp. 48-52.

Grdseloff 1951
B. Grdseloff, Nouvelles données concernant la tente de purification, ASAE 51, 1951, pp. 129-140.

Griggs 1985
C.W. Griggs (Edited by), Catalogue of the exhibition "Ramses II, The Pharaoh and his Time", Brigham 1985.

Grimal 1986
N.-C. Grimal, Les termes de la propagande égyptienne de la XIXe dynastie à la conquête d'Alexandre, MAIBL Nouvelle série, Tome VI, Paris 1986.

Grimal 1988
N. Grimal, Histoire de l'Égypte ancienne, Paris 1988.

Grimal 1990
N. Grimal, Storia dell'antico Egitto, (traduzione italiana di Grimal 1988), Roma/Bari 1990.

Grimal 1992
N. Grimal, A History of Ancient Egypt, (English translation by Ian Shaw of Grimal 1988), Oxford 1992.

Grimal 1998
N. Grimal (Édité par), Les critères de datation stylistiques à l'Ancien Empire, BdE 120, 1998.

Grimm, Schoske, Wildung 1997
A. Grimm, S. Schoske, D. Wildung, "Katalog zur Ausstellung Pharao. Kunst und Herrschaft im alten Ägypten", München 1997.

Grimm, Schoske 2001
A. Grimm, S. Schoske (Hrsg.), Das Geheimnis des goldenen Sarges, München 2001.

Guidotti 1991
M.C. Guidotti, Museo Egizio di Firenze. Vasi dall'Epoca Protodinastica al Nuovo Regno, Roma 1991.

Guidotti 2000
M.C. Guidotti (a cura di), Mal d'Egitto. Origini del gusto e passione scientifica nella Toscana dell'800, Livorno 2000.

Guiter 1998
J. Guiter, La stèle d'Ikhernofret, Egypte, Afrique et Orient 10, 1998, p.34-38.

Habachi 1954
L. Habachi, Grands Personnages en mission ou de passage à Assouan. I. Mey, attaché au Temple de Rê, CdE 29, 1954, pp. 210-220.

Habachi 1966
L. Habachi, The Qantir Stela of the Vizir Rahotep and the Statue "Ruler-of-Rulers", in: Will 1966, pp. 67-77.

Habachi 1969
L. Habachi, Features of the Deification of Ramesses II, ADAIK 5, Glückstadt 1969.

Habachi 1972
L. Habachi, The Second Stela of Kamose and His Struggle against the Hyksos Ruler and His Capital, ADAIK 8, Glückstadt 1972.

Hani 1976
J. Hani, La religion égyptienne dans la pensée de Plutarque, Paris 1976.

Hari 1965
R. Hari, Horemheb et la reine Moutnedjemet ou la fin d'une dynastie, Genève 1965.

Hari 1981
R. Hari, Sesostris et les historiens antiques, BSEG 5, 1981, pp. 15-21.

Harris, Weeks 1973
J.E. Harris, K.R. Weeks, X-raying the Pharaohs, London 1973.

Harris, Wente 1980
J.E. Harris, E.F. Wente, An X-Ray Atlas of the Royal Mummies, Chicago/London 1980.

Hawass 1999
Z. Hawass, The Queens of Ancient Egypt, Cairo 1999.

Hayes 1937
W.C. Hayes, Glazed Tiles from the Palace of Ramesses II at Kantir, The Metropolitan Museum of Art Papers 3, New York 1937.

Hayes 1953
W.C. Hayes, The Scepter of Egypt. A Background for the Study of the Egyptian Antiquities in The Metropolitan Museum of Art. Part I: From the Earliest Times to the End of the Middle Kingdom, New York 1953.

Hayes 1955
W.C. Hayes, A Papyrus of the Late Middle Kingdom In the Brooklyn Museum, Brooklyn 1955.

Hayes 1959
W.C. Hayes, The Scepter of Egypt. A Background for the Study of the Egyptian Antiquities in The Metropolitan Museum of Art. Part II: The Hyksos Period and the New Kingdom (1675-1080 B.C.), Cambridge 1959.

Hayes 1961
W.C. Hayes, The Middle Kingdom in Egypt. Internal History from the Rise of the Heracleopolitans to the Death of Ammenemes III, The Cambridge Ancient History (Revised Edition of Volumes I & II), Vol. I (Chapter XX), Cambridge 1961.

Helck 1958
W. Helck, Zur Verwaltung des Mittleren und Neuen Reichs, Probleme der Ägyptologie herausgegeben von Hermann Kees III, Leiden-Köln 1958.

Helck 1977
W.Helck, S.v. "Festleiter" in: LÄ II, Wiesbaden 1977, cc. 192-194.

Hermann 1938
A. Hermann, Die ägyptische Königsnovelle, LÄS 10, Glückstadt/Hamburg/New York 1938.

Hildesheim 1976
Katalog zur Ausstellung "Echnaton, Nofretete, Tutanchamun", Hildesheim 1976.

Hölscher 1941
U. Hölscher, The Mortuary Temple of Rameses III. Part I, The Excavations at Medinet Habu, Volume III, OIP LIV, Chicago1941.

Hölscher 1951
U. Hölscher, The Mortuary Temple of Rameses III.

Part II, The Excavations at Medinet Habu, Volume IV (OIP LV), Chicago1951.

Horne 1985
L. Horne (Edited by), Introduction to the Collections of the University Museum, Philadelphia 1985.

Hornemann 1957
B. Hornemann, Types of Ancient Egyptian Statuary II-III, Munksgaard 1957.

Hornung 1966
E. Hornung, Geschichte als Fest. Zwei Vorträge zum Geschichtsbild der frühen Menschheit, Darmstadt 1966.

Hornung 1971
E. Hornung, Ägyptische Unterweltsbücher, Zürich/München 1971.

Hornung 1982
E. Hornung, Der ägyptische Mythos von der Himmelskuh, Eine ätiologie des Unvollkommenen, OBO 46, Freiburg/Göttingen 1982

Hornung 1985
E. Hornung, Tal der Könige. Die Ruhestätte der Pharaonen, 3. Auflage, Zürich/München 1985.

Hornung 1996
E. Hornung, L'esprit du temps des pharaons, (traduction française de Geist der Pharaonenzeit, 1989), Paris 1996.

Hornung 1999
E. Hornung, Tal der Könige. Die Ruhestätte der Pharaonen, (6. Auflage), Düsseldorf/Zürich 1999.

Hornung, Bryan 2002
E. Hornung, B. Bryan (Edited by), Catalogue of the Exhibition"The Quest for Immortality: Treasures of Ancient Egypt", Washington 2002.

Houlihan 1996
P.F. Houlihan, The Animal World of the Pharaohs, London/New York 1996.

Houlihan 2001
P.F. Houlihan, Wit and Humour in Ancient Egypt, London 2001.

Huber 1998
B. Huber, Al-Kom al-Ahmar/Saruna : découverte d'une ville de province ", in: Eyre 1998, pp. 575-582.

Hüttner, Satzinger 1999
M. Hüttner, H. Satzinger, CAA Kunsthistorisches Museum Wien. Ägyptisch-Orientalische Sammlung. Lieferung 16: Stelen, Inschriftsteine und Reliefs aus der Zeit der 18. Dynastie, Mainz am Rhein 1999.

Iida et alii 1993
K. Iida et alii, Studies on the Palace of Malqata, 1985-1988. Investigations at the Palace of Malqata, 1985-1988, Papers in Honor of Professor Watanabe Yasutada on the Occasion of his 70th Birthday, Shinjuku Tokyo 1993.

Israelit-Groll 1985
S. Israelit-Groll (Edited by), Pharaonic Egypt: The Bible and Christianity, Jerusalem 1985.

Israelit-Groll 1990
S. Israelit-Groll (Edited by), Studies in Egyptology Presented to Miriam Lichtheim. Volumes I-II, Jerusalem 1990.

Iversen 1968
E. Iversen, Obelisks in Exile. Volume I: The Obelisks of Rome, Copenhagen 1968.

Jánosi 1996
P. Jánosi, Die Fundamentplattform eines Palastes (?) der Späten Hyksoszeit in Ezbet Helmi (Tell el-

Dab'a), in: Bietak 1996b, pp. 93-98.

Janot, Bourrier, Neveux 1999
Fr. Janot, P. Bourrier, A. Neveux, *Réplique et utilisation d'un nouvel instrument d'embaumement provenant d'un* instrumentarium *daté de la XXXe dynastie*, Vesalius V.2, 1999, pp. 72-78.

Janot 2000
Fr. Janot, *Les instruments d'embaumement de l'Égypte ancienne*, BdE 125, Le Caire 2000.

Janot 2001
Fr. Janot, *Incision de flanc, incision d'immortalité*, Vesalius VII.1, 2001, pp. 18-21.

Jelínková-Reymond 1956
E. Jelínková-Reymond, *Les inscriptions de la statue guérisseuse de Djed-Her-le-Sauveur*, BdE 23, Le Caire 1956.

Jéquier 1936
G. Jéquier, *Le monument funéraire de Pepi II. Vol. I. Le tombeau royal*, Le Caire 1936.

Jørgensen 1998
M. Jørgensen, *Ny Carlsberg Glyptotek. Catalogue Egypt II*, København 1998.

Junker 1943
H. Junker, *Gîza. Grabungen auf dem Friedhof des Alten Reiches bei den Pyramiden von Giza*, Bd. VI, AAWWien 72, Wien/Leipzig 1943.

Kaiser 1967
W. Kaiser, *Staatliche Museen Preußischer Kulturbesitz. Ägyptisches Museum Berlin*, [Berlin 1967].

Kakosi 1982
L. Kakosi, *S.v. "Mnevis"*, in: LÄ IV, Wiesbaden 1982, cc. 165-167.

Kaplony 1966
P. Kaplony, *Die Handwerker als Kulturträger Altägyptens*, Asiatische Studien 20, 1966, pp. 101-125.

Kemp 1978
B.J. Kemp, *The Harîm-Palace at Medinet el-Ghurab*, ZÄS 105, 1978, pp. 122-133

Kemp 1989
B.J. Kemp, *Ancient Egypt: Anatomy of a Civilization*, London – New York 1989.

Kemp 1995A
B.J. Kemp (Edited by), *Amarna Reports VI*, The Egypt Exploration Society Occasional Publications 10, London 1995.

Kemp 1995B
B.J. Kemp, *Outlying Temples at Amarna*, in: Kemp 1995A, pp. 411-462.

Kemp, Garfi 1993
B.J. Kemp, S. Garfi, *A Survey of the Ancient City of el-'Amarna*, The Egypt Exploration Society Occasional Publication, 9, London 1993

Kemp, Weatherhead 2000
B. Kemp, F. Weatherhead, *Palace Decoration at tell El-Amarna*, in: Sherratt 2000, pp. 491-523.

Kienitz 1953
F.K. Kienitz, *Die politische Geschichte Ägyptens vom 7. bis zum 4.Jahrhundert vor der Zeitwende*, Berlin 1953.

Kitchen 1982
K.A. Kitchen, *Pharaoh Triumphant: Life and Times of Ramesses II*, Mississauga 1982.

Kitchen 1986
K. A. Kitchen, *The Third Intermediary Period in Egypt (1100-650 BC)*, Second Edition, Warminster 1986.

Kitchen 1996
K.A. Kitchen, *Ramesside Inscriptions Translated and Annotated: Translations II*, Oxford 1996.

Klug 2002
A. Klug, *Königliche Stelen in der Zeit von Ahmose bis Amenophis III*, Monumenta Aegyptiaca VIII, Turnhout 2002.

Kozloff, Bryan 1992
A.P. Kozloff, B.M. Bryan, *Catalogue of the Exhibition "Egypt's Dazzling Sun: Amenhotep III and His World"*, Cleveland 1992.

Kozloff, Bryan, Berman, Delange 1993
A.P Kozloff, B.M. Bryan, L.M. Berman, E. Delange, *Catalogue de l'exposition " Aménophis III. Le Pharaon Soleil"*, Paris 1993.

Kuentz 1928
Ch. Kuentz, *La bataille de Qadech : les textes ("Poème de Pentaour" et "Bulletin de Qadech") et les bas-reliefs*, MIFAO 55, Le Caire 1928.

KRI I-VII
K.A. Kitchen, *Ramesside Inscriptions. Historical and Biographical*, Vols. I-VII, Oxford 1975-1989

Kriegér 1960
P. Kriéger, *Une statuette de roi-faucon au Musée du Louvre*, RdE 12, 1960, pp. 37-58.

Kruchten 1990
J.-M. Kruchten, *Une stèle signée dédiée à Aménophis I*er *et Ahmès Néfertari divinisés*, in: Israelit-Groll 1990, pp. 646-652.

Labrousse, Moussa 1996
A. Labrousse, A.M. Moussa, *Le temple d'accueil du complexe funéraire du roi Ounas*, BdE 111, Le Caire 1996.

Lacovara 1996
P. Lacovara, *Deir el-Ballas and New Kingdom Royal Cities*, in: Bietak 1996B, pp. 139-147.

Landström 1970
B. Landström, *Ships of the Pharaohs. 4000 Years of Egyptian Shipbuilding*, London 1970.

Lapp 1986
G. Lapp, *Die Opferformel des Alten Reiches, unter Berücksichtigung einiger späterer Formen*, SDAIK 21, Mainz am Rhein1986.

Lauer 1970
J.-Ph. Lauer, *Recherches et travaux à Saqqarah (campagne 1969-1970)*, CRAIBL 1970, pp. 484-503.

Lauer 1971
J.-Ph. Lauer, *Travaux et découvertes à Saqqarah (1970-1971)*, BSFE 62, Octobre 1971, pp. 30-48.

Lauer, Derry 1935
J.-Ph. Lauer, D.E. Derry, *Découverte à Saqqarah d'une partie de la momie du roi Zoser*, ASAE 35, 1935, pp. 25-30.

Lauer, Garnot 1958
J.-Ph. Lauer, J. Sainte Fare Garnot, *Rapport préliminaire sur les recherches entreprises dans le soussol de la pyramide de Téti à Saqqarah en 1951 et 1955-1956*, ASAE 55, 1958, pp. 253-261.

Leblanc 1989
Ch. Leblanc, *Ta Set Neferou. Une nécropole de Thèbes-Ouest et son histoire. I: Géographie - Toponymie historique de l'exploration scientifique du site*, Le Caire 1989.

Leblanc 1999
Chr. Leblanc, *Nefertari. " L'aimée de Mout"*, Paris 1999.

Leblanc 2001
Ch. Leblanc, *La véritable identité de Pentaouret, le " prince maudit "*, RdE 52, 2001, pp.151-182.

Leblanc 2002
Ch. Leblanc, *La Vallée des reines*, in : Weeks 2002, p.270-294.

Leblanc, de Cenival 1986
Chr. Leblanc, J.-L. de Cenival, *Rapport des activités scientifiques de l'UA 1064 du CNRS. Années 1985-1986*, Paris/Le Caire, 1986.

Leblanc, Fekri 1991
Ch. Leblanc, M. Fekri, *Les enfants de Ramsès II au Ramesseum*, Memnonia I, 1991, pp. 91-108.

Leca 1976
A.-P. Leca, *Les momies*, Paris 1976.

Le Caire 2002
Catalogue of the Exhibition" Parfums & Cosmetique, Dans L'Egypte Ancienne", Le Caire 2002.

Leclant 1972
J. Leclant, *Fouilles et travaux en Egypte et au Soudan, 1970 – 1971*, Orientalia 41, 1972, pp. 249 -291 (pl.).

Leclant *et alii* 1984
J. Leclant *et alii*, *Egypte*, Paris 1984.

Liverani 1990
M. Liverani, *Prestige and Interest. International Relations in the Near East ca. 1600-1100 B.C.*, History of the Ancient Near East Studies I, Padova 1990.

Lloyd 1988
A.B. Lloyd, *Herodotus Book II. Commentary 99-182*, EPRO 43/3, Leiden 1988.

Loprieno 1996A
A. Loprieno (Edited by), *Ancient Egyptian Literature. Hystory and Forms*, Leiden/New York/Köln 1996.

Loprieno 1996B
A. Loprieno, *The "King's Novel"*, in Loprieno 1996A, pp. 277-295.

Loret 1899
V. Loret, *Le tombeau d'Aménophis II et la cachette royale de Biban-el-Molouk*, BIE sér. 3, n. 9, 1899, pp. 98-112.

Lilyquist 1995
C. Lilyquist, *Egyptian Stone Vessels. Khian through Tuthmosis IV*, New York 1995.

Limme 1979
L. Limme, *Stèles égyptiennes*, Guides du Département Égyptien des Musées Royaux d'Art et d'Histoire 4, Bruxelles 1979.

Luft, Poetke 1977
U. Luft, G. Poetke, *Leben im ägyptischen Altertum. Literatur - Urkunden - Briefe - aus vier Jahrtausenden*, [Berlin] 1977.

el-Mahdi 1990
Chr. el-Mahdy, *Momies, mythe et magie*, Paris 1990.

Malaise 1966
M. Malaise, *Sésostris, pharaon de légende et d'histoire*, CdE XLI, 1966, p. 244-272.

Mariette 1857
A. Mariette, *Le Sérapeum de Memphis*, Paris 1857.

Marucchi 1898
O. Marucchi, *Gli obelischi egiziani di Roma*, Roma 1898.

Maspero 1874
G. Maspero, *Une enquête judiciaire à Thèbes au*

temps de la XXe dynastie : étude sur le Papyrus Abbott, MAIBL sér. 1, tome 8.2, Paris 1874, pp. 211-296.

Maspero 1882
G. Maspero, *La pyramide du roi Ounas*, RT 3, 1882, pp. 177-224.

Maspero 1883
G. Maspero, *Guide du Visiteur au Musée de Boulaq*, Cairo 1883.

Maspero 1884
G. Maspero, *La pyramide du roi Teti*, RT 5, 1884, pp. 1-59.

Maspero 1887
G. Maspero, *La pyramide du roi Mirinrî*, RT 9, 1887, pp. 177-191.

Maspero 1889
G. Maspero, *Les momies royales de Déir el-Baharî*, MMAF 1.4, Le Caire 1889, pp. 511-787.

Maspero 1892
G. Maspero, *La pyramide du roi Pépi II*, RT 12, 1892, pp. 53-95.

Maspero 1895
G. Maspero, *Histoire des peuples de l'Orient classique. Vol. I*, Paris 1895.

al-Masri 1983
Y. al-Masri, *Preliminary Report on the Excavations in Akhmim by the Egyptian Antiquities Organization*, ASAE 69, 1983, p.7-11.

Mathieu 1994
B. Mathieu, *Pharaons et rois de France. Profanation et résurrection*, in: Berger, Clerc, Grimal 1994.4, pp. 215-227.

Mathieu 1997
B. Mathieu, *La signification du serdab dans la pyramide d'Ounas. L'architecture des appartements funéraires royaux à la lumière des Textes des Pyramides*, in: Berger, Mathieu 1997, pp. 289-304.

Megally 1971
M. Megally, *Le papyrus hiératique comptable E. 3226 du Louvre*, BdE 53 Le Caire 1971.

Megally 1977
M. Megally, *Notions de comptabilité. A propos du Papyrus E. 3226 du Musée du Louvre*, BdE 72, [Le Caire] 1977.

de Meulenaere 1966
H. de Meulenaere, *Deux vizirs de Ramsès II*, CdE 41, 1966, pp. 223-232.

Michalowski 1994
K. Michalowski, *L'Art de l'Egypte ancienne*, Paris 1994.

Mojsov 1992
B. Mojsov, *The Sculpture and Relief of Ramesses III*. PhD. Thesis, New York University, Chicago University Microfilm 1992.

Monnet 1965
J. Monnet, *Remarques sur la famille et les successeurs de Ramsès III*, BIFAO 63, 1965, pp. 209-236.

Montet 1947
P. Montet, *La Nécropole royale de Tanis, tome premier : les constructions et le tombeau d'Osorkon II à Tanis*, Paris 1947.

Montet 1951
P. Montet, *La nécropole de Tanis, tome second : les constructions et le tombeau de Psousennès à Tanis*, Paris 1951.

Montet 1960
P. Montet, *La Nécropole royale de Tanis III. Les constructions et le tombeau de Chéchanq III à Tanis*, Paris 1960.

Montet, Yoyotte 1998
P. Montet, J. Yoyotte, *Lettres de Tanis 1939-1940. La découverte des trésors royaux*, Paris 1998.

Montréal 1986
Catalogue of the Exhibition "The Great Pharaoh Ramses II and his Time, Montréal 1986.

Moorey 1988
P.R.S. Moorey, *Ancient Egypt*, Oxford 1988.

Moret 1902
A. Moret, Le rituel du culte divin journalier en Egypte d'après les papyrus de Berlin et les textes du temple de Séti Ier, à Abydos, Paris 1902.

Müller 1969
H. W. Müller, Ein Siegelring Ramses' II, Pantheon 27. 5, 1969, pp. 359-363.

Müller 1989
H.-W. Müller, *Eine ungewöhnliche Metallfigur eines blinden ägyptischen Priesters*, AAWMun 5, 1989, pp. 5-33.

Müller, Wildung 1976
H.W. Müller, D. Wildung, *Staatliche Sammlung ägyptischer Kunst*, 2. erweiterte Auflage, München, 1976.

Müller, Thiem 1999
H.W. Müller, E. Thiem, *Gold of the Pharaohs*, Ithaca 1999.

Murnane 1995A
W.J. Murnane, *Texts from the Amarna Period in Egypt*, Writings from the Ancient World 5, Atlanta 1995.

Murnane 1995B
W.J. Murnane, *The Kingship of the Nineteenth Dynasty: A Study in the Resilience of an Institution*, in: O'Connor, Silverman 1995, pp. 185-217.

Murnane 1997
W.J. Murnane, *Three Kingdoms and Thirty-four Dynasties*, in: Silverman 1997, pp. ??? - ???.

Mysliwiec 1976
K. Mysliwiec, *Le portrait royal dans le bas-relief du Nouvel Empire*, ET 18, Warsaw 1976.

Mysliwiec 1988
K. Mysliwiec, *Royal Portraiture of the Dynasties XXI-XXX*, Mainz am Rhein 1988.

Nagel 1949
G. Nagel, *Le Linceul de Thoutmès III. Cairo, Cat. No. 40.001*, ASAE 49, 1949, pp. 317-329.

Nagoya/Boston 1999
Catalogue of the Exhbition "Art of the Ancient Mediterranean World", Nagoya/Boston 1999.

Naville 1892
E. Naville, *The Festival Hall of Osorkon II in the Great Temple of Bubastis (1887-1889)*, EEF Publications 10, London 1892.

Naville 1907
E. Naville, *The XIth Dynasty Temple at Deir el-Bahari. Vol. I*, EEF publications 28, London 1907.

Nelson 1981
H.H. Nelson, *The Great Hypostyle Hall at Karnak. Volume 1, Part 1: The Wall Reliefs*, OIP 106, Chicago 1981.

New York 1999
Catalogue of the Exhibition "Egyptian Art in the Age of the Pyramids", New York 1999.

Nicholson, Shaw 2000
P.T. Nicholson, I. Shaw (Edited by), *Ancient Egyptian Materials and Technology*, Cambridge 2000.

Obsomer 1989
Cl. Obsomer, *Les campagnes de Sésostris dans Hérodote*, Bruxelles, 1989.

Obsomer 1992
Cl. Obsomer, *Hérodote, Strabon et le "mystère" du labyrinthe d'Égypte*, in: Obsomer, Oosthoek 1992, pp. 221 - 333.

Obsomer 1995
Cl. Obsomer, *Sésostris Ier. Étude chronologique et historique du règne*, Connaissance de l'Égypte Ancienne 5, Bruxelles1995.

Obsomer, Oosthoek 1992
Cl. Obsomer, A.-L. Oosthoek (Édité par), *Amosiadès. Mélanges offerts au Professeur Claude Vandersleyen par ses anciens étudiants*, Louvain-la-Neuve 1992.

O'Connor 1980
D. O'Connor, *S.v. "Malqata"* in LÄ III, Wiesbaden 1980, cc. 1173-1177.

O'Connor 1991
D. O'Connor, *Mirror of the cosmos: the palace of Merenptah*, in: Bleiberg, Freed 1991, pp. 167-198.

O'Connor 1995
D. O'Connor, *Beloved of Maat, the Horizon of Re: The Royal Palace in New Kingdom Egypt*, in O'Connor, Silverman 1995, pp. 263-300.

O'Connor, Silverman 1995
D. O'Connor, D.P. Silverman (Edited by), *Ancient Egyptian Kingship*, Probleme der Ägyptologie 9, Leiden 1995.

Ollivier-Beauregard 1894
M. Ollivier-Beauregard, *La caricature égyptienne*, Paris 1894.

Omlin 1973
J.A. Omlin, *Der Papyrus 55001 und seine satirischerotischen Zeichnungen und Inschriften*, Catalogo del Museo Egizio di Torino, serie prima - Monumenti e testi 3, Torino 1973.

Oren 1997
E. Oren (Edited by), *The Hyksos: New Historical and Archaeological Perspectives*, Philadelphia 1997

Oren 2000
E. Oren, *The Sea Peoples and Their World: A Reassessment*, Philadelphia 2000.

Ortiz 1996
G. Ortiz, *In Pursuit of the Absolute. Art of the Ancient World. The George Ortiz Collection*, Berna 1996.

Paris 1982
Catalogue de l'exposition " Naissance de l'écriture, Cunéiformes et hiéroglyphes ", Paris 1982.

Paris 1987
Catalogue de l'exposition " Tanis, l'or des pharaons ", Paris 1987.

Paris 1990
Notices descriptives des objets présentés à l'Exposition "Mémoires d'Egypte. Hommage de l'Europe à Champollion ", Strasbourg 1990.

Paris 1997
Catalogue de l'exposition " Soudan. Royaumes sur le Nil ", Passau 1997.

Paris 1999
Catalogue de l'exposition "L'art égyptien au temps des pyramides", Paris 1999.

Parker, Leclant, Goyon 1979
R.A. Parker, J. Leclant, J.-C. Goyon, The Edifice of Taharqa by the Sacred Lake of Karnak, Brown Egyptological Studies VIII, Providence/London 1979.

Parkinson 1997
R.B. Parkinson, The Tale of Sinuhe and other Ancient Egyptian Poems 1940-1640 B.C., Oxford 1997.

Peck 1980
W.H. Peck, Dessins égyptiens, (traduction française de Drawings fron Ancient Egypt, 1978), Paris 1980.

Peet 1930
T.E. Peet, The great tomb-robberies of the twentieth Egyptian dynasty : being a critical study, with translations and commentaries, of the papyri in which these are recorded, Oxford 1930

Peet, Wolley 1923
E. Peet, C.L. Wooley, The City of Akhenaten. Part I, Thirty-Eighth Memoir of the EES, London 1923.

Pendlebury 1951
J.D.S. Pendlebury, The City of Akhenaten. Part III. The Central City and the Official Quarters. The Excavations at Tell El-Amarna during the Season 1926-1927 and 1931-1936, Forty-fourth Memoir of the EES, London1951.

Perdu en parution
O. Perdu, Le roi Roudamon en personne!, RdE 53, 2002 (en parution).

Pernigotti, Piacentini, Davoli 1988
S. Pernigotti, P. Piacentini, P. Davoli, L'Egitto antico, Imola 1992.

Petrie 1896
W.M.F. Petrie, Notice of a casket of Amenhotep II (XVIII dyn., c. 1430 B. C.) in the late Mr A. H. Rhind's Egyptian collection, now in the Scottish National Museum of Antiquities, PSAS 30, 1896, pp. 30-33.

Petrie, Brunton 1924
W.M.F. Petrie, G. Brunton, Sedment II, BSAE/ERA 35, London 1924.

Pezin, Janot 1995
M. Pezin, Fr. Janot, La pustule et les deux doigts, BIFAO 95, 1995, pp. 361-365.

Phillips 1994
J. Phillips, The Composite Sculpture of Akhetaten, Amarna Letters 3, 1994, 58-71.

Piccione 1981 - 1982
P.A. Piccione, The mḏȝ.t, "Peg", in Ancient Egyptian, Serapis 7, 1981-1982, pp. 75-86.

Pleyte, Rossi 1869
F. Pleyte, W. Rossi, Papyrus de Turin. Tome I, Leide 1869.

PM I.2
B. Porter, R.L. Moss (Edited by), Topographical Bibliography of Ancient Egyptian Hieroglyphic Texts, Reliefs and Paintings. Vol. I. The Theban Necropolis. Part 2: Royal Tombs and Small Cemeteries, 2nd Edition, Oxford 1973.

PM II
B. Porter, R.L. Moss (Edited by), Topographical Bibliography of Ancient Egyptian Hieroglyphic Texts, Reliefs and Paintings. Vol. II. Theban Temples, 2nd Edition, Oxford 1972.

PM III.1
B. Porter, R.L. Moss (Edited by), Topographical Bibliography of Ancient Egyptian Hieroglyphic Texts, Reliefs and Paintings. Vol. III. Memphis. Part 1: Abu Rawash to Abusir, 2nd edition, Oxford 1974.

PM IV
B. Porter, R. L. Moss (Edited by), Topographical Bibliography of Ancient Egyptian Hieroglyphic Texts, Reliefs and Paintings. Vol. IV : Lower and Middle Egypt, Oxford 1934.

PM VIII
J. Malek, D. Magee, E. Miles (Edited by), Topographical Bibliography of Ancient Egyptian Hieroglyphic Texts, Statues, Reliefs and Paintings. Vol. VIII. Objects of Provenance Not Known: Statues. Oxford 2000.

Polanyi 1975
K. Polanyi, L'économie en tant que procès institutionnalisé, in: Polanyi, Arensberg 1975, p. 239-260.

Polanyi, Arensberg 1975
K. Polanyi, C. Arensberg, Les systèmes économiques dans l'histoire et dans la théorie, Paris 1975.

Posener 1977 – 1980
G. Posener, Catalogue des ostraca hiératiques littéraires de Deir el-Médineh. Tome III : Nos. 1267 – 1675, DFIFAO 20, Le Caire1977-1980.

Posener 1956
G. Posener, Littérature et politique dans l'Egypte de la XIIe dynastie, Paris 1956.

Posener 1960
G. Posener, De la divinité du Pharaon, CSA 15, Paris 1960.

Priese 1991
K.-H. Priese (Hrsg.), Museumsinsel Berlin. Ägyptisches Museum, Berlin 1991

Quirke 1997
S. Quirke, The Temple in Ancient Egypt, London 1997.

Radwan 1961
A. Radwan, Die Darstellungen des regierende Königs und seiner Familienangehörigen in den Privatgräbern der 18. Dynastie, MÄS 21,Berlin 1961.

Radwan 1978
A. Radwan, Ramses II. und seine Mutter vor Osiris, SAK 6, 1978, pp. 157-161.

Ranke
H. Ranke, The Egyptian Collections of the University Museum, UPMB 15, 1950, pp. 21-109.

Redford 1967
D.B. Redford, History and Chronology of the Egyptian Eighteenth Dynasty: Seven Studies, Toronto 1967.

Redford 1984
D.B. Redford, Akhenaten: The Heretic King, Princeton 1984.

Redford 1992
D.B. Redford, Egypt, Canaan, and Israel in Ancient Times, Princeton 1992.

Redford 1995
D.B. Redford, The Concept of Kingship of the Eighteenth Dynasty, in: O'Connor, Silverman 1995, pp. 157-184.

Reeves 1990
C.N. Reeves, Valley of the Kings. The decline of a royal necropolis, London/New York 1990.

Reeves, Taylor 1992
N. Reeves, J.H. Taylor, Howard Carter before Tutankhamun, London 1992.

Reeves, Wilkinson 1996
C.N. Reeves, R.H. Wilkinson, The Complete Valley of the Kings. Tombs and Treasures of Egypt's Greatest Pharaohs, Cairo 1996.

Reiser 1972
E. Reiser, Der Königliche Harim im alten Ägypten und seine Verwaltung, Dissertationen der Universität Wien 77, Wien 1972.

Reisner 1923
G.A. Reisner, Harvard African Studies. Excavations at Kerma, Parts 4-5, Cambridge 1923.

Reisner 1955
G.A. Reisner, The tomb of Hetep-heres the Mother of Cheops. A Study of Egyptian Civilization in the Old Kingdom, (Completed and Revised by W.S. Smith) A History of the Giza Necropolis Volume II, Cambridge Massachusetts 1955.

Ricke 1932
H. Ricke, Der Grundriss des Amarna-Wohnhauses, Ausgrabungen der Deutschen Orient-Gesellschaft in Tell el-Amarna 4 = WVDOG 56, Leipzig 1932.

Robins 1993
Gay Robins, Women in Ancient Egypt, Cambridge Massachusetts 1993.

Roccati 1997
A. Roccati (a cura di), L'impero ramesside. Convegno internazionale in onore di Sergio Donadoni, VO Quaderno 1, Roma 1997.

Roeder 1926
G. Roeder, Ramses II. als Gott : nach den Hildesheimer Denksteinen aus Horbêt, ZÄS 61, 1926, pp. 57-67.

Roeder 1960
G. Roeder, Kulte, Orakel und Naturverehrung im alten Ägypten, eingeleitet und übertragen, Zürich/Stuttgart 1960.

Roehrig 2001
K. Roehrig, The Eighteen Dynasty Titles Royal Nurse (mn't nswt), Royal Tutor (mn' nswt) and foster Brother/Sister of the Lord of the two Lands (sn/snt mn' n nb ta3wy), (University of Berkley California 1990), Ann Arbor 2001

Roma 1992
AA.VV., Catalogo della mostra "Scavi italiani in Egitto e Sudan", Roma 1992.

Romano 1997
J.F. Romano, Sixth Dynasty Royal Sculpture", in : Grimal 1997, pp. 235-304.

Ronsecco 1996
P. Ronsecco, Due Libri dei Morti del principio del Nuovo Regno. Il lenzuolo funerario della principessa Ahmosi e le tele del Sa-Nesu Ahmosi, Catalogo del Museo Egizio di Torino. Serie Prima - Monumenti e Testi, 7, Torino 1996.

Rowe 1908
L.E. Rowe, Egyptian portraiture of the XX dynasty, BMFA 6, 1908, pp. 47-50.

Russmann 1981
E.R. Russmann, An Egyptian Royal Statuette of the Eighth Century B.C., in: Simpson, Davis 1981, pp. 149 – 155.

el-Saghir 1991
M. el-Saghir, Das Statuenversteck im Luxortempel, Mainz am Rhein 1991.

Sadek 1988
A.I. Sadek, *Popular Religion in Egypt during the New Kingdom*, HÄB 27, Hildesheim1988.

Saleh 1999
M. Saleh (a cura di), *Catalogo della mostra "Arte sublime nell'antico Egitto"*, Firenze/Milano 1999.

Saleh, Sourouzian 1987
M. Saleh, H. Sourouzian, *The Egyptian Museum Cairo. Official Catalogue*, Mainz am Rhein 1987.

Satzinger 1994
H. Satzinger, *Das Kunsthistorische Museum in Wien. Die Ägyptisch-Orientalische Sammlung*, Zaberns Bildbände zur Archäologie 14, Mainz am Rhein 1994.

Sauneron 1952
S. Sauneron, *Rituel de l'embaumement. Pap. Boulaq III. Pap. Louvre 5.158*, Le Caire 1952.

Sauneron 1953
S. Sauneron, *Le chef de travaux Mây*, BIFAO 53, 1953, pp. 57-63.

Scamuzzi 1966
E. Scamuzzi, *L'art égyptien au musée de Turin*, (Traduction française de *Museo Egizio di Torino*, Torino [1963]), [Paris 1966].

Schäfer 1910
H. Schäfer (Hrsg.), *Ägyptische Goldschmiedearbeiten*, Mitteilungen aus der Ägyptischen Sammlung / Königliche Museen zu Berlin1, Berlin 1910.

Scharff 1934
A. Scharff, *Alexander: Ein Denkstein des Vezirs Rahotep aus der 19. Dynastie*, ZÄS 70, 1934, pp. 47-51.

Schiaparelli 1887
E. Schiaparelli, *Museo Archeologico di Firenze: antichità egizie*, Catalogo generale dei musei di antichità e degli oggetti d'arte raccolti nelle gallerie e biblioteche del Regno, Serie 6.1, Roma 1887.

Schiaparelli 1923
E. Schiaparelli, *Relazione sui lavori della missione archeologica italiana in Egitto (anni 1903-1920). Vol. I: Esplorazione della Valle delle Regine nella necropoli di Tebe*, Torino 1923.

Schiff Giorgini 1961
M. Schiff Giorgini, *La quarta campagna di scavi a Soleb (Sudan)*, Levante 7, 1961, pp. 15 – 23.

Schiff Giorgini 1962
M. Schiff Giorgini, *Soleb, Campagna 1960-1*, Kush 10, 1962, pp. 152 – 167.

Schmitz 1976
B. Schmitz, *Untersuchungen zum Titel s3-njswt "Königssohn"*, Habelts Dissertationsdrucke. Reihe Ägyptologie 2, Bonn 1976.

Schoske 1992
S. Schoske, *Staatliche Sammlung Ägyptischer Kunst*, Münchner Jahrbuch der bildenden Kunst 43, 1992, pp. 175-185.

Schott 1992
S. Schott, *Les chants d'amour de l'Egypte ancienne*, (tradution française de P. Posener), Paris 1992.

Schulz 1992
R. Schulz, *Die Entwicklung und Bedeutung des kuboiden Statuentypus. Eine Untersuchung zu den sogenannten "Würfelhockern." Band I-II*, HÄB 33-34 Hildesheim, 1992.

Schulz, Seidel 1998
R. Schulz, M. Seidel, *Egypt. The World of the Pharaos*, Könemann 1998.

Schunck 1985
M. Schunck, *Untersuchungen zum Wortstamm xa*, Habelts Dissertationsdrucke, Reihe Ägyptologie, 5, Bonn, 1985.

Schwaller de Lubicz 1949
R.A. Schwaller de Lubicz, *Le Temple dans l'Homme*, Le Caire 1949.

Schwaller de Lubicz 1958
R.A. Schwaller de Lubicz, *Le Temple de l'Homme, Apet du Sud à Louqsor. Tomes I-III*, Paris [1958].

Scott III 1992
G.D. Scott III, *Temple, Tomb and Dwelling: Egyptian Antiquities from the Harer Family Trust Collection*, San Bernardino 1992.

Seipel 1989
W. Seipel, *Katalog zur Ausstellung „Ägypten. Götter, Gräber und die Kunst. 4000 Jahre Jenseitsglaube. Band I"*, Kataloge des OÖ. Landesmuseums Linz, Neue Folge, 22.I Linz 1989.

Seipel 1992
W. Seipel (Hrsg.), *Katalog zur Ausstellung "Gott-Mensch-Pharao"*, Wien 1992.

Seipel 2001
W. Seipel, *Katalog zur Ausstellung "Gold der Pharaonen"*, Milano 2001.

Settgast 1989
J. Settgast (Hrsg.), *Ägyptishes Museum*, Mainz am Rhein 1989.

Sherratt 2000
S. Sherratt (Edited by), *The Wall Paintings of Thera, Proceedings of the First International Symposium (Petros M. Nomikos Conference Centre Thera, Hellas 30 August - 4 September 1997). Vol. 1*, Athens 2000

van Siclen III 1996
C.C. van Siclen III, *Remarks on the Middle Kingdom Palace at Tell Basta*, in: Bietak 1996B, pp. 239-246.

Siliotti 1987
A. Siliotti (a cura di), *Padova e l'Egitto*, Padova 1987.

Silverman 1995
D.P. Silverman 1995, *The Nature of Egyptian Kingship*, in: O'Connor, Silverman 1995, pp. 49 – 92.

Silverman 1997
D.P. Silverman (Edited by), *Catalogue of the Exhibition "Searching for Ancient Egypt"*, New York 1997.

Simpson 1982
W.K. Simpson, *S.v. "Pap. Westcar"*, in: LÄ IV, Wiesbaden 1982.

Simpson 1987
AA.VV., *A Table of Offerings. 17 Years of Acquisitions of Egyptian and Ancient Near Eastern Art by William Kelly Simpson for the Museum of Fine Arts, Boston*, Boston 1987.

Simpson 1996
W.K. Simpson, *Belles lettres and Propaganda*, in: Loprieno 1996, pp. 435 – 443.

Simpson, Davis 1981
W.K. Simpson, W.M. Davis (Edited by), *Studies in Ancient Egypt, the Aegean, and the Sudan. Essays in honor of Dows Dunham on the occasion of his 90th birthday, June 1, 1980*, Boston 1981.

Smith 1960
W.S. Smith, *Ancient Egypt as represented in the Museum of Fine Arts*, Boston [1960].

Smith 1962
W.S. S[mith], *Some Recent Accessions*, BMFA 60, 1962, pp. 120-121.

Smith 1998
W.S. Smith, *The Art and Architecture of Ancient Egypt*, Revised with Additions by W. K. Simpson, Yale 1998.

Smither 1939
P.C. Smither, *The writing of* htp-di-nsw *in the Middle and New Kingdoms*, JEA 25, 1939, pp. 34-37.

Soukiassian 1997
G. Soukiassian, *A Govenor's Palace at 'Ayn Asil, Dakhla Oasis*, EA 11, 1997, pp. 15-17.

Soukiassian, Wuttmann, Schaad 1990
G. Soukiassian, G.-M. Wuttmann, D. Schaad, *La ville d'Ayn-Asil à Dakhla. État des recherches*, BIFAO 90, 1990, pp. 347-358

Sourouzian 1988
H. Sourouzian, *Standing Royal Colossi of the Middle Kingdom reused by Ramesses II*, MDAIK 44, 1988, pp. 229 – 254.

Sourouzian 1989
H. Sourouzian, *Les Monuments du roi Merenptah*, SDAIK 22, Mainz am Rhein 1989.

Sourouzian 1993
H. Sourouzian, *Statues et représentations royales sous Séthi I*, MDAIK 49, 1993, pp. 239 – 257.

Spalinger 2001
A.J. Spalinger, *S.v. "Festivals"*, in: OEAE I, Oxford 2001, pp. 521-525.

Stadelmann 1973
R. Stadelmann, *Tempelpalast und Erscheinungsfenster in den Thebanischen Totentempeln*, MDAIK 29, 1973, pp. 221-242.

Stadelmann 1985
R. Stadelmann, *Die Ägyptischen Pyramiden : Vom Ziegelbau zum Weltwunder*, Mainz am Rhein 1985.

Stadelmann 1999
R. Stadelmann, *Représentations de la famille royale à l'Ancien Empire*, in : Ziegler 1999, pp.169-179

Stadelmann 2001
R. Stadelmann, *S.v. "Palaces"*, in: OEAE III, Oxford 2001, pp. 13-17.

Strauss 1980
Chr. Strauss, *S.v. „Kronen"*, in: LÄ III, Wiesbaden 1980, cc. 811-816.

Stierlin, Ziegler 1987
H. Stierlin, Ch. Ziegler, *Tanis. Trésors des Pharaons*, Paris 1987.

Stierlin, Ziegler 1988
H. Stierlin, Ch. Ziegler, *Tanis. I tesori dei faraoni* (Traduzione italiana di Stierlin, Ziegler 1987), Milano 1988.

Strouhal *et alii* 1998
E. Strouhal *et alii*, *Re-investigation of the Remains Thought to be of King Djoser and those of an Unidentified Female from the Step Pyramid at Saqqara*, in: Eyre 1998, pp. 1103-1107.

Teeter 1997
E. Teeter, *The Presentation of Maat. Ritual and Legitimacy in Egypt*, SAOC 57, Chicago 1997.

Tefnin 1979
R. Tefnin, *La statuaire d'Hatshepsout. Portrait royal et politique sous la 18e Dynastie*, Monuments aegyptiaca 4, Bruxelles 1979

Thomas 1995
N. Thomas, *Catalogue of the Exhibition "The American Discovery of Ancient Egypt"*, [New York] 1995.

Thomas 1966
E. Thomas, *The Royal Necropolis of Thebes*, Princeton 1966.

Tiradritti 1998
F. Tiradritti (a cura di), *Tesori egizi nella collezione del Museo Egizio del Cairo*, Vercelli 1998.

Topozada 1991
Z. Topozada, *Une stèle de Horemheb retrouvée au Musée du Caire*, BIFAO 91, 1991, pp. 249 – 254.

Tosi, Roccati 1972
M. Tosi, A. Roccati, *Stele ed altre epigrafi di Deir el-Medina: n. 50001 - n. 50262*, Catalogo del Museo Egizio di Torino. Parte seconda: le collezioni. Vol I, Torino 1971.

Traunecker 1984
Cl. Traunecker, *Akhenaton et sa légende* ; in Leclant *et alii* 1984, p.159-185.

Traunecker 1986A
Cl. Traunecker, *Aménophis IV et Néfertiti. Le couple royal d'après les talatates du IXe pylône de Karnak*, BSFE 107, 1986, pp.17 – 44.

Traunecker 1986B
Cl. Traunecker, *Amon de Louqsor*, Dossiers Histoire et Archéologie 101, Janvier 1986, pp. 61-64.

Traunecker 1989
Cl. Traunecker, *Le "Château de l'Or" de Thoutmosis III et les magasins nord du temple d'Amon*, CRIPEL 11 (1989), pp. 89-111

Traunecker 1992
Cl. Traunecker, *Les Dieux de l'Egypte*, Paris 1992.

Traunecker 1995
Cl. Traunecker, *Le P. Spiegelberg et l'évolution des liturgies thébaines*, in : Vleeming 1995, pp. 183 - 201.

Traunecker 1998A
Cl. Traunecker, *Néfertiti, la reine sans nom*, Egypte, Afrique et Orient 14, 1998, p.34 – 38.

Traunecker 1998B
Cl. Traunecker, *Une famille de prêtres à Karnak aux 1er et 2e siècles avant J.-C.: les Horsaisis-Nekhtmontou*, dans *In Memoriam Jan Quaegebeur*. éditions Peters, 1998, pp. 1191-1230.

Traunecker 2001
Cl. Traunecker, *Gods of Egypt*, (version anglaise avec notes de Traunecker 1992), New York 2001.

Traunecker en parution
Cl. Traunecker, *Temple-Maquette ou maquette de temple dans l'Égypte ancienne*, Acte du colloque de Strasbourg 1998 (en parution).

Trigger *et alii* 1983
B.G. Trigger *et alii*, *Ancient Egypt. A Social History*, Cambridge, 1983

Troy 1986
Troy L, *Patterns of Queenship in Ancient Egypt Myth and History*, Boreas. Uppsala Studies in Ancient Mediterranean and Near Eastern Civilizations14, Uppsala 1986.

Tytus 1903
R. de Peyster Tytus, A *preliminary report on the re-excavation of the palace of Amenhetep III*, New York 1903.

Ucko, Tringham, Dimbleby 1972
P.J. Ucko, R. Tringham, G.W. Dimbleby (Edited by), *Man, Settlement and Urbanism. Proceedings of the Research Seminar in Archaeology and Related Subjects held at the Institute of Archaeology*, London 1972.

Uphill 1972
E. Uphill, *The Concept of the Egyptian Palace as a "Ruling Machine"*, in: Ucko, Tringham, Dimbleby 1972, pp. 721-734.

URK IV
G. Steindorff (Hrsg.), *Urkunden des ägyptische Altertums, Abt. IV : Urkunden der 18. Dynastie. Heft 1-16, bearbeitet von K. Sethe*, Berlin 1927-1930; *Heft 17-21*, bearbeitet von W. Helck, Berlin 1955-1958.

Valbelle 1998
D. Valbelle, *Histoire de l'État pharaonique*, Paris 1998.

Vandersleyen 1971
Cl. Vandersleyen, *Les guerres d'Amosis. Fondateur de la XVIIIe dynastie*, Monographies Reine Élisabeth 1, Bruxelles 1971.

Vandersleyen 1988
Cl. Vandersleyen, *Les deux jeunesses d'Amenhotep III*, BSFE 111, 1988, p. 9 - 30.

Vendersleyen 1995
Cl. Vandersleyen, *L'Égypte et la Vallée du Nil. Tome 2: De la fin de l'Ancien Empire à la fin du Nouvel Empire*, Paris, 1995.

Van de Walle 1969
B. Van de Walle, *L'humour dans la littérature et l'art de l'Ancienne Egypte*, Leyde 1969.

Van de Walle 1980
B. Van de Walle, *S.v. „Humor"*, in: LÄ III, 1980, cc. 73-77.

Vandersleyen 1971
Cl. Vandersleyen, *Les guerres d'Amosis. Fondateur de la XVIIIe dynastie*, Monographies Reine Élisabeth 1, Bruxelles 1971.

Vandersleyen 1983
Cl. Vandersleyen, *An Egyptian Figure Restored*, Arts of Asia 13.6, November/December 1983, pp. 80-81 (color ill.).

Vandier 1958
J. Vandier, *Manuel d'archéologie égyptienne. Tome III*, Paris 1958.

Vandier D'Abbadie 1937
J. Vandier D'Abbadie, *Catalogue des ostraca figurés de Deir el-Medineh. Deuxième fascicule*, DFIFAO II,2, Le Caire 1937.

Vandier D'Abbadie 1946
J. Vandier D'Abbadie, *Catalogue des ostraca figurés de Deir el-Medineh. Troisième fascicule*, DFIFAO II,3, Le Caire 1946.

Vandier D'Abbadie 1959
J. Vandier D'Abbadie, *Catalogue des ostraca figurés de Deir el Médineh. Nos 2734 à 3053*, DFIFAO II,4, Le Caire 1959.

Vandier D'Abbadie 1972
J. Vandier D'Abbadie, *Les Objets de toilette égyptiens au musée du Louvre*, Paris 1972.

Van Siclen 1999
C. Van Siclen, *S.v."Tell Basta"*, in: EAAE, London/New York 1999.

Vernus 1993
P. Vernus, *Affaires et scandales sous les Ramsès*, Paris 1993.

Vernus, Yoyotte 1988
P. Vernus, J. Yoyotte, *Pharaons*, Paris 1988.

Vleeming 1995
S.P. Vleeming (Edited by), *Hundred-Gated Thebes. Acts of a Colloquium on Thebes and the Theban Area in the Graeco-Roman Period*, Papyrologica Lugduno-Batava, 27, Leiden 1995.

Waddell 1980
W.G. Waddell, *Manetho*, London 1980.

Wallert 1967
I. Wallert, *Der verzierte Löffel. Seine Formgeschichte und Verwendung im alten Ägypten*, ÄA 16, Wiesbaden 1967.

Walzer, Higgs 2000
S. Walker, P. Higgs (a cura di), *Cleopatra regina d'Egitto*, Milano 2000.

Wamser, Gebhard 2001
L. Wamser, R. Gebhard (Hrsg.), *Katalog zur Ausstellung „Gold. Magie, Mythos, Macht – Gold der Alten und Neuen Welt"*, Stuttgart/ München 2001.

Warsaw 1997
Katalog zur Ausstellung "Geheimnisvolle Königin Hatschepsut. Ägyptische Kunst des 15. Jahrhunderts v. Chr.", Warsaw 1997.

Weatherhead 1992
F. Weatherhead, *Painted Pavements in the Great Palace at Amarna*, JEA 78, 1992, pp. 179-194.

Weeks 1971-1972
K.R. Weeks, *Preliminary Report on the First Two Seasons at Hierakonpolis. Part II: the Early Dynastic Palace*, JARCE 9, 1971-1972, pp. 29-33.

Weeks 2001
K.R. Weeks (a cura di), *La Valle dei Re. Le tombe e i templi funerari di Tebe Ovest*, Vercelli 2001.

Weeks 2002
K.R. Weeks (Édité par), *La Vallée des Rois*, (Traduction française de Weeks 2001), Vercelli 2002.

Wegner 2001
J. Wegner, *The Town of Wah-sut at South Abydos: 1999 Excavations*, MDAIK 57, 2001, pp. 281-308.

Wien 1994
Katalog zur Sonderausstellung "Pharaonen und Fremde. Dynastien im Dunkel", Wien 1994.

Wildung 1984
D. Wildung, *L'Âge d'or de l'Égypte. Le Moyen Empire*, (Traduction française de: Sesostris und Amenemhet. Ägypten im Mittleren Reich, 1984), Fribourg 1984.

Wildung 1992
D. Wildung, *Métamorphoses d'une reine. La tête berlinoise de la reine Tiyi*, BSFE 125, 1992, pp. 15-28.

Wildung 1997
D. Wildung (Édité par), *Catalogue de l'exposition " Soudan. Royaumes sur le Nil"*, Paris 1997.

Wildung 1998
D. Wildung, *Le frère aîné d'Ekhnaton. Réflexions sur un décès prématuré*, BSFE 143, 1998, pp.10-18.

Wilkinson 1971
A. Wilkinson, *Ancient Egyptian Jewellery*, London 1971.

Wilkinson 1999
T. Wilkinson, *Early Dynastic Egypt*, London/New York 1999.

Will 1966
AA.VV., *Festgabe für Dr. Walter Will, Ehrensenator*

der Universität München, zum 70. Geburtstag am 12. November 1966, Köln/Berlin/Bonn/München 1966.

Williams 1999
Elisabeth Williams, *S.v. "Tell el-Amarna, cult temples,"* in: EAAE, London/ New York, 1999, pp. 769-773.

Winlock 1924
H.E. Winlock, *The tombs of the Kings of the Seventeenth Dynasty at Thebes*, JEA 10, 1924, pp.217-277.

Winlock 1931
H.E. Winlock, *The Tomb of Queen Inhapi : an Open Letter to the Editor*, JEA 17, 1931, pp. 107-110.

Winlock 1942
H.E. Winlock, *Excavations at Deir el Bahri 1911-1931*, New York 1942.

Winlock 1945
H.E. Winlock, *The Slain Soldiers of Neb-hepet-rê' Mentu-hotpe*, PMMAEE XVI, New York, 1945.

Winlock 1947
H.E. Winlock, *The Rise and Fall of the Middle Kingdom in Thebes*, New York 1947.

Winlock 1948
H.E. Winlock, *The Treasure of the Three Egyptian Princesses*, Publications of The Metropolitan Museum of Art, Department of Egyptian Art X, New York 1948.

Yoyotte 1989
J. Yoyotte, *Le roi Mer-djefa-Re et le dieu Sopdou. Un monument de la XIVe dynastie*, BSFE 114, 1989, p. 17-63.

Zayed 1964
A.el-H. Zayed, *A Free-standing Stela of the XIXth Dynasty*, RdE 16, 1964, pp. 193-208.

Zampieri 1994
G. Zampieri, *Il Museo Archeologico di Padova. Dal Palazzo della Ragione al Museo agli Eremitani. Storia della formazione del Museo Civico Archeologico di Padova e Guida alle collezioni*, Milano 1994.

Ziegler 1977
Chr. Ziegler, *"Le sistre d'Henouttaowy"*, La Revue du Louvre et des Musées de France 27, 1977, pp. 1-4.

Ziegler 1990
Chr. Ziegler, *Musée du Luvre. Catalogue des stèles, peintures et reliefs égyptiens de l'Ancien Empire et de la Première Période Intermédiarie (vers 2686 – 2040 avant J.-C.*, Paris 1990.

Ziegler 1994
Ch. Ziegler, *Notes sur la reine Tiy*, in : Berger, Clerc, Grimal 1994.1, pp. 531-548.

Ziegler 1999
Ch. Ziegler (a cura di), *L'Art de l'Ancien Empire*, Actes du colloque organisé au Musée du Louvre par le Service culturel les 3 et 4 avril 1998, Paris 1999.

Ziegler 2001
C. Ziegler, *Les trésors de Tanis*, Paris, 2001.

Ziegler, Bovot 1999
Chr. Ziegler, J.-L. Bovot, *Art et archéologie : l'Égypte ancienne*, Paris, 2001.

Zivie 1976
Ch. Zivie, *Giza au deuxième millénaire*, BdE 70, Le Caire 1976.

Zonhoven 1979
L.M.J. Zonhoven, *The Inspection of a Tomb at Deir El-Medîna (O. Wien Aeg. 1)*, JEA 65, 1979, pp. 89-98.

Index

Credits

All the photographs of the finds from the Egyptian Museum of Cairo are part of a photographic campaign especially conceived by Sherif Sonbol, to whom the publisher particularly wishes to thank.

© Patrick Ageneau/Muséum de Lyon: pp. 21, cat. 5
Archivio RCS: pp. 192, 248-249
Ashmolean Museum: pp. 258, cat. 6
Berlino, Ägyptisches Museum und Papyrussammlung: pp. 140, 168, 290, cat. 69, 235
Berlino, Ägyptisches Museum und Papyrussammlung: Chr. Begall: p. 255; Margarete Büsing: pp. 60, 155, 168, 211, 219, 246, 247, 262, 338, catt. 16, 43, 74, 75, 78, 138, 144, 156, 202; Peter Garbe: p. 242, cat. 196; Jürgen Liepe: pp. 93, 103, 275, 312, catt. 23, 64, 100, 157, 194, 203, 231, 236; K. März: pp. 86, cat. 21; G. Stenzel: p. 253, cat. 201; Jutta Tietz: p. 106, cat. 121
Bibliothèque Nationale de France: cat. 225
Bruxelles, Bibliothèque Royale de Belgique: pp. 137, cat. 103
Chicago, The Field Museum of Natural History/Diane Alexander White: p. 243, catt. 135, 171
Collezioni egittologiche dell'Università di Pisa: cat. 15
Darmstadt, Hessisches Landesmuseum/Wolfgang Fuhrmannek: cat. 104
Araldo De Luca, Roma: pp. 24-25, 40, 68, 207, 344
Durham, The Oriental Museum-University Museum: pp. 278, 377, catt. 166, 175
Firenze, Museo Egizio: pp. 63, 125, 219, 283, catt. 18, 47, 50, 68, 111, 133, 158
Giraudon/Alinari: pp. 236, 266, 306, 310
Hannover, Kestner Museum/Michael Lindner: cat. 184
Béatrice Hatala: pp. 201, catt. 11, 14, 19, 26, 27, 28, 31, 32, 102, 119, 134, 141, 153, 155, 160, 161, 162, 164, 228, 229
Image Bank/Guido Alberto Rossi: pp. 9, 54-55
Image Bank/Giuliano Colliva: pp. 11-12, 190-191
Nasry Iskander: pp. 359, 360, 362, 366, 367, 368, 369, 370374, 375

Leida, Rijksmuseum van Oudheden: pp. 84, cat. 56
EPL-RMN-Poncet: pp. 147, catt. 34, 38, 62, 120, 163
Erich Lessing/Contrasto: pp. 20, 32-33, 35, 36, 44, 45, 56, 79, 174, 175, 181, 227, 298, 300, 301, 308-309, 311, 328-329, 330, 346, 347, 353, 354-355
Giacomo Lovera, Torino: pp. 53, 70, 77, 80-81, 89, 102, 146, 240, 242, 273, 274, 304-305, catt. 24, 25, 35, 59, 60, 61, 71, 94, 98, 130, 148, 151, 179, 180, 181, 197, 211, 212, 215, 234, 239
Laïla Menassa: pp. 226, 228
Museo Civico Archeologico di Bologna/ABC: pp. 90-91, 104, 212, 260, cat. 81, 146
© Monaco, Staatliche Sammlungen Ägyptischer Kunst: pp. 118, catt. 58, 140
Musée Royaux d'Art et d'Histoire de Bruxelles: pp. 215, 272, catt. 147, 214
© 2002, Museum of Fine Arts, Boston: pp. 37, 278, 280, 331, catt. 9, 86, 88, 110, 116, 167, 208, 209, 238, 251, 252, 253, 254, 255
© Ny Carlsberg Glyptotek: pp. 100, 247, catt. 36, 40, 182, 205
Padova, Museo Civico Archeologico: pp. 323, cat. 2
Photo RMN: p. 259, catt. 117, 152, 227; G. Blot/J. Schor: cat. 55; Chuzeville: pp. 18, 49, 93, 103, 119, catt. 22, 79, 170, 200; Ch. Larrieu: p. 34, catt. 8, 118; Hervé Lewandowski: pp. 26, 59, 61, 88, 130, 152, 210, 242, 244, catt. 7, 45, 84, 101, 105, 137, 195, 199; R.G. Ojeda: p. 255, cat. 193; Franck Raux: p. 224
Roemer und Pelizaeus Museum/PeterWindszus: cat. 39
Rainer Stadelmann: pp. 160, 162, 163, 166-167, 169, 170-171, 178, 185, 186-187, 189
The Brooklyn Museum of Art: pp. 28, 264, catt. 10, 65, 96
The Cleveland Museum of Art: pp. 148, cat. 44
© 1978, The Metropolitan Museum of Art: cat. 95
© 1979, The Metropolitan Museum of Art: cat. 233
© 1983, The Metropolitan Museum of Art: pp. 46, 139, 263, 334, catt. 92, 185, 186
© 1992, The Metropolitan Museum of Art: p. 277

© 1993, The Metropolitan Museum of Art: cat. 145
© 1994, The Metropolitan Museum of Art: pp. 57, catt. 13, 191
© 1996, The Metropolitan Museum of Art: p. 245
© 2001, The Metropolitan Museum of Art: p. 335, catt. 188, 189, 223
© 2002, The Metropolitan Museum of Art: pp. 96, 144, 263, 335, catt. 41, 49, 53, 115, 187, 190, 191, 198
The Royal Ontario Museum/Brian Boyle: p. 272, cat. 149
The Trustees of the British Museum: pp. 6, 52, 153, 205, catt. 3, 29, 37, 42, 51, 52, 57, 70, 77, 97, 132, 139, 142, 169, 210, 240, 246, 256, 257
© The University of Pennsylvania, Museum of Archaeology and Anthropology: pp. 105, 199, 284, catt. 4, 17, 73, 90, 91, 112, 113
The Walters Art Museum, Baltimora: pp. 197, 228, cat. 124
© Trustees of the National Museums of Scotland: pp. 64, 221, 254, catt. 46, 99, 108, 154, 226, 232
© Vienna, Kunsthistorisches Museum: pp. 101, 124, 152, 214, catt. 30, 63, 89, 168, 173
P. Zigrossi: p. 87

Maps and graphic reconstructions by Studio Margil.

If not otherwise specified, the photographs come from the museum where the corresponding works are conserved or their proprietors. The publisher wishes to apologize for any involuntary omissions; these will certainly be included in a subsequent reprint.

This volume has been published with the support of Cartiere Burgo and it is printed on R4 Matt Satin 150 g/m paper manufactured Cartiere Burgo

Printed in September 2002 by Bompiani Arte, Skira Group, Geneva-Milan
Printed in Italy

Pharaoh. If a word ever symbolized the power and mystery of Egypt, it is this one. Defying the millennia, it evokes the great figures who fashioned the history of antiquity: Cheops, Chephren, Akhenaton, Tutankhamun, Ramses… The term is mentioned many times in the Old Testament as the incarnation of one of the most terrible enemies of the elected people. Handed down from the Bible, "Pharaoh" is derived from the Egyptian "per-aa," "the great estate," which first designated the palace and only after was used to describe its owner. But at no time in Egypt was it used as a title for the sovereign, for whom the complete protocol included five distinct names; and its usage only became widespread during the first millennium BC.

When Palazzo Grassi entrusted me with the organization of an international exhibition on Egyptology, the project was included in the series of great projects dedicated to lost civilizations: the Celts, the Mayas, the Phoenicians, the Etruscans. However, it seemed impossible for me to present "the Egyptians" in Venice; the subject was much too vast. With respect to the other civilizations of antiquity, the Egyptian civilization was characterized by its extraordinary longevity, three millennia marked by terrific opulence and diversity. It was therefore necessary to choose a period or a specific theme, preferably an original one. For twenty years the Nile Valley has provided inspiration for great exhibitions that were very successful. These were conceived either from a historical perspective (a period, a king, a capital) or based on some particular themes: religion, funerary customs, or daily life. In order to better understand this legendary civilization, a new guiding principle came to mind: the pharaoh, that "divine king of multiple appearances" whose function and person dominated Egyptian history.

What is more evocative of this culture than the institution of the pharaoh? Ancient Egypt owes its exceptional stability and originality to him. Originating in the third millennium BC, the land of the pharaohs appears to be the oldest state of mankind. At its head was a monarch who reigned over an immense unified territory. It contrasted greatly with its contemporaries in the Near East and Africa, where city-states and principalities bordered on tribes and chiefdoms. Now that the nature of power has stimulated numerous studies, sociologists, political scientists and anthropologists have today joined forces with Egyptologists in order to take advantage of the mass of documents that designate the aspects of pharaonic power: his role is essential in Egyptian thought, which again placed man in the great course of the universe. All of society was articulated around the charismatic figure of the sovereign who was the heir of the gods, and the intercessor between the terrestrial and the divine worlds. The universe rested on the Pharaoh, who had been placed on Earth by the god creator in order to repel evil and chaos. Such was the concept of the world propagated by Egyptian power. In this context of communication between heaven and earth, in the center of the cosmos, the king naturally appears as the emblem of Egyptian civilization where nature and culture, religion and politics blend.

The son of the gods, the "living god," the pharaoh was the first priest of the land. His appearance derived from his divine nature: his emblems and his specific crowns, his diverse forms concurred to forge a magnificent and formidable image. One approached him with fear, prostrate and "smelling the earth," "dragging oneself on the ground," according to Egyptian texts. This reverence could reach giddiness, "while I was stretched out on my belly, I lost consciousness" recounts the noble Sinouhé.

As the owner of Egypt, the pharaoh managed, administered, and protected the country against internal disorder and foreign aggression. His colossal statues adorn the numerous temples that he had built and his likeness as a victorious fighter was sculpted everywhere. As chief of state and military chief, he appeared as a perfect being in the official texts. "The fear he inspires strikes the barbarians in their countries." His decisions were striking in their justice and the rapidity of their execution: "He is a god. He has no peers and no one (like him) has ever existed. He is a master of knowledge, excellent in his plans, magnificent in command." His benevolence was limitless: "Those who were hungry are satiated and joyful, those who were thirsty are refreshed. Those who were naked are again dressed in fine linen," chants a hymn that exalts royal beneficence. To maintain the proper course of the universe, to see to it that harmony—in Egyptian, Maat—vanquishes disorder is one of the fundamental duties of the sovereign. Each pharaoh was the master of a time reckoned from the beginning of the first year of his reign and ending with his death. The scribes dated events as "the year 23 of Tuthmose" or "the year 5 of Ramses." Any change of reign also constituted a threat for the cosmic equilibrium: the death of the king announced a return to primordial chaos. But by means of the coronation ceremonies, his successor renewed the original creation; equilibrium would be maintained by the regular celebration of rites, of which certain were particularly tied to the revitalization of the sovereign, such as the feast of Sed.

These official aspects of Egyptian royalty are the ones the public knows best. Still, it is necessary to provide proper keys for understanding them. This is what this exhibitions aims to do, by presenting the nature and function of the king of Egypt: his place in history, his divine origin, his various representations, his roles as a ritualist, builder, warrior, and governor... In order to illustrate these themes, the works have been deliberately limited to the period of the New Kingdom, one of the zeniths of Egyptian history, a period for which the testimonies are especially abundant and explicit. In order to exhibit the treasure of a royal tomb, the III Intermediate Period has also been included. The treasure of the kings of Tanis, the heirs of the New Kingdom kings, is, in effect, with that of Tutankhamun, the only funerary ensemble that bears witness to the magnificence of the *viaticum* that the pharaoh carried into the hereafter. It demonstrates that even at the end of his life, the pharaoh remained distinct from men, acceding to a celestial hereafter inasmuch as he was the son of the gods and a god himself.

Another aspect of the personality of the pharaohs is much less familiar to the public, one that this exhibition intends to reveal. The son of the gods was a man nonetheless and was incarnated in individuals. The visitor will find along a gallery of portraits the lineaments of those who governed Egypt. These singular faces adorned with symbolic attributes can, for some, be compared to the impressive series of royal mummies conserved in the Cairo Museum. During their lifetimes, these sovereigns were not spared either feelings or weaknesses. Therefore, we perceive through the historical texts, which were, however, animated by a spirit of propaganda, that they were familiar with doubt, fear, and failure. To mention just one example, the famous report of the battle of Kadesh, in which Ramses II opposed the Hittites, reveals to us that the pharaoh found himself isolated, the victim of a clumsy strategic error. Alarmed, he appealed to the gods who came to his aid. On the walls of the same temple, one can read the stereotyped formulas perpetuating the universal dominion of the sovereign alongside the text of the not very glorious treaty that he concluded with his enemy. One can easily image that for his contemporaries the image of the pharaoh was much less perfect than the one transmitted in official documents. Reality was much more prosaic. After all, the pharaoh was one of them. "Inspire love in everyone; a good character is remembered," counsels a king to his heir. Artists' sketches and ancient literature make it clear that the people of Egypt readily ignored the respect propagated by the dominant ideology: in a popular tale, one laughs at Neferkarê who secretly rejoined his favorite general; in another, a simple magician gives a moral lesson to the great Cheops. Enumerating the evils that overwhelm his country, the wise Ipour criticizes the weakness of an indolent king.

The texts and archeological vestiges are more than sufficient for presenting a picture of the pharaoh's daily life, which was divided between official journeys along the Nile, military and hunting expeditions, and sojourns at court. While there remains little from the splendid palaces that were spread across the country, the tomb furnishings give an idea of the extraordinary luxury of the court in which public events were accompanied by complex ceremonials: audiences, the presentation of honorary distinctions, royal appearances... The private life of the pharaoh, who was surrounded by a large family, unfolded not far from the official reception rooms. Flowering gardens, pools, and rich apartments equipped with every convenience formed the magnificent setting of a privileged existence. But the sovereign was subject to the same vicissitudes as other human beings. Illness and sorrow followed one another at court. The Egyptian archives make no mystery about harem intrigues, plots, and murders. The succession of kings shows that nothing was concealed: Egyptian history includes a number of usurpers.

God or king? The exhibition intends to present the twofold nature of the pharaoh, the opposition between the function and the person, a duality that is by now classic for Egyptologists but little known to the public. It is in this way that the sovereign established harmony between the gods and men.

Christiane Ziegler

Exhibition

Curator
Christiane Ziegler

Co-curators
Isabelle Franco
Francesco Tiradritti

Installation
Francesca Fenaroli
with Eliana Gerotto
for the scenography
Dario Zannier
with Fabio Zannier
for the graphic design

Lighting consultant
Piero Castiglioni

Press office
Mario Spetia, *Fiat press office coordination*

Lucia Pigozzo

Cairo Secretary
Annalisa Malaguti

In the preliminary phase of the project
Palazzo Grassi could count on the advisory
of Canali Associati s.r.l.

Catalogue

Catalogue editorial director
Mario Andreose

Coordinating editor
Marina Rotondo

Editorial collaboration
Giovanna Vitali

Editing
Paula Billingsley

Scientific revision of the translation
John H. Taylor

Graphic design
Marcello Francone

Cover
Dario Zannier

Layout
Sara Salvi

Iconographic research
Silvia Borghesi

Translations
Rhoda Billingsley
Paul Gookrick
Jeremy Scott
Susan Wise
John Young

Acknowledgments

Palazzo Grassi wishes to thank
the Accademia dei Lincei
for hosting the exhibition press conference;
the Istituto Veneto di Scienze Lettere e Arti
for hosting the meetings of the scientific
committee; the Italian Ambassador in Cairo
Mario Sica, and Francesco Cordano,
managing director of Fiat Auto Egypt,
for their cooperation.

Palazzo Grassi also wishes to thank

⏽BNL

for selling in its branches the exhibition's
tickets.

Contents

The Pharaohs and History

Günter Dreyer
Christiane Ziegler

The Predynastic Period

The First Kings of Egypt

The king lists of Abydos and Saqqara, the Turin Royal Canon and the compilation drawn up by Manetho, all mention a certain Menes as the first king of Egypt. Before him had reigned the gods and those mythical figures, "the followers of Horus" (*shemesu-Hor*). The Palermo Stone lists those sovereigns who ruled either over Upper or Lower Egypt alone (and thus governed only a part of the country) and then, immediately before the 1st Dynasty, gives a series of kings who had worn the double crown. Who was this Menes? Was he really the first king to establish his rule over both Upper and Lower Egypt? How did this "unification of the kingdom" come about? And who were those mythical demigods, "the followers of Horus"?

Menes cannot be identified with any certainty from contemporary monuments, as up to the end of the 3rd Dynasty the king lists do not give cartouches enclosing both the individual and reigning name of the monarch, but almost always simply use the Horus name. Our knowledge of this period is based essentially on the discoveries made at the temple of Hierakonpolis, the royal necropolis at Abydos and the great tombs of Saqqara (the latter often held to be royal burial places).

What emerges is that only two of the earliest rulers might be identified with Menes. These are Horus-Narmer and his successor Horus-Aha, who reigned in a period around 3000 BC. The famous votive Narmer Palette from Hierakonpolis is of key importance here. The central scene of this stone palette shows a vanquishing king wearing the white crown as he beats with a club an enemy he is holding by the hair. The ruler also appears in the form of a falcon, gripping an enemy who is identified as an inhabitant of the lower marshlands by the inclusion of the motif of papyrus reeds.

This palette has often been read as celebrating the unification of Upper and Lower Egypt under the rule of Narmer. However, his predecessor—a king named Scorpion (II)—was already depicted on a macehead found at Hierakonpolis in the performance of ritual acts taking place in Lower Egypt; similarly, "fiscal documents" from the period of the last kings of the Predynastic era—Horus-Qa'a and Irj-Hor—identify dues and deliveries from Upper and Lower Egypt. An ivory tablet recently found at Abydos confirms that the Narmer Palette is a reference to a particular event. In the upper right, it bears the Horus name of Narmer (silurid fish and woodworking chisel). Alongside, there is a repetition of the hieroglyphics for his name: the silurid holding a club and seizing by the hair an enemy whose head is surmounted by papyrus plants. Here, a further detail has been added: a small vase—the hieroglyphic rendering of the sound "nu"—which enables us to read the name "Tehenu." As the papyrus reeds make clear, these must be inhabitants of the western Delta. It is obvious that this is the same event as that depicted on the palette: a victory gained by King Narmer over the people of this region.

This victory probably marked the conclusion of a gradual subjection of the Delta to the authority of Upper Egypt—a process that took about one hundred and fifty years. Thus, the reign of Narmer marked the end of a period, rather than the beginning of a new era. This is confirmed by the archaeological evidence gleaned from the royal tombs of Abydos. Narmer's tomb is a very modest construction comprising two small rooms, and thus falls within the tradition of the late Predynastic period, while the mortuary complex for Aha is made up of three rooms that might already be considered as monumental; this is also the first such complex to be flanked by a series of smaller tombs. Thus the size of his mortuary complex, and the appearance of these satellite tombs, reveal a new status, which marks a clear break between Narmer and Aha. One sees the same phenomenon in the royal tombs that can be associated with transitions between later dynasties (the 2nd Dynasty characterized by tunnel tombs without annexed tombs, the 3rd by step pyramids, and the 4th by pyramids proper). This change between Narmer and Aha fits in well with the fact that the large niche tombs at Saqqara also make their appearance during the reign of the latter, when—for geopolitical reasons—he had transferred his royal residence to Memphis, at the junction between Upper and Lower Egypt.

The Cemetery U at Abydos is particularly rich in information relating to the process of unification during the Predynastic era. The cemetery was first used toward the end of the Naqada I period in Upper Egypt (around 3900 BC) and would then be used continuously right up until the Dynastic era.

1. Stele of King Djet, also known as the Serpent King. Early Dynastic period, 1st Dynasty. Paris, Musée du Louvre

2. The Narmer Palette, graywacke
(schist), from Hierakonpolis,
0 Dynasty, reign of Narmer.
Cairo, Egyptian Museum

Naqada itself and Hierakonpolis both have elite cemeteries that bear witness to their development as centers of power. At Hierakonpolis there is a tomb decorated with scenes of
war and hunting; and in the adjoining settlement an area of religious worship has been unearthed that contained imposing structures built using poles. Potters' kilns, facilities for the
drying of grain, and various workshops reveal that specialized centers of artisan crafts were
concentrated in these areas.

During the Naqada II period, local trade in agricultural and craft produce expanded to involve regions much further afield. The existence of trade relations with distant countries is
confirmed by the discovery within tombs of goods such as turquoise and lapis lazuli beads,
cylindrical seals and, above all, ceramics from Canaan—all imported to meet the needs of
the higher-ranking levels of society. These trade links also brought about the influx of cultural influences as well: The decorative motifs—for example, that of the rosette between two
entwined serpents (an emblem of order and chaos)—which appeared on the ivory objects,
seals and paintings in the princely tomb of Hierakonpolis reveal close relations with
Mesopotamia and Elam.

During the Naqada III period, Abydos' role was no longer limited to a regional context. The
tombs of Cemetery U were by then entirely in brickwork, and appeared to have housed only the eminent members of social elites. Most of the many-chambered tombs—together with
those large single-chamber tombs added a little later in the southern part of the cemetery—are no doubt to be seen as the burial places of Predynastic sovereigns. Tomb U-j, discovered in 1988, is of great importance here (fig. 5). Dating from around one hundred and
fifty years before the beginning of the 1st Dynasty (around 3200–3150 BC), it is unusual in
scale and comprises twelve chambers, the large one to the northwest undoubtedly serving
as the burial chamber (identifiable remains of a large wooden chapel were found on the floor).
The small openings linking one chamber with the next are particularly interesting. When com-

pared to the false doors present in numerous temples and tombs, the form and extant components of these openings reveal that they should be considered as some sort of model doorway. Hence, one can see the nine rooms linked up with the burial chamber as forming a sort of model of the house that the deceased will occupy in the afterlife. The layout of the rooms follows a rational plan: after the antechamber come two storerooms and a large central hall, while the private apartments lie beyond. With its own entrance, the corner room must have been intended for the servants.

The rich material found in the tomb comprised not only a large quantity of ceramics but also a number of objects in ivory, including a *heqa* scepter, which provides formal proof that this was a royal tomb. There were numerous inscriptions in ink on pottery vessels, as well as engraved labels from other containers. It is thanks to them that it was possible to provide a likely name for the monarch buried here: Like the ruler who, around one hundred years later, would commission the macehead found at Hierakonpolis, he was called Scorpion.

During the reign of this Scorpion (I) it is clear that trade with Palestine was on a certain scale. Three chambers of the tomb contain nothing but imported vases that had once held resinated wine; and in another room there were coffers in cedarwood, probably from the Lebanon. The indications of origin given on the labels often mention place-names in Lower Egypt, which justify the supposition that there were already very close links with the Delta; however, we cannot say if these links were those of domination or trade.

Certainly, there was armed conflict during the reign of King Falcon (Horus), Scorpion I's successor. In fact, on the so-called "Cities" or "Lybian" palette, the first in a series of animals shown destroying the enclosures around a number of cities is a falcon (fig. 7). This is, indeed, a list of the kings who, after Scorpion I gradually subjugated the Delta. The other animals destroying cities are: a second falcon (?), a lion, a scorpion and two falcons on shields. A seal (consisting of tree + lion) means that we can identify the lion as a royal name, while the scorpion is probably Scorpion II. Inscriptions on wine jars also bear witness to the existence of a ruler whose name was written with two falcons. The place-names written within the enclosures of the cities are largely impossible to identify, but they very probably refer to places in Lower Egypt.

The main motive for the extension of dominion over the Delta was undoubtedly the desire to protect trade routes to Palestine. This route would continue to be referred to as "The Road of Horus," which is sure proof that a King Horus was the first to truly exercise control over it.

One must also note how frequently—up to Menes/Horus-Aha, The Fighting Horus—the falcon appears as part of the name of the first kings. This preference might well be due to the particular importance of the hawk divinity, but could be explained by the exceptional position of the first king to bear that name, Falcon I, who initially undertook the conquest of Lower Egypt, a process that culminated in the ultimate unification of the country after Scorpion II and Narmer had subjugated the last regions of the western Delta.

This process of unification is the event that left the most indelible mark on the Egyptians, and played a fundamental part in determining how the role of the king was perceived. The achievement of unity was the key fact that marked the beginning of Egyptian history, and without fail was ritually played out again at each coronation. In effect, unification was the beginning of a new era, the era of dynasties, and those who lived through it must have felt this in a particularly strong fashion—so that King Falcon (Horus) who played an essential role therein would enjoy remarkable prestige. By adopting his name, future kings undoubtedly were attempting to imitate him, to identify themselves with him and also to exploit the power of the god who bore the same name. All of this would ultimately lead to the emergence of the pharaoh's "Horus name," with the falcon that appeared on palace façades not seen as a component of an individual's name but as a "surname," a title that expressed the "program" of the ruling monarch. One sees the same thing in those Roman emperors who added "Caesar" or "Augustus" to their own name.

So, the term "*shemesu-Hor*" used in the Turin papyrus to refer to the first sovereigns is to be taken literally; it means "followers of Horus." We do not yet have sufficient information about the number and order of the kings between Falcon and Narmer—those who today are classed as forming the "0 Dynasty"—but there is every reason to think that they are the ones

3. Scist statuette of a bearded man from Gebelein, Naqada I, Amratian period.
Lyon, Muséum d'Histoire Naturelle
cat. 5

4. Ivory plaque of King Aha, from
Naqada. Early Dynastic period,
1st Dynasty.
London, Petrie Museum

represented with the double crown on the stone of the annals, and are to be identified with those demigods who ruled before the advent of the 1st Dynasty.

The First Evidence of Writing
It is the objects found in Tomb U-j at Abydos that mark the most important contribution to our understanding of the development of writing in the Predynastic era, given that they include pottery jars with ink inscriptions and small engraved ivory labels.
Whether on ivory or pottery, however, these inscriptions comprise short texts mentioning the origin of deliveries from various places, and sometimes the quantity of goods involved. Clearly, they served in the control and direction of trade, and always consist of one of two motifs (the most frequent being a tree or plant and an animal). Given that all the containers were holding the same substance, the indications on the jars cannot have borne information about their contents; drawing a parallel with subsequent eras, it seems clear that the inscriptions refer to the place of origin of goods (tree = plantation) or foundations named after the kings who had established them (animal = name of king).
Writing developed because of growing organizational problems. It seems that, initially, it was enough to mark the origin and quantity of goods; hence it was possible to limit symbols to those which, by association, identified certain places or institutions (with simple images depicting human beings, animals, plants, emblems of the gods, mountains, irrigated land). However, as it became necessary to distinguish more and more places, economic establishments and administrative bodies, a system was required with a much higher number of different terms. To meet this end, the Egyptians very quickly adopted the rebus principle, using objects to indicate words of the same sound. This key phase was the basis for an ever more complicated system of writing.
The fiscal documents of the last Predynastic kings reveal the development of terms to dis-

tinguish different types of oil; by the 1st Dynasty, the names of specific functionaries begin to appear; and during the reign of Narmer, deliveries are dated according to year (using the "narrative infinitive," statement-as-title, which made it possible to refer to actions and events). However, the first known complete phrase dates from the end of the 2nd Dynasty. Given the very restricted nature of the extant source material, we know very little about the extent to which writing might have been used for other than administrative purposes.
(*Günter Dreyer*)

The Thinite Period

The Predynastic era was to end in a "pharaonic explosion." Linked with the Near East, whose products passed through the centers of Maadi and Buto, the sedentary farming-pastoral cultures of the North were assimilated within the sphere of influence of Naqada, which—in the South—saw not only the development of urbanization but also the emergence of a dominant class who brought with it a new ideology. Whether peaceful or violent, this assimilation led—around 3000 BC—to one of the first great states known to mankind. The regime was a monarchy, the basic characteristics of which would remain fixed for three thousand years. At the head of the country was a king of divine essence, the pharaoh, who guaranteed the equilibrium of the world and held all power in his hands. His tomb would differ from that of his subjects in both size and in the number of offerings that accompanied the dead man beyond the grave; the presence of great stone stelae placed the deceased king under the protection of the gods and proclaimed his own exceptional nature. This royal figure was already distinguished by certain rites of which brief mentions have come down to us: there was the coronation and the *sed* festival, during which the king magically renewed his powers. As one can see from the decoration of the extant tablets recounting the important events of a reign, the accent was always placed upon the pharaoh's victory over rebellious peoples who were the very embodiment of disorder.

The first two dynasties of pharaohs make up what is known as the Thinite period, the traditional homeland of these rulers being Thinis near Abydos. Recent excavations at Abydos have discovered traces of rulers pre-dating the 1st Dynasty (the so-called "0 Dynasties"), which

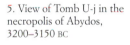

5. View of Tomb U-j in the necropolis of Abydos, 3200–3150 BC

following pages
6. Bracelets of King Djer, gold, lapis lazuli, turquoise and amethyst, from Abydos, Old Kingdom, 1st Dynasty.
Cairo, Egyptian Museum

7. "Libyan" palette, or palette showing the foundation of cities, schist, from Abydos. Protodynastic period.
Cairo, Egyptian Museum

8. Label with King Den's name, from Abydos, Early Dynastic period, 1st Dynasty.
Paris, Musée du Louvre

means that the date for the foundation of pharaonic power must be even earlier than has been thought. One of the most important innovations of this period was the emergence of a monumental architecture using firebrick; there were cities and palaces which today have disappeared, places of worship and tombs in imitation of a fortress (like those of the dignitaries buried at Saqqara). The Abydos site has yielded up a number of stelae with the names of rulers of the 1st Dynasty; while concentrated around them were the tombs of court officials. Royal and private tombs were then in the form of a mastaba, a trapezoidal construction over a cavity containing the deceased and abundant funeral furnishings and food for the afterlife. The resources of the land ruled by the pharaoh were exploited through a rigidly hierarchical administration which employed a new instrument of organization: pharaonic script. Newly-founded cities such as Memphis and Hierakonpolis gathered together a concentration of functionaries and artisans; and the general outlines of religious belief seem to have already been established. Although there is practically no extant image of them, the main deities who would be venerated in later periods are already mentioned in inscriptions: Horus, Seth, Hathor, Anubis, Min, Neith, Ra (the Apis bull, symbol of fertility, is depicted on a limestone shard in a manner that would remain characteristic for the next three thousand years). While no archaic temple has survived intact, the rare depictions of them—together with a few extant inscriptions (notably those referring to the rituals of foundation)—suggest that the essential features of religious belief and worship were already in place.

We have rather more information concerning funeral rites and customs, thanks to the necropolises of Abydos and Saqqara; their abundant funeral offerings suggest that in the afterlife man would be faced with the same needs as on earth: food, clothing, tools and weapons. What is more, there are also a number of stelae bearing images or written inscriptions extolling the virtues of the deceased in order to perpetuate his existence. Finally, in spite of the gaps in our knowledge, the works of the period reveal that the very elaborate skills of the craftsmen were already at the service of an art with rigorously-defined conventions. This can be seen for example, in the bas-reliefs at Hierakonpolis, or in the very first royal statues, such as that of Khasekhemwy, which in spite of its modest size already reveals the monumental air that would be characteristic of Egyptian art.

And while our actual knowledge of the work of this period is scanty, we do have archaeological evidence of works that are no longer extant: two pedestals and the fragments of feet bear witness to the existence of life-size wooden statues at the time of King Qa'a; and the first royal annals mention the existence of copper statues. In the field of the decorative arts, the tombs of Abydos, Saqqara or Helwan have yielded up a supply of masterpieces that testify to the genius of goldsmiths, jewelers and sculptors who were skilled in working even the hardest stone. Among the numerous examples: the precious jewels of King Djer; the enigmatic encrusted disks and the delicately-carved vessels from the tomb of Chancellor Hemaka; and various fragments of ivory furnishings (spoons decorated with the so-called "Thit" knot, small columns, the feet of beds in the form of bull's hooves).

The passage from the 2nd to the 3rd Dynasty seems to have occurred seamlessly, under the intermediary figure of a queen called Nimaathep.
(Christiane Ziegler)

Unlike the introduction of writing in subsequent civilizations, the *invention* of writing in Egypt does not mean the beginning of history, at least in the traditionally understood sense of production of informative documents. During the third millennium BC when the graphic code (already in the making during the preceding fourth millennium BC) became explicit, the primary purpose of these rare inscriptions seems to have essentially been "to exist" or "to make exist" those entities named therein, the basic intention undoubtedly being to perform in the same way as the oral language of the time. Among the principal realities designated by the inscriptions are the pharaohs' names, which were most certainly at the heart of the creative process of the complex expressive system that is now referred to as the Memphite civilization or age, or even the Pyramid age, after the most imposing monuments ever conceived. Of course this does not imply a lack of culture in the vast territories inside and around Egypt, however, we can only perceive culture at the sites of the Memphite or pharaonic power where an intentionally lasting, "eternal" tool was created and diffused that would later be used for obtaining direct data. Obviously, the world of the pharaohs in this remote era is a silent world. Pharaohs do not speak to their subjects, much less to their descendants; at the most they address their equals, the gods (and hieroglyphs in Egyptian are called "sacred words"). When, at the end of the 5th Dynasty (*c.* 2400 BC), the inside walls of the pyramids in which the pharaohs and then a few queens were buried began to be covered with writings, these endless, highly detailed inscriptions were not intended for anyone's eyes; they were to remain inaccessible forever, except to the buried pharaoh. Indeed, the situation they speak of has little to do with this world; it concerns instead the posthumous lives of those sovereigns who have ascended to heaven to join the gods amid the stars and the sun.

The Power of Speech and of Writing

Writing—and speech even more so—had to be used with circumspection. Not only were the figured symbols of writing animated and capable of doing harm, but even words were endowed like objects with a performative efficacy and required caution and protection. A special scribe (the so-called "lector priest") knew how to manipulate hieroglyphic writing and cope with its perils, or resort to formulas of well-wishing and defensive devices; for instance the pharaohs' names would soon (by the end of the 2nd Dynasty) be circumscribed within a protective rope, known as the cartouche. Like the signs of writing, art was highly symbolic in its reproduction of reality, as was architecture with masses partly based on naturalistic concepts (such as the columns that emulate the stems of certain plants) and probably also on abstract forms—like the pyramids—imitating visions of nature (sun rays?).

Conversely, writing could be used as an offensive device. The pharaoh's supreme power ideally spread over the entire inhabited globe, and his authority was ensured by rites more than acts of force. Detailed lists were drawn up of adversaries, rebels or enemies, including individuals, categories of peoples and even regions, who were neutralized by operations of homeopathic magic (breaking the figures, burning the writings, dissolving the clay on which they wrote in water, probably along with actual killings). Lists have been found of people and countries that were not under the Memphite sphere of power, but rather in conflict with it and probably represented equally important entities.

Just like rulers, officials and those close to them, statues also have names and architecture its own designation. For instance, the pyramid of Khufu is called "horizon of the sun" or "horizon of Khufu," automatically identifying that pharaoh with the sun-god. After Khufu, the pharaohs also assumed the title of "son of the sun," whereby their birth name was defined. This ideology proceeds from a long process that is already discernable in the 1st Dynasty, when a king was called Raneb ("the sun-god is [my] lord"). Later on it was presumably adopted by the priests of Heliopolis, the "city of the sun," near Memphis.

At first the pharaoh was identified with the god of heaven, (the falcon) Horus. This would remain the first name of a regal title, which in its fullest form contained up to five names, all endowed with a divine nature and therefore susceptible to worship. The Horus name was usually inscribed in an architectural frame symbolizing the royal palace, with a niched enclosure wall, a ritual symbol ever since prehistoric times that was borrowed for the profiling of the outside walls of the great mastaba tombs that were used at first by kings, and later in the decoration of sarcophagi; this iconography symbolized the lord in his palace.

1. *Sed*-festival statuette of Pepy I, alabaster, Old Kingdom, 6th Dynasty.
New York, The Brooklyn Museum of Art, Charles Edwin Wilbour Fund
cat. 10

2. Limestone statue of Djoser from
Saqqara, Old Kingdom, 3rd Dynasty.
Cairo, Egyptian Museum

The Private Vision

A great number of symbols of royal power were not exclusive to the sovereigns, but by royal consent were appropriated by the highest officials as well who were often members of the large royal family. Sarcophagi in pink granite (the sacred material of the sun-god), "false" doors with niches in the chapels, statues, mastabas and their decorations were offered as rewards by the pharaohs. Certain inscriptions explain the reason for the gift, indirectly providing us with "historical" information about the bestower sovereign. The elaborate titles of the mightiest personalities, necessarily connected with the royal family similarly reveal as much. We have evidence of a comparable situation from a dual point of view at the highest level of ceremonial expression, that of power and that of "privacy," which gradually breaks out of the rigid bonds of the central authority. The development of a greater autonomy and of available forms of expression to be used in a way that is not strictly subordinate appears by the end of the 5th Dynasty (c. 2400 BC) and grows in scope and variety of themes, especially in the regions outside of Memphis and also in more distant ones. The princes who availed themselves of these instruments tended to personalize their action, distinguishing it from the pharaoh's indifferent, anonymous central authority, and used them for contingent events of life, eventually marked by the reigns of the different pharaohs under whom they lived. These are the first references to precise facts, making an historical analysis possible.

Toward the end of the third millennium BC, there was a regionalization of the use of lasting forms of expression that gives the impression of a weakening of central authority, confirmed furthermore by a decrease in the size of the pharaohs' sepulchral monuments.

Then, alongside "sacralized" documents, that is those in hieroglyphs, were administrative documents written on papyrus scrolls in the non-figurative writing that the Greeks referred to as "hieratic." Such texts deal with accounting, records, and also the private realm, like letters, and only rarely refer to the pharaohs.

Later Sources

During the third millennium BC, the figure of the ruler is practically without a history, since everything that happens is attributed to mechanical forces like those of nature; knowledge of this sphere and of the pharaoh's role as the head of the state was inaccessible and had nothing to do with ordinary, personal experience. What a few individuals recount about their own lives only indirectly touches on the nature of power and aims essentially at dealing out personal praise, according to a genre that still exists in certain parts of Africa (like the *oriki* of the Yoruba). We might say that in this period there is a concept of action, but not a reflection on action, narration and description. The same can be said about the divine sphere, where we already notice—particularly in the Pyramid Texts—the essential ingredients of myths, however these are neither explained nor narrated. In other words, the Memphite pharaoh is a "ritualized," but not yet "thematized" ruler. History, according to Hornung's appropriate definition, is treated like a festival.

The introduction of the figure of the ruler in scenarios that had previously been used for the stories of private individuals occurred in the following millennium, in what we call the Middle Kingdom, when a large number of innovations led to a profound transformation of the values and customs not only of writing, but also of the oral speech reflected in it, and therefore of the things that are said and the ways in which they are said. This fact of extraordinary consequence can be defined as "textualization," and is at the origin of the sources of information that until then were absolutely nonexistent.

Thus, as the myths of the gods began to be recounted, the figures of several pharaohs of the third millennium (Old Kingdom) also appear in countless tales that at least in part continued the oral traditions. They were preserved in papyri of the Middle and New Kingdoms, the Late Period and then again by Herodotus and Manetho. These stories are presented as anecdotes, but they certainly have an authentic base, embellished by romantic actions inspired more by the assumed character of the royal figures than by actual events.

Many of these documents contain royal lists, which were drawn up especially during the New Kingdom and therefore reached to Herodotus and Manetho. These lists, too—among which the Papyrus of Kings or Turin Royal Canon (specifically a "canon") is unique because

3. The Step Pyramid of Djoser
at Saqqara, Old Kingdom,
3rd Dynasty

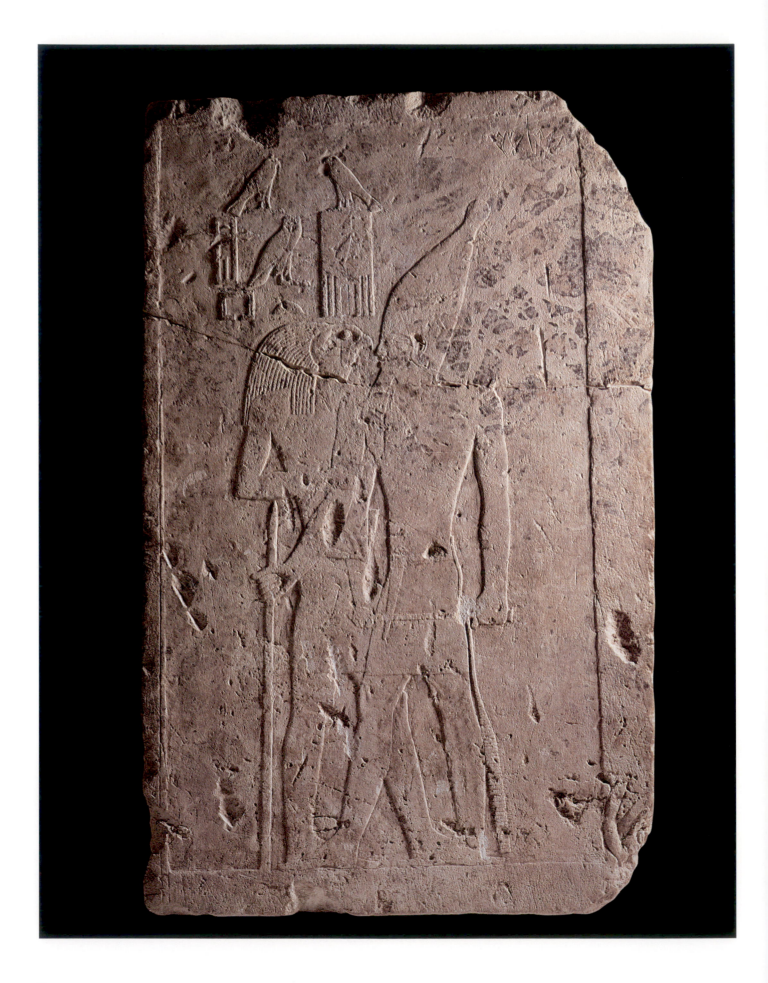

4. Limestone stele of King Qahedjet,
Old Kingdom, 3rd Dynasty.
Paris, Musée du Louvre
cat. 8

5. The Great Sphinx at Giza,
4th Dynasty

of its detailed character—are based on older documents. They give the sequence of the pharaohs that are to be found on the monuments of different periods, and sometimes they also specify a credible duration of their reigns. One of the prototypes was probably in the temple of Ptah at Memphis, and the largest fragment that has come down to us is presently in Palermo (the Palermo Stone).

Of course, regardless of its importance, such tradition cannot be taken literally, since it represents the official view of the political leadership of Egypt: the one belonging to a certain power during the Old Kingdom (the Palermo Stone, although some hold it to be a more recent copy, but still a replica); and the one official propaganda accredited to the leading classes of the New Kingdom. The later version in Greek basically relies on them.

As in the interpretation of myths, we do not find details of the overall history of Egypt in the third millennium in these successive works, but merely the image scholars of the later periods fashioned for themselves of that history, thus we should be very cautious in reconciling our few insights with the vast obscure areas of that remote period.

The Monuments

After all, we know about the pharaohs of the third millennium mainly from the impressive works they produced that have come down to us. The study of these amazing ruins is more eloquent than the long inscriptions with their improbable references to elusive facts. An example is the famous Narmer Palette unearthed at Hierakonpolis, a Protodynastic capital, whose symbolic value is far from clear (namely, to which territories did the crowns donned by the sovereign actually refer?).

The sepulchral monuments of almost all the pharaohs have been identified, and often these are the only thing known of them. Likewise, we know the sepulchers of the sovereigns (pharaohs?) not found in later lists. In the period coinciding with the first three dynasties we find royal sepulchral monuments in several areas in Egypt: at Memphis, at Abydos, and

6. Diorite statue of Khafra from Giza, Old Kingdom, 4th Dynasty. Cairo, Egyptian Museum

7. Alabaster face of King Khafra from Giza, Old Kingdom, 4th Dynasty. Boston, Museum of Fine Arts
cat. 9

again at Naqada (just north of Thebes), the site of the largest Protohistoric city in Egypt. It is unclear whether certain pharaohs possessed more than one tomb, or whether coeval sovereigns shared the territory of Egypt, which had not yet been formed and structured as it would be in the following millennia.

Some sepulchral monuments are better conserved and more easy to interpret than others. Thus the huge ensemble of Djoser, founder of the 3rd Dynasty, at Saqqara (*c.* 2650 BC), sums up centuries-old traditions, and makes extensive use of stone for the first time. The main building containing the sovereign's divine remains takes the form of a "step" pyramid for the first time, with underground rooms gorgeously decorated with multicolored panels. The cloaked statue of the ruler was placed in a small room on the north side with no exits but two openings in the wall at the eye level of the statue so it could contemplate the circumpolar stars at night, considered by the ancient Egyptians as "everlasting." The king wore the jubilee mantle of the *sed* festival whereby the pharaoh gained possession of his "active" powers, those of being "divine."

A large courtyard on the south side contained the stone "posts" that marked the boundaries of the king's ritual race that presumably took place at these ceremonies, whereas the wooden structures of the local sanctuaries of various regions of Egypt were reproduced in stone like sculptures around a smaller courtyard nearby. Other details are still a mystery to us. The entire ensemble that also contains a large "southern tomb" was surrounded by a high rectangular wall made of limestone ("The White Wall," the old name for Memphis) carved at intervals with niches, in keeping with the ritual symbolism of power present in several categories of monuments, from flat figurations to the reliefs on sarcophagi. This symbolism was certainly not meant to communicate an image of power to the population, but rather to reflect the image from which it stemmed on the individual therein.

Less than a century later, with the 4th Dynasty, the completed model of the pyramid as a royal tomb appeared. Constructional technology and symbolic meanings blend to form breathtaking works that still loom over the Giza plain. Here rise the three pyramids of Khufu, Khafra and Menkaura with their ritual annexes: a temple near the pyramid was connected by a long covered causeway to a "valley" entrance temple along a canal that was the landing-place. These pyramids also conserve such Protohistoric elements as a system of three chambers, whose role is unknown. The valley temples of Khufu and Menkaura already contained a series of statues of the sovereign in the company of divinities in different forms. Some of these were carved out of special stone that came from extremely remote quarries in the desert. Nearby rose the Sphinx: a colossal sculpture with the body of a crouching lion and the head of a pharaoh, for a long time identified as Khafra, but which may instead refer to Khufu.

Near the pyramid of Khufu, deep pits contained the dismantled planking of large boats, built out of Lebanon cedar, that tell us a great deal about the extent of the power of these rulers. The Menkaura pyramid, more modest in size than the two neighboring ones, was faced with blocks of granite brought from the distant quarry of Aswan (a river voyage of nearly one thousand kilometers). It would seem that a very vast space around these pyramids was supposed to remain vacant, before it was taken over by the cemeteries of later officials that gradually occupied all the available ground.

The 5th Dynasty moved to another area, to Abusir, between Giza and Saqqara, with smaller pyramids that were flanked, during the first six reigns, by a similiar monumental complex dedicated to the sun-god, with whom each pyramid was closely related. Later on the pyramids were probably replaced by obelisks, as we know them; but by the end of the 5th Dynasty (Unas, mid-twenty-fourth century BC), the main novelty was inside the pyramids, since from then on the burial chamber and the adjoining ones would be inscribed with the already-mentioned regal rituals of survival, the so-called "Pyramid Texts." They constitute the most extensive text in the history of humanity written in a legible form at a high level of literary elaboration. Since the written word at that time was held to be identical to the pronounced word, these texts echoed inside the pyramids as in a huge sound box.

The actions of many sovereigns were known even far from their burial places, which were certainly near their usual residences and therefore at the center of the kingdom. These were mainly mining regions, from the copper mines in the Sinai, where the pharaoh Djoser is first attested, to the granite quarries of the Etbai or the diorite quarries of Toshka, exploited since the days of Khufu, in the midst of the remote Nubian deserts.

Otherwise, the presence of the pharaohs was attested even farther away, with the discovery of stone vases made on the occasion of the jubilee celebrations, and sent as gifts of a great "magic" and symbolic value all the way to distant Ebla (fragments of vases of Khafra and Pepy I).

Although several private inscriptions mention the inevitable military expeditions, this is insufficient for a serious reconstruction of the political history of the period, however, the pharaohs' power speaks for itself.

The learned Egyptian Manetho lived during the reign of Ptolemy Philadelphus (285–246 BC), and the summary of his *Aegyptiaca* offers us a counterpoint reading of the history of ancient Egypt, painting a very different picture of the dynasties of the Middle Kingdom from that which emerges from archaeological research.

A native of Sebennytos, the writer reflects the view that was taken of the 11th to 14th Dynasties by what may be described as the "priestly" tradition. Although these four dynasties are generally referred to as composing the Middle Kingdom, there was in fact nothing transitional or intermediate in them; they form one of the most brilliant periods in Egyptian history, although one little represented by extant monuments (almost all the limestone used at the time ended up in the lime-kilns of the regions; while the granite of the Old Kingdom and the sandstone of the New Kingdom have survived). Indeed, one might say that the history embodied in the priestly tradition and the evidence patiently gathered by the last two centuries of archaeological and historical research offer us two complementary pictures of this period.

The epitome drawn up by Julius Africanus (fragment 31) tells us that:

"the eleventh dynasty [was made up of] sixteen Diospolite sovereigns, who reigned forty-three years. After these, Ammenemes [ruled] sixteen years."

As for the 12th Dynasty, the same version (fragment 34) gives us a much more varied picture:

"The twelfth dynasty [was made up of] seven Diospolite kings.
Sesonchosis, son of Ammenemes, [reigned] forty-six years.
Ammanemes [reigned] thirty-eight years; he was assassinated by his own eunuchs.
Sesostris [reigned] forty-eight years; he entirely subjugated Asia in nine years—from Europe to Thrace. Everywhere he had a record of the character of the various peoples engraved on stelae; the valorous were represented by the male sexual parts; the others without nobility by the female parts, in proportion as this man was considered by the Egyptians to be the first [king] after Osiris.
Lachares—who [reigned] eight years—is he who with great care constructed the Labyrinth in the name of Arsinoite *nome*—[that is], his own tomb.
Ameres [reigned] eight years.
Ammenemes [reigned] eight years.
Skemiophris, his sister, [reigned] four years.
Total: one hundred and sixty years."

Unlike his account of the 12th Dynasty, the Theban 11th Dynasty (2135–1994) as outlined by Manetho excludes the great sovereigns who made up what certain historians have correctly referred to as the First Theban Kingdom. However, the Turin papyrus (drawn up under the reigns of Sety I–Rameses II) brings these very rulers to the fore (col. V, fragment 84, 16–18). This earlier dynasty of the Mentuhoteps ("Montu is content"), who brandished the figure of the warrior-god Montu as their symbol, was dominated by the glorious Theban sovereign Mentuhotep II Nebhepetra (2065–2014), who reigned fifty-one years according to the Turin papyrus. After the wars of reconquest led by his three immediate predecessors—Intef I, Intef II and Intef III—against the northern powers of Herakleopolis, he would, around 2040 BC, finally bring down the "House of Khety" (the name certain contemporary biographers use in referring to the Herakleopolitan dynasty). However, one must admit here that the history of this period is pieced together from fragments that are still the subject of debate.

With a force composed of Theban veterans and *Medjai* mercenaries—a Nubian people originating from the area between the second and third cataracts and the desert to the east—Mentuhotep increased the power of the crown of Thebes. Not only did he successfully carry out the siege of Herakleopolis (2040 BC), he also extended the dominion of the South over the whole Delta area, which had traditionally become a region favored by Asiatic peoples. An examination of the bodies of Mentuhotep's soldiers, buried to the north of

1. *Sed*-festival statue of Mentuhotep II, painted sandstone, Middle Kingdom, 11th Dynasty. Cairo, Egyptian Museum

the funerary amphitheater of Deir el-Bahri—where the king had established his final residence—reveals that the fighting must have been fierce (though piously gathered from the battlefields, these bodies did not escape the ravages of vultures and crows). Unprecedented in the history of architecture, the extant fragments of the king's own funeral monument—together with the scenes that decorate the tomb of General Intef (Deir el-Bahri)—paint a picture of a period of continual fighting and war. Seen against the tombs of the Old Kingdom, there is no doubt that Deir el-Bahri is, indeed, the manifesto of a kingdom.

Mentuhotep II also reigned over the renaissance of Thebes itself. After having imposed peace on the country, the neighboring oases and Nubia, he gave a new impetus to building work. As a matter of fact, his reign breathed new life into a tradition that had not completely died out since the Old Kingdom but—especially in the provinces that were more distant from the important centers of intellectual life—had gone into sharp decline as the artistic and craft skills that had flourished under previous dynasties were gradually forgotten. In a certain sense it is true that the Middle Kingdom would never match the artistic output of the older Memphite kingdom, either in volume or in quality (the workshops were just being set up again; and, on the whole, they turned out works of rather poor composition and manufacture); however, the royal workshops did produce some strangely beautiful pieces—for example, the sarcophagi of the queens and concubines of Mentuhotep II, which were buried in the sovereign's funeral temple (their creation would seem to fit in with the biography of the artist Irtisen as recounted in the Louvre stele [inv. C 14], which offers a glimpse of the renaissance of the arts at the time). Indeed, the art produced under Mentuhotep II could be said to unite provincial charm and a certain echo of the art of Memphis.

All this took place as another era dawned. Egyptian society was emerging from the dark days of the First Intermediate Period. In more than one way, that period had brought about a profound change and development in the mentality and desires of the "middle classes," who were now anxious to see their different status recognized. And this slow process of development would reach its climax during the second part of the 12th Dynasty and the period of the 13th. The successor of Mentuhotep II Nebhepetra, Mentuhotep III Sankhkara, followed in his father's footsteps. However, in spite of a number of expeditions to Wadi Hammamat in the Eastern Desert —most notably, that undertaken by the treasurer Henu (the logistics of which were on an amazing scale)—this monarch did not make his mark on the Theban landscape to a similar degree. The 11th Dynasty would then end, under Mentuhotep IV Nebtawyra, in a period of troubles (though not even mentioned in the Turin papyrus, the fact that this monarch organized expeditions to the *bekhen*-stone [graywacke or siltstone] quarries of Wadi Hammamat and to the amethyst mines of Wadi el-Hudi, to the south of Aswan, reveals that he was a figure of some standing who died before his time). Nevertheless, this was one of those strife-ridden times in Egyptian history that are apparently inexplicable unless one invokes some sort of tragic destiny.

It seems highly unlikely that the figure which emerges from the inscriptions at Wadi Hammamat, a certain vizier Amenemhat, is anyone other than the 11th-Dynasty "Ammenemes" whom Manetho describes as having reigned sixteen years. And thus, while the writer leaves the Mentuhoteps nameless, the man who took over power after them suddenly emerges into the full light of day. Undoubtedly for historical reasons, Manetho's attention is entirely focused on the figure who served as a link between the 11th Dynasty and that which came after it.

As described by him, the 12th Dynasty becomes an astonishing period, mixing together historical facts and the names of rulers who subsequently became legendary in Egyptian tradition and were linked with the pharaohs of the New Kingdom. Behind the sovereigns mentioned by Manetho one glimpses a golden age, the memory of which lingered on in popular tradition. The dominant figure here is the legendary Sesostris—who should not be entirely identified with any of the sovereigns known by the Theban name of Senusret ("the man of the goddess Wosret"), of which Sesostris is the Greek transcription. Nevertheless, though there are some changes in the actual order of kings and events, Manetho's account of the 12th Dynasty is one to which one may profitably refer.

The vitality of the dynasty and the lengthy reigns of its sovereigns (from 1994 to 1781 BC) are outlined in the Turin papyrus (col. V, fragment 64, 19). Under the heading of the "Dynasty of Itjtawy "(Lisht), this gives the total reign of the eight pharaohs as two hundred and thirteen years, one month and seventeen days (Turin papyrus, col. VI, fragment 72, 3). In order to ward off dangers from the east, the founder of the dynasty, Amenemhat I (1994–1964), very quickly decided to move his capital to the north—midway between Herakleopolis, the power center of the 9th and 10th Dynasties, and Memphis, the administrative seat of the Old Kingdom. Thebes at this point became a spiritual metropolis under the priests of Amun, the powerful deity who had been the guiding force behind Theban victories, and the pharaohs themselves moved north, to el-Lisht, where the earliest phase of the royal necropolis was constructed (comprising the pyramids of Amenemhat I and Senusret I). The Arabic place name (el-Lisht) is in fact a contraction of "Amenemhat takes possession of the two lands" (Itjtawy), which underlines the dynamic role played by the dynasty's founder in the years of fighting that occupied the early part of his reign; with the support of such nomarchs as the nomarch of the Hare and of the Oryx, he would ultimately reunite the Two Lands—from Aswan to Pelusium—and drive the Asiatic occupiers out of the Delta (thence creating a string of fortresses that are traditionally known as the "Walls of the Prince").

The 12th Dynasty had obviously learned from the repeated crises of the First Intermediate Period, and most notably from the political division that was contemporary with the rule of the Herakleopolitan dynasty. The contents of the pseudo *Instruction for King Merikara*, a literary composition that very probably dates from the 12th Dynasty, were established on the basis of the Herakleopolitan tradition. Throughout the Middle Kingdom, its influence meant that political decisions were guided by the enlightened opinions and thoughts of King Khety, whose sententious and weighty words served as a reminder not only of an abhorred past in which attempts were made to destabilize established power, but also of what might result from civil war and its attendant horrors. The literature that appeared in the early days of the el-Lisht dynasty—most notably the *Instruction of Amenemhat* and *The Prophecy of Nerferty*—seemed to work as a sort of transmitter of propaganda throughout all levels of society. Imposing itself upon the accepted wisdom of the Old Kingdom, it invoked the need for a social savoir-vivre and—in the discussion of political themes—stressed the loyalty which all had to show to the sovereigns of the 12th Dynasty. The pharaohs became a sort of model, and their features—revealed in statuary—became familiar to one and all. What is more, from the reign of Senusret III onward, the idealized image of the pharaoh would actually give way to a more realistic portrait—a sign that the monarch was seen as bearing a role that left him marked by his burden of responsibilities. The text which may be taken as the manifesto of the early 12th Dynasty is the *Tale of Sinuhe,* which mixes together different historical periods and mentalities to recount the story of a man who has taken refuge in Canaan because he had unwittingly been witness to the intrigues which led to the assassination of Amenemhat I. The man continues resolutely to serve the interests of Senusret I, who during the first ten years of his reign had managed to reestablish peace and concord in a country that, once again, had been torn by strife and conflict (which, one assumes, was due to a reaction on the part of the supporters of the old dynasty of Herakleopolis). After a long life of roaming around Asia, Sinuhe returns to the pharaoh as the moment of his death approaches; he is the very symbol of Egypt's openness to Asia, and of the extension of the pharaoh's authority over Palestine thanks to the presence of Egyptian expatriates there. While Manetho's *Aegyptiaca* passes over the end of the 11th Dynasty in silence, the murder of Amenemhat I certainly does emerge from his work, in which a king Ammanemes is said to have been killed by his own eunuchs (the actual murder presented in the classic example of a palace intrigue). The assassination, which occurred while Amenemhat's successor was leading an Egyptian army against the Libyans of the Western Desert, created a situation of political unrest and uncertainty about the future that would leave a long-lasting mark on the Middle Kingdom, and force Senusret I to undertake reforms.

A key figure of the 12th Dynasty, Senusret I ("Sesonchosis" in Manetho's account) was an exceptional man. Thanks to his long reign of forty-five years, he managed to consolidate his father's work in both the religious and political spheres. From the very beginning of the 12th Dynasty, the site of the future Avaris in the north had been occupied in order to control the Pelusiac branch of the Delta, which was of strategic importance in fighting off Asian invaders, and during the reign of Senusret new trade routes were opened up: Nubia, which had been

2. The White Chapel of Senusret I
at Karnak, Middle Kingdom,
12th Dynasty.
Karnak, Open Air Museum

3. Detail of the decoration of one
of the pillars of the White Chapel:
Senusret I, followed by his *ka*, makes
an offering to Amun-Min, Middle
Kingdom, 12th Dynasty.
Karnak, Open Air Museum

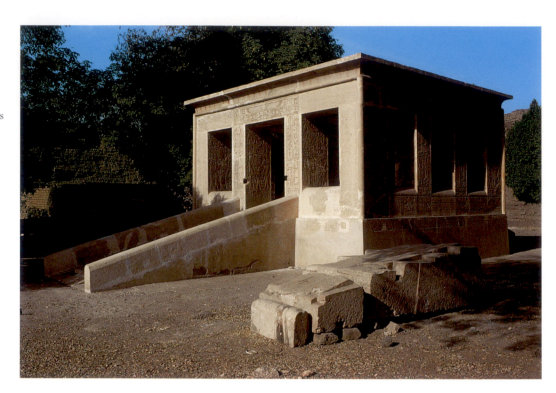

abandoned to itself, was now brought under Egyptian domination, as one can see from the
stele of the eighteenth regnal year from Wadi Halfa (now in the Turin Museum); thanks to
the logistic support provided by the fortress of Buhen on the second cataract, access was
gained to the gold mines of Wadi Allaqi; an important expedition to Punt was mounted, mention of which is still found in the inscriptions from Wadi Hammamat and the coastal areas
of the Red Sea. Indeed, traces of the military expeditions undertaken by this king and his
successors can be found all over the place—most notably at Serabit el-Khadim, in the areas
of the copper and turquoise mines, and in the various sites of the Eastern Desert where metal deposits were exploited (to obtain copper, galena and chrysocolla). The deserts to the east
and west were traversed by patrols of both police and explorers.

The sovereign also initiated a public building program intended to renovate the fabric of the
great metropolis and thus cover the effects of the civil war. The main cities involved were
Elephantine, Thebes and the four cities sacred to Montu that the Intefs and the Mentuhoteps had favored. In the Theban region various prestigious monuments were raised, most
notably the temple of Amun at Karnak. While a large part of these have disappeared, there
are fortunately numerous remains—such as the White Chapel (Karnak, Open-Air Museum)—which have survived intact within later monuments and thus can give us some idea of
the grandeur of the period. Other cities that received attention were Koptos and, in the north,
the Fayum, Heliopolis, Memphis and, of course, el-Lisht. However, it was the ancient religious city of Abydos, burial place of the great royal ancestors of the 1st and 2nd Dynasties,
which was the particular focus of building work. One reason was that this city—above the
bend in the Nile in the Koptos–Qena region—had been the site of the clashes between the
forces of Herakleopolis and Thebes during the first half of the 11th Dynasty; the other was
that, during the First Intermediate Period and the 11th Dynasty, the eschatological hopes of
the Egyptians had been focused on the god of Abydos, Osiris, identified with the local dog-
headed funeral deity, Khentimentiu. At this point, Osirian beliefs—adapted to all strata of
society—and their resultant implications for the burial of each individual, make their appearance in the religious life of Egypt, and remain part of it until the advent of Christianity. Abydos would become *the* holy city—both for local notables and for all the Egyptians who
came here to erect a cenotaph or a monument of devotional piety. Hence, the extant monuments in the area are an inexhaustible source of information on the names and dates of the
sovereigns of the Middle Kingdom, on the funeral beliefs and practices of the time, and on
the art favored by the middle strata of society. What is more, by giving new impetus to the

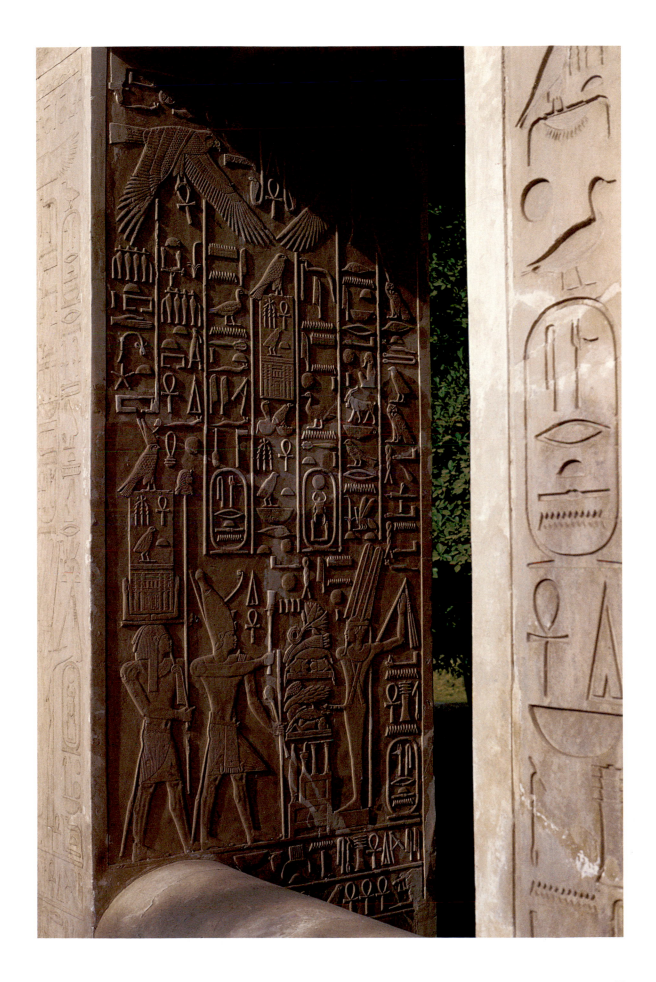

4. Diorite sphinx of Senusret III,
Middle Kingdom, 12th Dynasty.
New York, The Metropolitan
Museum of Art, gift of Edward
S. Harkness, 1917

royal building works, Senusret I stimulated developments in different schools of sculpture and architecture. While drawing inspiration from the models left by the 5th and 6th Memphite Dynasties, the el-Lisht pyramid and that which precedes it—together with the necropolis of courtiers and high functionaries—all give expression to new concepts in these fields. In size, el-Lisht reflects the pyramid cities of the Old Kingdom—and thus might be seen to continue, rather than break with, the principles of Memphis—however, overall, it seems clear that the sovereigns of the Middle Kingdom were aware of the futility of investing all their resources in the creation of royal burial complexes. Built on a smaller scale in brick and stone, these monuments left room for other important building projects throughout the country. The royal necropolis no longer commandeered all the energies within the nation; royal foundations now revealed a focus on economic activities. For example, a center like Diospolis Parva (Hiw) on the "elbow" of the Nile, which was founded by Senusret I and is known to us through the Reisner Papyri, would become a junction for trade with Upper Egypt and the Red Sea.

Senusret I's son, Amenemhat II, reigned for thirty-four years (1932–1898); however there are much fewer extant traces of the monuments erected during this time—and perhaps this has created a false impression of him. Nevertheless, the large inscription from Memphis, piously preserved in the wall of the Ramesside part of the temple of Ptah, reveals that sovereign's attentions to Asia. This was a turning-point in the history of the el-Lisht dynasty, which attempted to establish a protective glacis across southern Palestine by means of alliances with certain cities of Canaan. This large inscription bears witness to the arrival in Egypt of Asiatic craftsmen (and prisoners of war), who would be put to work on royal building projects. The booty mentioned in the Memphis inscription undoubtedly included the two caskets donated in the name of Amenemhat II to the foundations of the temple of Montu in Tod as a tribute to the god of war. Amenemhat II also reoccupied the site of Dahshur, where his pyramid and the necropolis of high-ranking court figures were constructed.

The reign of his successor, Senusret II (1900–1881), only appears to be relatively short; as a matter of fact, the nineteen years gave him time not only to construct his pyramid at el-Lahun, at the entrance to the Fayum—which the Egyptians then called Ro-henu—but also the large administrative city of el-Lahun alongside it. This city is remarkable because excavations have revealed it was divided up into residential districts—for viziers and city authorities—and other districts where craftsmen, workers and soldiers were housed. El-Lahun reveals itself to be a 12th-Dynasty foundation not only in its social structure but also by the fact that its layout shows a clear attempt at urban planning, with city blocks, access roads and open spaces all being designed to enhance living conditions for the majority of the population. This well-preserved city seemed to rest on a specific social contract between sovereigns and their subjects, since its model would be followed in various buildings at Abydos and at Qasr el-Sagha, on the northeast bank of the Birket Qarun in the Fayum.

Senusret III (1881–1842) undoubtedly served as the model for Manetho's "Sesostris," and his thirty-nine year reign was one of conquest in Asia and Nubia. His first move was to guarantee the exploitation of mineral resources in Nubia by setting up a veritable chain of fortresses stretching from Aswan to the second cataract and the forts of Semna, Kumma and Uronarti; the functioning of this defense system can be understood from the "Semna dispatches" that were discovered in a 13th-Dynasty tomb at the Ramesseum. According to a stele raised at Semna in year sixteen of the reign (and the duplicated one at Uronarti), Lower Nubia had at this point become an impregnable line of defense; and the king calls on his successors to allow no Nubian to infringe the line marked by the second cataract at Semna, which thus became the sole authorized junction for trade between Egypt and Nubia (important work was also being carried out at this time on the channel used to haul ships beyond the first cataract). It was, however, during the reign of Senusret III that growing unrest emerged on both the northern and southern borders of Egypt. This led to a policy involving a massive transfer of Nubian gold, which seemed to flow in an uninterrupted stream eastward in order to buy peace with Asia. Thus Senusret III kept the gold route open, and his memory was preserved in Nubia, where he became the object of religious veneration. This cult was, no doubt, also maintained at Abydos, where a cenotaph was raised to him. The pharaoh himself established his burial place at Dahshur, in the shadow of the pyramids of Sneferu—a site

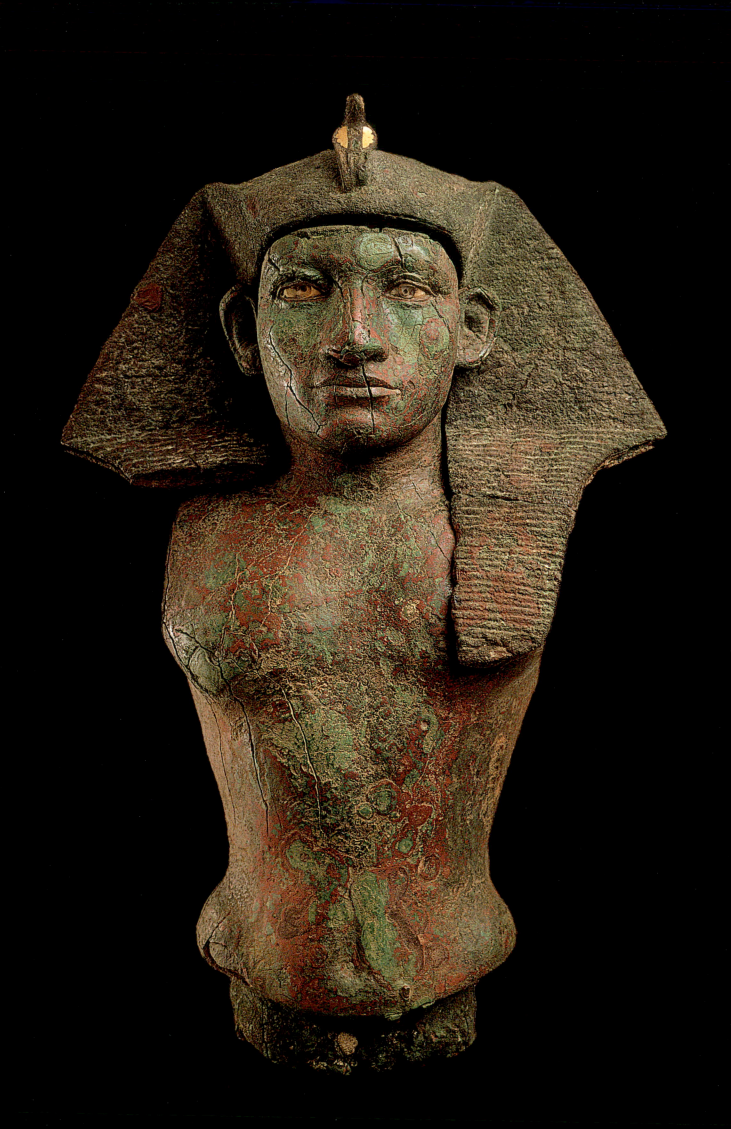

5. Bust of Amenemhat III, copper alloy, from Hawara, Middle Kingdom, 12th Dynasty. Collection George Ortiz
cat. 12

6. Small statuary group from Senpu, sandstone and soapstone, Middle Kingdom, 13th Dynasty. Paris, Musée du Louvre

that had already been chosen by Amenemhat II. Both of those later pyramids were looted. However, in 1894, Jacques de Morgan discovered the two treasures of Dahshur which revealed the burial places of the queens of both Amenemhat II and Senusret III. With its numerous corridors, the funeral monument is something like a palace, where—for the first time—the pharaoh was not totally separated in death from his queen.

The reign of Amenemhat III (1842–1794) was the most important of the 12th Dynasty. Reigning a total of forty-eight years, the pharaoh came to the throne as a very young man, after the short reign of the enigmatic King Awibra Hor (his are the sole tomb furnishings of the Middle Kingdom to have come down to us intact, giving us an idea of the standard of such adornments at the time). The reign of Amenemhat III marked a mutation in Egyptian foreign policy, particularly with regard to southern Palestine: whereas his predecessors had sought to strengthen their frontiers in order to avoid the mistakes of the past, he sought to establish collaboration and trade. Nevertheless, forces were as vigilant as ever in the eastern area of Avaris, where sphinxes used to stand bearing the name of Amenemhat III (these were later seized by the Hyksos and taken to Tanis during the 21st Dynasty). Further more, Amenemhat III developed the economic exploitation of the Fayum—a policy of which his predecessors (for example, Senusret II) had undoubtedly foreseen the utility. Many of the extant monuments to Amenemhat III are to be found in the vast depression occupied by Birket Qarun (then larger than it is today). Turning first to the past, the sovereign built himself a pyramid at Dahshur, a short way from that of his father Senusret III; then he turned to the future, raising his main monument at Hawarah, to the north of the Fayum, and making Shedyet–Crocodilopolis his capital and pyramid city. The energy of construction work at this period can still be felt in the letters discovered in the el-Lahun Archives which describe the deployment of work-teams here right up to the beginning of the 13th Dynasty. The funeral temple of Amenemhat III traditionally became known as the "Labyrinth" because of its large number of halls on two levels; it is considered one of the masterpieces of the ancient world. Attributed by Herodotus (II, 149–150) and Diodorus Siculus (Book I, LII) to "King Moeris"—the Greek name for Amenemhat III—the Fayum was a vast economic project that survived the pharaoh who had initially promoted it, earning him the divine name of Porramanres. Indeed, by creating a network of channels, the pharaoh made it possible to exploit the southern part of the depression. He also erected a temple at Medinet Maadi (Narmouthis), and extended the agricultural land of Egypt by providing a giant reservoir to meet possible future needs.

Archaeological evidence shows that, safeguarded from famine, the middle strata of Egyptian society clearly enjoyed a higher level of material well-being during the second half of Amenemhat III's reign. The funeral monuments dating from the rest of the 12th and the whole of the 13th Dynasties reveal that the craftsmen at work were divided according to family or professional groupings. These small monuments, mainly from the Abydos area, reveal new standards in tomb furnishings: works of art became "miniaturized" and bring to light an Egyptian society anxious to maintain family and professional links with those who had died.

The 12th Dynasty would come to an end with the reigns of Amenemhat IV and his sister Sobekneferu (Manetho's "Skemiophris"). Just like the 6th Dynasty, it opened with a monarch who was assassinated (Othoes and Amenemhat I respectively) and ended with the reign of a woman (in the case of the earlier dynasty, Nitiqret, whose beauty Manetho praises [fragment 20]).

The 13th and 14th Dynasties are undoubtedly less well known. After figures who might serve as veritable models of monarchy, the rulers become anonymous—as we can see from this account given by Manetho (fragments 38 and 41a):

"The thirteenth dynasty [is made up] of sixty Diospolite kings, who reigned for a total of four hundred and fifty-three years.
The fourteenth dynasty [is made up] of seventy Xoite kings, who reigned one hundred and eighty-four years."

Naturally, though the length of the total reigns given by Manetho is wide of the mark, the number of sovereigns he mentions does seem to be close to what can be worked out from the columns of the Turin papyrus (col. VI–X). As a matter of fact, this 131-year period (1781–1650) saw monarchs of different family lines take over from each other. There is a succession of short-lived and brusquely-terminated reigns; though sometimes the pharaohs do seem to have imposed some semblance of authority. A number of 13th-Dynasty kings passed under the name of Sobekhotep ("Sobek is content"); and certain families emerge, such as the sons of the divine father Mentuhotep (Sobekhotep III, Neferhotep and Sihathor). However, most of the real administrative power had passed into the hands of the aristocracy and the circle of the viziers. And while Neferhotep did actually publish an edict regulating the use of the Abydos necropolis—with the threat of death for those who infringed it—there seem to have been very few royal monuments (limited almost entirely to tombs). Nevertheless, some pharaohs did relaunch certain projects and even send expeditions abroad; but the efforts of the likes of Sobekhotep II and Sobkemsaf in Medamud strike us as pale copies of what had been achieved before. The monuments of royal propaganda also became smaller: this was the period that promoted the creation of scarabs bearing the names of sovereigns and members of their family (a practice that would last right through to the period of the Hyksos as being the sole efficient way of communicating the name of the ruler in the exchange of gifts and embassies).

Archaeological research has revealed that there were some disastrous Nile floods during the course of the 13th Dynasty. As a result, the structure of the pharaoh's power gradually lost solidity: Egypt's grip over Nubia was slowly relaxed, and shepherds from southern Palestine found less and less difficulty in getting across the eastern frontier of the Delta. The slow, inexorable erosion of Egyptian domains along the Pelusiac branch of the Nile had begun; trade in the east was now organized by the heads of Asiatic caravans. While the 14th-Dynasty (or Xoite) monarchs who were contemporaries of the 13th-Dynasty rulers—for example, Aasehre Nehsy (mentioned in the Turin papyrus, col. VIII, fragment 97, 1)—did establish a small Avarite kingdom on the Pelusiac branch of the Nile, thus maintaining some semblance of pharaonic power in the eastern Delta, archaeological evidence suggests that the direction of both trade and population movements was reversed. From Avaris outward, the region gradually became a base for the trade in Asiatic goods over a vast area from Palestine to Nubia (one of the most notable groups of products being those ceramic containers with distinctive decorated bellies that are rather simplistically lumped together as "Tell el-Yahudiya ware"). The reign of Didumes (Manetho's "Toutimaios," fragment 42) began around 1730 BC and marked the beginning of the Hyksos period, a totally unprecedented phase in Egyptian history. The Nile valley lay open to Asiatic warlords who promoted their own trade empires with—according to Manetho—the support of well-armed elite soldiers; and the 17th Dynasty—indeed, the 13th, but now transferred from el-Lisht back to the more southern Thebes—would have great difficulty in pushing these intruders out of its territory. Reduced to a small Theban nucleus resisting as well as it could through its network of fortresses and allies, an independent Egypt would have to find new resources within itself if it was to repeat the 11th Dynasty's ousting of the 10th. During the Second Intermediate Period an alien presence had become established in Egypt; new energy had to be found if the dynasty was to rid the country of this Mediterranean-style military force based on well-developed weapons and a different arsenal of economic concepts.

Despite its reliance on Nubian *Medjai*, the Middle Kingdom had been born out of a desire for national independence. Its end result, however, was the arrival of exogenous peoples, a mixed culture, and access to technologies, ways of thought and methods of economic exchange that had originated elsewhere (in the East and Mediterranean). All these were factors that would play a part in the great renewal that took place under the New Kingdom.

Bibliography
The general bibliography on the Middle Kingdom is extensive; one can get an overall sense of it in the following works: Winlock 1947; Hayes 1953; Hayes 1961; Aufrère 1980; Drioton, Vandier 1984; Wildung 1984; Grimal 1988; Vernus, Yoyotte 1988; Vandersleyen 1995. It is also worth consulting the articles on individual rulers in LÄ. For the chronology and royal names of the Middle Kingdom: Gauthier 1907, 1912; von Beckerath 1984. On the Turin papyrus, see Gardiner 1959. For Manetho's fragments: Waddell 1980. For the literature and politics of the period: Posener 1956; on the 11th Dynasty, see: Barta 1970; Winlock 1945; Aufrère 2000: on the 12th Dynasty: Obsomer 1995 (Senusret I); Delia 1980 (Senusret III); Obsomer 1992 (Amenemhat III); Aufrère 2001; on the 13th–14th Dynasties: Abd El-Maqsoud 1983; Yoyotte 1989. For a presentation of the archaelogical research at Avaris and the traces of the later Middle Kingdom, see Bietak 1996A (bibliography pp. 90–98). For the legendary Sesostris, see Malaise 1966; Hari 1981; Obsomer 1989.

1. Quartzite head of King
Amenhotep III, New Kingdom,
18th Dynasty.
London, The Trustees of the British
Museum
cat. 29

The history of the New Kingdom is marked by the appearance of several powerful royal figures whose distinctive personalities, beliefs, and actions greatly affected the direction that
Egypt's civilization took during this period of almost five hundred years (1550–1075 BC). Some
of these individuals had a profound effect on their immediate generation; others set the stage
for the following reigns; and one ruler introduced an innovative concept that, while not enduring in terms of ancient Egyptian culture, appears ultimately to have played a significant
role in the development of western religious thought.

The 18th Dynasty
The New Kingdom is comprised of three dynasties: the 18th, the 19th, and the 20th. The
pharaoh Ahmose (550–1525 BC) was responsible for reuniting the country which had been
ruled by rival factions during the turbulent time of the Second Intermediate Period (1650–1550
BC), and he began the dynasty that would consist of fourteen rulers (Some scholars suggest
fifteen, with Queen Nefertiti being given an independent reign.). He successfully completed the battles against the Hyksos, peoples of Asiatic origin who controlled the northern part
of the country from their base in the eastern Delta. His older brother Kamose was the leader
of the Theban (southern) faction, and he had led these struggles. He may have been killed
during a campaign, and Ahmose took over control and led the army to victory, and thus began the New Kingdom. A victory of the south over the north parallels earlier events at the
advent of the Middle Kingdom and the 1st Dynasty.
Both Ahmose I and his successor Amenhotep I (1525–1504 BC) had, out of necessity, to protect the borders of Egypt, especially to the east (the Asiatics) and the south (the Nubians),
and successful campaigns in these areas may have led to the imperialistic operations that became the hallmark of later rulers of the dynasty. Both of these pharaohs apparently followed

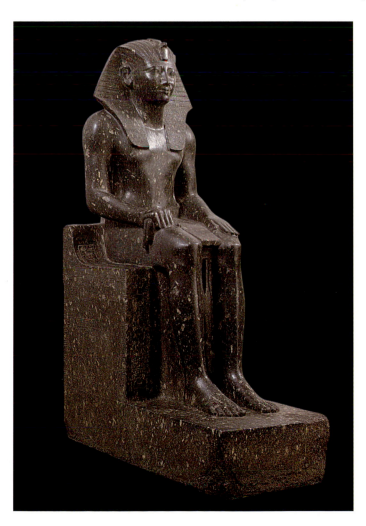

2. Diorite statue of Thutmose I
from Karnak, New Kingdom,
18th Dynasty.
Turin, Museo Egizio
cat. 24

following pages
3. Aerial view of the temple
of Hatshepsut at Deir el-Bahri,
New Kingdom, 18th Dynasty

the Theban tradition of the 17th Dynasty in choosing the necropolis of Dra Abu el-Naga as the site of their burial, but Amenhotep I made a fundamental change in plan, when he separated his mortuary temple from his tomb; this was a precedent that would become the rule with his successors. Records indicate that he was responsible for some building projects in the temple of Amun at Karnak, a structure that most of the pharaohs who followed him would add to as well.

Although the next king, Thutmose I, was not of royal blood, his marriage to the daughter of Ahmose I helped secure him the throne. An able military man, he was also active in restoring and adding to the temple at Karnak. It was his tomb that marked the move into the remote wadi, called in modern times the Valley of the Kings, and his successors would follow this practice. Thutmose II (1492–1479 BC) was the next to come to the throne, and he also had a wife, Hatshepsut, whose direct royal connections strengthened the power of her husband. His premature death left only a son, Thutmose III, to succeed him (1479–1425 BC). Too young to rule independently and born to a minor wife, Thutmose III had as coregent the reigning queen, Hatshepsut. An ambitious individual, she quickly assumed the full powers of the throne and took over the role of pharaoh (1479–1458 BC). She ruled as a king, was often depicted with male attributes in representations in two and three dimensions, and was often referred to in the masculine gender in texts. She recorded her divine birth in the scenes depicted in her magnificent mortuary temple at Deir el-Bahri, and, like her male predecessors, had a restoration inscription inscribed marking the order she had created out of chaos at the time of her coronation. Interestingly, her statements included her reconstruction of monuments desecrated by the Hyksos, who had in fact been expelled generations earlier. Although this may appear to be an exaggeration or even a fabrication to us, it instead reflects aspects of the Egyptian concept of kingship. This office was considered divine and eternal and its occupant was in theory so identified with it that he (or she) became the sum of all predecessors and successors and their accomplishments.

As Thutmose III matured, his "stepmother" held the primary power. When he came of age,

4. The temple of Hatshepsut at Deir el-Bahri, New Kingdom, 18th Dynasty

5. Head of a colossal statue of Hatshepsut as Osiris, from Deir el-Bahri, painted limestone, New Kingdom, 18th Dynasty. New York, The Metropolitan Museum of Art
cat. 13

the two appear to have had somewhat complementary roles. Years after her death, however, he embarked on a campaign to remove her name and images from monuments, thus preventing any memory of her to endure. Later lists of rulers in fact, omit her name, as well as that of other monarchs who had fallen out of favor. Thutmose III, however, is largely known for establishing the Egyptian empire and extending the borders of the country so that they reached well into western Asia and south into Nubia. His program marks the major imperialistic expansion of ancient Egypt, and he also erected temples to Egyptian gods in these areas to further emphasize the Egyptian presence. The success of his endeavors is indicated in part by the ease with which his successors were able to maintain his accomplishments and in some cases even expand on them. He was also involved in extensive building projects throughout Egypt, including a large temple built within the Karnak complex, where he also inscribed annals describing his military victories.

After Thutmose III was buried in a tomb hidden in a crevice in the upper part of the cliffs in the Valley of the Kings, his son Amenhotep II (1428–1397 BC) succeeded him and quickly had to deal with threats to the empire, first in Palestine, then in Syria, and later in Nubia. Successfully controlling these problems early in his reign allowed him to spend his later years

6. Sandstone bust of Akhenaten
from the temple at Karnak,
New Kingdom, 18th Dynasty.
Cairo, Egyptian Museum
cat. 71

in peace. Thutmose IV (1397–1387 BC) followed him to the throne, and his was a relatively calm reign, recorded so far by only a few military exploits, in Nubia and Syria. Both he and his father continued to stabilize the borders of the empire and the system of vassal states in western Asia, begun by Thutmose III.

When Amenhotep III became pharaoh (1387–1350 BC), he controlled the most stable and enduring monarchy in the ancient Near East. The domestic and foreign administrative structure that his ancestors had established proved to be durable, and thus the economy flourished. Fairly early in his reign, Amenhotep quelled some uprisings in Nubia, and he also continued to encourage the diplomatic ties his predecessors had set up with kingdoms in western Asia. The relative peace in the region allowed the king, who was ably supported by his powerful queen, Tiy (who was not of noble birth), to encourage the development of art, architecture, and literature. He had a royal palace complex built on a large scale at Malkata on the west bank of Thebes. It even boasted a huge man-made lake with its own harbor. The king was also responsible for considerable building projects throughout Egypt and added significant parts to the temples at Luxor (The colonnade and the "birth room"). Several of his accomplishments were recorded on a series of large scale scarabs. Inscribed on their underside, they deal primarily with the king's marriage, his athleticism, diplomacy, and building projects.

During his long reign of almost forty years, Amenhotep III apparently decided to devote some time to reviewing ancient Egyptian theoretical concepts, and it appears that kingship was one of his prime concerns. He focused to some degree on emphasizing the cult of the divine living king, and his interest in this matter can be seen in both the temple at Luxor, where his divine birth was recorded and the temple of Soleb, were divine statues of him were erected. The jubilee (*sed* festival) he celebrated late in his reign may also have been arranged to focus on his divinity. This trend, which was taken to new heights by his son Akhenaten and later by the 19th-Dynasty ruler Rameses II, may have originally been in part a result of Amenhotep III's concern over the rising power of the priesthood of Amun and its potential for competition with the monarchy. Such thoughts may well have been justified in light of the eventual vying for power that emerged at the end of the 20th and into the 21st Dynasty between royalty and clergy. There is also some indication that these interests of Amenhotep III also

7. Gold cup of General Djehuty,
New Kingdom, 18th Dynasty.
Cairo, Egyptian Museum
cat. 105

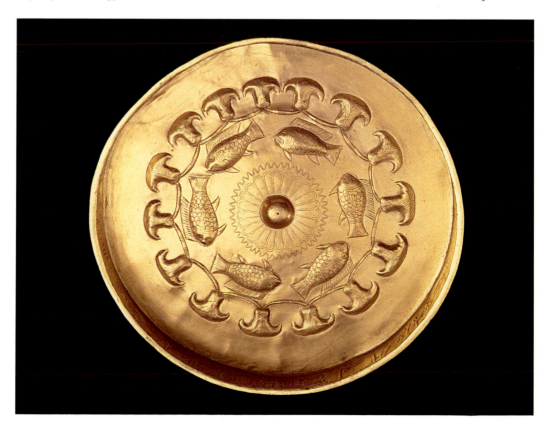

8. Portrait of King Akhenaten from
el-Amarna, plaster, New Kingdom,
18th Dynasty.
Berlin, Ägyptisches Museum
und Papyrussammlung
cat. 16

9. Gold seal ring with the name of
Horemheb, New Kingdom,
late 18th Dynasty.
Paris, Musée du Louvre
cat. 137

10. Colossal statue of Tutankhamun
usurped by Horemheb, from
Thebes, painted quartzite,
New Kingdom, 18th Dynasty.
Cairo, Egyptian Museum
cat. 1

focused to some degree on aspects of theology, with the king modifying the disk of the sun, the *aten*, into a more prominent aspect of the sun-god.

His son and successor, Amenhotep IV, ascended the throne (1350–1333 BC) to inherit a truly glorious realm. His queen, Nefertiti, like his mother, was not from the royal line, but she too apparently played an important role during her husband's reign; she even appears in a scene on a temple block as a victorious ruler smiting an enemy. It was not too long, however, before threats reached the northern frontier of Egypt's empire in Syria, in the form of the Hittites. A powerful force in their power base in Anatolia, the Hittites represented a potential challenge to the stability of the kingdom. Evidence of this situation has been documented in ancient diplomatic correspondence. Recorded on clay tablets these "Amarna letters" largely relate the difficulties that the vassal states and outposts in the western Asian area of the empire were experiencing. The pharaoh, however, was also occupied at the time with philosophical questions regarding the nature of kingship and his own relationship with the divine forces of the pantheon. Some scholars see this internal crisis taking precedence over external affairs, with the result that the empire was severely weakened. Others have suggested that these theoretical issues were in part a reaction to the rising power of the priesthood of Amun.

In any case, Amenhotep IV was in certain ways an iconoclast, and he began to shatter many of the traditional images of Egyptian beliefs that had already been in existence for almost two thousand years. He spearheaded a religious revolution that touched upon almost all the aspects of Egyptian civilization, when he replaced the multitude of deities in favor of a single god, a supreme power visualized as the disk of the sun. By year five of his reign, he had a radical style of art introduced, as well as a new type of construction. Along with these changes, he introduced a new style in the expression of royal inscriptions. He changed his own name to Akhenaten ("the one who is effective for the Aten") to reflect the focus of his new religion, the Aten, and he established the capital at a new site, Akhetaten ("the horizon of the Aten"). While his innovations have often been seen in modern times as the origin or forerunner of monotheism, it is clear that many of his modifications centered on the king and represented an attempt to elevate royal status, perhaps in an effort to make their relationship more balanced and equalized.

Whatever his motives, the "experiment" did not succeed, and he died within a few years, at which time the throne passed to Tutankhaten, who then changed his name to Tutankhamun (1333–1323 BC). The exact nature of the relationship between Akhenaten and him, as well as the identity of Smenkhkara, who does not seem to have had an independent reign, have been at the center of scholarly debate for decades. Tutankhamun, who came to the throne at a very early age, restored the orthodoxy and was guided apparently by Ay and Horemheb, two officials of high rank in the court. The young monarch, however, died after a short reign of ten years without a surviving heir. Today, he is more widely known as the owner of the most completely preserved royal tomb yet discovered in Egypt rather than as the restorer of traditional beliefs after a religious revolution.

A copy of a letter discovered in the Hittite archives records that, at the time of her husband's death, his wife Ankhesenamun had written to the king of that empire to find a husband among the Hittite princes. Although apprehensive, their ruler Suppiluliumas I sent a prince, who, it seems, was murdered before he could reach the Egyptian capital. Ay, who by this time must have been quite elderly, ascended the throne (1323–1319 BC), and it is he who is represented performing the funerary rituals for Tutankhamun on the walls of his tomb. After only four years he in turn was succeeded by Horemheb (1319–1291 BC), another influential senior member of the court. Although not of royal blood, Horemheb had excellent administrative credentials, and had been the commander of the army. Furthermore, he married the sister of Nefertiti, thereby securing a connection to the royal family. He reinforced his predecessors' steps toward the restoration of the ancient traditions that had been eliminated during the reign of Akhenaten. He built additions to the temple of Karnak and had scenes there and at Luxor carved to reflect his new position. He abandoned work on his tomb in Saqqara in the north, preferring to construct a grand burial place in the traditional royal cemetery in the Valley of the Kings on the west bank of Thebes. In constructing his pylon at Karnak he used as filler thousands of decorated blocks from the temple that Akhenaten had constructed at Thebes, which he had ordered to be dismantled. It is perhaps ironic that Horemheb's attempt to erad-

11–12. Ostracon with the portrait of Sety I from Qurna, recto and verso, New Kingdom, 19th Dynasty. Florence, Museo Egizio. *cat. 18*

icate the name and image of the "heretic" pharaoh from memory, inadvertently preserved for posterity a critical record of one of the world's first known innovative theorists.

In order to prevent ecclesiastical power from becoming a threat, Horemheb appointed former military men who were loyal to him to important clerical positions. While little remains to document his military exploits, it is clear that he did order at least one campaign in the South, and he reorganized the army into two divisions, one for the North and one for the South. With past traditions restored and a strong monarchy in power, Egypt could look forward to retaining its primary place as a significant power in the world of the ancient Near East.

The 19th Dynasty

Hormeheb may well have set Egypt on the course it would follow for generations, but he left no heir to succeed him when he died. The office of pharaoh fell to Rameses, who also came from a military background, and had served as the vizier, being one of the king's most trusted advisors. Clearly beyond middle age, Rameses I (1291–1289 BC) had no link to the previous dynasty. He is considered to be the founder of the 19th Dynasty. His wife, Satra was the first queen to be buried in a separate royal cemetery dedicated to royal wives, called today the Valley of the Queens.

Sety I, the son of Rameses I, was both vizier and general under his father, and he succeeded him upon his death (1289–1278 BC). He soon set about reestablishing Egypt's borders in the face of conflicts coming from all sides. He led successful campaigns into western Asia (Syria, Lebanon, and Palestine), he battled with the Libyans in the West, faced the threat of the Hittites from Anatolia, and also attended to situations in the South. Within Egypt, he concentrated on several building projects, including the magnificent temple to Osiris at Abydos, a site sacred to the deity. There, he also built a cenotaph. At Karnak, he had his military exploits recorded both in scenes and texts on the walls of the temple, and he began the construction of the hypostyle hall, a huge architectural masterpiece with a "forest" of one hundred and thirty-four columns. Each vertical support bore the weight of both a roof and clerestory level; their capitals flared out, obscuring from view the impost block upon which the roof rested. This architectural element gave the impression of a floating ceiling and reinforced its celestial symbolism.

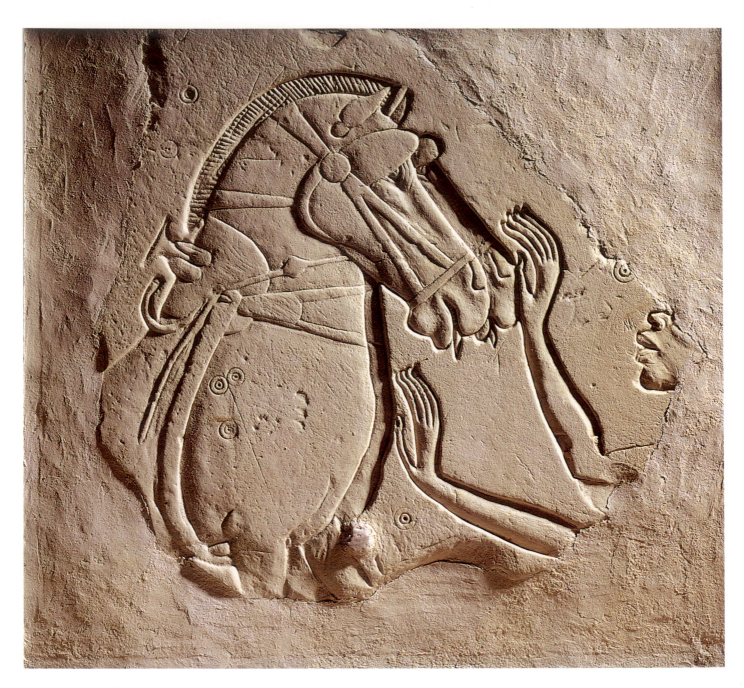

13. Stone relief with Nubian groom and two horses from Saqqara (?), New Kingdom, late 18th Dynasty. Edinburgh, The Trustees of the National Museums of Scotland
cat. 99

By the time Sety I died, his successor Rameses II (1279–1212) was old enough to have assisted his father at several levels and to have had a variety of experiences, for example: military campaigns, building projects, official protocol, and internal administration. It proved to be effective, since he became the pharaoh with the longest recorded reign, sixty-seven years, the one who fought more battles, produced more statuary and constructed more buildings than any other ruler of ancient Egypt. He was also the most prolific ruler, fathering more children that any other king. The apparent burial place of his princes, now in the process of excavation, appears to have been not only a unique structure, but also the largest multiple royal tomb. The rock-cut temple he built at Abu Simbel serves as a propagandistic statement close to Egypt's frontier with Nubia. A series of seated statues of the king are sculpted on the façade, and their monumental height, about 182 meters, makes them among the tallest ever produced, demonstrating for all to see the power that was pharaoh.

Within a very short period of time, Rameses II had to prove his mettle in Syria. Then, in his fifth year he initiated what was to become the most recorded military campaign in the history of the ancient Near East, the Battle of Qadesh, against the Hittites. While Rameses had it inscribed in texts and scenes on the walls of several temples throughout Egypt, as well as having copies inked on papyrus, it appears that he could not overcome the fact that his narrative and the accompanying illustrations greatly exaggerated his valor as well as the outcome of the conflict. It would seem, however, that Rameses probably underestimated his opponents, but fought valiantly, and managed to turn what might have been a disaster into a tie, with both sides claiming some element of victory. While the conflicts with the Hittites continued several more years, eventually, the warring nations agreed to the terms of peace, and a record of the treaty appears on the walls of a few Egyptian temples as well as on clay tablets in the Hittite archive. The agreement was a pragmatic solution, as the Assyrian empire had clearly become a threat, and it served both nations to join forces and support each other.

The rest of Rameses' reign was marked more by domestic building projects and diplomatic successes than by military activities, although the king occasionally sent a raid into Nubia. Rameses spent considerable energy in the construction of Piramesse, his new city in the Delta. For this work, he relied on labor forces acquired from his victories in the Near East, and it may have been here that the Hebrews labored on building projects for the pharaoh. In this location, as well as at other sites throughout the empire, the king had statues erected that represented him in his divine living form. The cult of the divine living king, associated with this image, received a new, enhanced attention under Rameses, and at Abu Simbel, one of these statues joins three other deities in the innermost shrine, "the holy of holies." The accentuation of the divinity of the living king certainly had roots in earlier periods, but it was perhaps first depicted in wall reliefs during the reign of Hatshepsut, in her mortuary temple at Deir el-Bahri. It clearly was an issue of importance to her successors, and especially to the pharaoh Amenhotep III. However, it was his son Akhenaten who brought this concept to its fullest form. Although Rameses II focused on his divinity, it is abundantly evident that the populace recognized the human element in the divine office then, just as they had seemed to do in earlier times. Indeed, a letter from the Ramesside period appears to refer to the ruler as the "old general," not the divine living king.

Often, Rameses II is referred to as the pharaoh of the Exodus, and sometimes that title is reserved for one of his successors. The Egyptian textual sources, which as a rule are verbose in their documentation, are mute on this subject. It is possible that the Egyptians did not consider the event to be of the type that they would record. It did not have any positive aspect in regard to them, their ruler, or their gods. Such negative texts rarely occur in hieroglyphs literally, as the "words of the gods." To do so would mean that such inscriptions and what they recorded would exist for eternity, like the deities themselves.

Rameses died in the sixty-seventh year of his reign, probably a few years after his ninetieth birthday. In terms of accomplishments, he may be ranked as one of the most important and effective rulers of the ancient world, and he clearly is worthy of the title accorded him in modern times, "Rameses the Great." He was indeed a hard act to follow, and managed to outlive many of his sons. It was his thirteenth son, however, Merenptah (1212–1202 BC) who succeeded him, but being of advanced age himself, he had a fairly brief reign. While the peace brokered during his father's rule extended after his death, the new pharaoh found hostile forces facing him, first in Syria and then in the area of the Delta and the western oases, in the form of Libyans and the Sea Peoples. In addition, he faced a major rebellion from the south, when the Nubians revolted against Egypt. He acted quickly against all of these foes and recorded his victories in inscriptions at Karnak and on stelae discovered in the Delta and in Thebes, at his mortuary temple. On his Theban victory stele, he recorded all the names of the peoples he conquered, including the only mention of Israel in an Egyptian text: "Israel is destroyed; its seed is no longer." Such a reference had led earlier scholars and others to assume that Merenptah was the pharaoh of the Exodus.

The succession after the death of Merenptah is somewhat unclear, as both Sety II (1199–1193 BC) and Amenmessu (1202–1199 BC) claimed the throne. Eventually, however, the latter, who may have been a usurper, lost out to the former, who was the intended heir, and Sety II became pharaoh. His short reign was followed by that of his son Saptah (1193–1187 BC) who was not yet of age to rule; so Sety II's major queen Tausret, ruled as regent with the support of the chancellor, Bay. She apparently took on the role of sole pharaoh herself after Saptah's death, and had an independent reign, claiming much of the prerogatives of royalty, as had her predeces-

14. Granite bust of a Ramesside king (Merenptah?) from Medinet Habu, New Kingdom, 19th Dynasty. Cairo, Egyptian Museum
cat. 125

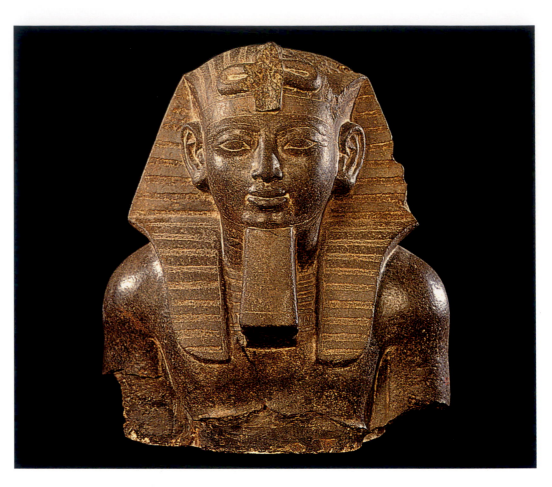

sor of the 18th Dynasty, Hatshepsut. Just exactly how the 19th Dynasty ended is a matter of conjecture, but it seems to have involved a dispute with supporters of at least two major factions. One of these groups, representing powerful members of the administration, seems to have backed an individual named Sethnakhte, and it was he who emerged as the next pharaoh.

The 20th Dynasty
While little is known of Sethnakhte, the first ruler of the 20th Dynasty (1187–1184 BC), the Great Harris Papyrus, a record written more than six decades later, documents that he successfully repelled the Asiatic rebellions and supported the operation of the temples in Egypt and assured their income. His son Rameses III (1184–1153 BC) served as coregent during the short reign of his father, and it is he who represents the end of the line of the successful military pharaohs of the Egyptian empire begun by Thutmose III. Rameses III ruled during a chaotic time in the ancient Near East and the Mediterranean world. While he spent his early years stabilizing his own country, by the fifth year of his reign, he was faced with hostility from the Libyan tribes of the west. Although he successfully repulsed this enemy, he soon had to deal with the Sea Peoples, a formidable group, including an assortment of peoples from the eastern Mediterranean, Asia Minor, and the Aegean, who had been migrating toward Egypt since the reign of Merenptah, with the apparent motive of settling in the western Delta. Although that pharaoh had successfully repelled them earlier, they continued to press forward, perhaps driven out of their homelands by invaders or forced out by disease or plague. So ferocious were they that the Hittites quickly fell victim to them. Rameses III recorded his conflict with the Sea Peoples on the walls of his temple at Medinet Habu on the west bank of Thebes. Unlike earlier battles, this one consisted of both land and marine components. The pharaoh eventually succeeded in driving the Sea Peoples beyond the borders of Egypt, perhaps as far as the Levant. With little time to recuperate from this onslaught, Rameses was soon faced with yet another incursion of Libyan tribes. Recorded on the walls of his mortuary temple at Medinet Habu, this victory of Rameses demonstrated the superior ability of the king

at the head of an extremely effective military force. These walls also document several other invasions that the king successfully repulsed, but there are clear indications that these claims were mere boasts, for they appear simply to be copies of exploits of his predecessors.

It is possible that the military exploits with which he was preoccupied and the efforts he made to prevent invading forces from taking hold of Egyptian territories took so much of Rameses' attention that for a time he was unaware of a plot that had developed in his harem to kill him. A minor wife Tiy, aided by several well-placed officials, conspired to murder the king and replace him with Tiy's son. According to the record on papyrus, the conspiracy was discovered before any harm to Rameses had occurred, and the plotters were tried before judges. They, as well as those who conspired with them, were condemned to death.

Rameses III survived the conspiracy, but he appears to have died prior to the end of the trial of the defendants. He was succeeded by Rameses IV (1153–1147 BC), the first of eight rulers, each of whom also took the throne name of Rameses. Records document expeditions sent to the Sinai as well as Nubia, but little else. Rameses V (1147–1143 BC) ruled even less time, and he was occupied during part of his reign with a lengthy civil disturbance. Rameses VI (1143–1135 BC) ruled longer than either of his two predecessors, but he seemed to be unable to maintain the territories of the empire in western Asia as well as its interests in the Sinai. Rameses VII (1135–1127 BC), who inherited the throne from his father, Rameses VI, ruled during a period of severe domestic problems and was faced with instability both within Egypt's borders and beyond them. He appears to have concentrated his administration in the Delta and may have experienced the weakened authority of his power in other parts of the country. The next king, Rameses VIII (1127–1126 BC) was not his son, but a son of Rameses III, and he held the throne for barely more than a year; these facts suggest a period of internal turmoil. Renewed construction under Rameses IX (1126–1108 BC) and a longer reign indicate that he perhaps was able to control the problems that had arisen under his predecessors. A series of papyri records that the royal tombs in the Valley of the Kings (and some temples as well) were being robbed. These documents, with their details of the investigations and the trials of the criminals, suggest that some domestic affairs were monitored well. Rameses X (1108–1104 BC) had a brief reign, and little information remains as to what, if anything, he was able to accomplish. The last pharaoh of the dynasty Rameses XI (1104–1075 BC) ruled a considerable length of time, but there are clear indications that the decline of Egypt in terms of its wealth, status and position in the ancient world, and its own internal stability had reached a severely low point. The Ramesside rulers following Rameses III were unable to maintain the empire, and deal with the strains of a rapidly changing external world and a continuously fractious relationship between the monarchy and the clergy. Evidence for this situation is abundantly clear during the latter part of the dynasty, and it is recorded to some extent in the *Report of Wenamen*, which details the travels of an emissary of Rameses XI who had to bring wood for the bark of Amun from Byblos. The treatment he received and the tribulations he faced during the journey present an Egypt with a very diminished image, in a world without the diplomatic ties and allegiances of the past. In addition, the power of the priesthood of Amun had increased to the point that the high priest in Thebes competed for control with the king. In fact, Rameses XI maintained power in the northern part of the country, while his counterpart, Herihor, the high priest of Amun at Thebes, essentially ruled the South. Herihor had assumed the highest civil titles as well, and evidence exists in the temple of Khons at Karnak that he even had himself identified as a pharaoh. This political situation and civil disturbance set the stage for a division of the country into two territories, the northern, with the pharaoh based in Tanis (in the Delta) and the southern, under the authority of the high priest of Amun at el-Hiba: this division marked the end of the New Kingdom.

Bibliography
General bibliography for history of the New Kingdom: Redford 1967; Habachi 1972; Kitchen 1982; Trigger *et alii* 1983; Redford 1984; Israelit-Groll 1985; Kitchen 1986; Dothan, Dothan 1992; Grimal 1992; Kozloff, Bryan 1992; Redford 1992; Clayton 1994: Baines 1995A; Baines 1995B; Murnane 1995B; O'Connor 1995; O'Connor, Silverman 1995; Silverman 1995; Redford 1995; Murnane 1997; Oren 1997; Silverman 1997; Oren 2000.

Mamduh el-Damaty
Isabelle Franco

The Third Intermediate Period

Rameses III, the second king of the 20th Dynasty, was the last of the great pharaohs of Egypt. His reign was followed by a great economic recession and a breakdown in sovereignty due to the weakness of the rulers that came after him. Those eight rulers, all named Rameses (IV to XI), who submitted to the high priests of Amun in Thebes, preferred to stay in the Delta, and far from the influence of the Theban priesthood throughout their reigns which lasted eighty years.

During the twenty-nine-year reign of the last king of this dynasty, King Rameses XI, the weakness of the central government resulted in the changing of the natural geographical regions in the north and in the south from administrative regions in semi-independent political units. The strength of the priesthood in Thebes contributed not only to the weakening of the rulers in the Delta but also to increasing the gap between the North and the South. During this period, Panehsy, viceroy of Nubia, gained control of Thebes and subjected the southern regions up to el-Hiba. The rule of Panehsy was disorganized and rather unstable until its collapse in Rameses XI's ninth regnal year. Later Herihor appeared, the high priest of Amun, commander of the army of Egypt and ruler of Nubia. Herihor began to date his reign as the first year of *wehm mesut*, the "renaissance period," which is also thought to be the nineteenth year of the reign of Rameses XI. This is how Herihor managed for the first time to control the military force, became the high priest of Amun, and rule over Nubia, and at times even hold the position of minister of the South. In the North, Nesbanebdjed (Smendes) was a successor of Rameses XI and a ruler whose authority was widespread in the North. According to the *Report of Wenamun*, Smendes was named "the foundation that Amun established in the north of the land." Wenamun reported to Smendes before he left for Syria and depended on him during his trip to Byblos. Therefore, it is difficult to believe that Smendes, who enjoyed all this authority in the North, held a less important position than the one Herihor had in the South. Smendes became the actual ruler of the city of Tanis. At the end of year nineteen of Rameses XI's reign, Egypt was divided into two regions each of which was ruled separately. The borders of those two regions were located near el-Hiba, near el-Minja. Thus a new political order began in the 21st Dynasty which lasted for more than three centuries.

The 21st Dynasty (1075–945 BC)

In the 21st Dynasty the political situation in Egypt started to change. Egypt lost its sovereignty in Asia and its influence in Nubia. Moreover, the country was governed by two ruling powers, one in the North which ruled over the Delta and Middle Egypt, and the other in Thebes. The activity of the northern kings was limited to the northern part of the country. It was due to the influence of Herihor and his fellow high priests of Amun that the South recognized the rule of the kings in the North in exchange for their letting them rule the South on their own. In fact this policy enjoyed a great success, and there was no conflict between the two ruling powers.

According to Manetho, this dynasty consisted of seven kings from Tanis who ruled for one hundred and thirty years as follows:

1. Smendes
2. Amenemnisu
3. Psusennes I
4. Amenemope
5. Osorkon the Elder
6. Siamun
7. Psusennes II

The ruling power in Thebes consisted of a group of priests, whose reign started with the high priest of Amun and King Herihor as follows:

1. Herihor
2. Payankh
3. Pinudjem I (as priest)
4. Pinudjem I (as king)
5. Masaharta
6. Djedkhonsuefankh

1. Gold and semi-precious stone pendant of Psusennes I with winged scarab, from the king's tomb at Tanis, Third Intermediate Period, 21st Dynasty.
Cairo, Egyptian Museum
cat. 265

2. Tanis, the royal necropolis of the pharaohs of the 21st and 22nd-Dynasties.

7. Menkheperra
8. Smendes II
9. Pinudjem II
10. Psusennes II

Kings of Tanis

Nesbanebdjed (Smendes I)

According to historical evidence and the writings of Manetho, Smendes ruled for nearly twenty-six years. But even though his reign was quite long, his accomplishments were very few. One of the most important of these was the restoration of the temple of Luxor after its destruction due to the flooding of the Nile. An inscription describing this work was found in Dibabieh near Gebelein. This same inscription also states that Smendes ruled over all Egypt in spite of the influence of Pinudjem I in the South. Indeed, the northern and southern ruling powers were allied, and as a result Pinudjem I married Henuttawy, daughter of Smendes and Tentamun. Thus the kings of Tanis ruled all over Egypt with the agreement of Thebes. In fact, this is also what led Manetho to call the 21st Dynasty "Tanite," reflecting the fact that Smendes lived and ruled from Djanet (Tanis) and may even have been buried there. One of the canopic jars bearing his name was found near Tanis, and since then the city of Tanis became the capital of the dynasty, an important trading port with eastern Asia as well as a shield against the threats coming from those areas.

Amenemnisu

Amenemnisu ruled after Smendes for a short period (nearly six years). He might even have shared the reign with his brother Psusennes, for an inscription with both their names was found on an the caps of an archer's bow in the tomb of Psusennes.

Psusennes I

Psusennes I is considered the most important king of this dynasty for he left behind the greatest number of monuments, and reigned for the longest period, one lasting nearly half a cen-

3. Lapis lazuli and gold heart-shaped amulet from the tomb of Psusennes I at Tanis, Third Intermediate Period, 21st Dynasty.
Cairo, Egyptian Museum
cat. 263

4. Gold embossed plaque with *wedjat* eye from the tomb of Psusennes I at Tanis, Third Intermediate Period, 21st Dynasty.
Cairo, Egyptian Museum

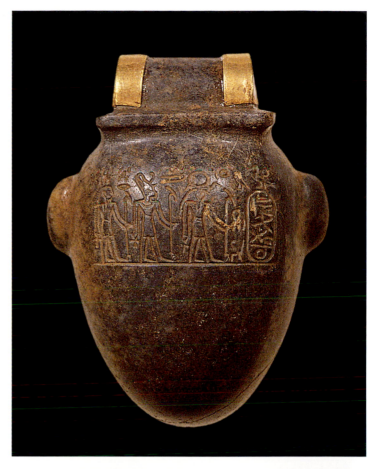

5. Gold and lapis lazuli ring with
a scarab inset, Third Intermediate
Period, 22nd Dynasty.
Cairo, Egyptian Museum
cat. 270

6. Gold and agate bracelet from the
tomb of Psusennes I at Tanis, Third
Intermediate Period, 21st Dynasty.
Cairo, Egyptian Museum
cat. 269

tury. He built a temple for Amun in Tanis, today unfortunately completely destroyed except for a few decorated stones. He built a tomb for himself near this temple made of granite and limestone. The tomb contained a burial chamber for both the king and his wife, and secondary rooms for the burial of the rest of the royal family. This tomb was discovered in 1939 by Pierre Montet. He noticed that both the outer red granite and the inner black granite sarcophagi had been reused. The first one belonged to Pharaoh Merenptah and the second to an unknown private individual. The funerary furniture, decorated with silver and gold, was also found completely intact.

Psusennes not only concentrated on the construction and prosperity of Tanis but he also built the temple of Isis (the lady of the pyramids) near the one of the third queen east of the pyramid of Khufu in Giza.

Psusennes was married to his sister Mutnedjmet and they both held various priestly titles. In this manner, both Psusennes and his wife were able to dominate the huge fortune and the numerous endowments coming from the temples.

Amenemope

Amenemope started his reign by sharing it with his predecessor Psusennes. His lasted for twelve years during which he continued the temple of Isis in Giza. His tomb was found in Tanis, and it contained a burial chamber in which were found a wooden gilded sarcophagus, a golden mask and a few bronze vessels.

7. Painted faience *shabti*s from the tomb of Psusennes I at Tanis, Third Intermediate Period, 21st Dynasty.
Cairo, Egyptian Museum
cat. 274

Osorkon
Osorkon ruled for six years. Nothing much is known about his reign except that he employed a priest in the temple of Karnak. This is known to us through a fragmented inscription. The tomb of Osorkon has not yet been found.

Siamun
He was the most active king of this dynasty. He ruled for nineteen years during which he built many constructions in Tanis, Khataanah and Memphis. His name also appears on several inscriptions in Thebes.

Unlike his predecessors, Siamun also carried on activities abroad. An example of these is to be found in southern Palestine. Historical evidence shows that he organized an expedition against the people of Philistia who had settled southeast of Palestine. This same expedition reached the city of Gezer in Canaan, located on the borders of Philistia and the land of the Hebrews. Siamun even signed an agreement with Solomon and consolidated it with marriage. His foreign affairs in Palestine were more commercial than military as he attempted to limit their commercial activities with Philistia.

Psusennes II
Although Psusennes II ruled for nearly fifteen years, little is known about him. The most important event in his reign was due to the influence of another dynasty ruled by "the great chief of the Ma" Sheshonq who succeeded in marrying his son Osorkon to Princess Maatkara, daughter of Psusennes II, which resulted in his taking over the throne and establishing the 22nd Dynasty.

The High Priests of Amun in Thebes
Herihor proclaimed himself king and ruled in Thebes. However, by then he was an old man and did not live long. Little is known about his reign in Thebes except that he paid considerable attention to the royal tombs that had been robbed by thieves. He ordered the reburial of a number of kings whose wrappings had been removed.

At Herihor's death, his son Payankh, once the ruler of northern Sudan, succeeded him. Payankh was the leader of the army and so could not assume the royal titulary like his father; therefore he kept the office of high priest of Amun. He recognized the royal institution's right to sit on the throne in Tanis.

The relations between the kings of Tanis and the priests of Amun increased as time went by. When Psusennes I succeeded Smendes, the relations between the two institutions were enhanced by the marriage of Pinudjem, the eldest son of Payankh, and Maatkara daughter of Psusennes. Indeed, when Psusennes died, Pinudjem declared himself king as Herihor had before him.

Pinudjem paid special attention to the mummies of the preceding kings that had been damaged and abused by the intrusions of thieves at the end of the 20th dynasty. He ordered the reshrouding and the reburial of Amenhotep I, Thutmose II, Amenhotep III, Rameses II and III. His activity was not limited only to this area, but extended to many other regions, from the island of Sehel in the south to el-Hiba in the north. Pinudjem also repaired and restored parts of the temple of Medinet Habu, and added his name to Rameses II's avenue of ram-headed sphinxes between the quay and the second pylon at Karnak.

When Pinudjem declared himself king, his authority was automatically shown on the monuments and administrative documents. Cartouches with his name appeared on the walls of the Karnak temple, on the offering table from Abydos, and on a slab from Koptos. Tanis itself recognized his authority and cartouches appeared with his name as well as that of Psusennes I on the stone blocks of a building constructed there. This has led to the assumption that Psusennes was a partner in the reign and that his royal headquarters were in el-Hiba, if not in Tanis itself.

Masaharta succeeded Pinudjem as high priest. Unfortunately, he did not survive for long, so his brother Menkheperra took over. This occurred during the reign of king Amenemope in Tanis between his sixteenth and twenty-fifth regnal year. The High Priest Menkheperra had a very strong personality, and cunningly managed to suppress a revolution in Thebes, exiling many of its people to the el-Kharga Oasis. He wanted to make peace with them before they returned to their homeland.

8. Gold and lapis lazuli ring
with *wedjat* eye and cartouche,
Third Intermediate Period,
21st Dynasty.
Cairo, Egyptian Museum
cat. 271

9. Gold toe-stalls from the tomb
of Psusennes I at Tanis, Third
Intermediate Period, 21st Dynasty.
Cairo, Egyptian Museum
cat. 273

The time came when Menkheperra declared himself king. According to some historians, Menkheperra called himself Psusennes II. After Menkheperra, came Smendes II, followed by Pinudjem II and finally Psusennes III. Relations between Tanis and Thebes ended during the 21st Dynasty, when the king lived in the eastern Delta and the high priest ruled from Thebes. There is no doubt that this unstable situation was deleterious in maintaining a stable condition and protecting Egypt.

There are very few extant documents regarding this era, and historians are uncertain about what they read. The excavations that started in 1939 in Tanis contributed a little in deciphering some mysteries. While they threw light on some questions, others are still waiting for the appearance of new discoveries or information.

The Libyan Rule (22nd Dynasty)

Rameses III made thousands of Libyan captives cross the Nile river, especially the Meshwesh tribes. They were brought to Egypt and settled in the eastern Delta around Bubastis, where they were granted land. As their numbers started to grow, some moved to other areas of the Delta. With the passage of time, the Libyans proved to be a strong and influential element in the political and administrative affairs of Egypt. The *Ma*'s power (an abbreviation for the word *meshwesh*) grew day by day under the weak kings of the 21st Dynasty. When King Psusennes II died without a legitimate heir, Sheshonq took over, and established the 22nd Dynasty of Libyan origin. He probably married his second son Osorkon to Princess Maatkara, the daughter of Psusennes II, in order to consolidate his legitimate right to the throne, thereby strengthening the relationship between the old and new royal families. For this reason he presided over the funerary ceremony of the deceased king who was not yet buried, a traditional tribute of the living king toward his predecessor.

There is no doubt that Sheshonq possessed a rare political sophistication, as can be seen by the policies that he applied conducting his administrative affairs in Egypt. He was farsighted enough to realize that the priests of Amun in Thebes were creating a state within state. As long as they enjoyed full power and authority, as was the case in the 21st Dynasty, they represented a threat to the new reign. The high priest was not only a religious power but also a military power, being the general commander-in-chief. Sheshonq therefore resorted to the same political tricks: they first would recruit members of the royal family and its supporters for leading positions in Thebes; they then would conclude marriages with prominent families there. Sheshonq soon saw to it that his second son Iuput became the high priest of Amun, and general commander-in-chief. He could therefore observe any opposition movement that might arise there. Meanwhile, the enormous treasures of the temple of Amun were also put under his control and benefit as a guarantee that they would not be used against him.

Sheshonq had an active foreign affairs policy with Nubia, Byblos, and Palestine, something that Egypt had not had for at least a century and a half. Nevertheless, Sheshonq's most important achievement was the expedition he led close to the end of his rule against Judah and Israel in Palestine. Our sources for this expedition are principally the Old Testament and the topographic list of the names of the cities that he had incised on the walls of the Bubastite Portal in the temple of Karnak, plus a slab found by Legrain in Karnak.

Sheshonq was obviously not about to risk an expedition into Palestine as long as King Solomon was powerful or at least appeared to be, and ruled a united kingdom. Nevertheless, he did not hesitate to grant Jeroboam, Solomon's enemy, refuge in Egypt. After Solomon's death, Jeroboam returned to Palestine defying the authority of Rehoboam and the only legitimate heir to the throne that divided the Hebrew kingdom into two enemy kingdoms. The first was headed by Rehoboam and included Judah's sons in the South, whose capital was Jerusalem; the other in the North, was headed by Jeroboam whose capital was Shechem.

With the division of the Hebrew kingdom, Sheshonq had the opportunity to dominate Palestine in the fifth year of Rehoboam's rule (the twentieth of Sheshonq's reign). He launched his expected expedition, as we learn from a stele found at Karnak, near Kem-Wer, the "Salt Lakes."

Sheshonq took over the "treasures of the house of God and of the house of the king. He took over everything and he took the shileds of gold that Solomon made".

After the king was assured of Judah's submissiveness, he moved north to make Israel submit. When he felt that King Jeroboam was getting close, he ran from his city to east of the Jordan River. Thus the cities of Israel became faire game for the Egyptian army, surrendering Beth-Shan, Taanach, Shunem, and Megiddo one after the other. The king took the last city as his operational center, sending forces to take over some regions east of the Jordan River. Sheshonq's expedition undoubtedly maintained Egyptian influence in Palestine in an absolute manner, so that Egypt benefited politically and economically. In addition to the trophies that the Egyptian army took from the Hebrew kingdom, commerce flourished with the Near East. Naturally, this had a positive influence on the economy of Egypt in the first part of the 22nd Dynasty, which was also reflected in their buildings and establishment in Tanis, Thebes, and Memphis.

The 23rd Dynasty
At that time Egypt was divided into several states due to the weakness of the royal family and the numerous revolutions at the end of the 22nd Dynasty. The kings' power decreased and the provincial princes became stronger as each strengthened himself fearing that his neighbor might overpower him or extend his property. Thus, Pedubastis was not greatly opposed when he set about creating a new ruling dynasty to govern in the north in Bubastis, while another king was in Tanis. It seems that Pedubastis ruled a large area of the western Delta (Sais) and received aid from the Theban priests while those in Memphis remained loyal to the old ruling establishment whose sphere of influence was in the eastern Delta and middle Egypt. Whatever the situation, the 22nd Dynasty remained on the throne for forty-seven years after the appearance of Pedubastis, and while it seems that the two ruling houses fought at first, they soon made peace. Both accepted the fact that Egypt had two ruling dynasties governing at the same time. Neither had total control over the cities governed by their own princes, for those princes were quite independent, each with his own army and court.
The high priest of Amun in Thebes, Harsiese, had also the right to write his name in a royal cartouche. Before the reign of Pedubastis ended, the days of Harsiese ended in Thebes, and someone else by the name of Takelot took over the priestly throne after him. The monuments of Takelot date to the sixth year of the reign of king Sheshonq IV, who probably came after king Pedubastis, followed by Osorkon III and others. In fact, considerable information is still lacking regarding the events in this mysterious and unstable period of Egyptian history. Despite the excavations in Tanis, it is still impossible to specify the succession of kings in the 22nd and the 23rd Dynasties, as well as the relations between them and one of those two branches of Amun priests.
The kings of the 23rd Dynasty left some monuments in Upper Egypt, especially in Thebes. The era of Osorkon III was renowned for two important events, the first of which was the great flood in Luxor that destroyed the front quay of the temple. The flood waters penetrated into the temple of Luxor and ruined much of it. As a result, king Osorkon ordered the restoration of the destroyed parts and the rebuilding of another quay. The second important event was that king Osorkon III did not follow his ancestors by making one of his sons high priest of Amun, but instead put his daughter Shepenwepet in that priestly role with the name of "god's wife of Amun" as a political and religious position. Soon, the influence of the "god's wife of Amun" increased, overpowering the influence of the high priests. Shepenwepet was the first of a series of women whose influence continued for two centuries.

The 24th Dynasty
The internal affairs of the country reached the bottom. Not only two royal institutions but several others claimed the throne. On the day King Sheshonq V died, several princes proclaimed their right to the throne, declaring themselves kings in Bubastis. One of the most important of these was the prince of the city of Sais, west of the Delta. Named Tefnakht, he founded a new royal institution, that of the 24th Dynasty. However, another king was competing with him in Herakleopolis, a second in Hermopilis, a third in Bubastis, and a fourth in Tanis. While all these catastrophes were underway in the Delta, the priests in Thebes continued to rule peacefully. Unlike his fellow princes, Tefnakht, was far more powerful and ambitious, and, desirous of making his title valid, he insisted on reuniting the states as they had

been before. He also insisted on making Egypt, with all its dynasties, into one empire as it had been in the times of its greatness.

Tefnakht succeeded in submitting all the states west of the Delta to his rule followed by those in the east, leaving each prince who recognized him as king in his position; eventually the whole of the Delta submitted to his rule. He then turned his attention to Middle Egypt, but things were different there. The poor conditions that led Tefnakht to try and save Egypt had apparently inspired others to do the same. In fact, King Piy (Piankhy) sent an army to liberate the country from the chaos it was in from Napata in northern Sudan. And so the army of Piy fought the army of Tefnakht, followed by the army of his son Bakenrenef (Bocchoris). The conflict ended with the victory of the southern army and the foundation of a new royal dynasty, the 25th, and a new era of renaissance for Egypt.

(Mamduh el-Damaty)

The Kushite Kings (25th Dynasty)

Egypt was torn by divisions during the first half of the eighth century that terminated in a period of political instability. It was then that the 24th Dynasty lived its last moments, as the conquerors who came from the south seized power. Their reigns constituted a transitional period between the two great periods of Egyptian history. Some historians consider it the last dynasty of the Third Intermediate Period, while others regard it as the first of the Late Period.

Far to the south, the ancient country of Kush had been under Egyptian rule for centuries; but, at the beginning of the eighth century BC, it underwent a radical reorganization, becoming a new kingdom under the capital of Napata. The holy mountain of Gebel Barkal housed an ancient sanctuary dedicated to Amun—a god who had very quickly been adopted by the local population—and hence the Kushite kings, like their eternal rivals to the north, styled themselves "sons of Amun."

As the power of the clergy at Karnak was crumbling, that of Napata was becoming more firmly established, and the political weakness of Upper Egypt offered the Kushite kings their chance to take revenge against the Egyptian pharaohs. It may even be true that the last of the great high priests actually sought refuge in Kush; what is however true, is that, when he

11. Statuette of Taharqo paying tribute to the god Hemen, 25th Dynasty.
Paris, Musée du Louvre

following pages
12. View of the remains of Taharqo's kiosk at Karnak, 25th Dynasty

13. Sphinx head of Shabaqo from the temple of Amun at Karnak, pink granite, 25th Dynasty. Cairo, Egyptian Museum

marched on Thebes, Kashta presented himself as a restorer of order in the name of Amun. His policy would be followed by his successors.

The first attempts to conquer Upper Egypt established only temporary control over the region. It was Piy who managed to establish Napata's firm grip on Thebes. Tefnakht, the king of Sais, put up a feeble resistance, which actually resulted in the Kushite forces marching further north (as far as Memphis). Piy then took steps to consolidate his control over Thebes, imposing his sister, Amenirdis I, as the new "god's wife of Amun." At his death, he was succeeded by his brother Shabaqo.

The new kings were hard put to establish their authority. Shabaqo had to fight Tefnakht's successor, Bakenrenef, whom he defeated. His nephews—Shabitqo and Taharqo—thereafter ruled through a period of relative stability, while their sister Shepenwepet II took over from Amenirdis I as the "god's wife of Amun." At the beginning of the seventh century BC, the authority of Shabitqo was sufficiently solid for him to intervene in the Near East, sending troops against the Assyrians—admittedly in a most *ad hoc* fashion.

Taharqo was undoubtedly the most striking monarch of this dynasty. Having ascended to the throne around 690 BC, he would rule for twenty-five years. During the early years of that reign Egypt enjoyed a period of peace, with the Delta almost entirely under Kushite control. Taharqo also followed up his brother's diplomatic policy, forming alliances with the old vassals of Egypt against the growing power of the Assyrians, whose advance was halted momentarily by some Egyptian successes in the field. However, in the end Taharqo could not withstand the increasing Assyrian might, and was crushingly defeated. At that point, he fell back towards Napata, while a new Assyrian-backed power was established in Sais.

Tanutamani, Shabaqo's son, took up the cause abandoned by his uncle and tried to reconquer Upper Egypt. The response was devastating: the Assyrian forces backing the Saite king crushed the Kushite troops and then seized and sacked Thebes in 663 BC. This marked the end of any hope for the restoration of the kingdom under the aegis of the Karnak deity of Amun.

In spite of their limited resources, the Kushite kings had tried to restore the ancient prestige of Amun; however, their contribution to the embellishment of Karnak was limited, and is known to us today mainly by the colonnades that they had built in front of the main entrances to the sanctuary of Amun (fig. 12). The "god's wives" also had several chapels built within the precincts of the temple; and the construction that Taharqo commissioned near the sacred lake carried on a tradition that dated back to the New Kingdom (it was intended to house rituals associated with Amun and Osiris and concerned with the renewal of royal power). However, in spite of their attachment to Thebes, the Kushite kings were buried in their land of origin, where one can see the remains of their pyramids in the el-Kurru necropolis downstream from the fourth cataract; Taharqo himself had his tomb built at Nuri, closer to Napata.

The kings of the Kushite dynasty are easy to recognize because of their distinctive iconography. In effect, they are shown wearing a simple skullcap or headband, and in both relief-sculptures and statues they are shown with a double *uraeus*, contrary to the usual single *uraeus* of the pharaohs. In fact, when the Saite dynasty came to power, the second of these divine cobras was eliminated from as many Kushite monuments as possible. Undoubtedly, the kings of the 25th Dynasty had doubled this traditional symbol of the Egyptian monarchy, combining it with another serpent, the symbol of the lands of the South (upstream from the first cataract). In doing so, they had failed to understand that the pharaoh's single *uraeus* was originally intended as one of the various symbols of the unity of Upper and Lower Egypt.
(*Isabelle Franco*)

Bibliography
On the history of the Third Intermediate Period, see Kitchen 1986. On the city of Tanis and the discovery of the tombs and their furnishings, see Paris 1987 and Stierlin, Ziegler 1987. On the kingdom of Kush, see Wildung 1997.

At the beginning of the seventh century BC, Nekau I, prince of Sais, succeeded in maneuvering between the two powers of Assyria and Ethiopia. To propitiate Taharqo, he married an Ethiopian princess with whom he had a son, Psamtek, the future pharaoh of reunified Egypt. As an Assyrian subject, we find him, after a stay in Nineveh, back in Sais, loaded with favors for himself and his son Psamtek who, raised at the Assyrian court under the name of Nabu-shezibanni ("Nabu protect me"), then obtained the principality of Athribis in the Delta. Nekau I died soon after returning to Sais, around 643 BC, about the same year as the demise of Taharqo, the Napatan king.

Psamtek (the name means "He of the mixed wine") is the founder of the 26th Dynasty, that Manetho calls "Saite" after the city of Sais, the family birthplace. His reign, lasting over fifty years (664–610 BC), enabled him to restore to Egypt its unity and political and economic stability (thanks to fiscal and administrative reforms, including the use throughout Egypt of the demotic script, formed in the bureaucracy of the Delta), along with an artistic renewal that looked back to the classical models of the Old Kingdom and the 12th Dynasty.

We are indebted to the History of Herodotus, the Greek historian and traveler who was in Egypt around 450 BC, for a great deal of information, often anecdotal yet not negligible, about Saite and Persian Egypt. For the beginning of the dynasty, we cannot ignore the passage in Herodotus' History (II, 152–153) about the "bronze men," whose arrival on the coast of Egypt had been predicted to Psamtek I, Nekau's son, by an oracle of Buto; these were Greek mercenaries from Ionia in Asia Minor, and Carians, inhabitants of Caria, who had a decisive importance for the Saite sovereigns, and became materially and culturally enriched in hospitable Egypt.

Further in the seventh century colonizers of various Greek origins founded the city of Naukratis in the western Delta, which was of such great importance for Phoenician traffic in the Mediterranean. Herodotus attributes a spirit of scientific curiosity to the Saite sovereigns that was probably that of the cultivated Greeks of the time. Supposedly Psamtek I (Herodotus, II, 28) had experimentally proven the abyssal depth of the two sources of the Nile at Elephantine, dropping a cable there thousands of meters long without touching bottom; and he was curious to find out (Herodotus, II, 2) which people had been the first to appear on earth, by verifying in what language two children raised in total isolation would pronounce their first word. The word was bekos, which the court experts identified as the word "bread" in Phrygian, so the pharaoh was convinced by the experiment that the oldest people were not Egyptian but Phrygian. According to Herodotus (IV, 42–43) Nekau II (610–595 BC) attempted to connect the Mediterranean with the Red Sea, commissioning Phoenician navigators to carry out the circumnavigation of Africa. The best-known episode during the reign of Psamtek II (595–589 BC) was the expedition (592 BC) to Ethiopia, testified by the countless graffiti engraved on the knees of one of the colossi of Abu Simbel, written by the members of the expedition in Greek (including the famous inscription of Potasimto), Carian and Phoenician.

Apries (589–570 BC) failed in his intervention to help Zedekiah of Judah, and was even more unfortunate in helping the Libyan king of Cyrene. The Egyptian army (Herodotus IV, 159) was crushed at Nasa, on the Libyan coast, and the general Ahmose, instead of appeasing the uprisings against Apries (who was accused of philhellenism), took advantage of them to be proclaimed king. In the civil war that ensued, Apries was defeated and died soon after. We know hardly anything about the family of the usurper Ahmose (570–526 BC) whom Herodotus says came from the city of Siuf in the vicinity of Sais; of plebeian birth, he was certainly an excellent pharaoh, a shrewd politician, and a good administrator (he made useful alliances with Cyrene, Samos, Lydia, and with the Greeks of the Ionian coast; and spread his rule to Cyprus, without seeking to intervene in Asia, where Persia was becoming a great empire under Cyrus II). It may well be that the amused, slightly scandalous portrait Herodotus left of Ahmose reflects the personality of the soldier turned pharaoh; hints of it also appear in Egyptian tradition in a story that has come down to us in demotic script on a papyrus dating from the Ptolemaic period.

The last pharaoh of the 26th Dynasty, Psamtek III (526–525 BC) was defeated and captured by the Persian king Cambyses, Cyrus' son, in the battle of Pelusium. That was in 525 BC. Egypt, with Cyprus and Phoenicia, then became part of the Achaemenid empire, the sixth

2. Graywacke head of General
Ahmose from Sais.
Berlin, Ägyptisches Museum
und Papyrussammlung
cat. 21

of the twenty satrapies. Manetho's 26th Dynasty, or "First Persian domination," includes Cambyses, who died in 522 BC in Syria on his way back from Persia, and in sequence, Darius I (521–486 BC), Xerxes I (486–465 BC), Artaxerxes I (465–424 BC), Darius II (423–405 BC) and Artaxerxes II (405–359 BC), who was acknowledged in Egypt at least until 404 BC. Cambyses meant to present himself to the conquered country as a pharaoh. He had an official protocol drawn up "as had been done for the preceding kings," choosing for his enthronement the name Mesut-ra ("scion of Ra"). In a significant legend, reported by Herodotus and Athenaeus, Cambyses became the descendant of the last legitimate king of the Saite dynasty, Apries, as the son of Cyrus and a daughter of the Egyptian pharaoh.

Between 525 and 522 BC, Cambyses remained in Egypt, occupied, according to the model of the Saite kings that inspired him, with three "African" campaigns: against Carthage, against the Libyan Desert oases and against Nubia, military expeditions that were complete failures. The Greek authors (Herodotus, Diodorus, Strabo, Plutarch) all agree in describing Cambyses' behavior in Egypt as insane, sacrilegious and cruel, yet direct testimonies that were contemporary with this sovereign should put such views in a proper perspective. Behind the anti-Cambyses tradition, and aside from an obvious resentment against the invader, we can discern the bitterness caused in the Egyptian sacerdotal class by a decree (an extract of it is transcribed on the demotic papyrus in Paris, Bibliothèque Nationale 215, from the Ptolemaic period), whereby Cambyses tried to reduce, with a prudent thriftiness, the royal subsidies to the Egyptian sanctuaries.

For Herodotus and Diodorus, Cambyses' death, brought on by a wound infected with gangrene, was punishment for his impiety, which was in contrast with the piety of his successor, Darius I (521–486 BC), whose virtue was praised; according to the Egyptian priests' reckoning, this meant his generosity toward the temples. It is not surprising to find on a stele (now in the Berlin Museum) good king Darius made divine and worshipped in the form of the falcon Horus, the major god of pharaonic royalty. Diodorus has good grounds for listing Darius I as the sixth and last legislator of Egypt: actually the Achaemenid ruler ordained, in the third year of his reign, the codification—that is, to set down in writing—in demotic of the regulations in force in Egypt until the forty-fourth year of Ahmose's reign, including private, religious and public law, having them translated concurrently into Aramaic for the satrap, who represented the power of the king of Persia in the provinces of the Persian empire. The satrap resided with his chancellery at Memphis, but he employed a great number of civil servants and soldiers of different nationalities all over the territory, reflecting the variety of the provinces of the Achaemenid empire, Persian, Median, Babylonian, Chorasmian, Judean, Aramaean, Phoenician, Syrian, Ionian, Carian, as well as Egyptian, since the overall administrative structure of the country remained the same. The military garrisons were on the borders of the country, at Marea, Daphnae, Elephantine–Aswan, as they had been during the Saite era. In order to increase contacts between Persia and the Egyptian satrapy, Darius I established a connection with the Red Sea by means of the old Nilotic canal that flowed into Lake Timsah (approximately present-day Ismailiya) and then through the Bitter Lakes, which made it possible to go from Bubastis all the way to the Red Sea in four days of navigation. All along the canal, Darius I had erected his colossal celebratory stelae with hieroglyphic, cuneiform and even bilingual texts. The visit Darius I undertook to the Egyptian satrapy in the twenty-seventh year of his reign (495 BC) may have been connected with the opening of the new waterway from Persia to the Nile valley.

The bilingualism in these commemorative monuments was certainly used as political propaganda; the same spirit also inspired the great statue of Darius I in Persian garb, covered with hieroglyphic and cuneiform inscriptions, that was discovered in 1972 at Susa (west-

3. Neophorous statue of Udjahorresnet, court physician of Cambyses and Darius I. Città del Vaticano, Museo Gregoriano Egizio

4. *Shabti*s of the pharaoh Hakor.
Paris, Musée du Louvre

opposite page
5. The temple of Darius in the
Kharga Oasis, Late Period, 27th
Dynasty

following pages
6. Relief representing Nectanebo I.
Bologna, Museo Civico Archeologico

ern Iran), which had been carved in Egypt out of stone from the quarries of Wadi Hammamat and probably taken to Persia by Xerxes.

The protection that Darius I "The Great" granted to the Egyptian temples and priests can also be observed in the construction of a grandiose temple dedicated to Amun at Hibis in the Kharga Oasis. The caravan routes of the Western Desert oases were of great importance in the Achaemenid era, much like maritime traffic in the Mediterranean. Exceptional proof of this can be found in a "Customs register" in Aramaic dated in the eleventh year of Xerxes' reign (475 BC) recently brought to the attention of scholars, in which are recorded the accounts of customs duty levied on the ships that stopped over at Tanis on the Canopic branch of the Nile, which was under the satrap's control. The boats arrived laden with gold, silver, wine from Ionia and Sidon, oil, wood, metal and wool, and departed with cargoes of Egyptian materials, especially natron, the Egyptian sodium carbonate that was highly prized in antiquity, in particular for making glass, which was widely produced in Asia Minor, especially in Phoenicia.

Under Artaxerxes I (465–424), the Lybian rebel Inaros, son of Psamtek, asked for Athens' assistance, and a fleet of two hundred Greek ships sailed to Memphis, conquering two-thirds of it. Memphis was then recaptured by Megabyzus, a satrap from Syria, and Inaros was seized

and killed (454 BC). Artaxerxes' reign ended peacefully, whereas Athens, after the Peace of Callias in 449, was forced to stay out of Egyptian affairs. We know little about the relationship between Egypt and Persia during the years of Darius II. A rich, but particular source from this period is the Aramaic Elephantine papyri, precious for providing insights into the affairs of the Judaic colony established there since the days of the Saite kings. Between 411 and 408 the disorders at Elephantine led to the destruction of the temple of Yahweh on the island, a temple that in any case, after the reconstruction of the temple of Jerusalem that Cyrus had granted to the Jews, was no longer legitimate.

Egypt won back and kept its independence during the 28th, 29th and 30th Dynasties. Amyrtaios of Sais (404–399 BC) is the only representative of the 28th Dynasty, that was followed by the 29th, founded by Nepherites (399–393 BC) from Mendes in the Delta. His successor Hakor, who, however, did not belong to Nepherites' family, occupied the throne for some time (393–380 BC). Then, royal power passed to Nectanebo I from Sebennytos, which gave rise to the 30th Dynasty, whose sovereigns were able to restore the country's stability and prestige, vigorously defending Egypt from Persian attempts at reconquest and engaging in complicated alliances with Greece.

Nectanebo I gained the support of the priests through a device related on the Naukratis Stele, that consisted of levying customs duty on merchandise arriving in the port of Naukratis and assigning ten percent to the temple of Neith at Sais. Teos, Nectanebo I's son, was even able to intervene militarily with some success in Syria, but his uncle's usurpation of the throne in favor of his own son Nectanebo, forced him to seek refuge at the Persian court in 360 BC. Nectanebo II, who was responsible for a considerable building activity in the Delta, organized his own cult during his lifetime under the guise of the falcon-god Horus; however, his opposition to the Persian invasion failed, and in 343 BC, vanquished by Artaxerxes III Ochus, he fled to Nubia.

The second Persian rule lasted but ten years; after the battle of Issus in which Darius III Codommanus was defeated, Egypt was ready to welcome Alexander the Great.

The Egyptian priests, creators of nationalistic legends during the Hellenistic era, declared that Alexander the Great, far from being a foreign conqueror, was instead the son of the last Nectanebo who, on fleeing to Macedonia, where he was hailed as a great magician, seduced Olympias, queen of Macedonia and wife of Philip II, under the guise of the god Amun, and thus was Alexander's father, a pharaoh in his own right according to the old pharaonic "theogamic" dogma. Alexander, who died of malaria in Babylon in 323 BC, was succeeded by his half-brother Philip Arrhidaeus (killed in 317), then by Alexander IV, the posthumous son of Alexander the Great and the Persian princess Roxana. In the Nile valley, the satrap was the old general and companion of the great Macedonian, Ptolemy, who took up the title of king of Egypt on November 7, 305 BC, founding the Ptolemaic dynasty. Ptolemy I took the byname Soter, which means "Saviour" in Greek.

Ptolemy I was the one who conveyed the remains of Alexander the Great to Egypt, whose first burial place was probably at the Memphite necropolis of Saqqara. If we are to believe Pausanias, it was Macedonian in style, that is, a tumulus mausoleum. The Macedonian's tomb in Alexandria, where his remains were transferred, perhaps in 285 BC, was also Macedonian in style (according to Diodorus and Strabo). Alexander's tomb was in the Soma, the Ptolemaic sovereigns' necropolis, where he was placed in a golden coffin until Ptolemy XI replaced it with one of alabaster. Alexander's tomb in the city that bears his name was visited in Roman times by Augustus, Caligula and other emperors, including Caracalla.

The dynasty of the Ptolemies ended with Cleopatra VII with the defeat of the Egyptian fleet at Actium by Augustus Octavian; on August 31, 30 BC, Octavian entered Alexandria.

Bibliography
Elgood 1951; Kienitz 1953; Curto 1981; Bresciani 1985; Boardman 1980; Lloyd 1988; Pernigotti, Piacentini, Davoli 1988; Vernus, Yoyotte 1988; Donadoni 1990; Grimal 1990; Clayton 1994; Bowman 1997; Gardiner 1997; Donadoni 1999; Bresciani 2000; Bresciani 2001.

7. Limestone relief with Nectanebo
adoring the Apis bull, from Saqqara,
Late Period, 30th Dynasty.
Paris, Musée du Louvre
cat. 22

8. Relief with Ptolemy III and
Cleopatra, from Karnak.
Berlin, Ägyptisches Museum
und Papyrussammlung
cat. 23

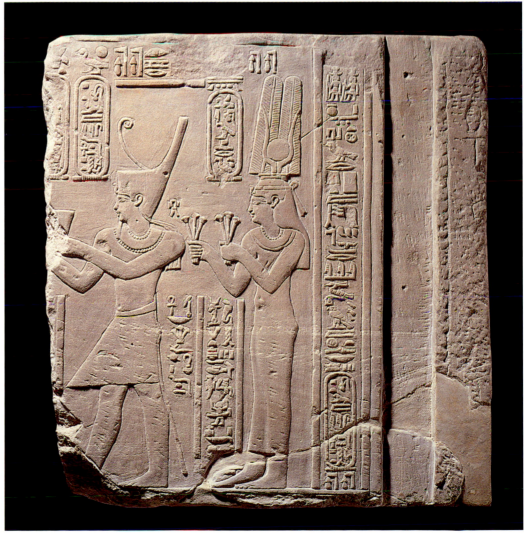

Pharaonic Regality. The Nature of Power

Introduction: Permanence and Development

The power basis of the Egyptian monarchy had certain original characteristics which ultimately made it into a model for numerous other states in the region. However, undoubtedly the most remarkable aspect of this monarchy was its durability: already part of a clear power structure at the beginning of the third millennium BC, it was only in the sixth century BC that it began to make way for foreign governments of different types—the Persian empire, the Ptolemaic monarchy and, finally, the Roman empire. Previous to this, although repeatedly destabilized as a result of internal or external factors, the Egyptian monarchy always managed to reemerge from its ashes in a form more suited to the geopolitical situation of the day. It could do this thanks to two advantages which, at first sight, might appear contradictory, but were really complementary: an in-built character of continuity and an ability to adapt. From the Thinite era onward, the ideology of monarchical power in Egypt contained certain key concepts that all successive pharaohs strove to maintain intact. This—together with the constant reference to the divine origins of the state rulers (or, at least, of the more orthodox of the pharaohs)—led the Egyptians to present their institutions as somehow immutable over time. However, throughout its long history, the Egypt of the pharaohs was closely bound up with the history of the region as a whole, and thus changing events meant that royal power had to develop new expressions of itself if it was to maintain a strong basis.

The prestige of the figure of the pharaoh helped to perpetuate this image of unchanging power both inside and outside the country. The Egyptian model would in effect be exported to Nubia and the Near East, where it would be adapted to local institutions in such states as Kerma and Byblos, which were most directly within the Egyptian sphere of influence. Subsequent conquerors of Egypt would recognize the specific nature of this monarchy and strive to understand it in order to administer it and preserve its more original characteristics (indeed, they would import homeward those features that served to reinforce their own authority).

The Royal and the Divine

The Origins of Egyptian Royalty

Complete or anecdotal, ancient or more recent, all accounts of the myth of the Egyptian state agree on one point: before human sovereigns, it was the gods who ruled on earth. The Heliopolitan cosmogony, having achieved a predominance that had since been unequalled, was the most often presented family of divinities invested with monarchic authority at the dawn of history. Ra, the sun-god Creator, begot Shu and Tefnut, who in turn begot Geb and Nut. This latter couple then had four children who formed two couples, Isis and Osiris and Nephthys and Seth.

The heir to the throne, Osiris, was murdered and dismembered by his brother, Seth. However, the victim's widow, Isis, traveled throughout Egypt to reassemble the scattered parts of his body and thence resuscitate her husband long enough to bear him an heir, Horus. The fate of Osiris, the god destined to die and be reborn, establishes a link between the world of deities and the world of mortals. Horus would initially pass on this paternal inheritance to hybrid creatures known as "the followers of Horus," but then his heritage would pass on to mortal sovereigns. Various lists of monarchs—for example, the Turin Canon and Manetho's *Aegyptiaca*—thus catalog the heirs to the throne of Egypt as comprising gods, spirits, demigods and finally mortals.

As a god of the heavens like Ra—the prototype of all gods—Horus was, at one and the same time, the god of origins, the patron of Hierakonpolis (one of the first principalities in the Nile valley) and the son of Osiris. The confusion of these deities—all of them represented by a falcon—made Horus into the link between the heavenly royalty of the gods and the terrestrial royalty of men. This is what is expressed, from the very earliest of the monarchs, by the "Horus name" attributed to the pharaohs. Their divine assimilation through the mechanisms of religion meant that these mortals could actually exercise power as Horus. This bestowal of royal status by the god Horus was one of the recurrent themes in the iconography of royal statuary, taking on various forms over the centuries. Hence, for example, the death of a sovereign was described in these terms—"This falcon has taken flight toward heaven"—and his successor would be said to ascend to "the throne of Horus among the living."

1. Faience "Golden Horus," from el-Ashmunein, 30th Dynasty. New York, The Metropolitan Museum of Art
cat. 41

2. Graywack triad of Menkaura
from the valley temple in Giza,
Old Kingdom, 4th Dynasty.
Cairo, Egyptian Museum

3. View of the *hwt-ka*
of Mentuhotep II.
Cairo, Egyptian Museum

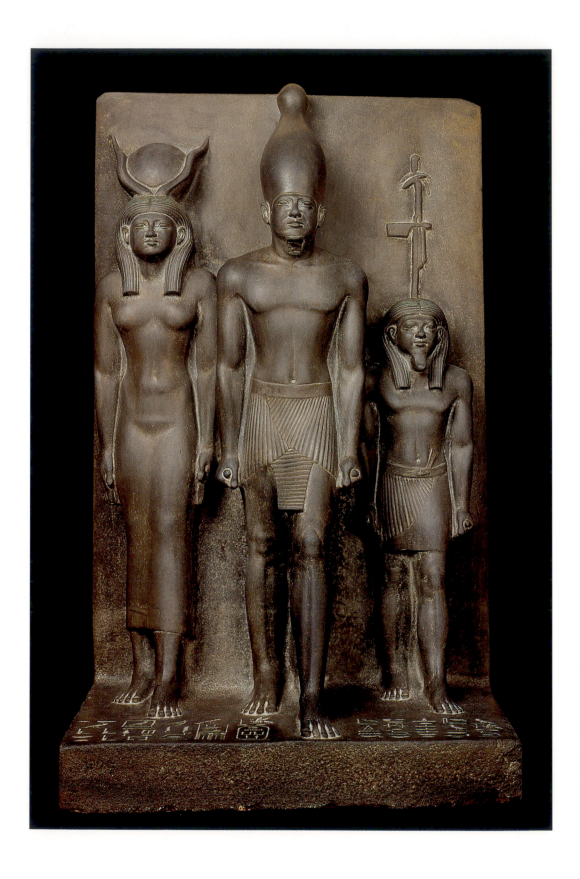

4. Sandstone relief with royal titulary of Amenhotep I, New Kingdom, 19th Dynasty.
Copenhagen, Ny Carlsberg Glyptotek
cat. 36

The Constant Reaffirmation of the Divine Character of Royalty
Literature and iconography from all periods of Egyptian history bear witness to the sacred character of the pharaoh's royalty. The name of "son of Ra," which is known to have been used from the 4th Dynasty onward, was one of the clearest demonstrations of this divine descent of the monarch. The sovereign was often presented as the child of some of the country's most important deities—Aten, Ra, Amun—or else as the heir to the throne of the gods. "It is my father. I am his son. He ordered me to take my place on his throne while I was in his nest. He begot me with the seed of his desire." Thus proclaims Thutmose III in the *Text of Youth* inscribed at the very heart of the temple of Karnak.

If the new king's rights of succession were not sufficiently indisputable, they might be strengthened by an appeal to divine conception: it was the god himself who had visited the queen to conceive the future heir. This principle was first used in the Middle Kingdom, occurring in one of the stories in the Westcar Papyrus to explain the origins of the 5th Dynasty. It later reappeared in the 18th Dynasty, at the temple of Deir el-Bahri to justify the royal status of Queen Hatshepsut, and in the royal *ka*-temple at Luxor to justify that of Amenhotep III.

The formal recognition of the new king by the dynastic god Amun within the context of oracular processions first occurred when Thutmose II died and both his widow Hatshepsut and his son Thutmose III laid claim to the blessing of the lord of Karnak.

There were also many other ways of expressing the divine nature of royalty and those who embodied it. In the Pyramid Texts, for example, the king appropriates to himself the various parts of the bodies of the gods; in succession he transforms himself into Atum, Horus and Anubis. Having died, he becomes Osiris, and—the papyri of Abusir tell us—a statue of him in the form of that god was worshipped in his funerary temple. During his lifetime, the pharaoh might associate his own effigy with that of the gods, and thus be worshipped at the sanctuaries of the main deities of the country. However, it was only much later—during the reigns of Amenhotep III and Rameses II—that the sovereign would, in the worship of his own image, see his effigy adorned with a tangible sign of deification: the horn of the ram.

The Principles of Royal Ideology
Maat
Although recounted in various different versions, the creation of the world primarily consisted in producing an organized universe from a turbid primordial ocean inhabited by beings of uncertain nature. The creation of the state came soon afterward, with the demiurge also being the founder of royalty. Subsequently, two essential but conflicting principles emerged: *maat* and *isefet*. The former described that harmony essential to the flowering of

5. Red granite statue of a praying baboon with a royal figure, from Memphis, 18th Dynasty (?). Vienna, Kunsthistorisches Museum
cat. 63

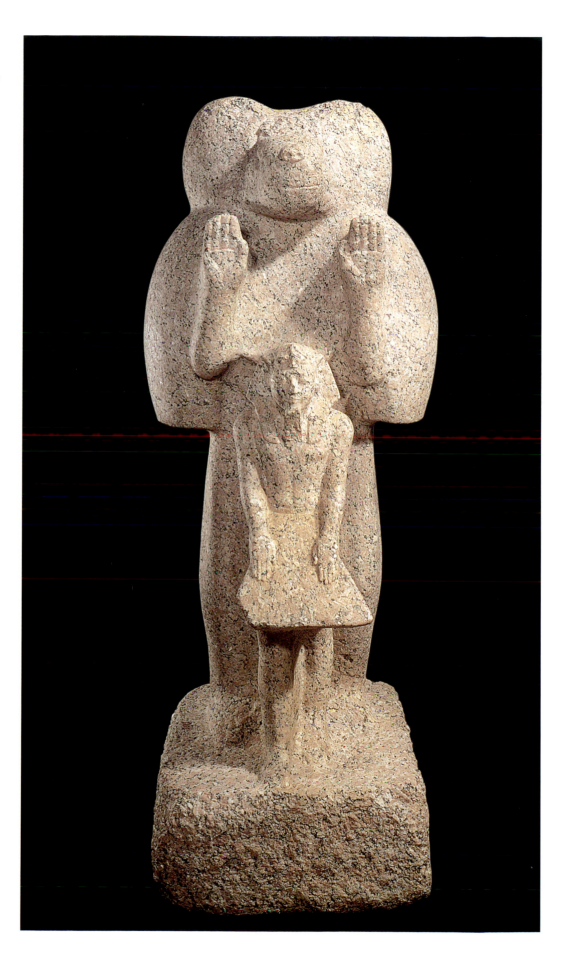

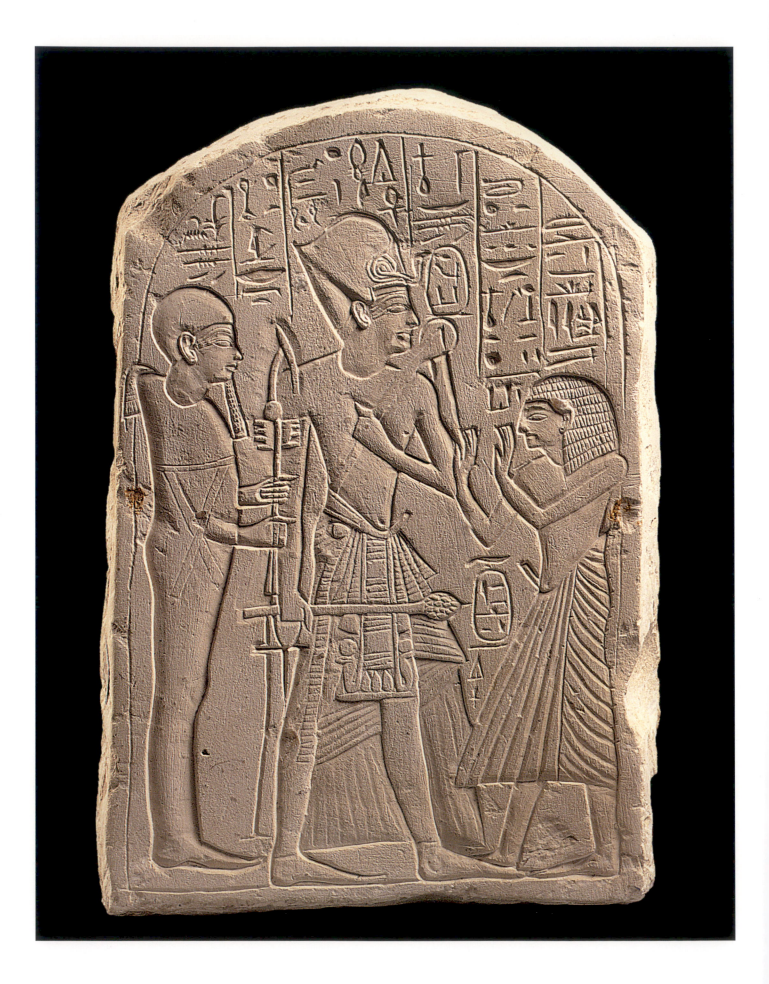

6. Sandstone votive stele from Deir el-Medina, New Kingdom, late 18th Dynasty.
Turin, Museo Egizio
cat. 60

7. Ramesside pharaoh making an offering of Maat, gold and silver, New Kingdom, 19th Dynasty.
Paris, Musée du Louvre
cat. 79

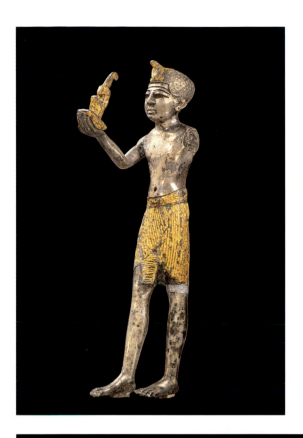

8. Granite statue of Amun represented as a ram protecting Amenhotep III, from Soleb, New Kingdom, 18th Dynasty.
Berlin, Agyptisches Museum und Papyrussammlung
cat. 64

9. Wooden decorative element in the name of Sehibra, 23rd Dynasty. Bologna, Museo Civico Archeologico
cat. 81

10. Limestone relief with Merenptah smiting his enemies, New Kingdom, 19th Dynasty.
The University of Pennsylvania, Museum of Archeology and Anthropology
cat. 91

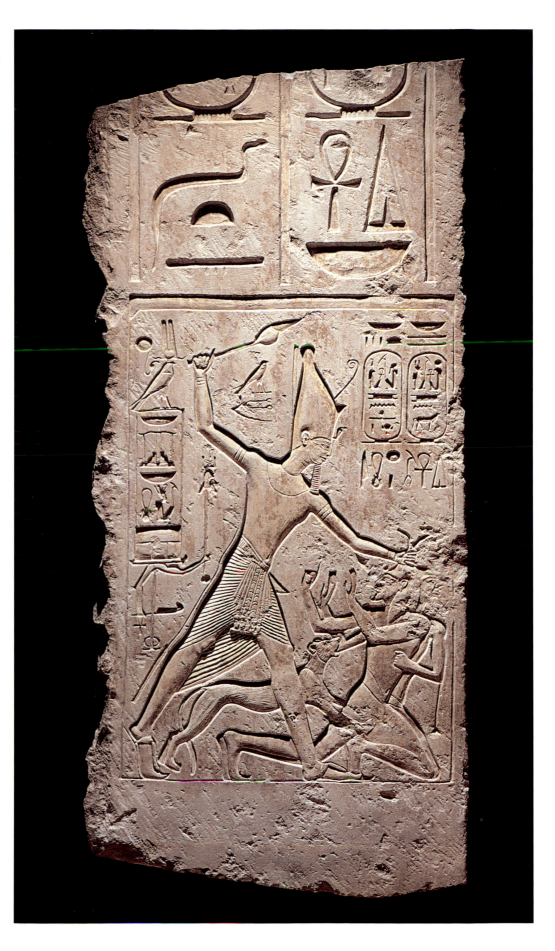

11. Ostracon with king carried
in a chair by porters from
Deir el-Medina, New Kingdom,
19th–20th Dynasties.
Berlin, Agyptisches Museum
und Papyrussammlung
cat. 121

the state, while the latter indicated all possible disturbances therein—be they natural or man-made (earthquakes, tempests, tidal waves, civil wars, epidemics, etc.). Thus one of the most sacred duties of the Egyptian monarch was to bring about the triumph of *maat* over *isefet*. The *Prophecy of Neferty* announced: "*Maat* will return to its place. *Isefet* having been driven out."

First mentioned in the 3rd Dynasty as an abstract concept, *maat* would from the Old Kingdom onward gradually take on the form of a female deity, adorned with a headband holding an ostrich feather. This latter detail indicated the notion of lightness and, therefore, of justice. It was doubtless this aspect of the goddess which led to the title "priest of Maat" being awarded to the directors of the "six great mansions," who functioned as "ministers of Justice" from the 5th Dynasty onward. The same feature was also developed in the moralistic texts of the private autobiographies written at the end of the Old Kingdom.

During the period of the First Intermediate Period, we encounter the expression: "Raise Maat toward the Great God, Lord of Heaven." Within a private context, this lays the bases for the ritual of the king's offering or presentation of Maat—something which would only make its actual appearance during the reign of Thutmose III (and thereafter become an essential function of the monarch).

As monarchical ideology developed, so did the meaning of the concepts associated with the goddess. Various hymns dating from the New Kingdom point out that both gods and kings live by *maat*. Hatshepsut declared: "I have glorified Maat which he [the god] loves, because I know he lives thanks to her. She is also my bread and I drink her dew, being of one body with him."

From the reign of Sety I onward, the offering of the goddess was regularly associated with the offering of the royal name.

History at the Service of Ritual

Accounts of the exploits of the gods occurred alongside the descriptions of historic events; hence texts and the iconography of Egyptian temples established close links between history and myth. A comparative study of the information relating to actual events and depictions that do not fit in with any actual political context raises the question of the significance of these references within a religious context. While the references to the pharaoh's campaigns abroad served to underline the power necessary to the ruler if he was to perform both his secular and religious functions, the depictions of Egyptian victories or the presence of certain countries in the lists of regions under the pharaoh's power did not necessarily have to correspond to a precise geopolitical conjuncture: victory was an intrinsic necessity of royal power, and hence ritual celebration thereof was performed regardless of the occasion. Raising doubts about such matters would be tantamount to admitting the legitimacy of chaos. This is why the Egyptians would continue to reproduce scenes of the massacre of their enemies from the dawn of their history to the very end of paganism—the oldest extant example being on King Scorpion's mace head, the latest on the pylons of temples dating from the Roman era. These show the sovereign seizing Egypt's enemies by the hair with one hand, while he wields a mace with the other. The iconography of the scene might be added to in time, but the initial content remained intact; this was in effect not the commemoration of a contemporary victory but the expression of an apotropaic ritual that protected the country against real or potential enemies. The accounts and detailed depictions of actual victories breathed new vigor into this ritual depiction, giving it a kind of veracity. Such depictions of real triumphs were only occasional during the period of the Middle Kingdom, but became more numerous as Egypt built itself an empire in Nubia and the Near East; whole walls at Karnak, the Ramesseum and Medinet Habu are dedicated to them.

Hunting was another expression of power in arms. From the Old Kingdom onward, the wall decorations in his funerary temple showed the dead monarch harpooning the hippopotamus, an animal that symbolized the forces of evil that threatened the monarchy and the peace necessary to its existence. Later, during the New Kingdom, Thutmose III, Amenhotep III and Rameses III became renowned as great hunters of elephants, lions and bulls respectively.

12. Fragment of painted sandstone relief with dignitaries, from Asasif (Thebes), New Kingdom, 19th Dynasty.
Cairo, Egyptian Museum
cat. 106

13. Basalt stele of the Vizier
Parahotep, from Sedment el-Gebel,
New Kingdom, 19th Dynasty.
Cairo, Egyptian Museum
cat. 131

The Expression of Power
The Image of the Sovereign

In bas-relief or three-dimensional sculpture, the image of the sovereign was omnipresent in ancient Egypt. Adorning the walls of temples and rock or standing stelae, this image proclaimed various aspects of royalty; and like the statues of the deities, it could become the object of religious veneration. In the temples of the Old Kingdom, the statues of deities and the monarch occupied alternate niches in the most sacred part of the sanctuary, and received the same physical attention as did the actual body of the pharaoh when alive: ablutions, unguents, incense, vestments and food. Strictly speaking, these practices did not signify that the king was considered as divine, but rather that his effigy, associated with those of the gods whom he had succeeded on the throne of Egypt, required the same ritual as those of the gods, if it were to perform its role properly in its present setting.

There were different sorts of royal statues—some monumental, some destined for sacred areas, and some reserved for the celebration of particular festivities. Each one had a specific form according to a specific function. While certain colossal statues—placed at the doorways to temples or in courtyards accessible to a large public—might serve as intercessors between the human and divine world, other smaller statues, in wood or rare stone, showed the monarch dressed in particular vestments or performing a particular rite. When they were not in use, these latter statues were deposited in crypts (groups of them are depicted at various points in the temple of Karnak, for example).

The iconography of king and falcon was particularly important in expressing the relation between royalty and divinity. During the Old Kingdom, numerous statues showed the king seated on his throne, receiving royal power and divine blessing from the god Horus (depicted in his usual form of a falcon, with outspread wings behind the king's head); the most famous of these statues is that of Khafra now in the Cairo Museum. During the Middle Kingdom, the king himself was depicted as a falcon, while during the Thutmoside regency he often bore the plumage of a falcon. From the New Kingdom onward, groups of statues depicted a falcon-god of variable identity (sometimes Horus, sometimes Montu) and small effigies of the monarch (shown walking, crouching or else mummified). The royal effigies here might be replaced by royal cartouches.

The Worship of the Sovereign

All these statues bear witness to the worship of the—living or dead—sovereign not as an individual but as the embodiment of the very principle of monarchy. Since they can be traced back to the Thinite rulers, it would seem that this worship was an integral part of Egyptian monarchy. The gradual development of the institution of the *hwt-ka* (the "*ka*-chapel")— the *ka* being that vital force animating all beings, be they divine, royal or simple mortals—ultimately led to the worship of the image of the living monarch within provincial sanctuaries of gods. The sovereigns of the 6th Dynasty instigated this worship as part of the celebration of their jubilees. As various indirect sources and architectural fragments indicate, this kind of worship was also extended to include members of the royal family and even some high functionaries (viziers, nomarchs or governors of the Dakhla Oasis). The only royal *hwt-ka* which has come down to us intact is the one Mentuhotep II had built within the chapel of Hathor during the 11th Dynasty.

While this institution became infrequent during the New Kingdom, another form of worship of the sovereign had already emerged during the Second Intermediate Period: that based on the Temples of Millions of Years. These foundations were either an entire temple or part of an existing temple. In the former case, the worship of the sovereign was associated with that of a particular deity (this was the statute governing the foundation of most of the temples on the west bank at Thebes). In the latter case, the chapels were integrated in the chosen temples in the same way as the *hwt-ka*; here, one might mention such varying examples as Thutmose III's *Akhmenu*, Sety I's hypostyle hall, the Bubastite Portal at Karnak, or the building raised by Rameses IV at the sanctuary of Hathor, which controlled the turquoise deposits on the plateau of Serabit el-Khadim.

Throughout history, Egyptian architects also designed other types of monuments to serve as the setting for ceremonies celebrating the unfailing power of the monarchy. As examples one might cite the Djoser complex at Saqqara, Amenhotep III's royal *ka*-temple at Luxor, or the *sed*-festival hall built for the 22nd-Dynasty rulers Osorkon I and Osorkon II at Bubastis. The important annual religious feasts also included celebrations of the monarchy, during which statues of past pharaohs and of the reigning monarch were carried in procession and included in some of the rituals of worship.

The Exercise of Power

The Functions of the Monarchy

As the heir of the gods, the pharaoh had duties he had to perform for the deities themselves, for his predecessors and for his subjects. The most important functions of the monarchy, therefore, were religious. As a rule, the pharaoh was the only person who could order the building of a temple. From the Middle Kingdom onward, this entitlement found expression in the rite known as "giving the house to its lord." Widespread during the New Kingdom, this ritual was represented by the depiction of a frontal view of a chapel surrounded by a ditch that defined the new territory dedicated to the gods; the sovereign was shown consecrating the building or else throwing grains of incense onto the site to purify it. This ritual offering was closely bound up with rituals of foundation practiced during the Old Kingdom.

The decision to build certain temples and the work thereon is described in literary texts, which are sometimes reproduced on the walls of the building itself. According to the Berlin Leather Roll, Senusret I declared: "Now I have become like an Horus. Having pondered at length and after having guaranteed offerings to the gods, I shall undertake work in the Great Mansion of my father, Atum. He will fix its extent in relation to that which he will enable me to conquer." Passages from two parallel texts are conserved on blocks at the temple of Karnak; they concern the king's command for the building of a Great Mansion of Amun, which was rebuilt during the reign of Thutmose III.

The sovereign was also the only one who could really officiate at worship as a priest, as one can see from the innumerable decorations on the walls of temples throughout Egypt. The offering expressed the "exchange" that had to take place between the gods and the ruler if his reign was to be a fruitful one; the legends to the scenes depicted comment upon what is happening in commercial terms. For example, the king offers wine to Amun, who in turn rewards him with power and victory over every country. The pharaoh also guaranteed the performance of all sorts of rituals—for example, that of "divine adoration, four times"—which served to satisfy the gods. In return, the deities permitted the monarch to perform all the functions expected of a king: provider, legislator and warrior. Lord of the land of Egypt, the king was responsible for the produce and resources that were indispensable to his subjects' survival. Not only had the gods bestowed upon him the power to create laws, but they also entrusted him with the protection of the land against any form of aggression.

Delegates and Substitutes

However, when it came to officiating at worship, administering the country or ensuring military protection of its borders, the pharaoh could not be everywhere at the same time. Hence he had to have people who could act in his name throughout the nation. With regard to the actual veneration of the monarch, his place could be taken simply by a statue; but when an actual agent was required, the monarch had to rely on the services of priests and dignitaries. Undoubtedly, the most delicate case here was that of the celebration of jubilees throughout Egypt; whereas he himself participated at one of the ceremonies, he had to be substituted at the rituals held at all the other sanctuaries throughout the country. The Brooklyn papyrus, which apparently dates from the early period of the Persian rule, gives us some idea of what happened on such occasions: the monarch's place at the commemorative celebrations was taken by a figure known as "the king's priest."

As for the administration of the country, it was the vizier who took the sovereign's place on a day-to-day basis. It was he who received information from all the regions of the country and then drew up regular reports for his master; it was he who oversaw the assessment and collection of taxes; he who appointed most of the other functionaries; he who implemented royal decrees and laws; he who represented the highest level of appeal in administrative legal matters or in those which directly involved members of the royal family. However, as needs varied, other people might be appointed to represent the monarch, especially in the regions farthest from the court. This was the case, for example, with the governors of certain oases, the viceroys of Kush and those sent on special missions in the name of the pharaoh (during which they enjoyed certain royal prerogatives).

It was less easy for the monarch to delegate his military role, given that here—more than elsewhere—it was the very fate of the country that was at risk. Throughout Egyptian history, the pharaoh himself was supposed to lead his troops in combat, and the iconography never fails to proclaim this responsibility. However, in certain circumstances this might not be possible: for example, if there were a number of campaigns going on at the same time; if the ruler was too young or too old; if the throne was occupied by a woman or by someone whose state of health made them unfit for military life, etc. In such cases, wherever possible, it was the heir to the throne who received the honor of leading the royal armies into combat. For example, Senusret I was leading the Egyptian army in a campaign against the Libyans when his father, Amenemhat I, was assassinated and the young prince had to return to court to replace him on the throne.

Theocracy

At the dawn of history, the gods had invested monarchical power in human kings; however, in times of particular trouble the nation could resort directly to the deities themselves. During the First Intermediate Period, when the sovereigns who should have been the heirs to those of the Old Kingdom had disappeared from the scene, the country was administered by regional authorities which fought among themselves for supremacy. With this temporary alteration in the power structure, the Egyptians turned to the gods, who—in each of the various regional contexts—occupied the place left vacant by the monarch. One gets a clear view of this from the use of formulae that invoke the name of a local god rather than a king, or from the appeals made to religious institutions rather than to the inadequate institution of the monarchy.

About a thousand years later, toward the end of the Ramesside period, the first prophet of Amun at Karnak took over certain royal responsibilities (for example, the sending of expeditions to the gold mines of Wadi Hammamat) and other responsiblities that had been reserved for the vizier (for example, overseeing work on the reigning monarch's tomb and the preservation of royal mummies). Ultimately, this prophet united the highest functions of the state in his own hands: the administration of the double granary, the high command of the army, the viceroyalty of Nubia and, finally, the position of vizier. This is how Herihor established a veritable kingdom of his own on the basis of his religious role in Thebes, and how one of his immediate successors—Pinudjem I—became king of Upper and Lower Egypt, ranking on a par with Smendes at Tanis (the power of the former extended from Aswan to el-Hiba, that of the latter being restricted to the north of the country).

This sharing of power did not result in a division within the country, because alliances guaranteed that the institutions of royal power were respected. However, the true ruler of the country at this point was Amun himself, whose oracles and decrees replaced royal laws and pronouncements. The high priest was simply the servant and interpreter of the deity. As a result, royal prerogatives were not limited to this high prophet alone; the entire clergy of Amun was enthroned in a ritual that was directly inspired by that of a royal coronation, with an "ascent" to the sanctuary of the god. Even several centuries later, "the god's wives of Amun" would still be making offerings of Maat or having their own jubilee feasts celebrated.

The Egyptian and foreign monarchs who occupied the throne of Egypt during the course of the first millennium did not fail to reinforce their position by laying claim to the support of Amun and the other great gods of the nations, such as Ptah. One sees this, for example, with Alexander the Great, who went to consult the oracle of Amun at Siwa, most likely, before having himself crowned at Memphis.

Bibliography
Bonhême, Forgeau 1988; Gabolde 1988; Assmann 1989; Hornung 1996; Roccati 1997; Valbelle 1998.

The State and Administration

The State and Administration

There is not the slightest doubt that the political regime of ancient Egypt was that of an absolute monarchy. The modern metaphor that compares the Egyptian society of the day to a pyramid—with the pharaoh at the summit and the subjugated peasants of the Nile valley at the base—is fundamentally correct; all that is missing is the inclusion of the class of the scribes or functionaries at the intermediate level of the structure, in order for the model to fully reflect what our sources tell us. However, one should be careful not to understand the term "absolutism" as indicating a political system analogous to that embodied in the European monarchies of the Early Modern Era (XVI–XVII centuries). The material, cultural and intellectual bases for the power that the pharaohs exercised over their people was very different from those upon which these monarchies were built.

The first part of this essay will try to trace the conditions that led to the appearance of royal power in Egypt and determined its specific characteristics. Thereafter, source material will be used to describe the intellectual model developed in Egypt as the justification of that power (I will carefully refrain from entering the debate as to which came first, given that ideology and the power structure were undoubtedly the mutually-interactive result of the same process). Finally, I will look at the administrative structure that enabled the kings of Egypt to implement their decisions.

The Bases of Political Power[1]

Climate, geography and the original settlement of the country all played key roles in the emergence of the Egyptian monarchy in the Archaic Period; and they would be equally important in maintaining it in a remarkably constant form for more than three and a half thousand years. Separated from the rest of the world by arid yet mineral-rich deserts, Egypt was as a matter of fact a closed world—an elongated oasis running for its entire length alongside a river, the Nile, that served as both a means of communication and a source of life. This dominant feature meant that from the very earliest days of its settlement, Egypt was a place of agriculture and trade. At the same time, the river was a factor of potential unity within a country whose thousand-kilometer length and patterns of settlement seemed predisposed to fragmentation.

Toward the beginning of the Predynastic period, semi-nomadic tribes of shepherds arrived from land which had been turned into arid desert by changes in the climate, establishing scattered settlements in the Nile valley where they gradually took up agriculture. The annual flooding of the Nile, which for several weeks every year covered the farmland, led to the concentration of these settlements in cities and villages built on natural and man-made elevations. Though they all originally shared a common "pastoral" culture, each of these groups also had its own traditions. Each, for example, venerated its own divinity, whose sanctuary—the center of social and political life—was surmounted by a religious emblem that served the tribe as a symbol of political belonging and, in some cases, would survive into the historical period as the standard or emblem of a particular province.

As well as causing a concentration of settlements, the Nile flood was naturally the key factor in the development of agriculture in this arid northeastern corner of Africa. However, as unpredictable as all natural phenomena—sometimes too slight, sometimes devastating—the flood could only be used to real advantage by raising enormous earthworks and by the construction and maintenance of vast networks of dykes and canals, all projects which implied the coordinated use of extensive manpower. This necessity meant that political power in Egypt took on the form of a "patriarchal" monarchy from its very beginnings, with the dignity of the ruler conceived as a patrimony that could be passed on from father to firstborn son. Seated in the urban centers, this monarchical power was responsible for the material well-being of the population through the organization of agricultural work and the control of its produce; acting in the name—and under the supposed supervision—of the local divinity, the monarch had the right to impose on each person the task and role he would perform for the good of all. Pressed by necessity, this social organization led to an early implementation of the system of economic redistribution: a system in which the political ruler, the highest proprietor of all the means of production in the territory under his control, was responsible for collecting all of the produce and then dividing it among the various members of society, according to their needs, after the deduction of resources for the

1. Quartzite statue of Hapy from the temple of Amun at Karnak, Ramesside period.
Cairo, Egyptian Museum
cat. 129

maintenance of the "non-productive" members of society (functionaries, soldiers, craftsmen, priests and servants) and the financing of collective work projects (agriculture, war, and the construction of monuments).[2]

A social organization of this kind naturally led to the emergence of a class of administrators whose work—essential to the correct functioning of society—had to be rewarded, and whose elevated social status was symbolized by the enjoyment of material goods of a higher quality than those enjoyed by the rest of the population: vast residences, monumental tombs, luxury furnishings, fine clothing, precious adornments, etc. This requirement explains why Egypt saw the early emergence of a palace architecture and of luxury crafts, under the strict control of the existing political power, which was the sole source of the resources they required. Trade—for which the presence of the Nile waterway was of crucial importance—thus developed as the heads of these prehistoric principalities in the valley sought either to exchange their agricultural surplus for finished products that could not be produced locally and for raw materials that might be used in local production, or else to export finished products and raw materials that were surplus to their own requirements. As this trade enriched them, certain regions of Egypt would, from the very earliest periods, become either specialists in a particular type of production or trade intermediaries. The latter was the case, for example, with the Koptos region to the north of Luxor, through which goods imported from the Eastern Desert and beyond crossed Wadi Hammamat and traveled into Upper Egypt.

Unlike other regions in the Near East where political fragmentation remained the rule in this period, the complex interplay of the above-mentioned factors would, from the end of the Prehistoric Period onward, lead to a process of unification in Egypt. This process initially started in various centers of Upper Egypt and then, in stages, brought about the establishment of a "national" monarchy. First, toward the middle of the Predynastic period, came the creation of three political bodies in Upper Egypt centered around Hierakonpolis, Koptos and Thinis; Koptos then was absorbed by Hierakonpolis and the latter by Thinis. By the dawn of history there was, therefore, a kingdom of Upper Egypt which, in conditions that are still unclear to us, had managed by c. 3200 BC to extend its sovereignty over Middle Egypt and the Nile delta. Without excluding the simple thirst for power as one of the motives of the rulers who brought about this change, there is no doubt that another consideration was the desire to obtain control over neighboring territories that would offer greater land resources, and thus enable them to raise the level of subsistence of their subjects and finance their own growing imports of luxury goods. Another clear consideration was the rulers' desire to conquer the very urban centers that produced or traded in those goods—and thus no longer have to pay either producers or middlemen. And finally, a third consideration was the princes' wish to conquer new outlets for the finished goods or raw materials that they already controlled.

One can already note within this process of unification another characteristic trait of the Egyptian monarchy: its recourse to both defensive and offensive war. Indeed, it is clear that the unification of Egypt was a violent process. When all other means failed (protectorate treaties and marriage alliances), an ambitious prince had little choice: to obtain control over the territory he desired, he had to go to war—and perhaps at the same time fight off similar attempts upon his own territory. As a result, the monarchy of the pharaohs maintained the idea that power was intrinsically bound up with the dynamics of conquest—an idea that explains not only the original unification of Egypt and its successive reunifications after the several "intermediate" periods in its history, but also the various protracted wars the monarchy waged beyond its own borders. However, it was part of the ethics of those prehistoric princes that their wars—like all their acts—were not to be seen as the initiative of some power-hungry leader but rather as directly inspired by the will of the divinity in whose name they held power in the first place. Their successors in later epochs would abide by the same notion.

Given that in all his actions the sovereign was seen as the agent of a divinity, political unification of different regions necessarily led to a process of cultural and religious unification. However, as reasons of social order made it advisable to maintain local beliefs, during the course of the Prehistoric Period the gods of conquered territories were gradually assimilated

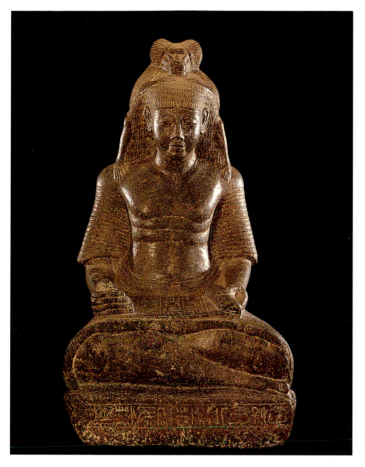

2. Granite statue of Ramessnakht
as a scribe, from the temple of
Amun at Karnak, New Kingdom,
20th Dynasty.
Cairo, Egyptian Museum
cat. 127

3. Limestone stele of Any
from el-Amarna, New Kingdom,
18th Dynasty.
Cairo, Egyptian Museum
cat. 109

into ever vaster theological systems, within which various articles of dogma enabled the god of the conqueror to maintain the dominant role—for example, that divinity might be conceived of as the head of a family comprising all the others, or else as the superior of a subordinated deity. When unification was complete, the sun-god Ra (later associated with Amun under the name Amun-Ra), the visible symbol of majesty and transcendence, gradually became the principal deity of the country. At some unspecified moment—probably as early as the Old Kingdom, although the phenomenon is generally dated later—the idea emerged that each of the deities of the country could be interpreted as the local form of a unique god—of which the sun, Ra, was the main manifestation—thus completing a process of religious synthesis which left a single monarch and a single god face-to-face (the latter, however, hidden behind an infinitude of forms).

By the dawn of history, the single monarch ruled over a country of such size and population that it was inevitable that a multiform administration would rapidly develop under the aegis of monarchy; and given the complexity and immensity of the tasks this administration had to face, it was—one might say—obliged within the space of a few short generations to invent writing. However, in spite of that discovery, administrative means remained generally archaic and incapable of exercising overall control over resources, and this must have led the monarch to delegate the autonomous administration of important sections of his territory and population to various institutions. As we will see below, the main institutions of this type served to guarantee the continuing worship of the nation's deities.

An Intellectual Model

A clear and succinct outline of the concepts behind the Egyptian notions of power and its exercise can be found in a short text which probably predates the oldest extant version known (an engraving in the Luxor temple, that dates from the reign of the 18th-Dynasty pharaoh Amenhotep III).[3] The inscription provides a conceptualized form for most of the features that were described in the previous section:

4. Limestone stele with a cult scene of the royal colossus, New Kingdom, 19th Dynasty. Munich, Staatliche Sammlungen Ägyptischer Kunst
cat. 58

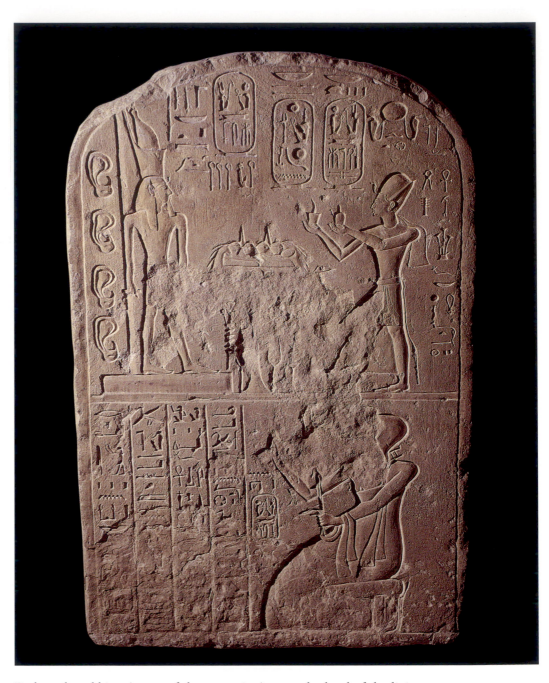

Ra has placed king (name of the sovereign) upon the land of the living,
for ever and ever,
to judge men and satisfy the gods,
to bring about *maat* and annihilate *isefet*,
while making offerings to the gods
and funeral offerings to the dead.

The name of king (name of the sovereign) is in the heavens as is Ra's,
and he lives on exaltation, as Ra-Horakhty does,
seeing him, the *pat* (notables) exult,
and the *rekhyt* (subjects) address him acclamations,
in his appearance as a new-born,
at the rising of Ra in the form of Khepri.

This text makes it clear that, whatever the personal origins of whoever happened to be

5. Limestone stele from the tomb of Intef, western Thebes, New Kingdom, 18th Dynasty, reign of Amenhotep III.
Paris, Musée du Louvre

king at a particular time in history, royal dignity stemmed from the fact that the sun-god Ra, creator of the world and supreme deity of the Egyptian pantheon, had delegated the power to command to the pharaoh; command being a divine attribute which, even after this act of delegation, was still only fully invested in Ra himself. Thus the Egyptian pharaoh was only the substitute, the earthly "lieutenant" of a god who had entrusted him with his creation as a lord might entrust his lands to a steward to administrate in his name and interest.

This distinction between a god who, in theory, remained the true lord of the country, but was content to rule in the heavens, and a king to whom he delegated the task of ruling and governing on earth, is justified by a myth contained in a text from some royal tombs of the New Kingdom: the *Book of the Heavenly Cow*. This book outlines the Egyptian version of the story of Original Sin: initially, the Creator resided on earth, ruling in person over a creation where nothing was lacking. However, unable to repress their instincts, men plotted against his authority. After having satisfied his initial thirst for vengeance by exterminating part of humanity, the Creator began, in spite of himself, to feel compassion for them,

6. Relief with the scene of the offering of *maat* to the Lord of Maat from the temple of Sety I at Abydos, New Kingdom, 19th Dynasty

7. Granite statue of Benermerut with Princess Meritamun from the temple of Amun at Karnak, New Kingdom, Ramesside period. Cairo, Egyptian Museum
cat. 172

and so resolved to punish them by distancing himself, removing himself to the heavens and leaving his son, the first pharaoh, to govern in his place.[4]

As expressed in our text, the extent and limits of the royal mandate are made clear by two double constraints: "judge men" / "satisfy the gods" (whose ranks also include the dead), and "bring about *maat*" / "annihilate *isefet.*" In other words, first, to "govern" and "celebrate worship," and secondly, to work on earth in order to bring about the restoration of *maat*—the perfect, harmonious order of the world and society which had been established by the Creator at the moment of creation (hence an intangible archetype for the imperfect world in which we live)—while fighting *isefet*—the disorder and ruin that threatens the creation both from within and without. According to the above-mentioned myth, when Ra left the earth, he took with him that divine perfection which made the world a true Garden of Eden before the Fall; handicapped by their own imperfections, men would henceforth be forced to work for their own health and survival. Note that these ideas reveal no difference in principle, in the exercise of power, between a secular and a religious component. Endowed with his power by the god, the pharaoh was both king and priest: a king who judged disputes while remaining impartial, imposing his law on all and rewarding each according to his merits; a priest—infact, the only priest in Egypt (all other officiators of worship being his substitutes)—who dedicated offerings, goods and acts of worship to the gods in order to obtain the approbation of deities who descended from their true home in heaven each day to "inhabit" the statues in which they were venerated. Thus, at an ideological level, government was not different from the celebration of worship—given that the former might be seen as the king's submission of his own acts of governance for the approval of the gods; and the celebration of worship was not different from an act of government: If the offerings made to the gods were held by them to be unsatisfactory, then the deities might abandon the earth as Ra had done after the Fall, and thus leave it to relapse into the chaos of barbarism. This identification of government and worship is given perfect expression in a scene that is frequently depicted in temples: the pharaoh is shown offering the sign *maat* to a god, who is identified as the "Lord of *maat*"—that is to say, offering an account to the god of his correct exercise of his own mandate on earth. Answerable to the gods for his acts, the king of Egypt may have been an absolute sovereign but, in theory, he could not act as a simple despot. Divine disapproval, expressed for instance through an oracle or the advent of catastrophic events, would deprive him of his charisma as heaven's appointed, which was essential for the exercise of his role.[5]

God's substitute on earth, the pharaoh also had to be the image of that divinity, dominating society as the sun dominates the earth, and thus obliging all members of society to recognize him as the supreme head of the nation. To this end, his contacts with others always had to comply with the forms laid down by a strict code of ritual. In our text, the metaphors relating to the heavenly position of the king's name—a name that almost always included the name of Ra—and the metaphor that exalts the person of the monarch through comparison with Ra-Horakhty (the sun-god shown with a falcon's head) are to be linked with the New Kingdom custom of always inscribing the pharaoh's name in the center of door lintels, or the much older custom of decorating those lintels with a winged solar disk. We also know that the king's only public appearances were at raised windows, from where he literally dominated the crowds gathered below. However, even though they were both thought to be equally under the dominance of the pharaoh, the two "classes" of Egyptian society, designated by the archaic terms of *pat* and *rekhyt* (the former indicating the category of state functionaries and royal agents, the latter that of the laboring classes), were not supposed to react to these public appearances in exactly the same way. Compared to Khepri, the young sun, each public manifestation of the pharaoh's person was supposed to stir a feeling of exultation in the functionaries that expressed their enthusiastic adhesion to his person and his politics, while the only reaction expected from the laboring classes was the noisy expression of their submission.

From the agents of its will, the monarchy expected active obedience, in which the intellect played its part; the workforce that carried out that will was simply required to passively perform its duties.

8. Granite statue of the vizier of
the South Paser, from the temple
of Amun at Karnak, New Kingdom,
19th Dynasty.
Cairo, Egyptian Museum
cat. 126

The Application of the Model[6]

If, in theory, the justification for the existence of any state power is that it guarantees the good of the population, and provides for the triumph of general interests over individual ones, we can see that in Egypt—unlike other civilizations—this role was not reduced to simply establishing (as far as possible) certain fixed rules which enabled everyone to earn some sort of living; the pharaoh was responsible for guaranteeing the material and moral well-being of each of his subjects. Summarized in the phrases "to bring about *maat*" and "annihilate *isefet*," this divine mandate of the monarch's implied responsibility for the apportionment of economic resources, the celebration of worship, the judgment of disputes, the prevention and punishment of crimes, and the military protection of the community (with the extension of its territory when necessary).

Along with his legislative power—which he exercised through straightforward public declarations—the pharaoh had two instruments to use in the performance of this mandate: the army and the administration, which reflected the fundamental division of all government duties into external and internal affairs (religious affairs formed a separate domain, which will be discussed later). External affairs were normally conducted by the king. In addition to the army—led by a "general-in-chief"—the pharaohs of the New Kingdom also had a "Ministry of foreign affairs," which had originally been nothing but the king's personal secretariat (as one can see from its name: "The office of the pharaoh's dispatches"). With its "envoys," this ministry supervised the Egyptian monarch's relations with his Asiatic vassals and other foreign monarchs, as well as seeing to the administration of functionaries working in the pharaoh's foreign possessions. Some of these latter functionaries were genuine "viceroys" with their own administration; this was the case, notably, with the "king's son of Kush," the governor of Egyptian territories in Nubia. In internal affairs, the pharaoh also had a "chief of works" directly under his orders, through whom he undertook the building or embellishment of temples. Similarly, only the pharaoh could command and organize expeditions abroad or into the mineral-rich deserts of Egypt itself in order to obtain either raw materials or finished products. The "king's spokesman" was responsible for a group of commissars from whom the pharaoh chose the leaders of these expeditions. These commissars might also serve as messengers, works inspectors, works managers or even as investigators of disputes and serious crimes. The royal personnel further comprised a whole body of administrators whose sole responsibility was the management of the vast possessions of the Crown itself.

The management of interior affairs was delegated by the pharaoh to a figure whom Egyptologists usually refer to as the vizier (sometimes there were two such figures, one for Upper and one for Lower Egypt). Though some have described the vizier as a "prime minister," his status and power were much less than that title presupposes in contemporary political organization. Answering solely to the pharaoh—indeed, sometimes described as his "second"—this figure was not supposed to determine policy, but simply to carry out royal directives (both standing and special) and then to report back on their implementation. His brief did not cover foreign affairs or large-scale works projects, but only the administration of resources, public safety and the application of justice. What is more, there were vast areas of territory—such as those owned by the Crown or those belonging to religious or funerary foundations—which enjoyed a special juridical status and thus did not come under his control.

However, despite these limitations, the vizier was a powerful figure. Just like every other functionary, his power to carry out the king's orders depended on the direct or indirect delegation of power from the monarch (a model that reflected the divine delegation of power to the pharaoh himself). In turn, each functionary could further delegate in ever more restricted fields; and in the case of the vizier this redelegation was extensive, given that he was responsible for nominating the whole body of state functionaries, meting out justice, punishing crimes, organizing the collection of taxes and the redistribution of the products in various sectors (most notably, agriculture). To this end, the vizier coordinated a variable number of "ministers," each responsible for a particular area of activity (alongside these ministers were others who answered directly to the king, and thus were outside the vizier's control). The most important and unchanging of the government departments was the "Treasury," which,

9. Limestone statue of the fanbearer
Thenuna from Thebes, New
Kingdom, 18th Dynasty.
Vienna, Kunsthistorisches Museum,
Antikensammlung
cat. 168

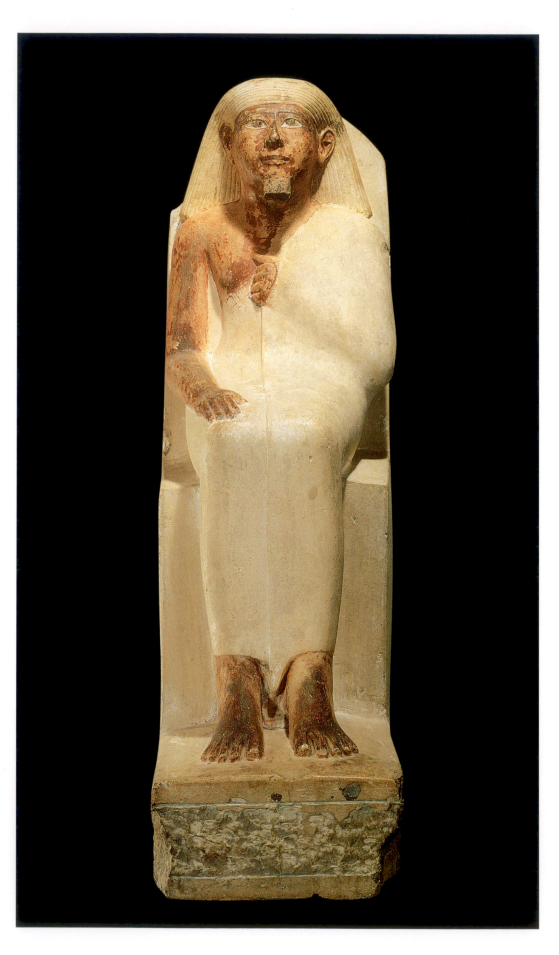

10. Limestone relief with scribes, from Saqqara, New Kingdom, 18th Dynasty, reigns of Tutankhamun and Ay. Florence, Museo Egizio
cat. 133

while managing actual treasures, also maintained archives pertaining to the size, nature and production of all the estates of Egypt, as well as to the changes or transfers that affected their ownership. During the Middle Kingdom, the only other "ministries" were those for the "Assignment of personnel"—a "human resources" ministry that provided manpower for large-scale works projects—and "Land," which organized such projects. With the advent of the New Kingdom, these bodies gave way to a "Ministry of livestock" and a "Ministry of the granary," responsible for herds and agricultural production respectively. It would seem that around the same era these were joined by another ministry, responsible for the administration of the clergy. One should also note that from the 18th Dynasty onward, the vizier (or the vizier of Upper Egypt, when such an official existed) was delegated by the king to oversee the team of workers at Deir el-Medina, and thus was responsible for the creation of the Theban tombs for the king and his kin.

From the point of view of local administration, the country was divided into two large regions—Upper and Lower Egypt—with capitals at Thebes and Memphis and, as already mentioned, each (at certain periods) with its own vizier (there was indeed a myth that, at the dawn of history, the nation had resulted from the union of the two separate kingdoms of Upper and Lower Egypt under the same monarch). During the Middle Kingdom, the size of Upper Egypt led to its division in two: The southern half—including the province of Thebes

125

and all the other provinces separating it from Elephantine—was known as "the extreme South" (literally: "the head of the South"). In turn, these large geographical entities contained smaller administrative regions which sometimes reflected the survival of prehistoric principalities. It is these regions or provinces (in Egyptian, *sepat*) that are, not without a certain anachronism, referred to as nomes (using the Greek name for an administrative district that was adopted during the period of the Ptolemies). A well-established tradition had it that Egypt was divided into forty-two provinces—twenty-two in Upper Egypt, twenty in Lower Egypt—but though these figures are often reflected in the lists of the provinces inscribed on monuments, they only rarely reflected historical reality. Some of those named had, by the time the lists were drawn up, disappeared into larger entities, while other new provinces, in the meantime, had come into existence.

During the period of the New Kingdom, each province was run by the governor (*haty-'*) of its main city, who was appointed by the vizier and was also responsible for the administration of the local clergy. Sometimes the position of governor was hereditary, and in periods when the central government was weakened, ambitious governors often managed to run their provinces in almost total independence. These provinces were themselves divided into a number of "districts" (in Egyptian, *u*), the heads of which were known as "district councillors." The urban centers in these districts were under the jurisdiction of subordinates of the governor known as *heqa-hut* ("chief of urban center"); alongside these there might also be governors of fortresses (if such existed in the province). The exploitation of farmlands and, more particularly, the maintenance of irrigation systems, were managed by a provincial "land director" and the district councillors under the governor's control. Each of these administrators had numerous subordinates: secretaries, police officers and local gendarmes. These local functionaries were flanked by representatives of the vizier known as *wehemu* ("reporters"), of which there would be at least one per province and per sizeable urban center. The main role of these officials was to provide notarial services: they legally registered changes of property ownership, established deeds, and transmitted them to the central government archives. When all those responsible for running a province gathered together, they formed its *kenbet*, "ruling council," whose members were required to present documented accounts of their administration to the vizier every four months. Finally, in each provincial capital and important urban center, bodies of local notables served as court and tribunal. Albeit imposing in character, this administrative apparatus did not directly administer the whole of Egypt. Various areas of the country and of its population enjoyed a particular juridical status which exempted them from common law and enabled them to administer themselves in perfect independence. Such bodies are generically known as "foundations," that is, complexes of buildings and property (lands, persons, buildings and objects of various kinds) that, by the will of a founder, formed an unalienable whole that was endowed with a collective identity and its own administration. These bodies, which corresponded more or less to a modern "trust," were intended to perform such perpetual functions as the veneration of the dead or a specific divinity, to provide for the maintenance of a specific category of people, or to fund a public service. Egypt itself was conceived as an institution of this kind: the supreme institution (which incorporated all others) had been founded by the Creator and then delegated to the monarch, who was responsible for maintaining and enhancing it. As the Creator's delegate, the monarch could in his own small way duplicate that act of creation through the foundation of an institution; and those in turn, who by statute or by the monarch's express wish were delegated to perform a task, again enjoyed the legal ability to set up such institutions. Just as kings strove to establish new cults of worship during their reigns—or else to extend the estates of existing cults—notables might, during the course of their lives, set aside part of their possessions to fund funerary rites and continuing veneration of their memory after their death. It is particularly worth noting that the celebration of worship depended entirely on the continual existence and incessant creation of such foundations by each new monarch; some of these foundations by the time of the New Kingdom—for example Amun's domain at Karnak—would own a sizeable proportion of Egypt's agricultural land and be responsible for the administration of a significant part of its population.

Even though the main aim in setting up such an institution was religious (the "satisfaction" of a god through the celebration of worship), these establishments could only continue in existence if they provided sustenance for the personnel attached to them—either by paying them in kind or allowing them to keep part of what they produced. Thus, the foundation of these institutions enabled the pharaoh to fulfil his obligations to both gods and men in one single political act. Hence, quite apart from their official purpose, these religious foundations were essential components in the general redistribution of goods and produce that the king was supposed to guarantee. Given the number of obstacles, it was generally preferable to implement such a large-scale system through collective bodies: while it was virtually impossible to organize the collection and individual redistribution of produce in a community of a million people, this task became much more manageable when there were a thousand communities, each one responsible for the administration of one thousand souls.

[1] For a general outline of the developments described in this section, see Wilkinson 1999, pp. 28–105.
[2] For the economy of redistribution, see the essential studies Polanyi 1975; Liverani 1990.
[3] Temple of Luxor, room XVII, east wall, Brunner 1979, pl. 65. Discussion: Assmann 1970. Other versions: Parker, Leclant, Goyon 1979, pl. 18 B and pp. 38–40.
[4] Hornung 1982.
[5] Gardiner 1958. On the iconography of this theme, see Teeter 1997.
[6] On administration, see in general Van den Boorn 1988, pp. 325–329. On the administration during the Middle Kingdom, see Hayes 1955, pp. 133–134. For the New Kingdom, see D. O'Connor, in Trigger et alii 1983, pp. 204–218. For a list of the main dignitaries in the country during the New Kingdom, see Gardiner 1947, pp. 24*–29* (nos. 85–98).

The Warrior Pharaoh.
The Conquest of the World

The Warrior Pharaoh. The Conquest of the World.
From an Empire to a Broken Reed

Egyptian history projects a monolithic image of itself, which seems to transcend time and space. The longevity of Egyptian institutions; the nation's occupation of an original and distinct geographical area which had no equals in the Mediterranean world or the Near East; the exceptional duration of Egyptian civilization when compared to its contemporary counterparts—all this serves to accentuate the impression of a disproportion in importance between the Valley of the Nile and its regional partners. And this impression is particularly clear-cut during the era covered by this exhibition—that is, from around the eighteenth century BC to the end of the first third of the first millennium—even if, ultimately, that period of around a thousand years would see regional empires emerge and decline as the result of slow developments and swift reversals, eventually giving rise to a new world order in which Egypt would have difficulty maintaining its status.

Things were very different in the third millennium; and even more so in the fourth, when the pharaohs were nurturing the emergent might of a kingdom whose unity was an integral part of their own notion of the created world (though one would now tend to qualify what was once said about the narrow borders of the Egyptian kingdom, which was long seen as defined by solely natural barriers, it is nevertheless true that the limits of the known universe were confined to a relatively small area).

Yet for all that "narrowness," we now have evidence of relations between the Nile valley and the Near East in the fourth millennium BC, and rather more information about relations between Egypt and the western fringes of Africa. Over the last thirty years increasingly detailed studies of the areas of settlement in the Western Desert (indeed, the Libyan oases) have thrown new light on the origins of civilization on the banks of the Nile. This new material means one can qualify a myth once solidly established in XX-century Egyptology, according to which Egypt was an entity that, from its very beginnings, was restricted to a valley that served as both the basis and framework of its cosmology.

Undoubtedly, the river's banks were the cradle of life, providing a model of a world in which annual floods made fertile land out of terrain which would otherwise have been arid desert. However, this model was far from static. Throughout the history of their civilization, the relations that the ancient Egyptians maintained with the outside world might be seen as predicated on this notion of rising water, of a natural flux whose range was determined by the nature and characteristics of the land over which it flowed.

Research over the last twenty years has produced extensive evidence of the appropriation of areas neighboring the Nile valley during the third and fourth millennia. In particular, it has become clear that the inhabitants of the valley, of sub-desert origin themselves, maintained and developed a deep knowledge of the arid areas that lay to the east and west, and could thus exploit the natural wealth of these regions. Agriculture and commerce probably developed in the western oases from the first half of the third millennium onward, and were incorporated within political and social frameworks that reveal the Egyptians to have considered these vast areas as an integral part of their country. The same things could be said of Sudanese Nubia up to the beginning of the second millennium, though here one must also add another point: The establishment of Egyptian mechanisms of administration was very soon accompanied by the creation of military structures capable of withstanding the pressure exerted by the societies of the southern Nile regions, which were also expanding—both southward and northward.

Recent research has, for example, cast extensive light on the dazzling civilization of Kerma, itself the origin of the future kingdom of Kush, which would be Egypt's main rival in the south and ultimately take over power in the land of its former conquerors. It was probably with regard to this African area that, in the initial centuries of the third millennium BC, the Egyptian first developed the very notion of foreign policy.

The fact that there is no archaeological evidence of military structures in the western oases during this period suggests that the Egyptians encountered no opposition or competition here (up to the first millennium—at the earliest—the oases did not form caravan stations for societies strong enough to threaten the established equilibrium).

The situation at this time on the other side of the valley—in an area extending as far as the shores of the Red Sea and the Sinai—was broadly comparable. The Arab mountain chain was less rich in water than the western oases, and thus without important settlements; how-

1. Bronze *khepesh* of Rameses II, New Kingdom, 19th Dynasty. Paris, Musée du Louvre
cat. 101

2–4. Painted wooden model boat
from the Valley of the Kings,
New Kingdom, 18th Dynasty.
Cairo, Egyptian Museum
cat. 261

ever, areas such as the Sinai were rich in minerals. Like the coast, these mountains had been crisscrossed by traffic from the very early days of antiquity, and the inhabitants of the Nile valley certainly knew their way around the region. The gold, galena, copper and turquoise from the East were an integral part of Egypt, whose sphere of influence would for many years extend as far as the Strait of Bab el-Mandeb (with the one exclusion of the mysterious Punt, the jewel of the "land of god").

Except for the South, the pharaohs' policy of conquest did not really start until relatively late: at the beginning of the second millennium BC. The absence of any adversaries who posed a threat to national integrity meant that, up to that point, the country had not had great difficulty in maintaining the identity of sphere of influence and known universe; deserts and mountains remained the limits of the world, large parts of which still maintained their mystery. From about the twenty-fifth century BC, the future Phoenicia formed an unchallenged coastal front, while the Syrian hinterland did not yet pose any threat. At the same time, Byblos makes its appearance on the walls of the funeral temple of King Sahura; yet his dealings in the areas were nevertheless restricted to a few tribes of bedouins.

This first period of regional domination would culminate in the twenty-first and twentieth centuries, after that great rupture at the beginning of the second millennium—a rupture which we now know affected not just Egypt but almost the whole of the Near East. During the reign of Senusret III (1881–1842), the princes of Byblos adopted an Egyptian style of life. This is also the period that saw the emergence of references to Jerusalem, Sekmem and Ashkelon, which suggests that in their foreign policy the pharaohs were soon concerned not only with protecting mineral resources and trade routes, but also with meeting the challenges posed by other powers that might play a role in the region.

The second phase in Egypt's exercise of centralized power—in the eighteenth century BC—was partially the result of a redistribution of settlements and population in the Near East. Marking the beginning of an era which would see the culmination of what is sometimes improperly called "the Egyptian empire," this is also—indeed, primarily—the period that saw the passage from the Early to the Middle Bronze Age, a characteristic feature of which was the sizeable population shift which brought about far-ranging economic and technological changes in the region. As the world around it seemed to draw closer, Egypt could impose its authority thanks to the economic and political strength which put it in a dominant position. Thereafter, in spite of its own lack of natural resources (a shortcoming which gave its rivals an advantage in the development of metal technologies) and, above all, that migratory flux which then hit the southern Mediterranean, Egypt would manage to coast along, maintaining its key role in the region's trade. However, it would encounter greater and greater difficulties and ultimately stagnate, a prisoner of the new forces that had superseded it.

The Egyptians give a very clear-cut image of their relations with their partners, be they in the Near East, east Africa or the southern Mediterranean. However, nowadays one cannot take this picture at face value; both archaeology and history make it possible to give a more nu-

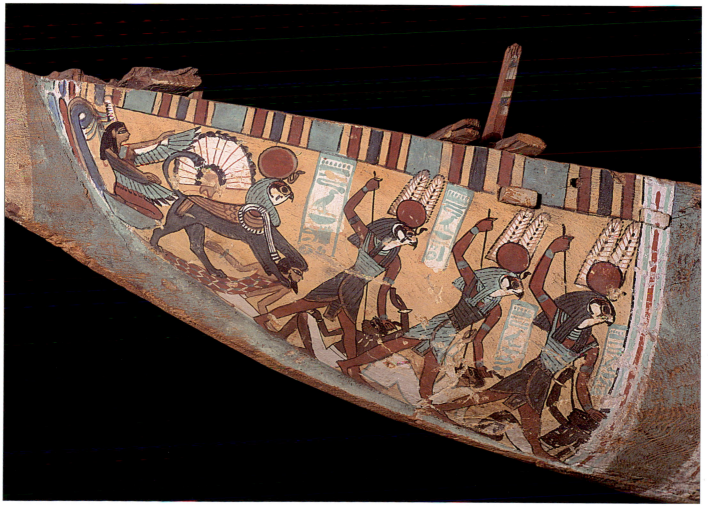

anced description of the glory of the pharaohs, especially thanks to two groups of discoveries that have cast important light on the outlying areas of this empire in recent years.
The first of these discoveries highlighted the importance of the pre-Hellenic Mediterranean world, and revealed that, right up to the middle of the second millennium, this world's role in eastern trade was much more important than scholars took it to be twenty years ago. Over the last thirty years, the digs carried out by Manfred Bietak and the Austrian Institute in the eastern areas of the Nile delta have repeatedly provided answers to questions that appeared insoluble in the 1960s; and two of the answers that have emerged have radically altered our historical perspective of the period. The first find to necessitate such a rethink was evidence that proved the presence on the same Tell el-Dab'a site of the capitals of the Hyksos kings and of Rameses II—namely, Avaris and Piramesse. What is more, an examination of the different archaeological layers has produced an unbroken stratigraphy for the site from the beginning of the twentieth to the end of the fifteenth century BC. This shows that not only were the above-mentioned eastern sovereigns present in Egypt for more than a century, but they maintained much closer links with Egyptian culture than one would suppose from reading the Theban inscriptions of those who emerged from the southern Valley of the Nile to conquer them. Similarly, thanks to the study of the abundant material (primarily ceramics) unearthed in the northern Sinai region up to Gaza, we can now see that a rather different reading should be made regarding what the pharaohs of the 18th Dynasty presented as the reconquest of territory that had historically been subject to Egypt. The Hurrians, in particular, seem to have played a far from negligible role in the balance of power within a region where, again in the fifteenth century BC, Thutmose III had to fight a twenty-year war to consolidate Egyptian power.
The other great revelation of the Tell el- Dab'a finds is the importance of the Minoans in the southern area of the Mediterranean basin. The presence on the site of a palace whose layout, materials and, above all, decoration reveal that it was not simply a local copy of a Minoan original has radically changed our view of the period. In the absence of archaeological evidence that this building was intended to serve some economic purpose—and given the presence of abundant material associated with the Egyptian royal chancellery—it is legitimate to posit the existence of political relations between the two states (with this "palace" serving some sort of diplomatic function).
While the influence of the Minoan civilization in the Near East was already known to us, its presence in Egypt is new. This enables us to paint a far more nuanced picture of the already quite well understood relations between the Nile valley and Cyprus and the Aegean area. One of the first things to crumble is that commonplace of an Egypt which before the first millennium BC was incapable of communicating directly with the Mediterranean world because it lacked a viable maritime interface. Even more importantly, a new vision of affairs emerges, with ongoing political and commercial links that seem to have come to an end only with the abrupt disappearance of the Cretan empire in the middle of the second millennium BC (a trace of these relations can be found in the slightly later lists that Amenhotep III had engraved on the pedestals of his statues at Kom el-Heitan; while their full magnificence emerges in the rich Theban tomb paintings that date from the reign of Thutmose III).
Those lists reveal that new arrivals—the Hellenes—took the place that had been left vacant, without however ever attaining to the importance of the Cretans. During the last two centuries of the second millennium, Egypt's relations with those it defined as "Sea Peoples" enable us to trace that movement, which would soon result in a radical shift of political and military initiative away from Asia Minor to the Aegean world and the eastern limits of what is now known as the Mahgreb. Nevertheless, Egypt still possessed enough power to absorb this influx, being affected only by the faint tail-end of it; the pride and glory expressed in the depictions of Rameses III on the walls of his temple at Medinet Habu are still in the same vein as those found in the triumphant decorations celebrating the great wars of Rameses II. However, this does not mean that the newcomers were simply crushed. Assimilated by the older civilization, which had always been a welcoming melting-pot, or else relegated to the very edges of the kingdom, they would gradually form their own communities. Just like the Hyksos, these groups were culturally acclimatized but never became truly Egyptian; ultimately, they would constitute one of the features that destabilized the institution of pharaonic pow-

5. Ostracon with lion devouring an enemy, from Deir el-Medina, New Kingdom, Ramesside period. Cairo, Egyptian Museum
cat. 54

er, placing it at the mercy of that series of conquerors who, from Napata, Persia, Macedonia and Rome, would take their place on the pharaoh's throne, which each "customized" to his own ends.

Another change in our image of the Egypt of the day can be found in the South, which used to be considered a quasi-province where the unchallenged power of the pharaohs was exercised solely in the imposition of peace. Our improved picture of the western sub-desert area and of Sudanese Nubia means that we can now add some light and shade to what was previously a starkly black-and-white picture of African areas unable to challenge the colonial power of an Egypt bearing peace and civilization into a chaotic region. The work of Charles Bonnet and Brigitte Gratien has revealed that—from as early as the end of the third millennium BC—there was a powerful native civilization from Kerma to Kush which was much more than the mere client of the pharaohs. In fact, recent work has discovered important installations of the Amarna period at Kerma, which reveal that the south of the third cataract was more than a simple *limes*. At the same time, this research gives us some idea of the distant roots of that process of cultural acclimatization in Nubia which, some one thousand years later, would result in the conquest of Egypt itself by those who constituted the 25th Dynasty. All these advances in research have made it possible to qualify what is still an oversimple picture of the Egyptian empire. Clearly, one can no longer hold that the empire was restricted to the immediate boundaries of the Nile valley; and, more importantly, one now has a more precise idea of the actual nature of the power the empire exercised, which Egyptian sources always depict as resting on undivided hegemony.

This is the case, for example, of the most extensive area of this "empire": the Near East, stretching as far as the borders of Anatolia and the Aegean—a region that is also the best known to us because of an abundance of cross-referenced source material dating from the beginning of the second millennium BC onward.

6. Sandstone stele with representation of foreign lands paying homage to the king, from the temple of Aten at Karnak, New Kingdom, 18th Dynasty. Cairo, Egyptian Museum
cat. 123

7. Sandstone fragment of bas-relief with painted enemies, New Kingdom, 19th Dynasty. Cairo, Egyptian Museum
cat. 93

The veritable starting-point for this empire was the moment when the Egyptians drove from their valley the only sovereigns that their historians would thereafter continue to refer to as "foreigners" (even if the country would subsequently be dominated by various foreign powers).

Indeed, at the beginning of the sixteenth century BC Asia Minor was not yet the tributary of a single great power. In Anatolia, there was the sixth era of Troy, as well as the last days of the ancient Hittite empire (these powers had always limited themselves to nearby territories, and thus had not come up against an Egyptian empire that was then only in the process of coming into being). At the same time, Ugarit had yet to arrive at its full glory, and—apart from Crete—there was no established power to oppose an Egyptian advance into Asiatic territory. That advance would start in the early days of the 18th Dynasty, by taking advantage of the Hurrians' move into Palestine, which dealt a decisive blow to the power of the Hyksos from a northern direction. Thus, perhaps already in the reign of Hatshepsut (1479–1458) and certainly sometime during the reign of Thutmose III (1479–1425), Egypt had established its suzerainty over the region of Gaza. Further north, repeated military campaigns had also given it control over that spread of principalities extending as far as the river Orontes, which for around fifty years would remain the effective limit of Egypt's direct sphere of influence. But this did not prevent the Egyptians from advancing to the east of the Euphrates—far from it. However, their possessions there were probably never long-term, as one can see from their concern in underlining the exceptional nature of those distant outposts with monuments both *in situ* and within Egypt itself (the former intended as what one would be tempted to call boundary-markers of the empire; the latter serving to celebrate the universality of the pharaoh's power).

For example, after taking Mishrife—and just before crossing the river which separated him from the Mitanni—Thutmose III underlined the exceptional character of this ultimate push into Asia by two things: a stele commemorating the exploits of his own grandfather, which are thus viewed as echoes of his own victories, and an elephant hunt, destined to illustrate his power over enemy territory. The royal annals of that year credit him with dominion over distant Babylon, Assyria and the land of the Hittites—all the fruit of this fictitious subjugation of the Mitannian empire, which naturally brought all its vassal states tumbling after it. In fact, the mutual—disputed—limit of Egyptian and Mitannian spheres of influence would for a long time be the region of Alep, in modern-day northern Syria. All the area to the south, extending as far as the frontiers of Egypt itself, would remain under Egyptian influence until almost the beginning of the twelfth century BC. Rameses II's military policy with regard to the Hittite empire, which after the collapse of the Mitanni had been a dominant force since the end of the fifteenth century BC, would once more give the pharaohs a regional control that would eventually be worn away by the advance of various dangerous rivals.

As one can see, even when overlooking the impropriety of applying the word "empire" to

8. Dagger of Kamose from Dra Abu el-Naga, bronze, silver and gold, Second Intermediate Period, 17th Dynasty. Brussels, Bibliothèque Royale Albert Ier, Cabinet des Médailles
cat. 103

ancient Egypt, the meaning of the term remains relative. If nowadays it is clear that the pharaohs did exert what might be called dominion over the regions occupying modern-day Syria, Jordan and Palestine at the middle of the second millennium BC, it would be wrong to continue the past usage of describing their relations with their more distant neighbors in the same terms. Such a reading takes the pharaonic language of power at more than face value, attributing objectives to it that were not its own.

As a matter of fact, when both Hattusilis III and Rameses II offer their respective accounts of the military and political outcome of the battle they had fought at Qadesh on the Orontes, it is difficult to accuse either of them of straining the truth, even though both claim to have been the victor. Each was operating within his own system of power, transcribing facts according to a view of reality that we would certainly be wrong in trying to measure by the scale of contemporary geopolitics. The best sign of this is the fabric of alliances that subsequently bound the two states together for more than a century up to the twelfth century BC.

Even when Thutmose III describes the two Retenu over which he had established Egyptian dominion in his Karnak temple, he never presents them as anything but foreign countries; in fact, he was happy to emphasize their specific peculiarities—as one can see in what has been called his "botanical garden," that extraordinary *wunderkammer* he had engraved in the antechamber to the Holy of Holies in his jubilee temple (a compendium that offers a veritable tetralogical inventory of the Other). Similarly, the court of Amenhotep III, which can be considered as coinciding with the high point of Egyptian expansion into the Near East, did not consider itself as exercising hegemony over the region. The court of the day saw itself as a junction at which the various parts of the universe ran into each other, drawing as much benefit from the wealth of Egypt as Egypt itself drew from the exploitation of their produce. The fact that this flow of trade was described in terms of the payment of tribute in what might well be seen as a military framework makes little difference here.

It is no coincidence that during the first century of the 18th Dynasty—and, especially, during the reign of Amenhotep III (1387–1350)—we first see clear evidence that the inhabitants of the Nile valley were beginning to reflect upon the world that enclosed them. The arrival at the Egyptian court of knowledge and skills from other parts of the known world had an effect upon the development of what were the most advanced expressions of the national genius. The age of the Thutmosides was one of magnificence and important advances in the intellectual, spiritual, technological and artistic fields, with the result that the very bases of Pharaonic civilization were subjected to a radical rethinking. And this self-questioning was undoubtedly due to a previously unparalleled degree of openness to an outside world which continued to get bigger and bigger and thus challenge received ideas.

Universalistic ideas became more and more common. During the peaceful reign of Amenhotep III, Egyptian influence extended as far as Crete, Mycenae, Aetolia, Assur and Babylon, and in his jubilee temple at Soleb (at the southern boundary of his empire, alongside the distant third cataract of the Nile) or on the pedestals of the statues adorning his Temple of Millions of Years at Thebes, the king had geographical lists engraved, showing a world comprising Achaeans, Babylonians, Mitannians, Hittites, Cypriots, Syrians, Nubians, Ethiopians, etc. Similarly, the cuneiform archives from Tell el-Amarna also bear witness to an intense diplomatic, economic and cultural activity which resulted in the sovereign covering his territory with monuments to his power. Indeed, these very records would become one of the models for Egyptian history—and would certainly be cited a century later by Rameses II when he set about reestablishing this lost empire.

In the intervening years, the regime of the pharaohs had been shaken to its very foundations by this very influx of influences. As a matter of fact, Amenhotep III's successor found himself in the bewildering position of ruling over an indefinitely extended universe, whose center of gravity could no longer be neatly transcribed within the banks of the Nile. His attempts to push the ideology of solar universalism to its extreme consequences would ultimately lead nowhere, and after what might simply appear as a generation-long parenthesis, the nation returned to its traditional structures of power and religion. Nevertheless, even if the only "inheritance" of the Akhenaten heresy is that claimed by some Christians with rather fanciful notions of history, its very existence reveals that there was a limit to what the theocracy of the pharaohs could absorb.

9. Painted sandstone relief with
conquered Asiatics, New Kingdom,
19th Dynasty.
New York, The Metropolitan
Museum of Art, Rogers Fund 1913
cat. 92

The final days of unchallenged Egyptian glory came at the end of the second millennium.
And the second peak here was marked by Rameses II's reestablishment of the framework left
by Amenhotep III. Indeed, political actors and political conditions were once more what they
had been. These made the reassertion of dominion—and the concomitant display of
wealth—possible, thus nurturing that flourishing period in the arts and sciences under Sety I (1289–1278) and Rameses II (1279–1212).
The end of the 19th Dynasty was marked by internal difficulties; and these—together with
the emergence of new powers in the regions neighboring upon those of an already weakened
Egypt—would quickly limit the pharaohs' field of action to the one defined by the original
borders of the New Kingdom. At the same time, the new populations driven here by whole-
sale migrations in the East would have a profound effect upon the Egyptian environment.
The migratory waves of the Sea Peoples unfurled upon the Egyptian coastline itself,
where—as had been the case in the past, and as would be the case in the future—the nation
managed to assimilate and metabolize this new input. However, the whole of the southeast
of the Mediterranean had changed. The Aegean world was expanding into new spaces
through a sort of peaceful campaign of conquest, and the result was that the leaders of Greek
cities—rough soldiers driven out because of the poverty of the territory over which they exercised dominion—would soon become as indispensable as those settlers who took to their
ships in order to sail southward and exploit the rich lands of the Nile valley and its oases.

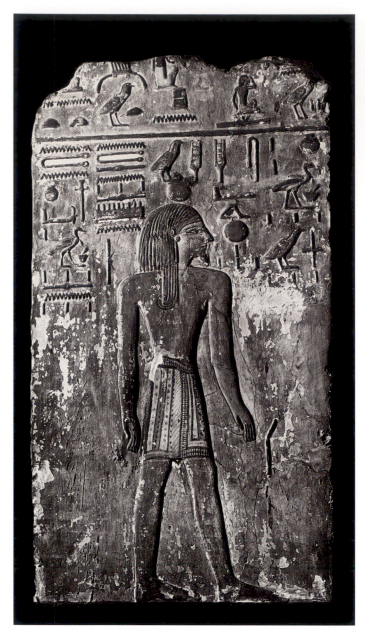 

10–11. Limestone bas-relief from a
royal tomb, from the Valley of the
Kings, New Kingdom, 19th Dynasty.
Berlin, Agyptisches Museum und
Papyrussammlung
cat. 235

What is more, over the early years of the first millennium BC, the Syria–Palestine area itself would gradually shake off Egyptian control. By 1010 BC, Israel under Saul had achieved a status that would continue to grow at the expense of a powerful neighbor embroiled in dynastic difficulties. It is true that the rivalry between Judah and Israel would allow the sovereigns of the 22nd Dynasty to regain some authority in the region, confirmed by Sheshonq I's victorious Palestinian campaign of 925 BC; however, Egypt would never recover the role it had played in the Levant some two centuries earlier. Thereafter, the two rival "renaissances" of Sais and Ethiopia would simply rebuild a semblance of national unity during the two hundred years that preceded the final loss of Egyptian independence—the first blow was struck by the Persians in 525 BC, and the *coup de grace* delivered by Alexander the Great in 332 BC. In conclusion one might say that, for around a thousand years, the pharaohs did manage to exert dominion over their entire region—but more as a result of circumstances than as the outcome of a deliberate political project. The driving-force behind this rule was the very capacity for expansion implicit in the Nile-based civilization; its limits were those that arose from the resistance on the part of the other peoples of the region who were themselves going through a phase of expansion.

By the turn of the first millennium BC Egypt had been left behind by a world in which the center of political gravity had shifted. Increasingly at the mercy of a succession of new conquerors, the nation had by the beginning of the seventh century BC become "this broken reed, which pierces the hand of him who tries to rest upon it"—to quote the mocking simile Sennacherib used when wryly summarizing the great past of Egypt for Hezekiah. And yet, whether under the yoke of Persians, Greeks or Romans, the fiction of the empire would continue: sources mention Darius "The Great" not only as the leader of the Persians but also as the son of Ra governing the universe; similarly, Rome is only rarely mentioned on the monuments that were raised in the Nile valley to commemorate Roman emperors who were dressed as pharaohs (when mentioned, it was only a distant city). And when, in his day, Hadrian wished to render the empire adequate to his own breadth of political vision, he would turn to Heliopolis, which—even in the second century AD, long after the period of the pharaohs—was the sole source of a universalistic vision that met the needs of a new master of the world eager to initiate a new era in history.

Thus over thousands of years Egypt was able to impose its image upon a world where—thanks to its key location as a crossroads—it continued to occupy an important position. As its culture spread along the southern banks of the Nile, Egypt managed to make Sudanese Nubia its own, and then ultimately fell prey to its own creation, which was an almost perfect example of the fusion between the nation's African roots and what it had drawn from the neighboring continent of Asia.

Far outlasting its historical rivals—and enjoying the additional advantage of an extensive population—the unique mix within Egypt meant that the aura of power around the country was based less on political and military might than on economic and cultural influence. Undoubtedly, Egypt could offer a much more powerful model than those at the disposal of the Greek newcomers, or of those Romans who were continually tempted by the call of the East—even if these two latter groups founded the Mediterranean world as we know it.

So was Egyptian supremacy in some sense a dream? It was undoubtedly real during the third and second millennia BC—even if limited by the expansion of rival civilizations. Thereafter, it survived the fortunes of war thanks to the unique place Egypt managed to carve for itself in international power politics, showing a readiness to surrender its own political independence when it was no longer capable of playing "in the big league." This continuing success was due to the fact Egypt was open to the Other, able to assimilate it without surrendering its own values. Perhaps we should look to this intelligent cosmopolitanism when trying to explain the origins of a myth that has survived the limits of time and space.

The Ritualist Pharaoh. The Religious Cult

The Pharaoh, a King or a God?

The pharaoh, it is said, was a god, and his people worshipped him as such. This idea, predominant in many of the studies of ancient Egypt, gives pharaonic royalty a certain aura of mystery—which some find appealing, some distasteful.

A lot has been said about the divinity of the king of Egypt; and in many cases, outsiders see no further into Egyptian civilization than this incredible claim that the ruler of the nation was of divine essence. Whether great or insignificant, whether part of an illustrious dynasty or a minor provincial usurper, the pharaoh was always declared to be the "son of Ra." Certain Western writers, both ancient and modern, have taken this much vaunted divinity of the kings of Egypt as a sign of a rather naive, unevolved society.[1] Certainly, there is no shortage of evidence that the pharaohs claimed a certain familiarity with the gods. On the walls of extant temples, it is the pharaoh—and the pharaoh alone—who is unceasingly shown in dialogue with Amun, Osiris, Ptah and numerous other gods. Whatever their ostensible purpose, even the slightest of royal stelae raised on the forecourts of temples begin with long litanies of praise that often take up most of the monument: "It is our seed that is in him," say the gods of Rameses II,[2] or again "it is Ra who set His Majesty in the world: it is he who has created his perfection."[3] But was the king really a superhuman being of divine essence, a blameless figure endowed with wonderful powers? How is one to reconcile such a claim with the vicissitudes of Egyptian history that are so clear from the extant documentation? Like all ancient civilizations, Egypt had no lack of usurpers, of incapable kings, defeated monarchs and even the victims of regicide. When one looks more closely, one sees the limits of the phraseology used in the religious documents. In 1960 G. Posener published a remarkable study entitled *De la divinité du Pharaon*,[4] a work which marks a turning-point in Egyptian studies and highlights all the various contradictions in the nature of a pharaoh who was, at one and the same time, "a divine king of multiple manifestations"[5] and a ruler subject to doubt and error. For example, at the very height of the Battle of Qadesh, as the result of a crude strategic error, Rameses II found himself threatened from all sides, at which point he called upon his father Amun. The gods came and inspired Rameses with the strength and courage necessary to reverse the situation. But, as G. Posener so convincingly shows, Rameses II—who, if ever there was one, was a king cherished by the gods, a chosen child destined for royalty—was also a man who, when surrounded by his enemies, gave way to fear and placed his hopes for salvation in the intervention of the gods. In fact, the terms he uses, and the way in which the gods intervene in the situation, are practically no different from those which might occur in the life of even his humblest subjects.[6] At most, the text suggests that the gods "talk" to the pharaoh, probably more a metaphor for an act of inspiration[7] than a description of a veritable intervention in the real world. There was no supernatural appearance, no demonstration of superhuman power in support of the pharaohs. If, by definition, they have the highest of human qualities, that is what they remain: human. G. Posener's study concludes that there was a sort of double personality to the pharaoh. "On the one hand, there was a being who embodied sacred power, who personified an institution of divine origin and who himself shared in that divinity; on the other hand, there was a Head of State, who fulfilled a terrestrial function within a human world. One figure was born and lived among the gods, his 'fathers,' and the other only knew the gods through sacred texts; only maintained intermittent contact with the heavens, approaching that world rarely and indirectly—in ways that differ very little from those used by ordinary mortals."[8]

So the king was a human being. Even if an individual, one hoped he had the perfection befitting a figure who represented humanity before the gods; and although he was pharaoh, the king nevertheless protected his bed with prophylactic images of the spirit Bes,[9] in order to drive off sickness and forces that might disturb his sleep. However, when—bedecked with all the insignia of divine royalty—the king officiated at ceremonies that were an ideological expression of pharaonic power, he was—for the duration of the rituals—the true interlocutor of the gods, their cherished child. Indeed, the double nature of the king reflected that Egyptian principle of an opposition between person and function. This is the key to a number of the particular features of Egyptian culture, and even applies to the gods themselves; Egyptian religion made a clear division between the personalities of the gods and the divine functions they fulfilled.[10] Nevertheless, with regard to the function of kingship, perhaps insufficient emphasis has been put on the importance of ritual in the basic mechanisms of pharaonic power.

1. Small ceramic sphinx representing Amenhotep III, New Kingdom, 18th Dynasty.
New York, The Metropolitan Museum of Art
cat. 49

2. Limestone stele of regal cult
from Deir el-Medina,
New Kingdom, 19th Dynasty.
Turin, Museo Egizio,
collezione Drovetti
cat. 59

The Recognition of the Legitimate Pharaoh

If the king is not a god, but an individual invested with a role of divine essence, what are the mechanisms whereby everyone can recognize his function as the representative of humanity before the gods, the legitimacy of the rites he performs? The true king of Upper and Lower Egypt was the man who bore the insignia that made his authority recognizable, and in Egypt these signs were essentially crowns. We know very little about the real nature of these crowns, about where they were kept or how they were used. We can, however, identify various types of regalia. The first that should be mentioned is the *uraeus*, the serpent rearing above the forehead of the king. This was a unique sign of royalty, worn on all occasions and in all circumstances, whatever other crown or headdress the sovereign might be wearing. Then there are the crowns of Upper and Lower Egypt, sometimes used separately, sometimes together; these symbolized the fiction of the Double Kingdom and were worn in either civic or more specifically liturgical ceremonies. Finally, on the walls of temples, the king is often shown wearing heavy ritual crowns which are often very complex combinations of various symbols. Here, it is legitimate to wonder if such headdresses were ever actually worn.

The Functioning of the Ritual Acts

A first definition of such acts would be that they were governed by specific norms; were often repetitive; and were of unquestionable efficacy (whether or not that efficacy could be objectively demonstrated). However, for a rite to be truly effective it had to be performed by someone with adequate knowledge, and this science of ritual was often presented as an ancestral heritage passed down from generation to generation.

There are three components to the ritual proper: Words and gestures whose efficacy cannot be judged by the categories that apply in the real world. For example, when the officiant touched the pile of food offered up to the god with his *sekhem* scepter, then the god truly came into possession and enjoyment of those offerings. The fact that the words of a ritual could be described as a "performative act"—that is, the saying of the word equalled the performance of an action—is very clear in these words the officiating pharaoh addressed to Amun: "Come in peace to your great offering."[11] But another factor has to be taken into account in this performative act: if the words are a sign of the efficacy of the ceremony within the field of the imagination, the physical action itself places that process within time. So—to go back to the example of the consecration of offerings—while the very preparation of foodstuffs within the temple kitchens implied that they would be consumed by the god, it was only at the precise moment

3–4. Faience amulets
of the crowns of Upper and
Lower Egypt, Late Period.
Paris, Musée du Louvre
cat. 34

5. Quartzite statue of Amenhotep III wearing a wig, New Kingdom, 18th Dynasty.
The Cleveland Museum of Art

when they were touched by the *sekhem* that their status really changed. Examples of such performative gestures, fixing an event in time, are not rare even in our own day. For example, during an auction, the lot is sold to the last bidder when the auctioneer's gavel hits the table; or again, a deal can be clinched by a handshake. Indeed, some notarial documents regarding the sale of property give not only the date but the very hour and minute in which the change of ownership occurs. So word and temporal setting are two factors that serve to guarantee the performative efficacy of the rite. Alongside these there is also the fact that the ritual is witnessed. Those who "witness" this ceremony can even be absent—for example, there can be a large audience or no more than the image of the deity to whom the ritual is addressed. In either case, the ritual is accomplished before a "public"; its performance is a witnessed act. Certain rituals, in fact, were performed by the king alone within the secrecy of the sanctuary. This was because they involved solely the pharaoh's divine father—creator of the world and the motive force animating creation—and the king himself, the ruler of a nation entrusted to his care by the gods. This was the case, for example, with the daily ritual to be performed before the statuette of the deity, which was both the recipient of—and access point to—divine powers.

But when it was a question of announcing the divine legitimacy of the king loud and clear, then the ritual had to be performed before a large public. On these occasions, the king appeared in all the glory of his insignia, and before his subjects performed the ritual gestures that established his relationship with the gods. This was the case, for example, with the coronation or the *sed* festival. This latter was a sort of repetition of the coronation—in theory, some thirty years after the original event—and was undoubtedly the event that most served to proclaim the ritual legitimacy of the king before his court, high functionaries and dignitaries. In the tomb of Kheruef, grand chamberlain to Queen Tiy, wife of Amenhotep III, it is claimed that the ritual (the king and queen navigating the river at evening, a metaphor for the celestial voyage of Ra and Hathor) was inspired by ancient texts, but never before had it been used in the celebration of a *sed* festival.[12]

6. Fragment of a stele of Horemheb,
New Kingdom, 18th Dynasty.
Cairo, Egyptian Museum
cat. 83

An Exemplary Ritual, or How to Defeat Death

It is a banal observation that death is one of the great generators of ritual, and that Egypt—with its mummies, pyramids and tombs—offers particularly abundant examples of this. In their desire to negate death, the ancient Egyptians set up a process intended to replace it. The deceased remained alive in an imaginary world because, on the one hand, he maintained his appearance (both in the form of a statue and a mummy) and, on the other, ritual served to restore his original vital functions to a stone form or to the dried flesh of a mummy. The officiant pronounced words which would open the mouth and eyes of the deceased so that he could regain these vital functions.[13] At the same time, in the presence of the family of the deceased, the officiant touched the stone, wood or plaster organs (the latter in the case of the binding of a mummy) with an adze. But who was the figure responsible for performing a ritual act that might befall every mortal? Dressed in a leopard skin that was the insignia of his function, he was—at least in theory—the eldest son of the deceased, thus someone who had lost his father. Hence, he would be the one to support his father's widow, and the title "pillar of his mother" (*iunmutef*) was bestowed upon him.[14] The figure who performed this ritual thus proclaimed his legitimate position as heir by publicly caring for his dead father. Obviously, in real life this liturgical role presupposed certain abilities and was taken over by specialists acting in the name of the son concerned—just as priests were delegated by the pharaoh to perform his duties in maintaining the images of the gods in the temples.

The performance of this ritual could thus fall to each male Egyptian—and to the pharaoh himself as an individual. There was nothing astonishing about the fact that the new king had to perform the funeral rites for his predecessor. In the Temples of Millions of Years built for New Kingdom sovereigns there is a chapel, sometimes a series of rooms, given over to the funeral veneration of the king's father.[15] But what happened when the natural father of the pharaoh was only a secondary figure in the royal family, someone who had never been raised to the dignity of kingship (as was the case with Thutmose I) or in the even more serious case where the reigning monarchy was the founder of a dynasty, the scion of a family that had been in more or less open opposition to the previous sovereigns? In these cases, the fiction of pharaonic power came into full play: each sovereign who wore the double crown was considered the natural legitimate heir of the previous kings. In a corridor of the commemorative temple to Sety I at Abydos there is a list of previous pharaohs, only the last one of whom was related to him by blood.

But things could be even more convenient. The mythical version of kingship was held by the god Horus, son-of-Isis (Horsaisis), the young and impetuous sovereign who took care of his father Osiris. His actions could be very abrupt, because he was a violent being, a fearsome fighter, the inspiration of the pharaoh when faced with his enemies: "He kills them all with his hand, just as before Horsaisis massacred his enemies."[16] But this young man was, above all, the figure who carried out the funeral rites for his father Osiris. Thus he was the officiant *par excellence*, the god who performed rituals. Horasaisis was the very model of a son faithful to his "functional" father—here, the god Osiris. This is how he would be depicted on the doors of the Theban temples of the Ptolemaic period.[17]

The King Performing Rituals for the Happiness of Mankind

From the end of the 3rd Dynasty onward an inscription that appears *ad infinitum* on Egyptian funeral monuments right up to the time of the Romans is "*nesut-di-hotep*," a phrase that poses certain grammatical problems of interpretation and has been the object of numerous studies.[18] One recent reading proposes the translation "May the king make it so that [the god or gods X] are satisfied," so that they will grant that the deceased N may enjoy the fruits of an incantatory offering.[19] The incantatory offering was a ritual performed by the family and by visitors to the tomb; the deceased and offerings were invoked, and perhaps a trickle of water was poured onto the offering table in front of the funeral stele; the dead person was thence considered to enjoy the benefits of these substances evoked by magic ritual. From the above-mentioned formula of introduction, it would seem that this ability to transfer real objects into the imaginary world depended on the mediation of the king with the gods. Here the king performs ritual in order to please the gods and set up a sort of trust and complicity with them. As the gods are so powerful, may they—thanks to the intervention of the king—grant each individual the power to perform with efficacy a magical ritual repeated in innumerable tombs throughout Egypt. According to G. Lapp, the origin of this ritual extension of royal action is to be traced back to the workings of the palace complexes of the Archaic Period. It makes reference to the provision of real foodstuffs by the king—foodstuffs that came either from the palace warehouses or, more probably, from the place of worship linked with the palace. We know, for example, that the solar temples of the 5th Dynasty provided the meat offerings for the funeral ceremonies of the sovereign. It is not impossible that they also played some role in the provision of food-stuffs for the royal residence. Here again, one can see that the ritual action of the king was fundamental in the economic working of complex systems on which large numbers of households depended for their survival.

From the 11th Dynasty onward, another of the titles that habitually preceded a sovereign's cartouche was the expression "lord of doing things."[20] This rather vague formula seems to refer to actions of ritual as they would have been seen by the laity. Not only was there the handling of symbolic objects, but also the recitation of texts and prayers in a language which, from the Ramesside period onward, was less and less understood by the uninitiated (eventually it was totally incomprehensible to them). It is no accident that this formula, which reveals the presence of an uninitiated public at the great royal ceremonies, should make its appearance in the era when, throughout Thebes, the reigns of Intef and Montuhotep were seeing the construction of a new theocracy, in which the epiphanies of the monarch within the settings of divine monuments were to play a key role.

The two above-mentioned examples show the king performing ritual for the benefit of all—either individually (through the monarch's sole ability to "activate" the incantatory formula) or collectively (by the performance of things that have to be performed before the gods and a public of initiated and non-initiated). These acts clearly assume that the officiating sovereign had certain powers. He was the one who, in principle, held the knowledge of divine forms and appearances. The oldest extant documents reveals to us that the craftsman responsible for the making of images—the very locus in which gods and men established contact with each other—were the first to work with the king in his role as a performer of ritual.[21] In the classical period, the king was the figure who not only stocked the storehouses of temples (through his wise government of the country and his vigorous prosecution of conquest) but also managed the distribution of these goods through his priests, those who were delegated with his liturgical powers. It was the king who ordered the creation of new images of the gods, obviously relying on the largely encyclopaedic religious knowledge of his clergy. It was he who—at least, theoretically (that is, in the depictions on the walls of temples)—consecrated the various implements of religious worship to the gods in that very ancient ritual of the "opening of the mouth." Thereafter, the stone, wood or metal object produced by craftsmen became an implement of divine power, a means whereby ritual acts impinged on the imagination. Thus for example, in a separate room at Karnak one sees Thutmose III "opening the mouth" of the boat of Amun, recently rebuilt using woods and precious metals won in his military campaigns. In the same room one also sees the erection of monumental pillars formed by the trunks of Cilician pines brought back from Lebanon.[22] Given his omnipotence, the king could not only delegate the performance of ritual but also the very initiation of ritual. Curiously enough, in the few cases where we have evidence of the pharaoh delegating a faithful follower to restore a cult of worship or institute a ritual, that follower is not necessarily a priest. For example, Ikhernofret, chancellor of Senusret III, was sent by his master to Abydos not only to restore the sacred holy image of Osiris with the gold brought back from Nubia, but also to perform the feasts of the god, reorganize his worship and make sure that these rituals were respected.[23]

In the above-mentioned examples, the action of the king as performer of ritual rested on manifestations that directly involve the individual. However, every day in every temple of Egypt, complex rituals were carried out in the secrecy of sanctuaries, lavishing upon the statue of the deity the same care one might lavish on an individual. The statue was the locus of a divine epiphany within our world, and at the same time the means whereby mankind might gain access to the world of the gods. Represented by his priests, the pharaoh came to awaken the statue from its nightly slumbers, to wash it, dress it and adorn it with jewels and protective amulets, and then present it with its morning repast. A series of papyri (now in Berlin[24]) have preserved collections of the phrases and responses that were part of this daily ritual in the Theban region in the eighth century BC. While the basic structure will have been the same in all

9. Faience plaque with figures of gods, Third Intermediate Period. London, The Trustees of the British Museum
cat. 37

7. Relief of Rameses II with his mother, New Kingdom, 19th Dynasty.
Vienna Kunsthistorisches Museum
cat. 89

8. Bronze censer from the Late Period.
Paris, Musée du Louvre
cat. 84

the temples of Egypt, there must also have been numerous variations suited to each of the deities concerned. Several temples have sequences of scenes depicting parts of this ritual; there is a relatively complete version (34 scenes) in the temple commemorating Sety I at Abydos.[25]

A particularly interesting aspect from our point of view is the fear shown by the officiant, the substitute for the king, when opening the cupboard which contained the image of the deity. What will be the divine power's reaction when it is disturbed from its sleep by this unknown human? "It is the king who has ordered me to see the god," announces the officiant.[26] The god is thus reassured, because the human priest who bursts into the darkness of his sanctuary is acting in the name of his beloved son. The decor of solar temples dating from the New Kingdom shows us the worship of the sun as it passes through the heavens during the course of the day; the king is depicted reciting a long hymn in which he presents himself as the priest of the sun, listing the extent of his knowledge: "The king N knows the secret words pronounced by the souls of the East . . . he knows their [hidden] appearance and their transformations . . . he knows where they are when Ra appears at the beginning of his journey. . . ."[27] The pharaoh who was a performer of ritual was also a learned scholar.

An Exception: Akhenaten, Object of his Own Ritual
It is worth halting for a moment to look at the case of Akhenaten, which might be said to reveal ritual taken to an extreme. Amenhotep IV promoted a theology of light and of the immediate world without, however, denying the ancient gods. The *talatat* blocks from Karnak reveal that the worship of Amun and Aten were not incompatible.[28] But while, as far as one can make out, Amenhotep IV took up the broad outlines of solar rituals and liturgies (with the presentation of food offerings on open-air altars), he also introduced a new form of hierarchy that centered on the royal couple, who was the transposition into this world of the celestial couple Ra and Hathor. Thus Akhenaten and Nefertiti were not only sovereign performers of ritual—only they could officiate on the altar of the eastern temple of el-Amarna—but they were also figures whose daily life took on a liturgical significance of its own. The *talatat* blocks of Karnak show us the king eating, washing and dressing, scenes which can only be explained if they were considered to have some sort of performative power. The places where Their Majesties ate, slept and ap-

peared before their subjects were, like the sites of contact with the divine, shown in representations with the sun-disk pouring forth its beneficent influence on mankind.[29] The great avenue across the city—linking the royal residence with the area of the temples and administration buildings—was not the creation of some inspired city planner but simply a processional route along which the royal couple advanced in a chariot, in full view of their people.[30]

The Ritualist Pharaoh Was There for All to See

In certain circumstances it was expected by everyone that the king would not resort to the use of delegation but himself perform the great liturgies of divine manifestation before the crowd of his subjects. This was an occasion to see the king, to see the gods in their divine boats, to follow the massive apparatus of pharaonic processions as they made their way along imposing sphinx-lined avenues that linked one temple with another. The greatest of these feasts were celebrated at Thebes. The Festival of Opet, for example, consisted of a procession of Amun from his temple at Karnak to the temple at Luxor, one of the places in which the world originated and home to the depiction of the god as a procreative power. During the course of the Beautiful Festival of the Valley, Amun passed through the necropolis—bringing new life to those buried there—visiting the Temple of Millions of Years of the reigning sovereign. On these occasions, the king opened the procession, bearing the sacred scepter of the god Amun as a standard behind which all followed.

Performing Public Ritual in the Absence of the Pharaoh

These annual festivals taking place far to the south of the nation were a problem for a pharaoh ruling the country from Memphis (from the reign of Thutmose III onward) or the eastern Delta (from the reign of the Ramessides). Certain of these festivals were politically important, occasions for a statement of the grandeur of pharaonic power in the very heart of its religious capital. However, caught up in the management of the country's political and military affairs, the king was sometimes unable to go south in person.

We have already seen how the ordinary daily business of rituals might be delegated from king to priest, but here the process goes much further. For the feasts combining the pharaoh's role as sovereign individual and officiant of ritual, the king would have resorted to new procedures. First of all, he might delegate one of his most faithful servants, a court administrator or general. Here, more than just the observation of ritual was involved; through the intermediary of a man who was recognized as an example of fidelity to the person of the sovereign, the very power of the throne was being demonstrated.[31] Nevertheless, the people also expected His Majesty himself; hence, once again, the Egyptians had to resort to images.

Standing in front of Sety II's bark shrine at Karnak are two colossi in quartzite of the king; striding forward, he is carrying before him the scepter of Amun, just as he would do in leading the procession.[32] What is more, the decor in the niches in the central sanctuary of this temple reveals that they also contained a life-size image of the walking king, bearing the cane and war club, just like any other pharaoh in procession to the temple. It is significant that this image shows the figure placed on a wooden sled, an iconographical detail which suggests that the statue of the king actually took part in the procession (drawn by priests). The image was the true substitute for the monarch. The colossal standard-bearers outside were the monumental, permanent—and, above all, external and visible—versions of this virtual presence of the officiating king. As the representative of the king, the person who now led the festivals became a sort of organizer of the whole event. As we know from extant papyri, these things could have important economic consequences. The idea of a surrogate image of the king would seem to offer the key to a correct interpretation of the magnificent standing statue of Amenhotep III (complete with sled) that was recently found in the court of the temple of Luxor.[33] It is a royal processional figure in stone, and is not to be read through some theological interpretation of the sled (the hieroglyphic sign which is a component of the name of the god Aten).

In the niches of Sety II's bark shrine, the officiant would perform his function in front of depictions of the processional statue of the pharaoh himself. This celebrant, therefore, clearly could not have been the king—already present—or an ordinary priest acting in his name. The difficulties of explanation posed here have been overcome by assuming the presence of a *Iunmutef* priest—that is, a son officiating in the veneration of his father (the officiant *par excellence*). The

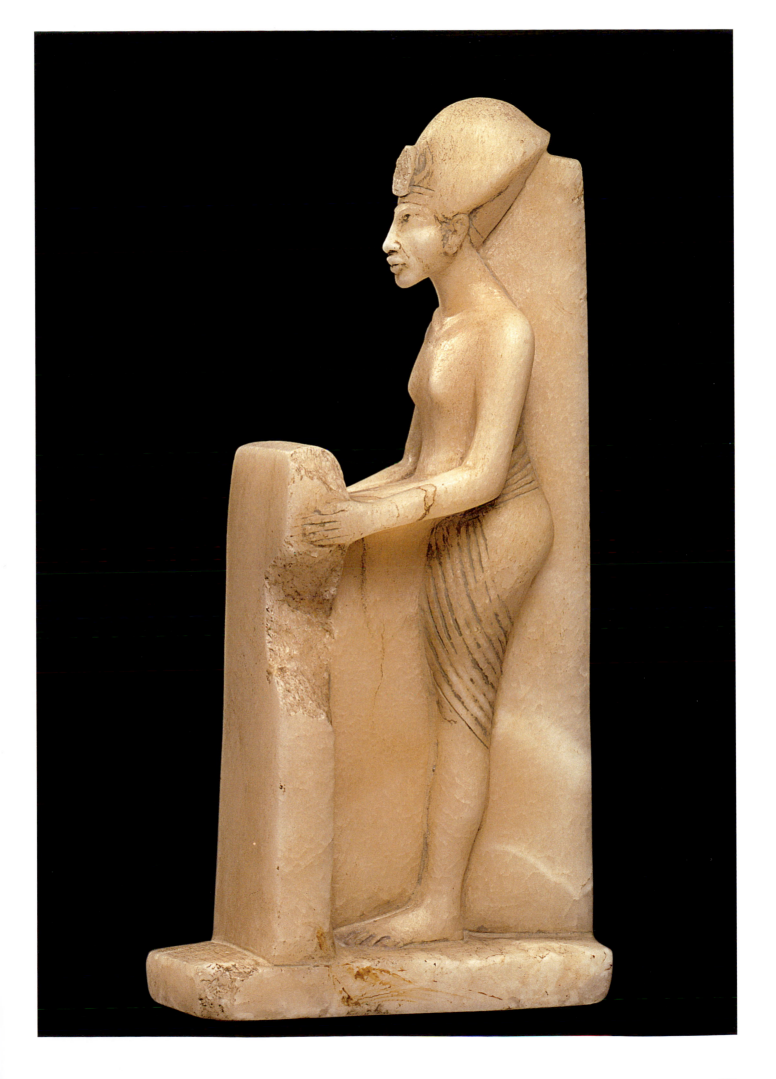

very same *mise-en-scène* appears on the bases of the colossi of Rameses II, in part "recycled" from those of Amenhotep III, in the court of the temple at Luxor. It is the *Iunmutef* priest who pronounces the formula of purification over the offerings "which come from the altar of Amun," and which are then to be placed before the royal statue for the enjoyment of the "*ka* of the Lord of the Two Lands."[34] The whole thing rests on the system of statue-as-substitute-for-dead-king, but here uses the statue as a substitute for an absent king—a living being who is monumentally present at the celebration of the liturgy. Here, there is a sort of reversal of roles: the absent king/officiant of ritual becomes—through the intermediary of his statue—the recipient of the ritual, addressed to his *ka*, as it would be before the statue of a dead pharaoh. Thus the ceremony became a means for "replenishing" the power of the king.

The Pharaoh: Ritual and Power
It is interesting to see how a weakening of power might affect the above-described mechanisms. In fact, the legitimacy granted by ritual was something sought after by all pretenders to the double crown. In the most straightforward of cases, the political power of the day simply took over the function of the celebration of ritual as it saw fit. At the end of the 20th Dynasty, General Herihor was commissioned by a rather weakened throne to carry out far-reaching reforms in the south of the country. His power for this was legitimized by proclaiming him the high priest of Amun through an oracle, and by granting him the prerogatives and insignia of pharaonic royalty: *uraeus*, cartouches and crowns. In fact, for his coronation name, the general simply enclosed his title of high priest within a cartouche.

During the Third Intermediate Period, the struggles between various royal families gave rise to the conflict over legitimacy, and the few extant documents reveal the liturgical implications of these rivalries. A story in demotic Egyptian—a sort of pseudo-historical parody—recounts the struggle between various factions for the privilege of leading the famous Valley Festival.[35] According to this tale, only the sovereign who each year brought Amun over to the west bank of the river (or who had the god accompanied by someone else) could be considered the true pharaoh. There was a struggle here between an old royal dynasty and a new power in the celebration of ritual claimed by a mysterious "priest of Horus"—a clear metaphor for the divine officiant Horsaisis. Thus the text reveals a new conception of the Theban festival emerging during the first millennium BC. Before, during the old times of the great monarchs of the New Kingdom—when the pharaoh, even if he had lived in the North, was always laid to rest in the Valley of the Kings—Thebes maintained a certain liturgical coherence. Each year Amun visited the sites that commemorated the kings, and all the dead profited from his vivifying presence alongside the dead king. However, when the sovereigns were buried in the necropolis of the North, Amun's visit to the left bank turned away from the Temples of Millions of Years to honor a divine figure, the deceased Kematef, "he who had completed his time."

From the 21st Dynasty onward a new theology began to emerge in the city of Amun, and a characteristic feature of it was the development of a religious geography. The right bank of Karnak was—and remained—the abode of Amun, living royalty, the true temporal sovereign. His procreative form at Luxor, Amun-Ope, took on the role of a divine officiant who was responsible for the pouring of a double libation of cool water onto the tomb of the deceased (in theory every ten days). On the left bank, at Medinet Habu, the old temple of the 18th Dynasty became the mortuary temple dedicated to Kematef, a dead mythical embodiment of Amun, a funerary transposition of the demiurge of primordial times. Known as the rites of Djeme, this funerary veneration of the dead god would undergo one last "burst of energy" when it served as a means of justifying and legitimizing the power of the pharaohs of foreign origin. The rites themselves involved the king in pouring a libation before Amun-Ope, the divine officiant *par excellence*; however, one might also find reference to Horsaisis, the very image of royal legitimacy associated with ritual. Sometimes the officiating king himself was known by this name; sometimes, more directly, he presented the royal crowns to Horsaisis in return for a recognition of the legitimacy of his pharaonic power by this divine heir.[36]

From the Saite period onward, the Theban priests responsible for the Djeme rites bore the title "priest of the White and of Horus, the great of the two crowns." In other words, they were considered as the guardians of the pharaonic crowns.[37] This liturgical function would develop further during the Ptolemaic and Roman periods, when Egypt was governed by sovereigns whose cultural background was non-Egyptian. Under Ptolemy VIII Euergetes II a small temple was built at Djeme and dedicated to Thoth (at the present-day Qasr el-Aguz[38]). Thoth therefore appears at the center of the dynastic worship of these sovereigns of foreign origin.

Thus, at the heart of the religious capital of the Pharaonic state, the king who performed or presided over these rituals acquired a legitimacy which was sanctioned by the theologians of Amun, who had been the very underpinning of pharaonic royalty from the 11th Dynasty onward. Whether these sovereigns were called Taharqo, Darius, Ptolemy or even Tiberius, whether they spoke Nubian, Greek, Persian or Latin, the rituals performed in their name were still capable of making them "the son of Ra, king of Upper and Lower Egypt." When the kings of Alexandria visited Upper Egypt, the local priests—who were the guardians of the ancient skills and traditions of pharaonic power—showed their sanctuaries to these foreign sovereigns. In a certain sense, this was the culmination of the doubling of pharaonic royalty referred to above: there was a virtual pharaoh fixed in stone and in the old religious writings that commemorated him, and a contemporary statesman, caught up in the affairs of the eastern Mediterranean. And when the occasion presented itself, ritual might momentarily reconcile these two facets of Egyptian royalty. Thus, for example, in 115 BC, when Cleopatra III and her recently-crowned son Ptolemy IX Soter II visited Upper Egypt, one can imagine that the young sovereign will have conscientiously performed the ancient rites of the pharaohs under the grave and watchful eye of the old primate of Thebes, the wise Horemheb, son of Nekhmontu.

---

[1] Hani 1976, p. 36.

[2] Grimal 1986, p. 95 (KRI II, 354.5–7).

[3] Grimal 1986, p. 104 (KRI I, 46.12).

[4] Posener 1960.

[5] Sethy I on the stele of west Gebel el-Silsila (KRI I, 80.13, Grimal 1986, p. 145).

[6] Posener 1960, pp. 79–81; Kuentz 1928, pp. 253–254.

[7] The Konosso stele of Thutmose IV alludes to the words of the god (URK IV, 1546, 2). See the study by Youri Volokhine in BIFAO 2002.

[8] Posener 1960, p. 88.

[9] Smith 1988, p. 165, fig. 56 and pl. 120 B.

[10] Derchain 1965; Traunecker 1992.

[11] Clère 1961, pl. 21.

[12] Epigraphic Survey 1980, pl. 32–40, URK IV, 1867.15–16.

[13] Goyon 1972, pp. 85–182; Traunecker 1989, p. 106ff.

[14] H. Te Velde in LA II 1980, col. 212.

[15] For example, the chapel of Rameses I in the temple of Sety I at Qurna. See also the temple of Queen Hatshepsut at Deir el-Bahri, with the veneration of Thutmose I and II.

[16] Gauthier, Sottas 1925, p. 34.

[17] See the examples cited in Traunecker 1995, pp. 197–98.

[18] Smither 1939; Barta 1968; Lapp 1986. According to A. Gardiner, the king gives and the gods give back.

[19] Grandet, Mathieu 1990, pp. 388–90.

[20] Barta 1986, p. 283.

[21] Kaplony 1966 and Traunecker 1995, p. 106.

[22] Traunecker 1995, pp. 89–111.

[23] Berlin Stele 1204. Guiter 1998.

[24] Berlin 3055 and 3053 +14. Moret 1902; Roeder 1960, pp. 72–142; Guglielmi, Buroth 1997, pp. 101–137.

[25] Traunecker 2001, pp. 497–503..

[26] Moret 1902, p. 55.

[27] Assmann 1970, p. 21.

[28] Traunecker 1986A, pp. 17–44.

[29] Traunecker 1998A, Traunecker 1984, p. 160.

[30] Chappaz 1987, pp. 118–19.

[31] Helck 1977.

[32] Louvre statue A24 and Turin 1383, see Chadefaud 1982, pp. 55–58.

[33] el-Saghir 1991, pp. 21–27.

[34] PM II, p. 313 (70). Schwaller de Lubicz 1958.II, pl. 46 and Schwaller de Lubicz 1949, fig. 11. See, above all, the text of the western colossus.

[35] Traunecker 1995.

[36] For a brief account of these rituals, see Traunecker 1986B; Traunecker 1992, pp. 92–93 or the English version, with notes, Gods of Egypt New York 2001.

[37] Traunecker 1998B.

[38] Monument undergoing excavation and study as part of a joint project involving Strasbourg University and IFAO.

The Builder Pharaoh. The Temples

Hourig Sourouzian
Rainer Stadelmann

The Temples of the New Kingdom

The Temples of the New Kingdom and of the 21st–22nd Dynasties

The New Kingdom, spanning almost five centuries from the middle of the second millennium BC until its close, witnessed one of the most glorious periods of architecture in ancient Egypt.

The rulers of Upper Egypt who had succeeded in freeing their land from sterile foreign dominion were also conscious of its cultural traditions, and managed to rebuild a unified and well-administered state. Agriculture and crafts quickly flourished once again. No sooner had the frontiers been secured and peace established with neighboring states to north and south, than tribute and trade goods began to flow into Egypt from the north, from Syria and Palestine, the islands of the Aegean, the Minoan-Cretan sea kingdom, the Peloponnese and the coasts of Asia Minor. To the south, Nubia was not only the land of gold, but also the place where all the exotic riches of Africa could be exchanged. Above all, the artists, architects and craftsmen of Egypt regained their magisterial command of nature and the environment and created, in every field of their endeavor, magnificent works which could bear comparison with the past achievements of the Old and Middle Kingdoms.

The splendid capital of the early New Kingdom was Thebes, "the Victorious," *No-Amun*, the "City of Amun," the only city of any size since the Middle Kingdom and since the Thutmosides. It was a genuine metropolis with governing quarters and city districts between the temples of Amun—Karnak today—and the "southern citadel," the temple of Luxor in the east and the great residential city of Hefthirnebes, "the city opposite her master," the palatial residence on the west bank. When Amenhotep IV/Akhenaten moved the residence to el-Amarna, there began a bleak period lasting a decade. Then the restoration of the traditional rituals under the Ramessides assured Thebes and the whole of Egypt southward as far as Nubia a new resurgence of art and architecture.

The Temples of Karnak and Luxor

In Thebes, the early 18th Dynasty leaned heavily on the example of the Middle Kingdom. The temple of Senusret I in Karnak continued for centuries to be the center of the temple complex, which now expanded layer by layer, eastward, westward and southward. The great king Amenhotep I restored the Middle Kingdom buildings, added his own alabaster vessel to the bark shrine and surrounded the court with a ring of chapels which his successor Thutmose I rapidly added to. The latter also endowed the temple precinct with its first masonry wall and erected two mighty towers to the west, pylons IV and V as they are termed today. These served as the entrance gate for more than a century, decorated with flagpoles and two obelisks standing 21.80 meters high. Between pylons IV and V he added an enclosed hypostyle hall, called Wadjet, the "hall of papyrus columns," the sacred hall of the election of the ruler and the coronation in the temple by the god Amun. On the north side of the hall must have stood the temple palace of the kings, known only from inscriptions. Niches in the walls of the hall carried outsized royal statues in the guise of Osiris, symbolizing the eternal renewal of the kingdom. Thutmose II added a walled enclosure with a smaller tower and obelisks in front of pylon IV. The walls of this enclosure were later decorated under Thutmose IV with colored reliefs showing processions and sacrifices. Both the compound and the tower were soon swept aside by the grandiose schemes of Amenhotep III, however, who had them demolished to make way for a giant pylon with eight flag poles. The earlier enclosure of Thutmose II was enlarged to serve as a ceremonial stage for processions to the temple of Luxor, the "southern citadel" of the god Amun, completely and magnificently rebuilt by Amenhotep III. The building stone from the demolished earlier buildings was carefully reused inside the new pylon.

Before this, Hatshepsut, the daughter of Thutmose I, had built a complex of rooms outside the temple of Senusret I and around the bark shrine of Amenhotep I, to serve as a resting place for religious objects and sacrificial items. She subsequently replaced the alabaster bark with one of her own made of quartzite, the "miraculous stone" from the sacred mountain of the sun-god at Heliopolis. The uninterrupted building activity, the use of costly building materials redolent with symbolic meaning and the erection of numerous obelisks in the temple itself, with the two largest inside the papyrus pillared hall: all these aspects underscore the efforts of the Theban kings to place their local divinity Amun on a par with the univer-

2. Karnak, the temple of Amun, the first pylon

sal sun-god Ra of Heliopolis, thus raising him to an imperial god, and to make of Thebes an even more extensive and magnificent city than Heliopolis in the north. Accordingly, Hatshepsut had a bigger enclosing wall built around the temple and erected a counter-temple against the outer face of the wall on its east side. This took the form of a grandiose image shrine in alabaster, with colossal, eastward-gazing effigies of the queen and of Amun, together with two obelisks sculpted with images of Amun. To the east of this, Thutmose III began work on a vast enclosure, intended to provide a setting for the largest obelisk, 34 meters in height. In all the above works Hatshepsut was represented as a reigning king, albeit closely followed as coregent at every stage of cult ceremony by her stepson Thutmose III, as yet a minor. After her death, the new pharaoh continued the queen's building schemes, but from the fortieth year of his reign his attitude toward his predecessor altered discernibly. This was probably essentially due to a change in religious dogma, which no longer viewed as orthodox the idea that a woman should take over the duties of the king; thus her name was erased, the plinths of her two obelisks in the papyrus pillared hall were walled up inside a new doorway, and even her sacred bark in red quartzite was replaced by a new one in granite bearing the name of Thutmose III only. In front of the bark shrine the king built a further small pylon, number VI, and replaced the original wooden plant emblems representing Upper and Lower Egypt with new ones in highly polished red granite. Thutmose also had the walls separating the bark shrine and the pylon decorated with scenes chronicling his two decades and more of victorious campaigns in Syria and Nubia.

It is remarkable how each successive king was so concerned to build in and make his mark on the confined space available in front of and around the bark shrine, conveying to us its significance as the holiest place of the temple. However, the constant construction also made the space increasingly confined and intricate, with the result that later rulers were unable to build there. Thus without doubt the most splendid monument to Amun founded by Thutmose III was his Festival Temple, built in the vast open courtyard to the east of the Middle Kingdom temple. Here there was enough space to erect an impressive basilica to house

3. Karnak, the temple of Amun, the Middle Kingdom court and the Festival Temple of Thutmose III

the ruler's jubilee ceremonies, with colonnaded aisles and two rows of ten giant "tent pole" columns in the nave. This huge ceremonial stone tent lay on a north-south axis; the sole entrance was in the southwestern corner, where there was also a small chapel, whose walls bore a royal list with the names of the kings that had founded Karnak and built there. There were very probably also statuettes of the kings, which would have been carried on ritual processions. The sanctuaries are ranged along the eastern side of the ceremonial hall, with that of Amun in the center, that of Sokar to the south, and the chapel of the sun-god to the north. The latter had a high chamber with representations of living nature, the so-called "botanical garden" and the chapels and altar of the Ennead, the original nine divinities of Heliopolis, plus a rooftop sanctum where the rising sun could be worshipped. This temple is thus strikingly similar to the scheme of the mortuary or memorial temple of the New Kingdom in west Thebes; indeed it is also called the Temple of Millions of Years in the temple of Amun. Thutmose III was thus the first king of the New Kingdom to create a memorial temple in east Thebes in the *temenos* of Amun, a kind of complementary temple for the start of processions to the western city. Lastly, the space left free between the outer walls and the inner temple precinct was occupied by large-chambered storage buildings and sacristies, extensively decorated with depictions of sacrificial goods and rituals of all kinds.

As early as the Middle Kingdom, the most important religious activities in Thebes were the bark processions of Amun to his "southern citadel," an ancient sanctuary on a hilltop thought to be the original Mound of Creation in what is now Luxor, and to Deir el-Bahri on the west bank of the Nile. The pomp and splendor of these excursions required the construction of ceremonial courts and processional ways. Since space was no longer available adjoining the bark shrine itself, these courts took the form of large enclosures with pylons laid out to the east and west, where the barks, standard-bearers of the gods, the royal court and military escorts could assemble.

Hatshepsut had already planned a first court with pylon VIII as a tower, decorating its façade with six colossal statues of Amenhotep I, Thutmose I and Thutmose II, of her coregent Thut-

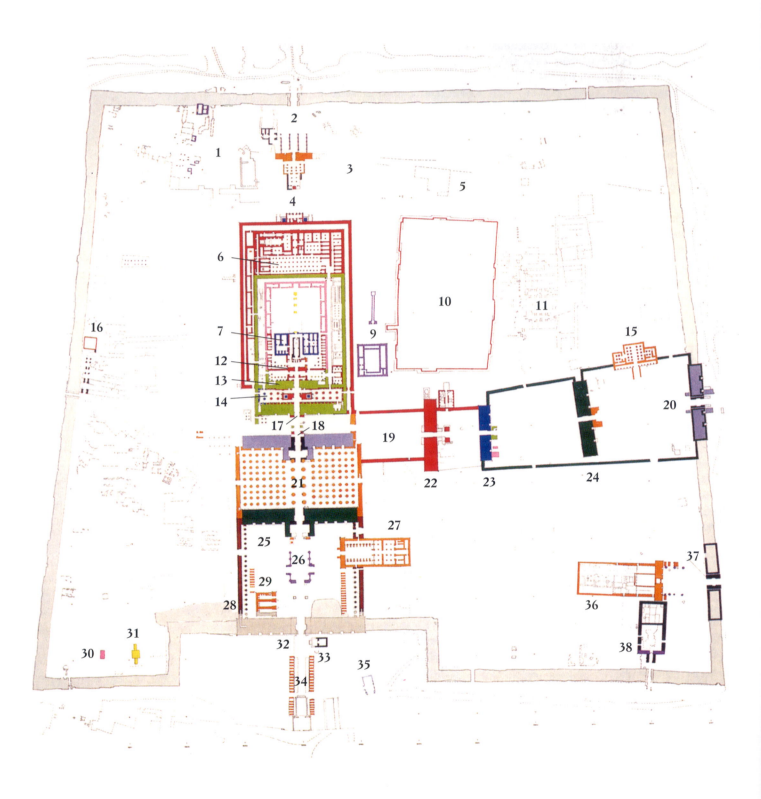

following pages
5. Karnak, temple of Amun, the
sacred lake and the eighth pylon

mose III and of herself. Thutmose III divided the court by placing another pylon, the seventh, in its center and by setting up two pairs of colossal statues and obelisks on its southern side. Amenhotep III laid new stress on the southern axis with a vast enclosure of more than 150 meters in length and the tenth pylon, 35 meters high, before whose entrance he placed a pair of statues which reached a height of more than 21 meters. This enclosure was later subdivided by the ninth pylon, built by Horemheb, in part using *talatat*, conveniently sized blocks, carved in relief, that had been removed from a building by Amenhotep IV. This earlier construction had been erected to the east of the temple of Amun by Amenhotep IV, during the first five years of his reign; it was dedicated to the sun-god Aten Ra-Horakhty and called *Gempaaten*, "Aten is found." In its broad, open compound stood the famous colossal statues of Amenhotep IV, in the mannerist style of his earlier years, when he was still resident in Thebes. In the extensive courts to the south, west and east of the temple of Amun stood statues of the kings and high-ranking dignitaries, who could thus take part in the divine festivals and processions for eternity. These processions led to neighboring temples: southward to that of the goddess Mut, probably a lioness-goddess in origin, who since the New Kingdom possessed her own precinct with an oval-shaped sacred lake, and beyond to the "southern citadel" of Amun, the temple of Luxor, in which Amun resided as one of the original gods. This was the destination of the annual bark procession with the god Amun of Karnak on the occasion of the Opet Festival, led by the king whose divine birth and rule were confirmed in the temple at Luxor. The bark of Amun rested in the central bark shrine as the god of Karnak was united with the original god of Luxor in the hindmost part of the temple. Amenhotep III remodeled the modest sanctuary of the Middle and early New Kingdom, giving it new magnificence and progressively expanding it. Between the shrine-chamber for sacred images and the bark shrine he added an enclosed chamber with twelve pillars, in which the daily course of the sun from east to west was mythologized and celebrated.

A sequence of chambers to the east of the bark shrine was decorated with scenes illustrating the divine procreation and birth of the king, a theme which belonged to the royal legend since the Old Kingdom. It had, for instance, been immortalized by Hatshepsut at Deir el-Bahri. Amenhotep III laid out a broad ceremonial court before the cult chambers. This had magnificent papyriform pillars, between which stood colossal statues. A number of group images of divinities from the time of Amenhotep III have recently been discovered there; these sculptures give us a very real idea of religious rites that were previously known only from reliefs. Lastly, in front of this peristyle court, Amenhotep III celebrated the jubilees of his reign by erecting the famous monumental colonnade with two rows of seven 21.20-meter-high papyrus pillars. During the early years of his reign, Rameses II expanded the temple still further with another peristyle court, and closed it off with a mighty pylon, before which he erected six colossal statues and two tall obelisks. The court of Rameses II is oriented both toward the temple of Karnak, with which it was joined by an avenue of sphinxes, and toward the Ramesseum, his mortuary temple in west Thebes. Between the peristyle pillars, Rameses again erected striding colossal statues, in part reusing pieces from the time of Amenhotep III that had been toppled by the henchmen of Akhenaten. For the façade of the pylon, Rameses II ordered scenes from the Battle of Qadesh, glorifying his campaign in Syria and the war with the Hittites.

The second great festival in Thebes was the Beautiful Festival of the Valley, a procession in which Amun and his fellow gods were carried from Karnak across the river to visit the funerary temples of deceased kings on the west bank, before remaining several days in the valley of Deir el-Bahri. The barks were collected beforehand in the enclosure in front of the pylons III and IV, which, however, soon proved too confined a space for this magnificent assembly, so that after the Amarna period Horemheb built a third pylon, number II, in front of pylon III. Sety I converted this court into a huge pillared hall, one of the wonders of the ancient world. It measured 104 meters in length and had a width of 52 meters between the pylons and the side walls. This now became the starting place for the processions of the great Theban festivals and was called "the temple of Sety-Merenptah shines in the house of Amun."

The sequence of pillars along the temple axis consists of two rows of six mighty pillars with open papyrus umbels. At 22.40 meters, the pillars are taller than the rest of the hall. The two

6. Relief of Thutmose III with
tutelary divinities from Elephantine,
New Kingdom, 18th Dynasty.
Berlin, Ägyptisches Museum
und Papyrussammlung

7. Ostracon with procession of the
boat of Amun from Deir el-Medina,
New Kingdom, 19th–20th Dynasties.
Berlin, Ägyptisches Museum
und Papyrussammlung
cat. 75

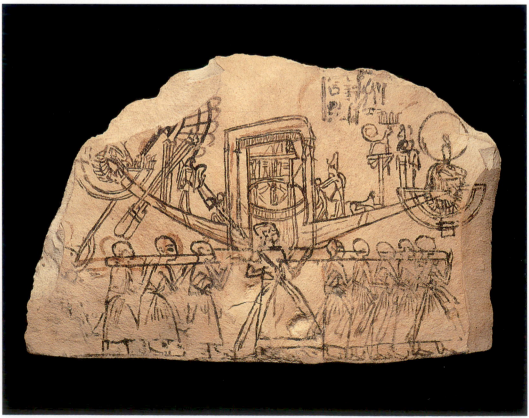

8. West Thebes, temple of
Amenhotep III, west portico
of the court.

following pages
9. Luxor, first pylon of the temple

side aisles of the pillared hall each have seven rows of pillars representing stylized bundles of stems, with closed capitals. Each row has nine pillars, except for the two innermost rows; these have seven, closed off by two square columns at the point where colonnade and vestibule meet. There is thus a total of one hundred and thirty-four pillars, representing a vast thicket of papyrus made eternal in stone. The pillars were not hewn from single blocks, but built up from massive drums; they rest on tall, round bases. They were topped by square abaci, on which rest the mighty architraves that bear the roof beams. Light could only enter through the stone latticework inserted in the raised, basilican main corridor. In the middle of the great pillared hall a diagonal axis in the right-hand corner runs to the main axis between gates in the southern and northern side walls, creating, in addition to the dominant east-west axis, a north-south axis to serve as a processional way between the temples of Karnak and Luxor.

When Sety I died shortly after entering the twelfth year of his reign, the still unfinished pillared hall and its pictorial program were completed by Rameses II. The northern half, whose mural decoration was carried out in high relief, was the work of Sety I, while the deeper-cut reliefs adorning the southern half of the walls were those finished by Rameses II. The pillar shafts are decorated with papyrus leaves below, while above they carry sacrificial scenes and cartouche friezes with the names of the royal founders. Later, these were mostly overwritten with the names of the last Ramessides. The inner walls of the halls are decorated with a variety of eventful scenes featuring many different figures. The pictorial sequences are laid out on a large scale, showing the king led by the Theban Triad of Amun, Mut and Khons, whom he worships, offering sacrifice. Representations of the liturgical purification of the king by the gods alternate with others of his coronation and enthronement in the temple, the handing over of the scepter and the inscription of the royal name in the leaves of the holy *ished* tree in the heavenly Heliopolis. The great significance of the processions in which the divine images were carried in sacred barks is attested to by their being depicted in the

principal registers both by Sety I and by Rameses II. In contrast to the inner walls, painted exclusively with scenes of ritual ceremony and festival processions, the outer walls carry depictions of the defeat of chaos through the king's victories over foreign enemies. The northern wall has the campaigns of Sety I against the Bedouins of Palestine and the Western Desert, the Libyans and the Hittites. The southern wall has reliefs of the famous battle fought by Rameses II against Hittite, Asiatic and Libyan forces at Qadesh. The great pillared hall is thus an illustration in stone of Egypt and its surrounding world: the sacred world of the gods and religious rites within; the threatening, chaotic world without, which the pharaoh must fend off again and again. The papyriform pillars themselves represent the "Black Land," Egypt flooded by the Nile, from which it resurfaces annually like the original mound of the creation myths.

From the pillared hall, an avenue of ram-headed sphinxes of Amun-Ra, named for Rameses II, led to a landing quay on a canal linking the temple with the Nile. To the north of this processional avenue Sety II later had a way-station built, a triple shrine where the barks of the Triad could be rested. Before it stood colossal statues of the kings shown as standard-bearers, now in the Louvre and the Egyptian Museum in Turin. Other, similar statues of almost life-size dimensions stood at the entrance of and inside the pillared hall and are now preserved in the museum in Cairo. Each king was required to lead the festival processions in person at least once, at the beginning of his reign, after which statues could serve as surrogates for his actual presence. Thus every king visited Thebes in his first year and built a memorial to make the memory of his presence eternal. At the outset of the 20th Dynasty, Rameses III had his own way-station erected to the south of the main axis of the processional way. This was a temple in its own right with a pylon flanked by standing figures of the king. Entrance to the sanctuary is through a forecourt, lined with Osiride pillars, and a vestibule. Again the way-station served as a resting place for the three divine barks and a place of sacrifice during the procession.

Sety I and Rameses II restored the old Festival Temple of Thutmose III, which lay to the east of the temple of Amun, erecting a single obelisk. Fragments of large sphinxes suggest there was an eastern processional way: in the broad, unencumbered space before it Rameses II built a temple for Ra-Horakhty, dedicated to the cult of the rising sun. At its entrance stood two large statues of Rameses II in the shape of Osiris. It was inside this temple that perhaps the most beautiful and certainly the most famous statue of Rameses II was found, sculpted in dark granite. The young pharaoh is shown enthroned; he wears the blue crown, a long pleated garment and sandals, and holds the scepter in one hand. The gentle smile characteristic of all original statues of Rameses II lights up his countenance. It can now be admired in the Turin Museum. The ritual significance of the many processions and their routes in the great temple precinct can be deduced from the fact that on both the outward and the return journey between the main and the eastern temples, the enclosing wall of Thutmose's temple had to be circumambulated by the procession. This was why Rameses II had the outer walls of this older temple decorated throughout with sacrificial scenes: The closed temple and its ritual practices thus became transparent and could be sensed from without by the participants in the procession.

There were also important temples to the north of the temple of Amun, outside the walls. A small, but highly sacred temple was that of Ptah on the north wall, built by Thutmose III. Beyond the great brick-built boundary walls of the Second Intermediate Period lay the temple precinct of the local god Montu. This god was largely superseded by Amun during the New Kingdom, but he possessed ancient, honored temples in the territory of Thebes, at Medamud and el-Tod in the east and at Hermonthis in the southwest, and these sites were joined to each other by processional routes.

The Mortuary Temples in West Thebes
Already during the Middle Kingdom, Mentuhotep II erected a funeral temple for himself in the valley of Deir el-Bahri, which at the same time served as a way-station temple for the visit of Amun of Karnak during the Beautiful Festival of the Valley. By the beginning of the New Kingdom this temple had fallen into such a state of disrepair that Hatshepsut decided to erect a new building beside the older structure. This new temple complex, called *Djeser-*

Djeseru, "the all-holiest," had a valley temple to receive the bark procession of Amun, an avenue of access flanked by sphinxes and a way-station temple. It now became the destination of the bark procession for the Beautiful Festival of the Valley, and remained so until the time of the Ptolemies. The new building reflected the styles both of Mentuhotep's earlier building on the site and of the terraced temples of the Middle Kingdom. Its architecture was probably the work of Hatshepsut's talented favorite, Senenmut, although the entire court and even the high priest of Amun, Hapuseneb, were involved in the execution of the project. Senenmut was able to leave his name in numerous, hidden places, even within the innermost sanctum; he also made a secret tomb for himself below the forecourt.

The forecourt, embellished by trees, ponds and flower beds, ends on the west side at a first terrace with a pillared façade, where gigantic statues of Osiris were placed at the northern and southern ends. On the west walls of this portico were depicted the deeds of Hatshepsut, including the transportation of two obelisks on an enormous ship, towed by twenty-seven boats with 864 oarsmen. A steep ramp leads up to the middle terrace, a broad court with a pillared façade is at its west end; in its southern hall the divine birth of Hatshepsut was portrayed, while the northern one illustrates the famous expedition to Punt, the exotic land of incense. The north end of the terrace has its own sanctuary of Anubis with a pillared entrance hall, while at the southern end is the highly sacred shrine of the goddess Hathor, emerging in the shape of a cow from the rock cauldron. A ramp with a balustrade wall in the form of a giant, coiling royal snake leads to the upper terrace. The façade consists of a portico with twenty-four Osiride statues, measuring more than five meters in height. The peristyle court has four rows of columns, between which numerous large statues of the queen stood or knelt, offering sacrifice. On the north side of the peristyle court is the sanctuary of Ra, an open enclosure with an altar and chapel niches for Thutmose I and his queens. On the southern side are an un-inscribed room with a window of appearance—a forerunner of the later temple palaces—and the mortuary chapels for Hatshepsut and her father Thutmose I. In the middle of the west façade, dominated by ten colossal Osiride statues, a granite door opens into the holy of holies in the mountainside, a bark shrine with a statue chapel, furnished with four figures of Osiris and representations of the bark and its ritual, plus portrayals of Hatshepsut's family. The layout of Hatshepsut's temple is one of the most original creations of Egyptian architecture: its scheme of allocating the center to a way-station temple of Amun, the north to a Ra sanctuary, and the south to temple palace and mortuary ritual chambers provided the model for all later royal mortuary temples in the New Kingdom.

The biggest and most magnificent mortuary temple was built by Amenhotep III right on the edge of the fertile section of the valley, so that each year when the Nile flooded, it rose out of the waters like the mythical mound of creation. Sadly, only scant remains of the temple have survived, since only a hundred years after its erection it served as a quarry for building stone for the later Ramesside kings, Merenptah and Rameses III. There were probably more than three hundred statues of all kinds in its courts and pillared halls, many of which were pillaged by Rameses II, Merenptah and Rameses III. In the early XIX century, however, the buyers for European collections still found rich pickings at the site: the magnificent quartzite colossal heads of Amenhotep III, the similar heads in pink granite in the Louvre and the monumental sphinxes in St. Petersburg once graced the halls and court of its vast peristyle. Only the famous Colossi of Memnon still rise to a height of over 14.5 meters outside the eastern entrance to the temple. The statues took their name from the northernmost pair, whose upper half fell after being shattered by an earthquake in 27 BC. Afterward, when the early morning sun warmed the stone, a murmuring sound of complaint or lamentation could be heard coming from the cracks in the stump. Greek travelers who witnessed the phenomenon were told the birth name of Amenhotep III, Nimmuria. This they confused with the noble Ethiopian monarch Memnon, who had died below the walls of Troy, but whose body, at the behest of his mother Eos, was carried back to his homeland by Zeus; they thought of the sound as the dead warrior's morning greeting to his grieving parent. More than a hundred poems are inscribed on the legs and plinth of the statue, mostly from the time of the Emperor Hadrian. In 199 AD the Emperor Septimius Severus ordered that the statue be restored. Though the work was never finished, enough was done to silence the song of Memnon for ever.

10. West Thebes, temple of
Amenhotep III, the Colossi
of Memnon

11. West Thebes, the Ramesseum,
mortuary temple of Rameses II,
detail of the second court's Osirid
pillars

Little has survived of the temples of the late 18th Dynasty. On the other hand, there was a new flowering under the Ramessides, an ambitious program aimed at the restoration of religious sites throughout Egypt, but especially in Thebes. The temple of Sety I at Qurna, a magnificent sandstone structure, is a veritable fortress of the gods and set the pattern for all subsequent mortuary temples. It was surrounded by a high, whitewashed brick wall with projecting rectangular towers, a return to the traditions of the Old Kingdom. There was also a mud-brick pylon, coated in white plaster and then colorfully painted, while the gate and entrance passageway were made from limestone and sandstone. The temple building was preceded by two courtyards with a ritual palace on the south side of the first court, where the reigning king could show himself in the window of appearance for the Beautiful Festival of the Valley; after his death a ritual statue lived on there and could participate in a royal bark in the various ceremonies and sacrificial rituals. The temple façade is a portico of ten closed papyrus sheath columns; originally a peristyle court was planned, but due to the untimely death of Sety this was never completed. The façade is decorated with a representation of the bark procession of the Theban Triad during the Valley Festival, accompanied by the barks of the deified queen Ahmose Nefertari and of the king. Three broad, tall gates in the façade gave entrance to the three main parts of the temple. The northern complex was dedicated to the worship of the sun, with a spacious open court, in whose center rose a sacrificial altar. The southern end of the temple housed the spaces dedicated to the royal mortuary cult; the forwardmost and better preserved part by Sety I held a chapel for his father Rameses I. The center of the temple was entirely dedicated to Amun and the Festival of the Valley. The processional route led into a pillared hall, off which six side chambers opened. One held the

royal bark; the one opposite has a representation of the dead king united with Amun, who thus becomes the god Sety-Amun of the temple. This is absolutely the most significant ritual act of the whole temple, one which encapsulates the function of the entire complex. A vestibule led to the bark shrine of Amun-Ra and the flanking chambers for Mut and Khons. The barks of these gods rested there after their arrival and received sacrificial offerings. At the far end was an adjoining chamber with four square pillars and a false door, which on the one hand showed Amun the path westward, while on the other it opened up an entrance for the dead king from the tomb into the temple, where he could receive daily sacrifices and take part in the ceremonial rites.

To the north of the temple were vaulted storerooms, separated by halls which were used for the division of sacrificial goods and offerings. The placing of such storerooms inside the walls of the temple enclosure was an innovation of the 19th Dynasty. Previously, all items for sacrifice were brought directly from the storehouses of the temple of Amun in Karnak; henceforward, the mortuary temples had their own separate administration and were also endowed with their own fields to provide produce, although they continued to be subject to the temple of Amun. In many ways, the way the temples were run and their productive role in society can be compared with the great monasteries of the Middle Ages in Europe.

Rameses II completed the complex begun by his father, at the same time planning and commencing his mortuary temple. For the first time on the west bank, stone pylons were erected. On the rear of the pylon to the first court, the Battle of Qadesh was depicted in lively reliefs as the major event of the early years of Rameses II's reign. In the same courtyard once stood the tallest of the colossal statues of west Thebes, reaching a height of 19 meters. Shattered into two parts, it now lies prone at the entrance to the second pylon. To the south was the ritual palace, of which only the bases of the columns survive. The scenes depicted on the pylon, the palace and the colossal statues show that the first court was dedicated to the celebration of the king's fame. Once again the peace treaty signed with the Hittites was included, this time as an afterthought. The second court was lined on the east and west sides by porticoes with Osiride pillars, while on the north and south sides there were double rows of papyrus sheaf pillars. The temple front with its raised portico is decorated with sacrificial scenes, including a festive procession of the king's sons marching into the temple. Three ramps, still preserved, lead to the three gates in the façade. These strongly suggest a tripartite division of the temple. At the sides of the middle ramp were two seated figures of the king. The magnificent head of the northern statue still lies in the court, while only the throne and the lower body of the southern figure have remained in the Ramesseum. The stunningly beautiful head and bust in fine-grained, light gray granite, tending to red in the upper parts, were carried off by Belzoni in 1816 on behalf of the British Consul General Salt, and sold to the British Museum, where they still attract intense admiration today as "Young Memnon." The main entrance in the façade opens into a magnificent pillared hall. The basilican nave has two rows of six tall papyriform columns with open umbel capitals, while the aisles each have three rows of six papyrus sheaf columns with closed capitals. This overwhelmingly impressive space—perhaps the most beautiful hypostyle hall in Egypt—derives its effect from the clear organization of space, the harmonious proportions of its pillars and the fine state of preservation of its vivid colors.

A sequence of three smaller rooms, their ceilings each supported by eight pillars, led to the now completely destroyed inner sanctum. In the first of these rooms, called the Astronomical Chamber because of the personified constellations depicted on its ceiling, the walls are decorated once again with the bark procession. The crown prince leads, followed by a train of the other royal children. On the right-hand west wall is the splendid image of the coronation of Rameses II in the celestial Heliopolis: The king is seated in the shade of the holy *ished* tree as Atum and Seshat inscribe his name on its leaves. The extensive vaulted storerooms that surround the temple are in a fair state of preservation and attest to the scale and wealth of goods that were stored there.

The only visible remains of the works of the successors of Rameses II in the 19th Dynasty are the ruins of the temple of Merenptah to the south of the Ramesseum. With only a few minor exceptions, the building follows the pattern of its predecessors. The complex was largely constructed with stone quarried from the neighboring structures built by Amenhotep III.

12. Schist statue of Rameses II holding the shrine of the temple of Karnak, New Kingdom, 19th Dynasty.
Cairo, Egyptian Museum
cat. 80

13. Faience foundation brick from the Ramesseum, New Kingdom, 19th Dynasty.
Cairo, Egyptian Museum
cat. 66

A century ago, the British archaeologist Sir Flinders Petrie found the Merenptah stele in the temple court. It records the pharaoh's triumphs over the allied armies of the Sea Peoples and Libyans that invaded Egypt in the fifth year of his reign. Very recent excavations have revealed what remained after the temple was largely dismantled in the XIX century to quarry limestone for local kilns and sandstone to obtain saltpeter. Some idea of its original magnificence may be gained from the great limestone blocks from the first pillared hall, decorated with depictions of the bark procession and sacrificial scenes, together with thousands of sandstone fragments from the walls of the halls and the inner sanctum, many still with traces of their original colors. The fragments of many statues, including the lower part of a bust found by Petrie over a hundred years ago, attest to the scale of the destruction. In the second court of the temple, large fragments from three groups of colossal statues were discovered, showing the king accompanied by gods. The sculptures were originally from the time of Amenhotep III, whose name was erased and replaced by that of Merenptah when they were used again. Further colossal statues of Amenhotep III, including jackals and sphinxes, plus a number of large limestone blocks from his temple with colored relief and magnificent scenes of the royal jubilee celebrations, were used in the construction of the foundations of Merenptah's temple and thus have been well preserved.

The last of the Theban mortuary temples was built by Rameses III at the southern extremity of the necropolis, in close proximity to a small temple that had been built by kings of the 18th Dynasty on the sacred site of the Theban creation mound. The well-preserved temple complex at Medinet Habu adds further scope to our understanding of the Temples of Millions of Years. Like the one of Sety I, the temple is surrounded by a wall with projecting towers, in other words it is conceived as a fortress of the gods. Some time later during the reign of Rameses III a considerably stronger and higher wall was built around the extensive magazines and administrative buildings that had clustered around the complex. Two bastion-like gates in the east and west gave access to the compound. The better preserved eastern gate shows clear signs that it was the nucleus of a royal residence built up over several floors, with a limestone gatehouse in the center and extensive brickbuilt wings flanking this, several storeys high. The central structure had high, airy state rooms with broad windows, of which the eastern one was the window of appearance. The exterior is decorated with scenes commemorating the victories of Rameses III over the Libyans and Sea Peoples, while the interior has

14. West Thebes, the Ramesseum, mortuary temple of Rameses II

more domestic scenes: the king playing the *senet* board game with his daughters, a game with a decidedly otherworldly character. Rameses III occupied both gatehouse palaces when he came to Thebes to take part in the Theban festivals; it was in one of the two that members of his *harim* carried out their plot to assassinate him.

The way along the temple axis to the temple forecourt leads on the right, to the older, immensely sacred creation mound sanctuary of the 18th Dynasty, which was held in high esteem and continually restored and expanded, as late as during the Roman period. On the left-hand side of the processional route, chapels for the "god's wives of Amun" were built during the 26th Dynasty, so that they could take part in processions and in the ritual of the sacred mound. It was, as always, the great processions of the gods which determined ritual practice at all temples in west Thebes.

The first pylon of the great temple is the best preserved in west Thebes. On its exterior wall is the traditional scene of the king "smiting his enemies" before Amun to the south and Ra-Horakhty in the north. The mural decorations of the first court glorify campaigns and victories against the Libyans and Sea Peoples, whose armies Rameses III, like Merenptah before him, could only repulse after bitter fighting by land and sea along Egypt's frontiers. On the north side the court is closed off by a pillared portico, which housed statues of the king in ceremonial garb. Across from this, the façade of the temple palace consists of a portico of papyriform columns with open capitals. At the center of the façade is the royal window of appearance, flanked by the two entrances to the palace. These lead first into a pillared hall, whose vaulted ceiling was supported by palmiform columns. Behind this are the throne room and adjoining chambers, a bathroom and bedchamber for the king, plus three small living rooms for princes or royal attendants. It is clear that this palace followed the pattern of a model royal residence, whose principal elements were, however, laid out with conscious spatial unity. At all events the palace can never have served as a real residential complex, because a number of essential amenities for a genuine palace, such as kitchens and stables, are missing. Furthermore, we may imagine that such a dwelling place would have been far too cramped for rulers so used to luxury as the Ramessides! Its first purpose must have been to provide a setting for the solemn appearance of the living king during the processions; after his death he continued to dwell in the temple palace in the form of a statue. A false door in the rear wall of the throne room allowed the spirit of the king to return from his tomb to observe the processions.

In a later period, the impoverished priest kings of the 21st Dynasty took over the building as an official palace, leaving their names inscribed on the gates.

A ramp leads through the gateway of the second pylon into the ritual court. The program of its mural decorations—whose colors are exceptionally well-preserved—is dedicated to the processions of the Beautiful Festival of the Valley, the feast of Min with statues of the dead kings, and the feast of Sokar. The pictures that have survived allow one to imagine how splendidly beautiful the original decorative scheme of the temple walls must have been in its entirety. A raised portico with broad and ponderous-looking, colored Osiride pillars, plus remarkably deep-cut lines of inscriptions, leads into a hypostyle hall with side chambers for the king's ancestors, guest divinities and the royal bark. Although the roof and the upper portions of walls and columns have fallen, the hall still seems gloomy and oppressive, doubtless mostly because of how tightly the massive pillars are ranked. Their bases almost touch one another and protrude into the passageways. The effect is far removed from the airy, spacious feel of the pillared hall of Sety I or of the splendid hypostyle hall in the Ramesseum, which nonetheless was the model for Rameses III in his temple. A dark, mystical heaviness pervades the inner sanctum. Rapid sequences of rooms lead to the sanctuary on the temple axis and to magazines at the side. To the north are the chambers of a narrow court dedicated to the cult of the sun, and to the south the rooms for the mortuary cult of the dead king, in both cases pressed tight against the high outer walls.

Between the inner enclosure wall of the temple and the walls surrounding the *temenos*, the magazines were joined by lodgings for the priests, administrative buildings, barracks, stables, ponds and gardens, all built and laid out during a second phase of construction. The water supply was ensured by wells and indicators of the levels of the Nile. During the period of unrest which followed the end of the Ramesside dynasties, this accommodation complex, together with the storehouses, barracks and the temple palace, eventually became the residential city of the priest kings of the divine state, initially restricted to Thebes and Upper Egypt. The high walls around the *temenos* protected the compound from attacks by robbers from the nomadic tribes. Thus the ideal fortress of the gods became at last a genuinely fortified residential city.

el-Amarna

In the fifth year of his reign Amenhotep IV changed his name to Akhenaten, abandoned Thebes and founded a new residence, Akhetaten, in Middle Egypt on a site untouched by cult practices at el-Amarna. The center of the city was formed by the extensive royal palaces and by the twin temples of the god Aten. The great temple, Per-Aten, was an immensely long—over 350 meters—but extremely narrow structure, only 32 meters wide. This part of the temple complex, with its seemingly endless open courts, furnished with 224 sacrificial altars, went by the same name as the earlier temple of Amenhotep IV in Karnak, *Gempaaten*, "Aten is found." Adjoining it is the sanctuary proper, the *hwt benben* or "house of *benben*." This consisted of a narrow peristyle and a sequence of three smaller courts with altars, in which stood two high altars and the *benben* stone, a mystic stone which originally belonged to the creator-god Atum in Heliopolis; in Amarna it may have taken the form of an outsized stele, before which a statue of Akhenaten performed sacrifice. The temple was preceded by a pylon with eight flag poles and a small ritual palace. A smaller temple to the south of the great one went by the name of *Tahutaten*, which allows us to surmise that it must have been the mortuary temple of Akhenaten-Aten, comparable to the Theban mortuary temples. Its architecture is in strict imitation of the great temple, with altar courts and a raised terrace with a high altar at the eastern end. We know from depictions of them that the temples of the queens and princesses in Amarna, called "sun shadows," also followed the same architectural pattern, perhaps exceptionally forming mortuary temples of a kind for the immediate members of the divine king's family. Thus the basic principle of the sanctuaries of Amarna becomes recognizable: courts, peristyle and numerous altars, with all spaces open so that they could be reached by the rays of the sun.

Abydos
The Temple of Sety I
Abydos, a place of pilgrimage and a cult center of the god of the dead Osiris, whose tomb was sought on the site, had been abandoned during the Amarna period. In order to make good this sacrilege, Sety I erected along the processional way, the "stairway of the great god" that led from the temple of Osiris to his tomb, the most beautiful temple of the gods in the land of the Nile, a Temple of Millions of Years for the royal ancestors from Menes to his own time and for all the great gods of Egypt, Osiris, Isis and Horus, as well as for the great gods of the kingdom, Amun of Thebes, Ra of Heliopolis and Ptah of Memphis. The plan of the temple is of the greatest simplicity, the architectural form faultless and the pictorial program is one of strict orthodoxy. The workmanship and artistic skill shown in carrying out the design are of the highest quality. This temple thus represents the high point of the flowering of the arts during the 19th Dynasty; moreover, the exceptionally well-preserved and exhaustive illustrations of the daily ritual of cults and image worship have also expanded our awareness of the religious concepts which lay behind the building.

A solemn stairway leads to the raised daïs-quay which was formerly linked to the Nile by a canal. Before the temple mansion there were two courts with pylons "that stretched up to the heavens." The first pillared hall is laid out as a portico with Osiride columns. Seven doorways open into seven sanctuaries, so that each sanctuary had its own separate door and axis. In the middle one, belonging to Amun-Ra, the barks of the Theban Triad are shown on the walls in glowing colors. To the right were the sanctuaries of Osiris, Isis and Horus; to the left those of Ptah, Ra-Horakhty and the deified Sety I. With the exception of Osiris' sanctuary, each chapel gave imaginary access through a false door in the rear wall to a cenotaph which lay below ground to the west of the temple. After his death Sety became Osiris and received his mortuary cult there. Only the sanctuary of Osiris actually opened into a complex of chambers beyond it, with two pillared halls, each with three chapels dedicated to the three Abydos divinities, Osiris-Sety, Isis and Horus. From the second pillared hall a gallery, decorated with a list of kings' names from the 1st Dynasty to Sety himself, led to the chapels of the Memphis gods and to sacristies in which statues, barks and processional paraphernalia were kept. To the south and east of the temple stood extensive brickbuilt storage magazines, as at the mortuary temples of Thebes. At the death of Sety I this extraordinary temple was still unfinished. The young Rameses II accompanied his father's funeral procession to Thebes in person, pausing on the way at Abydos. There he took a solemn oath to complete his father's temple and to raise the statues that still lay prone in the courts, and he was true to his word.

The Temple of Rameses II
Rameses II had his own temple built along the same processional way to the temple of Osiris. It, too, was a way-station and mortuary temple, no less lavishly furnished than that of his father, and it also included chapels for the gods of Abydos, Thebes and Heliopolis, and Upuaut. The mural decorations, which have survived in the splendor of their original colors. show solemn processions in the courts, the march hence of the Nile gods bearing gifts, representations of the gods in their chapels, and lastly, the festive procession during which the reliquary with the head of Osiris was brought from the temple of Osiris to the Early Dynastic cemetery in Umm el-Qaʿab.

Memphis
In Memphis the river bed of the Nile had moved further eastward during the New Kingdom, thus creating space for new 19th Dynasty buildings before the gates of the temple of Ptah.

15. West Thebes, Medinet Habu, monumental gatehouse of the temple of Rameses III

The first to be built was a processional way ending at the southern gate, where today the colossal statue of Rameses II in crystalline limestone lies, famous as the "alabaster" sphinx and the most perfect sculpture of the reign of Rameses II in the area of Memphis. Statues, temples and chapels, including one for Hathor, lined the new avenue. One fine small temple of the time of Sety I is dedicated to Ptah and the Memphite goddesses. The statue groups of this way-station sanctuary have survived intact and are unique: they repeat in the round the representations depicted in relief on the side walls.

On the west side of the great enclosure wall Rameses II erected a massive pylon, before which stood two colossal statues, flanking the entrance to a great pillared hall. At the northern gate was a dyad of Rameses II and Ptah-Tatjenen, now in the Ny Carlsberg Glyptotek in Copenhagen, and a colossal sphinx, now in the Philadelphia Museum. At the eastern gate stood the colossal statue in pink granite which in 1954 was moved to the square outside Cairo station—renamed *Midan Rameses* or Rameses Square for the occasion—to stand as a symbol of the new Egypt. The statue suffers badly from pollution damage in its new surroundings. A few hundred yards to the east of the Ptah enclosure lie the ruins of a further temple of Rameses II and of a building by Merenptah which was reached by a monumental gateway. There was also a splendid temple palace, whose walls and columns were decorated with ceramic tiles in many colors. The last Ramessides contented themselves with commemorating their own names on existing buildings. The practice was probably not so much an attempt to appropriate the monuments, as a tacit recognition of the fact that practically all the cult buildings were working perfectly, to the point where the religious foundations needed no more than continued royal assent and assurances.

Heliopolis

Heliopolis, once the center of intense building activities, today stands robbed of almost all of its monuments. They were either moved to other sites in Egypt or else carried off to oth-

16. Abydos, plan of the temple
of Sety I

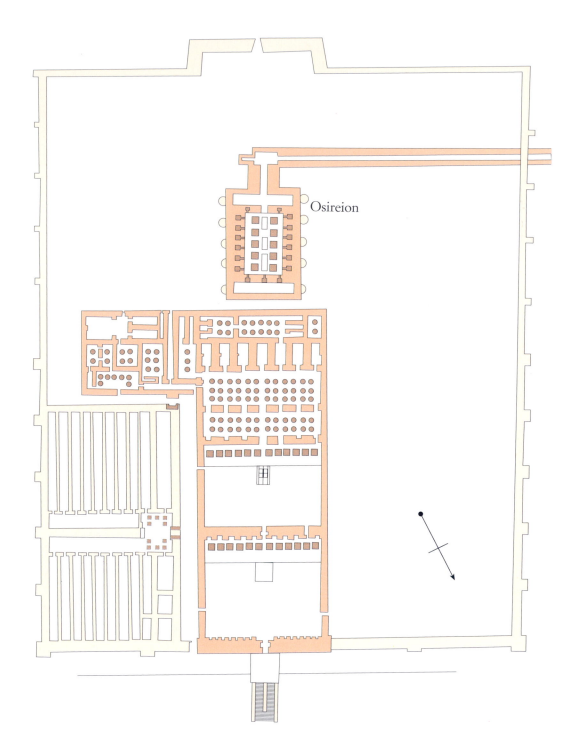

Osireion

er countries, from as early as the Greco-Roman period. Of the temples which we know of from documentary sources, dedicated to the sun-god Ra, Atum and Hathor, and of the great obelisks and avenue of sphinxes, we can now form only a vague notion on the basis of the model of the temple of Sety I that was found at Tell el-Yahudiya near Heliopolis and later reconstructed and set up in the Brooklyn Museum in New York. There remain on site only a few scant traces from the New Kingdom, found by recent excavations. These include a broad avenue, once lined by temples of Rameses II, before which stood royal statues. The avenue ended at a monumental gatehouse with papyrus sheaf columns, inscribed with the name of Rameses III, which in turn opened into a large temple. A short distance away stood a column of pink granite—now reerected—which bears an inscription from the fifth year of the reign of Merenptah, magnifying his victory over the Sea Peoples. This pillar very prob-

17. Tridimensional reconstruction
of the temple of Sety I at Qurna

ably served as the base for a statue and is thus a prototype for the monumental columns we
know from Greek and Roman times.

Piramesse

Papyri and stelae tell us of a great royal residence in the eastern Delta. Founded by Sety I,
it was extensively enlarged and enhanced by Rameses II, who gave it the name *Pi-Ramessu*,
"the victorious," the City of Rameses. The nucleus of the city was formed by the vast palace,
toward which were orientated, at the four points of the compass, the temples of the three
great gods of the kingdom, Amun, Ra, Ptah, and of the family god Seth. At the crossroads
before the palace, Rameses set up four colossal statues; from the surviving fragments it has
been calculated that these were the tallest free-standing statues ever erected in Egypt, reaching a height of more than 21 meters. We know what they looked like only from images on
stelae, which show them as objects of cult ritual and worship, the visible apparitions of the
gods in the person of the king. Through them an individual could make his plea to the gods.
When the statues were raised they were also endowed with goods and land to ensure the continuance of their cult, as recorded on commemorative scarabs. In order to conduct the appropriate celebrations for the many jubilees of his reign, Rameses II had vast ceremonial courts
laid out before the temples and palace, with a veritable forest of obelisks. However, the greater
part of the stone buildings of Piramesse were demolished during the 21st Dynasty and later periods, and their stonework carried off to be reused in the additions to the temple of the
new capital Tanis. Numerous decorated blocks with the names of Rameses II and the gods
of Piramesse have thus been found at Tanis, together with whole doorways in granite, parts
of architraves, numerous broken obelisks, columns and many fragments of colossal statues.
Some of the latter must have been enormous, when one considers that the eye of one of the

18. Tanis, plan of the temple complex.
1. Sacred lake
2. Temple of Khons-Neferhotep
3. Colossus of Rameses II
4. Royal tombs
5. Great temple of Amun
6. Old enclosure wall
7. Temple of Horus
8. Temple of Mut, Khons and Astarte

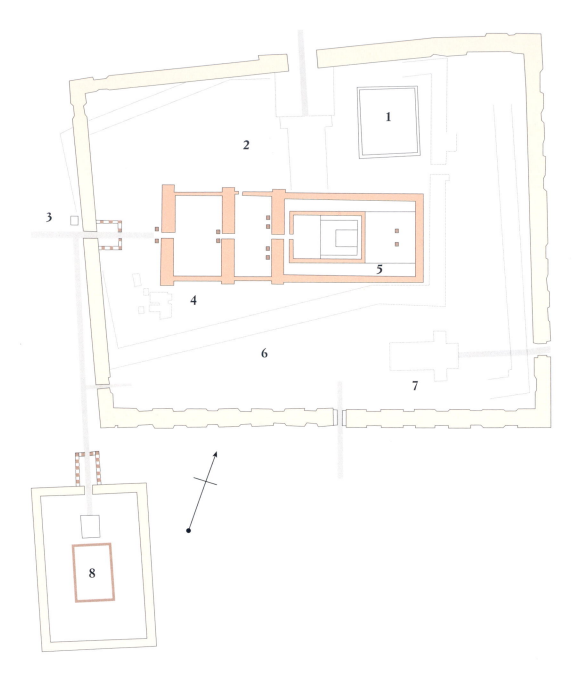

standing granite colossi measures 42 centimeters across, while one of the feet is over three meters long. Other colossi were made in sandstone, while numerous smaller statues, dyads and triads of the king were in granite, like the great sphinxes and colossal statues of the pharaohs of the Middle Kingdom which Rameses II or one of his sons had newly inscribed. Statues of priests and high-ranking courtiers were also dragged to Tanis. A total of more than fifty sculptures were removed from Piramesse to end up in other sites or museums around the world: a collection of free-standing sculpture which would have formed one of the most beautiful and impressive open-air museums anywhere, had it remained *in situ*. As things fell out, however, it is no surprise that scholars were long convinced that the great ruins at Tanis were also those of the famed Piramesse. But recent excavations have proved beyond doubt that the ancient site of Piramesse lay close to the place now called Qantir and stretched over an area of several square kilometers as far as Tell el-Dab'a, where the earlier residence of the Hyksos has been discovered and excavated. What little remains of the once splendid residence and its stately monuments lies scattered in the fields today.

19. Tanis, view of the site from the north

following pages
20. Tanis, the colossi of Rameses II in front of the monumental gate

The Temples in the Desert and in Nubia

During the New Kingdom, the desert regions on both sides of the Nile valley and the conquered land of Nubia were all incorporated into the religious practice of Egypt by the construction of temples and rock sanctuaries. Hatshepsut, Thutmose III and Amenhotep II restored cult centers in the Middle Kingdom fortresses lying far to the south. The temple on the holy mountain of Napata also dates back to the 18th Dynasty. But the most beautiful temple of all was the one erected by Amenhotep III in Soleb, an architectural gem that has an impressive vestibule with four 12 meter-tall palmiform columns, two peristyle courts and a hypostyle hall with twenty-four tall palmiform columns. Palms were assuredly the dominant trees of ancient Nubia! Rock temples were founded along the routes to the gold mines and at wells, like the one of Sety I in the Wadi Mia. They were also built in the mining areas themselves, where quarrying for the precious ores had often hollowed out ready-made sites, such as that occupied by Merenptah's chapel of Hathor at el-Babeïn.

Rameses II founded not less than six new temples in Nubia, each a jewel of its kind. All have preserved at least some of their former beauty and qualities. Beit el-Wali is famed for its finely carved reliefs, the temple of Derr for the polychromy of its mural decorations, the complex at Gerf Husein, now inundated by Lake Nasser, was renowned for its in-the-round triad sculptures on the walls of the court and in the pillared hall, and Wadi el-Sebua has a famously impressive avenue of sphinxes before its temple.

The artistic climax of these sites, however, is Abu Simbel, the ideal architectural embodiment of a Nubian rock-cut temple. In admiring this grandiose structure we can gain some idea of the greatness and gifted creative energy of the young Rameses II—barely fifteen years old

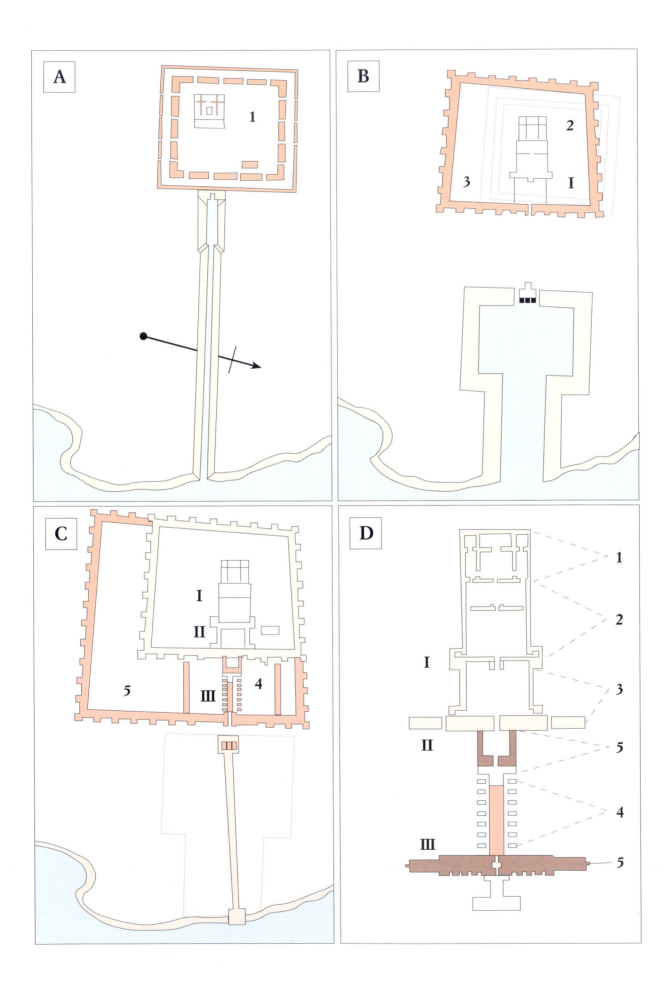

21. Soleb, the temple complex of Amenhotep III during the various phases of its construction. Arabic numbers refer to the historial periods, the Roman ones indicate the pylons. A: phase 1; B: phases 2 and 3; C: phases 4 and 5; D: overall scheme of the project

22. Soleb, the temple of Amenhotep III

following pages
23. The temple complex of Abu Simbel

at the time—when he commissioned the temple complex. It consists of two complementary sanctuaries. The great temple is dedicated to the cult of the three great gods of the kingdom, Amun, Ra and Ptah, and to the deified Rameses II; in the lesser temple Rameses is united with the goddess Hathor, embodied in the great royal bride Nefertari. The seated colossi before the great temple and the standing colossi against the façade of the lesser temple, surrounded by portraits of the royal children, served in this remote province as a display of the overwhelming power and greatness of the Egyptian gods and of the divine king and his family. In the interior of the complex, the depictions of sacrifices and festive bark processions show Egypt as a land inhabited and blessed by the gods, whose rule and divine world order are upheld by the pharaoh. Thus, as guarantor of that rule and order on earth, the pharaoh must guard Egypt against dangers from without: His performance of that role is illustrated by the depiction of the victory of Rameses II over the Hittites in the Battle of Qadesh. The broad, high rock-cut hall, with eight columnar statues of the king, narrows westward into the second pillared hall, leading downward to the inner sanctum, hollowed into a cave in the rock. Against its west wall sit the gods of the temple, Amun-Ra, Rameses, Ra-Horakhty and Ptah: the Ramesside gods of the kingdom united with the deified king himself. The temple is orientated in such a way that twice a year, on the 20th of February and the 20th of October, the rays of the rising sun illuminate all four statues—a much-touted publicity stunt at modern Abu Simbel. The idea that these two dates correspond to the days of Rameses II's birth and coronation is, however, a recent invention.

From 1964 to 1968 the two temples at Abu Simbel were the subject of a joint international effort, as unique as it was extraordinary, to save them from the rising waters of Lake Nasser, created by the Aswan Dam. The structures were dismantled and reerected on higher ground nearby. This feat of engineering matched their original construction under Rameses II. Nonetheless, the unique, romantic integration of the temple buildings in the Nubian river landscape, with its palms and farmsteads, was lost forever.

24. Abu Simbel, façade of the great
temple of Rameses II

The Temples of the Third Intermediate Period (21st–22nd Dynasties)

The temple building of the Third Intermediate Period in Upper Egypt was limited to the temple of Karnak. The temple precinct was surrounded by a mighty brick wall. In front of pylon II, Sheshonq I built a broad peristyle court, equipped with a gateway that was later replaced by pylon I. Herihor completed the temple of the moon-god Khons, begun during the 19th Dynasty south of the temple of Amun. Far more significant projects were undertaken in the Delta. Herodotus tells of a vast and splendid temple of Bastet in Bubastis. Because of the constant, large-scale theft of building stone, at best only the foundations and a few single architectural elements of these temples remain, such as Osorkon's *heb-sed* door. Tanis, the new residence of the 21st Dynasty, was built predominantly from the dismantled temples of Rameses' great city. The Delta kings were unstinting in their efforts to build a second Thebes in Tanis, dragging architectural elements, obelisks and colossal statues from far and wide to lend authenticity to their replica, which had the temple of Amun at its center, that of Mut (the Anat temple) in the south, a temple of Khons in the north, and an only recently discovered precinct in the south, which probably corresponded to the temple of Opet in Thebes. Little has survived of these temples, since they were largely brick-built and their stonework was repeatedly carried off and used elsewhere in the Delta.

Bibliography
PM II; Golvin, Goyon 1989; Kemp 1989; Aufrère, Golvin, Goyon 1991; Arnold 1992; Baines, Málek 1993; Arnold 1994; Quirke 1997; Brissaud, Zivie-Coche 1998; Smith 1998.

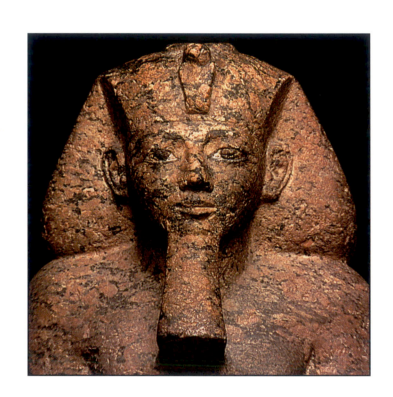

The Image of the Sovereign

1. Upper part of the colossus of Akhenaten from Karnak, sandstone, New Kingdom, 18th Dynasty. Cairo, Egyptian Museum
cat. 71

The central problem in the historiography of ancient Egypt is the lack of genuine ancient Egyptian historiography. It was the Greek historians who were the first to place the realm of the pharaohs in context, to look for causal links and make historical judgments. As they did not know the ancient Egyptian language and had to rely on others for information, their writings are in the final analysis secondary historical sources, the content of which requires particularly critical examination.

In the primary pharaonic sources, the historian is confronted with an atomized history, divided up into single items of information, which were recorded out of context and for which there is no common chronological framework. Ancient Egypt had no equivalent of *ab urbe condita* or BC, no beginning of time from which history unfolds in a straight line into an open future. Men experienced time and space as a closed system. The cycle of the sun's daily course, the yearly flood of the Nile were mirrored in the long line of pharaohs whose accession to the throne was perceived as a repetition of the creation of the world and their death as a brief return into a pre-cosmic chaos. Each reign marked the start of a new phase in world history with a new chronology starting from year one. The only continuous historical framework possible is one based on lists of kings, which record the succession of rulers and the length of their reign. Such lists have been preserved. Consisting simply of the names of successive rulers, they are found in temples and tombs; a more detailed version with the periods of reign indicated is contained in the fragmentary Turin Royal Canon.

The lists tell us nothing about the history of events. They provide a chronology purged of foreign rulers, usurpers and heretical kings, into which historiography can insert single events dated according to the period of a ruler. However, the events that the ancient Egyptians considered worth reporting do not correspond with our understanding of historical relevance, at least during the Old Kingdom. On the Palermo Stone, containing the annals of kings from the 1st to the 5th Dynasty, it is above all ritual acts that are mentioned as events serving to distinguish one year from another.

Religion and cults are predominant not only in the texts and depictions on royal monuments, but also in the picture sequences on non-royal tombs seemingly rich in information of all kind. In reality, the scenes from daily life are mostly devoid of biographical details. They portray an idealized, generally good world. Even uncommon scenes on royal reliefs from the peri-

2. Quartzite base with two prostrate figures, Middle Kingdom, 12th–13th Dynasties. Baltimore, The Walters Art Gallery
cat. 129

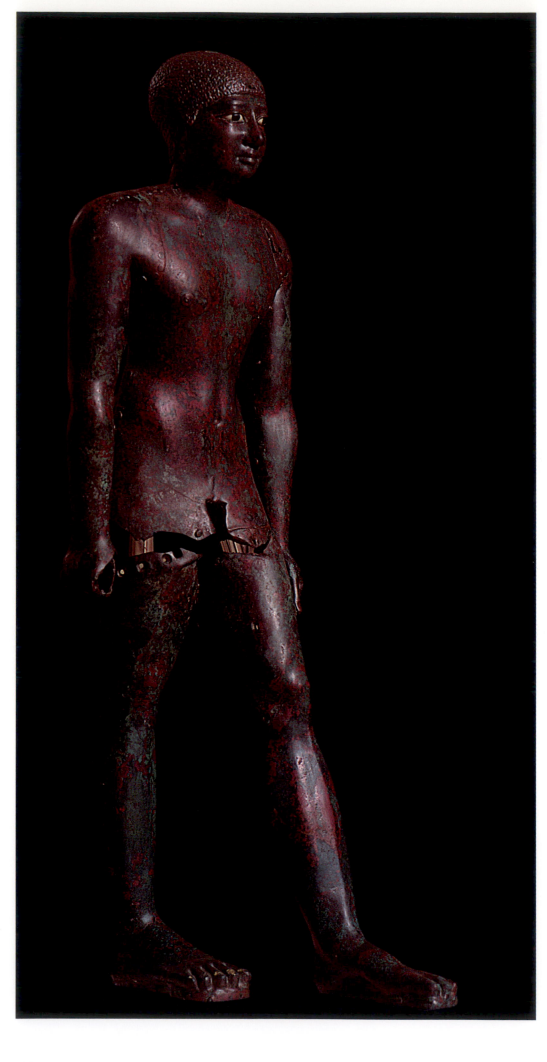

3. Copper statue of Pepy I
from Hierakonpolis,
Old Kingdom, 6th Dynasty.
Cairo, Egytpian Museum

4. Granite kneeling statue of
Hatshepsut, from Deir el-Bahri,
New Kingdom, 18th Dynasty.
Cairo, Egyptian Museum
cat. 76

5. Limestone statue of Rameses III,
New Kingdom, 20th Dynasty.
Philadelphia, The University of
Pennsylvania, Museum of
Archeology and Anthropology
cat. 73

od of the Old Kingdom—a famine or the subjugation of Libyans—turn up in practically identical detail in several temples at different times. They do not, therefore, reflect historical reality but act as pictorial devices for creating a political and cosmic order.

Once defined in the third millennium BC, the pictographs on the role of the pharaoh in the cosmic system kept their validity also in later eras, when Egypt became part of the global political network in the Near East and eastern Mediterranean. It is true that the political reality of the military confrontation with the city-states of the Levant and the Hittite empire is reflected in stirring battle scenes in the temple reliefs, but as in previous times the pharaoh is shown in the heraldic pose of slaying the enemy. The elevation of a single historical event to a generally valid cipher for victory also shapes the written description of the campaign. At the crucial point in the highly detailed war report, the description of the Battle of Qadesh, in which Rameses II encountered the Hittite king, turns into a hymn to the pharaoh, who is victorious thanks to direct intervention by the god Amun-Ra.

While in the thematic variety of the temple reliefs and the royal inscriptions, the person of the pharaoh is always interwoven in the ideologically pre-molded pictorial and textual pattern, the language sculpture in the round is even more restricted, at least in the formal structure and the choice of subjects.

Generally, the variety of possible postures is reduced to a few basic models in the representation of man in a three-dimensional statue. The stand-step-figure ("standing in walking and walking in standing" is Thomas Mann's precise formulation) takes as its theme the functional quality of the represented figure; its stepping posture, the raised shoulders, arms with tensed muscles, closed fists, head lifted high and slightly turned upper part of the trunk indicate readiness for action without depicting real action: They are pictorial symbols, pictographs of virtual movement. The sitting figure represents the enthroned subject as a transfigured deceased person raised above the everyday act of sitting. Both types of statue guarantee the essential preconditions for life after death: expendability of the earthly body and its transformation into a new eternal one. The squatting figure of the "scribe" is the graphic expression of the educated person's social position, who is destined for service to the state. The kneeling figure expresses submission in sacrifice and prayer to the deity. The cube statue, the first trace of which dates from the early Middle Kingdom, is the image of resurrection into eternal life. From this repertoire of forms, only three are used for the sculpture of kings: the stand-step, the sitting and the kneeling figure. This extreme reduction signifies that the purpose of the royal sculpture is not to convey the infinite variety of earthly existence, but to create an enduring medium in the statue that transcends the ruler's mortality.

The functional location of ancient Egyptian statues calls attention to the fact that the three-dimensional image has a higher status than the two-dimensional representation. In the temple's *adytum*, the deity was present in a statue at which the daily ritual of the cult idol took place. The bringing back to life of the deceased was carried out during the "opening of the mouth" ritual in front of a statue. Inside the tomb, the deceased was physically present as a three-dimensional image in the *serdab*, the statue chamber. In their statues, the gods took part in festive processions. Divine statues were lent to foreign rulers who asked the pharaoh for help from the Egyptian gods. In contrast to the differentiated vocabulary for describing fully plastic images, there are few terms in ancient Egyptian for denoting two-dimensional representations.

In Egyptian art, the two-dimensional and the three-dimensional images are not viewed as a unity. Within the variety of stylistic levels of the human image, they follow different paths between the idealizing and the individualizing manner of representation. In painting and reliefs, the regularity of the rigidly unified iconographic repertoire, the standard proportions, the period-linked style and the functional interweaving in the planned images for temples and tombs left little space for individuality in what was depicted and how it was depicted. When an entire temple or tomb was decorated, various persons were engaged in the single work phases—designers, sculptors, painters. The end result of this division of labor (reminiscent of assembly-line work) was a unified closed appearance, in which there was no place for individual variation. Being rule-bound this way, the two-dimensional image is formally and functionally very close to writing. And in ancient Egyptian art, the literal meaning of iconography is "writing in pictures." Just as the wall pictures can and have to be "read," so the signs in hieroglyphic writing are pictures. From a varied playing with writing up to a highly developed cryptography, the ancient Egyptian made use of this multilayered and ambiguous quality of writing and pictures.

The three-dimensional picture, sculpture, is on the contrary iconographically monotonous. Its predominant theme is the human figure. Human images in ancient Egyptian sculpture are functionally defined by the transcending of the represented subject's mortality. In this function of guaranteeing eternal life, we find the ubiquitous presence of the pharaoh in royal sculpture; he is physically present throughout the realm in his statues. At both functional levels, the sculpture creates a tangible reality, brings the dead back to life and makes the absent present. A third function is revealed in the three-dimensional divine image: the invisible is rendered visible.

This autonomy of sculpture takes the work of art beyond its commonly recognized function of illustrating history and makes it a primary historical source; one that stands on an equal footing with written and archaeological evidence and supplies the only authentic information on many historical figures.

The ruler's portrait also makes its presence felt beyond the language barrier, which stands in the way for the modern viewer, who as a rule is not familiar with ancient Egyptian. It is true that today translations of ancient Egyptian texts are of a very high linguistic and philological standard; nonetheless the authentic feel of the original language is never fully captured. Even the ancient Egyptian was faced with a similar obstacle, that of writing, since only a small part of the population could read and write. Then as now, visual communication provided direct and 'democratic' dialogue for everyone, which speech and writing cannot do. The biographical text and the biographical image possess the same authenticity and complement one another in their very different languages.

6. Polychrome sandstone of
Thutmose III from Elephantine,
New Kingdom, 18th Dynasty.
Paris, Musée du Louvre
cat. 14

Comparable to the portrait gallery of Roman emperors, the completeness of ancient Egyptian sculpture gives us a genealogy of the pharaohs over three thousand years. Within this unique historical dimension, the degree of continuity is so great that often it is very difficult for the non-expert to distinguish works created a thousand years apart. However, two components can be detected from which the king's portrait is constructed with differing emphasis. As the representative of the state-supporting institution of the monarchy he appears as a supertemporal idealization; as a mortal man he is portrayed with individual features. Between these two poles and in the interplay of tradition and innovation, ancient Egyptian art continually found new forms of expression in the course of its three-thousand-year history.

In the Old Kingdom, the function of the king's portrait is concentrated on the royal tomb. The earliest fully preserved life-size statue of a king, the sitting figure of Djoser (c. 2650 BC), stood in a statue chamber in his pyramid complex. The larger than life-size statues of Sneferu (c. 2550 BC) from Dahshur were found in a temple on the causeway to the Bent Pyramid. Khafra and Menkaura had a whole series of statues made for their pyramids at Giza. That the same must have also been true of Khufu, the builder of the Great Pyramid, and of the kings in the following 5th Dynasty (c. 2465–2323 BC), of whom we have only a few statues, is shown by the surprising discovery of several statues in the pyramid complex of the lesser known King Raneferef (c. 2420 BC) in Abusir.

Moreover, already in the Old Kingdom statues of kings were placed in temples all over Egypt. In the temple of the dynastic god Horus in Hierakonpolis, in Upper Egypt, two sitting figures of King Khasekhem from the Early Dynastic period (c. 2700 BC) were found as well as a pair of statues of King Pepy I (c. 2289–2255 BC). This pair of statues emphatically shows that Egyptian art cannot be encapsulated within plain, over-simple systems. As shown by a large figure of a falcon belonging to the same complex, copper was also used for statues, drawing attention to a highly developed technique of metalworking, which had previously only been known from the Middle Kingdom (c. 1800 BC). The individual features of kings also appear on Old Kingdom portrait statues as can be seen by this pair of statues. There is moreover the above-mentioned group of statues of Raneferef of Abusir, which clearly stands apart from the other 5th-Dynasty statues of kings, while already in the 4th Dynasty many statues of King Menkaura show him with a strikingly small head.

Nevertheless, the ruler's portraits at the time of the great pyramids in the Old Kingdom make the earthly king into a superhuman being, who is represented in direct contact with the gods. With its beard of the gods and in its style, which places it at an inaccessible distance, Khafra's statue with the falcon (imitated in a small figure representing Raneferef) is an equally valid image of the monarchy in the early Old Kingdom, as are the triads of Menkaura showing him in the embrace of the gods.

The new start after the political collapse of the First Intermediate Period (2150–1994 BC) brought to the forefront a region of Egypt that had remained peripheral during the Old Kingdom, the Nile valley in Upper Egypt. Rather than the texts, it is the sculpture of kings that underscores the independence of southern Egypt. The physiognomy and proportions of the statues of King Mentuhotep, who—starting from Thebes in Upper Egypt—led the country back to national unity around 2030 BC, are of a marked ethnic type revealing the proximity of Upper Egypt to Nubia.

When the royal residence moved from Thebes to the traditional location of Memphis at the beginning of the 12th Dynasty (c. 1960 BC), the Memphite art of the Old Kingdom underwent a renaissance.

There is a strong stylistic contrast between the cold smooth classicism of the king's statues in the pyramid complex of Senusret I in Dahshur and the highly original angular faces on the statues of the same king from Karnak. This instance of a new locally defined image of the ruler points to a trend that was to shape the king's portrait during the entire era of the Middle Kingdom (1994–1781 BC). Whereas in the Old Kingdom the representation of the monarchy as a divinely inspired institution lay at the heart of artistic endeavor, now it was the king as political authority that was expressed in his portrait. The royal statue as expression of the institution retreated into the background behind the individual personality. The portrait of Senusret III (1881–1842 BC) is echoed orally in a hymn to the king:

"Hail, Khakaura, our Horus, divine in incarnations!
who protects the land, extends its borders,
who subjugates the mountainous regions with his *uraeus*,
who clasps both lands with his hands,
who grips foreign peoples in his arms,
who kills the bow peoples without striking with a stick,
who shoots the arrow without pulling the bowstring,
whose dreadfulness beats the troglodytes in their lands,
whose frightfulness slew the Nine Bows,
whose horribleness caused thousands to die among the bow peoples,
tens of thousands of those who attacked his border,
who can shoot an arrow like Sekhmet,
to cut down thousands among those who misjudge his might.
It is his Majesty's tongue that daunts Nubia,
his utterances, they put the Asiatics to flight."
(el-Lahun hymn, from J. Assmann)

The stress on the king's word as an instrument of power gives us the key to understand the ruler's portraits. They are neither images of the brutal exercise of power nor, as so often assumed, a premonition of the rapid decline of the Middle Kingdom but rather psychographs of a king, "who speaks and acts" and of whom an inscription on a stele says: "What is planned by my heart is done by my hand. I am a king who strikes in order to grasp, who rushes off to a successful outcome, who does not rest while there is a plan in his heart." (Semna Stele, from S. Seidlmayer).

A few only could understand these words on a stele at the second cataract on Egypt's southern border, and only a small number would have heard the hymns to the king, which were sung in the palace. Still today, there is hardly any general awareness of the literary heritage of ancient Egypt. However, then as now the portraits of the ruler speak directly to the viewer; in those times at Deir el-Bahri, Karnak and Medamud, where they were placed in the courtyard in front of the temple, and at the present day in the world's museums, where the numerous portraits of Senusret III have found their definitive home.

In these portraits from the period of the Middle Kingdom, pharaoh no longer appears as the instrument of divine will but as the sole responsible actor who, like every man, must submit to a final judgment: "The judges are not lenient on that day when the wretches are sentenced, at the hour when the decision is carried out. Trust not in the length of the years; the judges see a lifetime as one hour. The man remains after his death, and his deeds are placed in a pile beside him. But eternity guarantees that one is there and that he is a fool who despises the Last Judgment. Whoever comes to them, however, without having sinned, he will there be like a god, striding free like the gods of eternity." (from the *Instruction for King Merikara*, from H. Brunner).

The reunification of Egypt starting in Thebes at the end of the First Intermediate Period had its counterpart at the beginning of the New Kingdom. Theban princes drove out the Hyksos kings, foreign rulers who had subjugated Egypt and reigned from their residence in Avaris in the Nile delta for one century (1650–1550 BC). Once again it is the typical Upper Egyptian style that characterizes the sculpture of the early New Kingdom (from 1550 BC).

The further stylistic development of the king's portrait in the 18th Dynasty (1539–1292 BC), however, then followed different lines from the portraiture of the Middle Kingdom. At the service of the policy of expansion followed in the early 18th Dynasty, which extended Egypt to the Euphrates and deep into northern Sudan, the king's portrait was now a self-representation expressing a claim to universal sovereignty. The portrait features on the king's statues are in fact still distinct, but they are subordinated to an idealizing image of the ruler. This "beautiful style" of the Thutmosides can suppress the personal aspect to such a degree that it is no longer possible to distinguish between Hatshepsut, a woman on the pharaoh's throne, and her co-ruler Thutmose III. The statues of the two ruling personages are first and foremost representations of the monarchy of their time.

As many inscriptions stated, the king does not act as his forefathers in the Middle Kingdom did "according to what his heart has planned" and it is not "his Majesty's tongue that daunts the Nubian"; the pharaoh is understood more as a tool in the hand of god. His individuality is fully integrated into the world order drawn up by Amun-Ra. In the inscription on the "poetic stele" of Thutmose III, Amun-Ra addresses the king:

"You are welcome, who rejoices at beholding my beauty,
my protector, Menkheperra, who lives forever!
For your sake, I rise
with a heart rejoicing at your coming to my temple.
My arms embrace your limbs in protection and life;
how sweet your gracefulness is against my breast!
I put you permanently in my dwelling, I work miracles for you:
I give you strength and victory over all foreign lands;
I leave proof of your power and fear of you in all lands
and allow dread of you to reach as far as the supports of the sky.
The princes of all foreign lands are in your grip,
I myself reach out so as to tie them to you.
I bundle up thousands and tens of thousands of Nubian troglodytes,
and from the northern lands prisoners of war in their hundreds of thousands.
You step into all foreign countries with a joyful heart,
while I am your leader when you move against them."

Guided by the king of the gods, the earthly king becomes god's replaceable governor on earth, who discharges his office, granted by god for a certain time. The continuity of the institution is the dominant factor characterizing the king's image. What should not be forgotten is an entirely pragmatic perspective regarding uniformity in the sculpture of kings during the New Kingdom. Sculptors' workshops received a huge amount of commissioned work. The numerous temples in Egypt and its newly acquired colonies had to be supplied with such a vast quantity of large-scale sculptures that division of labor, which had been maintained for reliefs, was also introduced in the making of statues. Furthermore, the technically perfect workmanship using the especially popular hard rocks—granite, diorite, quartzite, basalt and greywacke from the quarries in the Eastern Desert and the first cataract—required a lot of time. The dimensions of the statues grew to a monumental degree, reaching a peak in the Colossi of Memnon, eighteen meters high and weighing eight hundred tons.

Not only through their immense size but also through their functional location, in the temple courtyard, did these statues make an impact in profane public spaces and serve as elements in the ruler's self-staging. To this context belongs a type of statue, the figure of the sphinx, which already in the Old and Middle Kingdoms had represented a point of contact between god and king. It merges the body of the sacred animal with the head, or sometimes face, of the ruling sovereign and becomes a divine manifestation of the pharaoh. In the avenue of sphinxes in front of the divine temples, these statues denote the path from the profane to the sacred and the dogma of the king's position between man and god. At the end of this path, at the temple door, the pharaoh's divinity reaches its culmination in colossal statues. Under Amenhotep III (1387–1350 BC) these colossal statues took on an independent existence as divine beings, assumed their own names and were worshipped as sacred. Rameses II (1279–1212 BC) continued this deification of statues of himself in grand style in his residence in the eastern Delta of the Nile, in Memphis, in Thebes and in the temples on the kingdom's southern border with Nubia (Gerf Husein, Wadi es-Sebua, Abu Simbel).

The "beautiful style" of the early New Kingdom was interrupted around 1350 BC by the revolution of King Amenhotep IV. The abandonment of a conception of god with many forms and many names and the exclusive adoration of god in the solar disk, "Aten," confined the day to the period between morning and evening and a lifetime to that between birth and death. The three functional areas of sculpture became superfluous. The statue was no longer there to transcend mortality since life reached its completion under the beams of Aten. The ubiquitous presence of the pharaoh lay in the sun, and god no longer took on a form in statues, but revealed himself in his creation. Divine statues totally disappeared from the sculptor's

7. Sandstone falcon-headed sphinx
from the great temple of Abu
Simbel, New Kingdom,
19th Dynasty, reign of Rameses II.
London, The Trustees of the
British Museum
cat. 3

8. Faience statuette of King
Rudamon from Hermopolis Magna,
Third Intermediate Period,
23rd Dynasty. Private collection
cat. 20

repertoire, non-royal sculpture only appeared in a few small-size figures, and king's images projecting outward from the temples and cities of the kingdom no longer served any purpose. Only inside the sun temple and palaces, at first in Thebes, then—after the move to the newly built capital city—in el-Amarna, were statues of kings still to be found. In them is manifested the king's loving care for his divine father. As a part of creation, the king is depicted in a naturalistic fashion that is intensified to a caricature. This naturalism marked a complete departure from the traditional artistic styles and iconography and only the essential formal structure of Egyptian sculpture with its basic cubist principle was preserved. The representations of the members of the king's family—the king, who named himself now Akhenaten, the queen Nefertiti and their six daughters—resembled a new human image modeled on the king. The revolutionary nature of this short epoch is in no other area so directly recognizable as in its art. In the portrait of the king and of the queen is concentrated a vision of the world which sings the praise of Aten's creation:

"May you give to your beloved son,
while he lives in common with you for eternity,
while the king's great wife, whom he loves,
is at his side,
something to do, with which your heart is satisfied,
and let him see what you accomplish day by day."
(Hymn to Aten, from J. Assmann)

Soon after Akhenaten's death, the new art came to an abrupt end with the shutdown of the new capital city. Nonetheless, the king's portrait after the Amarna period remained marked by this brief revolutionary epoch. There was a tendency towards an impressionistic human image up to the end of the 18th Dynasty (*c.*1300 BC) and it can still be detected at the beginning of the Ramesside period (until *c.*1200 BC), although a phase now set in of a return to the classical past. The sculptures of Amenhotep III and those from the Middle Kingdom served as models for the statues of Rameses II, and many of the original statues from earlier times were reutilized by the Ramesside sovereigns. This recycling of sculpture from the past should not be described as usurpation; it was instead a reactivation and actualization of the past, a declaration of loyalty to tradition. As a consequence, the original inscriptions were not effaced, but often remained visible and new inscriptions were added; only in individual cases were the facial features of the original statues reworked so that they matched the appearance of the later model. The fundamental aspect in the sculpture of kings, which was to represent not the individual ruler but the institution of the monarchy, facilitated this repeated reuse of the statues of kings. As the identity of many statues is revealed in their inscriptions, it is possible to illustrate the list of the pharaohs of the Old, Middle and New Kingdoms almost entirely from the rulers' portraits, but it cannot be ruled out that in several cases they do not depict the king whose name they bear.

It was especially the pharaohs of the Third Intermediate Period following the New Kingdom (1075–664 BC) who reutilized the stock of statues of kings from the past. In art-historical research in Egyptology, there is a general methodological deficiency in the application of stylistic criteria for dating. In this still little studied epoch, this turns out to be a particular problem.

At the beginning of the Late Period (650–332 BC) the king's portrait was given a new boost. A ruling house from northern Sudan, based in Napata at the fourth cataract, conquered Egypt. The kings of this Kushite Dynasty can be recognized by their statues as "black pharaohs," characterized by a thickset neck and such typical facial features as a strongly pronounced chin, mouth, and low forehead. This foreign king's image fitted harmoniously into the formal structure of the traditional types of statues and, apart from new kinds of crowns and adornments, made use of the ancient Egyptian iconography of kings. Once again, continuity in ancient Egyptian art was maintained in the encounter with new stimuli.

After the Kushites withdrawal back to their African homeland, during the Saite period (664–525 BC) Egypt went through a phase of looking back on the nation's great past. Out of the "beautiful style" models of the New Kingdom, a smooth, cool perfection developed

9. Head of statue of Amenhotep III from the cachette court at Karnak, painted clay, New Kingdom, 18th Dynasty.
Cairo, Egyptian Museum
cat. 192

in the classical king's portrait, emphasized by a preference for the use of siltstone with its metallic effect. The last indigenous dynasty (380–342 BC) before Alexander the Great's conquest of Egypt (332 BC) continued to look back, carrying the tradition of an almost three-thousand-year-old art into the Ptolemaic dynasty (332–330 BC).

The deep gulf between the country's new rulers in their characteristically Greek capital city of Alexandria and the Egyptian motherland could not be bridged by art. Next to the purely Hellenistic portraits of the Ptolemaic rulers and their spouses, the archaically austere pharaoh statues stand like relics from a world of long ago.

One of the very last statues on the model of ancient Egyptian kings is that of the favorite of Emperor Hadrian (117–138 AD), Antinous, who, during the emperor's journey to Egypt in 130 AD, drowned in the river Nile. The classic statue of a king had become the embodiment of Egyptian culture, and in this alienated function it found its way via Roman Italy into the art of the Renaissance and into the mania for Egypt in the XVIII and XIX centuries.

When the pharaoh ascended the throne, he added to the name he had received at birth four others that expressed policy trends, concepts regarding the interpretation of royalty, devotion toward a particular god, or else the desire to draw inspiration for his own government from that of a predecessor. Although the most ancient periods of Egyptian history reflect this tendency, during the New Kingdom it won full acceptance. The five names forming the sovereign's complete titulary[1] were never used so widely to express the political options of the ruling pharaoh as during the period between the 18th and the 19th Dynasties.

In crucial moments, or else when a sudden change took place in the politico-social situation of Egypt, the ruler could decide to change his name to highlight the change. The most striking case is that of Amenhotep IV who, in the fifth year of his rule, altered his birth name to Akhenaten ("spirit of Aten," "he who is useful to Aten"), permanently sanctioning his complete break with the cult devoted to the Theban god Amun (Amenhotep actually means "Amun is content"). Instead, young Tutankhaten ("living image of the Aten") did the opposite once he ascended the throne, taking the name Tutankhamun ("living image of the Amun"). So these two changes sum up a whole period in which first the new cult devoted to the god Aten appeared, and then, the counter-reformation that marked the return to tradition and the worship of the Theban god.

The titulary can be seen as a preliminary description of the pharaoh and offers the image of himself he wanted to give to his contemporaries. Thus the great number of names Rameses II assumed in the course of his long reign, seen as a whole, renders the most stereotyped figure of the Egyptian ruler. Thus Rameses II is offspring of the gods ("mighty bull, son of Atum"[2]), who also chose him to become sovereign ("chosen by Ra"[3]).

On the other hand, countless references to the goddess of justice Maat ("rich of Maat is Ra,"[4] "beloved by Maat,"[5] "who delights Maat,"[6] "who upraises Maat"[7]) are used to describe Rameses II as the sovereign *par excellence*, in the most characteristic role ascribed to Egyptian royalty: that of upholding divine order (*maat*) on earth.

The situation of tranquillity, deriving from a proper maintenance of order, can be obtained only through the complete elimination of all the chaotic forces that permeate the orderly world (Egypt), and therefore many of the epithets Rameses II used describe his warlike abilities, nearly always in generic terms. Some of the Horus names chosen by the sovereign add to the recurrent "mighty bull" with epithetical forms describing him as "great in deeds of valor and one who fights with his strong arm,"[8] "Ra who crushes every foreign land under his sandals"[9] and, referring especially to those who in Rameses II's day were a concrete threat "who destroys the Asiatics."[10] Several "Golden Horus" names express the ruler's ability to destroy the enemy: "mighty in strength, who destroys the Nine Bows," "great in deeds of valor in every foreign land," "he who subdues foreign lands and destroys rebels."[11] The theme of the enemy's defeat, combined with that of the defense of Egypt, is instead expressed by the *nebty* name. Rameses II describes himself as "he who protects Egypt and subdues foreign lands,"[12] or else as "he who fights with his own arm and protects his army."[13]

The stereotyped image of the king is completed by his claim of deeds favoring the god: one of the many *nebty* names Rameses II chose describes him as "he who embellishes the monuments in the temple of Luxor for his father Amun, who placed him on the throne" and the

1. Limestone stele of Rameses II as a child, New Kingdom, 19th Dynasty.
Paris, Musée du Louvre
cat. 45

2. Westcar Papyrus, Second Intermediate Period.
Berlin, Ägyptisches Museum und Papyrussammlung
cat. 144

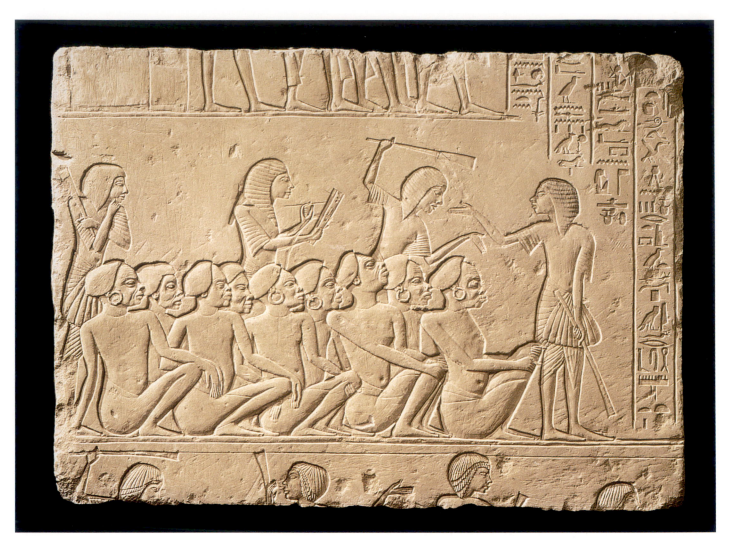

3. Limestone relief with Nubian prisoners.
Bologna, Museo Civico Archeologico

"Golden Horus" name that follows it, as "he who seeks useful things for the one who created him."[14] Here the titulary is used to emphasize the *do ut des* relationship closely binding the Egyptian sovereign to the god, and is expressed and reiterated quite monotonously, in all New Kingdom inscriptions: the god attributed royalty to the ruler so he would do something for him. The circularity of this relationship (a serpent biting its tail, an image inherent to Egyptian culture to express the everlasting[15]) is completed by very frequent sentences wherein the sovereign claims to have done something for the god in order to be given something in exchange:

"And you will double for me the long span of the life and the great reign of the King Usermaatra Setepenra [Rameses II], the great god . . . because I have done countless useful things for your temple. . . ."[16]

Thus, the ruler's names are used first to offer a description of the pharaoh while the titulary occasionally assumes a real literary *status*, becoming an integral part of the text. That, for instance, is the case in the inscription whereby Thutmose III describes his building activity in the temple of Amun-Ra at Karnak.[17] Within the part praising the ruler, the author of the text introduces all the names of Thutmose III, which he then extends, alters, and conceals in order to create a real panegyric:

"[He is the one (Amun) who perpetuated] my apparitions, writing my titulary.
He established my hawk on the *serekh*:[18] he made me as brave as a mighty bull and caused me to rise within Thebes [in this my Horus name of 'mighty bull rising in Thebes'].

He caused the Two Ladies to rise: he made my reign last as long as Ra's in heaven, [in] this my *nebty* [name] 'enduring of reign as Ra in heaven.'
He fashioned me like a golden Hawk: he gave me its might and its strength, magnifying me in its appearance in glory, in this my [Golden Horus] name 'mighty in strength, magnificent in appearing in glory.'
He made me rise like The One who belongs to the sedge and the bee,[19] to Upper and Lower Egypt: he perpetuated my forms like Ra's, in this [my] *nesw-bit* name, lord of the Two lands Menkheperra ['Stable of becoming is Ra'].
I am his son[20] who appeared before him, the image created like 'The first of Heseret' [Thoth].[21] He united each of my forms, in this my *sa Ra* name Djehutymes Semakheper ['Thutmose, who unites becoming'], lives perpetually and eternally!"

The titulary, in its canonical form, is also a way of introducing the protagonist into a text in which the pharaoh plays the leading role. As a matter of fact, it is occasionally preceded by the date of the sovereign's reign, at the beginning of documents glorifying the figure of the king, which, for that very reason, may be considered the products of royal propaganda. The definition of a category of propagandistic documents in the framework of ancient Egyptian culture is still today the source of lively discussion that generally involves the entire way of classifying and subdividing Egyptian written sources.[22] Regardless of such elements as form and content, I believe we can consider propagandistic all the texts that were produced by the royal chancellery, the central figure of which was the ruler, whose function was to inform his subjects of the events and significant works he accomplished. Therefore, these are written on pillars (stelae), rock, or temple walls in order to be accessible and read by the population (or part of it). These documents, actually based on a dual language (figurative and textual[23]), express both the civil and religious policies of the ruling sovereign, and can thus be considered, at least for the New Kingdom, an extension of the titulary adopted by the pharaoh on his ascent to the throne. Rameses II's titulary, mentioned at the beginning of this essay, is paradigmatic from this point of view.
When particular events occurred, nearly always of an unforeseen or exceptional nature (for instance, Hatshepsut's ascent to the throne, the battle Rameses II fought against the Hittites at Qadesh or the invasions of the Sea Peoples under Rameses III), the propagandistic document can become far longer, even covering entire walls of a religious building. The need to adapt the speech to events extraneous to the normal administration of the state also leads to disparities in the language used in the document: the greater importance given to the figuration by Hatshepsut, Rameses II and Rameses III echoes this necessity and finds its textual equivalent in the use of a language (neo-Egyptian) different from the one used by the royal chancellery (middle-Egyptian) in the documents written by Amenhotep IV-Akhenaten to support his socio-religious reform.
We can date the creation of a propagandist form of literature to the start of the Middle Kingdom, when the need to give the Nile valley a fresh unity engaged the state in an effort to give new credibility to royalty, that had nearly dissolved after the fragmentation of power during the First Intermediate Period. Thus, during the 12th Dynasty the stereotyped figure of the ruler was defined and remained practically unchanged in the texts of later periods.[24] When Sinuhe, the hero of the most famous story of ancient Egypt,[25] strives to exalt the greatness of Senusret I to Amuneneshi, the prince of Retenu who is questioning him about the future of Egypt after the sudden death of Amenemhat I, he portrays the sovereign in words that are practically the same as those in the royal texts of the New Kingdom and of later periods:

"He is a god. He has no equals and no one [like him] existed before him. He is the lord of knowledge, excellent in designs and splendid in commands. One comes and goes according to his orders. . . . He is truly a brave man who acts with his arm, a fighter who has no rival."[26]

Yet it was not until the 18th Dynasty that Egyptian royal propaganda became concretely formalized and contributed to casting an aura of constant glorification on the New Kingdom rulers, who were engaged not only in expanding their own dominion far beyond the borders of Egypt, but also in attributing a new organization to a constantly and swiftly evolving so-

4. Limestone bas-relief from the
tomb of Merira at Memphis,
New Kingdom, 18th Dynasty.
Vienna, Kunsthistorisches Museum,
Antikensammlung
cat. 173

5. Limestone stele of Mai from
Abydos, New Kingdom,
19th Dynasty, reign of Sety I.
Brussels, Musées Royaux d'Art
et d'Histoire
cat. 214

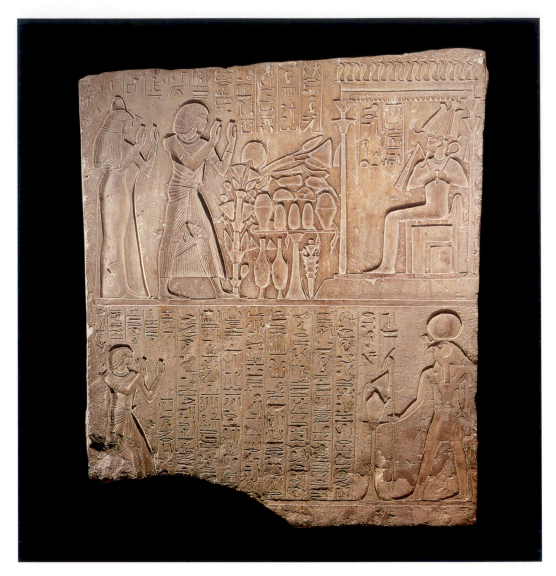

cial situation. The Nile valley, in the course of the five centuries (1550–1075 BC) ranging from
the beginning of the 18th to the end of the 20th Dynasty, underwent such radical and
painful changes that the very foundations of the state were shaken. Everything revolved around
the figure of the ruler, one that the texts desperately attempted to preserve intact, throughout all the social upheavals until the end of this period, whose achievements make it appear
to be the era of the greatest splendor of Egyptian civilization. But the Egypt of the New Kingdom was a serpent that was always changing skins: After several devastating evolutions, it
returned to being the same on the outside, albeit profoundly altered. In this critical situation, despite the image that the propagandistic documents tried to give of him, the pharaoh
was forced to play a central role, around which revolved the expectations and interests of
specific social classes that were constantly bickering, rather than represent the entire population. The nobility, army and clergy, depending on alliances only hinted at by documents,
alternately loomed behind the rulers of the 18th Dynasty, while the Ramessides (representatives of the army) were the only ones who were able to reestablish the totality and absolutism that had been inherent to pharaonic power ever since the birth of the Egyptian state.
Starting with Sety I, they would do so by using large-scale propaganda that tended toward
greater and greater monumentality. However, the Egypt of the 19th and 20th Dynasties was
a country open to the outside world (it had never really been so before), and the documents
of the last rulers, who in memory of their mighty and famous predecessor were all named
Rameses, did not fail to mention the problem of the delicate integration of foreign elements
that were increasingly being absorbed in Egyptian society:[27]

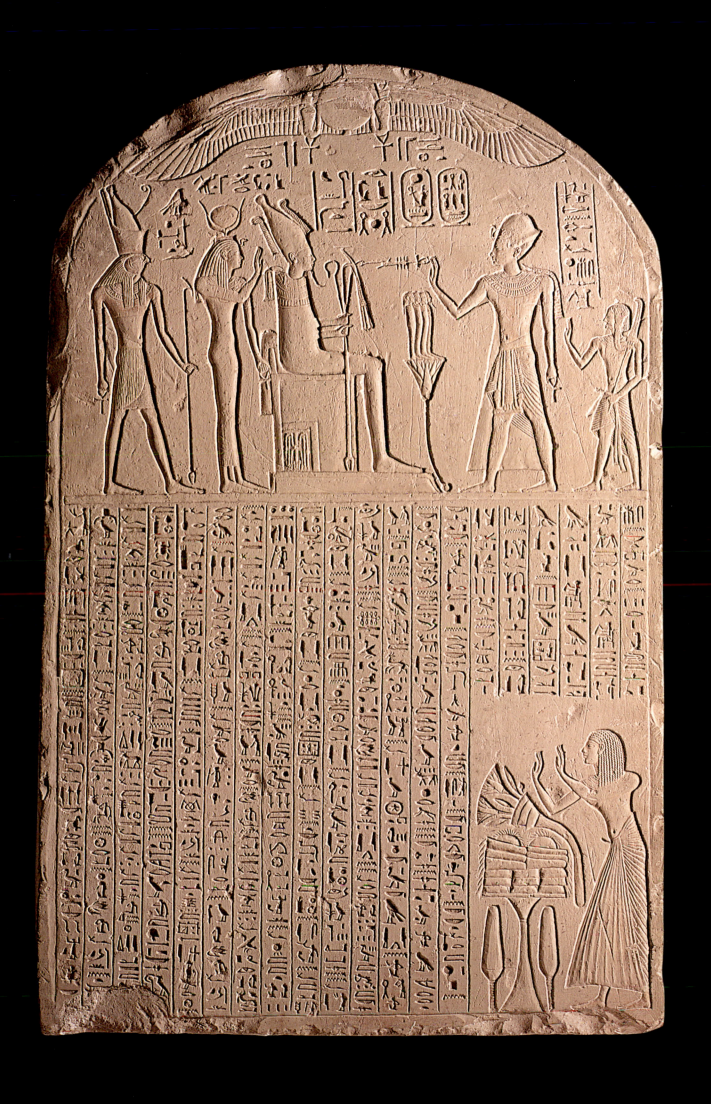

"He is the one [Rameses III] who sacked the foreign countries . . . the Libyans, the Meshwesh. He made them cross the rivers that lead to Egypt. They were locked up in the valiant ruler's fortresses, learned the language of the Egyptians in the sovereign's retinue. He exorcized their words and overturned their tongues. So they can go their way without being harassed."

Throughout this period, in spite of cultural and social changes, the royal propagandist documents seem to propose the image of a single ruler, whose figure has become a stereotype and is difficult to confirm by facts. The description of the pharaoh, whatever the main topic (construction of a temple, institution of offerings, expedition, military campaign, glorification of the divinity) motivating the emission of the document by the central chancellery, thereafter responded to a series of canonical themes that seem immutable at first. Thus, Ahmose, the sovereign who traditionally begins the 18th Dynasty, is described in these terms:[28]

"Son of Amun-Ra, of his own body, whom he loves; his heir to whom he attributed his own throne. The truly excellent god, there being no falsehood in that. . . . He who perpetuates justice [*maat*]. . . . He is a sovereign that Ra made rule and Amun made great. . . . He strikes terror in the Nubians, his war cry crosses the land of the *Fenekhu*."[29]

The sentences, from the many constituting this royal panegyric, insist on themes that are often expressed, in terms not very dissimilar, in the titulary of Rameses II. They describe Ahmose as a sovereign who is son of god (Amun-Ra), whose task is to perpetuate justice, who was chosen by the gods (Ra and Amun) to be king and who is able to destroy the enemies, in other words the chaotic elements that, without his intervention, might penetrate into Egypt, the land where divine order rules. With time, these same themes became formalized; and, classified according to a fictitious chronological sequence, succeeded in describing the ideal life of the ruler, as an introduction to the central topic, whatever that might be, that was dealt with in the propagandistic document. A hypothetical reconstruction of this series of events[30] (since they could not all be expressly mentioned in a single text) includes the birth of the king, sometimes anticipated by the claim of his predestination to the throne. Then comes the choice of the god, followed by the enthronement. At the end, the sovereign's ability to maintain (or reestablish) divine order on earth is asserted. This theme may be expressed or hinted at by the defeat of Egypt's enemies. A good example of this kind of development is given by the text inscribed on the stele that Amenhotep II had raised in honor of the Sphinx of Giza:[31]

"TITULARY Son of [Amun] whom [he] created for himself, progeny of Horakhty, splendid fruit, divine in limb. Neith created his form.
The primordial god [Ra] generated him to assume the government he assumed. He made him rise as a sovereign on the throne of the living. He reunited the black Land [Egypt] behind himself, the red Land [the desert] as his servant. He ordained for him a perpetual legacy and an everlasting royalty. He gave him the throne of Geb, the splendid function of Atum under the Two Lords [Horus and Seth], the part [belonging] to the Two Ladies [Wadjyt and Nekhbet], their years being in life and power. He placed his daughter [Maat] on his pectoral and perpetuated the *uraeus* on his brow.
He [Amenhotep II] crushed the Bedouins under his sandals; the peoples of the North kneel to his power and thus every foreign land fears him. He joined together the leaders of the Nine Bows; the Two Lands are in his hand. People revere him and all the gods love him."

The piece can be divided into three parts. The first introduces the sovereign, describing him as the son of various gods. Instead, in the second, the god in person (Ra) acts, first generating the sovereign and then placing him on the throne; the piece goes on, mentioning several images connected with Egyptian royalty, from the concrete (the union of the Two Lands) to the abstract (the mention of gods mythically associated with royal power: Geb, Atum, the Two Lords, the Two Ladies), to then return to the concrete (insignias of royalty: pectoral and *uraeus*). At this point, the subject of the action becomes the sovereign who, by crushing several enemies, at last wins supremacy over the entire earth, thus accomplishing the mission entrusted to him, which is to maintain (or reestablish) *maat* on earth. This last concept is just suggested by the love the gods have for Amenhotep II: indeed in the royal texts there are countless sentences claiming for the monarch:[32]

"Thou [Sety I] giveth them [the gods] Justice every day, because it is therein that they live."

The explicitness of these themes is instrumental in the presentation of the figure of the ruler in the propagandistic text as the legitimate holder of power (he is in charge because he is the god's son and because the god chose him). The image produced is that of a ruler predestined since birth to become such, but who is then chosen by the god in person to occupy the throne which should belong to him by right. These themes are expressed separately or appear one after the other, sometimes amplified with a reference to female divinities that supposedly suckled the sovereign when he was a babe. These are all concepts that can be related to the legitimacy of power, and such themes are in fact especially exploited by those who have no claim to the throne. Indeed, Queen Hatshepsut refashions the ideal life of the ruler, extending it both textually and figuratively to declare (despite evidence) her predestination to the throne. The iconic-textual cycle she dedicates to her presumed descent from Amun-Ra takes up a great deal of space in the queen's funerary temple at Deir el-Bahri.[33] The span of time attributed to the narration is so expanded that the moment of conception is practically described live:

"[Amun-Ra] turned himself into the Majesty of her [of the queen Ahmose] husband, the king of Upper and Lower Egypt Aakheperkara [Thutmose I] and found her [Ahmose] sleeping in the most hidden part of his palace. She awoke to the scent of the god and smiled to His Majesty. He rushed to her, desired her intensely and gave her his heart, appearing to her in his divine form, when he united with her. She delighted in seeing his beauty and desire for him ran through her limbs. Then the palace was permeated with the scent of the god, [who was similar] to all the fragrances [that come from] Punt."

The story of Hatshepsut's divine birth was slavishly imitated by Amenhotep III, who had it reproduced in the temple of Luxor. The ruler had no reason to do so, since he was the legitimate heir to the throne, and we almost have the impression that the claim to predestination to the throne, after Hatshepsut, had become part of the repertory of themes at the disposal of royal propaganda. Amenhotep III's father, Thutmose IV, the legitimate son of Amenhotep II, similarly felt obliged to repeat the concept. Yet he did it with a kind of narration in which he became a fairy-tale figure through an experience that went beyond the royal sphere. The text alludes to the youth of Thutmose IV, when he was not yet king. The young prince is vacationing at Giza and decides to rest in the shade of the Great Sphinx, at the time partly buried under the sand. In his dream, Khepri, the god the Egyptians at the time identified with the Sphinx, appears to him and predicts his sovereignty over Egypt and asks him to free him from the sand. The god's prophecy came true and Thutmose IV, as soon as he became ruler, complied with the god's request, even building a protective wall around the Sphinx.[34] In this case, the prophecy insists on the fact that Thutmose IV is the legitimate heir to the throne without, as in the case of Hatshepsut any need to claim it.

Thutmose IV saw his royalty announced in a dream, Hatshepsut was the fruit of the love between her mother Ahmose and the god Amun, Thutmose III and Rameses II routed the armies of the Mitanni and Hittite states practically without the help of soldiers, Sety I miraculously found water by the road in the desert. All this happened through divine intervention. In the propagandistic texts the god is thus led to play (when not the direct recipient of the sovereign's actions and undertakings) the role of magical assistant to the pharaoh. So the god is turned into a textual instrument (a real *deus ex machina*) who often intervenes in the ruler's life. "I did it for my father," "My father commanded me to do so," unanimously claimed the monarchs of the New Kingdom, as if seeking justification for their deeds in divine will thereby proclaiming their extraneousness to the facts. All in all, the textual image of the New Kingdom ruler is that of a passive personality, his fate marked by the inscrutable designs of the divinity.

In the propaganda, the pharaoh is the hero and the god his magical assistant. Without the

7. Bronze statuette of the goddess Isis suckling the king, Late Period, 600–400 BC.
Berlin, Ägyptisches Museum und Papyrussammlung
cat. 43

6. Pink granite statue of the cow Hathor suckling the Pharaoh Horemheb, New Kingdom, 18th Dynasty.
Florence, Museo Egizio
cat. 47

intervention of the second, the active force of the first would be interrupted: the story could not continue and, in some cases, not even begin.

This places the entire royal discourse in the realm of fables. Using the pattern of fables, the New Kingdom royal propaganda constructs the episodes to glorify the figure of the sovereign: narrative moments in which even the magical assistant (the god) is eliminated in order to add emphasis to the main character. In these fragments, the king is alone and it is precisely this solitude that enhances his greatness.

In the past, considerable prominence was given to the *Königsnovelle* (royal novel), dignifying it as an autonomous literary genre.[35] The plot is rather simple: the ruler faces an undertaking (nearly always through a communication), decides to act (usually choosing the most difficult, either real or metaphorical, road) and, in the end, carries out the undertaking. This sequence of events, which matches the course of a fable, should be viewed more as a literary mode than an authentic genre in itself.[36] The *Königsnovelle* is what most emphasizes the figure of the ruler, attributing to his image supernatural characteristics (the removal of the god left the place of the magical assistant vacant). In this frame, the world described by the propagandistic text undergoes a metamorphosis, time is dilated and space becomes concrete. The ruler is materialized in all his greatness and uniqueness. This last trait is precisely what the *Königsnovelle* most emphasizes. The king is unique, either by antonomasia or by opposition. Indeed, all of Egypt's enemies oppose him but, in the *Königsnovelle*, this also includes the circle of persons admitted to the ruler's presence. When Kamose decides to attack the Hyksos, he clashes with the aristocracy, who appear to entertain friendly relations with the future enemy. Thutmose III, before deciding which road to take to reach Megiddo, gathers the heads of the armed forces, who wisely advise him to surprise the enemy from the rear; furious at such a suggestion, he climbs on his battle chariot and penetrates the narrow Aruna gorge, sure of victory. The solitude of the ruler is also the basic theme of the entire Battle of Qadesh. This is the description of the terrible massacre scene, the climax of the clash between the Egyptians and the Hittites:[37]

"His Majesty completely annihilated the rebels of this vile enemy, the Khatti, with all their great chiefs and brothers and all the princes of every foreign land who had joined up with them. Their infantrymen and their charioteers fell on their faces, tumbling over one another. His Majesty killed them where they stood and they gathered around his chariot. His Majesty was alone, no one else was with him."

So the Battle of Qadesh can also be interpreted as a lengthy *Königsnovelle* and is perhaps the most fable-like of all the ones that Egyptian propagandistic literature has left us. The royal novel begins with two Hittite spies pretending to be traitors being led before the sovereign. In a normally developed *Königsnovelle*, Rameses II is not supposed to believe the words of the enemy (vile by antonomasia), and this is the astonishing novelty: the ruler puts himself against himself, against his nature as a superior being with boundless knowledge and, believing what the two Hittites tell him, behaves like a true fairy-tale character (who falls into the trap set for him, the examples are countless). This doubling of his personality, which places the sovereign-person in antithesis with the sovereign-stereotype, is merely a method to further emphasize the greatness of Rameses II, by creating a fearsome vacuum around him, a vacuum that comes from his wrong decision and leads to a terrible crisis. The consequences of Rameses II's decision are in fact, as in all tales, disastrous, and the Hittite armies storm the oblivious Egyptians' camp. Now the ruler is truly alone. Alone with himself and against himself. For the tale to reach its (certain) happy end (and here we have another disparity with the usual *Königsnovelle* plot), the intervention of the magical assistant (the god) is nonetheless necessary: The abyss Rameses II created around himself is too great to be filled by a mere mortal, even one possessing the divine function of royalty:[38]

"I invoke you, o my father Amun, while I am amid countless enemies whom I do not know. All the foreign lands have joined up against me and I am completely alone, without anyone by me. My numerous army has abandoned me, no charioteer protects me. If I cried out to them, not one of them would come."

Aside from stereotypes and particular cases, the image of the pharaoh traced by the New Kingdom propaganda was exactly the same: that of a unique, solitary ruler who drew his boundless greatness from his uniqueness and solitude. An obvious variation occurred during the 20th Dynasty, when the god's importance and supremacy became greater and the pharaoh was therefore less alone.

The rulers of this period, whose personalities appear lessened by the fact of their continuous use of the name Rameses, seemed to live in the aura of the memory of their predecessor. Their concerns were far from the battlefield (except for Rameses III) and the clash of arms that had been the background sound of the 18th and 19th Dynasties. The last Ramessides are mainly involved in seeking to confer a new social order onto a constantly evolving Egypt. Their efforts aimed at underlining their legitimacy to the throne and asking the god to continue their own line. Behind texts that reiterate the thundering, vainglorious tone of those of the preceding periods, can be sensed the image of a fragile sovereign.

The pharaoh was the icon of Egypt, and the fragility appearing in the propagandistic documents was a presage that the unitary state would soon shatter like a dropped mirror. The pieces, scattered along the Nile valley, would reflect the image of countless rulers.

[1] In the most ancient periods of Egyptian history, the sovereign's names were not all attested, and the royal titulary underwent significant variations before being permanently canonized. The monarchs of the first dynasties are mainly known by the name preceded by the Horus title, next to which, at the end of the 1st Dynasty, the *nebty* ("Two Ladies") appears. The first refers to the identification of the king with Horus, the falcon-headed solar god. The second displays one of the most characteristic roles of pharaonic royalty, that of sanctifying the union of Upper and Lower Egypt. This concept is expressed by the reference to the cobra-goddess Wadjyt, patroness of Buto in the Delta (located in the vicinity of Pe, the Predynastic capital of the North), and to the vulture-goddess Nekhbet, patroness of Elkab (in the vicinity of Hierakonpolis, the Predynastic capital of the South). The notion of the union of two different royalties (to which the latest research does not give a geographic connotation) is referred to by the title *nesw-bit* ("He of the sedge and bee") that, attested by the beginning of the 4th Dynasty, gradually moves up to being placed before the name chosen by the sovereign at the time of his enthronement and that, more than any other, proclaims the ruler's political intents. Instead the title *sa Ra* ("Son of Ra") claims the sovereign's descent from the solar divinity, and introduces his birth name; although it begins to appear under Djedefra (4th Dynasty), it is not until the 5th Dynasty that it is regularly attested. On the other hand, the so-called "Golden Horus," an epithet attested as of the rule of Djoser, increased in importance over the years, and finally became part of the king's canonical title. The most important names, *sa Ra* and *nesw-bit*, were written inside the "cartouche" (first attested under the reign of Peribsen), the mark of a knotted rope that played a protective role insofar as it separated the name from everything around it.

[2] Horus name on an obelisk originally erected in the capital Piramesse and later removed to Tanis (KRI II, 424.3).

[3] The introduction of the theme of the god's choice, connoting the claim to the legitimacy to rule, inside the throne name (*nesw-bit*), is not exclusive to Rameses II. We already find it as an extension in the throne names of Thutmose I, III and IV, Amenhotep III, Horemheb and Sety I. After Rameses II, and in emulation of him, many other rulers include in their own *nesw-bit* name.

[4] The first part of Rameses II's throne name that in full is Usermaatra Setepenra ("rich of Maat is Ra, chosen by Ra").

[5] This epithet appears more frequently as an extension of the Horus name that, as its first element always features the locution *ka-nekhet* ("mighty bull").

[6] Epithet used as an extension of the Horus name (Kanekhet Hayhermaat "mighty bull who delights Maat") in a seated statue of Rameses II from the temple of Karnak, now in the Egyptian Museum in Cairo (CG 42130), and as *nebty* name (Hayhermaat Miakhty "who delights Maat as 'The one who lives in the horizon'") in the text engraved on the west side of the obelisk placed in front of the temple of Luxor (KRI VI, 599.8).

[7] Extension of the Horus name (Kanekhet Utjesmaat "mighty bull who upraises Maat"), inscribed in the door of one of the north secondary rooms of the second pillared hall in the temple of Rameses II at Abydos (KRI II, 547.13).

[8] We also find it attested only as "mighty bull, who fights with his strong arm" (western obelisk of the temple of Luxor, presently in Place de la Concorde in Paris: KRI II, 603.3). Rameses II's claim that he personally took part in the warfare is most vividly illustrated in the Battle of Qadesh.

[9] Rhetoric stele from Tanis (Tanis V): KRI II, 294.10. The expression has an exact parallel on the base of the statues portraying the Egyptian ruler, on which are usually reproduced foreigners kneeling with their hands bound behind their back, or else nine bows, a metonymic representation of the enemies of Egypt (the enemy is represented by the weapon, while the number nine, plural of a plural, expressed the concept of totality).

[10] Temple of Luxor: east side of the western obelisk (KRI II, 602.15) and façade of the eastern mass of the pylon (KRI II, 605.15).

[11] Temple of Luxor: façade of the eastern mass of the pylon (KRI II, 605.15–16), east side (KRI II, 602.16) and south side (KRI II, 603.2–3) of the western obelisk.

[12] Rameses II's most widely used *nebty* name.

[13] KRI II, 605.15. Here the *nebty* name refers directly to one of the most dramatic moments of the Battle of Qadesh: Rameses intervenes to oppose the Hittites' attack when his army is in complete disarray. The text, in which the peculiar form of the *nebty* name appears, actually belongs to the version of the Battle of Qadesh figuring on the pylon of the temple of Luxor. Despite the reference to a particular event, the epithetical form can be identified with the protective role of the ruler with respect to Egypt on the grounds of a synecdochic relationship (the part for the whole) binding the army to Egypt.

[14] Temple of Luxor: façade of the eastern mass of the pylon (KRI II, 605. 11–12).

[15] The circularity of the relationship between ruler and god belongs to that recursive continuity ascribed to pharaonic royalty, which tends to consider each ruling sovereign as the incarnation of the god Horus on earth (the visible sun), whereas it ascribes to every deceased monarch the identity of Osiris (the invisible sun in the netherworld), and interprets the ascent to the throne as the rising of the sun (*kha*). The fate of the royalty on the Valley of Egypt is thus connoted by the perpetual daily rising of the sun. The concept of a circular, recursive infinity is often expressed in royal inscriptions by the term *djet*, in apposition with the term *neheh* that instead expresses the linearity of an infinity without beginning or end. The spelling of the word *djet* has the sign of the serpent over that of the earth. In the Hellenistic-Roman period, when the system of hieroglyphic writing underwent graphic alterations, greater visual immediacy was ascribed to this term, turning it into a serpent wrapped around a mummiform body. This image was very popular with late Antiquity authors, like Artemidorus Daldianus (II century) and Cyril of Alexandria (III–IV century) who interpreted it as a metaphor to express time. In Roman times, one of the representations of Aion is, on the other hand, an Egyptianizing figure (replaced by an obelisk on the "Parabiago patera," conserved in the Civiche Raccolte Archeologiche of Milan), wrapped in the spires of a serpent. Horapollo (see Boas 1950, p. 43) began his book on hieroglyphs by explaining the concepts of eternity and the universe, and claimed that the Egyptians used the figure of the serpent biting its tail in both cases. This image was to have a remarkable influence on European Renaissance culture and was to be used also in the Tarot card of the "World," as the symbol of the universe and everlasting time.

[16] Stele of Rameses IV for the gods of Abydos (KRI IV, 19.12–13). As we can see in this short fragment, the 20th Dynasty lives in the memory of Rameses II. The desire for emulation, explicitly expressed by Rameses IV is shared by all the rulers of the last part of the New Kingdom and many of the later eras, who would fashion their own titularies on those of their famous predecessor.

[17] The inscription is in the temple of Amun-Ra at Karnak, engraved on the north wall of the passage along the outer south side of the chambers (built by Hatshepsut, and then usurped by Thutmose III) that presently surround the sanctuary for Philip Arrhidaeus' divine granite boat. See PM II, p. 106 (328). I use the edition published in URK IV, 160. 10–161. 12. The parts in brackets are integrations suggested by K. Sethe.

[18] Ever since the remotest times of Egyptian history the Horus name has been written inside the schematic reproduction of a royal palace (the *serekh*) topped by a falcon.

[19] I translate the word *nesw-bit* by its literal meaning to show its difference with the following words that have a geographic connotation.

[20] Here the word *sa Ra* ("son of Ra") is concealed by the possessive pronoun, which ascribes the paternity of the sovereign to the god of Thebes Amun, whose solar aspect is manifested by the syncretism with Ra (=Amun-Ra).

[21] The birth name of Thutmose (*Djehuty-mes* "Thoth created him") is implicitly mentioned by placing the term *mes* ("create") before as an attribute of "image," followed by the reference to the god Thoth (*Djehuty*) by circumlocution: Heseret is in fact the necropolis of Hermopolis of which the god was the patron.

[22] See the most recent studies gathered in Loprieno 1996A, and, more particularly, the relationships between literature and politics, Assmann, Blumenthal 1999.

[23] At least as of the rule of Pepy I (stele with Decree of Coptos, see Klug 2002, p. 5), the royal document had two different parts: scene (above) and text (below). While the figuration does not constantly appear during the Middle Kingdom, it becomes an indispensable element of the royal propaganda document during the 18th Dynasty.

[24] Blumenthal 1970, p. 8.

[25] The *Tale of Sinuhe* is not to be considered a propagandistic document, since it is not centered on the figure of the sovereign. Instead, we can speak of a text having a didactic role, as the existence of countless copies produced in the scholastic context suggests. Supporting this interpretation is above all its moral intent, which instead is lacking in propagandistic texts. The fact that fragments borrowed from other literary genres are introduced in the story, such as in this case of the panegyric of Senusret I, should not surprise us. If the intention of its composition was didactic and intended for young scribes, then it is obvious that its composition meant to give them the broadest possible survey of the kind of texts they would be called upon to write. In the *Tale of Sinuhe*, we can immediately distinguish, aside from the panegyric devoted to Senusret I (Sinuhe, R 47–98), the title of the individual (Sinuhe, R 1–2), the *incipit* of the autobiography (Sinuhe, R 3–5), the prayer (Sinuhe, B 156–173), the ruler's order (Sinuhe, B 178–199), the letter (Sinuhe, B 204–235). For a discussion of the interconnections between literature and propaganda, see Simpson 1996.

[26] Sinuhe, B 47–52. Thutmose III, in the inscription dated to the twenty-third year of his reign, and inscribed on one of the pillars of the temple of Wadi Halfa, nearly literally borrowed the sentence used by Sinuhe: ". . . a sovereign who acts with his arm, a fighter who has no rival" (URK IV, 809. 1–2).

[27] Stele of Ramses III engraved in the sanctuary of Mertseger at Deir el-Medina. The quotation is published in KRI VI, 91.5–7.

[28] Stele of Ahmose found in front of the seventh pillar of the temple of Amun-Ra at Karnak and presently conserved in the Cairo Museum (CG 340021). For the hieroglyphic text, see URK IV, 14–17.

[29] Population of the Syro-Palestinian region. With the Nubians and the *Fenekhu*, the south and the north are mentioned in a typical expression of opposed duality, characterizing the entire world outside of Egypt.

[30] The succession of the themes suggested here generally reflects the treatment of propagandistic terminology adopted in Grimal 1986.

[31] URK IV, 1276.13–1277.7.

[32] Nauri decree of Sety I. (KRI I, 47.5–6).

[33] The entire cycle is inscribed on the rear wall of the north colonnade at the end of the second terrace of the temple. The text is published in URK IV, 219.11–220.6 and is integrated on the basis of the version Amenhotep III had carved in the temple of Luxor (URK IV, 1714.7–17).

[34] It is the so-called "Dream Stele" that can still be admired today between the paws of the Giza Sphinx. The hieroglyphic text appears in URK IV, 1539–1544.

[35] Whose existence was postulated for the first time by Hermann (1938).

[36] On the difficulty of attributing the *Königsnovelle* to a specific literary genre, see Loprieno 1996b, especially his conclusions, p. 295.

[37] KRI I, 121.11–122.10.

[38] KRI II, 39.13–41.5.

Bernard Mathieu

The Accession of a Pharaoh.
An Iconographical and Literary Theme in the Ramesside Period

Accession and Coronation

In ancient Egypt, the death of a pharaoh led to the immediate accession of his successor. Without resolving all the thorny questions of what constituted legitimacy—questions that recurred throughout Egyptian history and were tackled by a royal ideology admitting different modes of divine recognition (theogamy, predestination, designation through oracles, etc.)[1]—this institutional mechanism would, in principle, preserve the state from a dangerous power vacuum. Once the funeral was over and the body buried—that is, in theory, a total of seventy days after the death of the old ruler—the actual ceremony of coronation would take place.[2]

This time lapse between accession and coronation might be used by the scribe historians to draw up a balance of the past reign, applying certain fixed criteria inherited from tradition. Diodorus Siculus tells us: "On all of them [the kings], the priests had, from the earliest of days, kept archives in their sacred books which they then handed down to their successors, describing the appearance of each pharaoh, his character and what he had done during his reign."[3] The delay must also have allowed information to spread across the territory of the nation, informing the different levels of the state administration of key facts relating to the new sovereign—in particular, those which established his official status. Thus the country gradually learned of this change at the top; though, of course, the vast majority of Egyptians knew nothing about the pharaoh, or about his physical characteristics and intellectual qualities. The most that one can imagine happening—and this only in certain periods of Egyptian history—is that scribes, draftsmen and sculptors were sent from the royal household to provide a sort of reference model for those working in the various provincial workshops. While recognizing the gap between historical truth and official portraiture, I shall cite here some royal portraits in words or images that date from the Ramesside era and may be seen as relating specifically to the accession of a new monarch.

The Young King

During the New Kingdom most kings were very young when they came to the throne. Allowing for chronological imprecision and the sometimes complex debates relating to the length of specific reigns, one might estimate the age of accession of the monarchs of the 18th Dynasty as follows: Ahmose, 15; Amenhotep I, 25; Thutmose I, 20; Thutmose II, 13; Thutmose III, 5; Hatshepsut, 33; Amenhotep II, 18; Thutmose IV, 21; Amenhotep III, 10; Amenhotep IV (Akhenaten), 22; Merytaton, 15; Tutankhamun, 10. All in all, an average age of 17.

From the very origins of the Pharaonic state, the underlying mythologies of power led to the king being seen as a sort of earthly embodiment of the young god Horus, the protector of his father Osiris; and this—together with the youth of the new monarch—would seem to have profoundly affected the formation or consolidation of the official iconography. This is particularly true of the royal portraiture of the Ramesside period (19th–20th Dynasties), which we know owed a great deal to the burgeoning of the arts under Amenhotep III (in its turn, mediated through the complex modifications of iconography that took place during the Amarna period of Akhenaten).[4]

One might cite here the example of the remarkable black granite statue in the Egyptian Museum in Turin[5] which shows a young Rameses II wearing the blue crown or *khepresh*, the *wesekh* necklace and holding the scepter (*heka*) in his right hand—as was the custom during the Ramesside period (fig. 3).[6] This is undoubtedly a portrait of the young king produced in Thebes at his accession to the throne.

Wall decorations of the same period provide perfect parallels to this kind of representation of the king: for example, the scene of the coronation carved on the west wall of the Great Hypostyle Hall at Karnak, which shows Sety I, accompanied by Amun-Ra, Hathor and Thoth, wearing the *khepresh* while holding the *heka* and *nekhakha* scepters in his right hand.[7]

But alongside the masterpieces of royal statuary—whose exact provenance and attribution are often problematic[8]—and the multiple wall decorations in which the predominant weight of artistic conventions is undeniable, there are the decorated ostraca unearthed at the workmen's village of Deir el-Medina.[9] These contain some Ramesside "portraits"

1. Figurative ostracon 2569 from Deir el-Medina, New Kingdom, Ramesside period.
Paris, Musée du Louvre

2. Drawing of the granite statue
of Rameses II from Karnak,
New Kingdom, 19th Dynasty.
Turin, Museo Egizio

3. Granite statue of Rameses II,
from Karnak, New Kingdom,
19th Dynasty.
Turin, Museo Egizio

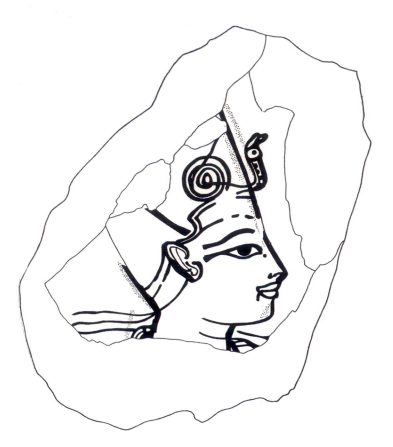

4. Figurative ostracon from
Deir el-Medina

5. Figurative ostracon 2568
from Deir el-Medina

which it is legitimate to suppose might represent the artists' attempts to familiarize themselves with the new codes to be applied in rendering the physiognomy of the monarch. One such piece shows a youthful-looking king wearing the *khepresh* (fig. 4).[10] First outlined in red, the drawing is then picked out in black; and various iconographical features—for example, the vertical line emphasizing the corner of the mouth; the double line indicating the creases in the neck; the pierced earlobe—reveal that this is a post-Amarna portrait. It could be Sety I (1290–1278 BC), his son and successor Rameses II (1279–1212), or even—bearing in mind that the profile does not seem to fit with that of these monarchs—a Ramesside portrait of an ancient king: perhaps Amenhotep I (1525–1504 BC), the patron of the workmen in the village.[11]

The Pharaoh in Mourning

Some of the ostraca portraits can be identified as relating to the specific period between accession and coronation because they show the monarch unshaven—not some royal slovenliness that the artists wished to record or criticize, but rather one of the outward signs of mourning (as Chr. Desroches-Noblecourt has so convincingly demonstrated).[12] The pharaoh was in mourning for his predecessor, whose seventy-day pre-burial period had yet to come to an end.

An ostracon now in Baltimore[13] is particularly interesting in that it seems, in the Egyptian manner, to lay down the canonical proportions to be respected in an official portrait (in this case, very probably that of Sety I) (fig. 6). Crowned with the *khepresh* bearing a frontal *uraeus* and adorned with the *wesekh* necklace, the pharaoh is shown unshaven and with a pierced earlobe. However, the royal face is also framed by a closed fist and a flat extended hand: the former to indicate the precise distance behind the back of the neck and the point of the chin; the latter that between the forehead and the shoulder.

One of the most beautiful depictions of the pharaoh in mourning is the limestone ostracon discovered in the house of the scribe Parahotep at Deir el-Medina, in which the enthroned figure is very probably the young Rameses II (fig. 5).[14] Again wearing the *khep-*

6. Figurative ostracon from Deir
el-Medina.
Baltimore, The Walters Art Gallery

resh with the frontal *uraeus*—the back of which is decorated with a symbol of the god Horus: a falcon with outstretched wings[15]—the pharaoh is shown turning to the left; his earlobe is pierced and his unshaven beard and moustache are picked out in dots. A unique detail here are the seven tears running from his eye, in demonstration of his mourning. While it shares certain characteristics (*khepresh*, pierced lobe, unshaven chin) with the above, the portrait on ostracon DeM 2569 reveals a very different profile (fig. 1).[16] The shape of the nose and the thickness of neck and chin (indicated by creases) lead one to suppose it might be a portrait of Amenhotep III (1387–1350), perhaps produced during the reign of Sety I or Rameses II, when references to this older king were common.

The Khepresh: the Crown of Accession?
Be they in the round or two-dimensional, all these portraits show the pharaoh with the *khepresh*[17]—a feature also systematically associated with the unshaven state of the figures depicted on the ostraca. All of which leads one to suggest that during the Ramesside dynasties—and perhaps already during the 18th Dynasty[18]—this was part of the iconography of a monarch who has ascended to the throne and is about to undertake the official ceremonies of coronation.

A text dating from the reign of Horemheb—which, in many ways, could be said to mark the beginning of the Ramesside period—bears out this interpretation. This is the famous "Coronation Inscription" on the back of the statues of Horemheb and Mutnedjmet now in the Egyptian Museum of Turin.[19] From Horus' sanctuary at Hutnesut, capital of Alabastronpolis or Kom el-Ahmar—the eighteenth *nome* of Upper Egypt[20]—the royal cortege passed to Thebes and thence to the temple at Luxor, and the text has the gods declare: "Behold, Amun has come unto the Palace, with his son [Horemheb] before him, to set his crowns on his head." (l. 17) The sign used to indicate the plural word "crowns" is precisely that of the *khepresh*, the only crown mentioned during this accession to the throne.[21]

Literary Works
The accession and the coronation were also the occasion for the composition and recital of special hymns. The Ramesside period is particularly full of royal eulogies of this type. Among the many royal hymns which start with the phrase "The perfect god" (*netjer nefer*)—the model for which can be traced back at least as far as the reign of Senusret I[22]—there is a particularly interesting example on a hieroglyphic ostracon dedicated to Rameses IV (1153–1147) and now in the Cairo Museum:[23] "The perfect god, image of Amun, creation of Ra himself, divine king who has produced the benefits of the Place of Truth, divine sovereign of Tatenen, king of Tamery [Egypt]. He of the gracious hands which bear the thurible to raise incense to his father. He who has brought about *maat* in all the lands, enlightening the entire country with his perfection. The king of Upper and Lower Egypt, Lord of the Double Land, Heqama'at-Setepenra, son of Ra, lord of the crowns, Rameses Maatymeryamun."

That phrase about "the gracious hands which bear the thurible to raise incense to his father" could well refer to the funeral ceremonies performed by Rameses IV in honor of his dead father Rameses III, and thus would make this the text of a coronation hymn.

A litany composed for Rameses VI (1143–1135) can also be set in relation to a specific event. After the accession of the new pharaoh, the royal fleet sails down from the north to put in at Karnak, where part of the coronation ceremonies are to be performed.[24] Four stanzas, each beginning "Praise be to you . . ." have survived:

"Praise be to you, who have come unto Amun, your fleet laden with acclamations! It is Ra who has given you the means to commission your ships; it is Iusaas who has brought you here! Your pilot is Aten, and your lookout is [the goddess of] heaven.

"Praise be to you, who has landed at Karnak and whose gods receive you! Whose monuments cry out and acclaim. The noise of your moorage bollard is pleasant! How pleasant is the noise of the maul of the valiant, of the master of force!

"Praise be to you, the riverbank of Thebes . . . ! The islands . . . for the plantation of Karnak; they are as numerous as the stars in the heavenly vault that lead the country to you!

"Praise be to you, who have come unto your father [Amun-Ra] with numerous victories before you, who is granted as many years as there are grains of sand, as many jubilees as there are constellations! The four monuments are fixed, one at each corner in all the districts of Egypt; all the countries are led toward you with tributes, and this House is happy!"

Also inherited from the Middle Kingdom,[25] and borrowed from hymns to the deities themselves, was a sub-genre of royal eulogy which began with the formula "Health to you . . ." A piece written on papyrus and dedicated to Rameses VII (1135–1127) is, in effect, a veritable coronation litany built up through a play on the sound of words:[26] "Health to you, who has appeared in the white crown (*hedjet*), so that everything pales (*hedj*) when you move across the heavenly vault! Health to you, who has appeared with the Two Mighty Ones [*sekhemty* = the *pschent*] [to exercise your power (*sekhem*) on . . .]! Health to you who has appeared with the *nemes*, so that the whole country advances (*nemes*) toward you . . . !"

The anniversary of the monarch's accession continued to be celebrated during his reign, as one can see from this fine hymn on an ostracon[27] that the scribe Amennakhte, son of Ipuy, composed in honor of Rameses IV in the fourth year of his reign:

"Happy Day, heaven and earth are filled with joy that you are the Great Master of Egypt! Those who had fled have returned to their city; those who had hidden have come out. Those who were hungry, have recovered and are content; those who were thirsty are drunk. Those who were naked, are dressed in fine cloth; those who were in rags are in white garments. Those who were in prison, are free; those who were detained are in joy. Those who had made trouble in the country have become calm. Great Niles have emerged from their cavern to flood the heart of men. The houses of widows are open; they receive travelers. Wet nurses rejoice in singing their lullabies, while they give the breast to male children born full-term. They will raise new generations who will say: 'O Prince (Life, Prosperity, Health), you are eternal!' The boats exult on a calm flood and draw close to land using wind and rudder. They have recovered from the storms since it was announced: 'The King of Upper and Lower Egypt, Heqamaatra Setepenra (Life, Prosperity and Health)!' In his turn he will wear the white crown, the son of Ra Rameses, and he will take up the royalty of his father. All the lands will say of him: 'Gracious is Horus on the throne of his father!' It is Amun-Ra, the protector of the prince (Life, Prosperity and Health) who has ordered it, who has brought all the countries."

Humorous Portraits?

Like the figurative depictions, the literary portraits are based on principles which have more to do with the dialectic interplay of conformity and innovation than respect for actual historical truth. Indeed, the enormous distance between the physical and psychological reality of the royal personage and the idealized description of him in words or images raises questions that relate more to sociology than aesthetics. There was a certain tension between respect for ancestral canons and the social or individual capacity for invention; a tension between slavish respect for the canons promulgated by the center of monarchical power and the desire to preserve provincial artistic traditions (perhaps more conservative than that central power itself). Indeed, there might even be tension between a lethargic ideological orthodoxy and a humorous or satirical intention that reveals the portraitists' ability to view their subject with detachment. There are various examples that seem to bear out this latter point; the ancient Egyptians revealed themselves to be skilled in the use of humor and irony.[28]

To illustrate this with regard to the presentation of Ramesside monarchs, I shall cite two portraits—one figurative, the other literary.

Among the ostraca showing the unshaven pharaoh in mourning, the limestone piece DeM 2072 occupies a special place.[29] Wearing the *khepresh* and the *wesekh* necklace, the king is shown facing to the right; the general appearance is like that in the already-mentioned works, except that here the line is more coarsely worked. Rather than viewing this as the artist's lack of skill or experience—an explanation that Egyptologists should always use sparingly—it seems to me that the best explanation is that this is a caricature of what was by then a conventional theme. Without making definite claims with regard to the corrosive humor intended here, one should note that there are other examples of satirical work among the Deir el-Medina ostraca dating from the 20th Dynasty: for example, a queen threatened by an animal that resembles a bear;[30] the king of Upper and Lower Egypt (identified as such by the inscription) depicted as a lion whose back paw is being bitten by a lioness (?);[31] or again, an astonishing battle between a pharaoh and an Egyptian queen, both perched in war chariots under a hail of arrows.[32]

The second example is a hymn of royal praise[33] written by the scribe Amennakhte, son of Ipuy, a work initially interpreted as a love song:

"The love of you, is the love of a bird; your face is the face of a child. Your perfume, your perfume is like that of mandragora; your life is consecrated to watching over life. O a gift for your . . . daily; your eyes sparkle [in seeing it]. Your arms reach down when your mouth adores in honor of the rising Ra. Your destiny is written on the . . . of god, inscribed by the lord of Hermopolis."

Quite apart from the literary play on one genre (love poetry) when writing in another,[34] one is quite justified in wondering what the actual intention of the writer was: a naive expression of courtly fawning or a knowing joke with his educated reader? From other works we know that Amennakhte was a skilled satirist,[35] and hence are led to believe that the metaphors here are tongue-in-cheek.

[1] See Grimal 1986, pp. 211–228.

[2] See M. Bonhême, Forgeau 1988, pp.247–248. The Egyptian language does not seem to have distinguished between accession and coronation, using the term (s)hʿw for both. See Grimal 1986, pp. 220–224; Cannuyer 1993, p. 19, who refers to Schunck's study (1985).

[3] I, 44, 4; translation Bertrac, Vernière 1993, p. 97.

[4] See Vandersleyen 1988 and the monographic studies by Kozloff, Brian 1992 and Cabrol 2000. See also Sourouzian 1993, p. 249, n. 45.

[5] Inv. 1380. See Vandier 1958, pp. 393–421, p. 407 and 415 and pl.CXXVI, 1, 3; KRI II, pp. 590–591; Kitchen 1996, pp. 387–388; Gratias 1999; Ziegler, Bovot 1999, pp. 228–229.

[6] In the 18th Dynasty the scepter was usually held in the left hand.

[7] Nelson 1981, pl. 150; Sourouzian 1993, p. 243, fig. 2.

[8] See for example Sourouzian 1988; Sourouzian 1993.

[9] Vandier d'Abbadie 1946, pp. 97–101.

[10] Bonnet, Valbelle 1976, pp. 335–336, fig. 8 (facsimile B. Privati) and pl. LIX.

[11] Adding the fundamental study by Cerny 1927; Altenmüller 1981; Kruchten 1990.

[12] Desroches-Noblecourt 1947, pp. 185–232. Along with the three examples examined here, one might also mention the Berlin ostracon 23674 (Desroches-Noblecourt 1947, pp. 190–191 and fig. 5) and the ostracon DeM 2579 (Desroches-Noblecourt 1947, p. 191 and fig. 6).

[13] Ostracon Baltimore 32.1 (Walters Art Gallery); Peck 1980, p. 104, fig. 31.

[14] Ostracon DeM 2568 (inv. 3658); Vandier d'Abbadie 1937, pp. 99, 116–117, pl. LXXII and LXXVI; Desroches-Noblecourt 1947, pp. 191–192, 220, and fig. 7.

[15] See Kriéger 1960, p. 55, n. 1. This iconography recalls the subject of the Horus-king, protector and legitimate successor of his father.

[16] Ostracon DeM 2569 (inv. 3037) = Louvre E 14318; Bruyère 1929, p. 28, fig. 71 (1); Vandier d'Abbadie 1937, p. 100, 117 and pl. LXXIII; Desroches-Noblecourt 1947, p. 195 and fig.10.

[17] For a general view, see Abu Bakr 1937; Mysliwiec 1976; Strauss 1980; Ertman 1993.

[18] The young Amenhotep II shown sitting on the knee of his wet nurse in the Theban tomb of Ken-Amun is wearing the *khepresh* and the *wesekh* necklace, and holding the *heka* scepter: Davies 1930, pl. 9.

[19] Inv. 1379. See Gardiner 1953 and pl. I–II; Vandier 1958, pp. 371, 373; Hari 1965, pp. 208–214 and pl. 60; Scamuzzi 1966, pl. XXXII; Bell 1985; Donadoni 1993, pp. 365–366; Murnane 1995A, no. 106, pp. 230–233.

[20] See Topozada 1991, p. 254, n. 34; Huber 1998 (with previous bibliography).

[21] Topozada, op. cit., p. 250, n. 6, simply observes that Horemheb is wearing the *khepresh* "in several scenes of royal offerings."

[22] Stele Cairo inv. no. JE 71901.

[23] Ostracon CGC 25202, p. 39 and pl. XXXIII.

[24] Turin papyrus 1886, verso (= Turin CG 54031); Ostracon DeM 1655, recto: Pleyte, Rossi 1869, pl. 20, col. I–II; Condon 1978, pp. 14–15 and pl. V; Posener 1977–1980, p. 94 and pl. 74.

[25] See the hymns from the Kahun papyrus dedicated to Senusret III.

[26] Turin papyrus 1892 (= CGT 54031), verso: Pleyte, Rossi 1869, pl. 86; Condon 1978, p. 16 and pl. VI.

[27] Ostracon CGT 57001, recto. See Bickel, Mathieu 1993, pp. 41–43.

[28] See in particular Ollivier-Beauregard 1894; Curto 1965; Van de Walle 1969; Omlin 1973; Van de Walle 1980; Houlihan 2001.

[29] Vandier d'Abbadie 1959, p. 213 and pl. CXLII.
[30] Ostracon Medelhaavsmuseet Stockholm inv. no. 14069; Houlihan, 2001, p. 118, fig. 130.
[31] Ostracon Cairo 25084; Houlihan 2001, p. 119, fig. 131.
[32] Ostracon Cairo 25125; Houlihan 2001, p. 120, fig. 132.
[33] Ostracon Hermitage 1125, recto. Text and translation in M. Matthiew, PSEL V, pp. 25–27; Bogoslovsky 1973, pp. 82–86; B. Van de Walle, *BiOr* 9, 1952, p. 108; Fox 1985, pp.347–348; Bickel, Mathieu 1993, pp. 44–45.
[34] The use of parody in erotic literature is illustrated by the *Adventures of Horus and Seth* (P. Chester Beatty I, recto = P. BM 10060) and the Ramesside tale in the Chassinat Papyrus III (= P. Louvre E 25353). See Barbotin 1999.
[35] See the satirical piece on the ostracon Gardiner 25, verso: Bickel, Mathieu 1993, pp. 40–41.

The Royal Family

The Queens of the New Kingdom

The extant texts dating from the New Kingdom paint a delightful picture of the queens of Egypt: "Enchanting under the two plumes of her headdress, she whose voice enraptures those who hear it, full of grace, pleasant of spirit, gentle in love, filling the palace with her wafting perfume . . . Queen of the Double Land, the beautiful one whose hands hold the two *sistra*. . . . The beloved who wears the crown. . . . Everything she requires is done for her, every fair thing arrives as her heart commands. . . ."

However, apart from Hatshepsut, who exercised absolute power and whom historians rank within the long succession of pharaohs, the queens of this glorious epoch were simply the mothers or wives of monarchs; we know nothing about the personality of most of them. All we have is a delightful image, in bas-relief or statuary—such as the famous "White Queen" which is a central attraction of this exhibition and which a recent study has identified as Meritamun, one of the numerous wives of the great Rameses, her own father. Nevertheless, there are a few queens of Egypt whose exceptional destiny is known to us in some slight detail.

Certain Grand Ladies

"Praise the Lady of the country, the queen of the banks of Hau-Nebut,
whose name is raised above all foreign countries,
who takes decisions regarding the people. Wife of a king, sister of a sovereign.
Life, health, strength!
Daughter of a king, venerable mother of a king,
Who knows the affairs of the country, who unites Egypt;
she has gathered together her notables, whose unity she guarantees;
she has brought home the fugitives; she has regrouped the dissidents;
She has pacified Upper Egypt; she has repulsed rebels;
Wife of the king, Ahhotep, long life!"

This is how Ahmose, founder of the 18th Dynasty, sings the praises of his mother, Ahhotep. Inscribed on a stele at the temple of Karnak, the text reveals the decisive role played by the queen when Ahmose was still young; undoubtedly, she held the regency during a troubled period in the country's history. Archaeological evidence confirms this written record: discovered in the XIX century, Ahhotep's tombs contained pendants in the form of golden flies—a badge of honor normally reserved only for the most valiant warriors. Ahmose's grandmother, Tetisheri, and his own wife, Ahmose Nefertari, made an even greater mark on Egyptian history. The latter, raised to the status of a deity after her death, was venerated throughout the New Kingdom alongside her son Amenhotep I; and in the ancient village of Deir el-Medina the craftsmen who worked in the Valley of the Kings looked upon her as their protector. The queen, in fact, seems to have taken an active role in the construction of numerous temples, and was the first to exercise the liturgical role of "god's wife of Amun." Exceptionally long-lived, she would survive both her husband and son.

Some hundred years later, the marriage of Amenhotep III and Queen Tiy did not pass unobserved. In his second regnal year, the young pharaoh issued a series of inscribed scarabs to commemorate their union. The royal couple had at least six children, including the future Amenhotep IV (Akhenaten), the artificer of the "Amarna Revolution." There can be no doubt that Queen Tiy was no ordinary woman; her slightly disdainful pout and determined expression render some of her extant statues all the more appealing. An educated queen—we have an *ex-libris* from the papyri in her library—she maintained a correspondence with the most important sovereigns of the day. A temple was dedicated to her in Sedeinga in Nubia—the pendant to that dedicated to Amenhotep III in Soleb. Surviving her husband, Queen Tiy would then live in the city of el-Amarna, where bas-reliefs show her sharing in the court life of Akhenaten and Nefertiti.

The latter is perhaps the most popular and best known of all Egyptian queens. Nefertiti was the most beautiful of all, and one can understand why her image is still used by advertisers; it is its very modernity that makes it so striking. A bust in Berlin shows her at the height of her youth adorned with a most original crown; long-necked and fine-featured, she seems to be staring toward some inaccessible dream. The statue was found in a sculptor's workshop on the site of el-Amarna, where one of the most beautiful utopias in history was created. Six

1. Wall-painting depicting Queen Nefertari, New Kingdom, 19th Dynasty.
Luxor, Valley of the Queens, tomb of Nefertari

237

2. Bracelet from the tomb of Ahhotep at Dra Abu el-Naga, gold, feldspar, cornelian and lapis lazuli, Second Intermediate Period, 18th Dynasty.
Cairo, Egyptian Museum
cat. 178

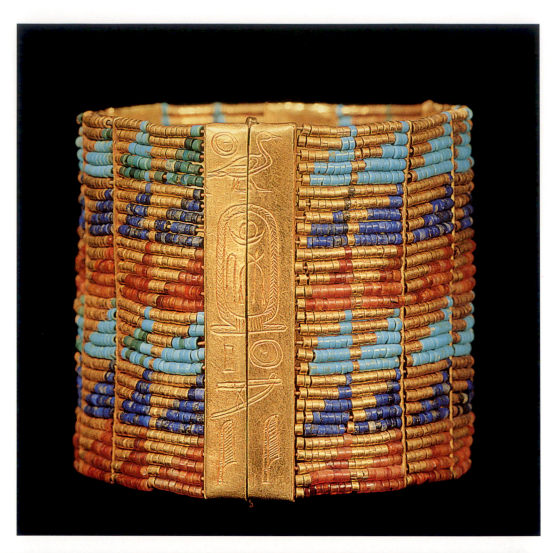

3–4. Gold and semi-precious stone necklace and gold necklace with fly-shaped pendants, from the tomb of Ahhotep at Dra Abu el-Naga, Second Intermediate Period, 18th Dynasty.
Cairo, Egyptian Museum
cat. 177

5. Fragment of furnishing with
Ahmose Nefertari and Amenhotep I
from Deir el-Medina, fretworked
and painted wood, New Kingdom,
18th Dynasty.
Turin, Museo Egizio
cat. 61

years after ascending to the throne, Amenhotep IV, Nefertiti's husband, left his capital of Thebes
to settle in a new city built on the site of Amarna in Middle Egypt. There he raised sanctuaries dedicated to a single god, Aten, the sun. This was a universal god, the source of all living beings, who accorded mankind both light and air. In the tombs of the city, the inscribed
hymns still render poetic homage to Aten for the awakening of nature and the beauty of the
world. The image of the royal couple was to be found everywhere; they were the incarnation
of the mother and father of humankind. Nefertiti was always shown alongside her husband
participating in the worship of the sun, whose extended rays end in human hands offering the
symbol of life. This was the trinity worshipped in the houses of Amarna. And on the walls of
temples and tombs the royal couple were depicted with their young daughters.

The last great female figure of the New Kingdom, Nefertari, is mainly known for her splendid tomb and for the two temples that her husband, Rameses II, had hollowed out of the cliffs
of Abu Simbel, where—just like today—the rays of the sun fell on the monumental effigies
sculpted on the façades to then penetrate right into the heart of the mountain. At the entrance,
where Rameses sits among the gods, Nefertari is shown occupying the place due her as royal wife and mother of the heir to the throne. On the façade of the small temple dedicated to
her, colossal statues of the queen are flanked by those of her children; inside, her image is omnipresent. Fine-featured and slim, she is identified with the goddesses Soped and Hathor and
invokes the annual renewal of the Nile floods. Texts describe Nefertari as "the beloved of the
king, gentle in love, splendid of face." She seems to have died shortly after the consecration
of these sanctuaries, and was buried in the most beautiful tomb in the Valley of the Queens;
recently restored, the dazzling colors and richness of its mural decoration have become all the
more striking.

The Pharaoh and His Family

6. Limestone stele of Amenhotep I
and Ahmose Nefertari, from
west Thebes, New Kingdom,
18th Dynasty.
Cairo, Egyptian Museum
cat. 174

The son of the gods, the pharaoh was also human, and the royal family played an extremely
important role in his life. The Egyptian monarchy was a court society, comparable perhaps
to that of the emperors of China or the sultans of Istanbul. Life unfolded according to an eti-
quette and protocol which maintained a theatrical aura around royalty, and the essential ad-

7. Gold fastener for hair (?)
of princess Ahmose,
New Kingdom, 18th Dynasty.
Turin, Museo Egizio
cat. 180

8. Enameled steatite scarab
of Amenhotep III, New Kingdom,
18th Dynasty.
Paris, Musée du Louvre
cat. 195

9. Limestone bas-relief with
the daughters of Amenhotep III,
from Thebes, New Kingdom,
18th Dynasty.
Berlin, Ägyptisches Museum
und Papyrussammlung
cat. 196

opposite page
10. Granite statue of Senenmut,
from Luxor, New Kingdom.
Chicago, The Field Museum of
Natural History, gift of Stanley Field
and Ernest Graham
cat. 171

11. Faience unguent jar,
New Kingdom, 18th Dynasty.
Paris, Musée du Louvre
cat. 199

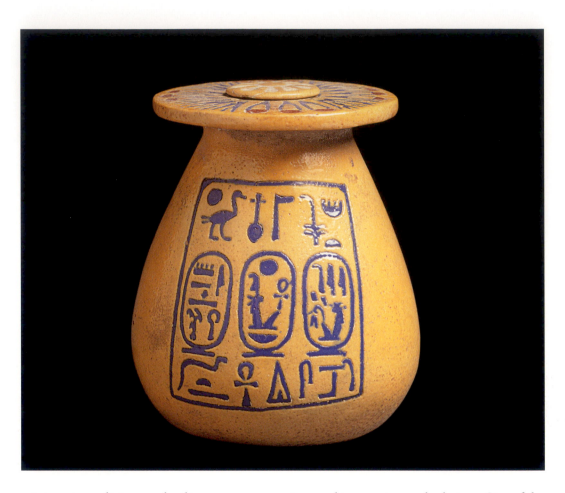

ministrative, religious and military powers were invested in courtiers and relatives. One of the words used to designate the king of Egypt was *nesut*, a term which referred to family ties and thus underlined the social character of a royal family network that served to reinforce social cohesion.

From the time of the pyramids, the family was organized around the figure of the reigning monarch. The terms of close family ties—"mother of the king," "wife of the king," "children of the king"—all referred to the present occupant of the throne without mentioning him by name. The sovereign was a unique figure; everything started all over again at his accession. When the pharaoh referred to his "father," he was referring neither to his predecessor nor to his biological parent, but to a god—more often than not, Amun of Thebes. Certain "sisters of the king" are known to us—for example, Tiaa, sister of Rameses II—but before the reign of Rameses III no dignitary was accorded the title "brother of the king" (even if there is clear proof that there were a number of princes in each generation). Perhaps the term was held to be dangerous, raising the specter of possible rivalry with the present occupant of the throne. Before the reign of Amenhotep III depictions of the full royal family are few and far between, with the royal children very rarely being shown in the company of their parents. However, the queens themselves always occupied a special position in royal iconography—a fact borne out by such remarkable works as the splendid statue of Menkaura in the company of his wife, the Middle-Kingdom royal groups showing Senusret III with his wife and mother, or the couple of Thutmose IV and his mother Tiaa. The royal princesses would seem to make their first appearance in royal iconography in that colossal group depicting Amenhotep III and his great wife Tiy. This family theme would then become a leitmotif of the Amarna period, with endless bas-reliefs of the royal couple and their daughters. Later, the walls of the Ramesside temples would be decorated with long carved processions of royal princes and princesses; and at the entrance to the temples of Abu Simbel stand the colossal statues of Rameses II with his queens and royal children, commemorating the memory of an all-powerful sovereign who was also the head of an immense family. These images are an expression of both fecundity and

12. Bracelet plaque of Queen Tiy as a winged sphinx holding Amenhotep III's cartouche, New Kingdom, 18th Dynasty. New York, The Metropolitan Museum of Art, gift of Edward S. Harkness

wealth; underlining the religious function of the royal family as a whole, they extended the role the queens of Egypt had played since the days of the very first dynasties.

The Women of the Royal Family

In the same way as the pharaoh, the monarch's mother and his "great royal wife" were distinguished from the rest of humanity by means of symbols borrowed from the deities themselves; their status was indicated by the *neret* crown, the *uraeus*, the double-plumed headdress, the sign of the *ankh*. However, did these attributes simply underline that the women of the royal family enjoyed a special intimacy with the sovereign, who was a son of the gods, or did they indicate that they themselves enjoyed a divine status in their own right? Recent studies would seem to have cast some light on this question. Texts and visual depictions dating from the reigns of various sovereigns—Amenhotep III, Akhenaten, Rameses II—reveal that the royal couple were seen as the terrestrial counterpart of the couple formed by the solar divinities Ra and Hathor–Maat. Far from being a mere anecdotal presence, the queen shown alongside her husband in the exercise of religious ritual or state power was an image of theological significance; the royal bride and pharaoh together were the guarantee of the equilibrium of the world. The female aspects of royalty emerge from the numerous official titles used in referring to the queens of the New Kingdom. The mythical origin of the figure of the queen can be seen in her qualification as "daughter of the gods," "companion of the god Horus" or "mistress of heaven"; the importance of her sexual role was recognized in such epithets as "gentle in love," "she who fills the palace with her beauty," and "she who delights the heart of the king"; her religious roles as priestess, celebrant and musician were also mentioned; her family tie with the pharaoh made her "mother of the king," "spouse of the king," "sister of the king" or "daughter of the king"; and finally her actual share in the exercise of royal power is recognized in such titles as "mistress of the Double Land," "sovereign lady of Upper and Lower Egypt."

One of the most significant emblems of the queen's status was the *neret* headdress, in which

13. Head of Nefertiti from el-Amarna, New Kingdom, 18th Dynasty.
Berlin, Ägyptisches Museum und Papyrussammlung

14. Faience bead showing Akhenaten and Nefertiti, New Kingdom, 18th Dynasty.
Copenhagen, Ny Carlsberg Glyptotek
cat. 205

15. Limestone stele with Akhenaten and Nefertiti holding their daughters on their laps, New Kingdom, 18th Dynasty.
Berlin, Ägyptisches Museum und Papyrussammlung
cat. 202

following pages
16. Façade of the small temple at Abu Simbel

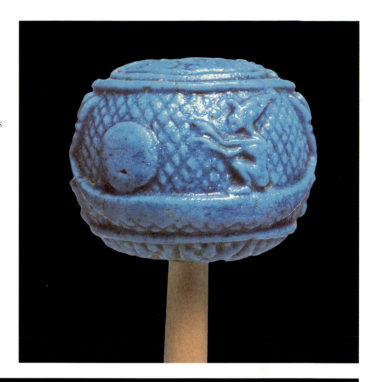

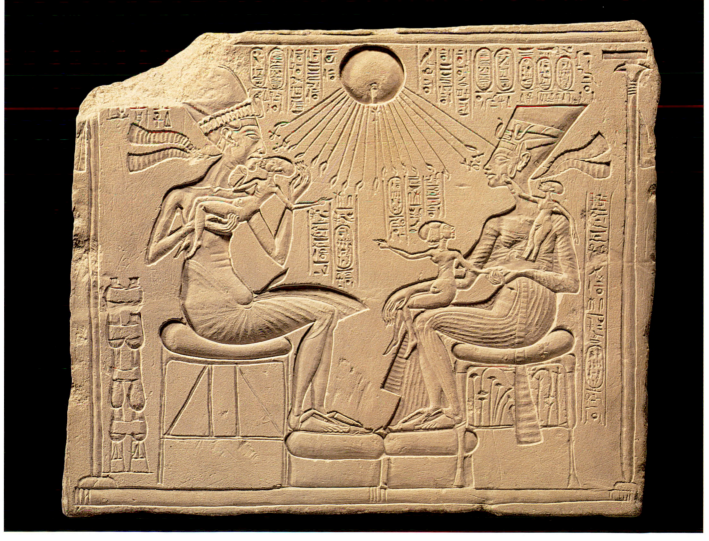

17. Brown quartzite head of an Amarna princess, New Kingdom, 18th Dynasty.
Cairo, Egyptian Museum
cat. 204

18. Double statue of a queen and prince from the cachette court at Karnak, schist, New Kingdom, 19th Dynasty.
Cairo, Egyptian Museum
cat. 213

the head of a vulture surmounted the forehead while its two wings enclosed either side of the face. Originally worn by Nekhbet, a goddess of Upper Egypt, this crown would over the centuries become the attribute of numerous female deities. First adopted by Egyptian queens in the 4th Dynasty, it would thereafter be worn throughout the period of pharaonic power. Sometimes the head of the bird of prey was replaced by that of a cobra (*uraeus*), the serpent being a symbol of the pharaoh's power and its use in headdress being restricted to sovereigns alone. The New Kingdom would see the emergence of different varieties of *uraei*: the "hathoric" *uraeus*, surmounted by a solar disk between two horns, and the double *uraeus*, in which the cobra appeared together with the head of the vulture. The queens could also avail themselves of other headdresses, for example, a double-plumed crown—associated with the two masculine deities, Min and Amun—or the two horns of Hathor and Isis–Sopdet bearing a solar disk. This complex iconography emphasized the solar nature of royalty and its identification with the goddess Hathor. As for the *ankh*, the sign of life, this was the preserve of kings and gods; it served to identify the women holding it as somehow beyond the realm of mere humanity. Just like their royal husbands, queens might also be depicted as less amiable characters—for example, Tiy is represented as a sphinx crushing her enemies underfoot.

The Ritual Role of Queens
Depictions of worship dating from the New Kingdom often show the queen officiating alongside the pharaoh. Using their charms to appease the gods, they might perform on such musical instruments as the *sistrum* (sacred chimes whose music soothed and delighted the gods) or the *menat* (whose rows of beads knocked together to make a sound pleasing to divine ears). Dedicated to the gods, these objects became a pledge of renewal, strengthening the seductive powers of their owners, who were described in texts as "mistress of the *sistrum*," "lady of the *menat*," "she whose pure hands hold the *sistrum* to charm her father Amun with the sound of its voice. . . ."
The *heb-sed*, or royal jubilee, was one of the major religious events. Certain rare extant de-

19. Limestone fragment of a stele with Akhenaten and Nefertiti, New Kingdom, 18th Dynasty. Berlin, Ägyptisches Museum und Papyrussammlung
cat. 201

pictions of this festivity—bas-reliefs from Thebes and Soleb (dating from the reign of Amenhotep III) and from Bubastis (from the reign of Osorkon II)—reveal that the royal spouse occupied an important role in the celebrations. Tiy, for example, appears behind her husband Amenhotep III "as the goddess Maat alongside the god Ra," the texts tell us. This parallel between the royal couple and the divine couple who presided over the creation of the world would be strengthened some years later during the Amarna period, when the beautiful Nefertiti was always shown alongside Akhenaten—be it in religious scenes (where, accompanied by their daughters, the royal couple seem to be co-celebrants), official scenes (where husband and wife together receive the homage of foreign lands) or domestic scenes (where the royal couple are shown tenderly embracing or exchanging kisses). This ostentation of the love uniting the couple here takes on universal meaning: it is the manifestation of the creative power of the demiurge, a guarantee of terrestrial renewal.

Two of the best-known temples dating from the New Kingdom—Deir el-Bahri and Luxor—contain a series of bas-reliefs in which the queen is a figure of key importance; blocks from the Ramesseum also indicate the existence of a similar cycle celebrating the birth of Rameses II. Indeed, all these works illustrate the union of the "great royal wife" with the god Amun, which results in the "divine" birth of the pharaoh. Clearly, not all these "theogamic" scenes have the same importance. It would seem that the scene of the "divine birth" at Deir el-Bahri served to give a certain legitimacy to Hatshepsut's power, while that relating to Amenhotep III (in Luxor) does not reflect any specific historical circumstances. Nevertheless, the scenes and the actors therein remain unchanged. Text and image describe the same sequence of events: the arrival at the royal palace of the god Amun, who appears to the queen in the form of the reigning pharaoh; the perfume of the god awakening the sleeping queen and revealing his divine nature; the love which seizes the queen's heart; their union; her pregnancy and the birth of the heir, who is then solemnly recognized by his father Amun. In this final form, the ritual of the royal birth involves the Theban god Amun and thus reflects this particular region of the country; however, its origins stretch far back into the earliest days of Egyptian history. A story set at the time of the pyramids has preserved the miraculous tale of the three first kings of the 5th Dynasty. Here it is the god Ra who uses a subterfuge to lie with the young wife of one of his priests. At the end of a difficult delivery, she gives birth to three sons, whom miraculous events identify as future sovereigns. Thus, in the New Kingdom, it was the queen of Egypt herself who served as the intermediary guaranteeing the double—human and divine—nature of the royal child and pharaoh.

The role of divine wife, theoretically held by the sovereign's mother, might also be taken by other female members of the royal family. During the 18th Dynasty, the title "god's wife" passed on from one royal wife to the next. Often accompanied by epithets such as "divine adorer of Amun" and "god's hand"—in reference to an Egyptian creation myth—this title designated a liturgical role. Ahmose Nefertari, wife of Ahmose and mother of Amenhotep I, was the first to take this priestess role as the terrestrial wife of Amun. Through music, song, dance and offerings, through rites of purification and devotion, she was supposed to "delight the heart of the god," helping to maintain universal order by driving off the forces of evil. Over time, the domain reserved to the "god's wife" increased, and ultimately this important figure had a whole college of priestesses to assist her in the celebration of ceremonies. The title was still borne by some of the queens at the time of the Ramesside pharaohs at the end of the New Kingdom. Chosen from among the king's daughters, the divine adorer would be married to the god Amun alone and thus dedicated to a life of chastity; she would choose her own "daughter" from among the princesses of the reigning house.

The Marriage of the Pharaoh

Dating from the reign of Rameses II, the so-called "Marriage stele" shows the arrival of a foreign princess, daughter of the king of the Hittites, at the royal palace. Received by the pharaoh, she becomes his "great royal wife." This work is interesting in a number of ways: it shows that the pharaoh contracted diplomatic alliances through marriages into foreign families; it brings out the polygamy that was widely practiced by the pharaohs of the New Kingdom; it highlights a hierarchical order that culminated in the "great royal wife," the female counterpart to the pharaoh and mother of the heir to the throne (though apparently unique,

20. Terra-cotta plaque with two female fanbearers, from Gurob, New Kingdom, 18th Dynasty. Edinburgh, The Trustees of the National Museums of Scotland
cat. 226

21. Graywacke statue of a queen, Ramesside period.
Berlin, Ägyptisches Museum und Papyrussammlung

22. Soapstone statuette of Tiy, New Kingdom, 18th Dynasty. Paris, Musée du Louvre
cat. 193

we know that this title was actually held by a number of women at the same time). Beneath these "royal wives" were various secondary wives, who in turn ranked above the innumerable concubines; as is to be expected, Egyptian documents tend to concentrate on the first two categories of this hierarchy.

Before going any further, one thing must be underlined: pharaonic power was never transmitted along the female line. This hypothesis was put forward on the basis of an analysis of the succession of queens of the 18th Dynasty, certain of whom bore the title "daughters of the king" and were chosen from within the royal family. However, this can be explained by the fact that certain pharaohs married their sisters or half-sisters, who then bore them children. The reason for these marriages was religious: Being divine, the pharaoh was permitted unions which, it seems, were forbidden to his subjects. These unions reenacted the creation of the world, when the first brother-sister couple created by the demiurge—the deities Osiris and his sister Isis—gave birth to Horus, the heir to the throne. There are also other mythical references that cast light on these marriages, examples of which are Amenhotep III and Satamon, and—probably—Akhenaten and two of his daughters, Rameses II and three of his. However, we also know of "great royal wives" who were not of royal blood. For example, Thutmose III married two commoners, one of which seems to have been the daughter of his wet

nurse. Even Tiy, the wife of Amenhotep III, and Tuy, the wife of Sety I, were simply the daughters of high-ranking soldiers.

Sovereigns married very young, and one can well image the court intrigues involved in arranging their marriages: For both powerful families and for relatives of the prince, such unions with the royal family were the best ways of promoting the interests of an entire clan.

Finally, there were a number of pharaohs who married foreign princesses. A rich treasure of silverware from the tomb of three of Thutmose III's secondary wives reveals that they bore names of Syrian origin. Documents from the New Kingdom, together with the *Annals of Thutmose III* and the diplomatic correspondence of Amarna, show that a large number of women from the East, daughters of the pharaoh's vassals, were sent to the court as pledges of their country's loyalty. "Send your daughter to the pharaoh, your master, and as a gift send twenty servants, carriages of silver and vigorous horses," orders a letter sent from Amarna. To win the pharaoh's good graces, some princelings would include women of humble birth among the tribute regularly paid to Egypt. "I have given twenty girls," writes Abdikheba of Jerusalem "as a gift to the pharaoh, my master."

Other alliances came at a higher price, for example, when the pharaoh treated with the kings of Babylon, of Mitanni and of Hatti as equals. However, a letter from Kadashman Enlil, king of Babylon, leaves us rather perplexed about the fate of these queens. "You want my daughter as a wife," he writes "while my sister, given to you by my father, is down there with you, even though up to now no one has seen her or knows if she is alive or has disappeared." Amenhotep III's reply is evasive; on the other hand, the fate of the first Hittite princess married to Rameses II was exceptional: she received an Egyptian name, Maathorneferura, and the title of "great wife." However, this was doubtless because her father had stipulated for this in the marriage contract.

The Queen's Residence: the Harim
Thus the pharaoh had a large female entourage. A scarab commemorating the marriage of Amenhotep III with Gilukhepa, daughter of his powerful neighbor the king of Mitanni, reveals that the princess was accompanied by "the very pick of her *harim*, 317 women." And we also know that Sety I granted his son Rameses numerous female companions before the latter's accession to the throne. What was the fate of this multitude of women? Undoubtedly the "great royal wives" lived in the capitals, alongside the pharaoh. On the west bank of Thebes one can still see the remains of the palace of Malkata where Amenhotep III and Tiy lived. The bas-reliefs from the tombs of el-Amarna show the royal couple of Amenhotep IV and Nefertiti distributing largesse in their Amarna palace or traveling through the city in a chariot accompanied by their daughters; there are also magnificent vivid paintings of royal feasts. And Rameses II's contemporaries praised the charms of Piramesse, the new city in which Nefertari and her royal husband stayed on numerous occasions. Queen mothers and "great wives" had their own rich domains and their own attendants; and it is likely that the royal favorites among the other wives had the same.

Most of the women of the household were grouped together in institutions habitually referred to as "*harims*." In its contemporary sense, the term is inaccurate, but I will use it for lack of a more precise translation. Based on the oldest extant examples, the *harim* (*ipet nesut*) constituted the private apartments of the king; it was not—as the modern word would lead one to believe—a place for the sequestration of concubines and eunuchs. Queens, princes and princesses lived there quite freely, in the company of ladies-in-waiting and "royal ornaments"—together with an entire army of servants, nurses, tutors, hairdressers and musicians (all of whom lived there with their own families). The texts of the New Kingdom reveal that there were numerous *harims* in the palaces of Upper and Lower Egypt. The transfers of the royal household and the administration of the *harim* were the responsibility of the "*harim* escort." The two most important institutions of this kind were at Memphis and at Mi-wer, on the site of the modern Medinet el-Gurob, at the entry to the verdant area of Fayum. The latter is the better known. A veritable city comprising temples, houses and a vast palace of unfired brick decorated with colonnades and enclosed within a wall, this was founded during the reign of Thutmose III and housed such important figures as Queen Tiy, then widow of Amenhotep III, and the Hittite princess Maathorneferura. The nearby cemetery contains var-

24. Pricesses Neferneferuaten Tasheri and Neferneferura, painting from the royal palace at el-Amarna, New Kingdom, 18th Dynasty. Oxford, Ashmolean Museum

ious rich tombs, including that of Prince Rameses-Nebuben, who died at the age of twenty; various precious objects, wooden statuettes and delicate objects of toiletry have been found here. We know that, richly endowed with lands and livestock, the palace had its own income and was managed by a swarm of male administrators, who are known to us through extant texts (particularly the papyri that have been found on the site itself). These administrators included such figures as "royal scribes of the *harim*," *harim* servants, the "director of the pharaoh's ladies," etc. The place was clearly the setting for a refined court life, with time being dedicated above all to the education of the royal princes and other scions of an international aristocracy, and to the perfection of accomplishments in foreign languages, music and dance. However, life for the servants, many of whom came from the neighboring districts, was very different.

Mi-wer was also a center of economic activity, and extant documents which record the supply details for the *harim* (managed by a figure known as the "governor of Mi-wer") reveal it to have been engaged in the spinning and weaving of precious linens and the creation of garments that were then sent to the capital Piramesse. It also seems to have produced work in wood, ivory, ceramics and brightly-colored glass.

From the times of the pyramids, the *harims* were also the breeding-ground for plots and conspiracies whose echo still survives. After all, what was at stake was the exercise of power.

Queens and Royal Children

Toward the end of the reign of Rameses III the court was shaken by a terrible scandal. A series of papyri has preserved the names of the culprits and the punishments inflicted upon them, without explicitly stating their criminal aim. In effect, the unpardonable had happened:

more than thirty people had conspired together to bring about a coup d'état which would have ousted the legitimate heir and replaced him with a prince whom the texts refer to under the pseudonym of "Pentaur." As far as we know, it would seem that the conspirators had not actually planned the assassination of the ruling pharaoh; it was his imminent death—his mummy shows clear signs that he was suffering from advanced arteriosclerosis—that led them to seize their chance to oppose the future Rameses IV.

The driving-force behind the conspiracy was a secondary wife named Tiy, Pentaur's mother. The plot was hatched in the *harim*, with the queen's followers rallying to the cause of their mistress, and the "director of the *harim* escort"—together with a number of his associates—either joining the conspirators or else turning a blind eye to their activities. Ultimately, the plot extended beyond the court to the highest levels of state government, with two ministers and various army officers becoming involved; one of the latter was the military governor of Nubia, whose sister was a lady-in-waiting to Queen Tiy. Various members of the pharaoh's own family, his cupbearers and "chief gentleman-in-waiting" then took part in inciting the population to rebellion; and sorcery too played its part, with priest magicians serving to circumvent the protection enveloping royalty and by creating small wax figures that would enable the conspirators to neutralize the royal guards. At this point, the conspiracy involved too many people for it to be kept a secret. Discovery led to defeat, and most of the conspirators were executed or committed suicide (including the six wives of the *harim* guards who had joined the plot); some did survive—minus nose and ears. However, we do not know what happened to Queen Tiy or to the ladies of the *harim*. The latter, in a last desperate attempt to win over their judges "played most subtly with them," as the Turin papyrus informs us; but after having succumbed to their charms, the judges themselves were condemned and mutilated—all except judge Hori, who was probably the one who reported his colleagues.

Although in each reign a number of different royal spouses gave birth to many possible heirs to the throne, the accession of the new pharaoh was not usually so dramatic. While extant documentation for the 18th Dynasty is too fragmentary to give us a clear idea of the rules governing this changeover, in practice it seems fair to assume that power went to the oldest surviving son of one of the "great wives"; and it is probable that the pharaoh himself nominated his successor. The title "eldest son of the king" was not sufficient to guarantee the throne, given that numerous pharaohs had several "eldest sons." The information we have on the sons who did not come to power is even more scant. A total of twenty-eight has been reckoned for

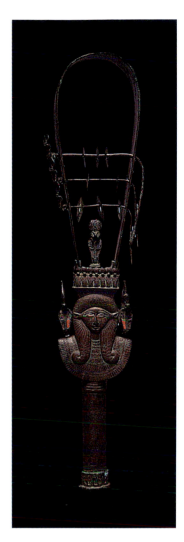

25. Gilded and inlaid bronze *sistrum*, Greco-Roman period. Cairo, Egyptian Museum *cat. 87*

26. *Senet* and other games belonging to Imenmes, New Kingdom, 18th Dynasty. Paris, Musée du Louvre *cat. 152*

27. Mirror handle in wood and ivory, New Kingdom, late 18th Dynasty. Bologna, Civico Museo Archeologico
cat. 146

28. Gold toiletry implement,
New Kingdom, 18th Dynasty.
New York, The Metropolitan
Museum of Art, gift of Lila
Acheson Wallace
cat. 233

this group during the 18th Dynasty, yet almost without exception we do not even know where their tombs are; perhaps in Memphis, close to what was the favored residence of such sons. The few documents that record them include such things as a series of labels from mummies in a Theban tomb, or the odd piece of tomb furnishing. In this period, royal princes were only very rarely depicted in temples or royal monuments (with the exception, that is, of those princes who were also high priests); it is private monuments—particularly those of their wet nurse or tutor—which preserve their name. There are a surprising number of such monuments claiming to commemorate those who brought up Amenhotep II. These touching bas-reliefs and statues are the first clear expression of a real affection between an individual and a member of the royal family: drawing milk from the breast of his wet nurse, sitting on the knees of his tutor, or practicing with bow and arrow, the prince is shown with the characteristic long lock of hair falling to the side of his head.

During the Ramesside period, the heir to the throne was known by the specific term of *repat*, and statues happily depict royal sons in the company of their parents. In temples, battle scenes show the young princes alongside their father in the assault on a fortress or in executing rebel leaders with their own hands. Multiple depictions of processions show the increase in the number of royal offspring. In fact, the number of children is amazing: Rameses II is credited with at least forty-nine. They have the distinctive hairstyle of princes and hold an ostrich feather in their hand, a symbol of their function as "fanbearer on the king's right hand." Their tombs are better known than those of their 18th-Dynasty counterparts—for example, the recently-explored tomb of the sons of Rameses II in the Valley of the Kings, or the richly-decorated tombs of the sons of Rameses III in the Valley of the Queens.

Raised in the company of young noblemen known as "the children of the Kap," the princes divided their time between intellectual and physical pursuits. In illustration of these two aspects, ancient texts mention two exceptional princes: Thutmose and Khaemwaset, who were not originally intended as heirs to the throne. The Dream Stele recounts how the former, accompanied by other royal sons and a troop of attendants, took pleasure in traveling all over the desert of Memphis "shooting his arrows at a metal target, hunting lions and wild game, driving his chariot; his horses were as swift as the wind." The second, who was the high priest of the god Ptah, is known for his great interest in things ancient; he took a concerned interest in the restoration of pyramids, and his reputation as a scholar versed in magic spells made him into a hero of tales dating from the end of the Pharaonic period. Princes such as these might serve as high priests, generals, leaders of cavalry, royal scribes or important administrators, but only during the reign of their fathers. Thereafter, they disappear from the scene. With their role in continuing the dynasty and their function in the nation's religious life, the daughters of the pharaohs are better known to us from the beginning of the New Kingdom onward; up to the Ramesside period, they would occupy an eminent place in official art. Thanks to numerous statues and temple decorations dedicated to them, we know their names and their appearance. Wearing a round cap with their long hair gathered in a single ponytail, they are

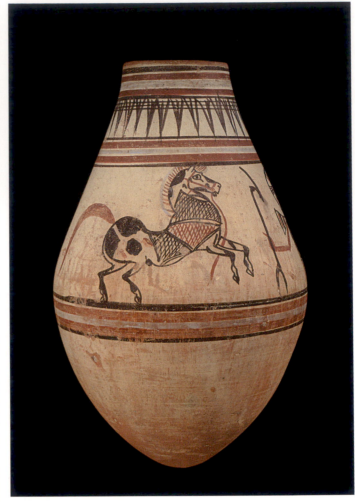

29. Black granite statue of Queen Nefertari as a standard-bearer, New Kingdom, 19th Dynasty.
San Bernardino, Harer Family Trust, California State University
cat. 85

30. Painted ceramic vase decorated with horses, New Kingdom, 18th Dynasty.
Berlin, Ägyptisches Museum und Papyrussammlung
cat. 156

31. Diadem with two gazelle heads, from Wadi Qubbanet el-Qirud New Kingdom, 18th Dynasty. New York, The Metropolitan Museum of Art, gift of George F. Baker and Mr. and Mrs. Everit Macy
cat. 186

32. Silver and gold foil mirror, from Wadi Qubbanet el-Qirud, New Kingdom, 18th Dynasty. New York, The Metropolitan Museum of Art, Fletcher Fund
cat. 189

33. Alabaster and gold cosmetic jar, from Wadi Qubbanet el-Qirud, New Kingdom, 18th Dynasty. New York, The Metropolitan Museum of Art, gift of Edward S. Harkness
cat. 191

shown bearing the ritual instruments of the *sistrum* and the *menat* (they often replaced their mothers in the celebration of religious rituals). The *migdol* or fortified door of the temple of Medinet Habu shows amazing scenes of family life: seated in a richly-adorned chair, the Pharaoh Rameses III is seen caressing his daughters, playing checkers with them and eating the fruit that they offer to him using his affectionate nickname: "to your health, Sese!" However, we know nothing of the personality of these daughters. Nothing more can be said of Neferura, the daughter of Hatshepsut, except that a dozen splendid statues show her seated on the knee of her tutor Senenmut. And what about of the delightful Satamon, daughter and wife of Amenhotep III; of Meritaton and Ankhesenpaaten, who appear as children in the bas-reliefs at Amar-

34. Statuette of Lady Mi.
New York, The Brooklyn
Museum of Art

35. Lid of Ahhotep's coffin,
wood covered with gold leaf,
New Kingdom, 18th Dynasty.
Cairo, Egyptian Museum

36. Gray granite statue of the queen
mother of Rameses II, from Tanis,
New Kingdom, 19th Dynasty.
Cairo, Egyptian Museum
cat. 224

na; of Bentanta, Isetnofret, Bakemut, Nebattauy, Meritamun and Nefertari who appear at the feet of the colossal statues of Rameses II on the façade of the temple of Abu Simbel? They were all part of that female world existing around the pharaoh, in which each king's daughter might become a king's bride and a king's mother. The intimacy that existed between the pharaoh and different generations of women belonging to his own royal family is undoubtedly to be explained referring to Egyptian myths: the association mother-wife-daughter was seen as a symbol of perpetual creation. In this sense, Egyptian queens played a fundamental role in the renewal of royal power and in the perpetuation of the pharaoh's existence in the afterlife.

The Tombs of the Queens of the New Kingdom
On February 5, 1859, a team of workers under the French Egyptologist Auguste Mariette discovered a magnificent sarcophagus in gilded wood that bore the name of Queen Ahhotep, wife of King Seqenenra Taa and mother of Ahmose, founder of the New Kingdom. The coffin was opened immediately. It contained a mummy which—the practice then—was brusquely unbound and thus destroyed. The body was adorned with marvelously-made gold jewelry, the numerous pieces of which totaled almost two kilos in weight. After a series of vicissitudes, the treasure—thanks to the good offices of Mariette—finally arrived in Cairo, where it is still preserved.
The queen had been buried on the west bank of the river at Thebes, at the foot of the Dra

37. View of a chamber of the tomb of Queen Nefertari, New Kingdom, 19th Dynasty.
Luxor, Valley of the Queens, tomb of Nefertari

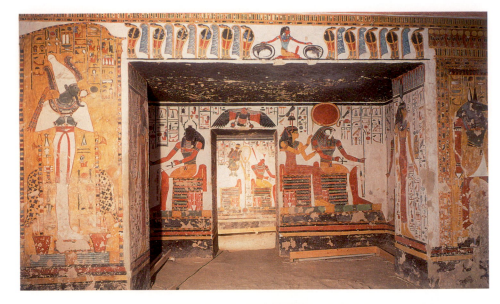

38. Wall-painting depicting Queen Nefertari,
New Kingdom, 19th Dynasty.
Luxor, Valley of the Queens, tomb of Nefertari

Abu el-Naga hills, between the Valley of the Kings and Deir el-Bahri—which is the same area that was chosen by the pharaohs of the 17th Dynasty for their burial ground.

During the New Kingdom, the west bank at Thebes continued to be the site chosen for royal tombs. Everyone has heard of the Valley of the Kings, a forbidding area of the Theban mountains which, from Thutmose I onward, became the elected burial place of most pharaohs. However, their wives do not seem to have been buried in the same place. Evidence concerning the queens of the 18th Dynasty is rare, even if archaeologists at Deir el-Bahri have discovered the tomb of Ahmose Meritamun, daughter of Ahmose and "great royal wife" of Amenhotep I (in the Cairo Museum one can now admire her enormous sarcophagus). We also now know that another queen, Meritra-Hatshepsut, wife of Thutmose III and mother of Amenhotep II, was buried in the Valley of the Kings itself. But since the discovery of these two tombs, little else has come to light about the final resting-place of the most famous queens of this period.

Things are very different when we come to the Ramesside period. To the south of the Theban mountains stands the Valley of the Queens, where the tombs of several "great royal wives" of the 19th and 20th Dynasties have been unearthed. Though not the sole necropolis of the royal family at this time—Rameses II's son and Queen Tausret are buried in the Valley of the Kings—it can be considered as a counterpart to the more famous earlier burial ground. An arid and desolate gorge, the Valley of the Queens comprises rock faces which are honeycombed with hypogea. The Egyptian term for it is *ta set neferu*, which should be translated as "the place of the royal children." In fact, from the 17th Dynasty onward this was the burial ground for the children of the royal family—a tradition that must have continued into the following era because the daughters of Rameses II and the sons of Rameses III are buried here, in tombs which are richly decorated in vivid colors. However, the most important tombs in the valley are undoubtedly those of royal mothers and "great royal wives." The oldest is that of Satra, wife of Rameses I. Among the more famous queens buried here is Tuya, mother of Rameses II, and Nefertari, one of that king's "great royal wives." The decor and inscription of these tombs, which were clearly envisaged as funeral apartments, is drawn from the Book of the Dead. Spirits and deities receive the dead woman, and protect and aid her during the trials she must overcome in order to reach the afterlife. At the end of this difficult journey, the queen is transfigured. She can now blend with the sun and gain access to eternity.

With its splendid decorations and its two levels of chambers, the tomb of Nefertari is certainly the jewel of this necropolis. The delicately-painted reliefs show the queen's journey toward the netherworld, her reception by Osiris and Anubis, the deities of death, and then the evil spirits who attempt to block her progress toward the "transfiguration" that will identify her with the sun. Facing the gods who protect her, she presents jars of wine and consecrates the morsels of meat and vegetables that are to be offered to them. All the brilliance of her royal beauty emerges from these images. Wearing the vulture headdress that symbolizes her sovereignty, she is shown dressed in a pleated linen shawl and an immaculate robe gathered at the waist with a dazzling purple girdle. Ears, neck and wrists are adorned with heavy gold jewelry.

Discovered in 1904 by the Italian Egyptologist Ernesto Schiaparelli, the tomb had already been looted in ancient times. All that remained of the magnificent trousseau that had accompanied the queen on her journey into the afterlife were thirty-odd funeral statues, a few pieces of furniture, a pair of sandals, a *djed* amulet, a few broken vases, and the shattered pieces of the pink granite sarcophagus. Today, the two pathetic mummified fragments in the Turin Museum are all that is left of the woman who was "the great royal wife, mistress of the Double Land, sovereign of Upper and Lower Egypt, Nefertari, beloved of the goddess Mut."

Bibliography
KRI I–VII; Winlock 1924; Winlock 1948; Radwan 1961; Blankenberg–van Delden 1969; Vandersleyen 1971; Reiser 1972; Schmitz 1976; Zivie 1976; Kemp 1978; Tefnin 1979; Gitton 1981; al-Masri 1983; Gitton 1984; Traunecker 1986; Troy 1986; Leblanc 1989; Dodson 1990; Bierbrier 1991; Desroches-Noblecourt 1991; Schott 1992; Wildung 1992; Grandet 1993; Robins 1993 (ample bibliography); Vernus 1993, pp. 141–157; Corzo 1994; Ziegler 1994; Feucht 1995; Arnold 1996; Capel, Markoe 1996; Berlandini 1997; Wildung 1998; Baud 1999; Fay 1999; Hawass 1999; Stadelmann 1999; Roehrig 2001; Leblanc 2002.

The Royal Palace.
Architecture, Decoration and Furnishings

The Royal Palace. Architecture, Decoration and Furnishings

1. Faience tile with *rekhyt* bird, New Kingdom, 20th Dynasty. Cairo, Egyptian Museum *cat. 217*

The palaces of Egyptian kings had multiple functions. They were the living quarters for the pharaoh and his family. They contained the audience halls where the king assembled his advisors and officers of state and decided on matters of state and religion. They were places of stately representation where the power of kingship was demonstrated both to Egypt's people and foreign envoys; and, since the pharaoh's role was to a large degree a religious one, ancient Egyptian palaces provided also the stage for ritual performances connected with the office of kingship. To provide for the welfare of the inhabitants of a palace and the ongoing events considerable economic institutions were attached to the palaces, and these institutions had their own spaces, personnel and administrative structure. Since the pharaoh was considered both human and divine, there was a sacred aspect to much that went on in the royal palaces; and this is well expressed in the most important ancient Egyptian word for "palace" *ah* which can also designate the shrine of a deity, although it is not the word most commonly used for "temple" which was *hwt netjer* "house of god." An alternative word for "palace" *per-aa* (the "great house" from which the designation for the king as "pharaoh" is derived) was solely used for the king's abode.

In reality, most palaces probably accommodated several of the above-listed functions just as some present day seats of government serve as residence for the head of state, chief administrative center and place for stately events. The ancient Egyptian king, moreover, had usually not just one but many palaces so that the royal power was represented in all the parts of the country, and at all places of royal interest. This included in the Old Kingdom, for instance, a palace at the site where the king's pyramid was built. Each palace had a name. For instance a palace near the pyramid of King Djedkara Isesi was called "Lotus flower of Djedkara."

Considering the multi-faceted character of the royal palace, it is especially regrettable that relatively few remains of such buildings have been excavated. There is, moreover, an unfortunate chronological imbalance, since most palace remains date from the late 18th, 19th and 20th Dynasties. Even concerning the New Kingdom we only know through literary sources about the palace built by Thutmose I at Memphis in which such important pharaohs as Hatshepsut or Thutmose III must have resided. Under these circumstances, a general picture of royal palace architecture in ancient Egypt must be pieced together from scattered remains, and use must also be made of other than purely archaeological evidence. Representations of palaces in wall reliefs and paintings, for instance, are invaluable for a reconstruction of the visual appearance and uses of royal palaces; and there is an additional—very typically Egyptian—source from which basic insights about the structures of Egyptian royal palaces can be deduced. The late 18th and 19th-Dynasty mortuary temples in western Thebes are provided with full-scale three-dimensional representations of royal palaces. These so-called "temple palaces" are always situated on the south side of the main temple with their axis at right angles to the temple axis. When first excavated, the temple palaces were believed to have served as rest-houses during visits of the ruling king to the mortuary temple. More recently, however, scholars have shown that most installations in these build-

2–3. Faience bowl with gazelle from the tomb of Maiherpri in the Valley of the Kings, New Kingdom, 18th Dynasty Cairo, Egyptian Museum *cat. 159*

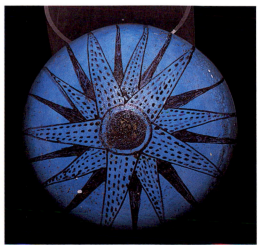

4. Folding ebony stool with ivory inlays and bronze pivot pins, New Kingdom, 18th Dynasty. Toronto, Royal Ontario Museum
cat. 149

5. Wooden stool with ivory inlays, from Thebes, New Kingdom. Brussels, Musées Royaux d'Art et d'Histoire
cat. 147

ings were not suitable for actual use. The temple palaces are, therefore, now understood as purely symbolic dwellings for the deceased pharaoh in whose honor the mortuary temple was built. However, since the temple palaces appear to reproduce real life structures, they can well serve to demonstrate properties of now lost real palace architecture provided one keeps in mind the symbolic nature of this source.

The Pharaoh's Living Quarters

Like all places of the living the king's residence was normally built of mud-brick with possibly some main doorways of stone. The walls, floors and ceilings were plastered and often painted, and columns and windows were of wood. More stone elements, such as columns and windows, were used in some temple and audience palaces as well as palaces for religious rites. The buildings had for the most part only one story with possibly some galleries as well as stairs to the roof. Furniture consisted of wooden (certainly often gilded and inlaid) chairs and beds (figs. 4–8) with blankets and cushions. Gate-legged stands supported terra-cotta vessels and served as tables; and lighting was provided by oil lamps on pedestals. Foodstuff and goods such as linen clothing were stored in chests and on shelves supported on painted mud-brick walls. As best seen in relief representations showing the palaces of King Akhenaten (figs. 10, 11) at el-Amarna, the royal living quarters comprised an entrance portico, various columned halls and rooms with shrine shaped doors. In the center the representations depict a large columned hall whose ceiling is higher than that of the surrounding rooms. This hall may have had clerestory windows just below the roof. Here cushioned chairs and a sumptuous meal await king and queen. The main hall is in most representations preceded by a portico, or several porticoes, one of which contains an ornate window, the so-called "window of appearance," about which more will be presently said. Behind—and at the

6. Wooden stool from Thebes with stuccoed and painted linen seat, New Kingdom, mid-18th Dynasty. Turin, Museo Egizio
cat. 148

7. Lid of painted wooden chest
from the tomb of Nefertari,
New Kingdom, 19th Dynasty.
Turin, Museo Egizio
cat. 211

8. Inlaid casket of Rameses IX
from Deir el-Bahri, New Kingdom,
20th Dynasty.
Cairo, Egyptian Museum
cat. 150

9. Wooden statuette of young girl
with a cat, from Abuzir el-Melek,
New Kingdom, 18th Dynasty.
Berlin, Ägyptisches Museum
und Papyrussammlung
cat. 231

10. Drawing of the bedroom and
harim in Akhenaten's palace from
the tomb of Ay at el-Amarna

11. Drawing of the living quarters of
Akhenaten from the tomb of Ay at
el-Amarna

12. A duck in the thicket, detail of the pavemet from the palace of Amenhotep III at Malkata. New York, The Metropolitan Museum of Art, Rogers Fund, 1920

side—of the large hall smaller rooms open to a narrow corridor. In the representations, most of the side rooms are filled with food supplies and boxes with goods.

In proximity to the king's bedroom some images from Amarna tombs depict columned chambers in which female musicians and dancers practice their art (fig. 10). In the corridors leading to these rooms men are seen standing, seated or talking to each other, while others prepare food and drink in adjacent rooms. It is tempting to interpret these representations as depictions of the king's *harim*. The presence in the abovementioned figure of foreign women with long curled tresses and "Syrian clothes" in their own separate room inside the musicians' quarters could be taken to confirm such an interpretation, because it is known that a number of princesses from countries in Western Asia and the Levant became minor wives of the Egyptian king. However, during the last twenty years serious doubts have been raised concerning the existence in ancient Egypt of an institution comparable to the *harim* in medieval Turkish palaces. Scholars have stressed the fact, for instance, that the term *khener*, often translated as "harim," actually identified a troop of dancers and musicians who performed at religious ceremonies. There appears to be no evidence that the members of this troop ever served in the role of royal concubines. In the light of this point of view the image (fig. 10) would have to be interpreted as an indication by the Amarna artists that the pharaoh went to sleep accompanied by soothing music performed by beautiful women.

The king's bedroom has one of the ingenious roof constructions with which the ancient Egyptians managed to funnel the cool north wind into rooms (fig. 11). In one representation, the

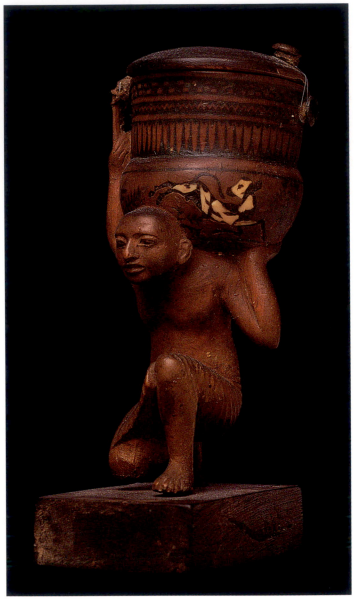

13. Statuette of a young girl holding a vase, wood, traces of paint, dyed ivory, gold and pigments, from Qurna, New Kingdom, 18th Dynasty.
Durham, The Oriental Museum
cat. 166

14. Dwarf carrying a jar, wood and ivory inlays, from el-Amarna, New Kingdom, 18th Dynasty. Boston, Fine Arts Museum, Helen and Alice Colburn Fund
cat. 167

floor of the bedroom appears to be painted with flowers and plants, and there is a similar painting on the wall. The bed stands on a dais or under a canopy (fig. 10) and is covered by a thick blanket. Queen Hetepheres, mother of Khufu, had her bed in a tent over which a linen curtain was probably hung for privacy and possibly against mosquitoes. In the el-Amarna palace representations, there is invariably only one bed in each palace representation, while there are two chairs in the dining hall, from which one is inclined to deduce that the king and queen shared the bed.

Remains of paintings from the walls, floors and ceilings of the palaces at Malkata and el-Amarna show that the rooms were mud plastered and decorated in intense colors such as dark green, deep yellow, dark red brown. A painting from the so-called "king's house" at el-Amarna, now in the Ashmolean Museum, Oxford, also provides a glimpse of the colored textiles that were used for chair and floor cushions. Again the colors are deep and intense, combining a dark orange background with yellow and dark blue patterns. The impact of this dense coloring on the walls and ceilings was effectively contrasted by the white and light blue colors of the floor paintings (fig. 12) and the translucent alabaster or light blue painted vases that stood in their (mostly white painted) wooden stands on the floors. Interior color schemes in the Ramesside palaces of the 19th and 20th Dynasties were—as far as can be ascertained—more somber, using brown and dark red colors on walls and columns and a cool light greenish-blue, dark brown and other dark colors in the faience tiles. No private apartments for king and royal family are, however, preserved from this period.

A number of bathrooms have been excavated. Like bathrooms in private mansions, they had a screen wall behind which a rectangular basin with a spout at one side is set into the floor. Here the king could take a shower under water that a servant poured from a jar. A royal bathroom at Memphis was decorated with "protective hieroglyphs topped by royal cartouches and a cornice" (David O'Connor's description). Some representations in el-Amarna tombs also show a pool in the residential compound with plants painted on the floor around it. King Akhenaten clearly preferred a river position (and river view) for his palaces. Both the large architectural complex that was most probably his major residential palace, the so-called "northern riverside palace," and the "great palace" in the city appear to have had terraces overlooking the Nile. We will deal below with the pools and water vegetation in the palace at Malkata and the parkland sanctuaries connected with Amarna queens.

It is remarkable how close the general layout of the royal living quarters was to that of the elite houses at el-Amarna. Herbert Ricke has described this in his famous treatise *Der Grundriss des Amarna-Wohnhauses*. Indeed, the front portico of the palace can be compared to the front rooms (broad halls) of the non-royal houses, while the palace's high main hall finds its direct counterpart in the square main hall of the typical el-Amarna house. Bedrooms and other private spaces lie in both types of buildings at the side and back of the main hall and thus removed from the entrance. That the king and his family essentially lived in a grandiose version of a nobleman's house makes sense. As far as physical needs were concerned every pharaoh was a human being, even if his special semi-divine qualities made privacy and seclusion a primary requisite.

Palace Economy Versus State Economy and State Administration

If we follow the evidence provided by wall reliefs at el-Amarna, food for the royal table was stored but not produced in the residential palace itself. In the non-royal mansions at el-Amarna, however, food production, workshops and storage areas were located at the sides and back of the main house; and the king's palace cannot have been entirely without such spaces. An impressive painting in the tomb of Rameses III in the Valley of the Kings at Thebes, for instance, allows a fascinating glimpse into a royal kitchen. It is clearly a huge place where—as a main feature—we see an ingenious device for the drying of meat. The cuts hang from a line that runs through two looped nails in the ceiling while the ends are tied to other loops in the floor.

Textual evidence also suggests a well-developed palace administration with hundreds of servants and their overseers who prepared the food and drink for the royal family. Provisions for the palace came from its own economic institutions and estates. In the same way there appears to have existed an elaborate economic and administrative structure for the female members of the royal family. Some excavated royal palaces, indeed, include spaces that have the typical shape of ancient Egyptian storage and production rooms. An example of such a building complex was found in the southeastern corner of the "great palace" at el-Amarna (fig. 18). Partly separated from the rest of the large palace complex by enclosure walls, the typical long corridors here are flanked by rows of elongated rooms. A courtyard provides open air space, and several columned and pillared halls were provided for the scribes and overseers to fulfill their administrative roles in the shade. It is, however, striking how relatively small this economic area was compared with the vast space that the rest of the palace occupied. Even the presence of other economic zones on the now destroyed north and west sides of the palace would not have changed this situation fundamentally. A look over to the opposite side of the Royal Road, on the other hand, reveals the presence there, outside the palace, of immense facilities for the storage and production as well as the administration of goods. Here, most of the provisions for the whole city of el-Amarna must have been stored, administered and distributed. In the same area were also the military stables and "barracks" for the troops, as well as offices for state affairs, such as the scribal offices and archives of foreign correspondence. The pharaoh was not entirely disengaged from all these affairs, on the contrary, he had a kind of "office" in the "king's house" which is situated in the center of the industrial and administrative area. The "king's house" was certainly not a

15. Faience frieze with lotus flowers from Tell el-Yahudiya, New Kingdom, 20th Dynasty. Cairo, Egyptian Museum
cat. 114

16. Limestone relief showing a palace interior, from el-Amarna, New Kingdom, 18th Dynasty. Boston, Museum of Fine Arts, Marilyn M. Simpson Fund
cat. 208

palace in the usual sense; besides large storage and administrative areas there was a royal "window of appearance" that opened into the large courtyard. It has been argued that the king communicated through this window with crowds of privileged people and awarded certain officials with the "gold of honor" for good conduct in office. The need for a separate building for such activities in the center of the storage and administration area forcefully underlines the fact that neither large-scale goods administration and storage, nor even some of the king's direct involvement in administrative activities had a place in the royal palace itself. The picture gained at el-Amarna of only a rudimentary presence of storage facilities and administrative spaces inside the royal palace is also true for most of the manufacture of goods not connected to food, what we would call objects of art. The excavations at el-Amarna, for instance, have shown that sculptors' workshops were predominantly placed at various points in the city, in some cases even in the compounds of private houses. This also appears to be true for the Ramesside residence at Piramesse in the eastern Delta. Again, not only the stables for the chariot horses, a New Kingdom pharaoh's most mighty military weapon, were located outside the palace itself, but also the faience and glass workshops. A similar situation is found at Malkata (fig. 21). The vast built-over area at this site to the south of the Theban necropolis is usually called "the palace of Amenhotep III at Malkata," but in reality there existed here at the mouth of a substantial ancient Nile harbor a veritable settlement comparable at least to the central part of the city of el-Amarna. Main features were a temple of the god Amun, a platform facing a large courtyard for official appearances of the king, several complexes that have been identified as palaces, groups of elite houses and various "villages for servants and workmen." Remains from the manufacture of faience and glass objects again were not found inside the palaces themselves, but in separate workmen's quarters such as the "South Village" and a workmen's quarter between the temple of Amun and the main palace. Seal impressions indicating administrative functions were discovered in a large building ("West Villa B") among the elite group of houses, not in the palaces.

In sum: the New Kingdom royal palace, although provided and cared for by its own outside economic institutions, did not house large-scale economic and administrative spaces. It is possible that the situation was somewhat different in the beginning of Egypt's history. The tombs of the pharaohs of the 2nd and 3rd Dynasties at Saqqara are accompanied by seemingly unending underground storage galleries filled—where the content is preserved—with tens of thousands of stone reproductions of storage vessels. It could well be that these funerary installations copied installations in the palaces of the living kings. If that was the case, the absence of large storage of goods in New Kingdom royal palaces, points to a somewhat different role of the pharaoh's palace in post-Archaic times.

Audience Halls and Other Stately Spaces

Based on new archaeological research in the royal cemeteries of Abydos, Gunter Dreyer has recently proposed the reconstruction of what appears to be the earliest Egyptian royal palace dating to the late Predynastic period (fig. 22). Considering the early date of the building, it is striking how similar this palace is to the much later New Kingdom stately halls in royal palaces (figs. 23, 24). Vestibule, throne room and side rooms equal the later arrangement; only the columns are missing. A famous Middle Kingdom description of an audience with King Senusret I serves to confirm the fact that the essential elements of such stately royal spaces may indeed have had a very long tradition in ancient Egypt. "I touched the ground between the sphinxes," relates the 12th-Dynasty official Sinuhe, while describing his reception in the royal palace after his long exile in foreign countries, "as the royal children stood in the portal [literally "thickness"], receiving me and the Friends who usher to the Pillared Hall. I found his Majesty on the great throne in the portal [again "thickness," here possibly canopy ?] of electrum."

The main parts of the audience palace described in the Sinuhe text are still present in the palaces of the New Kingdom that are either preserved as real examples or represented by symbolic "temple palaces." A gate into the temple palace of Rameses III at Medinet Habu, for instance, has been restored by the excavator Uvo Hölscher with representations of sphinxes trampling down enemies. Progress to the throne was then through a vestibule and columned hall and from there into the throne room (fig. 23). Behind the throne dais a double false door with images of the pharaoh proclaimed the king's presence, even when he was not there in person. The basic features of this room configuration are still essentially the ones of major rooms in a contemporary New Kingdom house for the upper ranks of society, but there is a much greater emphasis on movement along the central axis. When not attached to a temple, moreover, audience hall palaces were evidently equipped with additional spaces, including an open court and elaborate entrance structures.

The most impressive extant audience palace is the "palace of Merenptah" at Memphis (fig. 24). Here the broad vestibule in front of the throne room is preceded by a large open court surrounded on all four sides by columned porticoes. A pylon-like building forms the entrance to the whole building. David O'Connor has rightly pointed out how close this architecture is to the one of a typical New Kingdom temple. This close relationship between audience hall and temple makes perfect sense, because when appearing "on the throne of Horus," the pharaoh was clearly more than a human being; indeed, he was the incarnation of the god Horus, the "living Horus." One of many descriptions of royal audiences from the literature reads thus: "Appearance of His Incarnation on the throne of Horus in the palace [whose name is] 'Elevates Perfection.' Said His Incarnation to the privileged ones, the courtiers who were behind him, and the true scribes of hieroglyphs in charge of secrets: 'My heart has desired to see the writings of the first original time of [the god] Atum. Spread open for me for the great inventory.'. . ." At the end, such texts usually record a specific decision taken by the king on a matter of historical or religious importance. No question: the pharaoh made history "on the throne of Horus."

Remains of several daises have survived on which the thrones of Egyptian pharaohs once stood. A fairly well-preserved dais decoration comes from the royal palace at Qantir (Pi-ramesse). The Qantir dais (fig. 25) on which stood a throne of the great Rameses II was about 80 centimeters high and fully decorated with faience tiles. On the sides of the dais platform, figures of kneeling foreigners were depicted above a dado of "palace façade" emblems alternating with bushes of lilies and papyrus plants, signifying Upper and Lower Egypt. The foreigners are seen raising their hands to the pharaoh on his throne. On two sides, flights of stairs led up to the level of the throne. On the steps were figures of bound prisoners, and on the platform itself representations of the nine bows, symbolizing the subdued foreign countries. The stairs were accompanied by rising balustrades that ended at the foot in large figures of upright sitting lions that hold foreigners between their paws. The—now missing—heads of these foreigners were in the open mouths of the lions. The whole decoration is a powerful demonstration of the pharaoh's rule over Egypt and the surrounding countries; and similar motifs are found in paintings on walls and floors in all extant palaces.

The royal throne itself was either a simple block-shaped seat with a short back, or a chair with lion legs and lion heads at both sides of the seat. Seated thus between two lions the king would be understood as an incarnation of the rising sun, because in Egyptian mythology the horizon over which the sun rises is flanked by lions. Thrones were often decorated with symbols of the pharaoh's might such as the intertwined plants (papyrus and lily) that symbolized the union of Upper and Lower Egypt. On the arms of chair-like thrones sphinxes were seen trampling on figures of Egypt's enemies.

The Window of Appearance

In the above-described audience halls the architectural progression took its course from the entry toward the pharaoh on his throne. But the Egyptian pharaoh was not only approached by his subjects and foreign envoys, he also moved in person toward such an encounter. The place of contact in that case was the so-called "window of appearance." Windows of appearance are balcony-like openings usually in the center of the front wall of a palace. On the inside, steps lead up to the window which towers on the outside over the assembled subjects who look up to the ruler in the window from an open space, such as a courtyard. In the el-Amarna representations of royal living quarters (fig. 11) there is always a window of appearance to indicate that although the pharaoh's private apartments are inaccessible for most subjects, he is sure to keep contact with them by means of the window. In the temple palaces such as Medinet Habu (fig. 26) the window of appearance almost plays the role of a representation of the—absent—pharaoh, similar to the way in which a "false door" in Egyptian tombs of the Old and Middle Kingdom guaranteed the presence of the deceased. Windows of appearance were at least as richly adorned as the throne daises; and in the 19th and 20th Dynasties similar motives of power over foreign enemies were abundantly employed. At Medinet Habu, for instance, rows of fully sculpted three dimensional heads of foreigners were lined up below the window, while reliefs at the sides depicted the pharaoh smiting his enemies.

Elevated and Fortified Palaces

In the same way as the royal throne dais elevated the pharaoh above the assembled courtiers whole palace buildings could be elevated on substructures consisting of massive brick walls and sand and rubble-filled casemates. The result was an elevation of the building that far surpassed even the impression achieved by the otherwise often used massive brick foundation walls. While the foundation walls either served to level the uneven desert ground or to create terraces on the slope of a river bank, the casemate platform lent the palace a castle-like appearance; and the impression of heightened security was certainly not totally imaginary. In most cases where palaces of this type have been excavated only the substructures remain, and it is difficult to reconstruct the appearance of the actual palace building that stood on top of the platform.

17. Glazed faience goblet, New Kingdom, 19th–20th Dynasties. Florence, Museo Egizio
cat. 158

At the Upper Egyptian site of Deir el-Ballas, about 20 kilometers north of Luxor, the remains of two palaces are preserved. One (the "south palace") was built on a rocky natural elevation in the desert which made its sight even more impressive. It consisted of a lower platform on which a vast columned hall was built, and a higher, upper one behind on which stood a structure surrounded by a massive outer wall. Connection between the two platforms was through an imposing, broad flight of steps with a smaller one at its side. This is the only known instance of a monumental staircase in Egyptian architecture. Its existence between the large columned hall and further rooms suggests that it was over this staircase that one reached the king's throne room. The second, "northern palace" of Deir el-Ballas was located on the lower desert ground. The preserved traces suggest the existence of several large columned halls and a central tower-like structure (?). A few remains of wall paintings recovered from this building depict battle axes and the head of a man. Was a battle scene depicted here?

The Deir el-Ballas palaces date from the very beginning of the New Kingdom, and may have been built by the Theban kings of the late 17th Dynasty or early 18th who were at war with the Asiatic Hyksos kings who controlled the north of the country from their imposing capital at Avaris, close to the later Ramesside residence of Piramesse. Recent excavations at Tell el-Dab'a—as the area of Avaris–Piramesse is called today—have revealed the remains of a similar elevated palace from the time of the Hyksos rulers and two elevated palace structures dating to the early 18th Dynasty when Egyptian kings were again in command of the region. Rooms of in these latter palaces were decorated with Minoan frescoes. Later, the main palace at Piramesse was also built on an elevation, although here the substructure appears to have been a hill of sand and rubble surrounded by a massive brick wall. The still later 26th-Dynasty palace of King Apries at Memphis was again elevated on a casemate platform. Its

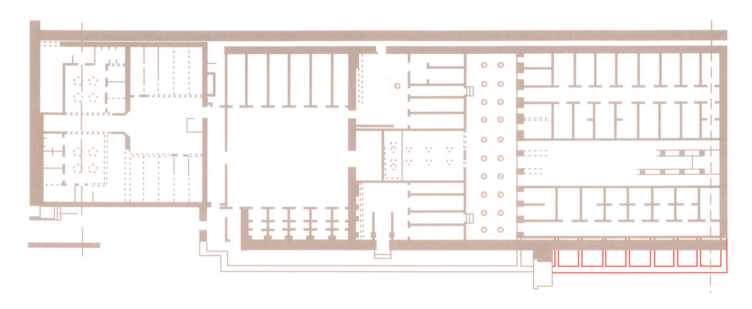

18. Plan of the administrative rooms in the "great palace" at el-Amarna

19. Window of appearance from the palace of Merenptah, New Kingdom, 19th Dynasty. Philadelphia, The University of Pennsylvania, Museum of Archaeology and Anthropology
cat. 113

20. Glazed faience tile with a fish, from a Ramesside building at Qantir, New Kingdom, 19th Dynasty. Cairo, Egytpian Museum
cat. 216

21. Malkata, the central part of Amenhotep III's palace.
1. central residential area on the west
2. western villas
3. central palace
4. temple of Amun
5. storerooms
6. workmen's village
7. audience pavilion
8. *harim* (king's palace)
9. storerooms
10. southern palace
11. southern village
12. northern palace
13. Birket Habu hills
14. B building
15. unexcavated area

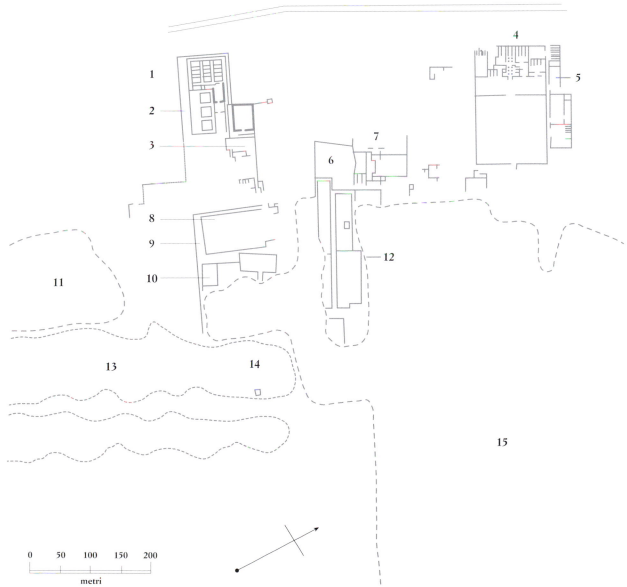

0   50   100   150   200

metri

massive substructure may have superseded a palace already built by Thutmose I (also on a platform ?) that was in use by pharaohs until Sety I.

Other methods of fortifying a royal palace are known from early Egypt. This at least seems to be indicated by the emblematic banner, called *serekh*, on which Egyptians used to write the pharaoh's so-called "Horus name." The *serekh* consists of the representation of an ornate façade with an enclosed rectangle above it. On top of the rectangle sits a falcon figure signifying the god Horus. The full explanation of this complex pictogram is still under discussion. But it is possible that the ornate architectural façade at the base depicts the niched enclosure wall of a building from the Archaic period. In the famous stele of King Serpent in the Louvre, this façade is further elaborated by three towers that are considerably higher than the rest of the building; and it has been suggested that this is an image of the king's fortified palace. Part of a real palace wall of Archaic date was excavated at Hierakonpolis. Among the here described palaces of the New Kingdom the "northern riverside palace" of King Akhenaten at el-Amarna was surrounded by a wall fortified at equal distances with rectangular towers. Whether this was a real and "working" fortification or just a show-off and an allusion to the castles of Archaic kings, has to remain open. The same question has been raised concerning the walls and castle-like gateways of the mortuary temple of Rameses III at Medinet Habu. Uvo Hölscher has convincingly argued that "in the construction [of these "fortifications"] the aim was for an imposing reception of processions rather than for protection against attack. . . . The mighty gates especially were triumphal in character." Some scholars have suggested that the upper stories of the gate towers were the places of repose for the pharaoh when visiting the temple. Representations of the king in intimate conversation with a number of royal females seem rather to suggest that we see here another artificial creation of Egyptian builders aimed at depicting a paradisiacal state of existence under the eyes of the gods. However that may be, the reconstructions of the Medinet Habu "fortifications" convey as much as anything else the use that Egyptians made of a castle-like appearance of the royal abode in order to express the pharaoh's power. For the ordinary people of Egypt, such a view of a royal palace from the outside was probably all they would ever be granted to see.

The Royal Palace as a Stage for Religious Festivals
It was a fundamental belief of the ancient Egyptians that life depended on the pharaoh's up-

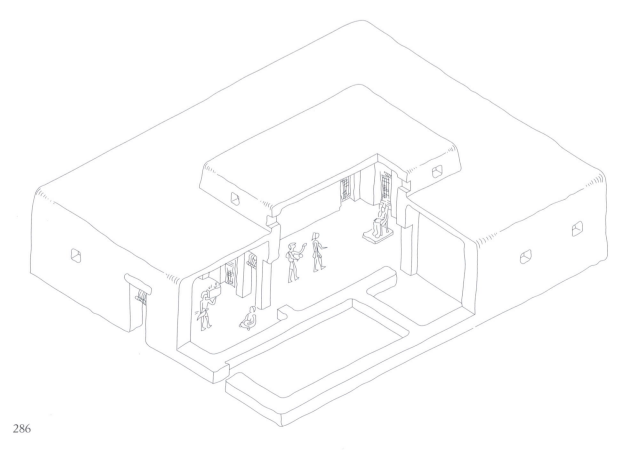

23. Reconstruction of the columned hall in the temple palace at Medinet Habu

24. Plan of the palace of Merenptah at Memphis

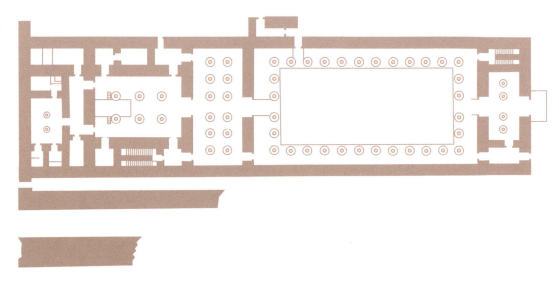

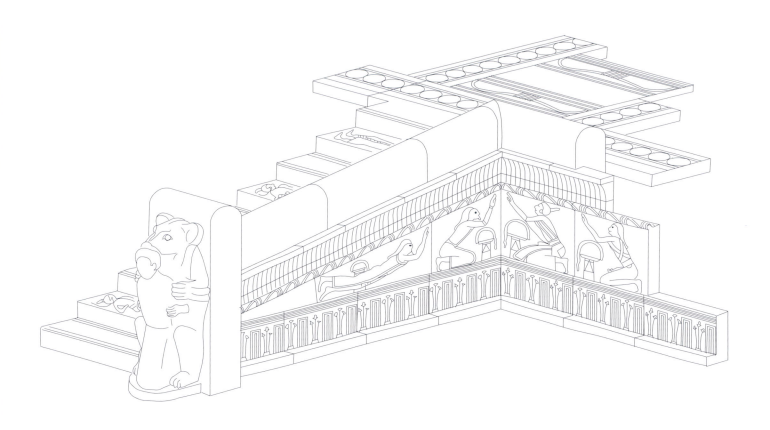

25. Reconstruction of the throne dais of Rameses II, from Piramesse

holding right, justice and balance in the world. In the proper fulfillment of this role the king was supported by rituals and ceremonies. A number of these were certainly performed in the country's temples and sanctuaries, but there is evidence that palaces must also have served as the settings for such rituals. Indeed, Erik Hornung has demonstrated that the whole life of a pharaoh was in a sense a ritual celebration ("history as ritual"). This function of palaces as places for the ritual of kingship must have had considerable consequences for their architecture and decoration. An instructive example of a primarily ritually used royal palace is, in this author's opinion, the so-called "*harim* palace" of Malkata.

The usual interpretation of the main palace at Malkata (fig. 28) as a royal *harim* does not stand up under close scrutiny. The building's most striking feature are the two lines of four, practically identical, individual compounds on each side of a central columned hall which itself is connected with a royal throne room. If the eight compounds were indeed the living quarters of eight ladies of the royal *harim*, their direct connection to a throne room clearly contradicts the evidence of *harim* representations at el-Amarna (fig. 10), since all those representations showed the female quarters to be situated at a considerable distance from the main hall of the palace.

Some details of the eight compounds at Malkata are admittedly reminiscent of installations in el-Amarna private houses. In the anterooms of each compound, for instance, is a stone lined basin with an outlet for water. The original identification by the excavators of these anterooms as bathrooms was rightly rejected by the Waseda University scholars who worked more recently at the site. Comparing the basins with similar water receptacles in el-Amarna houses they identified them as emplacements for water jars. This interpretation, however, does not explain why the water receptacles in the eight compounds were not positioned in the main "living rooms" but in the antechambers. Why would anybody want to drink water on the way from a royal hall into a private apartment?

It is, furthermore, possible that one, maybe even two, of the compounds included a bedroom at the innermost end of the structure. But the rest of the compounds lack bedrooms. Sleeping, therefore, cannot have been a main function of the compounds. The most conspicuous room in each, on the other hand, is a fairly large, elongated storeroom lined with short projecting brick walls that once supported shelves. Relative to the available space in each compound these storerooms occupy as much as a third of the whole. There can be no doubt, therefore, that the storerooms were of paramount importance for the function of the spaces; a fact that is further corroborated by the painting of the shelf supports with vivid images of calves in full gallop and stands with baskets full of fruit. In the central rooms of each compound, moreover, stood a dais; and considering the close proximities of the rooms to a throne dais of the king, it appears improbable that anybody but the pharaoh would have sat on these thrones. Putting storerooms and throne daises together leads one to suggest that the eight compounds were used for the investments of the king with eight different sets of garments and insignia that served during an important ritual performance.

A scrutiny of the remains of wall paintings and other decoration in the "*harim* palace" also reveals the dominant role of the king in his capacity as pharaoh and ruler, not as a pleasure seeking potentate. The ceilings of central hall H (fig. 28) as well as the large "king's bedchamber" were decorated with flying vultures, protective goddesses to the king, and his official names and titles. On the south wall of hall H a figure of the king on his throne was painted with subdued prisoners at his feet. In the "king's bedchamber" was a dado of "palace façade" motifs alternating with imposing hieroglyphic emblems for life and protection. Above the dado, figures of the god Bes were depicted, a deity who appears both in the context of the king's divine birth and the various rituals connected with kingship. The only evidence for a role played by a female comes from hall F which is somewhat removed from the so-called "*harim*" compounds. In hall F, the remains of wall paintings were found depicting a larger than life size female figure. However, a closer look at the preserved fragments from the head and knee of the woman shows that her elaborate flower headdress is the one of a lady of high rank officiating at an important ceremony. A window grill in the same room, moreover, comprised the figure of a striding royal sphinx and on the wall behind the throne dais desert animals were painted. None of these decorations seems suitable for a *harim*. Ceilings

26. Reconstruction of the window of appearance of Rameses II at Medinet Habu

27. Ostracon with window
of appearance from Thebes,
New Kingdom, 19th–20th Dynasties.
Berlin, Ägyptisches Museum und
Papyrussammlung
cat. 122

in the eight individual compounds to the side of hall H were, as far as one can ascertain, not decorated with vultures or royal names; beside scroll designs, which are also found in the main royal rooms, grape vines, flying ducks and flying pigeons decorated the ceilings of the square rooms L in compounds 4, 2 and 1 respectively. El-Amarna reliefs show the last motif as the decoration of columns supporting a royal pavilion. To send out birds was an Egyptian custom at the coronation of a king. More depictions of plant and animal life were spread over walls, ceilings and pavements in halls F and E (fig. 12).

Hundreds, if not thousands of inscriptions on storage jars provide evidence that the royal complex at Malkata was built and used on the occasion of Amenhotep III's thirty-year jubilee festival (*heb-sed*) which was celebrated three times by this king, in the first instance after the customary thirty years of rule with the two others following at shorter intervals. Various monuments attest to the fact that the king and country understood these festivals to be extremely important religious and political occasions. The age-old *sed* festival comprised a complex series of rituals whose celebration stretched over a number of days and involved, beside the king and royal family, most members of the elite and at certain points possibly also the population at large. The ancient Egyptians believed that the festival rites had the power to rejuvenate the king physically and mentally, and reconstitute his reign in full strength and effectiveness. It is extremely unlikely that a primary building in the palace complex that was built and used at these festivals would have been dedicated to the king's *harim*. It is much more probable that all the important palace buildings at Malkata were dedicated to the celebrations of the *heb-sed*. Observed in the light of such considerations, it is striking how closely the plan of the so-called "*harim* palace" resembles the famous *heb-sed* court of King Djoser at Saqqara (fig. 30). The resemblance is all the more astonishing, since King Djoser predates Amenhotep III by over a millennium. It is, however, known that Amenhotep's officials had gone to old archives and studied the previous celebrations of the *heb-sed*. In both monuments a central north-south oriented space (an open courtyard at Saqqara, a columned hall at Malkata) is flanked on both long sides by separate compartments. At the south end is the

following pages
29. Fragment of a painted floor
from el-Amarna, New Kingdom,
18th Dynasty.
Cairo, Egyptian Museum
cat. 207

king's throne, and behind it to the southwest a number of private apartments are located: the so-called "Temple T" at Saqqara, the "king's bedchamber" suite at Malkata. Beyond the private apartments in the south (southwest at Saqqara) is a large open court, and in the north other courts and halls are attached.

The striking similarity of the Malkata main palace and the *heb-sed* installations of King Djoser needs further in-depth study. Suffice to point out here that based on comparisons such as this an alternative explanation for the Malkata main palace would be that during the *heb-sed* celebrations the king entered various separate spaces to be invested with appropriate insignia and in addition perform certain rites. The parallel arrangements of rooms in the Djoser complex and the halls and separate compounds at Malkata would suggest that perhaps the small room P in each of the Malkata compounds was really a chapel in which an image of a certain deity was deposited during the festivities. The necessity for the king to purify himself at the entrance into the compounds would then be understandable, although ablutions would also make sense prior to each of the robings that would have occurred while the king sat on the throne in room K. Attendants would then bring insignia and garments from the storeroom M and invest the king. If indeed a deity image was present in chapel P, the king would then have celebrated certain rites in the chapel. While the celebrations were underway, the king would have slept, or rested, in the "king's bedchamber." The other bedroom of royal size in the northern part of the palace (B) would have served him during rites performed in that part of the building. Indeed, the arrangement might have been for rites concerning Lower Egypt in the northern part, and rites concerning Upper Egypt in the southern with one bedroom for the king in each. The much smaller bedroom(s) in compound 5 (and possibly 1) may have provided a resting place for the king during the ceremonies. One should not forget that one aim of the *heb-sed* was the king's rejuvenation. Sleep was always considered an important means to reach that goal. All rites in the "*harim* palace" would have been secret rites without the presence of anyone but the necessary attendance. We know that at times during the festival the king left the palace in order to appear to larger crowds of people. For that purpose the "audience pavilion" at Malkata was prepared (fig. 21).

28. The so-called *Harim* Palace
of Amenhotep III at Malkata
H. central hall
I. throne room
S. court
T. king's bedchamber
M. storerooms
P. chapels

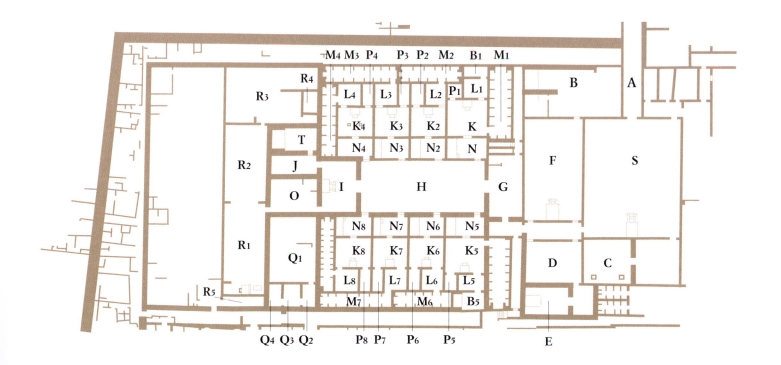

30. Plan of the *heb-sed* court in the pyramid complex of Djoser

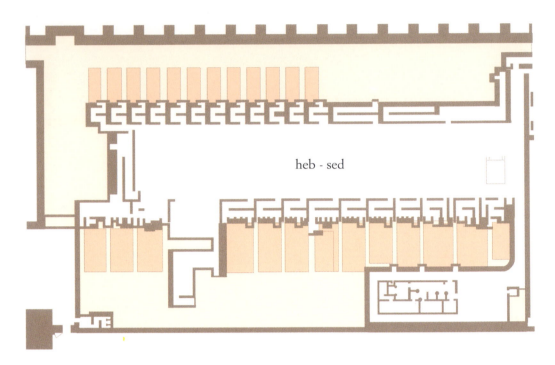

heb - sed

Whether one accepts the above interpretation of the Malkata main palace or not, there can be no doubt that the Egyptians built palaces in order to have a stage on which to perform various state rituals. Another example of such palatial stage architecture was most probably the "great palace" at el-Amarna. Barry Kemp has recently described "the monumental formality" of its stone-built central part as, on the one side, "suited for display to a large gathering," while the inner part may have been again a stage for the *heb-sed*. Kemp ended his description by stating: "This connection [with the *heb-sed*] can be no more than a suggestion, but it illustrates the most profitable direction for explanations for the plan of the "great palace" to take: that it is a vast setting for processional rituals of kingship."

Gardens, Parklands and Zoos
We have above briefly pointed out that a most desirable part of Egyptian palaces and mansions was a pool and garden. Already the early 4th-Dynasty official Metjen boasted in his tomb inscription that he owned an estate "200 cubits long and 200 cubits wide with a wall equipped and set with good wood, a very big pool made in it, and planted with figs and grapes." No doubt, like their present day descendants, the ancient Egyptians, loved gardens and pools. Living in a river oasis surrounded on all sides by desert and depending totally on the water of the Nile as source of life, the inhabitants of the valley saw in water and vegetation indeed more than just a means to gain pleasure and recreation. Water and vegetation were the most potent symbols of life. Water receptacles and gardens were, therefore, parts of most temples and many tombs; and if they also abounded in the royal palaces both as real pools and gardens and as themes of relief representations, paintings and architectural decoration, they also served there as an affirmation of life and underlined the role of the pharaoh as guarantor not only of a stable political condition, but also of the proper functioning of the natural world.
Considering the especially important role played by nature in the time of Akhenaten, it is no surprise that the remains of a number of veritable parkland estates have been excavated at el-Amarna. They were situated at the outskirts of the city in the desert and shielded by high walls. Inside were pools, trees and flower gardens as well as small sanctuaries. Some of the buildings in these gardens, however, may well have served as temporary resting places for the king and his family. Significantly, most of these parklands were connected by inscriptions with the female members of the royal family. No wonder, because the Amarna religion put unprecedented stress on the importance of royal women as counterparts to the king in the great scenario of the daily renewal of creation under the tutelage of the god Aten. Ordinary

Egyptians, of course, might just have taken this for a secularized version of the idea that the tree goddess was procuring water for the deceased in the necropolis. In another architectural complex at el-Amarna, the so-called "north palace," not only water and plants but also animals (cattle, fowl and birds) were kept in close proximity to sanctuaries and a few rooms that may have been used by the royal family. A large painting in one of the rooms is the most lush depiction of marshland nature in the whole of Egyptian art. Earlier and later pharaohs also had zoos in which lions above all were kept as symbols of the king's might.

The Metropolitan Museum of Art owns a wooden drawing board on which a scribe has drawn in careful, straight lines the plan of a tree garden in the proximity of water and some architectural structures and walls. It has been suggested, probably rightly, that the architectural structures on this board were parts of a sanctuary or sacred processional kiosk. But a plan for a royal garden would presumably not have looked much different. In fact, the very uncertainty as to whether we are seeing a sanctuary or part of a palace underlines the fact that the affirmation of life gained through gardens and pools was a feature shared by sanctuaries (temples and tombs) and palaces in ancient Egypt. The ancient plan demonstrates the care taken by Egyptians in laying out such gardens, and their essentially formal character. We are firmly reminded by this plan's ordered structure that the ultimate function of all the vivid depictions of nature in the palaces as well as the real plants, trees and animals in their gardens and parklands was to confirm the pharaoh and his people in the conviction that human beings can indeed control the world. Through the ages this has been a belief, albeit illusionary, of palace builders and landscape architects, but it has also been, then and later, the source of much beautiful art.

Bibliography
General: Badawy 1968, pp. 26–55; Uphill 1972; Arnold 1982; Stadelmann 2001. *Temple palaces*: Stadelmann 1973. *Amarna representations of palaces*: Davies 1903, pls. 18, 26; Davies 1906, pl. 8 (with lake); Davies 1908, pls. 4, 17. *Furniture of Queen Hetepheres*: G.A. Reisner 1955, pp. 23–35, pls. 5b, 26, 28, 29. *Harim*: Reiser 1972; Robins 1993, pp. 39–40, 120. *Story from Papyrus Westcar*: Parkinson 1997, pp. 102–127, passage here quoted: pp. 109–110. *Palaces and Amarna private houses*: Ricke 1932, pp. 58–63. *Palace administration*: Helck 1958, pp. 252–268. *Amarna "great palace" and "king's house"*: Pendlebury 1951, pls. 13A–16. *Palace of governors of Dakhla Oasis*: Soukiassian, Wuttmann, Schaad 1990, pp. 348–350 with plan on p. 351; Soukiassian 1997; Cherpion 1999, p. 95, fig. 2b. *Palace of a govenor of the eastern Delta, Bubastis*: van Siclen III 1996. *Palace of a local ruler, Tell el-Dab'a*: Eigner 1996. *Palace of the mayor of Wah-sut, Abydos*: Wegner 2001. *Location of administrative buildings and workshops at el-Amarna*: Kemp, Garfi 1993. *Palace and city of Piramesse*: Dorner 1999, pp. 77–83 with map 2. *Sinuhe text*: Parkinson 1997, p. 40. *Medinet Habu palace*: Hölscher 1941, pp. 37–59. *Palace of Merenptah at Memphis*: O'Connor 1991, pp. 167–190. *"Throne of Horus" text*: Neferhotep Stele: Breasted 1906, pp. 332–337, this translation by James P. Allen. *Qantir dais*: Hayes 1937. *Palaces of Deir el-Ballas*: Lacovara 1996. *Palace on platform at Tell el-Dab'a*: Jánosi 1996. *Palace wall at Hierakonpolis*: Weeks 1971–1972, fig. 13. *Medinet Habu walls and fortified gates*: Hölscher 1951, pp. 1–13 (quote on p. 11). *Reliefs in Medinet Habu gates*: Epigraphic Survey 1970, especially pls. 630–654. *"History as a Celebration"*: Hornung 1966. *Metjen inscription*: Translation by J.P. Allen in: Arnold, Ziegler 1999, p. 213 no. 7. *Malkata*: O'Connor 1980; Iida *et alii*1993 (in Japanese with English captions, abstract and extensive bibliography). *Woman in Malkata painting*: Tytus 1903, p. 17, fig. 10. *Parkland sanctuaries at el-Amarna*: Kemp 1995B. *Paintings in palaces at el-Amarna*: Kemp, Weatherhead 2000.

The Royal Tombs

The onset of the New Kingdom brought about radical changes in the conception of Egyptian royal tombs. The form of the pyramid with its cult structures was abandoned in favor of royal rock-cut tombs, with a completely new kind of decoration. At the same time the spaces reserved for burial and for cult purposes were separated. The temples for the permanent cult of the dead kings, also dedicated to the cult of the god Amun, stood on the edge of the fertile land of west Thebes, while their tombs were hollowed out of the limestone in the isolated valley of the Western Desert called the Valley of the Kings.

Two principles above all were influential for the further development of the royal tomb:

1) A kind of "escalation" which led to the constant enlargement of the tombs and extension of their decoration. The pharaohs vied with each other in magnificence, each attempting to outdo his predecessor in both his tomb and the important temple attached to it, thus "extending the borders of Egypt." Even Rameses I, who ruled for little more than a year, felt obliged to incorporate a series of new motifs in the decoration of his very limited tomb.

2) The strictly hierarchical layout of the tombs, with the royal tomb uppermost, the tombs of queens and princes in the second rank and those of non-royal members of the court in the third. This hierarchy extended to the form and plan of the tombs, as well as their size and decoration. Thus a small number of court officials were buried in the Valley of the Kings, but only in very modest shaft tombs, entirely unadorned and with wooden coffins in place of sarcophagi. Members of the royal household (such as Yuya and Tuyu, the parents-in-law of Amenhotep III) were given only plain corridor tombs, again undecorated. Columns with a diameter of two cubits (= 1.05 meters) are met with only in true royal tombs, while those in other tombs are conspicuously smaller in diameter. In the later 18th Dynasty "royal" measurements of 5 x 5 cubits were also developed for the height and width of the corridors.

The rhythmical alternation of stairways and corridors were features of royal rock-cut tomb building from the outset, while the use of two pillared halls and a shaft before the upper chamber became established from the reign of Thutmose III. Whereas the Middle Kingdom had no specific royal decoration, the New Kingdom once again built up a corpus of religious texts which were destined exclusively for royal use with only a very few exceptions. In contrast to the Pyramid and Coffin Texts of earlier times, these so-called "Books of the Afterlife" were richly illustrated, thus accounting for the particular attractiveness of the tomb decorations in the Valley of the Kings.

The earliest royal rock-cut tombs were very modest affairs at first, but were gradually expanded from reign to reign, irrespective of the length of the reign itself. The curved or bent axis typical of the later Middle Kingdom reappeared, the straight axis being restored only by Akhenaten. The adornment of the tombs was initially concentrated on the burial chamber: until Amenhotep III its walls depicted the *Amduat* with its description of the underworld. The earliest complete examples to have survived are in the tombs of Thutmose III and his vizier Useramun. The book narrates the nightly journey of the sun-god through the "hidden space" of the underworld, divided into twelve parts by the twelve hours of the night.

Another key subject in the decoration is the depiction of the pharaoh before the gods who were crucial in determining his fate in the afterlife: next to Osiris, ruler of the dead, we see Hathor, goddess of regeneration, and Anubis, who is responsible for mummification and in general for the continued existence of the body. These scenes that record the entry of the pharaoh into the world of the gods are usually found on the pillars of the burial chamber, although later they may also appear in the shaft and antechamber.

Amenhotep II split the burial chamber in two. The resulting six pillars in the first section are painted with scenes showing the king before Osiris, Anubis and Hathor. In the second, furthermost section stands the sarcophagus, while the walls of the whole chamber are once again decorated with the *Amduat*. This is missing, however, in the case of Thutmose IV, whose artists painted only the walls of the shaft and antechamber with divine scenes. However he added to the plan a further stairway and the antechamber between the two pillared chambers, increasing the total of passages from seven to nine.

With Amenhotep III we find the first instance of shaft, antechamber and sarcophagus chamber, together with their pillars, being completely decorated: the pictorial program is now extended around Nut, goddess of the sky, and the goddess of the "West," in other words

1. Wall-painting with monkeys, New Kingdom, 18th Dynasty. Valley of the Kings, tomb of Tutankhamun.
Leiden, Rijksmuseum Van Oudheden

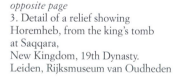

2. Burial chamber and sarcophagus of Pharaoh Tutankhamun. Valley of the Kings, tomb of Tutankhamun

around the personifications of the two spheres of the afterlife to which the dead pharaoh belongs. The plan also includes several rooms behind the sarcophagus chamber.

The subsequent Amarna period brought the religious revolution of Akhenaten and with it a crisis in beliefs about the afterlife that also interrupted the development of royal tombs. Akhenaten himself laid out his rock-cut tomb in el-Amarna as a family tomb, foregoing the customary decorative scheme. His successors Tutankhamun and Ay sought to work out a new conception, blending previous decorative elements with motifs from the tombs of court officials; their tombs are thus much shortened, lacking pillars and royal dimensions, and concentrated on the sarcophagus chamber and its offerings, which in the case of Tutankhamun have survived in all their splendor.

Only with Horemheb was there a return to the earlier line of development, clearly evoking Amenhotep III in the architecture, the axis being slightly displaced, but not bent. Horemheb once again decorated shaft and antechamber with scenes of the gods, including several deities that had not previously been portrayed—above all Horus-Son-of-Isis, Isis herself, and the Memphite gods Ptah and Nefertem. For the first time, there also appeared the goddess Maat in the entrance to the sarcophagus chamber personifying Order, Law and Harmony. Her portrayal was to become increasingly important under Sety I and his successors. One important innovation was the introduction of a painted raised relief, a technique which had been developed in tombs for court officials since Amenhotep III, in particular the new necropolis for nobles and courtiers at Saqqara, where Horemheb had had his own tomb prepared before his accession to the throne. In the sarcophagus chamber, the *Amduat* was now replaced by a new book of the underworld, the *Book of Gates*, again describing the nightly passage of the sun through the underworld in twelve night hours.

Initially, Sety I followed the example of Horemheb in his plan, before deciding on a totally new concept which was decisive for further developments until the end of the New Kingdom. Not only the prominent areas, but all the walls and pillars were now decorated with painted raised reliefs, while the ceilings were painted with stars, and there were astronomical scenes above the sarcophagus itself. Since the resulting decorated surface was far more extensive, the pictorial program could be expanded accordingly. Several books of the un-

opposite page
3. Detail of a relief showing Horemheb, from the king's tomb at Saqqara,
New Kingdom, 19th Dynasty.
Leiden, Rijksmuseum van Oudheden

derworld and related texts were included: the "opening of the mouth" ritual, the "astronomical ceiling" in the sarcophagus chamber and a wealth of portrayals of the gods. Henceforth, certain objects of the burial equipment were also depicted on the walls, which had long been a common practice in the tombs of officials and on sarcophagi.

With the *Litany of Ra* in the first two corridors, and the subsequent depiction of hours from the *Amduat* and the *Book of Gates* spread throughout the tomb, the dead pharaoh was now involved from the start in the nocturnal journey of the sun, automatically rejuvenated and renewed by daily regeneration in the depths of the underworld and the primordial waters of Nun. Through the *Litany of Ra* the pharaoh was identified with the sun-god Ra and his course: the first scene of the tomb decoration shows him in prayer before the falcon-headed Ra-Horakhty, who promises the fullness of time to his reign. On the rear wall of the first pillared hall, the king is led by Horus before the enthroned Osiris, ruler of the dead, into whose identity he now enters. The third deity to receive him, at the entrance to the lower half of the tomb, is Hathor, who represents all the aspects of regeneration. The clothing of the goddess bears hieroglyphs wishing the king millions of *sed* festivals, so that his constant renewal, as invoked by such "jubilees," is prolonged into the afterlife.

Subsequent tombs tended to follow the example set by Sety I—so much so, indeed, that we can reconstruct some of the destroyed parts of the tomb of Sety himself from parallels with the tombs of his successors. Only after Rameses II was there again a fundamental innovation in tomb conception. Rameses II reshaped the sarcophagus chamber, giving it eight pillars and a deeper-lying central nave for the sarcophagus. There was a further important innovation in the antechamber: here, in addition to the previous scenes of gods, Spell 125 of the Book of the Dead was used together with the depiction of the judgment of the dead, as found in earlier courtiers' tombs. Under Merenptah the judgment scene disappeared once more, but the pleading before the judges of the dead, which the pharaoh himself had to face, continued until Rameses VI. The façade of the tomb was also decorated and, from the end of the 19th Dynasty, the scenes depicted became increasingly representative: the entrance and the inner chambers were closed off by large wooden doors. From the time of Sety II the tombs descended less steeply into the ground while after Saptah there were no longer stairways of any kind.

For Nefertari, the favorite queen of Rameses II, the often only hinted at hierarchical gradation became clearly stated. The decoration of her tomb in the Valley of the Queens is clearly dependent on the new concept of royal tomb as realized for Sety I and Rameses II. The layout of the sarcophagus chamber follows the innovations of Rameses II, but has only half the number of pillars and is smaller than the royal dimensions. Like the pharaoh, the queen appears before several deities, but her wish is not to rule in the world beyond, as in royal tombs, but to be admitted to and cared for in the afterlife.

Nefertari adopted the star-bedecked ceilings of royal tombs, but had no truly royal texts, although she came as close as she could. For her burial chamber she used the spells on the gates from the Book of the Dead, instead of the *Book of Gates* itself, and for a side chamber a scene with the Hathor-cow in the western mountains instead of the *Book of the Heavenly Cow*. The "unified" image of the king and Osiris in a single figure (with the mummy figure of Osiris and the ram's head of the night-time sun) illustrates a central message of the royal *Litany of Ra*, while the prominence of the goddess Maat in Nefertari's tomb reflects her growing importance in royal tombs—from Sety I she appears in virtually all corridors and from Rameses II she is also shown at the entrance to the tomb, with protective wings. In tomb KV5, a polytaph or collective tomb for the numerous sons of Rameses II, decoration was used for the first time in a princely tomb, as was later the case for the sons of Rameses III (KV3) and Rameses IX (KV19).

The tomb of Queen Tausret (KV14) of the late 19th Dynasty is a special case, since it was begun for a queen but completed as a tomb for a king, after the queen became the reigning pharaoh following the death of her son Saptah. The layout avoids royal elements entirely until the first pillared hall, tending to follow the examples of the Valley of the Queens; but the decoration of the pillared hall is entirely in keeping with a royal tomb, featuring the *Book of Gates*, an "astronomical ceiling" and deities on the pillars. As in the earlier case of Merenptah, motifs from the *Book of Caverns* and the *Book of the Earth* are also included. The dimensions, on the other hand, are still far from the royal scale, which is reached only beyond this hall. A second hall was initially planned as a royal burial chamber but never finished.

Under Rameses III at the outset of the 20th Dynasty, the systematic expansion of the ground plan and decorative scheme reached its apogee: the "escalation" in the magnificence of tombs had reached its limit. His successor Rameses IV forewent pillars, shaft, side chambers and part of the previously established decoration (above all the scenes of the gods), but nonetheless once again increased the height and width of the corridors (from 5 by 5 to 6 by 6 cubits) and the royal sarcophagus.

Rameses VI took over a tomb that had been begun by his predecessor, enabling him almost to finish another imposing monument—with a nearly complete set of the major "books of the netherworld"—despite his relatively short reign of some seven to eight years. The effort to bring the journey of the sun into the tomb and involve the king is here once again particularly clear: the *Book of Gates* and *Book of Caverns* make up two complete cycles which unfold from the entrance to the rear wall of the first pillared hall, accompanied by the *Books of the Heavens* on the ceilings. With the *Amduat* and the new *Book of the Earth* in the sarcophagus chamber, the second part of the tomb has two further cycles of the nightly journey of the sun, again combined with the *Books of the Heavens*.

After Rameses VI there began a concluding phase in the Valley of the Kings, during which only Rameses IX produced a more richly conceived tomb. He was also the last pharaoh that was actually buried there as far as we know, since there is much evidence to suggest that the last two kings of the 20th Dynasty, Rameses X and XI, were laid to rest in the north of the country, at the new residence in the eastern Delta called Piramesse. Nonetheless, tombs were prepared for them in the Valley of the Kings (featuring a gigantic shaft in the case of Rameses XI), though work on their decoration was soon abandoned. The Amun priests of the 21st Dynasty brought tomb-building to an abrupt end, removing the royal mummies to two collective caches. Rather earlier, the new royal necropolis had already been transferred from Piramesse to nearby Tanis. This new necropolis at Tanis has been known to scholars since 1939. Situated in the southwestern corner of the precinct of the great temple of Amun, it has seven tombs from the 21st and 22nd Dynasties, in which princes and high-ranking officials were buried alongside kings. Only three of the tombs were decorated. The two largest belonged to Psusennes I from the 21st and Osorkon II from the 22nd Dynasty and were both conceived as family tombs with a number of chambers, while the remaining tombs all had a single chamber. The rich treasure of Psusennes' tomb survived intact, as did, in large part, that of Osorkon II. Both tombs were decorated with reliefs inspired by New Kingdom models, featuring motifs from the Book of the Dead, the "opening of the mouth" ceremony, hymns to Amun-Ra and his Triad, while for Osorkon there were also excerpts from the "books of the netherworld" (*Amduat, Book of the Earth*) and the *Books of the Heavens*.

The "god's wives of Amun" ruled over Upper Egypt as representatives of the king from around 750 until the Persian conquest in 525 BC. Along with many other royal prerogatives, they took over the contemporary form of the royal tomb in the temple precinct. These tomb buildings have been well preserved above ground in the forecourt at Medinet Habu, the mortuary temple of Rameses III. They did not, however, use the funerary royal texts that we find at Tanis. On the other hand, a fragment recently acquired by the Louvre shows that the *Amduat* was used again in the royal tombs of the 26th Dynasty in Sais; until now this later royal necropolis had been known only from Herodotus' account of it. Further royal burials in the temple precinct have been ascertained only at Mendes for the 29th Dynasty and at the Siwa Oasis for local "kings" in the 30th Dynasty, but the burial sites of the Ptolemaic dynasty probably continued in Alexandria.

The planning of a royal tomb probably began immediately after the accession to the throne of the new ruler. The site for the new tomb was located in the first year of the reign. In the late 19th Dynasty, work on the tomb often began within months of the start of the reign; the project also had to be completed within a matter of years. The design embraced not only the architecture and the decoration of the tomb, but also the sarcophagus and the required burial outfit, which had to be ready for the burial ceremony. After the king's funeral his tomb was sealed and subsequently only opened for inspections. The rites of the dead were performed in parts of the temple set aside for that purpose.

following pages
4. Aerial view of the Valley of the Kings

We can only suppose that the designs were the responsibility of the highest-ranking court officials, together with a number of specialists; we do not know whether the king was involved in the process. Control over the work as it progressed lay with two overseers and a series of scribes; there were also occasional inspections carried out by the nominally most senior official, the vizier, who also supervised the ceremony at royal burials. The king never entered his tomb in his own lifetime and was not present at the funeral of his predecessor.

Plans were drawn up for the design and its execution, and a number of these have been preserved, such as the Turin papyrus for the tomb of Rameses IV, complete with a scale of measurements. Given the ever-growing number of tombs, it became increasingly difficult to avoid encroaching on earlier excavation work: there were a number of instances of collisions with earlier tombs, as in the case of Saptah, Rameses III and Rameses VI.

The mummy of the king was itself the most significant content of the tomb. From the 3rd Dynasty on, it was laid in a stone sarcophagus, though given further protection by several wooden coffins. In the 18th Dynasty a "solar" stone was chosen for the king's sarcophagus, either quartzite or granite, thereby underlining once again his identification with the sun-god; in the 19th Dynasty, we also find outer sarcophagi of granite and inner ones of alabaster. In this period, under Sety I, there was also a fundamental change in the decoration: Anubis and the Sons of Horus as guardian gods were replaced by the "books of the netherworld" and spells from the Book of the Dead. In the tomb of Tutankhamun, four gilt wooden shrines, decorated with religious scenes and texts, were also found surrounding the sarcophagus; how-

5. Nefertari playing a game of *senet*, wall-painting from the tomb of Nefertari in the Valley of the Queens

following pages
6. View of the tomb of Rameses VI
with the remains of the king's
granite sarcophagus,
New Kingdom, 20th Dynasty.
Valley of the Kings,
tomb of Rameses VI

ever the tomb plan of Rameses IV now in Turin shows that similar shrines existed in other royal tombs, too.

While only a few fragments of mummies remained in the pyramids of the Old Kingdom, the mummified bodies of the majority of the pharaohs of the New Kingdom have survived. After being moved several times during the 21st Dynasty by the Amun priesthood, the royal mummies found their last resting place in two underground caches. The larger of these occupied an older tomb in the vicinity of the temple of Hatshepsut in Deir el-Bahri, while a smaller group of mummies remained in the tomb of Amenhotep II (KV35), where they were discovered by Victor Loret in 1898; later the mummy of Tutankhamun was also found. The cache in Deir el-Bahri was discovered by local people in 1881, its contents were removed and taken to the Cairo Museum. There the mummies were unwrapped and underwent a scientific investigation whose main focus was to ascertain the pharaohs' age at death and the presence of signs of disease. Determining the age of royal mummies could be a vital tool for resolving chronological and genealogical questions, but so far the techniques used have not been sufficiently accurate. An additional problem is that during the many removals, coffins and inscriptions were exchanged, so that the identification of many of the kings' mummies is by no means certain.

During the embalming process the internal organs (except for the heart and kidneys) were removed from the body and preserved in four stone vessels called canopic jars, kept in a canopic chest. From the time of Amenhotep II four goddesses stood guard over the chest, while the jars themselves were consigned to the protection of the four Sons of Horus.

After death the pharaoh (like all the dead) required a wealth of burial outfits to grant him care, assistance and protection in the afterlife. Since other burial sites were looted of all or most of their contents, it is the complete treasure found in the tomb of Tutankhamun which allows us to clearly grasp the sheer abundance and variety of royal tomb goods. These included various foodstuffs and beverages in inscribed jars, chests with fabrics and complete sets of clothing, wigs, sandals and even gloves (for the king to drive his chariot), furniture of all kinds, from the simple stool to the three stately beds decorated with animal heads, which were also depicted, at least, in the tomb of Sety I. There were ornate lamps and weapons, to fend off darkness and enemies. Staves and scepters symbolized power, but there were no kingly crowns.

By ancient tradition there were numerous boats to facilitate the journey into the afterlife, already found in the very earliest burials; in the New Kingdom these were complemented by richly decorated chariots. Cosmetic items such as oils, ointments, eye makeup, mirrors, combs, razors, etc. intended to ensure that the living freshness of the king be maintained or restored. Objects for the "opening of the mouth" ritual were provided, to enable him to recover the use of his sense organs. Board games worked out a symbolic path through the netherworld, while musical instruments like those used in religious ceremonies propitiated the gods and the hoped-for regeneration.

The burial treasure of Tutankhamun included lavishly gilded wooden statuettes of gods, some of which portrayed very particular deities and sacred animals, thus completing the pictorial program on the walls and strengthening the divine presence in the tomb. Sety II had such figures painted on the walls of his antechamber in place of real statues. They include figures of the king himself with his insignia, above all the still mysterious motif of the king atop a panther. Stone statues were not placed in royal tombs, but stood in the temples dedicated to the on-going funeral cult of the pharaoh.

The burial treasure of many kings and courtiers of the New Kingdom included the so-called *shabti*s—small mummiform figures of the dead which were at once effigies and servants, intended to perform any labors that might be required in the afterlife, such as the irrigation, clearing and manuring of fields. Made from a great variety of materials (wood, stone, faience, even bronze), they have been found by the hundreds in the royal tombs, one or even two obviously being provided for every day of the year. They were especially numerous and well-preserved in the tombs of Tutankhamun and Sety I.

Spells from the Book of the Dead point to the significance of certain amulets, so it is far from surprising that tomb treasures included many amulets, often, in the case of royal burials, made from the most precious materials. Some were wrapped into the mummy bandages, ensur-

7. Painted limestone relief showing
Sety and Hathor, from the tomb
of Sety I in the Valley of the Kings,
New Kingdom, 19th Dynasty.
Paris, Musée du Louvre

8. Alabaster ointment jar in the shape of a lion, New Kingdom, 18th Dynasty.
Valley of the Kings, tomb of Tutankhamun

9. Lid of a canopic jar from the tomb of Tutankhamun, painted alabaster, New Kingdom, 18th Dynasty.
Cairo, Egyptian Museum

ing the closest possible contact with the dead body. The preferred and most common types were the *ankh*, or the symbol of life, and the *djed (Tet)* pillar sign which symbolized duration and stability. The *wedjat* eye, believed in myth to be restored whenever damaged, was also popular, symbolizing the regeneration of the sun and the deceased alike.

The most popular amulet of all, however, was the scarab beetle, which embodied the rejuvenated, renewed sun and thus became the most powerful symbol of rebirth, new life and regeneration. The scarab was usually the centerpiece of the pectoral, as in the famous examples preserved in the burial treasures of Tutankhamun and Psusennes I. Its worship by Isis and Nephthys suggests that during the New Kingdom, Osiris, too, became an aspect of the sun-god, who now universally guaranteed that the pharaoh would live on in the hereafter.

Bibliography
Thomas 1966; Abitz 1995; Reeves, Wilkinson 1996; Hornung 1999; Weeks 2001.

The Space-Time of Night

The daily disappearance of the stars was a mystery to the Egyptians. As they reappeared in perfectly regular order on the other side of the earth, their period of invisibility was conceived of as a voyage through an inaccessible space, to be described only through images which took into account two phenomena. Take, for example, the sun: it appeared to get weaker at the end of each day, and its setting might well be compared to a death. When it touched the horizon, the star seemed to be disappearing beyond the limits of the world, sinking into an invisible realm. However, each morning it rose again, recharged with an energy and power that it poured out over the world. Hence, the domain passed through during the night was the locus of both displacement and regeneration.

To render these two observations in a symbolic fashion, the Egyptians drew on the models and images that were part of their daily life. As they lived on the banks of the Nile, it was the river that represented the most obvious means of communication, and a boat the most obvious means of transport from one place to another. This is why in the Valley of the Kings, the sun is depicted in a boat that passes along an imaginary waterway. The journey of the sun is rendered in simple images that do not aim to offer a scientific explanation of its daily disappearance, but merely acknowledge the existence of such a phenomenon.

The second aspect of the sun's nocturnal voyage to be rendered was the notion that it rose again rejuvenated. Here, the Egyptians borrowed various images from nature. Looking to the animal world, they compared the disappearance of the sun to a period of gestation; hence, the space in which this occurs was conceived of as a womb, and the divine power embodied therein as a female deity. Turning toward the plant world, the sun's period in the earth could be compared to that of a seed, from which a new shoot then arises. In this case, the deity which personified the phenomenon was Osiris, who represented the great mystery of life's perpetual rebirth. "Death" here is nothing but an apparent hibernation that is the prelude to the appearance of a new existence. In order to be reborn, the sun each evening follows the same fate as Osiris; in its voyage through the night, it is assimilated to the god of perpetual renewal, undergoing all the metamorphoses that will make its regeneration possible.

This temporary fusion of sun and Osiris was made possible by the idea that the Egyptians had of the spiritual part of any individual, be they mortal or divine. The *ba* represented the dynamic component of a personality which made it possible to move into the afterlife, but also to communicate and change. In written script, the ideogram for the *ba* could be the icon of the ram. This is why, in the Valley of the Kings, the solar god appears as a ram-headed figure. The image, to be read as a hieroglyph, refers to the union of the *ba* of Osiris and that of Ra. During the night, the sun—Osiris-like—is led from apparent death to a new existence.

The Litany of Ra

The compilations unearthed in the Valley of the Kings have only rarely maintained their original title; usually they are known by the names that Egyptologists have given them. The ancient name for the so-called *Litany of Ra* was, in fact, "The Book to adore Ra in the West." The introductory vignette to this text is divided into three parts: At the center, the ram-headed man, a representation of the sun at night, is accompanied by a scarab, which is both symbol and hieroglyph for the general concept of "becoming." Here, it expresses the passage of the primordial force of the creator into an active, visible state. When Atum, the demiurge, undertook to create the universe, he took on the form of the sun, whose rays drove off the shadows of chaos. The coleopteran beetle serves to announce the permanent triumph of the sun at dawn. In the two other parts of the vignette there is a serpent and a crocodile, images representing the dark powers present in land and water respectively. Shifted away from the center of the picture, over which flows the power of the sun, these two seem to have been pushed aside by the light. Two hartebeest heads mark the boundary between the real world and the netherworld.

The so-called *Litany of Ra* proper is a list of the seventy-five forms of the sun itself (fig. 3). In reciting them, the dead king gradually identified himself with the god-star, and at the same time moved toward the reconstitution of the divine entity. Indeed, the forces of the solar demiurge must be scattered across the universe if they are to engender creation; and therefore,

1. Papyrus of the *Amduat*, New Kingdom, 20th Dynasty. Berlin, Ägyptisches Museum und Papyrussammlung *cat. 236*

if this process is to be repeated daily, they must first be gathered together again. One finds the same phenomenon in the myth of Osiris, whose body had been torn to shreds that were then scattered throughout Egypt; the reassembly of his divine cadaver reestablished his unity and thence brought him back to an active state. The similarity in fate here certainly facilitated the fusion of the two gods in an account of the permanent renewal of creation.

The Book of Amduat

The oldest description in the Valley of the Kings regarding the nocturnal voyage of the sun was *The Book of the Hidden Chamber* (the chamber in question being the underground abode where divine metamorphoses—and the metamorphosis of Osiris in particular—took place); its present name is due to Gaston Maspero, and is based on one of the Egyptian terms for the netherworld, *dwat*. The text appears for the first time in the tomb of the vizier Useramun, a high functionary during the reigns of Hatshepsut and Thutmose III. However, its full form would only come in royal tombs, though thereafter—in the Third Intermediate Period—it might well be written out on papyri that accompanied normal individuals beyond the grave.

The most complete form of the *Book of the Hidden Chamber*, or the *Amduat*, is to be found in the funerary chambers of Thutmose III and Amenhotep II. In what seems like an enormous papyrus unfurled across the walls of the chamber, the composition relates the twelve hours of the nocturnal journey of the sun. During this voyage, the god gradually rebuilds his strength, helped by various entities which are distributed along the banks of the imaginary river. Certain of these figures are shown in the leotard that identifies them as the avatars of Osiris; others bear easily recognizable insignia of royalty, such as crowns and scepters—thus associating the fate of the dead sovereign with the process that enables the sun to regenerate itself. In fact, at the moment of his burial, the king, too, blends his fate with Osiris and becomes part of life's permanent cycle of renewal.

Various sections represent crucial stages in the journey. In the fourth hour (fig. 5), the

2. The *Litany of Ra* from the tomb of Merenptah, New Kingdom, 19th Dynasty.
Valley of the Kings, tomb KV8

3. The *Litany of Ra* from the tomb of Thutmose III, New Kingdom, 18th Dynasty.
Valley of the Kings, tomb KV34

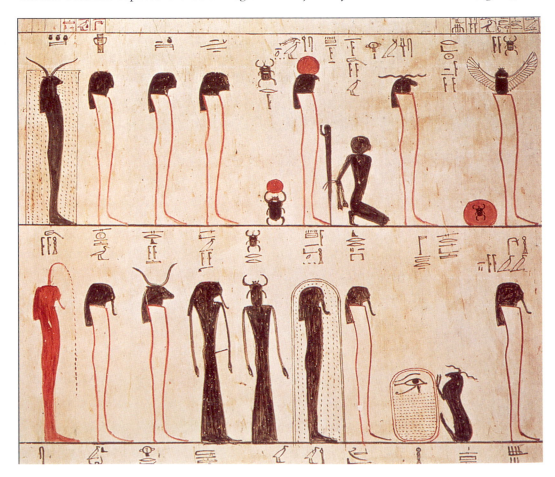

cortege of the sun approaches the most intimate regions of the netherworld, the crucible of the great mystery behind the perpetual renewal of life. The most secret area of the *dwat* is dedicated to the god Sokar, who embodied the process of royal rebirth from generation to generation since the earliest days of antiquity. The space dedicated to this key moment is divided by a barrier that runs through its three sections. In the middle is a portal, through whose open door the divine boat will be able to reach the deepest part of the earth.

At the heart of the fifth section of the *dwat*, a hillock shelters the locus of supreme mystery (fig. 6). The text here tells us that one is at the end point of the created world, beyond which reign the dense shadows of chaos. The hillock represents both the tomb itself and that mound which was the basis from which the world was created. In both cases, life flows from the knoll that occupies the lower section. The oval that serves as a receptacle for the life to come is flanked by two lion heads which evoke Aker, the divinity that governs the depths of the earth. The head that emerges from here indicates that this space is personified, assimilated to the body of Osiris himself, of whom Sokar is only a manifestation. At the edge of the upper section, a scarab heralds the final transformation that, at the end of the voyage, will enable the solar deity to regain his visible form and his active strength. Finally, above, there is a sandy hillock flanked by two birds; this scene recalls the tomb of Osiris and the form taken by Isis and Nephthys when mourning for their brother. Having gone beyond this end point, the solar boat seems to undertake a slow climb toward the horizon. At the seventh hour (fig. 7) the forces of chaos are placed in check. The upper section contains the traditional image of the enemies of Egypt, used over and over again in all places where there are representations of the power of the pharaoh and the universal domination of divine order that he embodies. The magical power of the image is believed to check the negative power embodied in all adversaries of cosmic harmony. More mythological in content, the middle section here reveals the same unfailing concern for defusing the power of anything that might interfere with the smooth functioning of life's cycles of renewal. Even if the real enemies of Egypt are well known, and concrete depictions of them are used in magical practices designed to conjure

4. Papyrus of the *Amduat*, New Kingdom, 20th Dynasty. Berlin, Ägyptisches Museum und Papyrussammlung *cat. 236*

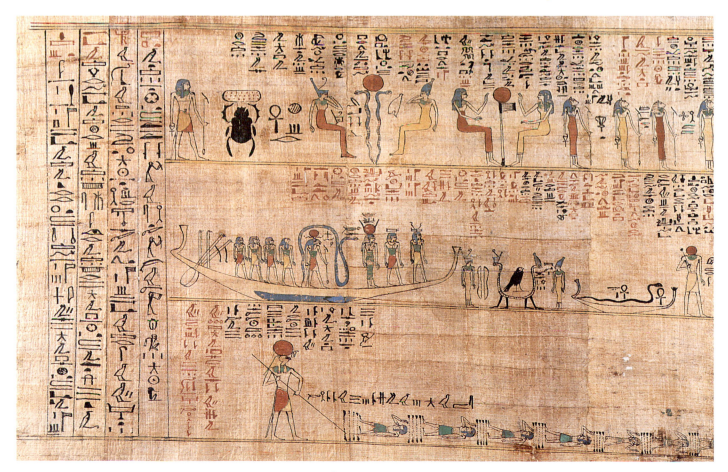

5. Fourth Hour in the book of
Amduat, tomb of Thutmose III,
New Kingdom, 18th Dynasty.
Valley of the Kings, tomb KV34

6. Fifth Hour in the book of
Amduat, tomb of Thutmose III,
New Kingdom, 18th Dynasty.
Valley of the Kings, tomb KV34

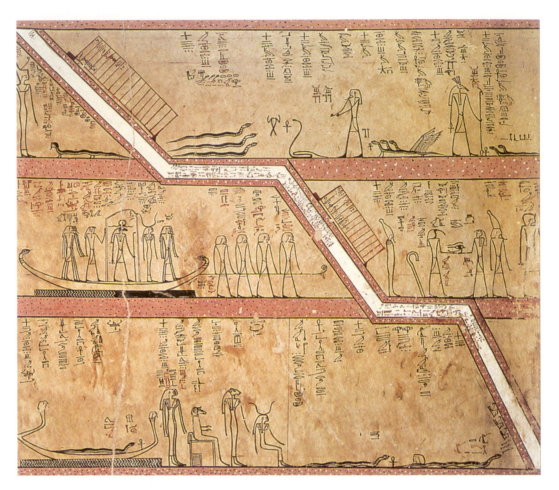

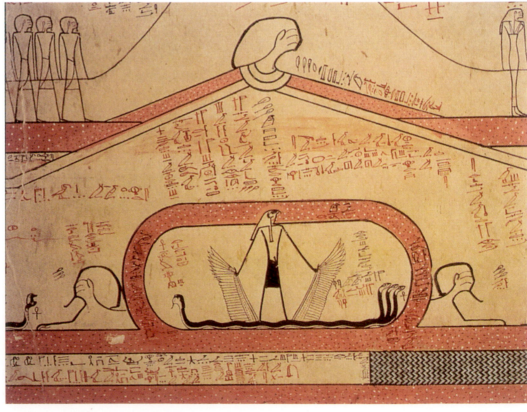

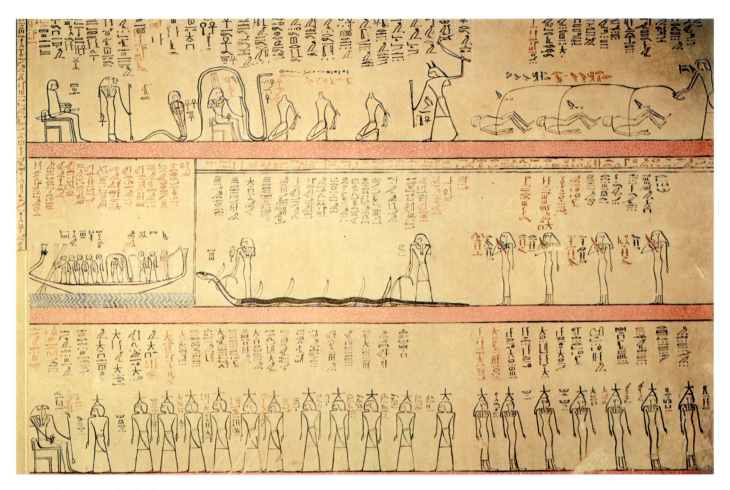

7. Seventh Hour in the book of *Amduat*, tomb of Thutmose III, New Kingdom, 18th Dynasty. Valley of the Kings, tomb KV34

away the threat they pose, those depictions cannot be used to represent the ineffable forces at work in the invisible world of the gods. The interruption of the journey of the sun would mean the annihilation of the world, and the forces of darkness that might hinder that voyage are embodied in a serpent, Apophis, whose undulating body recalls those sandbanks which posed a danger to boats as the Nile flood receded. Here, the gods render this malefic reptile harmless. However, just like their positive counterparts, the forces of destruction are always at work; they can never be destroyed but only momentarily neutralized.

The triumph of the reborn sun unfolds in the frame of the twelfth hour of the *dwat* (fig. 8). At the end of its journey of regeneration, the creating sun is on the point of taking on visible form once more, and manifesting itself to the world. This passage from a passive, invisible state to a glorious state of existence is embodied by Khepri, shown as a scarab. In the lower section, the mummy evokes the chrysalis of Osiris, which is the very crucible within which this mysterious alchemy of renewal has been played out; provisionally abandoned by the god at the point of his rebirth, it will nevertheless once more have a role to play when he returns to the netherworld at the setting of the sun.

Later, when the pharaohs had their hypogea decorated with other theological compositions, the book of *Amduat* was never completely abandoned; the essential hours—those that describe the arrival in the abode of Sokar—would always appear in a prominent place in the corridors of their tombs.

The Royal Tomb of el-Amarna

During the 18th Dynasty, Amenhotep IV/Akhenaten would, during the so-called "Amarna period," champion a profound change in religious iconography and in the very concept of the plurality of divine forms. This is not the place to go into the theological debates and concerns of that era; suffice to point out that Aten—the sun-disk—was considered the sole visible form of the divine, and the only image used in religious worship. The multiplicity of cre-

8. Twelfth Hour in the book of
Amduat, tomb of Thutmose III,
New Kingdom, 18th Dynasty.
Valley of the Kings, tomb KV34

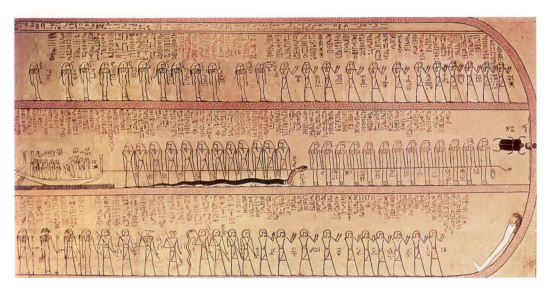

ative functions that had before been embodied in the gods was now concentrated in the person of the pharaoh himself and his wife. The ruling couple were the agents for the earthly diffusion of the forces of life emanating from the sun.

Contrary to what is often claimed, the tombs of the pharaoh and court dignitaries at Tell el-Amarna in no way reveal a lack of interest in the other world. The very existence of the tombs—with their furnishings, *shabti*s, etc.—reveal the presence of a belief in an existence after death. However, it is true that we have very little information on the Amarna concept of the netherworld. The most obvious changes to be noted are in the layout of the tombs (the access corridors are perfectly straight, with multiple chambers suggesting these were envisaged as family tombs) and decor (a shift away from mythological concerns, with an emphasis on the humanity of the king). One of the best-known scenes in this syrinx is the emotionally-powerful depiction of the sorrow felt by the royal couple as they mourn before the body of their dead daughter Meketaten. The innumerable figures of the book of *Amduat* have disappeared.

It would seem to have been Akhenaten's intention to simplify the iconography regarding the active role of the gods and focus on the reigning monarchs as performing the same functions. To give only one example: the goddesses usually shown at the corners of the sarcophagus watching over the body of the dead monarch are replaced by four images of the "great royal wife," who thus takes over fully the role of the female principle of creation.

The Amarna "reform" was short-lived. All it has left us are a few traces regarding the burial rituals intended to facilitate the king's passage into the afterlife, but very little information on what that existence beyond the tomb was like (it is, however, very likely that it reflected contemporary ideas of the divine). Nevertheless, the period left a durable mark on religious thought, and the *Book of Gates*, a Valley of the Kings text which dates from slightly later, reveals the influence of these new ideas.

An Original Decor: the Tombs of Tutankhamun and Ay

Having returned to Thebes—to the very bosom of Amun—Akhenaten's successors once more began to have their tombs built in the Valley of the Kings. As far as the tomb of Tutankhamun is concerned, so much has been said about it that it may appear pointless to return to the subject of a burial place whose furnishings bear witness not only to the magnificence of royal funeral rites but also to the accoutrements of magic that were supposed to be part of the sovereign's final resting-place.

However, what is striking is that the tomb of this young king certainly does not conform to the classical pattern of tombs in the royal necropolis. If it is true that Tutankhamun did die "young," it is also the case that he ruled over Egypt for a dozen or so years. Having quickly returned to Thebes after the abrupt end of the Amarna period, he would have had plenty of time to prepare a tomb that was quite different from the one known to us today. For example, Rameses I, who reigned a few decades later, was on the throne for a total of less than eighteenth months, yet his tomb is much more imposing than that of the pharaoh who restored the worship of Amun. Anxious as he was to show himself as the—albeit indirect—successor to his grandfather, Amenhotep III, one would have expected Tutankhamun to have his tomb dug near that of his ancestor, in the western vale of the Valley of the Kings—the so-called Western Valley or Valley of the Monkeys. Curiously enough, Ay, who succeeded the young king and ruled for just four years, occupies a vast tomb situated in that very valley (though with a long single corridor reminiscent of an Amarna syrinx that is much closer to the hypogea of the beginning of the 18th Dynasty in its general layout).

While still only a high-ranking functionary under Akhenaten, Ay did have an important tomb cut for himself into the rock of Amarna, but then—having remained in the service of Tutankhamun—he, like other figures close to the Crown, was privileged with a tomb in the Valley of the Kings. It is tempting to think that once having ascended to the throne in turn, he actually appropriated the tomb of his predecessor, whom he had buried in a grave more suitable for a private individual, perhaps originally dug for Ay himself. This is only an hypothesis, but it would explain the anomalies in the tomb of this young son of the "heretic" Akhenaten.

Tutankhamun's tomb was completed rather hastily, and only the sarcophagus chamber itself is decorated. The walls show scenes of the royal burial—from the towing of the catafalque to the tomb, up to the ceremony of the "opening of the mouth," which restored to the dead man (and images of the dead man) the use of those senses that had enabled him to communicate with the world of the living. The priest shown awakening the dead king is his successor, Ay, who was far from being a young man at this point yet is depicted as such here; it is also interesting that he is the spitting image of the dead king. There was no family link between the two men, so this concern to twin them off undoubtedly arose from an anxiety to use the magic of iconographical artifice to underline that the new monarch was the legitimate heir—even if the dead man had, in fact, been the last surviving member of the reigning dynasty.

Ay himself would manage to have all of his tomb decorated with an iconographic scheme that contains not only elements from the book of *Amduat* but also some more specific features: For example, the marshland hunting scene is more appropriate to the decor of a private tomb than to that of a sovereign. However, certain wooden statues found in the tomb of Tutankhamun show the king brandishing a harpoon and are a three dimensional rendering of the same theme—that is, the deceased's triumph over the forces of chaos. The depiction of the various stages in the mystical journey of the dead man obviously finds a counterpart in the effigy of the young king shown standing on a feline; associated with arid countries, this animal would carry the deceased beyond the deserts, another area filled with danger.

Above a lintel in his tomb, Ay is depicted as the four Sons of Horus, figures traditionally associated with the preservation of the viscera after death and thus with the deceased's subsequent reacquisition of vital energy. Generally shown with human or animal heads, they are depicted here as kings of Upper and Lower Egypt. Spells 112 and 113 of the Book of the Dead tells us, in fact, that two of these scions of divinity were associated with the Nile valley and two with the Delta. The association with the Sons of Horus is made clear here by the fact that two of these effigies of the dead king wear red crowns, and two white ones.

Though noticeably different from those of the early 18th Dynasty, these tombs are interesting because they were created at a key moment in the development of Egyptian religious ideas, when priests were rethinking their world in response to the notions that had emerged during the Amarna period.

The Book of Gates

These latter reflections are not explicitly expressed in the *Book of Gates*, which—replacing the *Amduat*—appears in the Valley of the Kings as part of the decor of the tomb of Horemheb and the first ruler of the 19th Dynasty, Rameses I. Thereafter, one finds extracts from both books used together, as if to complete each other. During the Ramesside period, other descriptions of the afterlife would emerge; and it was undoubtedly due to lack of space that the two fundamental books of *Amduat* and *Gates* were abridged. A complete text of the *Book of Gates* is to be found in the tomb of Rameses VI.

Like the *Amduat*, the *Book of Gates* is divided into three-level sections that give a general account of the nocturnal journey of the boat of the sun. What is new here is the introduction of a scene of judgment and the use of cryptography (the latter had, however, already been used in the gilded shrines of Tutankhamun). The two scenes at the beginning and end of the solar voyage are also original. In fact, the main characteristic of the *Book of Gates* is the presence of twelve portals, which represent the hours of the night. The *dwat* itself accounts for eleven divisions, with two supplementary scenes that serve as a sort of prologue and conclusion to the description of the solar journey.

The giant portals that punctuate the different stages in the voyage are clearly inspired by an essential feature of Egyptian architecture. Like the gateways in a royal palace or temple, they seem to lead the voyaging sun toward the heart of an architectural space. The end vignettes of the *Book of Gates* refer to the two horizons, hence indicating that the sun progresses from west to east—something which reflects the course followed by all visitors to a sanctuary such as Karnak. The officiating priests must move beyond various gateways before they reach the *naos*, the locus in which the god manifests himself (just as the east is the place where the sun rises).

The portals in the *Book of Gates* serve to enclose the different sections of the *dwat*; they are like so many locks that open up at the passage of the divine cortege to then close hermetically, refusing entrance to intruders. In this way they seem to mark the passage of the hours. One has the impression that these portals depicted on the walls reflect those that—at least in Ramesside tombs—marked out the length of the corridor leading to the burial chamber. Thus, the decor bears out the idea that the tomb itself was conceived as a reflection of the *dwat*. As a matter of fact, the chamber, with its annexes and doorways, was merely an icon, a sort of complex three-dimensional hieroglyph for the netherworld. This use of the burial space to represent both the imaginary geography of the afterlife and the progress of the dead king toward rebirth could already be found in the pyramids of the Old Kingdom.

The introductory scene in the *Book of Gates* shows the entrance into the *dwat*. The solar boat is in the center, about to pass between two hillocks that undoubtedly recall the double mountain used in writing the word "horizon." The first portal is seen as a sort of gateway to the other world, which opens up on the borders of the desert. The gateway is guarded by an immense serpent, whose task is to open the gate at the approach of the sun and his royal suite. When one looks carefully at the sections of the *Book of Gates* one immediately sees a key difference from the *Amduat*: the over ninety figures that appeared in the different levels of the earlier work are here replaced by somber corteges. The participants in the voyage are considered in groups and act collectively. Even the numbers shown have a symbolic meaning: For example, the groups often comprise twelve figures (the temporal divisions of the day or the year), nine (the divine ennead) or four (the directions within the created world).

The same simplification can be seen in the crew of the divine vessel. The nocturnal sun is now accompanied by only two entities: Hu (the creating word) and Sia (divine knowledge). These two were the instruments used by the demiurge in giving birth to the world—either the "First Time" or during the daily renewal of the cosmos. The concerns expressed in the accompanying texts are here much more human in focus than those of the book of *Amduat*. For example, in the section after the third gate, time is symbolized by a serpent enclosing twelve female figures—a personification of the hours, the offspring of the serpent. In fact, the accompanying commentary described these hours as destructive.

The fifth gate opens into a very special space. The gateway itself seems to be extended into a sort of tribunal hall where Osiris presides. This cannot but recall to mind those records we have of royal audiences, with the sovereign seated within the frame of a portal. This scene of judgment is not a common feature of the iconography used in the Valley of the Kings, but seems to be part of the rituals intended for simple mortals (Spell 125 of the Book of the Dead). At the very heart of the necropolis—in a description of the course followed by the sun—there is another expression of this idea that the gods (just like the dead king who is part of their cortege) have to justify their existence.

This is not the place to go into all the subtleties of a text which is full of allusions to the fact that all entities—be they human or divine—are involved in a process of degradation by their passage through the created world. This corruption was considered an inherent part of a material universe that was open to direct assault by chaos; certain elements here would later be developed by the Gnostics. This new conception of the terrestrial world was undoubtedly influenced by Amarna thought, which had perceived nature "as it was." The last image in the *Book of Gates* describes the birth of the sun (fig. 10). Once the gates of the twelfth hour have been closed, the sun takes wing. Isis and Nephthys, in the form of cobras, again evoke the Osirian aspects of the metamorphosis that has just occurred. Just as Atum, the god of origins, distinguished himself from Nun, the primordial liquid, to then beget the universe, so the last stage in the sun's nocturnal journey passes through the waters of rejuvenation. Nun raises the solar vessel to make it reemerge into the world. The scarab Khepri expresses this transformation of the god into a visible active agent. In the upper part, the human body is formed into a loop—a personification of the *dwat*, which also plays a part in bringing this regenerated sun into the world.

The Book of the Heavenly Cow

This important text differs little in content from the accounts of the nocturnal voyage of the sun. However, it focuses on the creation of the world. Its distinguishing feature is the presence of a majestic silhouette of a large celestial cow, symbolizing the womb of the universe that gives birth daily to the world star and to that crowd of the "justified" deceased who accompany it. This text is already to be found on one of the gilded shrines of Tutankhamun, but its best-known version is in the tomb of Sety I.

The mythological tale recounts two essential stages in the creation of Egypt; behind features that seem purely legendary, it offers a broad outline of the pharaonic concept of the universe. When the gods still inhabited the earth, Ra ruled over all creatures. A part of humanity rebelled against his rule and then sought refuge in the desert. The Sun decided to send his daughter, Hathor, in pursuit of them; the goddess is the incarnation of the solar rays that destroy all those who disturb the divine order. Ra greets the success of his daughter by proclaiming how "powerful" she is (in Egyptian *sekhmet*). This word was unfortunate, because the words of the creating sun had a performative force: henceforth Hathor would incarnate the fearful aspects of the divine rays in the form of the goddess Sekhmet; even after the rebels had been defeated, it was impossible to extinguish the murderous rage of those rays, and thus the whole of humanity was threatened. The gods had to use a trick to placate the goddess, who fell drunk after drinking a red beverage she had taken for blood, and thereafter regained

9. Fourth Hour in the *Book of Gates*, tomb of Rameses I, New Kingdom, 19th Dynasty

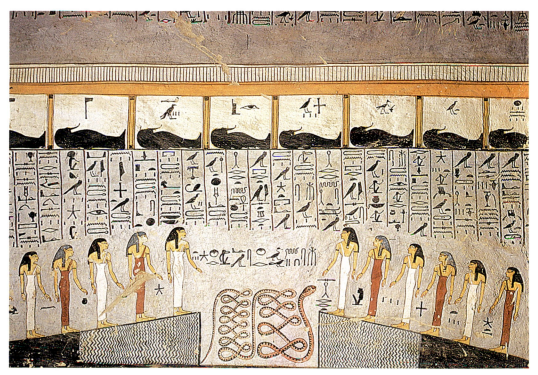

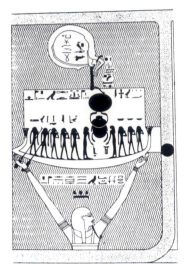

10. Final vignette of the *Book of Gates*: the birth of the sun

her clemency. After having given orders that this event in the foundation of the world be celebrated by human rituals, Ra leaves the earth and retires to heaven on the back of the goddess Nut. The latter takes the form of a cow, with four pairs of different entities bearing her up (two at each hoof), thus assuming the familiar role of the supports on which the heavens rest.

The account of the tribulations caused by Sekhmet—and her subsequent appeasement—served to sanctify a sort of pact that henceforth united men and gods. While it is impossible to exist without the rays of the sun—whose power is felt so clearly—it is equally impossible to survive on the banks of the river without the floods, the first waters of which are made red by the alluvium of the Atbara. The rituals whose origin is described in the text are those actions by means of which mankind can remind the sovereign sun of its clemency. After Ra's departure for lands inaccessible to mortals, the gods leave men to take the fate of the country into their own hands—with the king as their intermediary.

The Book of Caverns

This text appears at the beginning of the Ramesside period, with the first complete version appearing on the cenotaph of Sety I at Abydos, and a passage later occurring in the tomb of Merenptah. The final scene—which is particularly rich in meaning—is to be found not only in the tomb of that king but also in those of Queen Tausret and Rameses III. Subsequently, it would be partially recopied in the royal tombs of the 20th Dynasty, but a—final—complete version of the text is only to be found in the hypogeum of Rameses VI. Like other compositions initially intended solely for the tombs of kings, the *Book of Caverns* would—from the Third Intermediate Period onward—appear (in fragments) on the burial papyri and coffins of court functionaries.

The title of the Egyptian text remains unknown; its present name comes from the fact that it divides the space of the *dwat* into two parts of three sections, each considered to be some sort of cave or grotto. Here again one finds the distribution of divine entities over different distinct levels. The lower level of the text is, on the whole, dedicated to the enemies of the sun and to the means used to prevent them from doing their evil work. The mythological tale of the text focuses on the transformations of the god in a process of becoming; these occur within an essentially chthonic space and involve two of the gods of earth, Geb and Aker. The latter occupied the middle level of the third "cavern" in the form of a double-headed sphinx. The solar boat plays no part in the composition, except in the last scene. The succession of hours to be seen in the books of *Amduat* and *Gates* disappears; the "voyage" is now a series of metamorphoses which the sun undergoes during the night.

The sun is generally depicted as the familiar ram-headed figure. In the final scene, however, it takes on forms that hint at its imminent rebirth, which is shown in the upper left-hand corner. The scarab indicates that it is about to regain its visible active role, while the infant symbolizes the young vigor of the being about to be born.

11. Graphic reproduction of the *Book of Caverns*, tomb of Rameses IX

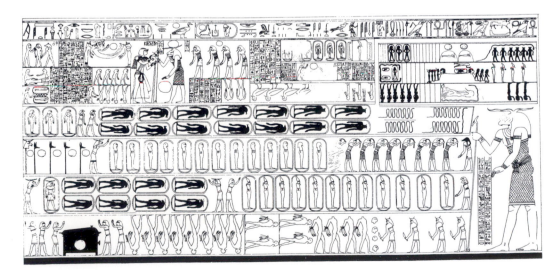

12. Diorite statue of Sekhmet,
from the temple of Mut at Karnak
(?), New Kingdom, 18th Dynasty.
Padua, Museo Civico Archeologico
cat. 2

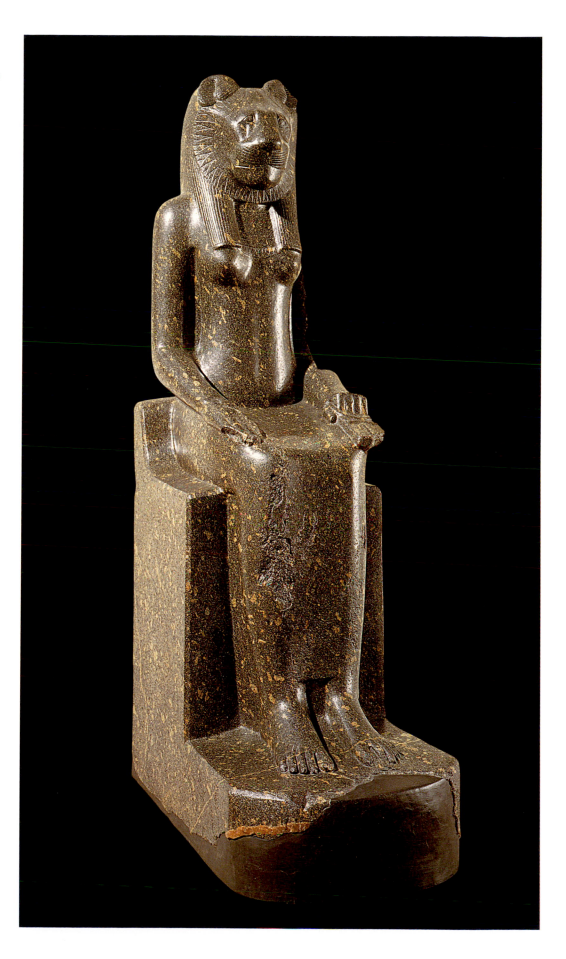

The Books of the Heavens

These are also known as two distinct compositions entitled the *Book of Day* and the *Book of Night*. They appear on the ceilings of the corridors and certain chambers in the tombs of Ramesside pharaohs. Over the sarcophagus of Sety I is a mythological account of the night sky, with the stars forming constellations that take on the shape of various tutelary divinities. The *Book of the Heavens* emphasizes the notion of gestation and birth. The celestial space is personified by the goddess Nut, who swallows the sun in the evening and keeps it in her breast before restoring it to the world each morning. The same phenomenon occurs during the day, except that this time it is the stars that move within the body of the divine mother during the time that they are invisible to man.

The double image of the goddess on the ceilings represents the two cycles: one image shows the body of Nut scattered with small solar disks, the other with stars. Against the dark blue background are depictions of the decans and the various deities that play a role in facilitating the progress of the sun and the stars.

Completing the texts of the book of *Amduat* and the *Book of Gates*, these descriptions of the heavens emphasize the permanent renewal of time, which draws along with it all those entities that are destined to be reborn.

The Book of the Earth

The last—and most sophisticated—of the compositions in the Valley of the Kings exists in complete form only in one hypogeum, covering the entire wall space of Rameses VI's tomb. The first person to publish it, Piankoff, entitled the text *The Creation of the Disk of the Sun*—on the basis of the images which recount the multiple aspects of the sun's daily renewal—whereas Hornung preferred the title *The Book of the Earth* because the main characters in this generation of the sun are three terrestrial figures: Geb, the personification of fertile soil; Tatjenen, the personification of the earth in movement (the earth as lifted up during the process of creation, but also each time a seed puts forth a shoot) and Aker, the embodiment of the very entrails of the *dwat*.

This book develops a theme that had already appeared in other compositions found in the Valley of the Kings. It makes its first, partial, appearance in the tomb of Merenptah, and so is contemporary with the other texts examined. Here, the priests are more concerned with the milieu within which the nocturnal metamorphoses of the sun occur, rather than with the idea of a passage of the hours.

The book of Aker is only apparently complex; all the elements here are to be found in other compositions, but in the chamber of Rameses VI they are concentrated in four immense scenes, each one occupying an entire wall. The idea of a composition divided into sections is abandoned, and the birth of the god is described "at a single stroke." Here again we find hillocks representing both the tomb and primordial mound of the world—both of which suggest the idea of life on the verge of renewal. The figures in the ovals represent the multiple forms of the solar entity undergoing transformation, and at the same time embody the ineffable mystery of the renewal of all existence.

The two main compositions, which occupy the largest walls of the burial chamber, deal with the same subject, but offer different descriptions of the gestation of the sun. They are to be read from bottom to top. In both, the lower part deals with the mysterious crucible from which the new entity will emerge. On one side the body of Aker—represented by the double lion head—has been cut in half, with the sun-disk in the middle borne by two arms which seem to reach up out of nowhere. One can interpret these as the hieroglyphs of action arising out of the unknown, from beyond a threshold that the human mind cannot even begin to describe. From the body of Aker there also emerge two boats, which symbolize the moment of departure in the course the sun will follow. The end of the cycle comes at the top of the composition, with a renewed Aker now embodied in a double sphinx, which one can read as representing the horizon, that holds up the frail skiff of the sun. Within the vessel, one has no difficulty recognizing the triumphant sun embodied in the form of a ram-headed figure.

On the other side of the tomb, the same phenomenon is described, with the milieu in which the whole process originates here embodied in a female entity stretched out in the lower part of the composition. The other scenes develop the theme of the metamorphoses leading to rebirth. Here, too, are the enemies of cosmic order, again shown reduced to impotence; bound or cut to pieces, by means of magic they are unable to hinder the course of life. The scene in the middle of the arch also depicts divine renewal, this time framed by two female figures; the stars and the suns which seem to form a chain represent the hours of the day and night, thus indicating that the return of time is also a renewal of the cosmos.

The decor in the tomb of Rameses VI is one of the most successful in the Valley of the Kings, and the *Book of the Earth* described above is complemented by the *Books of the Heavens* on the ceiling, with the double body of the goddess Nut. Hence, the burial chamber itself represented an image of the cosmos, enclosing the body of the dead king within an effective model of the permanent process of creation that would lead to his rebirth. At the heart of this symbolic depiction of the universe, he finds his place within the unfailing process of the sun's renewal.

Bibliography
The texts from the tombs in the Valley of the Kings have been translated and published by Erik Hornung: Hornung 1971 and Hornung 1985 contain a detailed bibliography. Franco 1993 (pp. 276–277) has references to the more recent publications. On the pyramid chambers, see Mathieu 1997. On the architecture of the royal funerary chambers in the light of the Pyramid Texts, see Berger, Mathieu 1997.

Anna Maria
Donadoni Roveri

The Funerary Equipment

1. Gold funerary mask of Psusennes
I from Tanis, Third Intermediate
Period, 21st Dynasty.
Cairo, Egyptian Museum
cat. 275

The longing for survival inherent in Egyptian civilization, which has made it possible for its testimony and significance to come down to us, also has a bearing on the symbol of society in ancient Egypt, the monarch.

The royal tomb, in the various forms it was given over thousands of years, was the object of public concern and differed ostensibly from those of ordinary mankind. Yet they were alike in being less a sign of exclusion than of change with respect to the world of the living. Since the grave was the house of the deceased, as such it had to provide him with the implements for his new, second life.

This meant that the grave had to contain all the things that allowed the "personality," the *ka*, of the deceased to preserve its value and vital efficiency. Therefore, the very identification requirements of a personality as complex as the sovereign implied that it boasted grave goods of special relevance, variety and value.

Yet in that last word lurks what would nearly always be the fate of these burial goods that featured riches removed from circulation, and that tended—owing to the grave-robbers' constant activity—to return to circulation. In antiquity Egyptian tombs were nearly all looted, especially the royal ones.

While the royal tombs that were found intact can be counted on one hand, this does not mean we do not have a large number of different elements enabling us to appraise situations that continued to evolve over the large span of time of Egyptian history.

In the oldest periods, the pit graves furnished with just a few goods—vases or simple trinkets—usually did not provide elements suggesting a hierarchical difference between individuals, so a wooden scepter (or something looking like one) found in a grave in el-Omari dated the fifth millennium BC is considered an exception.

For the late Predynastic and the Protodynastic periods, the royal necropolis of Abydos is particularly relevant, since it gathers several tombs in a typologically coherent complex and a number of excavation campaigns have gradually given us a better definition of their characters and dating.

Distinguishing them from ordinary graves were their dimensions and increasingly intricate structures, as well as the fact that their equal rank implied special furnishings.

The successive raids in antiquity deprived them of nearly everything of an intrinsic value, and excavations that were carried out in separate and random periods have in part obscured their appraisal.

But thanks to a thorough revision of the known information in a final, highly accurate archeological exploration we can assess the remaining artifacts. They are essentially vases, earthenware or stone, the former offered for the afterlife, the latter for ostentation. The inscriptions carved or painted in ink on the earthenware vases give the name of the owner of the grave, usually written in the *serekh*, that is the mark of the royal palace, and in some cases the manner and provenance of the goods it contained, thus providing us with an idea, if not an estimate, of the economic structures supporting royal power. Inscribed plaques—generally ivory—recalling specific events, help to date, by designating their use, specific objects they were attached to and that now have been lost.

This material gives an idea of the opulence of the goods, although a more specific, albeit rare, mark of royalty is only occasionally indicated. Thus in two graves of the late Predynastic period we have stone reproductions of a scepter, the "pastoral staff" that was typical of deities and sovereigns in the historical era. And when we find a whole fleet of boats by a Protodynastic grave buried in the ground nearby we are certainly dealing with a rite that places articles that can only be of use in the afterlife among the goods of the dead king.

The Protodynastic period ended spectacularly with the building of Djoser's Step Pyramid at Saqqara. The exploration of the galleries concealed inside has revealed parts overlooked by the robbers and diggers of old. Thousands of vases, earthenware but especially stone have come to light. The former were the usual offerings, but the latter have their own value, and their huge number is even more meaningful, since many of them are inscribed with the names of ancient rulers as their owners or beneficiaries. In other royal tombs as well similar furnishings from older periods can be found; these are said to be articles from an older deposit that were handed down and enriched at later rulers' courts. But here we have had to assume that the entire store of stone vases had been removed to the galleries of the grave to enrich

following pages
2. The pyramids of Khafra, Khufu,
and Menkaura at Giza